THE PRESIDENTS
OF THE CHURCH

JOSEPH SMITH, JR.
(1830-1844)

JOSEPH SMITH III
(1860-1914)

FREDERICK M. SMITH
(1915-1946)

ISRAEL A. SMITH
(1946-1958)

W. WALLACE SMITH
(1958-1978)

WALLACE B. SMITH
(1978-   )

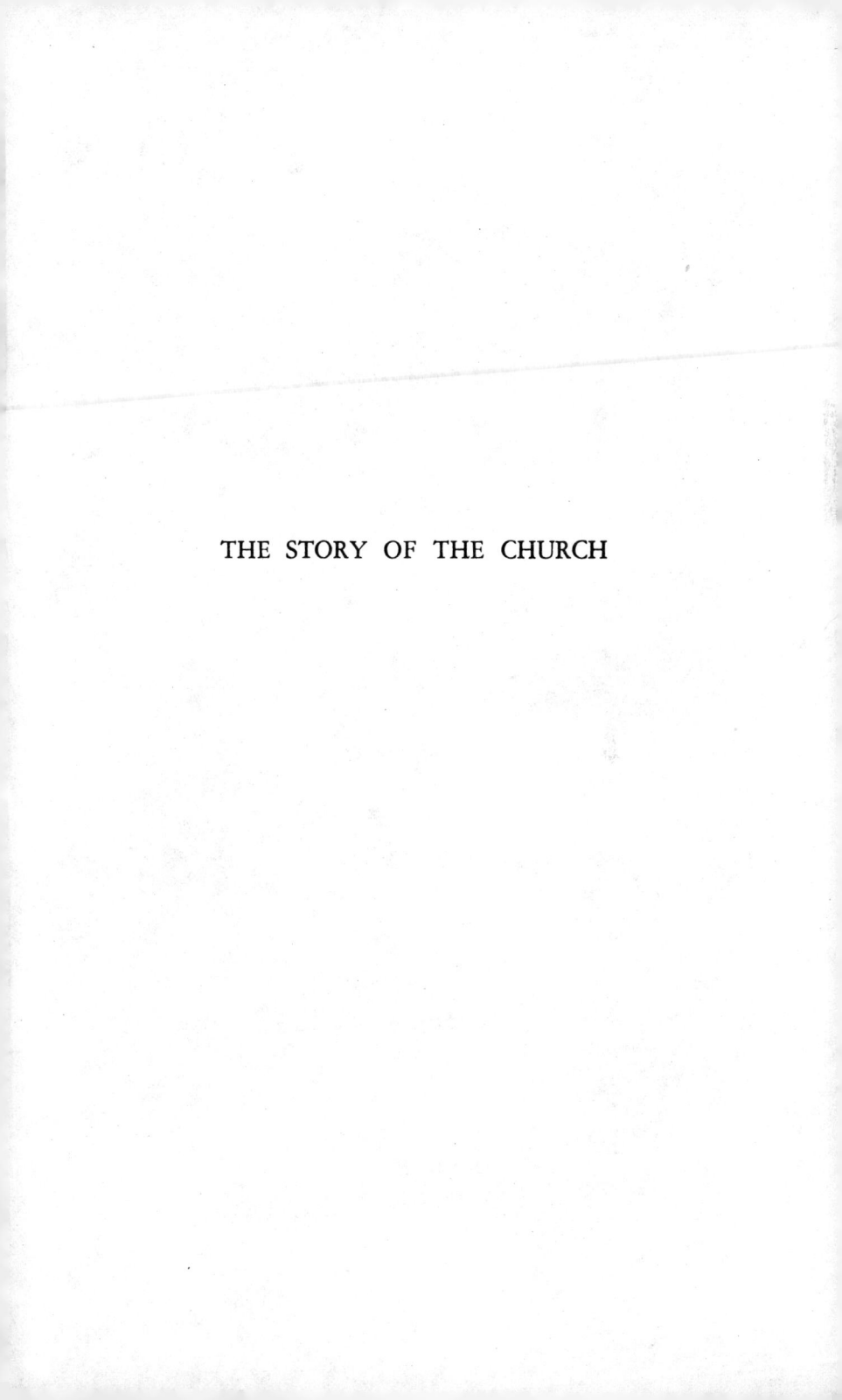

THE STORY OF THE CHURCH

THE *Story of* THE CHURCH

By INEZ SMITH DAVIS

A history of the Church of Jesus Christ of Latter Day Saints, and of its legal successor, the Reorganized Church of Jesus Christ of Latter Day Saints

ELEVENTH EDITION

HERALD PUBLISHING HOUSE
INDEPENDENCE, MISSOURI
1983

THE STORY OF THE CHURCH
Copyright, 1943
Sixth Edition (Second Revision) Copyright, 1959
HERALD PUBLISHING HOUSE
Independence, Missouri

All rights in this book are reserved. No part of the text may be reproduced in any form without written permission of the publishers, except brief quotations used in connection with reviews in a magazine or newspaper.

First Edition, 1934
Second Edition, 1938
Third Edition, 1943
Fourth Edition (Revised), 1948
Fifth Edition, 1955
Sixth Edition (Second Revision), 1959
Seventh Edition, 1964
Eighth Edition (Third Revision), 1969
Ninth Edition (Updated), 1977
Tenth Edition (Updated), 1981
Eleventh Edition (Updated), 1983

Printed in the United States of America

DEDICATED
to the memory of
my father
HEMAN C. SMITH

"Through such souls alone God stooping, shows sufficient of his light for us in the dark to rise by."—Browning.

ACKNOWLEDGMENTS

The thanks of the author are due to Samuel A. Burgess, and to F. Henry Edwards for their valuable suggestions in the compilation of the material, and their careful and painstaking help in the preparation of the manuscript of this story of the church.

FOREWORD

The task of writing a *brief* history of an organization whose record covers an expanse of one hundred years is more difficult than writing one of unlimited length, for there is the necessity of selecting the incidents or events one would record, and the choice is not always easy, because many events parallel each other in importance. The briefer writing, therefore, might well have a central theme as a guide to selecting the material to make up the volume. Such a central theme is always present in the development of our church, for the social philosophy which revolves about the idea of Zion and her redemption has always been present among the factors determining church movements or activities. The author has happily chosen this theme as the guiding star in writing this brief history. She brings to her task especial qualifications. Her maternal and paternal ancestors were connected with the church in its formative period and lived through the varied and colorful experiences which have brought it to its present state. As the daughter of a former historian of the church, she has from her infancy lived in the atmosphere of the student of history. To the manor born, her heritage has been one of sympathetic support of the church as a worker. By her assiduity as a student she has added to this equipment in attaining scholastic rank above the average of college students, having won honors nationally recognized. Her heritage and attainments augment a deep-seated love for the church and this combination she has brought into play as a writer of history to produce a book which all members of the church will read with great interest, and which will be valuable to anyone seeking a terse survey of our interesting history, for these factors have united to give her a distinct urge to write our history.

The pleasure I have found in reading the manuscript will, I am sure, be matched by the pleasure the Saints will find in perusing the book.

Frederick M. Smith

1934

FOREWORD TO FIFTH EDITION

"The Story of the Church" has given such general satisfaction that it is with genuine pleasure that we now present this edition which has been brought up to date and improved in a number of details.

"The Story of the Church" reminds us that our message has a significant historical setting. We stand where we do because of the experiences which we and our fathers have shared in the years now past. It is therefore eminently fitting that a book which tells the story of our history so accurately and in so interesting a manner should receive the widespread acclaim which we feel sure will continue with this fifth edition as it was with those that went before.

Israel A. Smith

Independence, Missouri

CONTENTS

CHAPTER

I	Background	11
II	The Great Revival	18
III	The Revolt Against Creeds	23
IV	The Golden Plates	31
V	Joseph Smith	42
VI	Friends	50
VII	The Book of Mormon	55
VIII	The Book of Mormon Witnesses	69
IX	Organizing the Church	76
X	The First Great Mission of the Church	88
XI	Sidney Rigdon	101
XII	The Church Moves West	112
XIII	Pioneering in the West	125
XIV	Slavery in Missouri	138
XV	The Militia	145
XVI	The Church Grows	148
XVII	Doctrinal Development	168
XVIII	The Storm Breaks	172
XIX	Missions to Canada and the East	186
XX	Governor Dunklin Takes a Hand	193
XXI	The High Council	205
XXII	Zion's Camp	208
XXIII	The Missionary Quorums	217
XXIV	The Doctrine and Covenants	220
XXV	The Kirtland Temple	224
XXVI	After the Endowment	230
XXVII	The Panic of 1837	239
XXVIII	The First Foreign Mission	245
XXIX	The Mission to New York City and the "Voice of Warning"	257
XXX	Far West	261
XXXI	Nauvoo	287
XXXII	The Gospel of the Kingdom	308
XXXIII	Enemies in Camp	315
XXXIV	A Mission to the South Sea Islands	321
XXXV	The Last Days of the Prophet	332
XXXVI	The Deserted City	344

CHAPTER

XXXVII	The Parting of the Ways	355
XXXVIII	The Good Ship "Brooklyn"	363
XXXIX	The Texas Colony	374
XL	The Community at Preparation	387
XLI	Jason W. Briggs and the Beloit and Waukesha Branches	390
XLII	Zenas H. Gurley and the Yellowstone Branch	396
XLIII	Reorganizing the Church	405
XLIV	William Marks	415
XLV	A Mission to Young Joseph	425
XLVI	Granville Hedrick and the Crow Creek Branch	431
XLVII	"The True Latter Day Saints' Herald"	436
XLVIII	William Marks Receives an Important Letter	440
XLIX	Young Joseph	442
L	Amboy, 1860	450
LI	Friends and Otherwise	454
LII	Welding the Fragments	459
LIII	England and Wales	469
LIV	The First Mission to the West	489
LV	The Fight Against Polygamy	486
LVI	Reinforcements	491
LVII	Plano Days	499
LVIII	Switzerland and Germany	507
LIX	Pioneering for the Gospel in the West	516
LX	"Te Atua Speaks Again"	523
LXI	Australia	529
LXII	Scandinavia	535
LXIII	Canada	541
LXIV	Lamoni and the Order of Enoch	546
LXV	The Saints Return to the Goodly Land	557
LXVI	Island Missions	562
LXVII	Development and Progress	568
LXVIII	Frederick M. Smith	576
LXIX	Israel A. Smith	583
LXX	W. Wallace Smith	594
LXXI	Wallace B. Smith	598B
	Appendix	599
	Index	631

I. Background

Little more than a century ago our church had its beginnings in the pioneer village of Palmyra in western New York. The history we have made in the succeeding years has been vivid, colorful, and distinctive; so much so that thousands of writers have piled up books, pamphlets, magazine articles, sermons, novels, stories, and plays in such number that it would take a library to hold them all. Collectors to whom the ecclesiasticism of the church has meant nothing have seized upon its early publications with avidity, until book dealers issue special catalogues of "Mormona" in fabulous figures. Zealous ministers of almost every other faith under the sun have added their rabid contributions and kindled many a fire, the acrid smoke of whose burning still obscures the clear facts of history. Peeved and disgruntled dissenters from our own ranks have occasionally added gossipy exposés, some of which have run into many undeserved editions. And eager but undiscriminating students have enriched the world with their "scientific" and psychological studies of "Mormonism." Even the novelist, eschewing the drab toils of religious controversy as the plague, has persistently distorted the history of this much maligned people to suit his own ideas of romance.

Out of the resulting mass of conflicting ideas, of counter statements and irrelevant debris, it becomes our pleasant task to sift the grains of truth. Says Matthew Arnold, "The mass of mankind will never have any ardent zeal for seeing things as they are; very inadequate ideas will always satisfy them." But to the few who may, lost in the maze of what has been said, earnestly wonder what men have seen in this strange religion which has made it seem worthy to live and to die by (sometimes all too literally); to those who, schooled in half-truths, have honestly asked why thousands of their fellow creatures have chosen to believe in it, rest in it, and give their lives for it, a re-telling of the story may be worth-while.

The institution which is the subject of this history has meant many things to many people, a mighty imposture, the dizzy dream of a master fanatic, the queer structure of a megalomaniac, the eternal plan of salvation. The artist, whose vision is always clearer than he knows, has seen there the stuff of drama: suspense, crisis, human error and disappointment, high hope, sterling courage, black despair. All the elements of real drama are there, and to those who know the story best, back of it all, inspiration and motive, the inspiration of the gospel restored, and motive—the Zionic ideal, that like the *leitmotif* in a Wagnerian opera comes singing up in every generation, over and over again, perhaps only to fade away in discordant notes. Our critics have missed more than all else this Zion-melody in their telling, perhaps because its notes have not been clear enough, but the fact remains that without it, the story would scarcely be worth telling, for the greatest heritage we have from our fathers who wrote the story of their faith in blood and tears, is the belief that this *leitmotif*, this plea for universal brotherhood, will someday rise at last to a grand triumphal chant—the glorious finale which has been the dream of our youth, the goal of maturity and the heart's longing of our aged ones through three long generations—"the redemption of Zion."

No malicious people ever enthroned in their philosophy as their highest ideal the belief that God is love and that all men are brothers. Such a philosophy comes from the hearts of poets, enthusiasts, prophets, "saints." To have missed the central faith and purpose of our belief is to have failed to know it at all; and the history of our church movement comprises, at its core, the more or less sporadic attempts of a people—incapacitated by human stupidities, human fears and prejudices, but actuated by lofty aspirations and glorious dreams—to frame their convictions into a system that will eventually regenerate the souls of men.

The origin, evolution, principles, and exceptionally rapid growth of the Latter Day Saint doctrine and belief can be best understood in connection with religious and economic conditions in the American commonwealth at the close of the eighteenth and beginning of the nineteenth centuries.

The people had passed through a war of seven years' duration, and moral and religious decadence almost invariably follows war. A toppling over of the Episcopal Church in America was the natural result. Forced into compromise or silence by the war, Episcopal services became, according to Bishop Meade, "brief and most unimpressive." Many of the clergymen had migrated to Canada, followed by the British part of their congregation. In Virginia, the stronghold of the mother church, where in 1776 there were seventy-one Episcopal clergymen, there were in 1783 but fifteen.

The year 1783 marked the closing of the Revolution, and left the people drunk with the idea of "liberty"—a liberty which needed to be interpreted to be made usable in the formation of a new government. The political struggles of that epoch required the best thought and attention of the great men of the new nation. Other considerations took second place. A measure of success was hardly achieved in self-government before quarrels with England again fanned the flames of parental hatred into another war.

Throughout all our troubles, France had been our friend, or was so considered. The French Revolution found many partisans in the new republic. Everyone began to talk and write the new "liberty" jargon that was fashionable at the time. License, anarchy, infidelity were part of that jargon, even as the French fashions, the white cockade, and the address of "Citizen." France was frankly atheistic.

When Theodore Dwight became president of Yale College in 1795, only five or six students were members of any church. Similar conditions existed in the College of New Jersey (Princeton); William and Mary's; Transylvania (Kentucky University), which had been founded by the Presbyterian Church, had frankly passed into the hands of "unbelievers." In the early part of the nineteenth century only one student at Bowdoin College was willing to be known as a Christian. Chancellor Kent, who died in 1847, said that in his younger days there were few professional men who were professed "believers." Lyman Beecher in his autobiography, speaking of that period said: "It was the day of the Tom Paine school when boys who dressed flax in the barn read Tom Paine and believed him." Lyman Beecher was graduated from Yale in 1797, and he tells us that the members of his class were known to each other by the names of "Voltaire," "D'Alembert," "Rousseau," and other French atheists. Prominent thinkers honestly predicted the Christian religion would soon be discarded.

In 1800 only one Congregational Church in Boston remained loyal to the orthodox faith. When the Reverend E. D. Griffith became pastor of the Park Church in 1811, the feeling against orthodoxy was so intense that men who went to hear him went in disguise for fear of ridicule.

Intemperance was the rule. To become drunk was not a breach of decency, nor did such indulgence particularly injure any man's reputation. Liquor was in every home. Total abstinence was scarcely known. Few ministers preached temperance sermons, or even knew that intoxication was an "evil" to be denounced by Christians. Members of the church in high standing drank to intoxication at social functions. Wine was served as a matter of course at religious ceremonies, christenings, marriages, funerals, and even ordinations. The physician was offered a drink as a matter of course when he called on a patient; the minister was accorded like hospitality by members of his congregation. One pastor in New York, as late as 1820, deplored the fact that it was difficult to make pastoral calls for a day and duly observe the social amenities without becoming in a measure intoxicated. The Reverend Daniel Dorchester, D. D., quotes a minister of the period as saying he could count among his ministerial acquaintances

BACKGROUND

forty who were either drunkards or so addicted to the use of liquor that their usefulness was seriously impaired[1]. This man says he was present at an ordination where two aged ministers were literally drunk.[2]

The legislature of Kentucky, at this time, by vote dispensed with the services of a chaplain. The pioneer States were marked by general disregard, even contempt, for religion and religious institutions. The Lord's Day in such communities was only distinguished from other days by greater noise, more amusement, and dissipation. Often on the western frontier there were no houses of worship, even in towns of considerable size.

It is not at all strange that the most intelligent and tolerant men in a community made no profession of faith, for so many religious people were so narrow and fanatical that they would be intolerable to the people who profess to belong to the same denominations today. "The most pious people in the beginning of the present century in the United States entertained a faith so unlike the belief of evangelical Christians as to almost create the impression that their religion was not the same religion we now have, and in which we now believe."[3]

Doctor Wayland tells of an early experience in his ministry in a small community in Massachusetts. He had in his congregation a highly intelligent gentleman who had an interesting but "worldly" family of young people. He expressed to this man his desire to speak to his sons and daughters on the subject of their "personal piety." The father objected strenuously—if his children were of the elect, God would save them in his own due time; and if they were not, such a conversation as Doctor Wayland proposed might make them hypocrites! There was no power in the written word, or for that matter in the spoken word, to

---

[1] *Christianity in the United States From Its First Settlement Down to the Present Time* (1888), by Reverend Daniel Dorchester, D.D., New York; Phillips and Hart.
[2] In his *Background of Mormon Word of Wisdom* reprinted from the *Scratch*, Brigham Young University, Volume 2, No. 2, page 56, March, 1930, M. Wilford Poulson tells of the beginnings of the temperance movement in the United States.
[3] *Ibid.*

produce a saving faith in anyone. Such faith, or "regeneration" as it was then called, was a gift from God, a miracle with which he transformed the hearts of his elect.[4]

At the beginning of the last century there were few, if any, Sunday schools in the United States. The American Bible Society was not organized until 1810 or after. Antislavery agitation had scarcely started, the crusade for temperance barely begun, nor was the orthodox attitude towards these movements, when they did start, often one of approval, or even toleration. Missions, Sunday schools, Bible societies were all opposed under the avowed belief that they "conflicted with the sovereignty of God in the kingdom of Christ." As late as 1836 the Baltimore Association of the Baptist Church resolved that it would not hold fellowship with such churches as united with these and other societies of a benevolent, religious, and philanthropic character. The names of congregations co-operating in mission work, in Sunday school work, in distribution of the Word of God through Bible societies were erased from the minutes of that association.[5] The same attitude prevailed in other denominations. Whole congregations zealously bound themselves together by oaths and covenants of the rankest intolerance, such as the "solemn league and covenant" taken by one church "to oppose Rome, the pope, and popery with all their anti-Christian ways."

Economic brotherhood was as foreign to the thought of this day as religious brotherhood. The majority of the laboring class, caught in the aftermath of financial stringency following the wars with England, knew fare that was mean and scant in the extreme. A laborer was fortunate indeed if he drew four dollars a week for the support of his large family. His home boasted no carpets, no glassware, but few bits of china, no pictures—not even cheap chromos for the wall. His clothing was a pair of leather breeches,

---

[4] Wayland, on *Notes on the Principles and Practices of the Baptists.*
[5] *History of the Baptists,* by Thomas Armitage.

a flannel jacket, a rusty felt hat, shoes of neat's skin, and a leather apron. The bare necessities of today were luxuries in that era.

Into such a world, French ideas of "liberty, fraternity, equality" flowed like a flood, which even as its radicalism ebbed away left behind it notions of economic liberty, equality before the law, and denial of titled aristocracy. Of such ideas, was born the new state, a government in which "freedom" and "liberty" were to become magic passwords, a government completely and permanently separate from any and all churches. At the same time religious people were shaking off the shackles of outgrown thought in rebellion against "creeds and confessions of faith" and ushering in the days of the "Great Revival," in which old denominations were to go through the throes of a new birth, and in which many new religions were destined to come forward.

II.—The Great Revival

A "REVIVAL" MOVEMENT among a people who had previously shown such little interest in religion and had indeed fostered assiduously an attitude of antipathy to it is one of the strangest chapters in American religious history. Perhaps stranger still was the fact that those most affected by the movement were in many cases the most unimaginative, phlegmatic, and common-sense backwoodsmen. A swing of the pendulum back from the reign of French atheism early in the century marked the beginning of a feverish emotional reaction, which psychologists are still attempting to explain, for though in a general sense, the high tide of the "great revival" slowly subsided, actually it was never over. The revival, the camp meeting, the protracted meeting, by whatever name it may be called, became a permanent American institution, which never entirely lost its appeal, especially to rural folk, an appeal still wholly mysterious to many minds.

This movement had its beginning in the South, Kentucky and Tennessee, with the labors of certain Presbyterian ministers, prominent among whom was one James McCready. Cataleptic seizures and strange agitations which had formerly appeared under Whitfield (in England) were here witnessed for the first time in "camp meeting." Those under the spell of "the spirit" were suddenly stricken and lay motionless for hours. No age or condition was immune from these strange manifestations which were popularly conceived to be visitations from God. The person affected almost invariably regained consciousness in an agony of repentance that soon changed to an ecstasy of joy.

The revival spirit spread like wildfire through the West, and extended eastward. Revivals and camp meetings were held everywhere. From a people to whom the very mention of religion was anathema, in one mad moment the whole country was converted to one where religious controversy was the one main topic of the day. One minister after another succumbed to the new hysteria, but the excitement reached its height in the long line of western frontier, and perhaps justly so, for if the hardened in sin were in need of revival, here was a field ripened for harvest.

In August, 1801, Barton Stone introduced the movement into Cane Ridge, Kentucky, and held one of the most famous camp meetings of all time. More than twenty thousand people attended. Methodist and Baptist ministers aided the Presbyterians, several preaching at once in different parts of the mammoth camp meeting. At these famous Cane Ridge meetings not less than one thousand persons, many of them previously infidels, were stricken down with these peculiar manifestations and presumably "saved."

Other Presbyterian ministers, McNamar, Thompson, Dunlavy, Marshall, David Purviance, began to hold similar services. "The people appeared," says Stone, "as just awakened from the sleep of ages; they seemed to see for the first time that they were responsible beings."[1]

A revival was at first synonymous with a "camp meeting." A place was selected in the forest near a spring, for wood and water were the two great essentials for the pioneer. Trees were felled, benches built, a bower thatched for shelter, and, most significant of all, in front of the rude platform chosen to serve as a pulpit, was arranged the "mourners' bench." This was a rectangular space inclosed by a rail and provided with seats. Into this inclosure the penitent were invited to assemble after the sermon, a vociferous lengthy discourse redolent of the fires of hell and the wrath of God. The ground was well strewn with straw, and all was in readiness for the camp meeting. The meeting was scheduled to last for days. All work on farms and clearings was suspended for

---

[1] *Autobiography of Barton Stone.*

the period, while whole families gathered from miles around by every means of conveyance. Rude cabins and tents were erected and preparations made for cooking on an even more primitive housekeeping plan than the log cabins at home afforded. The occasion was a social one, as well as a sober religious duty, and time was found somehow between services for friendship, hospitality, and courtship, and all the community activity dear to the heart of the lonely pioneer.

A trumpet was sounded at daybreak for rising, a second blast for prayer in the tents, a third for call to public prayer on the ground. Breakfast was then served and all was in readiness for a first service at eight, followed by meetings at eleven, three in the afternoon, and "early candlelight." All the "meetings" followed one general plan. First the sermon with its exhortation and warning of the briefness of life, the danger of sudden and unprepared death, and the pains of hell, followed by pleading to sinners to repent. During the exhortation men, women, and children pressed up the straw-strewn aisles to the mourners' bench. There were usually many of these penitent. At the mourners' bench workers waited and proceeded to "lay their sins heavily" upon those who answered the call. This was called "a class," and so long was the sermon, the exhortation, and the class that the services just missed overlapping. But short church sessions were neither known nor desired in that day.

Singing and shouting were always prominent features of the camp meeting. Men, women, and children fell down in trances and suffered other strange seizures. As the movement reached fever heat, new manifestations appeared; one of the weirdest was known as the "jerks," in which the victim's head would be jerked back and forth at a rapid rate. The famous itinerant preacher, Peter Cartright, thus describes the "jerks" in his memoirs: "To see these proud young gentlemen and young ladies in their silks, jewelry, and prunella from top to toe take the jerks, would often excite my risibilities. The first jerk or so, you would see their fine

THE GREAT REVIVAL

bonnets, caps, and combs fly; and so sudden would be the jerkings of the head that their long loose hair would crack almost as loud as a wagoner's whip."[2] The "jerks" affected saints and sinners, credulous and skeptical alike, and the spectators would often dance, run, or pray to avoid it, but try to restrain themselves as they would, they still continued to jerk. Sometimes to add to the general hysteria, victims barked like dogs or howled like wolves. Many saw visions, and claimed divine authority for them, and many new movements sprang up in the wake of the great revival.

"In the supercharged atmosphere of the evening meetings, when the strident tones of the evangelist rang through the straw-strewn pavilion and died away in the echoes of the dark and silent forest,"[3] the revival was most successful. "And it was among the young and most impressionable that the greatest number of converts were made."

"It was not theological abstractions, nor yet the simple gospel of love with which the itinerant Samsons slew their tens of thousands. It was with the fires of hell, and the vengeance of God that they accomplished it."[4]

"Thundered at with all the stentorian verbosity of the primitive evangelist . . . they listened in awed stupefaction until their nerves failed. The demonstration of the camp meeting was not so much a product of emotionalism as of emotional collapse . . . without this element of hysteria, the camp meeting would have been a failure."[5]

The heroes of these pioneer meetings were the itinerant preachers such as Asbury, Peter Cartright, Lorenzo Dow, and others. Often these men, as brave as they were zealous, traveled many miles through the most dangerous and lonely forest on foot or on horseback, hazarding all sorts of weather and every danger of the trail in order to meet appointments made fully a year in advance.

---

[2] *Autobiography of Peter Cartright*, pages 48, 49.
[3] *From Frontier to Plantation in Tennessee*, by Abernathy
[4] *Ibid.* [5] *Ibid.*

As he left each cabin in the woods, the preacher made his appointments often for months ahead, and the pioneer family knew as that day approached, that at the time specified, the "preacher" would ride into the clearing, tired, harried by the uncertainties of the trail, but ready for a meeting in the cabin that night. Many a child on such nights shivered by the fireplace, afraid to go to bed after listening to tales of judgment and God's vengeance. In stockades and schoolhouses, log cabins and camp meetings, these men lifted up their warning voices, never too old, too ill, or too self-seeking to spend themselves.

For many years these revivals were general all through the trans-Allegheny region, continuing with unabated zeal through the depression of 1837. For a time the denominations co-operated in saving souls, each agreeing to avoid all proselyting. But as the force of emotionalism began to recede, discussions began to break out among denominations, and even more generally within the ranks of each denomination, and the issue at stake was "creeds and confessions of faith." The conservative faction of each denomination clung to the old creeds and confessions of faith in which they felt was crystallized the wisdom of the ages; the radical wing viewed these statements of faith as a pernicious obstacle to Christian union.

III.—THE REVOLT AGAINST CREEDS

THE MOVEMENTS AND COUNTER movements running through the history of Christianity have taken their courses like currents in the sea. Every great movement has its antecedents. Back of every flower is a seed, and all ideas, however wonderful, like all living things grow. Back of Copernicus was Pythagoras; and after him his theories found fruition in Kepler, Galileo, and Newton.

So for more than a century in Europe, and for a less length of time in America, religious thinkers visioned the rise of a "new" movement in religion. Protestantism had not brought peace, but "bitter and incessant strife,"[1] and for a time it seemed that it would devour itself by strife and multiplicity of division.[2] The Roman Catholic orator, Bossuet, predicted that very thing with the continuation of the Protestant policies of that period—a "complete disintegration and disappearance of the entire Protestant movement."[3]

Each prophet that appeared with a new gospel was tried at the bitter and fickle court of public opinion and suffered the calumny of him who differs from the masses. Of one of the greatest of these, John Wesley, we are told by Canon Farrar:

"We might think it strange that the desire to preach the gospel of Christ should invoke such deadly opposition, alike of the so-called respectable and religious classes, and of the rude and ignorant multitude. Yet so it was . . . Every form of opposition, we are told, was tried against him. Milldams were let out; church bells were jangled; drunken fiddlers and ballad singers were hired; organs peeled forth; drums were beaten; street venders,

---
[1] *Origin of the Disciples of Christ*, by Peter Ainslee, Revell, New York.
[2] *Ibid.*
[3] *History of Variations of the Protestant Church*, by Bossuet.

clowns, drunken fops, and papists were hired, and incited to brawl or blow horns, so as to drown his voice. He was struck in the face with sticks; he was cursed and groaned at, pelted with stones, beaten to the ground, threatened with murder, dragged and hustled hither and thither by drinking, cursing, swearing, riotous mobs who acted the part of judge, jury, and executioner. 'Knock him down and kill him at once,' was the shout of the brutal roughs who assaulted him at Wednesbury. On more than one occasion, a mad or a baited bull was driven into the midst of his assemblies; the windows of the houses in which he stayed were broken, and rioters burst their way even into his private rooms. 'The men,' says Dr. Taylor, 'who commenced and continued this arduous service—and they were scholars and gentlemen—displayed a courage far surpassing that which carries the soldier through the hailstorm of the battlefield. Ten thousand might easily be found who would confront a battery than two, who, with the sensitiveness of education about them, could (in that day) mount a table by the roadside, give out a Psalm, and gather a mob.

"To face all this, and to face it day after day, and year by year, in England, in Scotland, in Wales, in Cornwell, in Ireland, required a supreme bravery and persistence. Yet it needed even greater courage to meet hurricanes of abuse and tornadoes of slander. Wesley had to face this also on all sides. The most popular actors of the day held him up to odium and ridicule in lewd comedies. Reams of calumny were written against him; shoals of pamphlets, full of virulence and falsehood, were poured forth from the press. The most simple, the most innocent, the most generous of men, he was called a smuggler, a liar, an immoral and designing intriguer, a Pope, a Jesuit, a swindler, the most notorious hypocrite living. The clergy, I grieve to say, led the way. Rowland Hill called Wesley 'a lying apostate, a designing wolf, a dealer in stolen wares,' and said that he was as unprincipled as a rook, and as silly as a jackdaw, first pilfering his neighbor's plumage, and then going proudly forth to display it to a laughing world.' Augustus Toplady said among floods of other and worse abuse, that 'for thirty years he had been endeavoring to palm on his credulous followers his pernicious doctrines, with all the sophistry of a Jesuit and the dictatorial authority of a Pope,' and described him as 'the most rancorous hater of the gospel system that ever appeared in England.' Bishop Lavington of Exeter denounced the Methodists as a dangerous and presumptuous sect, animated with an enthusiastical and fanatical spirit, and said that they were either innocent madmen or infamous cheats."[4]

Wesley suffered all this in law-abiding England, and men of vision have received similar treatment since. But Wesley did not believe the gospel he preached had reached its full fruition in his ministry:

"The times which we have reason to believe are at hand (if they are not already begun), are what many pious men have termed, the time of 'latter-day glory'—meaning, the time wherein God would gloriously display his power and love, in the fulfillment of his gracious promise that 'the knowledge of the Lord shall cover the earth, as the waters cover the sea,' "[5] and

"What could God have done which he hath not done, to convince you that the day is coming, that the time is at hand, when he will fulfill his glorious promises; when he will arise to maintain his own cause, and set up his kingdom over all the earth?"[6]

Even Luther had preached that one would come who was to do a greater work than he: "I cannot tell what to say of myself. Perhaps I am Philipp's (Melanchthon's) forerunner. I am preparing the way for him, like Elias, in spirit and in power."

The amazing spread of the great revival in the new world led many to believe that this time spoken of by reformers had ar-

---
[4] Archdeacon Farrar, in the *Contemporary Review*. Quoted in *Church History*, Volume 1, pages 109, 110.
[5] Wesley, *Sermons*, Volume 2 (2), sermon 71. See *Church History*, Volume 1, page 2.
[6] *Ibid.*

rived, but as the spirit of emotionalism began to ebb, men who thought for themselves began to analyze and meditate over their Bibles after the hour of ecstasy at the penitent form, and they discovered that their new light had brought them little but confusion. They could no longer believe in "total depravity"; that men could do nothing of themselves to bring about their own salvation until God by some mysterious power had quickened and enlightened and regenerated the heart and prepared the sinner to believe in Jesus. Any reasoning man could plainly see that if God did not do this regenerating work for all, it must be because he chose to do it for some and not for others, as this was the doctrine so plainly taught and linked with "unconditional election" and "reprobation," as taught in the *Winchester Confession of Faith.* Men like Barton Stone in reading the Scriptures and comparing them with the confession of faith, became convinced "that God did love the whole world, and the reason why he did not save all was because of their unbelief,"[7] and immediately began the assault upon creeds and authoritative systems of religion which followed in the wake of the great revival as inevitably as night follows day.

For early in the day of Protestantism, either because they felt they must do so to cope with the dogmatic theology of the Roman Catholic religion, or because, accustomed to dogmatism, they felt at sea without its anchor, the reformers had established their own systems, as positive and creed bound as the one they had renounced, and as years went by became more and more involved in the arduous task of exacting uncompromising loyalty, not to Christ but to the systems they had evolved, an ever increasingly difficult task.

Early in the century, in different places, and in unrelated and even in antagonistic sects, arose men who declared that all creeds and systems must be abandoned and the Scriptures alone become

---
[7] *Autobiography of Barton Stone.*

the simple rule and guide of Christian life. As early as 1793, on Christmas Day, James O'Kelley and his courageous little band of dissenters seceded from the Methodist Church in North Carolina, declaring they would have no creed or discipline but the Bible. Early in the century Abner Jones and Elias Smith in Vermont formed a fellowship, rejecting "sectarian names and creeds" and adopting the Bible as their only standard of faith and practice.

The situation among the Presbyterians will illustrate what was happening in many communions. They had been caught unexpectedly in the vortex of the great revival, and now that its inadequacies became apparent, they were carried into a whirlpool of uncertainty and confusion. For a time they co-operated valiantly with the Methodists and the Baptists in the South in the camp meetings which seemed to produce such glorious results, protecting themselves by the usual "agreement to avoid proselyting" and harmony was sustained until about 1804, when the force of emotionalism began to wane slightly. Dissensions began to break out among the denominations but even more seriously within their own ranks. The Cumberland Presbytery had gone enthusiastically and wholeheartedly into the new movement. In the general excitement young men had gone forth to preach who did not meet the previously established qualifications of the denomination, and these had even been licensed as ministers. The erring Presbytery was brought for these and other indiscretions under the censure of the synod of Kentucky. Finally in 1810, after six years of wrangling and dissension the Cumberland Presbytery, led by William McGee and others, seceded from the organization and formed the Cumberland Presbyterian Church. The new body made an earnest effort to compromise between old and new. They renounced the doctrine of predestination, but retained a belief in the "perseverance of the saints," and especially espoused the evangelical tendencies acquired during the great revival, and provided that candidates for the ministry be examined in no language but English.

Among the various denominations there was considerable discussion of the meaning and manner of administering the various rites and ceremonies of the church. There was the matter of baptism. Many had come to think that baptism was in some way connected in the Scriptures with conversion. For some time the reformers had been dissatisfied with their infant baptism, and as the Baptists would not baptize except on condition of union with their organization, many of them were reduced to the same expedient resorted to by Roger Williams and reasoned that if they were commissioned to preach they were commissioned to baptize, and therefore baptized each other. Baptism by immersion was growing rapidly into favor, but was still looked upon as a means of admission into the church to be obeyed by those already converted, and very seldom preached or talked about except when someone was going to be baptized.

The religious awakening had for some time engrossed the minds of all to the practical exclusion of baptism, but as one by one the reformers sensed that it must play some part in the scheme of conversion, it became once more a subject of controversy. Once indeed Barton Stone in the early days of the revival dimly recognized its true place. There had been a great meeting and the mourners were duly invited to the mourners' bench, and prayed over without receiving at once the expected manifestations. "The words of Peter at Pentecost," says he, "rolled through my mind, 'Repent and be baptized for the remission of sins, and ye shall receive the gift of the Holy Spirit.' I thought, were Peter here, he would thus address these mourners. I quickly arose and addressed them in the same language and urged them to comply."[8] The invitation, however, had the reverse effect of what he intended. The penitents, familiar with the tactics of the revival, were disappointed and confused. This was something new and strange, and they were wholly unprepared. Barton Stone's sensi-

---

[8] *Autobiography of Barton Stone.*

tive mind quickly saw that what he had said had produced a "chilling effect."[9] He had often been thrilled by the warmth of the emotional reaction to his words on such occasions, and he was disappointed. He declined to repeat the experiment.

Some years later Walter Scott, an ardent and excitable man, though naturally timid and vacillating, came to the conclusion that the Bible plainly set forth the idea that baptism was for "remission of sin." He had studied long, "about the discordant and confused ideas relating to conversion"[10] and in spite of all he could do "baptism seemed to present itself as in some way intimately connected with the personal enjoyment of the blessings of the gospel,"[11] but he "was unable to perceive its exact position . . . in relation to other requirements."[12] Once he tentatively spoke in a sermon of baptism as "designed to be a pledge of the remission of sin."[13] Being very much given to analysis and arrangement he soon placed the "various items of the gospel" in a consecutive order that appealed to him as scriptural: (1) faith; (2) repentance; (3) baptism; (4) remission of sins; (5) reception of the Holy Spirit. This arrangement he said seemed to him almost like a "revelation." Perhaps it was one. He longed to present this "clue to the labyrinth in which they were involved in relation to conversion," but his timid nature made him fear to introduce more disorder. At length he ventured to do so, and though his efforts met failure at first, he was surprised at his second invitation to receive a candidate for baptism in the person of William Amend,[14] who on November 18, 1827, was baptized by immersion at New Lisbon, Ohio, "for the remission of sins." From then on such baptism became general in the Western Reserve.

Other ideas were advanced. A peculiar sect called the Restorationalists actually revolted against eternal damnation and taught an infamous heresy (according to the orthodox believer): that

---
[9]*Ibid.*
[10]*Memoirs of Alexander Campbell,* by Richardson, page 207.
[11]*Ibid.*   [12]*Ibid.*   [13]*Ibid.*
[14]This is the same William Amend who united with the Latter Day Saints in Ohio, and whose descendants are now numbered with the church.

the wicked would "be restored to grace" after a due amount of punishment.[15]

Thus did the revival shake to its foundations the religious structure of the West. Conservatives clung to the old creeds, the crystallized thought of the ages; radicals demanded they be thrown into the scrap heap, and a return made to the simple truths of the New Testament.

One of the chief reformers of the day, that indomitable Scotchman, Alexander Campbell, voiced the spirit of his time when he declared he would dissolve the whole superstructure of the church and go back to the simplicity of apostolic times. "Christian union," he said, "can result from nothing short of the destruction of creeds and confessions of faith, inasmuch as human creeds and confessions have destroyed Christian union."[16]

And Barton Stone applauded his statement in a letter to him, declaring that he had watched him "with the arm of a Samson, and the courage of a David tearing away the long-established foundations of partyism, human authoritative creeds, and confessions."[17]

---

[15] The Restorationalists of Ohio did not believe in the restoration of the gospel as preached by the Latter Day Saints, but in a restoration of the wicked to divine favor.
[16] *A Short History of the Christian Church*, by John F. Hurst, page 557.
[17] *The Christian Baptist*, early in 1827.

IV.—The Golden Plates

*A*LTHOUGH THE GREAT REVIVAL was a significant result of the reaction that swept over America in the early part of the nineteenth century (and it was "noteworthy that in the contemporary literature of the first forty years of this century, no subject so engrossed the interest of the Christian public as did these revivals,")[1] its "most brilliant decade, between 1830 and 1840"[2] was marked by several remarkable events; for this re-awakening, as had been the case in no previous intellectual revival, spread into practical, utilitarian, and commercial channels. This decade saw the establishment of the railroad, the electric telegraph, and the ocean steamship.

On the 6th day of April, in the first year of this "most brilliant" decade of American history (1830) the Church of Jesus Christ of Latter Day Saints was organized at Fayette, New York, just seven months before the first American railroad train, the diminutive and experimental forerunner of modern methods of transportation, made a trial trip from Schenectady to Albany in the state of New York, a distance of seventeen miles (November 2, 1830).

The organization of the church was the result of a series of most unusual happenings in western New York, then a pioneer state. The revivals started in the South had spread northward through the trans-Allegheny region, and had reached their peak in New York in the early twenties. In and near the post-township of Palmyra, in what was then Ontario (later Wayne) County, a series of revivals had been held by the Presbyterian, Baptist, and Methodist Churches uniting, as was then the custom, in a non-

---
[1] *The Frontier Spirit in American Christianity*, by Peter G. Mode, Macmillan, 1923.
[2] *The Erie Canal Proceedings of New York State History Society for 1926*, by Noble Whitford, A.B., page 214.

proselyting attack upon the emotions of the community, a part of the general movement of that period, for "it spread from town to town, from county to county, and from state to state."[3]

Says William Smith, "The people in our neighborhood were very much stirred up with regard to religious matters by the preaching of a Mr. Lane,[4] an elder of the Methodist Church and celebrated throughout the country as a great 'revivalist preacher.' "[5]

Attending these revivals with most of his father's family was a country lad of about fourteen years by the name of Joseph Smith. The family had but one year before, after a few years' residence in the village of Palmyra, taken up some "new land on Stafford Street near the line of Palmyra."[6] "During the time of great excitement," he later wrote, "my feelings were deep," but after the height of the revival began to subside "notwithstanding the great love which the converts for these different faiths expressed at the time of their conversion, and the great zeal manifested by the respective clergy, who were active in getting up and promoting this extraordinary scene of religious feeling, in order to have everybody 'converted' as they pleased to call it, let them join what sect they pleased; yet, when the converts began to file off, some to one party, and some to another, it was seen that the seemingly good feelings of both the priests and the converts were more pretended than real, for a scene of great confusion and bad feeling ensued; priest contending against priest, and convert against convert, so that all the good feelings, one for another, if

---

[3]From a sermon by William Smith at Deloit, Iowa, June 8, 1884, *Saints' Herald*, Volume 31, page 643.
[4]Reverend George Lane, who since 1808 had been in charge of a circuit embracing all of the State of New York west of the Genesee River. Mr. Lane did the first Methodist preaching in the counties comprising the "Holland purchase." The courage, faith, zeal, and capacity for self-denial of these old-time circuitriders can hardly be overestimated. For incidents in Reverend Lane's ministry, see Gregg's history of Methodism as within the bounds of the Erie Annual Conference, as quoted in *History of Chautauqua County, New York*. Andrew W. Young, Buffalo, New York, Matthews and Warren, 1875, page 107.
[5]From *William Smith on Mormonism*, pages 6, 7, by William Smith, Herald Press, Lamoni, 1883.
[6]*History of the Pioneer Settlements of Phelps and Gorham's Purchase*, etc., by O. Turner, Rochester, 1851.

they ever had any, were entirely lost in a strife of words, and a contest about opinions."⁷

This young man's mother, his sister, and two of his brothers were soon won by the Presbyterian faith, and joined that church, but he himself "became somewhat partial to the Methodist sect,"⁸ and "felt some desire to be united with them,"⁹ and yet "found the confusion and strife among the different denominations" so great that "it was impossible for a person young as I was and so unacquainted with men and things, to come to any certain conclusion who was right and who was wrong. My mind at different times was greatly excited, the cry and tumult was so great and incessant. The Presbyterians were most decided against the Baptists and Methodists, and used all their powers of either reason, or sophistry to prove their errors, or at least to make the people think they were in error; on the other hand the Baptists and Methodists in their turn were equally zealous to establish their own tenets and disprove all others."¹⁰

"Considering that all could not be right, and that God could not be the author of so much confusion, I determined to investigate the subject more fully, believing that if God had a church, it would not be split up into factions, and that if he taught one society to worship one way, and administer in one set of ordinances, he would not teach another principles which were diametrically opposed. Believing the word of God, I had confidence in the declaration of James: 'If any of you lack wisdom, let him ask of God, that giveth to all men liberally, and upbraideth not; and it shall be given him,'¹¹ I retired to a secret place in a grove and began to call upon the Lord; while fervently engaged in supplication, my mind was taken away from the objects with which I was surrounded, and I was enwrapped in a heavenly vision and saw

---
7 *Times and Seasons,* Volume 3, page 727.
8 *Ibid.*   9 *Ibid.*
10 *Ibid.*
11 James 1:5.

two glorious personages who exactly resembled each other in features and likeness, surrounded with a brilliant light which eclipsed the sun at noonday. They told me that all religious denominations were believing in incorrect doctrines, and that none of them were acknowledged of God as his church and kingdom. And I was expressly commanded to 'go not after them,' at the same time receiving a promise that the fullness of the gospel should at some future time be made known unto me."[12]

Several days after, the boy was talking with one of the ministers who had been active during the revival, and told him all about the wonderful vision he had seen. To his surprise, the man, to whom he had looked as a spiritual adviser treated his communication not only lightly, but with contempt. For then, as now, "Pretensions to miraculous powers, . . . excited not only in persons of intelligence but in most men of sober thought, indignation or contempt."[13] The story spread among his friends, and the boy was subjected to all kinds of ridicule, and the cruelest kind of torment.

"Until after the angel appeared . . . it was never said that my father's family were lazy, shiftless, or poor,"[14] said his brother many years later. "The hand of fellowship was extended to us upon all sides,"[15] his mother tells us, and a contemporary of his grudgingly admits, "Joseph had a little ambition and some very laudable aspirations, and his mother's intellect occasionally shone out in him . . . especially when he used to help us solve some portentous question of moral and political ethics, in our juvenile debating club, which we moved down to the old red schoolhouse on Durfee Street, to get rid of the annoyance of critics who used to drop in upon us in the village; and subsequently after catching a spark of Methodism in the camp meeting down in the woods

---
[12]Letter of Joseph Smith to John Wentworth, *Times and Seasons*, Volume 3, pages 706, 707.
[13]*Theology Explained and Defended*, by Theodore Dwight, President of Yale College, page 153.
[14]William Smith in sermon preached at Deloit, Iowa, June 8, 1884, *Saints' Herald*, Volume 31, pages 643, 644.
[15]*Joseph Smith and His Progenitors*, by Lucy Smith, page 73.

THE GOLDEN PLATES

on the Vienna Road, he was a very passable exhorter in evening meetings."[16]

But now these days were over. No one could forget that young Joseph claimed to have seen a vision. "But strange or not, so it was, and was often cause of great sorrow to myself. However, it was nevertheless a fact that I had had a vision. I have thought since that I felt much like Paul when he made his defense before King Agrippa, and related the account of the vision he had when he 'saw a light and heard a voice.' . . . He had seen a vision, he knew he had, and all the persecution under heaven could not make it otherwise; and though they should persecute him unto death, yet he knew and would know unto his latest breath, that he had both seen a light, and heard a voice speaking to him, and all the world could not make him think or believe otherwise. So it was with me, I had actually seen a light, and in the midst of that light I saw two personages, and they did in reality speak unto me, or one of them did."[17]

He could not forget it. The things he had heard while alone that day in the woods would not down. Though he no longer mingled with the religious activities of the community, he pondered in his own heart over what had happened. It was, he said, "a great sorrow" to him, and yet he dare not disobey. Moments of temptation and rebellion were followed by hours of contrition, and at length on the evening of September 21, 1823, upon retiring to bed, he prayed for forgiveness for his rebellion and folly and also asked for a further manifestation of his standing before the Lord. He tells us that he had full confidence that he would receive an answer to his petitions, and he was not disappointed. His prayers were answered while he was still on his knees. Years after in answer to a letter of inquiry from John Wentworth of the *Chicago Democrat* he retold the story:

---

[16] *History of the Pioneer Settlement of Phelps and Gorham's Purchase*, etc., by O. Turner, Rochester, 1851.
[17] *Times and Seasons*, Volume 3, page 749.

"On the evening of the 21st of September, A. D., 1823, while I was praying unto God, and endeavoring to exercise faith in the precious promises of Scripture on a sudden a light like that of day, only of a far purer and more glorious appearance, and brightness burst into the room, indeed the first sight was as though the house was filled with consuming fire; the appearance produced a shock that affected the whole body; in a moment a personage stood before me surrounded with a glory yet greater than that with which I was already surrounded. This messenger proclaimed himself to be an angel of God sent to bring the joyful tidings, that the covenant which God made with ancient Israel was at hand to be fulfilled, that the preparatory work for the second coming of the Messiah was speedily to commence; that the time was at hand for the gospel in all its fullness to be preached in power unto all nations that a people might be prepared for the millennial reign.

"I was informed that I was chosen to be an instrument in the hands of God to bring about some of his purposes in this glorious dispensation.

"I was also informed concerning the aboriginal inhabitants of this country, and shown who they were, and from whence they came; a brief sketch of their origin, progress, civilization, laws, governments, of their righteousness and iniquity, and the blessings of God being finally withdrawn from them as a people was made known unto me: I was also told where there were deposited some plates on which were engraven an abridgment of the records of the ancient prophets that had existed on this continent. The angel appeared to me three times the same night and unfolded the same things."[18]

The next morning in the field Joseph told his father what he had seen. His father believed him, as did the rest of the family, and he was advised to follow the directions of the angel and find the plates. Accordingly he left the field and says he went im-

---

[18]*Times and Seasons*, Volume 3, page 707. See Volume 3, pages 727, 728, 748, 749.

mediately to the place pointed out in the vision. "Convenient to the village of Manchester, Ontario County, New York, stands a hill of considerable size, and the most elevated of any in the neighborhood; on the west side of this hill not far from the top, under a stone of considerable size, lay the plates deposited in a stone box: this stone was thick and rounding in the middle on the upper side, and thinner towards the edges, so that the middle part of it was visible above the ground, but the edge all around was covered with earth. Having removed the earth," he says, "and having obtained a lever which I got fixed under the edge of the stone and with a little exertion raised it up, I looked in and there indeed did I behold the plates, the Urim and Thummim and the Breastplate, as stated by the messenger. The box in which they lay was formed by laying stones together in some kind of cement; in the bottom of the box were laid two stones crossways of the box, and on these stones lay the plates and the other things with them."[19] He tells us he made an attempt to take them out, but was forbidden to touch them. We are elsewhere told that he had already laid some of the plates by his side upon the ground, when the idea, natural to a lad of less than eighteen, came to him that there might be treasure buried with them. He stooped to look in the box when the plates were returned to the box, and he was forbidden to take them again. The plates could not be had for the purpose of making money.

"I remember how the family wept when they found Joseph could not get the plates at that time,"[20] said his brother, William as an old man. "The circumstances that occurred and the impressions made upon my mind at that time I can remember better than that which occurred two years ago. We were all looking forward for the time to come, father, mother, brothers, and sisters."[21] William was twelve years old at the time.

---

[19] *Times and Seasons*, Volume 3, page 771.
[20] Sermon of William Smith at Deloit, Iowa, June 8, 1884, *Saints' Herald*, Volume 31, pages 643, 644.
[21] *Ibid.*

Joseph was no longer in doubt as to his mission, nor unsatisfied with what he considered his destiny. Annually on the anniversary of this event he visited the spot on the hill, and reported to the assembled family all that had occurred. Never during the next four years, he told them, had the angel failed to meet and instruct him there.

Work on the homestead continued from day to day, much as it did with many of their neighbors. "After my father's family moved to New York State, in about five years they cleared sixty acres of land and fenced it. The timber on the land was very heavy. Some of the elms were so large that we had to 'nigger' them off. They were too large to be cut with a crosscut saw." The three elder boys of the family, Alvin, Hyrum, and Joseph, bore the burden of the work. When there was extra expense or the family income was low, one of the younger boys "worked out" as most farm boys of their time did to help with the common expenses.

"Yes, sir: I knew all of the Smith family, well," said an old neighbor, Orlando Saunders, "there were six boys, Alvin, Hyrum, Joseph, Harrison, William, and Carlos, and there were two girls; the old man was a cooper, they have all worked for me many a day; they were very good people. Young Joe (as we called him then) has worked for me, and he was a good worker; they all were. I did not consider them good managers about business, but they were poor people, the old man had a large family." So far as young Joseph was concerned, Saunders went on to insist he knew him "just as well as one could very well; he has worked for me many a time, and been about my place a great deal. He stopped with me many a time, when through here, after they went west to Kirtland; he was always a gentleman when about my place."[22]

---

[22] From a series of interviews made by Wm. H. and Edmund L. Kelley with old settlers in and around Palmyra, N. Y. For all this interesting series, see *Saints' Herald* for 1881; or *From Palmyra to Independence*, pages 341 to 378. The quotation from Saunders appears on pages 360, 361. Saunders was not a Latter Day Saint, had seen the Book of Mormon but never read it; "cared nothing about it."

THE GOLDEN PLATES 39

In the summer of 1823,[23] the boys with Alvin in charge began to replace the family log cabin with a "frame dwelling house," that badge of prosperity of the pioneer. It was a proud moment for them all. But Alvin died before the new house was finished, a never-forgotten sorrow to the entire family. His last request to his brothers was that they finish the new home for their mother. This they did but much of the joy of moving into it had vanished.

Pioneer life, except for the promise of the "golden plates," continued much the same after Alvin was gone. The Smiths dispensed hospitality in the new house as they had in the log cabin.[24] One of the regular visitors was a prosperous miller, Joseph Knight, from Colesville, Broome County, where he owned a gristmill on the Susquehanna River. Although blessed with three sons of his own and four daughters, there were times that farm and millwork required an extra hand, and Knight had several times hired young Joseph Smith. The young people in the Knight home were pleasant, and he enjoyed going there. They liked him, too. Mrs. Knight treated him as her own son. Mr. Knight was not a church member though he favored the "Universalist doctrine."[25] "Faithful and true, evenhanded and exemplary, virtuous and kind, never deviating to the right hand or the left,"[26] the erstwhile young millhand characterized him in later years. And the Knight boys with whom he wrestled and played in his young days, were his tried and trusty companions down the tempestuous years to the

---

[23]Earlier editions of this book gave the date 1824. This date was used since it agreed with the date of Alvin's death (November 19, 1824) as recorded in Joseph Smith, Jr.'s autobiography in *Times and Seasons*, Volume 3, page 772, and with Lucy Smith's *Joseph Smith and His Progenitors*. Recent research, however, indicates this is in error. The Wayne County *Sentinel* of Palmyra, New York, on September 25, 1824, carried a notice signed by Joseph Smith, Sr., to the effect that there being a rumor that Alvin's body had been disinterred, he, with friends, had opened the grave and found the body undisturbed. This proves conclusively that Alvin died prior to that date. On the tombstone at Alvin's grave in the old cemetery across from the Catholic Church in Palmyra is an inscription showing date of death as November 19, 1823.
[24]Since the entire Smith family agrees that the frame house was not finished at the time of Alvin Smith's death, and that almost the last words he uttered admonished his younger brothers to finish the new house for which the logs were hauled, we must conclude that any spiritual manifestations given before November 19, 1823, to Joseph Smith must have been received in the old log house. This includes the vision of September 21, 1823.
[25]*Millennial Star*, Volume 19, page 756.
[26]*Ibid.*

end of his life. "I record their names," he once said, when he was tortured and hunted far from those peaceful Susquehanna hills, "with unspeakable delight, for they are my friends."[27]

Once a year it was the custom of Joseph Knight to visit the farmers in neighboring counties and contract for wheat to be delivered at his mill in the fall. Upon some of these visits he was accompanied by an old friend, Josiah Stoal, from Bainbridge, New York. The old gentleman had conceived the idea of searching for an ancient silver mine, supposed by neighborhood tradition to have been opened by the Spaniards somewhere in the hills, near Harmony,[28] in Susquehanna County, Pennsylvania. Spanish treasure was in those days the popular myth with all classes of society. Upon recommendation of his friend Knight, Stoal secured the services of young Smith, and took him to Pennsylvania and put him to board with other "hands" at the prosperous farm home of Isaac Hale in Harmony.

The Spanish treasure never materialized, and the disappointed treasure seeker was finally persuaded to abandon the quest, but not before young Joseph Smith had found time during moonlit nights on the Susquehanna to embark on a more successful treasure hunt of his own. Emma, dark-eyed daughter of the Hales, found it easy to like the young stranger from New York, but the story of Joseph's visions had followed him, and canny old Isaac Hale was doubtful of the sort of farmer that could be made from a young man who saw and heard such unusual sights and sounds. Having once determined what he wanted, it was never easy for Joseph Smith to give up because of obstacles, and he records in this case he was "under the necessity of taking her elsewhere, so we went and were married at the house of Squire Tarbell in South Bainbridge [now Afton], Chenango County, New York." The marriage occurred on January 18, 1827, and the young couple

---

[27] *Millennial Star*, Volume 19, page 756.
[28] Now called Oakland. This is not the Harmony where the Rappite colony existed, as is popularly supposed. There were two Harmonys in Pennsylvania. The other famed for the Rappite community was in Butler County, across the State from Susquehanna County.

went immediately to Manchester where they lived with the elder Smiths for a year.

Later in the year on the historical date of September 22, when Joseph Smith made his annual visit to the hill of promise, he took his wife, and borrowed a horse and carriage from a miller from Colesville, Joseph Knight, who happened to be there that evening. The trip was taken secretly, but Joseph knew he was welcome to the horse and traveling equipage of this old friend. Joseph and Emma left sometime after midnight, and that morning[29] he brought back the cherished plates.

But the longed-for adventure had only begun. The story of the golden plates spread abroad in the neighborhood; they must be protected from theft and danger. There was a book to be translated and published, and Joseph was uneducated and poor.

---
[29] Letter to the *Saints' Herald* from Catherine Salisbury, sister to Joseph Smith. She wrote from Fountain Green, Illinois, March 10, 1886. *Saints' Herald*, Lamoni, Volume 33, page 260. Catherine says, "He was commanded to go on the 22d day of September, 1827, at 2 o'clock." See also *Joseph Smith and His Progenitors* by Lucy Smith, Chapter XXIII, and Andrew Jensen's *Biographical Encyclopedia*, Volume II, pages 772-73.

V.—Joseph Smith

Joseph Smith was the fourth child and third son of Joseph Smith and Lucy Mack Smith,[1] and was born December 23, 1805, at Sharon, Windsor County, Vermont. He had the usual training and background of the New England boy of that period. His parents though poor, had perhaps more than the average common school education, as both were schoolteachers at one time or another in their native Vermont. As a business man, Joseph, Sr., evidently, was not a success. He worked hard all his life, but had more than once been a victim of overconfidence and shrewd speculators. His son inherited that overconfidence, and suffered for it. Though with the charm peculiar to those who have no thought of commercialism, he drew to his side many tried and true friends who would stay with him to the finish, yet to the end of his life the younger Joseph was never able to cope with the insidious advances and devious tactics of wily speculators and sycophants. After a series of crop failures in Vermont, many farmers became discouraged and moved to the newer State of New York, the Smiths among them.

The place selected was Palmyra, a post-township in what was then Ontario County (now Wayne County), a place fifteen miles north of Canandaigua, and about two hundred twenty-three miles west of Albany. Here in what was known as Phelps and Gorham's Purchase was much "new land" and at the same time "the settlements were of such a date as to give farming ease and independence to the inhabitants."[2] Palmyra itself was a "place of considerable business,"[3] the business evidently being that of weaving, for

---

[1] *Ancestry and Posterity of Joseph Smith and Emma Hale*, by Mary Audentia Smith Anderson, Independence, Missouri, 1929, contains a detailed account of ancestry of Joseph Smith.
[2] *A Gazeteer of New York*, by Horatio Gates Spofford, Albany, 1813, page 27.
[3] *Ibid.*

the town boasted a yearly output of 53,719 yards of cloth. There was also a "handsome collection of houses"[4] in 1810, housing a population of 2,187 souls, grouped in 355 families, with 290 heads of families able to qualify financially as senatorial electors. There was a "large meeting of Quakers, and one Episcopal church"[5] and a "competent number of common schools."[6] Through the full length of the little town from west to east ran Mud Creek "affording fine advantages for mills" and "of some little use for navigation"[7] (Palmyra was later to become an Erie Canal town.) The main road from Canandaigua to Sodas Bay led across the east part of the town, with "many other roads in different directions,"[8] truly no mean pioneer village.

Upon the enigma that was the real Joseph Smith, writers will probably never even approach agreement. To his six feet in stature, his physical strength, his fair hair, and his blue eyes, perhaps all might agree, but beyond that, no man has ever been characterized so variously. For who has yet analyzed the mysterious elements of flamed genius? Who can deny some of the attributes of genius to this dynamic young man? Though his life was snuffed out before he reached his meridian, from the day he made claim to a revelation from God to the end of his brief career, he dominated his surroundings so powerfully for fourteen years, that the story of the making of the West cannot be told without tribute to him and that "peculiar" people who, under his leadership became exponents of a philosophy of life that set them apart from others of their kind.

To such spirits as his, restless, tragic, but always spiritually free, vitalized by some perennial inner spring of imagination, courage, and self-faith, belong the youth of every new movement. When he said of himself that his name would be known for good and evil among all people, he spoke truly. Some have called him weak. Yet nature allotted to him that gift no training can emulate, to

---

[4] Ibid. [5] Ibid. [6] Ibid. [7] Ibid. [8] Ibid.

call men to his side and keep them there, through scenes that tried the sturdiest souls. Alexander W. Doniphan, who knew him so well in Missouri, used whimsically to say that Lyman Wight was the bravest man he ever knew; Sidney Rigdon the greatest orator, but no one else could have them all working together, but Joe Smith. "Ah," remarked David Whitmer in his old age, "Joseph was a good man, but he had a hard task to manage with the people in the early days of the church. They were sectarian . . . and came in with all of their own views, and were hard to manage."[9]

And yet, in a little more than a decade he drew and held to his standard over 200,000 of these diverse personalities, and that too in spite of the most severe persecution:

> I don't think the man ever lived who was more beloved by his people; they would have interposed their own lives to shield him. The world knew him not. In the palmy days of Nauvoo, visitors were constantly arriving, with curiosity sharpened by Madam Rumor, to interview the man of whom so much was said. They beheld a beautiful city, where once was a stagnant, fever-breeding locality; a well-ordered community of 25,000 persons, as busy and industrious as bees, gathered from all quarters through the influence of the gospel, and presided over by a man whom all loved, and whose lightest wish was respected . . . . In those days I never saw a drunken person staggering on the streets, nor heard a profane oath uttered by any of the multitudes daily met there.[10]

"David Whitmer," says a reporter to the Chicago *Tribune* in 1886, "always asserted that Joseph Smith, as he knew him, was a righteous, God-fearing man." "I was well and intimately acquainted with the Prophet Joseph," said Lucius Merchant, one of the pilgrims from the loved city, after more than sixty years had passed, and he lay upon his deathbed. "I saw and heard him, both in private and public. I never heard him say an immoral word or *do an unkind act*. We loved him deeply, and when he was mar-

---

[9]Letter of E. C. Briggs in *Saints' Herald*, Volume 31, page 397.
[10]Letter of Edward Page in *Saints' Herald*, Volume 3, page 36.

tyred, you may be sure the mourning and distress can never be imagined; known only to those who were there."[11]

Even the children remembered him, and carried the memory of his kindness down into their own old age.

I can remember (I shall never forget) the day when Joseph and Hyrum were assassinated at Carthage. It was the darkest day of my life [wrote one white-haired old lady, telling of a life more than full of pioneer danger and adventure], no scene before nor since has struck such terror to my heart. Joseph, when living, often patted my head and said, "You're a little Ephraimite." How I loved that man! And I know now even as I knew then, that he was a man of God, a true prophet.[12]

Again she speaks of him as a man who "would divide his last loaf with his brethren."[13]

He particularly loved children, always noticed them as he went along the street, and found time from a very busy life to play with them, recorded ofttimes the clever sayings of his own children in his journal, told of taking his children for a ride in the new carriage, and of "sliding on the ice with little Frederick."

He seldom passed a group of boys playing ball on the green, but he took turn at the bat. After two or three rounds, batting the ball over the fence, he would say, "Over the fence is out," and go on to his office or council meeting, with the adoring eyes of his small companions following him admiringly.

Among animals, horses and dogs were favorites with him, but he could hardly endure to see cruelty to any creature. He did not like to see a man kill even a snake needlessly, and at one time a reprimand from him to a surly follower who kicked a stray dog nearly provoked a church court. His black horse Charley receives an honorable mention in his journal, as if he were a human friend. And was not such a horse as "Charley," companion of so many of his wanderings, really a friend? A second favorite horse called by some whim "Joe Duncan" after a political arch-enemy, was commonly addressed as "Governor" in mild derision

---
[11]Chicago *Tribune* for December 15, 1885;*Saints' Herald*, Volume 33, page 14. *Testimony of the Past*, by Alma Fyrando, *Journal of History*, Volume 3, page 252.
[12]"Autobiography," Sylvia C. Webb, *Saints' Herald*, March 24, 1915, page 290.
[13]*Ibid.*, page 291.

of the gubernatorial aspirations of his namesake. Then there was his great mastiff Major, who faithfully served and protected him all his life, and would have followed him to his death if he could. "Beware of a man whom children and dogs do not like," has often been said. Not always perhaps a safe standard of judgment, and yet what is a greater measure of a man's humbleness than his kindness to the weak and helpless?

Throughout his life he kept open house, alike to friend and stranger. Says one, "I have found Joseph Smith living in a tent, having given up his home as a hospital for the sick."[14] His home was always filled with the ill, the lame, the unfortunate; and many are the stories told of his sacrifice of self, his kindness to the poor, his sympathy for the unfortunate, and his perhaps too ready forgiveness for the erring.

He has been called unscrupulous. In his journal, intended for no eyes but his own, he once wrote, "My heart is full of desire today, to be blessed with prosperity, until I will be able to pay all my debts; for it is the delight of my soul to be honest. O Lord, that thou knowest right well."[15] When states and cities were repudiating the debts caused by the depression of 1837, he and his church were attempting to meet their obligations, despite the universal financial wreckage about them.

In an age where intemperance was the rule, he preached temperance. "The statesman of the thirties who did not drink heavily was a rarity. Just as whisky, brandy, gin, and wine were served in great decanters on the tables at hotels, at the boarding houses every guest had his bottle or interest in a bottle."[16] At the national capital among the leading men of the nation, temperance was as rare as drunkenness is today:

On the way to the capitol the statesman could quench his thirst at numerous bars—and often did. And in the basement of the capitol

---

[14]"Autobiography," Moses Nickerson, *Saints' Herald*, Volume 17, page 424, *seq.*
[15]*Church History*, Volume 1, page 586.
[16]*Figures of the Past*, by Josiah Quincy.

building whiskey could be had. Never in American history have so many promising careers been wrecked by drunkenness as during the third decade; frequently national celebrities would appear upon the floor of the House or Senate in a state of intoxication, and at least on one occasion, the greater part of the House was hilariously drunk.[17]

At such a time in the history of the country, before anyone ever dreamed of prohibition, Joseph Smith wrote: "O my God! how long will this monster intemperance find its victims on the earth? Methinks until . . . Christ's kingdom becomes universal."[18] He was one of the first thinkers to associate temperance with religion.

Unschooled, he was all his life an eager student. Forced by reason of his position to write much, he longed to sprinkle his letters with the foreign phrases so favored by rhetoricians of his time, an ambition he was at length able to indulge, with little improvement to his naturally plain English diction. As long as he lived he was taking lessons in something. Very early in his life he confided to his Journal:

> My soul delights in reading the word of the Lord in the original, and I am determined to pursue the study of the languages until I shall become master of them, if I am permitted to live long enough. At any rate, so long as I do live, I am determined to make this my object; and with the blessing of God I shall succeed to my satisfaction.[19]

He has been called a bigot. History shows him tolerant. He "wept over the mob of Missouri and Philadelphia alike," says Lyman Wight, when in a race riot against the Negroes in 1834, thirty houses were destroyed, a church pulled down, and several killed in the "city of brotherly love." Joseph Smith, referring to the burning of the Ursaline Convent near Boston in 1834, wrote:

> The early settlers of Boston (the Emporium of New England) who had fled from their mother country to avoid persecution and death, soon became so lost to principles of justice and religious liberty as to whip and hang the Baptist and the Quaker, who, like themselves, had

---
[17] *Party Battles of the Jackson Period*, by C. G. Bowers, page 19.
[18] *Church History*, Volume 2, page 31.
[19] *Ibid.*, page 26.

fled from tyranny to a land of freedom; and the Fathers of Salem, from 1691 to 1693, whipped, imprisoned, tortured, and hung many of their citizens for supposed witchcraft; and quite recently, while boasting of her light and knowledge, of her laws and religion, as surpassed by none on earth, has New England been guilty of burning a Catholic convent in the vicinity of Charlestown [1834], and of scattering the inmates to the four winds; yes, in sight of the very spot where the fire of the American Independence was first kindled, where a monument is now erecting in memory of the battle of Bunker Hill, and the fate of the immortal Warren, who bled, who died on those sacred heights, to purchase religious liberty for his country; in sight of this very spot, have the religionists of the nineteenth century demolished a noble brick edifice, hurling its inhabitants forth upon a cold, unfeeling world for protection and subsistence.[20]

He has been called lazy and shiftless. His journals show days filled with more activity than the average man could encompass in twice the time. Men who were his employers in his boyhood were numbered among the most enthusiastic of his followers, Josiah Stoal, Joseph Knight, Ezra Thayre,[21] and all unite in praising his honesty and industry.

He was a man and had a man's faults, but his motives and ambitions were pure. He was not a thief, a libertine, or a charlatan. When a man has a "yellow streak," it goes all the way through. He was fitted for leadership by nature. He had never studied psychology; never heard of the expulsive power of new affection, but when the depression of 1837 hit the church in Kirtland, burdened as was the rest of the country with the collapse of overspeculation, he said, "God revealed to me that something *new* must be done for the salvation of the church," and he approached the young church, threatened with destruction by internal strife, proposed the church's first foreign mission, and sent off to England, after nine days of preparation, the first missionaries to another land! Six men, limited financially to a gift of five dollars from a young lady, Mary Fielding, but unlimited in spirit because of a boundless faith and a great courage. And the mind of the church, unhappily rent

---
[20]*Church History*, Volume 2, pages 81, 82.
[21]A bridge, dam, and mill builder near Palmyra. See *Memoirs*, W. W. Blair, pages 39, 40.

by a national crisis, united with renewed zeal on the first foreign mission of the church. From a human standpoint it was a bold stroke, a foolhardy one; from the standpoint of prophetic vision it was more than justified. The mission was a success—a great success!

Perhaps as Edward Page said, "The world never knew him!" Perhaps his life and character have yet to be properly appraised. And yet even in his own time Josiah Quincy gave him almost too extravagant praise:

> It is by no means improbable that some future textbook, for the use of generations yet unborn, will contain a question something like this: What historical American of the nineteenth century has exerted the most powerful influence upon the destinies of his countrymen? And it is by no means impossible that the answer to that interrogatory may be thus written: Joseph Smith, the Mormon prophet. And the reply, absurd as it doubtless seems to most men now living, may be an obvious commonplace to their descendants. History deals in surprises and paradoxes quite as startling as this. The man who established a religion in this age of free debate, who was and is today accepted by hundreds of thousands as a direct emissary from the Most High—such a rare human being is not to be disposed of by pelting his memory with unsavory epithets. Fanatic, impostor, charlatan, he may have been; but these hard names furnish no solution to the problem he presents to us. Fanatics and impostors are living and dying every day, and their memory is buried with them; but the wonderful influence which this founder of a religion exerted and still exerts throws him into relief before us, not as a rogue to be criminated, but as a phenomenon to be explained . . . . Joseph Smith, claiming to be an inspired teacher, faced adversity such as few men have been called to meet, enjoyed a brief season of prosperity such as few men have ever attained, and, finally, forty-three days after I saw him, went cheerfully to a martyr's death.[22]

But in 1827 back in New York, before the world had anything to say about him, he was but an inexperienced youth, with confidence in his mission and a bundle of golden plates inscribed in an unknown language, sadly in need of help, and nowhere to turn for it. He did as he had done before in his life. He depended upon the Lord, and the Lord did not fail him.

---

[22]*Figures of the Past*, by Josiah Quincy, pages 376, 377, quoted in *Church History*, Volume 1, page 3.

VI.—Friends

ONE OF THE OLDEST AND MOST comfortably situated of the pioneer families of Palmyra was that of Nathan Harris, for he had come early to that locality. With other children was a small son, Martin, born May 18, 1783, in Eastown, Saratoga County, New York. Although he did not know it then, all of Nathan's claim to future public recognition rested in that boy. Perhaps he never knew it. Probably if he had been asked the greatest moment of his life, he would have told of a day in 1792 "when he drew a net across Genargau Creek . . . and caught eighteen large salmon." Fishermen are like that, and Nathan Harris was the greatest hunter and fisherman in all Palmyra.

He was a jovial man, open-hearted and hospitable. Nature had been kind to him and given him plenty, and he dispensed it generously. The parties at the pioneer home of the Harrises in those early days, while the Government of the United States was still in its infancy, have gone down in the contemporary annals of the period as times when pioneer hospitality fairly outshone itself in its lavish scale of entertainment. One very old book gives a graphic account of a "husking frolic" at Nathan Harris's in 1796:

> We had a pot pie baked in a lard kettle, composed of thirteen fowls, as many squirrels, and due proportions of beef, mutton, and venison; baked meats; beans and large pumpkin pies. Hunting stories, singing, dancing on a split basswood floor; snap and catch 'em; jumping the broomstick; and hunt the squirrel, followed the feast.[1]

Just when or how Martin Harris became interested in Joseph Smith is not known. He was a man of middle age when he began to take an interest in the unusual events centering around the

---

[1] *History of the Pioneer Settlement of Phelps and Gorham's Purchase*, etc., by O. Turner, Rochester, 1851.

golden plates—"an honorable man; one of the first men of the town."[2] He had married a daughter of his father's brother, his own cousin, rather a sharp-tongued lady we have been told. Perhaps she was honestly skeptical, and did not like to see good Harris money going into visionary schemes. Anyway, she was in the habit of demanding value received for what went out, and seeing that she got it, which was apt to involve Martin in all sorts of predicaments as time went on. Martin had been guilty of acts of overgenerosity at other times in his life, and Lucy Harris was practical, thrifty, and saving.

Certain it is that so far as Joseph Smith was concerned, nothing could ever convince him that the Lord had not moved upon the heart of this well-to-do neighbor to help him in his hour of need. He says:

> The excitement, however, still continued, and rumor with her thousand tongues was all the time employed in circulating tales about my father's family, and about myself. If I were to relate a thousandth part of them it would fill up volumes. The persecution, however, became so intolerable that I was under the necessity of leaving Manchester, and going with my wife to Susquehanna County in the State of Pennsylvania. While preparing to start (being very poor and the persecution so heavy upon us that there was no probability that we would ever be otherwise), in the midst of our afflictions we found a friend in a gentleman by the name of Martin Harris, who came to us and gave me fifty dollars to assist us in our afflictions. Mr. Harris was a resident of Palmyra Township, Wayne County, in the State of New York, and a farmer of respectability. By this timely aid I was enabled to reach the place of my destination in Pennsylvania.[3]

Whatever may have been his purpose at that time, Martin Harris soon cast in his lot wholeheartedly with the new work. In the years that came he lost his farm, his money, his wife, and children for the sake of the "angel message," but he remained unshaken in his allegiance to the last.

---

[2] Interview of Edmund L. Kelley and Wm. H. Kelley with Orlando Saunders, an old settler in Palmyra, published in *Saints' Herald* (1881); also *From Palmyra to Independence*, by R. Etzenhouser, page 361, Ensign Publishing House, Independence, Missouri, 1894.
[3] *Church History*, Volume 1, page 18.

THE STORY OF THE CHURCH

Joseph Smith was to have another trusted friend, young Oliver Cowdery,[4] who came to teach school on Stafford Street near where the Smith family resided, and Oliver boarded in the Smith home.

Oliver had not been in the Smith family long, before they told him the strange story of a young man of the household, now gone with his young wife to her father's home in Harmony, Pennsylvania; of gold plates; and miraculous angelic visitations. He liked the Smiths and believed their story, or almost believed it, for he had found them honest. Sometime previous to this Oliver had taught school in Fayette, New York, some twenty-five miles distant. Here he had met and made his friends, the entire family of the Pennsylvania German farmer, Peter Whitmer. There were seven children in the family, five sons and two daughters. David, the fourth son, was his especial friend and companion. Catherine Whitmer, the older sister, was married to Hiram Page; and the winsome Elizabeth Ann, the youngest child of the family, was everybody's pet.

Peter Whitmer, Sr., was a hard-working, God-fearing man, a strict Presbyterian, and had brought his children up with rigid sectarian discipline. David was born January 7, 1805, at a small trading post near Harrisburg, Pennsylvania, and was brought in his infancy with his three older brothers to the farm in Fayette Township, two miles from Waterloo, seven from Geneva, and twenty-five from Palmyra, where he had since lived. The Whitmers were thrifty and prosperous.

David tells his own story:

I first heard of what is now termed Mormonism in the year 1828. I made a business trip to Palmyra, New York, and while there stopped with one Oliver Cowdery. A great many people in the neighborhood were talking about the finding of certain golden plates by one Joseph

---

[4]In the fall of 1828, a young man by the name of Lyman Cowdery came to the Smith neighborhood, and applied to Hyrum, who was one of the board of trustees for the school, to teach the following winter. Hyrum called together the trustees and they hired Cowdery. But the following day, he came to them and said circumstances made it necessary for him to disappoint them, but brought with him his brother Oliver, whom he wished them to accept in his stead. Oliver Cowdery was born, October 3, 1806, in Wells, Rutland County, Vermont, but his father soon moved to the neighboring town of Poultney. In 1825 he followed his older brothers to western New York, where he clerked in a country store, then taught school in various places, until he made contact with Joseph Smith and the church.

Smith, junior, a young man of that neighborhood. Cowdery and I, as well as others, talked about the matter, but at the time I paid but little attention to it, supposing it to be only the idle gossip of the neighborhood. Cowdery said he was acquainted with the Smith family, and he believed there must be some truth in the story of the plates, and that he intended to investigate the matter. I had conversations with several young men who said that Joseph Smith certainly had golden plates. . . . These parties were so positive in their statements that I began to believe there must be some foundation for the stories then in circulation all over that part of the country. I had never seen any of the Smith family up to that time, and I began to inquire of the people in regard to them, and learned that one night during the year 1823, Joseph Smith, junior, had a vision and an angel appeared to him and told him where certain plates were to be found and pointed out the spot to him, and that shortly afterward he went to that place and found the plates which were still in his possession. After thinking over the matter for a long time, and talking with Cowdery, who also gave me a history of the finding of the plates, I went home, and after several months Cowdery told me he was going to Harmony, Pa.—whither Joseph Smith had gone with the plates on account of the persecution of his neighbors— and see him about the matter. He did go, and on his way stopped at my father's house, and told me that as soon as he found out anything, either truth or untruth, he would let me know. After he got there he became acquainted with Joseph Smith, and shortly afterward wrote to me, telling me that he was convinced that Joseph Smith had the records, and that he (Smith) had told him that it was the will of heaven that he (Cowdery) should be his scribe to assist in the translation of the plates. . . . Shortly after this Cowdery wrote me another letter, in which he gave me a few lines of what they had translated, and he assured me that he knew of a certainty that he had a record of a people that inhabited this continent, and that the plates they were translating gave a complete history of these people. When Cowdery wrote me these things and told me that he had revealed knowledge concerning the truth of them, I showed these letters to my parents, brothers, and sisters.[5]

And on another occasion David Whitmer said:

Before I knew Joseph I had heard about him and the plates from persons who declared they knew he had them, and swore they would get them from him. When Oliver Cowdery went to Pennsylvania, he promised to write me what he should learn about these matters, which he did. He told me that Joseph had told him his (Oliver's) secret

---

[5] Account given by Whitmer to a reporter for the Kansas City *Journal*, published there June 5, 1881. *Saints' Herald*, Volume 28, pages 197-199.

thoughts, and all that he had meditated about going to see him, which no man on earth knew, as he supposed, but himself.[6]

All of the Whitmer family became more or less prominent in the work. All went to Missouri. Oliver Cowdery and many of the Whitmers are buried near the village of Richmond in Ray County, Missouri. They never forsook their original story of how they came in touch with the work of translating the Book of Mormon and organizing the church.

---

[6]An interview with Orson Pratt and Joseph Smith, *Millennial Star*, Volume 45, page 538.

VII.—THE BOOK OF MORMON

*P*ERHAPS FROM THE STANDPOINT of literary critics there never has been a greater literary puzzle than the Book of Mormon. A number of "rational" explanations for it have been set forth by students, but of them all, none will bear critical examination. The one offered by those who really knew and played the star roles in the strange story, though often challenged, still stands untouched by any evidence of untruthfulness or fraud. Simple, straightforward, incredible as when they first told it, the three "witnesses" to the Book of Mormon, David Whitmer, Oliver Cowdery, and Martin Harris reaffirmed their testimony all through their ministry in the church; unchanged as years passed, though misunderstandings estranged them from Joseph Smith and the church; still unchanged down into old age; and each when death was imminent, with his last breath declared that he truly had seen the plates of gold, and heard the voice of an angel.

One of the first detailed descriptions of the "golden plates" to be published was given in February, 1842, in a letter from Joseph Smith to John Wentworth, editor of the Chicago *Democrat*. He said:

> These records were engraved on plates which had the appearance of gold, each plate was six inches wide and eight inches long and not quite as thick as common tin.
> They were filled with engravings, in Egyptian characters, and bound together in a volume, as the leaves of a book with three rings running through the whole.
> The volume was something near six inches in thickness, a part of which was sealed.
> The characters on the unsealed part were small and beautifully engraved.
> The whole book exhibited many marks of antiquity in its construction and much skill in the art of engraving.

With the records was found a curious instrument which the ancients called "Urim and Thummim" which consisted of two transparent stones set in the rims of a bow fastened to a breastplate.[1]

Two others (at least) of the men who claimed to have seen these curious records and the "Urim and Thummim," that "most mysterious thing in the Old Testament,"[2] have left their descriptions on record. Martin Harris in 1853:

> And as many of the plates as Joseph Smith translated, I handled with my hands, plate after plate.
> [Then, describing their dimensions, he pointed with one of the fingers of his left hand to the back of his right hand and said], I should think they were so long [or about eight inches] and about so thick [or about four inches] and each of the plates was thicker than the thickest tin.[3]

In 1881, David Whitmer gave his description as follows:

> They appeared to be of gold, about six inches by nine inches in size, about as thick as parchment, a great many in number, bound together like the leaves of a book by massive rings passing through the back edges. The engraving upon them was very plain and of very curious appearance.[4]

One of the very earliest published accounts of what the records were and the incidents connected with their discovery, coming from other than those who had received the story enthusiastically with all its implications, is that of O. Turner in his *History of the Pioneer Settlement of Phelps and Gorham's Purchase*.[5] Turner was well acquainted in the vicinity of Palmyra, and refers to one of the most generally accepted theories of the emergence of the Book of Mormon:

---

[1] *Times and Seasons*, Volume 3, page 707.
[2] John M. Zane, in *A Rare Judicial Service of Charles S. Zane*, Illinois State Historical Publications, 1826. For Urim and Thummim in the Old Testament, Ezekiel 28: 30; Leviticus 8: 8; Deuteronomy 33: 8; Ezra 2: 63; Numbers 17: 21; Nehemiah 7: 65; I Samuel 28: 6.
[3] *Millennial Star*, as quoted in the *Myth of Manuscript Found*, pages 88, 89.
[4] *Kansas City Journal*, June 5, 1881. See *Church History*, Volume 4, page 362; *Saints' Herald*, Volume 28, page 198.
[5] *History of the Pioneer Settlement of Phelps and Gorham's Purchase and Morris Reserve*, embracing counties of Monroe, Ontario, Livingston, Yates, Steuben, and parts of Orleans, Genesee, and Wyoming, 1851. Rochester, New York.

THE BOOK OF MORMON

It is believed by those who were best acquainted with the Smith family and most conversant with all the Gold Book movements that there is no foundation for the statement that the original manuscript was written by a Mr. Spaulding of Ohio . . . . The book itself is without doubt a production of the Smith family aided by Oliver Cowdery, who was a schoolteacher on Stafford Street, an intimate of the Smith family and identified with the whole matter.

His (Harris') version of the discovery, as communicated to him by the Prophet Joseph is well remembered by several respectable citizens in Palmyra to whom he made early disclosures. It was in substance as follows:

The Prophet Joseph was directed by an angel where to find, by excavation at the place afterwards called Mormon Hill, the golden plates; and was compelled by the angel, much against his will, to be the interpreter of the sacred record they contained and published it to the world; that the records contained a record of the ancient inhabitants of this country "engraved by Mormon, the son of Nephi"; that on top of the box containing the plates "a pair of large spectacles were found, the stones or glass set in which were opaque to all but the Prophet"; that these belonged to Mormon, the engraver of the plates, and without them the plates could not be read. Harris assumed that himself and Cowdery were the chosen amanuenses, and that the prophet curtained from the world and them with his spectacles read from the gold plates, what they had committed to paper . . . Harris had never seen the plates.[6]

This account written by one very adverse to the whole movement gives Harris' story so nearly in accord with all the versions of the principals, and vouching for its being Harris' disclosure to early inhabitants before the translation of the book and before he (Harris) had ever seen the plates, seems peculiarly corroborative, considering the length of time that had elapsed between 1827 and 1851 (date of publication) and the tendency of neighborhood tradition to increase in inaccuracy with age.

Letters were infrequent events in the log cabins of pioneers of that day, but the Smith household though humble, was different in this respect. An ordinary letter cost either its sender or recipient

---
[6]*History of Pioneer Settlement*, etc., O Turner, pages 214, 215.

twenty-five cents postage, which could be prepaid, or collected at the other end, nevertheless Lucy Smith, who loved to write, kept in communication with her family back in Gilsum, New Hampshire, and with her eldest brother's family in Michigan. Peculiarly enough one of these letters escaped the ravages of time, one written to her brother Solomon in Gilsum. On these yellowed bits of parchment, the carefully penned words of this pioneer mother, still remain, postmarked and dated—to give the lie to many a theory of the origin of that strange book. The letter to Solomon Mack under date of January 6, 1831, was written from Waterloo, and addressed to her brother and wife:

> Dear Brother and Sister: . . . By searching the prophecies contained in the Old Testament we find it there prophesied that God will set his hand the second time to recover his people the house of Israel. He has now commenced this work; He hath sent forth a revelation in these last days, and this revelation is called the Book of Mormon. . . . Perhaps you will inquire how this revelation came forth. It has been hid up in the earth fourteen hundred years, and was placed there by Moroni, one of the Nephites; it was engraven upon plates which had the appearance of gold . . . . Joseph after repenting of his sins and humbling himself before God, was visited by an holy angel whose countenance was as lightning and whose garments were white above all whiteness who gave unto him commandments which inspired him from on high; and who gave unto him, by the means of which was before prepared, that he should translate this book.[7]

Mother Lucy Smith also gives a very similar account in her book, *Joseph Smith and His Progenitors,* written in her last years, a very graphic and detailed account, though told in the garrulous manner of old age.

Standing in the pulpit at Deloit, Iowa, in 1884, the last venerable representative of the family who witnessed the coming of the "golden plates" into that lowly pioneer home in the forests of New York, William Smith told his plain, unvarnished story with the simplicity and fervor of an old man going back in memory to

---

[7] From a letter given to Joseph F. Smith of Salt Lake City, Utah, by Mrs. Candace Mack Barker of Keene, New Hampshire, granddaughter of Solomon Mack, published in *Scrapbook of Mormon Literature,* published by Ben E. Rich, Volume 1, pages 543-545.

his youth. The scenes he called to mind happened when he was just sixteen. They seemed plainer, he told his hearers, than things which had happened two years before:

> The time to receive the plates came at last. When Joseph received them, he came in and said: "Father, I have got the plates." All believed it was true, father, mother, brothers, and sisters. . . . Father knew his child was telling the truth. When the plates were brought in they were wrapped up in a tow frock. My father put them into a pillowcase. Father said, "What, Joseph, can we not see them?"[8] "No, I was disobedient the first time, but I intend to be faithful this time; for I was forbidden to show them until they are translated, but you can feel them." We handled them and could tell what they were. They were not quite as large as this Bible. Could tell whether they were round or square. Could raise the leaves this way (raising a few leaves of the Bible before him.) One could easily tell that they were not a stone or even a block of wood . . . . They were much heavier than stone, and very much heavier than wood. . . . I am a little too old a man to be telling stories. . . . I expect to stand before angels and arch angels and be judged for how I have told it.[9]

Joseph Smith had removed to his father-in-law's in Harmony, Pennsylvania, less than three months after he received the plates. Martin Harris had been overly enthusiastic; he had talked to many. Some of the family perhaps had been similarly indiscreet. Everybody in the vicinity had heard the story; buried gold of any sort meant fabulous wealth. The three months remaining in the year 1827 were filled with a hectic struggle to keep the plates hidden where they could not be stolen. The family resorted to all sorts of expedients. Once Emma took a long horseback ride to warn Joseph who was working some distance from home. It was apparent that the plates could not be translated in peace and quiet at Palmyra, so a change was imperative.

In February, 1828, Martin visited Joseph and took a carefully copied transcription of the characters to a professor in New York.

---

[8] Joseph's sister, Catherine Salisbury, in a letter from Fountain Green, Illinois, March 10, 1886, and published in the *Elders' Journal*, Chattanooga, Tennessee, Volume 4, page 60, says, "We had supposed that when he should bring them home, the whole family would be allowed to see them, but he said he was forbidden of the Lord. They could only be seen by those who were chosen to bear their testimony to the world" (*Saints' Herald*, Volume 33, page 260).
[9] Sermon by William Smith, Deloit, Iowa, June 8, 1884, as reported in the *Saints' Herald*, Volume 31, pages 643, 644.

Martin was still intent on proving to his neighbors in Palmyra that his confidence had not been misplaced. He asked Professor Anthon for a "certificate addressed to the people of Palmyra."

> Sometime in this month of February the aforementioned Mr. Martin Harris came to our place, got the characters which I had drawn off the plates, and started with them to the city of New York. For what took place relative to him and the characters, I refer to his own account of the circumstances as he related them to me after his return, which was as follows: "I went to the city of New York and presented the characters which had been translated, with the translation thereof, to Professor Anthon, a gentleman celebrated for his literary attainments. Professor Anthon stated that the translation was correct, more so than any he had before seen translated from the Egyptian. I then showed him those which were not yet translated, and he said that they were Egyptian, Chaldaic, Assyriac, and Arabic, and he said that they were the true characters. He gave me a certificate, certifying to the people of Palmyra that they were true characters, and that the translation of such of them as had been translated was also correct. I took the certificate and put it into my pocket, and was just leaving the house, when Mr. Anthon called me back, and asked me how the young man found out that there were gold plates in the place where he found them, I answered that an angel of God had revealed it unto him.
>
> "He then said to me, 'Let me see that certificate.' I accordingly took it out of my pocket and gave it to him, when he took it and tore it to pieces, saying that there was no such thing now as ministering of angels, and that if I would bring the plates to him, he would translate them. I informed him that part of the plates were sealed, and that I was forbidden to bring them. He replied, 'I cannot read a sealed book.' I left him and went to Doctor Mitchell, who sanctioned what Professor Anthon had said respecting both the characters and the translation."[10]

Martin returned crestfallen, without his certificate, but still secure in his belief that he could yet convince his wife and friends of Joseph's sincerity and the genuineness of what he had told them. He arranged his business in Palmyra, returned to Harmony, and acted as scribe for Joseph Smith from April 12 to June 14.

The work progressed very slowly, but Martin Harris was pleased as the pages mounted until he had written 116 pages of foolscap. He wanted to take the manuscript back to Palmyra to

---

[10] *Church History*, Volume 1, page 19.

show just a very few whom he desired so much to convince that he was not being ridiculous in his adherence to this strange work. But Joseph had been forbidden to let anyone see it. Harris pleaded. He would show it only to his wife, his brother, his mother and father, and his sister-in-law, and bring it right back. After all Joseph felt keenly he could have done nothing without Harris' aid, and it seemed such a small thing to yield to him in this one particular that meant so much to the peace of the home of his great benefactor. Joseph wavered and yielded. True, he bound Martin Harris with a "solemn covenant" which Martin did not intend to break, but in his desire to convert others, the manuscript was lost and never recovered.

It was a time of darkness and discouragement to Joseph. The days passed and Harris did not return. Joseph was censured by revelation for his disobedience. His wife became ill, almost died. His first-born son died at birth and was laid to rest in the family burial lot. Watching by Emma's bedside day and night, he pondered over the fate of the precious manuscript. He tried not to show his anxiety, but at length with that curious intuition women are said to possess, she sent him on a trip to his father's, to find out what had become of Martin. Harris was duly contrite, but the manuscript was gone, irretrievably gone! The plates had temporarily disappeared, and with them went the gift to translate. At length, after humble repentance and forgiveness, the precious commission returned, and he was bidden to translate. Emma was weak and frail from her long illness. Her father, a prosperous farmer, had become convinced during the production of the lost 116 pages of foolscap that his son-in-law was hopelessly lazy, or he would not sit in the house working over his foolish task, in the busiest time of the year on the farm. Joseph was trying to redeem himself with Isaac Hale by working long and arduous hours on the little place they were buying from Emma's father. Upon him lay the heavy consciousness of duty undone, but he could not farm and do the work assigned him, too. Emma helped him as best she could in what time she could spare from her household duties. He dared not trust again to Martin's vacillating hand. Months went by, and then one day in April, Joseph thought it was the 15th, Oliver says the 5th of April, 1829, the Palmyra schoolteacher appeared at the little farmhouse in Harmony. Some strange urging had forced Oliver to follow up the youth with the golden plates and find out the whole story.

Oliver was more than satisfied with what he saw and heard. Several years later, he wrote:

> Near the time of the setting of the sun, Sabbath evening, April 5, 1829, my natural eyes for the first time beheld Joseph Smith the Prophet. He then resided in Harmony, Susquehanna County, Pennsylvania. On Monday the 6th I assisted him in arranging some business of a temporal nature, and on Tuesday the 7th commenced to write the Book of Mormon. These were days never to be forgotten, to sit under the sound of a voice dictated by the inspiration of heaven, awakened the uttermost gratitude of this bosom! Day after day I continued, uninterrupted, to write from his mouth, as he translated, with the Urim and Thummim, or, as the Nephites would have said, "Interpreters," the history, or record, called The Book of Mormon.[11]

He immediately wrote his friend, David Whitmer, enthusiastically of his reception and David told his family. They all had confidence in Oliver Cowdery, the confidence of long acquaintance. Joseph was happy in what he considered another mark of God's providence. Henceforth he was to be no more alone, but companioned by a man young like himself, as divinely commissioned and converted to his share of the work, as Joseph was to his. There was but one growing cloud on the horizon. Isaac Hale was becoming more and more disgusted with his seemingly worthless son-in-law, for Joseph at the very time of spring planting wished to spend hour after hour closeted with this young schoolteacher, working upon a book, not only impractical, but perhaps even harmful to the peace of his family. Joseph, always sensitive to

---

[11] From a letter written W. W. Phelps, and dated Norton, Medina County, Ohio, September 7, 1834, and published in the *Saints' Messenger and Advocate,* Kirtland, Ohio, October, 1834 (first number of that publication).

THE BOOK OF MORMON

criticism, felt this growing antipathy. Oliver talked often of his friends, the Whitmers, of the peace and comfort of their fireside. Perhaps David had answered his letters with friendly confidence. One day Joseph told Oliver he had received directions to go to Fayette and continue his work there. Whitmer said:

> Soon after [Cowdery went to Pennsylvania] I received another letter from Cowdery telling me to come down to Pennsylvania, and bring him and Joseph to my father's house, giving as a reason therefor that they had received a commandment from God to that effect.[12]
>
> I did not know what to do, I was pressed with my work. I had some twenty acres to plow, so I concluded I would finish my plowing and then go. I got up one morning to go to work as usual and on going to the field found between five and seven acres of my ground had been plowed during the night. I didn't know who did it, but it was done just as I would have done it myself, and the plow was left standing in the furrow. This enabled me to start sooner. When I arrived at Harmony, Joseph and Oliver were coming towards me, and met me some distance from the house. Oliver told me that Joseph had informed him when I started from home, where I had stopped the next night, how I read the sign at the tavern, where I stopped the next night, etc., and that I would be there that day before dinner, and this was why they had come out to meet me; all of which was exactly as Joseph had told Oliver, at which I was greatly astonished.[13]
>
> The next day after I got there, they packed up the plates, and we proceeded on our journey to my father's house, where we arrived in due time, and the day after we commenced the translation of the plates.[14]

The month of June, 1829, was one in which heaven came very near to earth for a little group of sincerely devoted ones, toiling away day after day in the "story and a half log house" of the prosperous Whitmer family. There could have been no more beautiful location for this quiet farm that figures so tranquilly in the beginnings of the church, for the township of Fayette lay between Lake Seneca and Lake Cayuga. Here those who were doing the work that seemed so important to them found peace and quiet. It was a month of miraculous happenings. Hardly a night fell on the farmhouse that someone did not have a new

---

[12]Kansas City *Journal*, June 5, 1881; *Saints' Herald*, Volume 28, page 198. (See *Church History*, Volume 4, page 362.)
[13]*Saints' Herald*, Volume 26, pages 6, 7. Quoted from *Deseret Evening News*.
[14]Interview with David Whitmer, Kansas City *Journal*, June 5, 1881; *Saints' Herald*, Volume 28, page 198.

spiritual experience to relate, the restoration of the priesthood, the wonderful experience of the "Three Witnesses to the Book of Mormon," all the marvelous events leading up to the finding of the plates, Oliver Cowdery's inspired call to go to Pennsylvania, David Whitmer and the plowing that was done in the dark of nighttime, how Joseph saw him in vision leave Fayette and make the two-day journey to Harmony. One evening the faithful mother of the family clasped her toil-knotted hands in her lap, quiet for once from her work, and told how when she had gone to the barn that night to milk, she, too, had met the mysterious messenger and was shown the golden plates.

At times all of the Whitmers, Emma Smith, Oliver Cowdery, and Martin Harris were present in the room (taking part in the humble prayer that preceded each session[15] of translating). They all agree that Oliver Cowdery wrote as dictated by Joseph Smith, who sat at the same table, and with eyes darkened and using the Urim and Thummim slowly enunciated the words that were to form the Book of Mormon. Before it was finished all knew the story that was written there.

In this important and interesting book the history of ancient America is unfolded, from its first settlement by a colony that came from the tower of Babel at the confusion of languages to the beginning of the fifth century of the Christian era. We are informed by these records that America in ancient times has been inhabited by two distinct races of people. The first were called Jaredites, and came directly from the tower of Babel. The second race came directly from the city of Jerusalem, about six hundred years before Christ. They were principally Israelites of the decendants of Joseph. The Jaredites were destroyed about the time that the Israelites came from Jerusalem, who succeeded them in the inheritance of the country. The principal nations of the second race fell in battle towards the close of the fourth century. The remnant are the Indians that now inhabit this country. This book also tells us that our Saviour made his appearance upon this continent after his resurrection, that he planted the gospel here in all its fullness, and richness, and power, and blessing, that they had apostles, prophets, pastors, teachers, and evangelists; the same order, the same priesthood, the

---

[15]Chicago *Tribune* of December 15, 1885, report of interview with David Whitmer, also *Saints' Herald*, Volume 33, page 12.

same ordinances, gifts, powers, and blessings, as was enjoyed on the eastern continent, that the people were cut off in consequence of their transgressions, that the last of their prophets who existed among them was commanded to write an abridgment of their prophecies, history, etc., and hide it up in the earth, and that it should come forth and be united with the Bible for the accomplishment of the purposes of God in the last days.[16]

Several of the Whitmer brothers, especially John and Christian, Martin Harris, and Emma Smith, assisted in writing for Joseph, but the great burden of the work fell upon Oliver Cowdery. "That book is true," he said in later years. "Sidney Rigdon did not write it. Mr. Spaulding did not write it. I wrote it myself as it fell from the lips of the Prophet."[17]

In the manuscript which has been preserved, all these various handwritings have been recognized. Alexander W. Doniphan was requested at one time to identify the handwriting in this old manuscript. He knew Cowdery well, and was acquainted with his penmanship. On July 13, 1884, he wrote to Heman C. Smith:

> Some eight years ago I was requested by some persons to accompany them to the residence of David Whitmer, Sr., in this village [Richmond, Missouri]. When we arrived quite a volume of manuscript was lying on the center table, and I was requested to state whether I recognized the handwriting. I had not been told the purpose of our visit before. I began to turn over the pages. It was an old looking document, but in a good state of preservation, as if it had been well cared for. After sketching it over in various parts, I felt sure it was the handwriting of Oliver Cowdery, although I had not seen it for many years; and said that I believed it was his. In the further examination I found a few pages here and there in two other hands, and so pointed them out. Those present then asked Mr. Whitmer as to the various handwritings. He said that I was correct, the manuscript was almost entirely written by Cowdery. The other parts were written by Emma, wife of Joseph Smith, and Christian Whitmer, merely to relieve Cowdery when tired. I still believe the handwriting to be Cowdery's.[18]

On the 11th day of June, 1829, the title page of the new book was deposited with R. R. Lansing, clerk of the United States Dis-

---
[16] *Times and Seasons*, Volume 3, pages 707, 708.
[17] *Church History*, Volume 1, page 50.
[18] *Church History*, Volume 4, page 451.

trict Court in northern New York. The book was still unfinished. In order to protect himself under the law, against such a loss as he had met the year before, Joseph signed his own name as "author and proprietor" as provided by act of Congress. In order not to deceive anyone as to the nature of the book, he also put on the front page, a description of the work taken from the book itself, as Joseph Smith explained.

THE BOOK OF MORMON

An Account Written by the Hand of Mormon upon Plates Taken from the Plates of Nephi.

Wherefore, it is an abridgment of the record of the people of Nephi, and also of the Lamanites; written to the Lamanites, who are a remnant of the house of Israel; and also to Jew and Gentile; written by way of commandment, and also by the spirit of prophecy and of revelation. Written, and sealed up, and hid unto the Lord, that they might not be destroyed; to come forth by the gift and power of God unto the interpretation thereof; sealed by the hand of Moroni, and hid up unto the Lord, to come forth in due time by the way of Gentile; the interpretation thereof by the gift of God.

An abridgment taken from the Book of Ether; also, which is a record of the people of Jared; who were scattered at the time the Lord confounded the language of the people, when they were building a tower to get to heaven: which is to shew unto the remnant of the house of Israel what great things the Lord hath done for their fathers; and that they may know the covenants of the Lord, that they are not cast off for ever; and also to the convincing of the Jew and Gentile that Jesus is the Christ, the Eternal God, manifesting himself unto all nations. And now if there are faults, they are the mistakes of men; wherefore, condemn not the things of God, that ye may be found spotless at the judgment seat of Christ.

By Joseph Smith, Junior,
Author and Proprietor.

Palmyra:
Printed by E. B. Grandin, for the Author, 1830.

David Whitmer says the work of translating was finished about July, and that it was in process at his father's for about a month.[19]

---

[19] Interview with David Whitmer, Kansas City *Journal*, June 5, 1881. *Saints' Herald*, Volume 28, page 198.

Mr. John H. Gilbert of Palmyra, New York, who claims to have set the type for the Book of Mormon, says, "The manuscript was put in our hands in August, 1829, and all printed by March, 1830."[20] Mr. Egbert Grandin in Palmyra agreed to print five thousand copies for the sum of three thousand dollars.

Oliver Cowdery continued his vigil over the manuscript to the end, taking only a few pages to the printer at a time, remaining with them, proofreading, and seeing that they were correct.[21] In April, 1830, the book was sent into the world to fight its own battles. The young men instrumental in its publication sought diligently, it is true, to sell these copies, while they also preached the restoration of the gospel (for they felt it was not only necessary but right to reimburse Martin Harris as much as possible for the expense of their printing, which had involved him heavily),[22] at the same time they felt no one who could not buy should be deprived of a copy, and gave them away freely.

More than a century has passed. The Book of Mormon has been printed in over a hundred editions, and in fifteen or more languages. It has made its own place in the sun and has kept it. Carlyle has said:

> I will allow a thing to struggle for itself in this world, with any sword, or tongue, or implement it has, or can lay hold of. We will let it preach and pamphleteer and fight, and to the uttermost bestir itself and do, beak and claw, whatsoever is in it; very sure that it will in the long run, conquer nothing which does not deserve to be conquered. What is better than itself cannot be put away, but only what is worse. In this great duel, Nature herself is umpire and can do no wrong; the thing which is deepest rooted in nature, which we call truest, that thing and not the other will be found growing at last.

But who will believe such a ridiculous, such an incredulous, such a chimerical tale? Thousands upon thousands of people

---

[20] *Saints' Herald.* Volume 28, page 166.
[21] *Saints' Herald,* Volume 31, pages 396-397, and *Church History,* Volume 4, page 448.
[22] Martin Harris states that every penny he advanced for the publication of the Book of Mormon was repaid.

have believed. And today, after more than a hundred years have passed, missionaries of the gospel restored are still handing this book to those who will hear, and telling them its story as romantic as a fairy tale, as unbelievable as a New Testament miracle. And today after more than a hundred years, men and women are reading it, praying over it, as did these young men of long ago, and coming forward to say with Oliver Cowdery:

"The book is true."

VIII.—THE BOOK OF MORMON WITNESSES

SOMEWHERE IN EVERY BOOK OF MORMON that has ever been printed one may read the testimony of eleven men who saw the gold plates[1] from which it was printed. The names signed there include the names of almost every man over twenty connected with the giving to the world of that mys-

---

[1] THE TESTIMONY OF THREE WITNESSES:
Be it known unto all nations, kindreds, tongues, and people, unto whom this work shall come, that we, through the grace of God the Father, and our Lord Jesus Christ, have seen the plates which contain this record, which is a record of the people of Nephi, and also of the Lamanites, their brethren, and also of the people of Jared, who came from the tower of which hath been spoken; and we also know that they have been translated by the gift and power of God, for his voice hath declared it unto us; wherefore we know of a surety, that the work is true. And we also testify that we have seen the engravings which are upon the plates; and they have been shewn unto us by the power of God, and not of man. And we declare with words of soberness, that an angel of God came down from heaven, and he brought and laid before our eyes, that we beheld and saw the plates, and the engravings thereon; and we know that it is by the grace of God the Father, and our Lord Jesus Christ, that we beheld and bear record that these things are true; and it is marvelous in our eyes, nevertheless, the voice of the Lord commanded us that we should bear record of it; wherefore, to be obedient unto the commandments of God, we bear testimony of these things. And we know that if we are faithful in Christ, we shall rid our garments of the blood of all men, and be found spotless before the judgment seat of Christ, and shall dwell with him eternally in the heavens. And the honor be to the Father, and to the Son, and to the Holy Ghost, which is one God. Amen.

Oliver Cowdery.
David Whitmer.
Martin Harris.

AND ALSO THE TESTIMONY OF EIGHT WITNESSES:
Be it known unto all nations, kindreds, tongues, and people, unto whom this work shall come, that Joseph Smith, Jr., the translator of this work, hath shewn unto us the plates of which hath been spoken, which have the appearance of gold; and as many of the leaves as the said Smith has translated, we did handle with our hands: and we also saw the engravings thereon, all of which has the appearance of ancient work, and of curious workmanship. And this we bear record with words of soberness, that the said Smith has shewn unto us, for we have seen and hefted, and know of a surety, that the said Smith has got the plates of which we have spoken. And we give our names unto the world, to witness unto the world that which we have seen; and we lie not, God bearing witness of it.

Christian Whitmer.
Jacob Whitmer.
Peter Whitmer, Jr.
John Whitmer.
Hiram Page.
Joseph Smith, Sen.
Hyrum Smith.
Samuel H. Smith

terious book. This privilege was limited necessarily to the several families who had part in the work. Joseph had intrusted his secret fully to no one except the members of his own family, the Whitmer family, and his two friends, Martin Harris and Oliver Cowdery.

One day in that memorable month of June, 1829, as he was working on the translation in the presence of those usually in the room and also Martin Harris, who frequently made the twenty-five-mile trip from his home in Palmyra to watch the progress of the work, they discovered that three special witnesses were to be chosen, who would eventually see not only the plates, but the angel who had first shown them to Joseph. Immediately Harris, Cowdery, and David Whitmer began to importune him for the honor, and no others had so certainly earned the distinction. Joseph consented to place the matter before the Lord, and the four accordingly withdrew to the woods, which previously had been the sanctuary of the young prophet on more than one occasion. Here kneeling in the solitude of the forest, each man prayed in turn, that they might be blessed by the vision promised to "three others." But as the last voice died out in the stillness of the forest, nothing happened. Joseph Smith prayed again; each of the others followed in turn. Again, the silence of the dim forest was their only answer.

Slowly Martin Harris rose, the man to whom this vision would have meant more than to all others, and told them he must be the cause of their disappointment, and offered to withdraw. When he had gone, and each man prayed again, in turn, Joseph tells us:

> We . . . had not been many minutes engaged in prayer when presently we beheld a light above us in the air of exceeding brightness, and behold an angel stood before us; in his hands he held the plates which we had been praying for these to have a view of: he turned over the leaves one by one, so that we could see them, and discover the engravings thereon distinctly. He addressed himself to David Whitmer, and said, "David, blessed is the Lord, and he that keeps his commandments." When immediately afterwards, we heard a voice

from out of the bright light above us, saying, "These plates have been revealed by the power of God, and they have been translated by the power of God; the translation of them which you have seen is correct, and I command you to bear record of what you now see and hear."[2]

More than once in the many interviews David Whitmer gave to the public, he has described this scene even more minutely.

> It was June, 1829, the latter part of the month . . . the angel showed us the plates. We not only saw the plates of the Book of Mormon, but also the brass plates, the plates of the book of Ether, the plates containing the records of the wickedness of the world and the secret combinations of the people of the world down to the time of their being engraved, and many other plates. The fact is, it was just as though Joseph, Oliver, and I were sitting just here on a log, when we were overshadowed by a light. It was not like the light of the sun, nor like that of a fire, but more glorious and beautiful. It extended away around us, I cannot tell how far, but in the midst of this light about as far off as he sits [pointing to John C. Whitmer, sitting a few feet from him] there appeared as it were a table, with many records and plates upon it, besides the plates of the Book of Mormon, also the sword of Laban, the directors, and the interpreters. I saw them as plain as I see this bed [striking the bed beside him with his hand] and I heard the voice of the Lord just as distinctly as I ever heard anything in my life, declaring that the records of the Book of Mormon were translated by the gift and power of God. . . . Our testimony as recorded in the Book of Mormon is strictly and absolutely true, just as it is here written.[3]

Six years later, in another interview he said:

> In June, 1829, I saw the angel by the power of God. Joseph, Oliver, and I were alone, and a light from heaven shone round us, and solemnity pervaded our minds. The angel appeared in the light, as near as that young man (within five or six feet). Between us and the angel there appeared a table, and there lay upon it the Sword of Laban, the Ball of Directors, the Record and the Interpreters. The angel took the record and turned the leaves, and showed it to us by the power of God. . . . My testimony in the Book of Mormon is true; I can't deviate from it.[4]

---

[2] *Times and Seasons*, Volume 3, page 898.
[3] Interview given by David Whitmer in a hotel in Richmond, Missouri, in the presence of a number of witnesses on September 7 1878. *L. D. S. Biographical Encyclopedia*, page 266. *Saints' Herald*, Volume 28, page 198.
[4] Interview with E. C. Briggs and R. Etzenhouser at Richmond, Missouri, April 25, 1884. *Saints' Herald*, Volume 31, page 396.

Immediately after, Joseph went in search of his friend Martin and found the old man in the woods praying alone. Joseph joined him, and the vision seen by Whitmer and Cowdery was repeated.

Two or three days after this, Joseph showed the plates to eight others, his father, Joseph, Sr.; his two brothers, Hyrum and Samuel Harrison Smith; David Whitmer's four brothers, Christian, Peter, Jacob, and John, and brother-in-law, Hiram Page.

From that day, Harris, Whitmer, and Cowdery looked back upon that scene in the woods as the supreme hour of their lives; they felt that the sharing of that unusual privilege had bound them together with an insoluble tie, as Oliver Cowdery said six years later in his charge to newly ordained Twelve Apostles, "You are bound together as the three witnesses were; you, notwithstanding can part and meet, and meet and part again, until your heads are silvered over with age."

These men were not visionary in the ordinary sense of the term. They were not given to seeing remarkable, supernatural things. One of them, Oliver Cowdery, practiced law practically all his life. As years passed, all three became estranged from Joseph Smith and the church he organized, and yet they all affirmed and reaffirmed their knowledge of the events that occurred at the beginning of his ministry and the principles they all once believed. Their paths separated far, but they held firm to their testimony.

Oliver Cowdery went back to Ohio in 1838 and entered the practice of law. He is said never to have spoken to his business associates of his connection with Joseph Smith, hiding his disappointments in his own heart, but ten years later at a conference at Council Bluffs, Iowa, touched by a spark of the old time fire we hear him saying:

> Friends and Brethren, my name is Cowdery—Oliver Cowdery. In the early history of this church I stood identified with her, and one in her councils. True it is that the gifts and callings of God are without repentance. Not because I was better than the rest of mankind was I called; but, to fulfill the purposes of God, he called me to a high and holy calling. I wrote with my own pen, the entire Book of Mormon (save a few pages), as it fell from the lips of the Prophet

THE BOOK OF MORMON WITNESSES   73

Joseph Smith, as he translated it by the gift and power of God, by the means of the Urim and Thummim, or, as it is called by that book, "holy interpreters." I beheld with my eyes and handled with my hands the gold plates from which it was translated. I also saw with my eyes and handled with my hands the "holy interpreters." That book is *true*. Sidney Rigdon did not write it. Mr. Spaulding did not write it. I wrote it myself as it fell from the lips of the Prophet.[5]

On the 31st of March, 1850, at the home of his old friend David Whitmer, now for many years his brother-in-law (for Oliver had married the youngest of the Whitmers, Elizabeth Ann), Oliver Cowdery died. His last words were, "Brother David, be true to your testimony to the Book of Mormon."[6]

Martin Harris, still a prosperous farmer, resided on a farm near Kirtland for many years. Finally in 1870 he joined members of his own family in Utah and died there July 10, 1875, a very old man.[7] His son says his last words concerned the Book of Mormon. He had previously testified many times, "The angel did show to me the plates containing the Book of Mormon."[8]

David Whitmer, the young man to whom the angel addressed himself in 1829 in the Fayette woods lived on for many years, the last remaining witness to the Book of Mormon. He resided in the same town, Richmond, Missouri, for about half a century, one of the most remarkable men ever connected with the history of Ray County. "No man ever lived here who had more friends and fewer enemies. Honest, conscientious, and upright in all his dealings, just in his estimate of men, and open, manly, and frank in his treatment of all, he made lasting friends who loved him to the end."[9] He gave many interviews and wrote many letters. It would take a book to hold them all. When E. C. Brand visited him on the 8th of February, 1875, David Whitmer, then a white-haired old man told him he would rather suffer death than deny his testimony. "I did see the angel of God," he said "and was commanded to

---

[5] *Myth of Manuscript Found*, by George Reynolds, pages 79, 80.
[6] David Whitmer's *Address to All Believers in Christ*, page 8.
[7] "The Ogden Junction," quoted in *Saints' Herald*, Volume 22, page 542.
[8] *Church History*, Volume 1, page 51.
[9] Richmond *Democrat*, January 26, 1888, quoted in *Saints' Herald*, Volume 35, page 94.

testify concerning these things, and they are true."[10] A month later he wrote to Mark H. Forscutt.[11]. (See reproduction, page 75.)

An editorial in the Chicago *Times,* December 15, 1885, asks:

> Do people in general want to know the truth about Joseph Smith? . . . Apparently they do not. . . . At last accounts, David Whitmer, the last of the original testifiers of the existence of the golden plates from which the Book of Mormon was translated, was approaching death at his home in Richmond, Missouri. He went to that state over forty years ago. . . . His neighbors of every sort of political and religious predelictions unite in giving him an exceedingly high character for honesty, truthfulness, and courage. No man, it is said, ever doubted his word in regard to any ordinary matter. Why should not the testimony of a man so truthful, so honest, so courageous, be accepted in relation to the golden plates and the character of the man who professed to find them?[12]

Whitmer did not die at that time, but as his few remaining years passed, and he knew he had not long to live, he wrote the inscription, "The record of the Jews, and the record of the Nephites are one. Truth is eternal," to be placed on his tombstone, which he designed to be an everlasting memorial, of what he had loved to declare upon earth. He died at Richmond, January 25, 1888, reaffirming his life-long testimony with almost his dying breath.

Over half a century before, he had heard an angel speak. He had never forgotten those words: "David, blessed is the Lord and he that keeps his commandments." No other words on earth had ever sounded so sweet to him. He asked that his funeral sermon be preached from Revelation 22, "Blessed are they that do his commandments, that they may have right to the tree of life, and may enter in through the gates into the city."

---

[10] Mark H. Forscutt's scrapbook, page 18. Heman C. Smith collection. Original pasted in book.
[11] Mark H. Forscutt's scrapbook, pages 16, 17. Heman C. Smith collection. Original pasted in book.
[12] Chicago Sunday *Times* for December 15, 1885, republished in *Saints' Herald,* Volume 33, page 1.

Richmond, Missouri, March 2d, 1875.

Mr. Mark H. Forscutt

Dear Sir:

My testimony to the world is written concerning the Book of Mormon, and it is the same that I gave at first and it is the same as shall stand to my latest hour in life, linger with me in death and shine as gospel truth beyond the limits of life, among the tribunals of heaven, and [that] the nations of the earth will have known too late the divine truth written on the pages of that book is the only sorrow of this servant of the Almighty Father.

David Whitmer.

IX.—Organizing the Church

THE TRANSLATION AND publication of the Book of Mormon, although looked upon as a sacred responsibility by Joseph Smith and those who helped him, was by no means the most important task that awaited the young prophet. From the very hour of his first vision he had continued to receive what he looked upon as divine direction. There had been several years of confusion and strife in the religious world. There was a definite move to abolish creeds and return to the old paths. Joseph Smith as a youth said an angel had told him the creeds of men were an abomination[1]; the reformers had said that and more. The angel had said a marvelous work was about to come forth in the world, the reformers had predicted that for a generation or more. All through the United States reformers were slowly formulating compromises with departures from their mother churches. An unlettered farm boy comes forward to say that not reform but restoration was the thing needed; that the gospel was once again to be restored in its completeness from God himself, the author of the plan of salvation. Reformers were struggling over who had the power to ordain, to baptize, to preach the gospel; this daring country lad told them the authority to minister in the things of God must be restored from heaven itself by those who held the keys of divine authority; that no one must take this honor upon himself, unless he was called of God as was Aaron.

The translation of the Book of Mormon he said was but a manifestation of the power of God to communicate his mind and will

---

[1] Perhaps no other statement of Joseph Smith's has received more bitter criticism than this. Students of religious thought of that day have no difficulty in understanding it. Creeds and confessions of faith, were they to be retained or was the religious world to go back to the Bible for inspiration? That was the burning religious question of his time. That was undoubtedly one of the questions upon which Joseph Smith sought divine answer.

to the sons of men as he had done in ancient times. Even in the days at Harmony when two young men, mere boys in point of years, were struggling against odds with a gigantic task, they were not lacking in assurance, for to Joseph Smith his projects were crystal clear. In the midst of confusion, he spoke authoritatively.

Oliver Cowdery was no less eager. He said:

> No men in their sober senses could translate and write the directions given to the Nephites, from the mouth of the Saviour, of the precise manner in which men should build up his church, . . . without desiring a privilege of showing a willingness of the heart by being buried in the liquid grave, to answer "a good conscience by the resurrection of Jesus Christ." . . . We only waited for a commandment to be given, "arise and be baptized."[2]

There in the woods on the Susquehanna River that was their temple, these two young men visioned a great organization that would be nothing less than a restoration of the original Christian church. They had no money; they had no education, or very little at most; they had not even the humblest country church in which to tell their story, but they had faith in their mission, and the moral and physical courage to carry out what they believed their divinely appointed duty. There was no timidity, no vacillation. They were ready to speak out regardless of scoffers, of false witnesses, of difficulties, or depression. There was nothing that could turn them aside from what they saw as a divinely appointed objective. What better preparation could a man have for a pioneer of any movement?

Joseph Smith tells the story:

> We still continued the work of translation, when in the ensuing month [May, eighteen hundred and twenty-nine] we on a certain day went into the woods to pray and inquire of the Lord respecting baptism for the remission of sins, as we found mentioned in the translation of the plates. While we were thus employed praying, and calling upon the Lord, a messenger from heaven descended in a cloud of

---

[2] Letter of Oliver Cowdery to W. W. Phelps, dated Norton, Medina County, Ohio, Sabbath evening, September 7, 1834, published in *Saints' Messenger and Advocate*, October, 1834. (Volume 1, pages 15, 16.)

light, and having laid his hands upon us, he ordained us, saying unto us, "Upon you, my fellow servants, in the name of Messiah, I confer the priesthood of Aaron, which holds the keys of the ministering of angels, and of the gospel of repentance, and of baptism by immersion, for the remission of sins; and this shall never be taken again from the earth, until the sons of Levi do offer again an offering unto the Lord in righteousness." He said this Aaronic priesthood had not the power of laying on of hands, for the gift of the Holy Ghost, but that this should be conferred on us hereafter; and he commanded us to go and be baptized, and gave us directions that I should baptize Oliver Cowdery, and afterwards that he should baptize me.

Accordingly we went and were baptized. I baptized him first, and afterwards he baptized me, after which I laid my hands upon his head and ordained him to the Aaronic priesthood, and afterwards he laid his hands on me, and ordained me to the same priesthood, for so we were commanded.

The messenger who visited us on this occasion, and conferred this priesthood upon us, said that his name was John, the same that is called John the Baptist, in the New Testament, and that he acted under the direction of Peter, James, and John, who held the keys of the priesthood of Melchisedec, which priesthood he said should in due time be conferred on us—and that I should be called the first elder, and he the second. It was on the fifteenth day of May, eighteen hundred and twenty-nine, that we were baptized, and ordained under the hand of the messenger.

Immediately upon our coming up out of the water, after we had been baptized, we experienced great and glorious blessings from our heavenly Father. No sooner had I baptized Oliver Cowdery than the Holy Ghost fell upon him and he stood up and prophesied many things which should shortly come to pass. And again, so soon as I had been baptized by him, I also had the spirit of prophecy, when, standing up, I prophesied concerning the rise of the church, and many other things connected with the church, and this generation of the children of men. We were filled with the Holy Ghost, and rejoiced in the God of our salvation.

Our minds being now enlightened, we began to have the Scriptures laid open to our understandings, and the true meaning of their more mysterious passages revealed unto us, in a manner which we never could attain to previously, nor ever before had thought of.[3]

Oliver Cowdery's ecstatic account shows the effect of a positive declaration upon a mind that had tasted of the uncertainties of the religious controversies of the time—a positive declaration that to Oliver was a revelation from the very courts of glory itself.

---

[3] *Times and Seasons*, Volume 3, pages 865, 866; *Church History*, Volume 1, page 34.

The Lord, who is rich in mercy, and ever willing to answer the consistent prayer of the humble, after we had called upon him in a fervent manner, aside from the abodes of men, condescended to manifest to us his will. On a sudden, as from the midst of eternity, the voice of the Redeemer spake peace to us, while the vail was parted, and the angel of God came down clothed with glory, and delivered the anxiously looked for message, and the keys of the gospel of repentance! What joy! what wonder! what amazement! While the world was racked and distracted—while millions were groping as the blind for the wall, and while all men were resting upon uncertainty, as a general mass, our eyes beheld—our ears heard. As in the "blaze of day"; yes, more—above the glitter of the May sunbeam, which then shed its brilliancy over the face of nature! Then his voice, though mild, pierced to the center, and his words, "I am thy fellow servant," dispelled every fear. We listened—we gazed—we admired! 'Twas the voice of the angel from glory—'twas a message from the Most High! And as we heard we rejoiced, while his love enkindled upon our souls, and we were rapt in the vision of the Almighty! Where was room for doubt? Nowhere; uncertainty had fled, doubt had sunk, no more to rise, while fiction and deception had fled forever!

But, dear brother, think, further think for a moment, what joy filled our hearts and with what surprise we must have bowed (for who would not have bowed the knee for such a blessing?) when we received under his hand the holy priesthood as he said, "Upon you my fellow servants, in the name of Messiah, I confer this priesthood, and this authority, which shall remain upon earth, that the sons of Levi may yet offer an offering unto the Lord in righteousness."

I shall not attempt to paint to you the feelings of this heart, nor the majestic beauty and glory which surrounded us on this occasion; but you will believe me when I say, that earth, nor men, with the eloquence of time, cannot begin to clothe language in as interesting and sublime a manner as this holy personage. No; nor has this earth power to give the joy, to bestow the peace, or comprehend the wisdom which was contained in each sentence as they were delivered by the power of the Holy Spirit! Man may deceive his fellow man, deception may follow deception, and the children of the wicked one may have the power to seduce the foolish and untaught, till naught but fiction feeds the many, and the fruit of falsehood carries in its current the giddy to the grave; but one touch with the finger of his love, yes, one ray of glory from the upper world, or one word from the mouth of the Saviour, from the bosom of eternity, strikes it all into insignificance and blots it forever from the mind! The assurance that we were in the presence of an angel; the certainty that we heard the voice of Jesus, and the truth unsullied as it flowed from a pure personage, dictated by the will of God, is to me, past description, and I shall ever look upon this expression of the Saviour's goodness with wonder and thanksgiving while I am permitted to tarry, and in those mansions where perfection dwells and sin never comes, I hope to adore in that day which shall never cease![4]

After a few days they began "to reason out of the Scriptures" and inform their friends "what the Lord was about to do for the children of men." Some were baptized, among them Samuel Harrison Smith, a younger brother of Joseph, who visited them in Harmony.

Joseph Smith, now removed to Fayette, New York, wrote:

Meanwhile, we continued to translate at intervals, when not necessitated to attend to the numerous enquirers, that had now begun to visit us; some for the sake of finding the truth, others for the purpose of putting hard questions, and trying to confound us. Among the latter class were several learned priests who generally came for the purpose of disputation: however, the Lord continued to pour out his Holy Spirit, and as often as we had need, he gave us that moment what to say; so that unlearned and inexperienced in religious controversies, yet were we able to confound those learned rabbis of the day, whilst at the same time, we were able to convince the honest in heart, that we had obtained (through the mercy of God) to the true and everlasting gospel of Jesus Christ, so that almost daily we administered the ordinance of baptism for the remission of sins, to such as believed. We now became anxious to have that promise realized to us, which the angel that conferred upon us the Aaronic priesthood had given us; viz., that provided we continued faithful we should also have the Melchisedec priesthood, which holds the authority of the laying on of hands for the gift of the Holy Ghost. We had for some time made this matter a subject of humble prayer, and at length we got together in the chamber of Mr. Whitmer's house in order more particularly to seek of the Lord what we now so earnestly desired; and here to our unspeakable satisfaction did we realize the truth of the Saviour's promise; "Ask, and you shall receive, seek and you shall find, knock and it shall be opened unto you"; for we had not long been engaged in solemn and fervent prayer, when the word of the Lord came unto us in the chamber, commanding us that I should ordain Oliver Cowdery to be an elder in the Church of Jesus Christ, and that he also should ordain me to the same office, and then to ordain others as it should be made known unto us, from time to time. We were, however, commanded to defer our ordination until such times as it should be practicable to have our brethren, who had been and who should be baptized, assembled together, when we must have their sanction to our thus proceeding to ordain each

---

[4]*Messenger and Advocate,* Volume 1, pages 15, 16. See *Church History,* Volume 1, pages 37-39.

ORGANIZING THE CHURCH

other, and have them decide by vote whether they were willing to accept us as their spiritual teachers, or not, when also we were commanded to bless bread and break it with them, and to take wine, bless it and drink with them, afterward proceed to ordain each other according to commandment, then call out such men as the Spirit should dictate, and ordain them, and then attend to the laying on of hands for the gift of the Holy Ghost upon all those whom we had previously baptized; doing all things in the name of the Lord.[5]

Oliver Cowdery later says, "I was also present with Joseph when the higher or Melchisedec priesthood was conferred by the holy angel from on high. This priesthood was then conferred on each other, by the will and commandment of God."[6] In one of the revelations received by Joseph Smith occurs the statement, "Peter, James, and John, whom I have sent unto you, by whom I have ordained you and confirmed you to be apostles and especial witnesses of my name,"[7] and in a letter to the church written September 6, 1842, Joseph Smith refers to the "voice of Peter, James, and John in the wilderness between Harmony, Susquehanna County, and Colesville, Broome County, on the Susquehanna River, declaring themselves as possessing the keys of the kingdom, and of the dispensation of the fullness of time."[8] But by some chance, details of this experience have not been left to us.

In this manner did the Lord continue to give us instructions from time to time, concerning the duties which now devolved upon us, and among many other things of the kind, we obtained of him the following, by the Spirit of prophecy and revelation; which not only gave us much information, but also pointed out to us the precise day upon which, according to his will and commandment, we should proceed to organize his church once again upon the earth. (See Doctrine and Covenants 17, and *Church History*, Volume 1, page 67.)

All through the winter of 1829-30, the preparations for organization continued. "Whilst the Book of Mormon was in the hands of the printer, we still continued to bear testimony and give information, as far as we had opportunity; and also made known to

---
[5] *Times and Seasons*, Volume 3, page 915.
[6] *Myth of Manuscript Found*, by George Reynolds, page 80.
[7] Doctrine and Covenants 26:3.
[8] *Times and Seasons*, Volume 3, page 936, *Church History*, Volume 1, page 64.

our brethren that we had received a commandment to organize the church, and accordingly we met together for that purpose at the house[9] of the above-mentioned Mr. Whitmer (being six in number) on Tuesday, the sixth day of April, A. D., one thousand eight hundred and thirty"—

> Having opened the meeting by solemn prayer to our heavenly Father, we proceeded (according to previous commandment) to call on our brethren to know whether they accepted us as their teachers, in the things of the kingdom of God and whether they were satisfied that we should proceed and be organized as a church according to said commandment which we had received. To these they consented by a unanimous vote. I then laid my hands upon Oliver Cowdery and ordained him an elder of the "Church of Jesus Christ of Latter Day Saints," after which he ordained me also to the office of an elder of said church. We then took bread, blessed it and brake it with them, also wine, blessed it and drank it with them. We then laid our hands on each individual member of the church present that they might receive the gift of the Holy Ghost; and be confirmed members of the Church of Christ. The Holy Ghost was poured out upon us to a very great degree. Some prophesied, whilst we all praised the Lord and rejoiced exceedingly.[10]

The newly ordained ministers began from that time forth to spread the gospel throughout the neighborhood where they lived. Many believed.

"In 1830," says E. Douglas Branch, "the Book of Mormon was published. Its philosophy of history exacted no more credulity than the cosmogony of Genesis; its faith was the old-time religion brought up-to-date without being modernized."[11]

Preaching services were held around Manchester and Palmyra, at Fayette [12] and at Colesville in Broome County, where the entire family of Joseph Knight and others had very early aligned them-

---

[9]This house is no longer standing. See *Latter-day Saints Biographical Encyclopedia*—Vol. I, page 282, Salt Lake City: "There [in Fayette Township] he [Peter Whitmer, Sr.] built a story and a half log house, the one in which the church was organized April 6, 1830, and where Joseph Smith received a number of important revelations. The house was torn down many years ago, but when Elder Andrew Jensen visited the place in 1888, he found several of the logs which once constituted a part of the building lying in a ditch near by."
[10]*Church History*, Volume 1, pages 76-77.
[11]*Westward*, by E. Douglas Branch, page 411.
[12]Preaching services were held in 1830 and 1831 in (1) Peter Whitmer's house, (2) at "Whitmer School," in District No. 17, Fayette (northeast from Whitmer's, near Martin Miller's and the Junction of Military lots 3, 4, and 13). This school district was annulled in 1841, and the schoolhouse moved. (3) Schoolhouse in District No. 15 (now No. 7) in locality known as the beach. *History Sketch of Fayette*, by Diedrich Villers, page 48.

selves definitely with the new movement. Knight was the genial miller, so often a guest in the Smith home in Palmyra, as he traveled through the neighborhood contracting wheat for his mill. He had already given the young prophet substantial pecuniary aid while he was working on the translation.

The first conference convened at Fayette on the first of June with thirty members of the church and many others present. A glorious time was reported by all, although the services partook too much of the ecstatic scenes that had marked the great revival. The "meeting" was in the Whitmer home, and as was common in pioneer times, in order to accommodate a large family, beds were a part of every living room's furniture, and "some were so overcome that we had to lay them on beds, or other convenient places."[13] To the participants in meetings like these one hundred years ago, such manifestations[14] were neither strange nor unexpected but something which accompanied all religious gatherings of any pretension to spirituality. In the new church they were generally discouraged, and eventually disappeared altogether.

Members soon began to be added to their number in what seemed almost miraculous ways. After translating the Book of Mormon, Joseph, Oliver, his father, and brother, Hyrum, were preaching near Auburn, New York, when they were pleased to see the face of an old-time friend, Ezra Thayre, who had been a bridge, dam, and mill builder in and around Palmyra, and had many times employed Father Smith and his sons, including Joseph. It was Sunday.

> He said that on reaching the double log house where the meeting was held, he pressed his way through the congregation and took his seat immediately in front of these new preachers, listened to the broken remarks by the three others, and then Joseph taking the Book of Mormon in his hand, proceeded in his unlearned manner, to tell the history of its coming forth, and explained how he had received the golden plates at the hands of the angel, and how he had translated the book

---
[13] *Times and Seasons*, Volume 4, page 23.
[14] (While often objectionable, such a state has its counterpart in Biblical history, as in the case of the trance of Peter, Acts 10: 10; 11: 5; of Paul, *Ibid.*, 22: 7, and of Paul's conversion and of other cases in the Bible.)

by the gift of God, with other marvelous matters connected with its coming forth, and Thayre said that immediately upon Joseph beginning these statements a new and heavenly power fell upon him filling his entire being with unspeakable assurance of the truth of the statements, melting him to tears. When Joseph concluded his recital, he said he eagerly stretched forth his hand and said, "Let me have that book." It was handed to him and Brother Thayre kept it, esteeming it a heavenly treasure indeed.[15]

Sometime in the month of August a young man of twenty-three sold all his earthly possessions (though they happened to be few) to get enough money to go back to his home place and preach the gospel, upon which he believed he had found new light.

Parley P. Pratt, third son of Jared and Charity Pratt, was born April 12, 1807, in Burlington, Otsego County, N. Y. He worked at farming in various places, until 1826, when at the ripe age of nineteen, he came to the conclusion "to bid farewell to the civilized world—where I had met with little else but disappointment, sorrow, and unrewarded toil . . . and spend the remainder of my days in the solitudes of the great west." The spot chosen was thirty miles west of Cleveland, Ohio, where he had built a cabin in the woods and made one trip back "to the civilized world" for a boyhood sweetheart, Thankful Halsey. He had never heard of Joseph Smith or the Book of Mormon, but in this western home had come in contact "with a kind of reformed Baptist"[16] by the name of Sidney Rigdon. He was astonished to find Rigdon preached "repentance toward God, and baptism for remission of sins, with the promise of the gift of the Holy Ghost to all who would come forward, with all their hearts and obey this doctrine!"[17] Parley P. Pratt felt "swallowed up in these things . . . constrained to devote his time to enlightening his fellow men on these important truths, and warning them to prepare for the coming of the Lord." He was on his way back to Columbia County, New York, with his young wife, Thankful, and all the money his earthly possessions would bring.

---
[15]*Memoirs of William W. Blair*, pages 39, 40.
[16]*Autobiography of Parley Parker Pratt*, Chicago, 1888, page 31.
[17]*Ibid.*

The young missionary made his way to Cleveland, thirty miles, then took a schooner for Buffalo, and the captain being short of hands permitted him to work his way, which proved to be a very good thing, for when he attempted to engage passage on the new Erie Canal to Albany, he found it took not only their money, but some of their clothing as well to pay their way. Fortunately that included board. The packets furnishing board, however, were large and fine and could cover one hundred and fifty miles in a week!

There was a tiny cabin in front with five or six bunks for the crew. Next a small room used by women for washing and for dressing, then the women's cabin where ladies could retire and where all women slept at night. In the center was a large, general compartment which might be forty-five feet long, which was used as a general assembly room. Bunks were suspended on iron brackets, the ends of which on one side were pushed into the wall and the other ends hung by ropes from the ceiling. Such shelves were six by three and a half feet, arranged in tiers three feet apart. When all bunks were filled, surplus men slept on the floor. A small mattress and filthy blankets completed the equipment. These bedclothes were rolled in a corner of the room during the day and seldom washed. During the day all the passengers read, talked, sewed, played games, and dozed in this room. Some parcels were stored here, large ones on the deck. Meals were served on planks supported by wooden trestles. Back of this room were the kitchen and the inevitable bar. The cook was also the bartender and worked both day and night. The rest of the crew consisted of a captain, two steersmen and two drivers, who alternated each other in six-hour shifts. Sometimes the men would exercise by walking along the tow path with the driver.

No wonder the tedious routine of the boat became irksome to young Pratt, and he finally announced to his young wife that he would like to leave the boat, though his passage was paid, and preach a while to some friends in Wayne County. He had two uncles in that county, where he had visited some years before and made friends. Leaving his wife to get the benefit of the luxurious passage on the canal packet, he left the boat at Newark about daybreak one morning and walked ten miles to the home of a friend by the name of Wells. As was the custom of itinerant preachers then, he lost no time, but proposed a meeting that night.

He and Wells set out to collect a crowd, or at least announce their meeting, and church services of any kind were largely attended in those days. Among others they visited an old Baptist deacon by the name of Hamlin. After hearing of the appointment for the evening, he told his visitors of a "book, a strange book, a very strange book" in his possession, which had just been published. After listening to the circumstances of its translation and publication, young Pratt had a curiosity to obtain one, and was told by the old man that although he would not like to part with his copy, he would be pleased to permit Pratt to read it at his house, if he could call there. Early the next morning after filling his appointment the night before, Pratt went to Hamlin's and read the entire day, but failed to finish the book. His mind was now made up to visit Palmyra and see for himself. For as he read, "the Spirit of the Lord was upon me, and I knew and comprehended that the book was true, as plainly and manifestly as a man comprehends and knows that he exists."[18]

He walked the thirty miles to Palmyra, inquired for Joseph Smith, and was told that he lived two or three miles from the village. As he approached the neighborhood of the place near the close of the day, he overtook a young man a few years older than himself driving some cows, and asked him about Joseph Smith. He was informed that Joseph now lived in Pennsylvania, but pointed out the home of his father, and introduced himself as Joseph's brother, Hyrum. Pratt informed him of his new-found interest in the Book of Mormon and was invited to Hyrum's home, where they spent most of the night in conversation. Early

---

[18]*Autobiography of Parley Parker Pratt*, page 38.

in the morning Pratt felt he must hasten back to fill another appointment that evening. As he was leaving, Hyrum presented him with a copy of the Book of Mormon.

When the young minister had traveled long enough to require a rest, he sat down by the roadside, found the place where he had left off reading at Hamlin's, and was soon absorbed in the account of the personal ministry of Christ upon this continent. He continued on his journey when he had finished that part of the book, and kept his appointment to preach that night and the next. The people begged him to continue, but he no longer felt satisfied with his authority to preach. The next morning found him walking back the thirty miles to the home of Hyrum Smith to demand baptism. For some reason Hyrum did not comply, but after one night's rest, they both started to walk to Fayette, a distance of twenty-five miles. During the long walk, Pratt heard anew of the strange happenings attending the "angel message."

It was evening when they arrived at Whitmer's which had now assumed something of the properties of a hospitable inn. He was made welcome and on the next day (the first day of the second conference of the church) was baptized by the hand of Oliver Cowdery in beautiful Lake Seneca. That night at the evening meeting he was confirmed and ordained an elder, and continued on his way to his people in Columbia County.

Such conversions were so frequent that the recital of all that have been preserved in history would be impossible. Pratt says that at the time of his baptism there were three branches, Manchester, Fayette, and Colesville, and about fifty members. By the month of October he had returned to Manchester and was preaching with Joseph Smith in the Smith home, to two large rooms full of the Smith neighbors. This was his first meeting with Joseph, who apprised him of the news that he was one of the men chosen to undertake the first long mission of the church.

X.—The First Great Mission of the Church

Shortly before the September conference, a division appeared for the first time among the members of the church and threatened serious trouble. In a world where men's opinions differ, these things must come soon or late. This controversy, arising over the finding of a stone by Hiram Page, young husband of Catherine Whitmer, through which he, too, was giving "revelations" to guide the church, found the Whitmer family naturally sympathetic, and also Oliver Cowdery. Joseph Smith faced the difficult problem of correcting this error, which, if carried to its ultimate conclusion might wreck the young organization, and at the same time of maintaining at high level the faith and zeal of these loyal friends and brethren who had so stoutly defended him through the trying months just past. Again, the young man sought his altar in the woods, and came before the people with a masterly solution, a new project that dwarfed in significance the threatened division among them. He proposed a missionary trip to the very borders of the civilized world, with its object the conversion of the Indians, or the Lamanites as the church now called them (for they were so known in the Book of Mormon). All differences of opinion were soon dropped in the excitement of preparation for the first great mission of the church that promised hazards enough to test the mettle of the most courageous.

From the time the Puritans landed in New England, the conversion of the Indian had been a project dear to the heart of pious New Englanders, and to those who had accepted the Book of Mormon that ambition now shone with new luster. For they were going to offer to the Indian, the book of books, the record of his forefathers. Those chosen for this work were Parley P. Pratt, Oliver Cowdery, Peter Whitmer, and Ziba Peterson. The call came in October, and before the month passed they were on their way. Pratt's young wife, Thankful, was to spend the winter with the Whitmers, where there seemed to be always room for one more. The other young men were unmarried. They left Fayette on foot and made their way to Buffalo. The autumn weather was beautiful, and they were used to much walking. Many travelers went on foot in those days. Near the town of Buffalo they had their first experience in meeting the "Lamanites," the Catteraugas tribe near Buffalo. They stayed only part of the day, as they had some difficulty in making themselves understood, but they were treated well and left two copies of the Book of Mormon with those of the tribe who could read English.

Two hundred miles now lay between Pratt and his most longed-for objective—to meet and win the orator of the Western Reserve, Sidney Rigdon, to the new faith. Rigdon was known far and near for his eloquence and personal magnetism. He could chain the imagination of the most prosaic listener, and draw him to a cause in a way no other minister Pratt had ever met could do. Thus in his eagerness Rigdon's house was the first one entered in Mentor:

> After the usual salutations, [they] presented him with the Book of Mormon stating that it was a revelation from God. This being the first time he had ever heard of or seen the Book of Mormon, he felt very much prejudiced at the assertion, and replied that "he had one Bible, which he believed was a revelation from God, and with which he pretended to have some acquaintance; but with respect to the book they had presented him, he must say that he had considerable doubt." Upon which they expressed a desire to investigate the subject, and argue the matter; but he replied, "No, young gentlemen, you must not argue with me on the subject; but I will read your book and see what claim it has upon my faith, and will endeavor to ascertain whether it be a revelation from God or not." After some further conversation on the subject, they expressed a desire to lay the subject before the people, and requested the privilege of preaching in Elder Rigdon's church, to which he readily consented.[1]

The preaching appointment was published from house to house and "a large and respectable congregation assembled. Oliver Cowdery and Parley P. Pratt severally addressed the meeting. At the conclusion Elder Rigdon arose and stated to the congregation

---
[1] *Times and Seasons*, Volume 4, page 289.

that the information they had that evening received, was of an extraordinary character, and certainly demanded their most serious consideration: and as the apostle advised his brethren 'to prove all things, and hold fast that which is good,' so he would exhort his brethren to do likewise, and give the matter a careful investigation; and not turn against it, without being fully convinced of its being an imposition, lest they should, possibly, resist the truth."[2]

About two miles from Rigdon's home a group of members of his church, *viz.*, Lyman Wight, Isaac Morley, and Titus Billings, had "all things common,"[3] and the missionaries went to present the gospel to them. The community had been started in February of 1830, when Wight moved to Kirtland and into the same house with Isaac Morley. Eight other families later joined them, and Lyman Wight says they lived "in great peace and union" and "began to feel as if the millennium were close at hand."[4]

Along about the first of November five families in the town of Mayfield, about seven miles up the Chagrin River, concluded to join them. As these families owned good farms and mills there, it was decided to organize a branch of "The Family" as it was called there, instead of moving the five new families to Kirtland. Lyman Wight was appointed to take charge of the new branch and had his goods about loaded when Pratt, Cowdery, Whitmer, and Peterson came along. "I desired they would hold on till I got away, as my business was of vital importance, and I did not wish to be troubled with romances nor idle speculators," said Lyman Wight. "But nothing daunted, they were not to be put off, but were as good-natured as you please. Curiosity got uppermost, and I concluded to stop for a short time."[5] And this curiosity changed the course of many lives.

A meeting was held that very afternoon before sundown, for the sun was still an hour high when Lyman Wight left for his

---
[2]*Times and Seasons*, Volume 4, pages 289, 290.
[3]Lyman Wight's Journal as quoted in *Church History*, Volume 1, page 153.
[4]*Ibid.*
[5]*Ibid.*

THE FIRST GREAT MISSION OF THE CHURCH 91

new home, a bit provoked because he would not arrive in Mayfield before dark. "But I amused myself by thinking the trouble was over, and that I would not see them again for a long time, supposing they would start the next morning for the western boundary of the State of Missouri; but in this I was very much disappointed."[6] For seven weeks the missionaries remained in the vicinity, thronged with visitors, preaching every night in various places. They occasionally visited Rigdon, who was reading and praying over the new book. On November 14, Lyman Wight and his family, Sidney Rigdon, and others were baptized. By the end of their stay those converted to their cause numbered one hundred and twenty-seven souls, so that the church in the West[7] had a larger membership than the church in New York State.

But the missionaries felt they could no longer delay their departure as winter was closing in upon them. On the way west a Book of Mormon accidentally left in the home of Simeon Carter some fifty miles west of Kirtland was to do missionary work of its own as the missionaries traveled on, their number augmented by one Doctor Frederick G. Williams, one of the Kirtland converts. Continuing on foot to near Sandusky, they spent a few days with a tribe of Indians, Wyandottes, near that place and were well received. Then they went on to Cincinnati where they spent several days preaching, but with little success. About the 20th of December they took passage by steamboat to St. Louis but arriving at Cairo, Illinois, found the Mississippi River so blocked with ice that the steamboat could not proceed farther. Unwilling to wait until spring, the missionaries walked the two hundred miles between them and East St. Louis. Inclement winter weather had now taken away all the pleasure of walking through the forests. Every ounce of courage and stamina was demanded for the journey ahead. The country was just entering upon the

---
[6] Lyman Wight's Journal as quoted in *Church History*, Volume 1, page 153.
[7] *Autobiography of Parley Parker Pratt*, page 50.

coldest winter in history. No one suggested turning back or waiting until spring.

Christmas came and went unnoticed while the youthful missionaries waited anxiously for a severe storm of snow and rain to abate, but another storm of similar character followed a few days later, until snow lay two and a half feet deep on the prairie. But still the storms were not at an end. On the 5th of January another two feet of snow fell.[8] Preaching had helped to pass the tedious days, but all felt that longer delay was useless, so they plunged into the trackless wilds of snow, anxious to proceed on to their destination.

How they ever crossed Missouri that season was perhaps as miraculous as any in the series of unusual and exciting events that had thrilled them thus far in the restoration of the gospel church. But walk they did the entire distance, and arrived safely over snowfields that the bravest settler dared not attempt, although local writers admitted that "many strangers must have attempted such journeys and perished, as proved by the findings of bodies of strangers in many places when the snow went off in the spring."[9]

Among the weather features of early days, probably none has received more attention than the "deep snow" of the winter of 1830-31. Settlers lost their way in going three miles in the snowstorms of that winter. Following the December storms, the weather was continuously cold, and what little melting occurred was balanced by later snowstorms, so the depth on a level of four feet was maintained practically up until the last of February. Not before the middle of January were some of the settlers able to break roads sufficiently to get away from their homes at all. Fatalities from lack of fuel and food were narrowly averted in places. Wild animals found life difficult. At first, while the snow was soft, wolves were handicapped, and farmers on horseback could run them down. But the tables turned early in January when a

---

[8] *The Winter of the Deep Snow*, by Eleanor Atkinson. *Illinois State Historical Society Proceedings*, 1909, page 47, seq.
[9] *Record and Historical Review of Peoria*, by Drown.

driving rain, freezing as it fell, was covered by a few inches of soft snow. Then the wolves were practically lords of the snow-covered creation. Deer, buffalo, and elk could not get through the snow to forage on grass beneath, nor get about to browse on shrubs and twigs of trees, while the snow could now hold up the wolves, and they preyed upon the deer and buffalo, helping the famine to destroy them in large numbers. That winter the elk were exterminated from the plains of Missouri and Illinois, never again to return.[10]

The *American Journal of Science* for 1831-1832, later recharted and published in the *Smithsonian Institute Journal of Science*, says, "The winter months were attended with a degree of cold found only in Arctic regions."

In the memory of the oldest inhabitant of the new country of Missouri, the winters had been uniformly mild and open—grass and pasture fairly abundant until January, then light falls of snow, an occasional storm with zero temperatures that moderated in a few days; thaws to start the pastures and a fairly early spring. Cattle were pastured in the open the greater part of the year, with little or no shelter provided; wheat and corn left standing in the fields to be husked when needed. Now the shocks of grain were under the frozen snow, the limbs of the trees lay on the surface of the ground, making it impossible to drive horses into the woods, where at best their feet broke through the frozen crust with every step. No morning dawned for many days when the thermometer registered less than twelve degrees below zero. This storm visited the whole length of the United States. The icy crust was not quite thick enough to support a man's weight; on top of this was a layer of snow as "light and fine as ashes, and as hard as sand. Then a bright, cold sun shone on the dazzling landscape to threaten the eyesight. To add to these difficulties a strong northwest wind arose, to fill the air with flying snow, so

---
[10] "The Climate of Illinois—Its Permanence," by M. L. Fuller, forecaster of the weather bureau at Peoria, writing in *Illinois State Historical Society Proceedings* for 1912.

stinging, blinding, and choking that men could not make headway against it."[11] Often it was not easy to determine whether new snow was falling or only the old surface snow was being driven before the icy blast. For nine weeks snow covered the ground to the depth of forty-eight inches. Mail was not carried for many weeks at a time. Newspapers suspended publication.

On January 8, 1831, the *Missouri Intelligencer* of Columbia, although newspapers of the day were usually supremely indifferent to such ordinary affairs as weather reports, stated: "We are informed that the snow in the upper counties of Missouri is forty-one inches deep, and what is more remarkable, the falling was accompanied by frequent and tremendous peals of thunder and vivid blue streaks of lightning. It was an awful scene indeed." January 15, the paper was only a half sheet. The little settlement in the western wilds was cut off from the world by a blanket of snow. "Have no news," the editor said briefly. "Last mail brought only one Washington newspaper, no paper from Jefferson City [thirty miles]. Saint Louis *Times* reports eight to ten inches of snow in last storm. Here it is not less than twenty inches, and most of it remains, for the weather has been intensely cold." The Edwardsville (Illinois) *Advocate* for February 28, 1831, says, "We have issued no paper for the last two weeks, owing to excessively cold weather, and our office being too open to resist the rude attacks of the northern blasts." "The few roads were blocked, and no one pretended to go abroad except on horseback."[12]

Parley P. Pratt leaves the only record of this perilous journey in one paragraph in his journal. He was much more concerned with theology than with physical discomforts. "In the beginning of 1831 we renewed our journey; and, passing through Saint Louis and Saint Charles, we traveled on foot for three hundred miles through vast prairies and through trackless wilds of snow—no beaten road; houses few and far between; and the bleak north-

---
[11] *Winter of the Deep Snow*, by Eleanor Atkinson.
[12] *History of Clay and Platte County, Missouri*, page 122.

THE FIRST GREAT MISSION OF THE CHURCH 95

west wind blowing in our faces with a keenness which would almost take the skin off the face. We traveled for whole days, from morning till night, without a house or fire, wading in snow to the knees at every step, and the cold so intense that the snow did not melt on the south side of the houses, even in the midday sun, for nearly six weeks. We carried on our backs our changes of clothing, several books, and corn bread and raw pork. We often ate our frozen bread and pork by the way, when the bread would be so frozen that we could not bite or penetrate any part of it but the outside crust. After much fatigue and some suffering we all arrived in Independence, in the county of Jackson, on the extreme western frontiers of Missouri, and of the United States."[13]

We know from other accounts that it was all human power could do, perhaps more than human power could do, to ward away during that journey the twin specters of cold and starvation, as they kept their course without a beaten road over a wilderness of snow, the few stake and rider fences, corn shocks, low outbuildings completely buried, and streams only traced by the half buried lines of woods. All familiar features of the landscape were obliterated in a blur of blinding snow.[14]

One writer asserts that the missionaries upon their arrival from Ohio "sought and found shelter at the home of Colonel Robert Patterson, over toward the state line"[15] and remained there several days. Of this we do not know, but two of the missionaries were soon established as tailors in Independence. One of the first patrons of the new tailor shop was a tall young Kentuckian, Alexander W. Doniphan, who rode thirty miles from Lexington in order to have a suit made in the latest eastern style by Peter Whitmer.[16] The other missionaries passed over the line, through the Shawnees, and preached for a short time among the Dela-

---
[13] *Autobiography of Parley Parker Pratt*, pages 54, 55.
[14] Ida M. Tarbell in her *Life of Abraham Lincoln* states that old settlers for many years dated events by the "Winter of the Big Snow." Hay and Nicolet in their history of Lincoln give two pages to the description of the great snow of this winter.
[15] William W. Harris in Kansas City *Star* for Sunday, March 19, 1933.
[16] Interview with Doniphan published by Kansas City *Journal* in 1881—*Church History*, Volume 4, page 360.

wares, until forced to leave by the Indian agent, Major Richard W. Cummins.[17]

The copies of the Book of Mormon had all been sold or given away, and someone was needed to go back to report the success of their mission. A meeting of the five was held in Independence on February 14, and Pratt was selected as the emissary to return to civilization, get more books, and report the mission. The snow had begun to melt, the great rivers were breaking up, but the "snow turnpikes that had been made along main-traveled roads remained long after the great body of snow had melted—shining ribbons of white across the green spring prairie."[18]

After Pratt had gone, the other missionaries continued their efforts. Oliver Cowdery, when he wrote on May 7, 1831, to his brethren in the East, speaks of a missionary trip east into Lafayette County. He and Ziba Peterson had made this trip, forty miles, and "in the name of Jesus, called upon the people to repent." They found many earnestly "searching for truth," and Oliver "prayed that they might find that precious treasure." Apparently his prayer was answered. Forty-four were baptized in Big Sni Township, Lafayette County, at a point about three miles west of Lexington.

Ziba Peterson married one of these converts, and also among them was a young couple by the name of Francis and Mary Case. These were to follow the fortunes of the church on down through all its joys and sorrows. Mary Case died in the Old Folks Home in Lamoni at a very old age, and saw her children and grandchildren working in the church. Two of her grandsons, Oscar and Hubert Case, became missionaries for the church, and Hubert has probably baptized more people into the faith than any other man. He often heard his grandmother tell of her baptism by Oliver Cowdery. Little did those two missionaries know, as they took that forty-mile trip into the wilderness, how many

---

[17] William W. Harris in Kansas City *Star* for Sunday, March 19, 1933.
[18] *Winter of the Deep Snow*, by Eleanor Atkinson.

THE FIRST GREAT MISSION OF THE CHURCH 97

would find that "precious treasure" as a result of their efforts.

The Indian mission had not been forgotten, although they had been refused admittance to the Indian country about them. Cowdery had been partaking of the excitement that was then pervading Jackson County, which was to connect the fame of the little village of Independence forever with the great saga of the Santa Fe Trail. "I am informed of another tribe of Lamanites lately," wrote Oliver Cowdery, "who have an abundance of flocks of the best kinds of sheep and cattle, and they manufacture blankets of a superior quality. The tribe is very numerous; they live three hundred miles west of Santa Fe, and are called Navajos."[19]

One cannot but mark in the early writings of the Latter Day Saints, an unusual tolerance and kindliness, which later persecutions slowly changed into a bitterness that is wholly understandable, if not pardonable. Cowdery, speaking of difficulties that were being met in the East, wrote, "God forbid that I should bring a railing accusation against them, for vengeance belongeth to him who is able to repay; and herein, brethren, we confide."[20]

Pratt took immediate leave of his fellow missionaries and the friends they had made in Missouri and started on foot to St. Louis, a distance of around three hundred miles, which he made in nine days, then visited with friends near East St. Louis (the same place and with the same friends they found when snowbound just before Christmas). Another week accomplished the trip by steamboat from St. Louis to Cincinnati. It was March, 1831, and the "big snow" had at last melted, leaving as Pratt said "the whole country inundated as it were with mud and water."

He started, in spite of the mud, and walked two hundred and fifty miles towards Kirtland, but as the journey stretched out ahead, he became unaccountably weak and weary. About sundown, some days after he left Cincinnati, he came into the village

---

[19] Letter of Oliver Cowdery, written May 7, 1831, from Kaw Township, Missouri, as published in *Times and Seasons*, Volume 5, pages 432, 433.
[20] Letter of Oliver Cowdery, *Times and Seasons*, Volume 5, pages 432, 433.

of Strongville, Ohio. Pratt was so ill, he felt he could go no farther. Kirtland was only forty miles away, so he inquired for Latter Day Saints, and was directed to the Coltrin home. He knocked at the door and asked if they could entertain a stranger who had no money.

Even in pioneer times, when all strangers were made welcome, "Brother" Coltrin's slight hesitation might have been excusable, for there stood "a weary, weather-beaten traveler; soiled with the toil of a long journey; besmeared with mud, eyes inflamed with pain, long beard, and a visage lengthened by 'sickness and extreme fatigue.'" And Mrs. Coltrin had "ladies in to tea!" Our church history records only this one mention of Sister Coltrin, but what a gracious lady she must have been. "She received me with a smile of welcome, and immediately insisted upon my sitting down to tea with them," Pratt says.

Although he felt deathly sick, Pratt summoned every force to be agreeable. "You look so weary, stranger," Mrs. Coltrin said, as after making himself as presentable as possible he took his place at the table, "you must have traveled a long distance?" When he told them where he was from, all was animation immediately.

"Did you hear anything of the four great prophets out that way? . . . four men, four strange men, who came through this country, and preached, and baptized hundreds of people; and, after ordaining elders and organizing churches, they continued on westward, as we suppose, to the frontiers on a mission to the Indians; and we have never heard from them since."

Someone else hastened to add to the description: "They were dressed plainly and comely, very neat in their persons, and each one wore a hat of a drab color, low round crown and broad brim; after the manner of the Shakers, so it is said, for we had not the privilege of seeing them."

"They had neither purse nor script for their journey, neither shoes, nor two coats apiece," added a third.

THE FIRST GREAT MISSION OF THE CHURCH

Pratt admitted he had seen them.

"Will they return soon? Oh, who would not give the world to see them!"

Pratt laughed. "My name is Parley P. Pratt, one of the four men you have described, but not much of a prophet, and as to a sight of me in my present plight, I think it would not be worth *half* a world."

Pratt had fallen among brethren, which was well, for on the following morning, he could not lift his head from the pillow. He had the measles, but the long exposure in rain and mud had so aggravated what might be a very simple disease, that he almost died. But he was "watched over night and day, and had all the care that a man could have in his father's house." As soon as he had recovered sufficiently, he was provided with a horse to finish the trip to Kirtland.[21]

He found the church in Ohio had increased to "more than a thousand members, and those in New York, to several hundred."[22] He also heard from his wife in New York, whom he had not seen for six months, with the "news that the whole church in the State of New York, including herself (for she had joined the church during my absence) was about to remove to Ohio in the opening spring."[23] He concluded to go no farther eastward, but await their arrival.

His young brother, Orson, whom he had baptized shortly after he himself had been baptized and ordained, had also become a missionary. The boy was but nineteen when he was baptized on his birthday. Less than a year had passed, and Orson had walked from New York to Ohio, preaching and baptizing by the way. Lyman Wight, who had been ordained before the missionaries left Kirtland on November 20, 1830, had traveled six hundred miles in Ohio and Pennsylvania and baptized three hundred and ninety-three persons (by June 14, 1831).

---
[21]*Autobiography of Parley Parker Pratt*, pages 61-64.
[22]*Ibid.*, page 64.
[23]*Ibid.*

He learned that Simeon Carter from near Amherst, in whose home he had accidently left a Book of Mormon, had read it, believed, and made the trip of fifty miles to Kirtland for baptism, confirmation, and ordination; that he had then returned to his home and was preaching and baptizing.

But perhaps the most outstanding change was the call of Edward Partridge to be Bishop, and to look after the financial concerns of the church which had occurred very shortly before he left Missouri to come east (February 4, 1831). Edward Partridge had become interested in the work while the missionaries were in Kirtland, but being of a conservative turn of mind, he, in company with Sidney Rigdon, had made a trip to New York to see for himself. They had found Joseph Smith at Fayette, and Partridge had become convinced of the truth of the message and was baptized by Joseph in the Seneca River, December 11, 1830. In the revelation which called him to great responsibility in the church he was likened to "Nathanael of old in whom there is no guile."[24]

Partridge was born in Pittsfield, Berkshire County, Massachusetts, on the 27th of March, 1793. He was a hatter by trade, living, when the gospel found him, in Painesville, Ohio. He had not united with any church in his younger days, being unable to reconcile the popular preaching of the wrath of God with his own ideas of the mercy and kindness of a Supreme Being. Eventually he became a restorationalist, as the belief in a universal restoration of the wicked to divine grace was much in accord with his tolerant and forgiving disposition.

Rigdon and Partridge brought to the church a ripened experience that was much needed in the new organization at the time. Both were thirty-seven years of age, scarcely six months between their dates of birth, and both were rich in the knowledge of humanity, Partridge as a business man, Rigdon as a minister of no ordinary ability.

[24] Doctrine and Covenants 41: 3.

XI.—Sidney Rigdon

The mission to Kirtland resulted in bringing to the church many brilliant men who played active parts in its destiny, Sidney Rigdon, Frederick Granger Williams, Orson Hyde, Lyman Wight, Luke and Lyman E. Johnson, Newel K. Whitney, and others. But of all these none created such a stir throughout the whole Western Reserve[1] as the conversion of Sidney Rigdon, the minister of the most popular church in Mentor, who was universally recognized as "the great orator" of the Reform Baptist Movement in Ohio, then in process of evolution into what has since been called the Disciples of Christ.

All who knew Rigdon spoke of him as "eloquent," as an "orator," and his oratory was of the kind that kindled a fire in his hearers' hearts, like to that with which his very soul was glowing. His enthusiasm brooked no delay, and he was impatient of obstacles. He disliked discussion, his mind leaped to its conclusions, rather than arriving at them by slow process of cold logic. Once during a conference, while he was associated with Campbell, Scott, and Bentley, he interrupted a long, monotonous debate in which he had taken no part with this short speech, "You are consuming too much time on this question. One of the old Jerusalem preachers would start out with his hunting shirt and moccasins, and convert half the world while you are discussing and settling plans."[2] That speedily brought the argument to a close.

After the arrival of the missionaries and the transfer of many of his congregation to the new faith, an event described by his

---

[1] "Western Reserve" was a term applied to a large, fertile, and remarkably level portion of northern Ohio, which had been reserved in the original grant of territory by the Government in reference to certain military claims.
[2] *History of the Disciples in the Western Reserve*, by A. S. Hayden, page 174.

former associates as "That overflowing scourge[3] of Mormonism" and the missionaries who brought it "like the four evil messengers from the Euphrates" (Revelation 9: 15), the people in the vicinity of Kirtland "were shaken as by a tempest," but Rigdon, aflame with a message as never before, continued to draw men to him. Of the peculiar winning power of Rigdon's oratory, a story is vouched for by John Barr of Cleveland, well versed in the history of the Western Reserve:

"In 1830 I was deputy sheriff, and being at Willoughby on official business determined to go to Mayfield, which is seven or eight miles up the Chagrin River, and hear Cowdery and Rigdon on the revelations of Mormonism. Varnem J. Card the lawyer, and myself started early Sunday morning on horseback. We found the roads crowded with people going in the same direction. Services were opened by Cowdery . . . he was followed by Rigdon . . . ." A baptism followed the service: "The place selected for immersion was in a clear pool in the river above the bridge, around which was a beautiful rise of ground on the west side for the audience. On the east bank was a sharp bluff and some stumps, where Mr. Card and myself stationed ourselves. The time of baptism was fixed at 2 p.m. Long before this hour, the spot was surrounded by as many people as could have a clear view. Rigdon went into the pool, which, at the deepest, was about four feet, and after a suitable address with prayer, Cahoon came forward and was baptized. Standing in the water, Rigdon gave one of his most powerful exhortations. The assembly became greatly affected. As he proceeded, he called for the converts to step forward. They came through the crowd in rapid succession to the number of thirty and were immersed, with no intermission of the discourse on the part of Rigdon.

"Mr. Card was apparently the most radical, stoical of men—of a clear, unexcitable temperament, with unorthodox and vague

---

[3]*Ibid.*, page 207.

religious ideas. While the exciting scene was transpiring below us in the valley and in the pool, the faces of the crowd expressing the most intense emotion, Mr. Card suddenly seized my arm and said, 'Take me away.' Taking his arm, I saw his face was so pale that he seemed to be about to faint. His frame trembled as we walked away and mounted our horses. We rode a mile toward Willoughby before a word was said. Rising the hill out of the valley he seemed to recover and said, 'Mr. Barr, if you had not been there I certainly should have gone into the water.' He said the impulse was irresistible."[4]

Such was the man Rigdon, who was so profoundly to influence the church in the years to come. The enthusiasm, kindled by the fire of his words, was no transient thing, but something that remained with the hearer through life. There are those who would have us believe that Sidney Rigdon as a lad on the farm planned with the most deceitful cunning to erect upon theft and lies the whole superstructure of the Latter Day Saint Church. His was not the life of an impostor. As the years passed he suffered all kinds of sorrow and disappointment for the church's sake, and at sixty years of age, we find him, working as a shingle-packer in Friendship, Allegheny County, N. Y., near his boyhood home. He was silent about his connection with the church for the most part, but the fire had not died. There was life in the embers yet, ready to be fanned into flame, should the right moment come. He wrote to Lyman Wight. "Old friend," he called him and referred to himself as an "exile," and said, "But should that day arrive which I have longed for and desired above all other events in the history of the world when Zion shall be redeemed; I hope then to meet to be driven . . . no more."[5]

Says A. S. Hayden, one of his fellow ministers in that movement: "Whatever may be justly said of him after he had sur-

---

[4] "The Early Days of Mormonism," by Frederick G. Mather, *Lippincott's Magazine*, 1880, page 206.
[5] Letter from Sidney Rigdon to Lyman Wight in Texas. Dated Friendship, Allegheny County, New York, May 22, 1853. *Lyman Wight Letter Book*, Heman C. Smith collection.

rendered himself a victim and a leader of the Mormon delusion, it would scarcely be just to deny sincerity and candor to him, previous to the time when his bright star became permanently eclipsed under that dark cloud."[6]

Sidney Rigdon was born in Saint Clair Township, Allegheny County, Pennsylvania, February 19, 1793, the youngest son of William and Nancy Rigdon. His father died when he was but seventeen, and he continued on the home farm with his mother until he was twenty-six years of age, when he went to reside with a Baptist minister by the name of Andrew Clark, as he had the year previous united with that denomination. He studied with this man until March, 1819, when he received his license to preach from the Regular Baptist Society, and leaving his native state two months later went to the West (Trumbell County, Ohio). There in the town of Warren, he made his home from July of that year with Adamson Bentley, another Baptist minister, until on the 12th of June, 1820, he married Phoebe Brook, a sister of Bentley's wife. The two brothers-in-law, always great friends, became more and more united in their work.

> Through this now thickly settled region, quite a number of Baptist churches had already been formed, and Mr. Bentley had induced a number of their preachers to hold annually what was known as "ministers" meetings for the purpose of conversing upon the Scriptures, and upon their own religious progress, and improving each other by criticisms upon each other's sermons. In these meetings he acted as secretary, and contributed largely to render them profitable and interesting. It was also agreed that the churches should form an association and on the 30th day of August, 1820, . . . the messengers appointed by the churches met and constituted the Mahoning Baptist Association.[7]

Through other Baptist ministers, Rigdon and Bentley learned of one Alexander Campbell and read his debate with a man named Walker. Both became intensely interested in his views. Campbell himself tells the sequel of the story:

---
[6]*History of the Disciples in the Western Reserve*, by A. S. Hayden, page 192.
[7]*Memoirs of Alexander Campbell*, by Richardson, Volume 2, page 44.

In the summer of 1821, while sitting in my portico [in Bethany, West Virginia] after dinner, two gentlemen in the costume of clergymen, as then technically called, appeared in my yard, advancing to the house. The elder of them on approaching me, first introduced himself saying, "My name, sir, is Adamson Bentley; this is Elder Sidney Rigdon, both of Warren, Ohio." On entering my house, and being introduced to my family, after some refreshment, Elder Bentley said, "Having just read your debate with Mr. John Walker of our State of Ohio, with considerable interest, and having been deputed by the Mahoning Baptist Association last year to ordain some elders and to set some churches in order, which brought us within little more than a day's ride of you, we concluded to make a special visit, to inquire of you particularly on sundry matters of much interest to us as set forth in the debate, and would be glad, when perfectly at your leisure, to have an opportunity to do so." I replied, that, as soon as the afternoon duties of my seminary [Alexander Campbell conducted what he called a high school for boys, which was to all intents and purposes a religious seminary] were discharged, I would take pleasure in hearing from them fully on such matters.

After tea, in the evening, we commenced, and prolonged our discourse until the next morning. Beginning with the baptism that John preached, we went back to Adam, and forward to the final judgment. The dispensations—Adamic, Abrahamic, Jewish, and Christian—passed and repassed before us. Mount Sinai in Arabia, Mount Zion, Mount Tabor, and the Red Sea and the Jordan, the passovers and the Pentecosts, the law and the gospel, but especially the ancient order of things and the modern occasionally engaged our attention.[8]

From that time forward Adamson Bentley, Sidney Rigdon, and Alexander Campbell, and a Baptist minister by the name of Walter Scott, to whom Campbell introduced them in Pittsburgh, became active exponents of what was then known as a reformed Baptist movement.

Upon their return to Warren, Bentley and Rigdon perfected the Regular Baptist communion, for their new ideas by the means of these gatherings were effectively scattered over all the nine counties that comprised the 3,000,000 acres of the Western Reserve.

These meetings were conducted in the following manner: A, B, C, and D, were appointed to address the public assembled on the occasion

---

[8]*Millennial Harbinger,* 1848, page 532.

[usually at a conference]. A at a given time delivered an address; B succeeded him. In the evening all the speakers and other ministers met in an appointed room and in the presence of the more elderly and interested brethren, and those looking forward to public positions in the church, the discourses of A and B were taken up and examined by all the speakers present, and were somewhat strictly reviewed as to the manner of them, the form of them, and the mode of delivering them. Doctrinal questions and expositions of the Scripture occasionally were introduced and debated. The next day C and D addressed the assembled audience, and so on until all were heard, and all had passed through the same ordeal.[9]

In these ministers' meetings Rigdon figured prominently, and, by means of the minutes left of them, we are able to trace his movements with remarkable detail through the ensuing years of his Baptist ministry. The last meeting of the Mahoning Association was at Austintown in 1830, and its historian, Hayden, places the date "about two months previous to the fall of that star [Rigdon] from heaven."[10]

In 1822, Campbell was much interested in a Baptist Church in Pittsburgh, many of whose hundred members, he considered were in favor of "reformation." Naturally he desired a pastor there who was fully in sympathy with his reform ideas. "Through Mr. Campbell's influence, Sidney Rigdon was induced to accept a call from the church to become the pastor. He was a man of more than ordinary ability as a speaker, possessing great fluency and a lively fancy, which gave him great popularity as an orator."[11] The church prospered under Rigdon's care, and he had the opportunity of cultivating the acquaintance of Campbell, whom he greatly admired.

Early in October, 1823, Campbell arranged for a debate on baptism, with a Reverend McCalla of Washington, Kentucky, and Sidney Rigdon went with him to take notes for publication. As the Ohio River was too low that year for navigation, they made

---

[9] *Memoirs of Alexander Campbell*, by Richardson, page 46.
[10] *Early History of the Disciples in the Western Reserve, Ohio*, by A. S. Hayden, pages 297, 298.
[11] *Memoirs of Alexander Campbell*, by Richardson, pages 47, 48.

the trip on horseback. They rode the three hundred miles in safety, arriving at Washington four days before the debate, so had ample time to rest and prepare. The debate ended on October 22, and they preached at Mayslick, Bryant's Station, and Lexington before returning home. Upon their return, they were busily engaged for several weeks in preparing the notes for publication.

The reform movement in the meantime proceeded to gain adherents and enemies in Pittsburgh until a division was effected in the Baptist Communion in 1824, the reform adherents of the two churches in Pittsburgh uniting, and those who remained in the conservative wing being recognized as the only "legitimate Baptist Church" in Pittsburgh. The united church in 1825 came under the pastorship of Scott, the older of the two reform pastors in Pittsburgh. Scott was teaching school there and able to sustain himself. Rigdon obtained secular employment until such time as he could return to Ohio. After two years' labor as a tanner, he removed to Bainbridge, Geauga County, Ohio, and from there to Mantua, and then to Mentor, raising up large followings in each place. He was at Mentor when the gospel found him, at the height of his fame as an orator in the Western Reserve. He believed and for the second time stepped down from his position as a minister and accepted the lot of a struggling pioneer in a new and untried movement. There is no antagonism so bitter as that found among "religious" people; no man considered so base by his former associates as he who secedes from them. Once again came the bitter separation from friends and associates. True, some of them went with him, but Alexander Campbell, whom he loved as a father, became a bitter enemy; and his brother-in-law, Adamson Bentley, grew so hostile that the intimacy of these two more than brother ministers was completely and finally severed.

In 1834, E. D. Howe, editor of the Painsville *Telegraph*, incensed because his wife and other members of his family had united with the church, published the first rabid exposé of the church, *Mormonism Unveiled,* which was to become the model for a long series of such works. Among other things, Howe, aided by that perennial troublemaker, Doctor Hurlbut, advanced an ingenious theory accounting for the origin of the Book of Mormon. The claim made was that the manuscript was derived from a romance written by one Solomon Spaulding in the year 1812; that this "Manuscript Found" was submitted to Robert Patterson, a printer in Pittsburgh, Pennsylvania; and after some time was returned to its owner; that Spaulding later removed to Amity, Pennsylvania, and died there in 1816.[12]

"Supported by an abundance of conjecture, but by very little positive evidence"[13] *Mormonism Unveiled* expressed the theory that Rigdon working as a printer for Patterson, either copied or stole the manuscript, and in collaboration with Joseph Smith produced the Book of Mormon some fifteen years later. The public eagerly accepted this fabrication, and it soon became an American tradition, copied as a matter of course in all non-Mormon literature and many leading histories and encyclopedia. Rigdon's family, mother and brothers advanced the unrefuted testimony that Sidney was never a printer; that he never lived in Pittsburgh until 1822, eight years after the Spauldings moved away, and that he then went there as a pastor of a leading church. Nor has there ever been any proof that Rigdon ever saw Joseph Smith until he saw him in Fayette, in December, 1830. Nevertheless the story would not down.

All through the years, denials of the story have been made by those who are in a position to know, and after his death the family of Rigdon continued to deny that he participated in such a fraud. Mrs. Nancy Rigdon Ellis, although but eight years old

---
[12]For a discussion of this theory from a nonpartisan viewpoint, read an article by James H. Fairchild, at one time president of Oberlin College, first published as Tract No. 77 by the Western Reserve Historical Society of Cleveland, and republished in the *Saints' Herald,* August 21, 1918, Volume 65; also in *Journal of History* (L. D. S.), Volume 17 (1924).
[13]Fairchild in Tract No. 77, Western Reserve Historical Society.

at the time the missionaries came to her father's home in Mentor, Ohio, says she has a distinct remembrance of the occasion:

> "I saw them hand him the book, and I am as positive as can be that he never saw it before. He read it and examined it for about an hour and then threw it down, and said he did not believe a word in it." She further stated that her father in the last years of his life called his family together and told them, as sure as there was a God in heaven, he never had anything to do in getting up the Book of Mormon, and never saw any such thing as a manuscript written by Solomon Spaulding.[14]

To a reporter from the *Pittsburgh* (Pennsylvania) *Leader*, Mrs. Ellis gave this statement: "I will say this, that my father, who had the respect of all who knew him, and at a time when he had but little hope of living from one day to another, said to the clergymen around him, of which there was a number belonging to the various denominations. These were his words: 'As I expect to die and meet my Maker, I know nothing about where the manuscript of the Mormon Bible came from.'"[15]

In 1905 his son John W., though an infant at the time of the coming of the missionaries to his father, had this to say of what happened:

> I determined to ascertain from my father whether he knew anything in regard to the origin of the Book of Mormon other than had been made public, and if such were unfavorable to the church [John W. Rigdon was a member of no faction of the church at this time] I should make it known. My father was then in his last years, and I found him as firm as ever in declaring that he himself had nothing whatever to do in writing the book, and that Joseph Smith received it from an angel. On his dying bed he made the same declaration to a Methodist minister.... My sister [Athalia, wife of George W. Robinson] some nine years older than I, testified to me a few months ago that she also remembers when the book was first seen by our father. My mother has also told me that Father had nothing whatever to do with the writing of the book, and that she positively knew that he had never seen it until Parley P. Pratt came to our home with it. These testimonies have clung to me ever since, and I could not forget them.[16]

---
[14]Nancy Rigdon Ellis in an interview with Wm. H. and E. L. Kelley, May 14, 1884, at Pittsburgh, Pennsylvania, *Church History*, Volume 4, pages 451, 452.
[15]Nancy Rigdon Ellis as reported in *Pittsburgh Leader*, May 18, 1884, *Church History*, Volume 4, page 453.
[16]*Elders' Journal*, Chattanooga, Tennessee, Volume 2, pages 267, 268.

Over his own signature while he lived, Rigdon made repeated denials, writing in 1839 from Nauvoo to the Boston *Journal* when thoroughly incensed over the persistence of the story. He said emphatically, "It is only necessary to say, in relation to the whole story about Spaulding's writings being in the hands of Mr. Patterson, who was in Pittsburgh, and who is said to have kept a printing office and my saying that I was concerned in the said office, etc., it is the most base of lies, without a shadow of truth . . . . If I were to say that I ever heard of the Reverend Solomon Spaulding and his hopeful wife until Doctor P. Hurlbut wrote his lie about me, I would be a liar like unto themselves."[17]

Many an old time Saint remembers how he stood in the pulpit and in his eloquent and dramatic style carried conviction, as was the way of Rigdon, to their very souls.[18]

In the spring of 1833 or 1834, at the house of Samuel Baker, near New Portage, Medina County, Ohio, . . . we did hear Elder Sidney Rigdon in the presence of a large congregation say he had been informed that some in the neighborhood had accused him of being the instigator of the Book of Mormon. Standing in the doorway, there being many standing in the doorway, he, holding up the Book of Mormon said, "I testify in the presence of this congregation, and before God, and all his holy angels up yonder (pointing upward) before whom I expect to give account at the judgment day, that I never saw a sentence of the Book of Mormon, I never penned a sentence of the Book of Mormon, I never knew there was such a book in existence as the Book of Mormon, until it was presented to me by Parley P. Pratt in the form that it now is."[19]

Years passed, and Howe sold the Painsville *Telegraph* with type, press, old books, manuscripts, and papers to Mr. L. L. Rice. Much of this material was not destroyed by Rice but carried with him, unexamined in an old trunk for many years. In 1884 Mr. Rice lived in Honolulu in the Hawaiian Islands, and had as his guest President James H. Fairchild of Oberlin University. In looking over these papers, they discovered the long-lost Spaulding

---
[17]*Church History*, Smith & Smith, Volume 1, page 144, 145.
[18]*Saints' Herald*, Volume 31 page 339.
[19]Statement of Phineas, Hiel, and Mary Bronson.

romance which had been in Mr. Rice's possession, unknown to him, for over forty years.[20] These men, both disinterested so far as Sidney Rigdon is concerned, unhesitatingly absolve him from all responsibility. Rice says, "No one who reads this manuscript will give credit to the story that Solomon Spaulding was in any wise the author of the Book of Mormon. It was unlikely that anyone who wrote so elaborate a work as the Mormon Bible would spend his time in getting up so shallow a story as this . . . . Finally I am more than half convinced that this is his only writing of the sort, and that any pretense that Spaulding was in any sense the author of the other, is a sheer fabrication."[21]

Dr. Fairchild, who had only a scholar's curiosity concerning the whole subject, said: "Mr. Rice, myself, and others compared it with the Book of Mormon, and could detect no resemblance between the two, in general or in detail. There seems to be no name or incident common to the two . . . . Some other explanation of the origin of the Book of Mormon must be found if any explanation is required."[22]

---

[20] Now in library of Oberlin College at Oberlin, Ohio.

[21] Letter from L. L. Rice to Joseph Smith, March 28, 1885. L. L. Rice was formerly a prominent antislavery editor of Ohio and later for many years was state printer in Columbus, Ohio. He later (May 14, 1885) wrote Joseph Smith as follows: "Two things are true concerning this manuscript in my possession: First, it is a genuine writing of Solomon Spaulding; and second, it is not the original of the Book of Mormon. My opinion is from all I have seen and learned, that this is the only writing of Spaulding, and there is no foundation for the statement of Deming and others, that Spaulding made another story, more elaborate" etc. *Bibliotheca Sacra*, Volume 42, No. 165, January, 1885, page 173; *Manuscript Found*, pages 7-8. (See *Saints' Herald*, Volume 32, page 177.)

XII.—The Church Moves West

By December, 1830, plans were being made for the church in New York to remove to Ohio. According to a statement of Joseph about this time, the church from "Colesville to Canandaigua, New York, numbered about seventy members." The eventful year of 1830 ended amid preparations to move as a body westward and await in Ohio the return of the missionaries.

At the Conference in Fayette, January 2, 1831, the last General Conference in New York, direction was given concerning the move to Ohio, and promise of a great endowment there was given. Therefore about the last of January, Joseph Smith, his wife, Sidney Rigdon, and Edward Partridge started for Kirtland, arriving there the first of February, where for "several weeks" Joseph Smith and his wife were pleasantly received and entertained by the genial merchant of the little town, Newel K. Whitney. "With a little caution and some wisdom," writes Joseph Smith, "I soon assisted the brethren and sisters to abandon some of the notions that had crept in among them." "The plan of common stock which had existed in what was called 'the family,' whose members generally had embraced the everlasting gospel, was readily abandoned for the more perfect law of the Lord."

On Friday, February 4, 1831, Edward Partridge was called to take charge of the financial affairs of the church, and the people were promised on condition of their assembling with prayer and faith, that a law should be given "that ye may know how to govern my church, and have all things right before me."

The people were looking forward not only to a spiritual, but also to an economic brotherhood, which came to be called after the city of old, where all men lived in righteousness and equality, and there were no rich and no poor, "Zion," which was defined to mean "the pure in heart."

The people from the East were gathering into Kirtland as spring progressed. When the majority of those who were experienced in such matters considered that the spring was "open" enough for travel, the Saints from that region assembled at the home of Joseph Smith, Sr., who now occupied a rented house near the Erie Canal, on the Seneca River in Waterloo, and prepared to make the long trip to Kirtland. To most of the people gathered there, it was an event of great importance, for few of them had been many miles from home, except those who had migrated years before from New England, and from Pennsylvania to Fayette in the German immigration early in the century. They had planned with a foresight that later marked the Saints in matters of immigration to go together, chartering a canal boat for their own use and thus saving expense. When all was prepared it was found that there were eighty souls present, each with his small belongings, and most of them with what food was considered sufficient for the trip.

The Methodist minister's boat had been rented for the occasion. Doubtless it was a "line" boat, and not one of the luxuriously appointed and gaily painted packets that plied the canal. Even on these humble line boats, the fare without board was two and a half cents per mile, so that the cost of transportation for the entire group would have been around two dollars a mile. They were rejoiced to be saving money on the trip. Neighbors thronged the little boat and the now nearly empty house of the Smiths, saying good-by. One kind friend put into the hands of Mother Smith seventeen dollars, which, although she had plenty for herself and her own children,[1] came to good use later in supplying food for those who had not brought an ample supply. Canal travel, even though it was upon little more than a large ditch, had some hazards. The famous Erie Canal was but forty feet wide at the top, twenty-eight feet at the bottom, and only about four

---

[1] There were eight of the Smith family, mother Lucy Smith, her daughter Sophronia Stoddard, husband and child; Catherine, William, Don Carlos, and Lucy. The father and other sons had preceded them to Kirtland.

feet deep. The locks were ninety by twelve feet, and the largest boat they would hold would be only one hundred tons. One of the most common mishaps was for the canal to "break," which stopped all progress down the canal until it was repaired. This happened on this occasion, but "Mormon" preaching was always in demand among the curious, and one of the neighbors where the boat was held up came on board and asked if there were any preachers there. As there was a beautiful green near the boat, Elders Humphrey and Page preached to a good congregation gathered there, and were invited to make another appointment for the next day, but that night at eleven the canal was repaired, and the little band of pilgrims continued on its way. They made good time, arriving at Buffalo just five days after leaving Waterloo. Here they met the Colesville Saints who had come ahead of them, and were still in Buffalo, held up by four feet of ice on the lake.

All shipping was laid up, and rooms in the city of Buffalo were at a premium. Mother Smith could find none, and supplies and money were limited. She was anxious to reach her destination. Then she remembered her brother Stephen Mack's former partner, a lake captain, and fortunately found him in port. He told her to bring her party on board his boat and remain there until the ice broke. She tells of how the little band of pilgrims knelt in prayer upon the deck, and how almost immediately the ice broke, opening up a channel, which soon closed behind them, and how for almost three weeks no other boat left port.[2] The trip was long and stormy, the most stormy Captain Blake had seen in his thirty years upon the lakes. The boat was reported lost, and the members of the family in Kirtland almost despaired of seeing those who were on her. But at last, worn and weary with wind, rain, and storm, the little band disembarked at Fairfield, eleven miles from Kirtland. Young William Smith and another young man

---

[2] See *Joseph Smith and His Progenitors,* also letter of Catherine (Smith) Salisbury, written from Fountain Green, Illinois, May 16, 1886, *Saints' Herald* for 1886, Volume 33, page 404.

by the name of Jenkins Salisbury started to walk to Kirtland in search of their father and brothers, who on hearing the news hastened to Fairfield to conduct the rest of the family home. The reunion was a happy one, and the breakfast at Edward Partridge's, the first regular meal they had had in weeks, was so enjoyed, especially by the young members of the company, that they remembered it even down to old age.[3]

By similar journeys the Saints poured into Kirtland from the East. Although practically the entire membership had migrated to Kirtland, New York still continued to be one of the most fertile fields for missionary efforts for many years to come.

Kirtland had never been intended for more than a temporary stopping place for the Saints in their pilgrimage west to the Zion that was to be built on "the borders by the Lamanites." It was now planned that practically all the elders in Kirtland who could travel were to make the trip to Zion, two by two, and upon their arrival the place where the city should begin would be pointed out to them.

A more effective missionary campaign could hardly have been devised. Fifteen pairs of men (see D. and C. 52) traveling through that sparsely settled western country, might easily cover all the main roads to Missouri. These men were to be Sidney Rigdon and Joseph Smith, Lyman Wight and John Corrill, John Murdock and Hyrum Smith, Thomas B. Marsh and Ezra Thayre, Isaac Morley and Ezra Booth, Edward Partridge and Martin Harris, David Whitmer and Harvey Whitlock, Parley P. and Orson Pratt, Solomon Hancock and Simeon Carter, Edson Fuller and Jacob Scott, Levi Hancock and Zebedee Coltrin, Reynolds Cahoon and Samuel H. Smith, William Carter and Wheeler Baldwin, Newell Knight and Selah J. Griffith, Joseph Wakefield and Solomon Humphrey. Edson Fuller, Jacob Scott, and William Carter dropped out. Ezra B. Thayre could not prepare in time, and Newell Knight was required to stay home to help superintend the proposed re-

---
[3] William Smith on Mormonism, Lamoni Herald Press, 1883.

moval of the Colesville Branch en masse, as the community experiment attempted at Thompson by the Colesville Branch was not working out as anticipated. Therefore Thomas B. Marsh was mated anew with Selah J. Griffith, and Wheeler Baldwin occupied himself with missionary work near Kirtland.

The fact that little time was spent in preparation was characteristic of our early missionaries. These men were called to go on a mission at the conference of June 6. In less than two weeks the majority of them, probably all of them, had said good-by to their families and taken up their journey on foot to the unknown West. The entire saga of these early missionary travels would be as thrilling as a tale of adventure, but unfortunately only a few written lines remain to tell the story.

Just as Joseph Smith was about to leave, one of the many inquirers from the East called at his house and having learned of the latest missionary project was anxious to go along. That man was William Wine Phelps. He was promptly baptized, ordained, and provided with a traveling companion in the person of Joseph Coe. Thus it happened three of the missionary pairs made the journey together. With them was a partner of Newell Knight in his mercantile venture, Algernon S. Gilbert, who was accompanied by his wife. Gilbert was to establish a new store in Independence.

These went by wagon to a point where they could take the new canal to Cincinnati; Ohio had a few years previously entered upon a program of canal building intended to link the Erie Canal to the Ohio River, for travel in this era was mainly by water. This was part of the magnificent scheme of state improvements, for which six years later the people of Ohio with the rest of the citizens of the United States were asked to pay the piper in the panic of 1837. It took superlative courage and optimism (not to say rashness) to plan the building of such an immense system of canals, the first one alone of which was estimated to cost one tenth of all the taxable property in the State of

Ohio ($5,700,000). The first of these two canals, the Ohio-Erie Canal, ran from Cleveland on Lake Erie and down the Scioto to Portsmouth on the Ohio River; the second, the Miami Canal, followed the historic route from Cincinnati to Toledo on Maumee Bay. These canals, or such portions of them as were finished, figured largely in the migrations of the early Saints to and from Missouri. The missionary party consisting of Joseph Smith, Sidney Rigdon, Edward Partridge, Martin Harris, W. W. Phelps, Joseph Coe, and the Gilberts took the Miami Canal which had been finished as far as Dayton two years before, and arriving in Cincinnati had a few days to wait for a steamer to Louisville. Joseph Smith and Rigdon took the occasion to visit Rigdon's old friend of Pittsburgh days, Walter Scott, but they were bitterly repulsed.

From there they took a steamboat to Louisville, Kentucky, and down to Saint Louis. At Saint Louis, after some parley, the party separated. Mr. and Mrs. Gilbert with Sidney Rigdon, whose previous life and over two hundred pounds of avoirdupois unsuited him for walking, took a Missouri River steamboat. Now any river pilot of that day could tell you that the Missouri was temperamental; that navigation on the Mississippi was child's play compared with taking a boat up the Missouri. "Of all the variable things in creation the most uncertain are the action of a jury, the state of a woman's mind, and the condition of the Missouri River."[4] And yet the river in the heyday of steamboating was navigated twenty-three hundred miles above Saint Louis. So while the Gilberts and Rigdon waited for a boat, their brethren started to walk and beat them to Independence!

As the five men walked along, they talked over the gospel and made it a practice to read a chapter from the Bible and have a prayer every day. Arriving in what is now Kansas City, the party camped near the site of the historic old spring which is now directly at the foot of the extension of Charlotte Street. The

---
[4]Sioux City *Register*, March 28, 1868.

earth on top of what was once the cave's mouth forms the union of what is now Charlotte Street and Gleed Terrace.[5] The old cave and the spring which flowed from it were well known to frontiersmen long before Kansas City was built. It was located near the old Independence-Westport Road, a part of which now forms Gillham Road. The Santa Fe trade that traveled the route from Independence through Westport had established a watering place there for the wagon caravans which passed. In the days when Joseph Smith and his missionary party camped here, a stream of crystal clear water ran from this spring and fed a good-sized creek, which flowed southwest and made a junction with another creek, running down the present side of Oak Street.

Joseph Smith's impression of the people was not reassuring, for the Missourians were as uncongenial to the people from the East as the "Mormonites" were to them. He says: "Our reflections were great, coming as we had from a highly cultivated state of society in the East, and standing now upon the confines or western limits of the United States and looking into the vast wilderness of those that sat in darkness. How natural it was to observe the degradation, leanness of intellect, ferocity and jealousy of a people that were nearly a century behind the time, and to feel for those who roamed about without the benefit of civilization, refinement, or religion!"

He was greatly pleased with the country as a whole, and thought that by encouraging the people to bring with them a better grade of stock, grain for planting, and implements for farming, and the will to establish and maintain schools, conditions

[5] In Carrie Westlake Whitney's *Kansas City, Missouri, Its History and Its People, 1808-1908*, Volume 1, pages 55-56, it is stated that Joseph Smith the Mormon prophet established a school one hundred yards northeast of the cave's mouth two years before Westport was platted. The school was abandoned when the Mormons left the county in 1833. This would place the date as 1831, since Westport was platted in 1833. Joseph Smith was present in Jackson County only for a very short time in 1831—from the middle of July to August 9. The only possible incident, if any, referring to the school's establishment is one recorded in Joseph Smith's notes which reads: "August 2, I assisted in laying the first log for a house as the foundation of Zion in Kaw Township, twelve miles west of Independence. The log was carried and laid in place by twelve men in honor of the twelve tribes of Israel." We have no record of this property ever belonging to the church. However, at the same time, the church dedicated the site for the temple to be built in Independence on land they did not own, but acquired by purchase some months later.

would improve, and the land would become indeed the promised land of their highest hopes.

The union with the brethren who had left Fayette nearly nine months before was an unmixed pleasure.

W. W. Phelps, a member of the church now for nearly a month, was the chosen speaker the Sunday after the arrival of the missionaries, speaking to a mixed congregation of white pioneers, Negroes, and Indians. Two were baptized that day. It was now the middle of July. Few of the missionaries had arrived. The next week the Colesville Branch[6] came, Sidney Rigdon, A. S. Gilbert and wife, and the first of the missionary teams, Isaac Morley and Ezra Booth. The settlement of Zion had begun!

And by special protection of the Lord, Brother Joseph Smith, Junior, and Sidney Rigdon [wrote John Whitmer, historian of the church], in company with eight other elders, with the church from Colesville, New York, consisting of about sixty souls, arrived in the month of July, and by revelation the place was made known where the temple shall stand and the city should commence. And by commandment twelve of us assembled ourselves together, viz., Elder Joseph Smith, Junior, the Seer, Oliver Cowdery, Sidney Rigdon, Newel Knight, William W. Phelps, and Ezra Booth who denied the faith.

On the second day of August, 1831, Brother Sidney Rigdon stood up and asked, saying, Do you receive this land for the land of your inheritance with thankful hearts from the Lord? Answer from all, We do. Do you pledge yourself to keep the laws of God on this land, which you have never kept in your own land?[7] We do.

---

[6] In the Kansas City *Star* for March 19, 1933, in an article "Westport Won the Santa Fe Trade from Independence" by William W. Harris, we are told, "The first large settlement [of the Saints] was established in the valley of Brush Creek from the state line eastward a mile or more between the Ward homestead and Westport, where they entered and bought several thousand acres. The families occupied ten or twenty acre tracts of land which had been secured in 1831 by Bishop Partridge and held as common property." The old records in the courthouse in Independence bear out the fact that Edward Partridge did hold considerable land in the valley of Brush Creek. In the summer of 1933, W. O. Hands made a blue print showing these land descriptions superimposed upon a modern map of Kansas City. The Saints of Colesville probably occupied these tracts, or a part of them, particularly the part indicated by Harris. Five tracts of this land following modern boundaries as nearly as possible were (1) Beginning at state line and 47th Street, east to Holly, south to 55th, west to state line, north to place of beginning; (2) Beginning at Summit and 51st, east to Wornall Road, south to 55th, west to Summit, north to 51st (This tract comprises all of Jacob L. Loose Memorial Park); (3) Beginning at 47th and Broadway, east to Main, south to 50th, west to Broadway, and north to 47th; (4) Beginning at 51st and Main, east to Holmes, south to 55th, west to Main, and north to 51st; (5) Beginning at 51st and Troost, east to Woodland, south to 55th, west to Troost, and north to 51st.

[7] Probably referring to the new economic order about to be instituted among them.

Do you pledge yourselves to see that others of your brethren who shall come hither do keep the laws of God? We do. After prayer, he arose and said, I now pronounce this land consecrated and dedicated to the Lord for a possession and inheritance for the Saints (in the name of Jesus Christ, having authority from him). And for all the faithful servants of the Lord to the remotest ages of time. Amen.

The day following eight elders, viz., Joseph Smith, Junior, Oliver Cowdery, Sidney Rigdon, Peter Whitmer, Junior, Frederick G. Williams, William W. Phelps, Martin Harris, and Joseph Coe assembled together where the temple is to be erected. Sidney Rigdon dedicated the ground where the city is to stand, and Joseph Smith, Junior, laid a stone at the northeast corner of the contemplated temple in the name of the Lord Jesus of Nazareth. After all present had rendered thanks to the great Ruler of the universe, Sidney Rigdon pronounced this spot of ground wholly dedicated unto the Lord forever. Amen.[8]

The spot for the temple was about a half mile from the straggling little village of Independence, a short distance south of the road. As yet these people did not own one foot of ground!

The purpose for which they had come now being fulfilled, the missionary party made ready to go back to Kirtland. On the 4th, all attended a conference at the home of Joshua Lewis,[9] one of the Missouri converts to the church, near what is now 35th and the Paseo in Kansas City.

All the way west, Polly Knight, wife of Joseph Knight, Sr., who had mothered young Joseph Smith in the old days at Colesville, had been steadily failing. It was her one great wish to live to see the "land of Zion." Now less than a month after she had arrived with all her family, she passed away. Joseph Smith

---

[8] *Manuscript History of John Whitmer; Journal of History*, Volume 1, page 59.
[9] For many years it was assumed that Joshua Lewis was one of the Colesville Saints, and that if and when his home was located, we would know the location of the "Colesville Settlement." Mr. Rolland Brittain finally located the Joshua Lewis homestead by means of a tax title. For many years we called this the site of the Colesville settlement, but we now know definitely that Joshua Lewis was *not* a member of the Colesville Branch but a convert made by the earliest missionaries to Missouri. His farm was actually in the Whitmer settlement as shown by Whitmer deeds on record in the courthouse at Independence, and by other accounts which definitely place the Lewis farm near the Whitmer settlement on the Blue. Briefly, evidence leading us to the conclusion that Lewis was not one of the Colesville settlers is as follows: The Kansas City *Star* of Tuesday, February 3, 1931, speaks of him as one "who was believed by his relatives at the time to have disgraced his family by joining the then persecuted sect." Parley Parker Pratt in his autobiography says he was "a most faithful pilot, an old resident of the country, who knew every crook and turn of the different paths." The Colesville Saints had only arrived a few days before this conference. And lastly and most conclusively he is listed as a voter in Jackson County in 1828, before the Latter Day Saints ever came to Missouri.

delayed his departure until after her funeral. Hers was the first death in the church in the land of Zion. Tradition is silent upon the place of her burial.

On the day of Sister Knight's funeral, August 7, 1831, directions were given for keeping the Sabbath Day, for to the New England bred elders a town without a church, and a community where Sunday was just another day represented a barbarous condition. In every small village in New England little white churches lifted a spire heavenward, and the Sabbath Day was most religiously unprofaned.

On the 9th day of August, the little party of eleven elders set out in canoes from Independence Landing, to return to Kirtland. The first day they went as far as Fort Osage (now Sibley). At this pioneer outpost of civilization they were made welcome with a dinner of wild turkey. The night of the third day they encamped at McIlwain's Bend. On the 13th some of the elders on their way to Zion met with this party just returning and had a joyful reunion, recounting experiences of the road. The party divided here, some going by water, others by stage back to Kirtland, where they arrived August 27.

In the meantime the little group left alone in the "wilderness" were trying faithfully to adapt themselves to pioneer life. They found much different conditions than they had in their home in the East. The frequent arrival of the missionaries created some diversion, but the summer of 1831 had been as unseasonal as the previous winter, dark, cold, and stormy from the time spring opened with waters "higher than they had been since Noah's flood."[10] The summer had been one succession of floods and disasters, until people were afraid to venture on the water. The scientific papers of the Smithsonian Institute show torrential rains that summer such as were known only in the tropics. At last in August there came a "killing frost," nipping the corn so severely that it did not fully mature. Only a few grains were ripened, so

---

[10] *Pioneers of Mason and Menard*, by T. G. Omstot.

that seed for the following year's spring planting was scarce and very expensive. Many of the vegetables counted upon for winter stores failed, so the gathering Saints, who had no crops, found supplies hard to obtain as the season advanced. Deer and wild game still abounded, so there was no danger of actual starvation.

Three days after the missionaries started east, Lyman Wight came on foot, saying he had left his companion John Murdock fifty miles behind, very ill. Wight borrowed a horse of one of the Saints, rode back to where he left Murdock, and brought in the sick man, walking beside him all the fifty miles to support him in the saddle.

They had come from the faraway outpost of Detroit, after a visit to Pontiac and other points on the way. They reported the conversion and baptism of many, including some names later familiar in Latter Day Saint history, such as James Emmett and Morris Phelps. From the very beginning, Mother Lucy Smith had most earnestly desired the opening of a mission in Michigan, for it was here where her second brother, Stephen Mack, had gone before the War of 1812 and made a fortune for himself. Since Stephen was one of the eldest of the family and Lucy the youngest, she hardly knew him, but still he was the pride of the family. She had heard all her life of his success "merchandising" in Michigan, of his trading posts there and elsewhere, how he had six clerks in one store and mills and boats on the lakes and trading posts even as far east as Ohio.[11] True, her brother had died without hearing the gospel, but there was a duty Lucy felt she owed to his widow, Temperance Mack, and the rest of his family. Therefore, two pairs of missionaries were to go by way of Detroit and Pontiac, and Lucy was to accompany them on a visit to her sister-in-law. These four were Lyman Wight, John Corrill, John Murdock, and Hyrum Smith.

They went by boat to Detroit, and hence to Pontiac, where they found Temperance Mack and her family in enjoyment of an

---

[11]Stephen Mack built "the turnpike road" from Detroit to Pontiac, known now as Woodward Avenue. Mack Avenue in Detroit is named for him.

estate of fifty thousand dollars, free of encumbrance, left by Stephen when he died. There were stores, farms, a mill at Rochester, and considerable other property.[12] Such an interest was raised here that Jared Carter was sent out from Kirtland to follow up the work of the first missionaries. He soon baptized seventy people in Pontiac, which may well be known as the cradle of the Latter Day Saint work in Michigan.

Toward the latter part of August about fifteen elders met in Zion. All had not yet arrived from their missions, for wherever they had found an interest, they had remained to preach, baptize, confirm, ordain, and organize branches. Many of the converts simply came along with the missionaries as they traveled. One of these, William McLellin, had come Zionward with the first elders he met, Samuel H. Smith and Reynolds Cahoon, and was baptized by Hyrum Smith on the 29th of August in Colesville settlement, and immediately ordained an elder.[13]

The Pratt brothers did not arrive in Zion until September. They were fast becoming two of the most able preachers and prose-

---

[12] The present church of Reorganized Church of Latter Day Saints stands on a portion of the old Mack estate.

[13] William McLellin was a rather eccentric character. He was born in Tennessee, probably in 1806. His joining the elders in their trek westward leaving his store to its own devices was characteristic of his impulsive behavior. He became one of the first Quorum of Apostles in February, 1835. In March he was carrying on a famous debate with Reverend J. M. Tracy of the Christian Church at Huntsburg, Geauga County, Ohio, and defended his position well enough to earn the admiration of those outside as well as in the church (*History of Geauga County, Ohio*, page 751). In August, 1836, he wrote to the Presidency that he was withdrawing, as he had lost confidence in the leaders. Two years later the church took action expelling him from the church. He was later connected for brief periods with different factions. Perhaps his latest venture was when he was received by vote into the Church of Christ (Temple Lot) on June 5, 1869 (*Old Record Church of Christ*, page 28). On November 3 of the same year, he withdrew from their fellowship (*Ibid.*, page 33) and just 18 days later wrote to Davis H. Bays, "As to Brighamism, Young Josephism, or G. Hedrickism, I have no use for either of them.... I do not believe in plurality of Gods, nor women; in baptism for the dead, in two priesthoods in the gospel church. Not I. But say you: 'Do tell what you do believe?' I believe David Whitmer was legally and properly appointed and ordained on the 8th day of July, 1834, by Joseph Smith, in a kind of general assembly of all his camp-followers, and all the ministerial authorities of Zion met together three miles west of Liberty, Missouri" (from a letter to D. H. Bays, printed in the *Saints' Herald*, Volume 17, page 291). McLellin lived, practiced his profession of medicine, and died in Independence, near the square. His grave is in Woodlawn Cemetery, beside that of his faithful wife, who cast her fortunes with the Reorganized Church. One of the noteworthy characteristics of the Restoration of the gospel is that those who once partook of its spirit never forsook its basic principles. These principles were as firmly implanted in Dr. McLellin's heart in his lonely old age as they were in his impetuous youth, when he walked out of his business establishment to follow two strange men with a strange story into the western wilderness. Dissenting with almost all his former colleagues [except David Whitmer] he wrote his crusty criticisms to all and sundry but signed them, "Yours in the love of the pure truth."

lytizers of the new faith. Leaving Kirtland in June they had traveled on foot through Ohio, Indiana, Illinois, and Missouri, preaching, baptizing, suffering many hardships: hunger, thirst, fatigue, but with the record of many baptisms and new branches organized in various parts of Ohio, Illinois, and Indiana. Almost immediately upon arrival, Parley P. Pratt, much weakened by the hardships he had endured, fell a victim to that curse of settlers in new country, fever and ague.

He was tended by the old friends in Colesville Branch, who were struggling under difficulties to make a home in the new surroundings. He writes of those days:

>   They had arrived late in the summer, and cut some hay for the cattle, sowed a little grain, and prepared some ground for cultivation, and were engaged during the fall and winter in building log cabins, etc. The winter was cold, and for some time about ten families lived in one log cabin, which was open and unfinished, while the frozen ground served for a floor. Our food consisted of beef and a little bread made of corn, which had been grated into coarse meal by rubbing the ears on a tin grater. That was rather an inconvenient way of living for a sick person; but it was for the gospel's sake, and all were very cheerful and happy.
>   We enjoyed many happy seasons in our prayer and other meetings, and the Spirit of the Lord was poured out upon us, and even on the little children, insomuch that many of eight, ten or twelve years of age spake, and prayed, and prophesied in our meetings and in our family worship. There was a spirit of peace and union, and love, and good will manifested in this little church in the wilderness, the memory of which will be ever dear to my heart.[14][15]

---

[14]*Autobiography of Parley Parker Pratt*, pages 76, 77.
[15]The author was criticized in the former edition of this book for use of this quotation as not representative of true conditions, but further study does not convince her that Pratt's testimony should be rejected. In an article, "Elder John Brush," by two friends, as published in the *Autumn Leaves*, Volume 4, page 22, we find, "To this period Brother Brush looks back with the deepest pleasure; for although the Saints were poor, being new settlers and so away from mills and manufactories, they were very happy; and there were no quarrelings or dissensions among the masses that he knew of. The officers of the branch at this settlement visited the Saints regularly every two or three weeks; the priests enlightening and counseling the families; the teachers rooting out, smoothing away, and helping to settle the very beginnings of difficulties among members; the deacon attending to the wants of the needy, assisting them to obtain that wherein they lacked. It is his testimony also that the Saints were discreet in their intercourse with nonbelievers, and that they did not disobey the laws of the land. That they did not obey perfectly *all* the commandments of God is probable, but the character of their social and religious relations when thus in their gathered condition was so far above anything he has before or since seen, that he cannot but look back to those times with the tenderest emotions."

XIII.—Pioneering in the West

Progress during the last century and a half has been so rapid that it is quite literally true that men who live their allotted span are born in one world and die in another. Therefore if we would understand the struggles of our church fathers, we must make an effort to reconstruct the world in which they lived. To do this we should dismiss from our homes the telephone, the telegraph, the phonograph, electricity as a servant, with all its contribution to the comfort of modern life, and of course the radio and television, which were undreamed of by the ordinary person a few years ago.

We must take up all our railroads, live without our daily paper, let stoves and furnaces be as rare as log cabins today, let our only fuel be wood, for even the river steamboats fired their engines with green cordwood procured on the river banks. We must light our homes by dipped candles, whale oil lamps or a saucer of lard with a bit of rag for a wick.

Into each home we must bring two spinning wheels, one for wool and one for flax, and let the principal industry of the women be the making of homespun, home-dyed and homemade garments for the men, women, and children of the large families. Shoes must be made by shoemakers to order (both shoes alike, no left and no right). We must tear down most of our colleges, and abolish our high schools and substitute academies, which were private enterprises for pay, and hold our common schools in log cabins with curriculum and length of term dependent upon the caprice or opportunity of the settlers.

We would have to restore slavery with all its inhumanities, local bickerings, and political strife. We must cut down the number of the States of the Union to twenty-four, all east of the Mississippi except Missouri and Louisiana, and count the whole population of the United States at less than ten million. To Mexico must be returned the States west of the Rocky Mountains except Washington and Oregon, which were merely wild wastes where as Bryant intimated, one might "lose oneself in the continuous woods where flows the Oregon and hear no sound save its own dashing." To them also would go States immediately east of the Rockies, except Montana and Idaho and part of Colorado and Wyoming.

We must cover again the gold mines of California and the silver mines of Colorado, and return to the time when the owner of a gold watch was a person of opulence, and the woman who owned a set of silver spoons was in a class set far apart from the common herd.

Having stepped back over the centuries into this world of our pioneer fathers, we might attempt to take a trip to Independence on the wild frontier of the world with Washington Irving and his friend, Charles Joseph Latrobe, the year after the Colesville Branch came to the western wilds. The party was a most eminent one, including Colonel Ellsworth, Indian Commissioner to the Pawnees, Count de Pourtales, a young Swiss nobleman, and Paul L. Chouteau of Saint Louis. Latrobe was an Englishman traveling in America, and found much to amuse and entertain him in the manners of his partly civilized American cousins. He published his observations in *The Rambler in North America,* and should be competent to be quoted with impunity, as no future complications with the people of Missouri could possibly give him a prejudiced bias.

> The town of Independence was full of promise [he tells us] like most of the innumerable towns springing up in the midst of the forests of the West, many of which, though dignified by high-sounding epithets, consist of nothing but a ragged congeries of five or six rough log huts, two or three clapboard houses, two or three so-called hotels, alias grog shops; a few stores, a bank, a printing office, and barn-like church. It lacked at the time I commemorate, the three last edifices,

but was nevertheless, a thriving and aspiring place, in its way; and the fortune made here already in the course of its brief existence, by a bold Yankee shopkeeper, who had sold $60,000 worth of goods here in three years—was a matter of equal notoriety, surprise, and envy.[1] It is situated about twenty miles east of the Kansas river, and three south of the Missouri, and is consequently very near the extreme frontier of the State. A little beyond this point, all carriage roads cease, and one deep black trail alone, which might be seen tending to the southwest, was that of the Santa Fe trappers and traders. . . . On the morning of one of the days spent here in expectation of our friends' arrival—mounted on Methuselah, an old white horse of the innkeeper, I left my comrades and our horses to their repose at the town, partly for a morning pigeon-shooting, and partly with the purpose of going down to the ferry on the Missouri, to inquire if any intelligence had come up the river with reference to the expected steamboat.

After missing the path, and an hour's rough scramble in the thick forest, during which I found means to insinuate my steed, gun, and person through many a tangled jungle of ropevine, bush and creeper, much to my own astonishment and that of the grave old quadruped which I bestrode, I descended the bluff, which here rises, precipitously from the bank of the Missouri, and reached the ferry.[2] I met with no intelligence, but with an acquaintance from the town above who proposed to me that we should ride together six or seven miles down the river, and call upon one of his friends, whose "clearing" was situated at a point where the current is unusually narrow, and of difficult navigation. To this I readily acceded, as it would give me a better opportunity of observing the phenomenon connected with this stupendous stream than I had hitherto enjoyed. . . . Having rounded a noble, and expanded bend of the river, in about an hour's time, we heard by the barking of dogs, and the clatter of many voices, that we were approaching the farm in question. From the prominent appearance of a long table covered with dinner apparatus, which appeared arranged in the open air, a few steps from the door, a number of dogs sniffing and whining around it, and the unusual bustle among the Negro dependents toiling about a small fire in advance, we suspected that something extraordinary was going on. A young Negro took our horses with that affection of extreme politeness and good breeding, which is so highly amusing in many of his color, and which inclines me to think that they appreciate the character of a "fine gentlemen" more than any other part of the community. . . .We were met by the settler with the frank unceremonious bearing of his race. He informed us that his wife had got a number of her neighbors with her for a "quilting frolic," and made us heartily welcome. The interior of the log hut presented a singular scene. A square table was seen to occupy a great

---

[1] Very probably referring to Algernon S. Gilbert, as he was in all probability the only Yankee merchant. And the attitude expressed is typical.
[2] Wayne City Landing near Liberty, previously known as Duckers Ferry.

part of the floor. It was surrounded by a compact body of females, whose fingers were occupied with all diligence upon the quilt which lay stretched out before them, and which, though neither the smartest nor the costliest, promised—judging from the quantity of cotton or wool which I saw stuffed into its inside, and the close lozenge-shaped compartments into which the latter was confined by rapid and successful gobble-stitching, to be of real utility and comfort to the matron who presided, during the coming winter. . . .

The meal which followed was plentiful and homely, and was dispatched first by the female and then by the male visitors, with the marvelous rapacity which is generally observable in the West; and, as I sat apart waiting till our turn should come, I was much amused with the bustle of the scene. I watched the plates run the gauntlet from the table to the washing-tub, among a set of little Negroes of all shapes and sizes, who all strove to act as preliminary scourers, much to the disappointment of the dogs, who whined, whimpered, scratched, and pushed their sable competitors, and not less to the annoyance of the fat Negress who acted as cook, and who, with lustrous visage and goggle-eyes, flourished her dishclout over the tub in a fume of impatience.[3]

While Latrobe amused himself by visiting the typical settlers of this western land, Washington Irving wrote his sister, Mrs. Paris, from the hotel:

We arrived at this place [Independence] the day before yesterday, after nine days' traveling on horseback from Saint Louis. Our journey has been a very interesting one, leading us across fine prairies and through noble forests, dotted here and there by farms and log houses, at which we find rough, but wholesome and abundant fare and very civil treatment. Many parts of these prairies of the Missouri are extremely beautiful, resembling cultivated countries, rather than the savage rudeness of the wilderness.

Yesterday I was out on a deer hunt in the vicinity of this place, which led me through some scenery that only wanted a castle, or a gentleman's seat here and there interspersed, to have equaled some of the most celebrated park scenery of England.

The fertility of all this western country is truly remarkable. The soil is like that of a garden, and the luxuriance and beauty of the forests exceed any I have ever seen. We have gradually been advancing, however, to rougher and rougher life, and we are now at a straggling little frontier village that has only been five years in existence. From hence in the course of a day or two, we take our departure southwardly, and shall soon bid adieu to civilization and encamp at nights in our tents.[4]

---

[3]Quoted from *Centennial History of Independence*, W. S. Webb, author and publisher, pages 95-98.
[4]Letter of Washington Irving, written September 25, 1832. See *Centennial History of Independence*, Webb.

These were the scenes which seemed to eastern-bred Joseph Smith nearly a century behind the times. They depict the original settler as he appeared to his contemporaries. It is a common failing of the American people to place the pioneer upon a pedestal and worship there. The virtues of the father always exceed the virtues of the son; we always sigh for the good old days and the good old ways, which would prove intolerable to us if we could bring them back. Our grandsires are great and noble. It is sacrilege to assign to them the commonplace sins and failings. Our grandmothers are universally virtuous, self-sacrificing, and industrious, possessing virtues we may never attain.

> Long ago George Washington lost his human semblance and arose to the rarified air of empyrean. The apotheosis of Abraham Lincoln has already taken place before the very eyes of the present generation. Already his long shanks are resting on a throne in the skies beside the divine George. How uncomfortable both these men who were so human in all that made up their characters must feel as they sit there weighed down by their golden crowns and their royal mantles![5]

In both secular and church history, we demand perfection in our heroes. We church members may easily fall victim to all the sins and faults to which human flesh is heir, but our church history must possess the unblemished page of faultless virtue and heroism, or our faith is shattered, and we must perforce turn to infidelity. Shakespeare, who more truly saw life whole than any of us probably ever will, said, "Men are as the times are." Turning back the pages of history to the time in which the Saints went to Missouri, we see a state of civilization not very unlike the one pictured by Service in his poems of the far northwest, or such tales of the frontier as existed within our own memories, well-known to be anything but a picture of virtuous simplicity:

> On the border the uncultivated, the illiterate, and the desperado rubbed shoulders with the virtuous farmer, the college graduate, and the missionary. Here there were some fine examples of noble self-

---
[5]Clarence W. Alford, in *The Centennial History of Illinois,* State Historical Society of Illinois, 1918, page 81.

sacrifice; but here also were instances of selfish greed easily paralleling anything we know today. The frontier afforded a freedom which thrills the imagination of a more stifled generation; it allowed also a lawlessness and license which would be intolerable to the modern man.[6]

As far as Independence of that day was concerned, if we may trust the pen of unprejudiced writers, conditions were far from ideal. "Around Independence it was not unusual to see whole families dressed in skins; buildings were generally without glass windows and the door stood open in winter for light . . . and this remote region . . . was as innocent of all refinements and even the comforts of life as a Siberian Ostrog."[7,8]

When the Colesville Saints made their settlement twelve or fifteen miles west of Independence in 1831, there was no Kansas City. That did not come until eight years later. An old settler describes the present site of Kansas City:

A clearing or old field of a few acres lying on the high ridge between Main and Wyandotte and Second and Fifth Streets, made and abandoned by a mountain trapper. A few old girdled dead trees standing in the field, surrounded by a dilapidated rail fence. Around on all sides a dense forest, the ground covered with impenetrable brush, vines, fallen timber, and deep, impassable gorges. A narrow, crooked roadway winding from Twelfth and Walnut Streets, along down on the west side of the deep ravine towards the river, across the public square to the river at the foot of Grand Avenue. A narrow, difficult path, barely wide enough for a single horseman, running up and down the river under the bluff, winding its way around fallen timber and deep ravines. An old log house on the river bank at the foot of Main Street, occupied by a lank, cadaverous specimen of humanity, named Ellis, with one blind eye and the other on a sharp lookout for stray horses, straggling Indians and squatters with whom to swap a tin cup of whisky for a coonskin. Another old, dilapidated cabin below the Pacific depot. Two or three small clearings or cabins in the Kaw bottoms, now called West Kansas, which were houses of French mountain trappers. The rest of the surroundings was the still solitude of the native forest, unbroken, only by the snort of the darting deer, the barking of the squirrel, the

---

[6] Clarence W. Alford in *The Centennial History of Illinois*, Illinois Historical Society and Transactions, 1918, pages 81, 82.
[7] Warren Watson in *Kansas City Globe Souvenir*, reprinted in *Saints' Herald*, Volume 37, page 203.
[8] Ostrogoth—East Goth.

howl of the wolf, the settler's cowbell, and mayhap the distant baying of the hunter's dog, or the sharp report of his rifle.[9]

Westport was not laid out until 1833. Westport Landing was three miles below the city.

Independence was a real town, but its recent emergence from the forest was testified to by a town square thickly studded with stumps of trees.

The typical pioneer was of the rough and ready type. Physical courage was inordinately admired. Deeds of personal valor and strength in the hunt, the Indian fight, or in personal combat were the principal boast of the pioneer. "If two men had a quarrel, they would meet and fight it out, and then make friends and take a drink, thus quickly and easily settling their difficulty,"[10] says one old-timer with evident admiration for the system. The same author tells of a very glorious fight that took place on Christmas Day, 1819, when the young men of Franklin crossed the river on the ice for the purpose "of cleaning out Boonville." The author details the scene which though "bloody" had no one "killed or fatally wounded" with evident enjoyment, and ends up the story on a religious note, evidently the product of later years, but showing the absolute lack of malice inspired by the event. "The most of them have left this world of trouble, strife, and turmoil, and gone, it is hoped, to a better and brighter world beyond the vale. Alas, time will tell. It waits for no man. Peace be to their ashes. But these heroes will live in history and in grateful remembrance as long as time shall last."[11]

There was in those early days a Missourian who has been the hero of more than one singular story. This man was Martin Parmer, who because he so designated himself in moments of extreme gaiety was generally called the "Ring-tailed Painter." This man at one time was sent to Jefferson City as state senator.

---
[9] J. C. McCoy at an Old Settlers' Reunion, December 30, 1871, as published in *History of Jackson County*, by W. Z. Hickman, page 243.
[10] *History of Cooper County*, by Levins and Hyde, page 120.
[11] *Ibid.*, page 129.

Like most Missourians he loved a fight, and being on the street one day when Governor Hugh McNair was about to interfere to settle a fight, the "Ring-tailed Painter," although a perfect stranger, promptly collared the Governor and backed him out of the circle. "A governor is no more in a fight than any other man," he later explained, "and he was like to spoil the prettiest kind of a fight."[12] This man's great-grandsons, as the famous James boys, would have furnished him plenty of diversion had he lived to see them.

This attitude of the fighting Missourian was as inexplicable to the staid New England Latter Day Saints, as their tendency to reason things out without the aid of fists was to the Missourian. To the majority of pioneers, there could be but one reason for not fighting out a quarrel, and that was cowardice. To the early Saints, Lyman Wight's tendency to refuse to turn the other cheek was a grievous fault. Old settlers invariably spoke well of him. Other "Mormons" might be cowards, but "Old Wight was brave as a lion." They would have let him go free, if only he would renounce "Joe Smith" and his "Mormon religion." Such a fighter was too good to waste.[13]

These rough old settlers did not tolerate "drunkenness," they said, but one who refused to drink as did the rather effeminate "Mormonites" was anything but a good fellow well met with them. "Just before Christmas," in the year 1818, says one of them, reminiscing, "the boys of the school had determined to turn the teacher out, and force him to treat the scholars, by taking him to the creek and ducking him. This proceeding, though showing little respect for the dignity of the teacher, generally had the desired effect. The fear of it, in this case, had the desired effect,

---

[12] *History of Clay County,* by W. H. Woodson, page 89.
[13] The impetuous Lyman Wight, with whom I was well acquainted, wanted to fight the mob, giving it as his opinion that it would be only a breakfast spell to whip the Missourians. Lyman was a brave and good man, knowing not what fear was. When told by one of the mobocrats that he would be shot the next morning if he did not betray Joseph Smith, he replied, "Shoot and be damned, for that is what you will get anyway." It is to be hoped that the recording angel dropped a tear on the little swear word and thus blotted it out forever. Testimony of Elder Levi Graybill, *Journal of History,* Volume 4, page 106.

for the teacher, hearing of the plans of the scholars, voluntarily gave them a week's holiday, and on New Year's Day treated them to a keg of whiskey. This no doubt will sound strange to most of our citizens at this day, but it is nevertheless true. It must not be thought that this was a terribly demoralized community, for it certainly was not, but on the contrary one of the most refined in the country."[14]

Racing and gambling were two other manly sports of those years, nor were they confined to the western wilds. Gambling was as universal as drinking. Even the nation's capital was not immune.

> The racing on the national course near the city made it difficult to maintain a quorum in Congress, and the statesmen mounted their horses to ride to the track to cheer their favorites and bet their money. Even the President entered his horses and lost heavily on his wagers. There Jackson and a goodly portion of the cabinet, and a formidable sprinkling of the leaders of the opposition from Clay to Letcher, might be seen backing their judgment as to horse flesh with their purses. And when it was not horse racing it was cock fighting, with the President entering his own birds from the Hermitage and riding with his friends to Bladensburg to witness the humiliation of his entries. It was a day of gambling, when statesmen, whose names school children are now taught to reverence, played for heavy stakes for days and nights at a time, with Clay and Poindexter losing fortunes and an occasional victim of the lure blowing out his brains.[15]

And the Latter Day Saints as time went on had a "Word of Wisdom" and insisted on their members obeying it. Could anything appear more wild and fanatical to the men of the time who considered themselves properly red-blooded!

Almost everybody realized the importance of learning from books, but in the press of other and seemingly more essential things education was often neglected. Some of the wisest and most common-sense judges of western Missouri in that day were unable to read or write. Now and then some person started a school and charged each pupil a reasonable amount for tuition,

---
[14]*History of Cooper County*, by Levins and Hyde, page 193.
[15]*Party Battles of the Jackson Period*, by Bowers, page 18.

such as perhaps a dollar a month. The schoolhouses, when an enterprising community did build one, were quite often without any floor but earth, or puncheon, with no window sash or glass, merely a hole cut in the log wall which was covered by a plank at night, not as a precaution against thieves—there was nothing in a schoolhouse anyone would wish to steal—but as a protection against wild animals. There were even schools consisting of two logs in the woods, the pupils occupying one, and the teacher another, facing them.

The Saints immediately started schools, the first in Jackson County. Oliver Cowdery and Parley P. Pratt were both teachers, the first schoolteachers in Jackson County. Ziba Peterson is reported to have opened a school at Lone Jack.

The settler did not have to raise meat. Buffalo, bear, and deer were plentiful, and wild turkeys were to be had in abundance. Bread was oftenest made of ground corn mixed with water and baked. No other grain was grown. The process of making meal before mills were erected is described by one of the pioneers as follows:

> We first made mortars, by burning or cutting out the end of a log twelve or fifteen inches deep, bringing it to a point at the bottom, then making a pestle by putting an iron wedge in the end of a stick, with a band or cord around the end to keep it from splitting where we drove in the wedge; then we had what we call a hominy mortar, in which we pounded our corn as fine as we could, then sifted it, and took the finest for bread, and the coarse for hominy, which did very well, though the process was slow and hard. We soon invented another style for making meal—took two flat stones about four inches thick, dressed them up, mill-stone style, fitted the bedstone into a hollow gum, cutting the upper stone, or runner, about an inch less than the bedrock, so there would be room for the meal as we turned to be carried around the spout, drilling a hole in the top stone so as to put in a handle, to turn the mill with one hand and feed with another. This was much better than a mortar. But the rock or mill stone was too soft, so our meal had more or less grit in it, which made it rather unpleasant, yet we preferred it to the mortar and pestle. We were not destitute of inventive talent, we soon had another fitted up in a frame

with trunnel head, cogs, and wheels, which was run by a crank on each side of the frame, with a hopper and shoe to take the corn to the runner.[16]

This was all very well for settlers who had been used to nothing better, but among the Colesville Saints were some particularly good millers. Old Joseph Knight and his sons had made flour on rather a large grist scale in Colesville, and they soon were operating a mill which was patronized by the settlers as well as the Saints.[17]

Far from being dissatisfied with their pioneer fare, most of the pioneers looked back to those days with longing. Perhaps in memory the wild turkeys seemed fatter, the honey sweeter, and the bear's oil less pungent, but a prominent judge of Clay County, looking backward says:

> The turkeys certainly surpassed all other birds. They were very large and fatter than I ever saw tame ones on the farm. They were truly delicious when properly prepared for the hunter's table, which was a blanket spread upon the ground. The best way to prepare them is to dress them nicely and stick them on a stick stuck in the ground before a good camp fire, turning them around until they are browned, but not burned, salt well rubbed in them before you begin with a little bear's oil poured over while roasting. This with a trough of honey is better than a king's table affords. Of all the dishes I ever ate, give me venison stewed in a camp kettle or spit before the fire with bear's oil, and plenty of good honey in the comb for bread.[18]

Even in the matter of money the Yankee and the Southerner counted differently. The Yankee reckoned by shillings and pence but in the South and West, and hence in Missouri, the Spanish dollar and its fractions were used. In this locality the eighth of a dollar was a bit, and the large Spanish dollar often circulated in the literal form of its fractions, although all too often could the dollar ever have been reassembled there would have been found to be nine "bits" in it instead of eight. Prices were almost invariably given in the form of two bits, four bits, or

---
[16] Judge Josiah Thorpe in *Early Missouri Days*, Letter No. 4.
[17] Newel Knight's Journal in *Scraps of Biography*, Salt Lake City, 1883.
[18] *Early Missouri Days*, by Judge Josiah Thorpe.

six bits, and the settlers it has been said would refuse seventy-five cents for an article and insist upon "six bits." So the Saints who came West had to drop the fo'pence and ninepence for the bit and the picayune. The eighth of a dollar was also known as a New York shilling, because in the Revolutionary War, the credit of New York State fell so low that eight shillings equaled a dollar. In 1844, the post office department started demanding postage in its own coin, and banned the use of foreign coin.

The usual wear for men was buckskin with fringe on the seams, but in the very earliest days after the homespun trousers and calico dresses of the original settlers wore out, clothing was made of nettles. "The low flats along the rivers were covered with a thick growth of nettles about three feet high, sometimes standing in patches of twenty acres or more. These were permitted to remain standing until they became decayed in winter, when they were gathered. They were broken up, spun into long strings, and woven into cloth, from which the garments were made."[19] "Little children generally wore a leathern shirt (long) over their tow shirt." "The lint [from the nettles] was bright, fine, and strong, and made splendid shirts and pants for summer wear."[20]

As time went on, it was possible to import fashionable clothes from the East. Two of the Latter Day Saint missionaries had been tailors, and were kept busy supplying the men of the new town of Independence and the vicinity for several miles around with fashionable apparel. It was the thing in those days for "gentlemen" to wear high, stiff coat collars, padded with buckram, reaching half way up the back of the head, with five or six cravats covering the neck, and tall "stove-pipe hats," wide at the top and tapering downwards. The ladies wore long sunbonnets, projecting about ten inches in front of their faces, or if they really wished to reflect the eastern styles, "leghorn" hats and with tortoiseshell combs making a semi-circle on the back of the head.

---

[19] *History of Cooper County*, by Levins and Hyde.
[20] *Early Missouri Days*, by Judge Josiah Thorpe.

Even the language used by the settlers differed from that the "Yankees" had learned in their native State. No one ever said "there," but "thar." If a sick neighbor was very ill, she was "powerful weak," or "mighty sick." They heard their neighbors speak of a "right smart chance"; toothache was "misery in the teeth." It was never quite comprehensible to eastern minds, why a bridegroom of less than twenty spoke of his sixteen-year-old bride as "my old woman," and she called him "my old man." When school was dismissed, the children shouted, "School is broke." Forenoon was all "morning," and anytime after midday dinner was "evening."

But perhaps all might have gone well in spite of so many differences in temperament had it not been for slavery. The gentry of New York had slaves, a few even in Fayette had a bond servant or two, but the keeping of slaves in large numbers was new to the Saints. They would have indignantly denied they were that hated thing known as an "abolitionist," but at the same time these eastern people were Yankees; they owned no slaves, and in spite of denials, they were suspected of being abolitionists, whether they were or not. There was an attitude of almost fraternizing with the blacks, of treating them much as they treated white people, which was to say the least, enough to make any slave-owner distinctly uneasy.[21]

And the Saints heard the stories that were passed about. There was one of a runaway Negro man who was chained overnight to an anvil in a blacksmith shop as he was to be publicly whipped the next day, and in the morning he was dead, still chained to the anvil, with no marks of violence, perhaps died of terror.

The Saints could not help but shudder a bit when they met the patrol on the village streets after nine o'clock at night.

---

[21] There is evidence to intimate that after extensive missionary campaigning in the South, a few slaveholders with their slaves moved into Nauvoo, perhaps even in Caldwell County, Missouri. Slavery existed in a limited degree in the Utah Mormon church previous to the Civil War. But it may safely be said that the predominant sentiment was against it. Doniphan cites it as the chief cause of the Jackson County troubles.

XIV.—Slavery in Missouri

In the days of slavery, it was considered unwise and unsafe to let Negroes, male or female, go about the country in the nighttime, without a written permit from their owners or masters. County courts usually named patrols for each neighborhood in the country, and when they failed to name the patrols, the citizens of the neighborhood would name them. It was the duty of the patrol to watch the roads, byways, and places where Negroes were likely to be or congregate, and when found after nine o'clock without a written pass or permit, the Negro or Negroes were punished there and then, the patrols administering a sound thrashing. Ghosts and hobgoblins were no greater terror to the average Negro than the patrols (Negroes called them paterrollers). When old Uncle Rastus prayed, he said, "O Lord, we thank thee for the New Jerusalem, with its pearly gates and its golden streets, but above all we thank thee for that high wall around the great big city, so high that a paterroller can't get over it."[1]

There lived in Independence a large slave population. . . . One of the first ordinances passed by the first city council was a brief one specifying the number of lashes to be laid upon a Negro.[2]

IN 1808 IN MISSOURI THERE were about eleven thousand slaves, constantly increasing in number. There can be no doubt that there was a considerable slave population in the territory in the days when Missouri's statehood was before the country. "Perhaps Taylor of New York was inclined to exaggerate when he said, 'A negro man is bought in Africa for a few gewgaws or a bottle of whisky, and sold in New Orleans for twelve to fifteen hundred dollars,'[3] but nevertheless the slaveholders of Missouri who contended for statehood in 1820 were fighting not for a mere political principle actually but for property, and a considerable amount of it. If Missouri in 1820 was simply a battleground for selfish, southern purposes, there would be some

---
[1] *History of Clay County*, by W. H. Woodson, Historical Publishing House, Topeka and Indianapolis (1920), pages 85, 86.
[2] *Centennial History of Independence, Missouri*, by W. L. Webb, published by author 1926, pages 187, 188.
[3] *Annals of Congress*, Volume 33, page 1175.

evidence of loose economic conditions or at least stray hints that the system was ill-adapted to so northern a country. But business seems to have been sound, and the tone of all the papers gives the impression that these were 'booming' times for Missouri."[4]

On December 12, 1820, the General Assembly enacted a law that a tax be levied "on all lands . . . dwelling houses . . . and improvements at the rate of twenty-five cents on every one hundred dollars of value thereof, on all slaves above the age of three years and livestock at the same rate."[5]

The continual fear of insurrection, in Missouri as elsewhere, caused somewhat drastic laws to be passed restricting the slaves' right to bear arms or to go hunting. The Law of 1724 provided that no slave should carry a weapon or even a heavy stick unless sent to hunt game by his master who must supply him with a written permission. The laws of O'Reilley condemned a slave to thirty lashes for bearing firearms, and he could be shot when found armed if he could not otherwise be captured. These provisions were included in the Laws of 1804. For a slave or a mulatto to carry "a club or other weapon whatsoever," any number of lashes not exceeding thirty could be given "on his or her bare back well laid on." But as Missouri was in the territorial period a frontier community, and as Indian incursions were often feared, a slave in the outlying districts might bear weapons if so licensed by a justice of the peace.[6]

The overshadowing fear of insurrection and of property loss caused the enactment of stringent provisions against the slave who was found off his master's plantation. The Code of 1724 forbade slaves assembling in crowds for any purpose; the first offense being punished by whipping, the second by branding, while capital punishment could be exercised under "aggravating circumstances." . . . According to the Laws of 1804, no slave was to leave his master's "tenements" without a pass or other token of authority. A justice was to punish such slave "with stripes," and it was "lawful for the owner or overseer of such plantation [on which the slave had trespassed] to give or order such slave ten lashes on his or her bare back for every such offense." Riots, unlawful assemblies, and seditious speeches by slaves were to be punished with stripes at the discretion of a justice of the peace. Any slave "conspiring to rebel or murder" was to be executed after convic-

---

[4]"Slavery in Missouri Territory," *Missouri Historical Review*, Volume 3, page 182, by Harrison A. Trexler.
[5]*Ibid.*, pages 184, 185.
[6]*Ibid.*, page 187; *Territorial Laws*, Volume 1, sections 4 and 5.

tion without benefit of clergy. Any master or mistress of slaves knowingly permitting slaves or others to remain upon their property for more than four hours without the consent of the owners was to be fined three dollars and costs, and for permitting more than five slaves to assemble "at any other time" was fined one dollar per slave so assembled. Negroes with passes could meet for worship or on "any other lawful occasion." Any white, free negro, or mulatto meeting with a seditious slave or aiding such was fined three dollars if such seditious slave was not exposed, and on failure to pay this should "receive on his or her bare back twenty lashes well laid on." Any justice failing to act within ten days when informed of an unlawful meeting of slaves was to be fined eight dollars and costs, and a sheriff four dollars and costs for the same offense.[7]

The Law of 1724 condemned a slave to branding and loss of ears for the first offense in being away from the plantation for more than a month; the second and third offenses being punished by hamstringing and death, respectively.[8]

At Cahokia in 1779, a negro was sentenced to twenty lashes, "since he used very bad language and threatened to revenge himself on those who should undertake to seize him."

From the criminal legislation against the blacks, we can decide that there was more fear of the slave selling his master's goods or of running away than any of his committing private crimes.[9]

That the master might not abuse his slaves, legislation was also passed to guarantee what was then considered humane treatment.

Every slave was to "receive the barrel of corn provided by the usage of the colony; and was also to be given the use of waste lands." "The slave who has not a portion of waste land shall receive punctually from his master a shirt and trousers of linen in summer, and a great coat and trousers of wool for the winter." It was also provided that "every slave should be allowed one-half hour for breakfast, two hours for dinner; their labor shall commence at break of day, and shall cease at the approach of night."[10] Sundays off except in time of harvest.

As to the treatment of the Missouri slave . . . a correspondent of Niles *Register* thus pictures the state of the institution in the St. Louis country: "The condition of their slaves, when compared with most countries, where slavery is tolerated, is not hard or severe. Their labor is not great, or painful, they are allowed many privileges, and are well clothed and fed." But the editor, however, seems suspicious of the veracity of this statement, for he adds in parentheses, "Better information satisfies me that this encomium is unmerited."[11]

---

[7]"Slavery in Missouri," by Harrison A. Trexler, from *Missouri Historical Review*, Volume 3, pages 187-189.
[8]*Ibid*. 189. [9]*Ibid*., 191, 192.
[10]*Ibid*., 194
[11]*Slavery in Missouri*, by Trexler, pages 194, 195.

Naturally the great majority of slaveholders were kind to their slaves according to their own estimate of kindness and humanity, and the story is told of one slaveholder near Independence who was so tenderhearted he could not bear to sell a slave, consequently they "ate him out of house and home." He was regarded with good-natured tolerance as one might a tenderhearted spinster who could not bear to dispose of any of a household of cats.

We may conclude that slavery as it existed in Missouri in 1820 was a fairly well organized system. It is true there were but a few thousand negro slaves in the Territory, but were chiefly massed along the Mississippi and Missouri Rivers, the only portions of the Territory then well settled. We have seen that special slave codes were enacted, and special slave taxes were levied, and the ratio between the races was about five to one.[12]

Slave property was the most valuable possession of the Missouri pioneer. The first instrument of writing recorded in Platte County was a bill of sale for a slave, from Felix B. Mullikan to Zadoc Martin, the money consideration being $200 and the slave a Negro man, Willis, aged about thirty-three years. It was dated May 11, 1839, and recorded two days later. The first deed for real estate had been executed March 2 of the same year, one eighth of lots number 383 and 382 for $12.50.[13]

This is even more forcibly shown by the appraisement of Archibald Holtzclaw's estate in 1829 in Clay County, which reads:[14]

Jincy, a crippled slave girl, 30 years old	$100.00
Anthony, a child, 1 year old	$100.00
Susan, a slave, 14 years old	$300.00
Henry, a slave, 13 years old	$336.00
Isaac, a slave, 25 years old	$460.00
George, a slave, 13 years old	$316.00
Horse and side saddle	$ 40.00
Cow and calf	$ 7.50
Sow and five pigs	$ 1.50
Sheep, each	$ 1.00

[12]*Ibid.*, pages 197, 198.
[13]*History of Clay and Platte Counties*, National Historical Company, 1885, p. 581.
[14]*History of Clay and Platte Counties*, National Historical Company, 1829, page 115.

Flax wheel	$ 3.00
Cotton Wheel	$ 3.00
Flag bottomed chairs, each	$ .50
Bible and hymnbook	$ 1.50
Skillet	$ 1.25
A good horse	$ 25.00

As was natural when so much of their property was tied up in slaves, the slaveowners used every means in their power to see that no menace to that property was allowed to exist in the community.

There was but one Yankee in Clay County. His name was Humphrey Smith, but so unusual was a northerner in that section that he was never called anything but "Yankee." Why he elected to live for the most part of his life where he knew he was not wanted is hard to understand. Perhaps it was merely Yankee perversity. He was born in New Jersey in 1774, and came to Howard County, Missouri, where he resided for three and a half years. He was all his life an avowed abolitionist. He declared frankly that human slavery was a sin at all times and under all circumstances. Driven by a mob out of Howard County to Carroll, and from Carroll to Clay, he still persisted in making his home among slaveowners, where he knew he was not only unwelcome but profoundly hated. Clay County was, fortunately, although very proslavery in feeling, dominated by men of education, tolerance, and wisdom, who used their influence against mob violence, therefore Yankee Smith was permitted to found in comparative peace the town of Smithville, by building his log cabin, and his mill (at first nothing but a corncracker) where he thought he could catch the trade from not only the settlers, but the government agencies in Platte County. No sort of threatening, denunciation, or raillery ever deterred him from speaking his mind.

Often some rough character, wishing to have a little fun, would approach him and say, "Smith, are you an abolitionist?"

"I am," was the invariable reply.

The next moment he would be knocked down. Smith would calmly arise, brush the dust off his clothes, and remark dryly, "Oh, that's no argument."

He died in June, 1857. His neighbors believed that he got smallpox from an abolitionist paper. As he died he made one request: "Never let the men stealers know where I am buried until my State is free, then write my epitaph, 'Here lies Humphrey Smith, who was in favor of human rights, universal liberty, equal and exact justice, no union with slaveholders, free states, free people, union of states, and one and universal republic.'" Perhaps in no other county in the State would he have been permitted to live and die as peacefully as he did.

George S. Park, editor of the *Eastern Luminary* in Parkville and W. S. Patterson who was associated with him were less fortunate. "Their editorials became so outspoken in favor of free soil, and in aiding eastern abolition societies . . . that they attracted the attention of the Platte County Self Defense Association. This was an association composed of citizens of that section of the State who favored slave-soil. About two hundred members of this association met at Parkville, on April 14, 1855, and proceeded to the *Luminary* office. The editors heard them coming and hid a large amount of the type in the garret. This type was afterwards taken to Kansas and used in publishing a free-soil paper. The mob secured the press and remaining type. A procession was formed, a banner carried aloft and, with songs and shouts, the procession started for the Missouri River—the grave of more than one Missouri press whose owner gave too free expression to views not held by a majority of his readers. Sentence of banishment was pronounced upon the editors, and a resolution passed 'if they go to Kansas to reside we will follow and hang them wherever we can take them.'"

"George S. Park . . . went to Illinois, invested what remained of his property in land. He prospered, and, returning to Parkville at the close of the [Civil] War, founded Park College. He was buried at the place where the sentence of banishment had been pronounced upon him, and a magnificent monument to his memory overlooks the very spot where the Missouri River received his press and type."[15]

To our so-called enlightened age, the economic system under which these people lived savored of barbarism, but conscientious and religious people held these opinions and made these laws. It is not at all improbable that one hundred years from now, our economic system will seem as antiquated and our political treatises as quaint as that of Governor Reynolds of Illinois as late as 1860. This man, who was possessed of enough culture, education, and popularity to become governor of the State of Illinois, wrote "a rather remarkable pamphlet entitled *Balm of Gilead,* which he termed 'An Inquiry Into the Right of Human Slavery.' . . . He compares the cohesion of the abolitionists to the religious organization of the Mormons, and the followers of John Brown are declared to be the same class as those in the French Revolution who 'fraternized on pikes, and feasted on blood.' His conclusion was that 'we, of the United States at this day, with slavery, enjoy the most perfect and the most free government on earth, and I pray that it may be continued forever!' "[16]

---

[15] See *Annals of Platte County,* by W. M. Paxton, page 171, seq. "History of County Press of Missouri," by Minnie Organ, in *Missouri Historical Review,* Vol. 4, pages 258, 259.
[16] "Literature and Literary People of Early Illinois," by Isabel Jamison, in *Transactions of the Illinois State Historical Society,* 1908.

XV.—THE MILITIA

ON ACCOUNT OF THE near-by Indian frontier, the law in many of the border States was that every able-bodied citizen must train for military service.[1] This law was new to the Latter Day Saints, and they had no desire to take part in ceremonies which many times were out of accord with their own standards of behavior, for "muster days," especially in pioneer communities, were a round of celebration from daylight until dark, and long after.

From the organization of the government of the State of Missouri until the year 1847, there existed a militia law, requiring all able-bodied male citizens, between the ages of eighteen and forty-five years, to organize into companies and to muster upon certain days. They had during the year at different times, a company, a battalion and a general muster. A company muster was a drilling of the members of one company; a battalion muster consisted in the drilling of the companies of one-half a county; and a general muster was the meeting of all the companies of a county.

Muster day was for a long time after the commencement of the custom a gala day for the citizens, and was looked forward to with considerable interest, especially by the different officers who appeared in full military dress; captains and lieutenants with long red feathers stuck in the fore parts of their hats, and epaulettes upon their shoulders, and fine cloth coats, ornamented with gold fringe, rode around among the men and gave orders, making themselves the "observed of all observers." Also the vendors of whiskey, ginger cakes, apples, and cider took no small interest in the anticipated muster day, for on that day, every person being excited, bought more or less of these things. Always on muster day, after the muster was over, the rival bruisers of the neighborhood tried their strength upon one another, thus furnishing a great deal of amusement for those attending. The little folks were also happy in the anticipation if not the enjoyment of being presented with ginger[2] cake and an apple on that day.[3]

---

[1] The organization of companies of militia among Latter Day Saints has been greatly misunderstood because of ignorance of this law. Jason W. Briggs and Zenos H. Gurley, Jr., bitterly arraigned the early church for this when they withdrew from the church and even the late Joseph Smith in his splendid "The Situation" in *Saints' Herald*, Volumes 18, 19, (see *Church History*, Volume 3, page 676) deplored the raising of a military organization by the church.

[2] Our grandmothers called gingerbread "muster bread" because of its being so generally sold on muster days.

[3] *History of Cooper County, Missouri*, by Levins and Drake, Perrin and Smith, Saint Louis, 1876.

Citizens were compelled to pay a fine of one dollar for absence from muster. These militia adopted names according to their fancy, such as the Liberty (Missouri) Blues and Carthage (Illinois) Greys. Of the militia of Clay County, many of whom later distinguished themselves in the Mexican War, one of the old-time judges in writing of the past says:

> In the early days of Clay County the people had great zeal for keeping up military organizations; and the military laws of the State required that they should organize. They took quite a pride in complying with the law, and the Indians being immediately upon the border, from past experience a great many of us, knowing their treachery, were actuated from purposes of self-protection as well as due respect for the law, soon organized ourselves into companies with a full set of officers, each company having its stated time and place for drilling, or muster, as it was termed. We generally met three times a year for company drill—spring, summer, and fall. We had in addition regimental and battalion muster once or twice a year. . . . At our big musters, our officers vied with each other in going through all the tactics known in military discipline. . . . The people enjoyed themselves on these occasions. All hands being of a genial, social disposition, they ate, drank, and were merry, and some would drink essence of corn until they were so drunk they would be feeling upward for the ground.

When first urged to organize into a company of state militia, the Saints demurred, telling Governor Dunklin it was "by no means agreeable to the feelings of the church." The governor's reply was: "Should your men organize according to law, which, they have a right to do (indeed, it is their duty to do so, unless exempted by religious scruples), and apply for public arms, the executive could not distinguish between their right to have them, and the right of every other description of people similarly situated."

After Caldwell County, supposed to be exclusively Latter Day Saint, was organized, a military organization was, of course, compulsory, but Joseph Smith, Sidney Rigdon, and others took advantage of legal exemption, as clergymen. However, in Nauvoo, some years later, forced to the wall by a series of heartbreaking events, Joseph Smith took his place with all other citizens in a military organization, that, while fulfilling the requirements of the law, was also a matter of great pride, for it was second to none in the state. While the "Nauvoo Legion" with its handsome arsenal on the hill, its uniforms, its military drills, and sham battles may seem rather foolish to us today, we must remember that these exercises were a part of the life of every frontier town of that period.

The state of affairs in a community where every man was a soldier and one in every dozen an officer had its complications. The task of determining whether or not a group of men were acting in official capacity brought about all manner of complications. Rioting was not uncommon as in the case of the killing of Major J. Logan Forsythe during a muster at Boonville. When some of the citizens of Independence forced all the Latter Day Saints to surrender their arms, Governor Dunklin, after an investigation, decided that these men were not acting as militia, but as a mob, and ordered the arms returned. Finally, in the late forties, this law was abolished.

XVI.—The Church Grows

*I*N THE MEANTIME, THE organization of the church was expanding to meet the needs of a rapidly growing people. At the conference of June 6, 1831, at Kirtland, Ohio, high priests had been ordained for the first time in the church, and the elders receiving this ordination felt an added power and increased assurance.

> It was already evident [says Joseph Smith] that the Lord gave us power in proportion to the work that was to be done, and strength according to the race set before us, and grace and help as our needs required. Great harmony prevailed; several were ordained; faith was strengthened; and humility so necessary for the blessing of God to follow prayer, characterized the Saints.[1]

The priesthood of the church was on the eve of still further important organization, which occurred during the succeeding years as fast as the necessities of the church arose and men came forward to fill the positions of trust thus created.

The special blessings of this conference, the confidence that meeting with those of kindred spirits inspired, was to be a stay and consolation to those departing on perilous journeys to Missouri where they would ofttimes find themselves alone in the midst of those who were not friendly to their work. It took courage and confidence to endure those long weeks and months before they would again be privileged to meet with those of their own faith.

Joseph Smith and his party, after their short visit in Independence and vicinity, were back in Kirtland by August, 1831, but many of the missionaries did not see their homes until months later, some not for a year or more. Joseph Smith and Sidney

---

[1] *Times and Seasons*, Volume 5, page 416.

THE CHURCH GROWS

Rigdon now took up a project planned and barely commenced in that memorable summer of 1830, the revision of the Scriptures. They needed a quiet place for study and work far from the many visitors and inquirers that thronged Kirtland. They found it in Hiram, a little village some thirty miles from that place.

Sidney Rigdon moved his family there, and Joseph Smith and his wife, Emma, and their twin babies, now almost five months old, found a peaceful shelter at the home of John Johnson and his wife, Elsa, where they were made welcome by the host and hostess and their family of young people, who also became interested in the work of the church. Two of their sons became members of the First Quorum[2] of Twelve, and one of their daughters the wife[3] of another of the same body. Lyman E.[4] was a youth of not quite nineteen when he was baptized by Sidney Rigdon in February, 1831. Four years later when the Quorum of Twelve was organized, he was its youngest member, and the first chosen. After some three years of active missionary work, he was forced out, with many of the younger men of the church, accused of "merchandising" in 1838. He later took up the practice of law in Davenport, Iowa, and still later went to Keokuk and practiced there. He was always friendly to the church, and often visited at Nauvoo. He met his death by accidental drowning at Prairie du Chien, Wisconsin, in 1856.

In June following Lyman's baptism, his brother Luke,[5] his senior by four years, was baptized by Joseph Smith. He also became one of the Twelve, and was disaffected at the same time as his brother, John F. Boynton, the Whitmers, and Oliver Cowdery. He later returned, although he never became very active in church work again.

---

[2] Our use as a church of the word adheres more closely to the Latin derivation of the word, than the one in commonest use among us. See Webster's unabridged dictionary, "a specially select or selected body."
[3] Marinda N. Johnson, wife of Orson Hyde.
[4] Lyman E. Johnson, son of John and Elsa Johnson, was born in Pomfret, Windsor County, Vermont, October 24, 1811.
[5] Luke S. Johnson, son of John and Elsa Johnson, was born in Pomfret, Windsor County, Vermont, November 3, 1807. He went to Salt Lake City with Brigham Young's movement and died there December 9, 1861.

Perhaps what first attracted the Johnson family to the church was the famous healing of Mrs. Johnson's crippled arm. A. S. Hayden, a Disciples minister, describes this incident, and puts his own explanation upon it:

> Whatever we may say of the moral character of the author of Mormonism, it cannot be denied that Joseph Smith was a man of remarkable power—over others. Added to the stupendous claim of supernatural power, conferred by the direct gift of God, he exercised an almost magnetic power—an irresistible fascination—over those with whom he came in contact. Ezra Booth of Mantua, a Methodist preacher of much more than ordinary culture, and with strong natural abilities, in company with his wife, Mr. and Mrs. Johnson, and some other citizens of this place, visited Smith at his home in Kirtland in 1831. Mrs. Johnson had been afflicted for some time with a lame arm, and was not at the time of the visit able to lift her hand to her head. The party visited Smith partly out of curiosity, and partly to see for themselves what there might be in the new doctrine. During the interview, the conversation turned on the subject of supernatural gifts, such as were conferred in the days of the apostles. Someone said, "Here is Mrs. Johnson with a lame arm. Has God given any power to men now on earth to cure her?" A few moments later, when the conversation had turned in another direction, Smith arose, and walking across the room, taking Mrs. Johnson by the hand, said in the most solemn and impressive manner: "Woman, in the name of the Lord Jesus Christ, I command thee to be whole," and immediately left the room.
> The company was awe stricken at the infinite presumption of the man, and the calm assurance with which he spoke. The sudden mental and moral shock—I know not better how to explain the well-attested fact—electrified the rheumatic arm—Mrs. Johnson at once lifted it up with ease, and on her return home the next day she was able to do her washing without difficulty or pain.[6]

The Johnsons had a different explanation for this miracle. They really believed it to be a manifestation of the power of God, and immediately threw in their fortunes with the Latter Day Saints. At their hospitable farm home the Smiths found a quiet haven such as had been theirs in the Whitmer home in Fayette. They moved to Hiram in September, and by the first of October, with

---

[6] Hayden's *History of the Western Reserve*, pages 240, 250. *Church History*, Volume 1, pages 90, 91.

THE CHURCH GROWS   151

the aid of Rigdon, Joseph Smith was hard at work upon the revision of the Scriptures.

This work was interrupted rather frequently by conferences, councils, and short missionary trips. At one of these conferences, it was determined to publish a paper in the town of Independence, to be called *The Evening and the Morning Star*. W. W. Phelps, who was on his way back to "Zion" in the West, was to purchase a press and type as he passed through Cincinnati. This was an expensive and forward-looking venture for the young church, busy as they were in collecting enough money to buy western lands upon which to locate the people who were thronging into the church, anxious to take part in the new experiment in the West. But the revelations received through Joseph Smith were still in manuscript form, and could only be interpreted by the people as they passed by word of mouth from one to the other, or were handed about in rare copies. As these revelations contained important direction to the church, it seemed that some means of making them accessible to everyone was almost imperative. These revelations were to be published in the proposed *The Evening and the Morning Star* and also in book form for general distribution. This latter publication was to be known as the *Book of Commandments*.[7]

The first Sunday in October, Orson Hyde,[8] a young clerk in

---

[7] The *Book of Commandments* as printed during the following months is still extant, though but few copies of the book are in existence. It is generally believed that the pages of the book were scattered through the streets of Independence when the press was destroyed July 20, 1833. William McLellin of the original Quorum of Apostles, told Robert M. Elvin that he "gathered up the leaves as they blew about the street to compile his book." Some factions of the church maintain that the book was complete at the time of the destruction of the press, and use the *Book of Commandments* and condemn all later publications. The *Book of Commandments* (whether complete or not) was used as reference up to the time the Doctrine and Covenants was accepted officially by the church.

[8] Orson Hyde was the son of Nathan and Sally Hyde. Born in Oxford, New Haven County, Connecticut, January 8, 1808. His mother died when he was seven, and he was "taken to raise" by Nathan Wheeler who took him to Kirtland, Ohio, when fourteen. Although only twenty-six years old when he began his career in the church, he was not without experience as a minister. Becoming a Methodist convert and class leader at nineteen, he later was attracted by Rigdon's preaching, and under the spell of that "eloquent tongue that never stammered" became a minister of the "Reformed-Baptists" (as then called) organizing churches throughout Lorain and Huron Counties, Ohio. He at first refused to follow Rigdon into the Saints' church, and opposed it openly and publicly, but later was baptized by Rigdon on October 31, 1831.

Whitney's store, was baptized. He was another of those destined to be numbered among the first Quorum of Twelve Apostles.

The work on the Scriptures was temporarily suspended early in November, while Joseph Smith made haste to correct and prepare the material for the *Book of Commandments* that the manuscript might be taken by Oliver Cowdery and John Whitmer to Missouri for publication, mails being far too uncertain for such valuable papers. From November 1 to November 12, a number of the brethren sat in council constantly preparing this work. And even then they later considered that their work had been too hurried for absolute accuracy.

The brethren left with the precious papers about the middle of November, and the work on the translation, or rather revision of the Scriptures was resumed, to be continued all through the winter, though with rather frequent interruptions due to missionary activity and church business.

In the meantime, under the able direction of Edward Partridge, the experiment in Missouri was progressing quite satisfactorily, in spite of occasional discouragements and disagreements. After only a few days in Independence, on August 3, 1831, Joseph Smith went out into the woods, pointed out a beautiful location, and said, "Here is where the temple is to be built." At this time the church did not own a foot of this land. It is doubtful if they knew who did own it. Certainly it did not matter. They were so sure of themselves, so positive of their mission, they knew without shadow of doubt that this consecrated spot would become their own. On December 10, 1831, for "the consideration of one hundred and thirty dollars," Bishop Partridge bought for the church, from Jones H. Flournoy and wife, a tract of land, including the spot dedicated for the temple, which has ever since been known as the Temple Lot. Upon this tract near the northeast corner he erected his own house, where meetings were often held when the weather did not permit their being held in the open on the

Temple Lot. He also secured some two thousand acres of land, some by purchase, and some by original entry.

The student of history who for the first time looks upon the plat showing original entries of land in Jackson County, and recalls the race for land that so often caused trouble and bloodshed in early days, receives no uncertain light on events that came so soon after. Here he sees a large acreage of choice land marked Edward Partridge, next to it one labeled Lilburn W. Boggs, again and again the names appear in close proximity, foretelling a rivalry that was all too soon manifest.

Partridge's rather enormous purchases of land were not for himself, but to be allotted as inheritances to the Saints who came up to Zion to aid in the establishment of the new economic system, variously known as the "United Order," the "Zionic Plan," and the "Order of Enoch."[9]

Theirs was not an isolated example of the awakening of public conscience. Similar religious trends marked the beginning of a movement for public morality. Only two years later in 1833 John Joy Shipherd and Philo Penfield Stewart founded the Oberlin Colony in the forests of Northern Ohio, declaring their purpose to serve God, and to hold no more property than each could manage, operating that property as a divine trust. This idea is very much akin to the Latter Day Saint theory of stewardships, promulgated from the inception of the church until today.

To the Saints from the East, where large families were successfully reared and reasonably well educated on snug little farms of forty to sixty acres, the cry of the long-sided Kentuckians for "elbow-room" was incomprehensible and showed at the least, greed and lack of thrift, while the gregarious tendency of the

---

[9] It is said that Edward Bellamy, noted socialist and author, conceived the theories expressed in his *Looking Backward* by a study of this economic principle advanced by Latter Day Saints. John Henry Evans makes this claim in his *Joseph Smith, an American Prophet,* page 244; and it is confirmed by the Arizona historian, McClintock, in his *Mormon Settlements.* Warren Watson in *Kansas City Globe Souvenir* compares Joseph Smith's plan to the "mild lunacy" of Edward Bellamy.

Latter Day Saint colonies was equally baffling to the original settlers.

A disinterested writer says, "It was late in the summer when the Saints arrived, but they immediately went to work. . . . Notwithstanding the belated season they cut hay for their cattle, sowed a little grain and carried forward the work of building log cabins. Winter came and found them somewhat unprepared, but cheerfully content to bear its inclemencies for the glory of the church. The season was an unusually cold one and there was some scarcity of food and clothing, but the devotees huddled together, sometimes with as many as ten families in one cabin, whose floor was the frozen ground, and withstood every hardship without a murmur. Their food consisted of beef and cornmeal . . . and their drink was cold water—for Joseph Smith was the first prohibitionist.[10] . . . Notwithstanding the trials of the first year, the Mormons acquired property from the first. While the Gentiles suffered around them, they prospered constantly. They openly boasted that heaven was on their side . . . and these [neighbors] in their turn roundly declared that it was Satan who thus favored . . . the Mormons. Perhaps both were wrong—an agnostic can only guess in such a dilemma—perhaps the prosperity of the Mormons was the result of combined efforts toward one end.[11] With this self-styled agnostic conclusion, most Latter Day Saints will heartily agree.

Meanwhile in Kirtland on February 10, 1832, while working upon the revision of the Scriptures, Joseph Smith received the revelation upon the "glories," showing how provision was to be made in the next world for all men, according "as their works should be," and delighting the hearts of those former Restorationists, such as Edward Partridge, who clung to their original faith in "universal restoration."

---

[10] Perhaps a pardonable exaggeration in Missouri in 1832.
[11] Warren Watson in *Kansas City Globe Souvenir*, reprinted in *Saints' Herald*, Volume 37, pages 203, 204.

THE CHURCH GROWS

The Johnson home in Hiram had proved a quiet retreat for study and work, and Emma Smith joined her husband there, and Sidney Rigdon temporarily moved his family to the little village on the hill. In March the Smith twins,[12] and all the little Rigdons developed measles, and nursing them became a real task. At the Johnson home, Emma Smith and her husband took turns watching by the bedside of the little ones. Along about midnight on March 25 (1832) Emma Smith rose (for she could never sleep long in her anxiety for the babes) and insisted upon Joseph lying down upon the trundle bed. He was awakened by her scream as he was borne out of the room by a mob of angry men. Led by a minister of another denomination they proceeded to "tar and feather" both Joseph Smith and Sidney Rigdon. Terrified, the Saints gathered at the Johnson home that night, and willing and loving hands of brethren helped to remove the tar from the flesh of the victims, but nothing could be done for the innocent baby martyr to this exhibition of cruel and barbaric folly. Little Joseph lingered for only four days. The wintry wind blowing upon the feverish little body had brought on a relapse, from which the child never recovered.

A trip to Missouri had been planned on account of certain important developments in the organization of the church, namely, the ordination of Joseph Smith at a conference at Amherst on January 25 to be president of the high priesthood (which should be ratified by the church in Missouri). Sidney Rigdon was very ill from exposure on the night of the mob, and continued delirious. Joseph was quite recovered (although bruised and lacerated) and had preached in Hiram on the day following the mob, but he was concerned over Rigdon's condition. Mrs. Rigdon was afraid to be alone, so in spite of his illness and that of the chil-

---

[12]These twins, Joseph and Julia, were adopted by Joseph and Emma Smith, when their own newborn children did not survive their birth. They were the children of John and Julia (Clapp) Murdock, whose mother died at their birth. They were born on the same date as the Smith babies, April 30, 1831.

dren, the whole family was taken to Kirtland, where they would be among friends.

On Friday, March 30, baby Joseph died on the eve of his birthday, for the twins would have been eleven months old next day, and on Sunday, April 1, the father, who could delay his trip to Missouri no longer, was forced to bid his wife and remaining child good-by, and start on his long trip westward.

Sidney Rigdon had been so weakened by his recent experience that the party did not plan to walk to the Ohio River as usual. Instead a brother of the church, George Pitkin took Joseph Smith, Newel K. Whitney, Peter Whitmer, and Jesse Gauze from Hiram to Steubenville, Ohio, in his wagon. They were joined at Warren by Sidney Rigdon, who left Chardon the same morning. They made the trip in two days, stopping at Wellsville the first night.

The purpose in going to Steubenville, instead of Cincinnati, was that they might call at Wheeling, West Virginia, for paper. Indeed this was one of the primary purposes of the westward trip. W. W. Phelps had written that the new printing press was all set up, and they were ready to go ahead with the printing as soon as paper could be brought from the East.

The little party took passage on a steam packet to Wheeling, from whence, having secured a stock of paper and had it loaded on the "Trenton," they were ready to start, when on the night before their departure, the boat was partially destroyed by fire. After some parley, the boat was considered fit to travel as far as Louisville, so on they went. What was their surprise on changing their precious paper to the "Charleston" at Louisville to meet Titus Billings and a band of Saints "going up to Zion." Amid happy associations the whole company made the trip to St. Louis, where on account of so many delays, Joseph Smith felt it imperative to make the journey in shorter time than usual, and leaving the party at St. Louis, took the stage for Independence, carrying as cargo his load of paper. He records with satisfaction that he made the trip by the 24th of April! Only twenty-three days from Kirtland!

A special conference had been called for April 26. On that day his ordination at Amherst, Ohio, as president of the high priesthood was formally acknowledged by the church in Missouri. The brief mention of this ordination is one of the strange slips that historians sometimes make. We do not know who ordained him, doubtless someone ordained him to a higher order in the priesthood than he himself held, as this had been done before in the history of the organization. Joseph Smith had ordained Oliver Cowdery to the Aaronic priesthood before he himself had received that priesthood, and elders had officiated the summer before in the ordination of high priests. In this emergency those involved felt the command of God was sufficient authority.

On the next day he was occupied with church business, mainly directed toward greater unity among the brethren of the church, for he felt that such unity must eventually characterize those who would establish the "United Order." "It was my endeavor," he says, "to so organize the church that the brethren might eventually be independent of every incumbrance beneath the celestial kingdom, by bonds and covenants of mutual friendship and mutual love."[13]

Two days were taken off from council meetings to visit the old friends of the Colesville Branch. "The Colesville branch, in particular, rejoiced as the ancient saints did with Paul."[14] Of this event Newel Knight writes joyfully in his journal:

> Brother Joseph did not forget his old friends of Colesville Branch, and he came the twelve miles to visit us. We welcomed him heartily, and were greatly rejoiced to see his face once more, and shake him by the hand. He remained with us two days and returned on the 30th to Independence.[15]

On the sixth day of May, the President of the church "gave his

---
[13]*Times and Seasons,* Volume 5, page 625; *Church History,* Volume 1, page 248.
[14]*Ibid.; Church History* Volume 1, page 249.
[15]Newel Knight's Journal in *Scraps of Biography,* Salt Lake City, 1883.

parting hand to the brethren in Independence, and, in company with Brothers Rigdon and Whitney, commenced a return to Kirtland, by stage to Saint Louis, from thence to Vincennes, Indiana, from thence to New Albany, near the falls of the Ohio River." Here Bishop Whitney, in attempting to jump from the stagecoach, caught his foot in the wheel and had his leg broken so they were obliged to remain in Greenville, Indiana, at the inn of a man by the name of Porter. Rigdon went on to Kirtland, but Joseph Smith stayed with his associate, who otherwise was in perfect health, but on account of this compound fracture of his leg could not be moved for four weeks.

While the two were whiling away the tedious hours as best they could, the mysterious forces, that seemed to be bringing forward at the right time just the man needed, were at work in the far northern frontier to bring to the church another who was to fill a place in the forthcoming quorum of apostles. David Wyman Patten was thirty-one years of age, stood six feet and one inch in height and weighed over two hundred pounds, a man of great physical strength, absolute fearlessness, and in a day of great faith, noted among his brethren as the possessor of the most unquestioning faith of all. No one of the apostles was more loved. He was the man who was in his future ministry to enter thousands of cabins in the woods, walk to the sickbed of those who lay dying and tell them with assurance to rise and walk, that God could heal them today, even as Jesus healed the multitudes in Galilee. Literally thousands of miracles took place under the hands of this mighty man with his simple, unquestioning, childlike faith. Alone among hostile bands, he strode through the woods, and preached his powerful sermons in country churches, schoolhouses, and frontier cabins. He did not feel alone, faith was on his right hand, and courage on his left—the two great dominant characteristics of David Patten.

In 1830 he had seen a Book of Mormon, probably in Jefferson County, New York, but held it in his hands only long enough to read the title page and the testimony of the witnesses. Two years had elapsed since then, and he was living in the wilds of Monroe County, Michigan, a devout Methodist. He had married a Michigan girl, Phoebe Ann Babcock, and they had a comfortable cabin and clearing in the woods. One day in May, 1832, he received a letter from his brother, John Patten of Fairplay, Greene County, Indiana, telling of the Book of Mormon and the restoration of the gospel. He received the letter on Sunday, and spoke of it in the Methodist prayer meeting that day. The next morning early (for Latter Day Saints had not learned to procrastinate)—

> He mounted his old gray mare and started alone through the woods on a journey of three hundred miles. That country in those days was little more than a wilderness. The roads by which settlers had come from their eastern homes ran in the main, east and west, so that David's way to the south led him over hills, through valleys, and across rivers by paths almost unknown to the white man; but nature was in her glory, the birds made melody the day through, and more than all else, his own heart, swelling with gratitude, kept time to the music of the spheres . . . arrived at the home of his brother at Fairplay, he found him, before an infidel, now a devoted Christian.[16]

On the 15th of June, his brother, John Patten, baptized him, and on the 17th of June, Elisha H. Groves ordained him, and he was appointed on a mission to Michigan with another recent convert, Joseph Wood. David Patten lost no time in entering into his labors. On his way back to Michigan he stopped at a house to ask for his dinner, as was the custom of travelers at the time, and, finding a very sick child, explained the gospel to the parents, and saw the child instantly healed under his hands. He was not surprised.

Until the latter part of September, David spent his time in southeastern Michigan, forming a group of his converts on the River Indiana into a "branch" of the church. People came to his meetings from miles around, bringing their sick to be healed. In

---
[16]*Life of David W. Patten,* by Lycurgus Wilson, *Deseret News,* 1924.

September he determined to go on to Kirtland, as he had as yet seen but few of the church people. He preached his farewell sermon and was starting on in haste to be on his way by sundown, when he was told there were two children sick of fever and ague who had been brought to the place of meeting by the parents, who had hoped they might be healed. Patten turned back at once and, after talking to the parents concerning his faith, administered to both children, and they were instantly healed.

Arriving in Kirtland sometime in October, after preaching by the way, he found the Prophet was absent in Indiana, and would not be back until November. Rather late, he reflected, looking at the unharvested Smith crops. And since he could not meet the man, whom above all others he desired to meet, he might as well be busy. So while he waited, he spent the weeks intervening in digging the unharvested potato crop of a man he had never seen.[17]

About the time Patten was making his way south to inquire about the new faith, another traveler, now almost a seasoned veteran after two years in its service, arrived in Kirtland to greet his young wife, after an absence of nearly eighteen months. Parley P. Pratt had not seen his wife, Thankful, since he left her at Whitmer's in the fall of 1830. True he had come back to Kirtland, expecting to wait until she came overland from New York and meet her there, but before her arrival, he had been called to make his way westward again in the missionary campaign of 1831. What could he say to this call that he believed divine? He went, trusting soon to be back in Kirtland, as many of his brethren did. Instead, he was detained all winter in the Colesville Branch in Missouri, laid quite low with the dreaded fever and ague.

Spring came and some of the brethren were going east—going home. He resolved to go with them, though he could scarcely stand alone. His resolution was strengthened by a rumor that

---

[17]*Life of David W. Patten*, by Lycurgus Wilson, *Deseret News*, 1924.

had reached him from Kirtland. His wife was ill of that dread disease tuberculosis, and she would not be there to meet him if he did not go quickly. She had kept her own condition from him in her infrequent letters: he had only read there her anxiety for him. He must go to her at all costs.

It had been a fearful journey. He started in February with Levi Hancock.

> I gained strength at every step, and the second evening after wading through the snow about six inches deep for some ten miles, I was enabled to address a congregation for the first time in several months.
>
> I now parted with Levi Hancock, and had John Murdock[18] for a fellow traveler. We passed down the south side of the Missouri River, among a thin settlement of people—mostly very ignorant, but extremely hospitable. Some families were entirely dressed in skins, without any other clothing, including ladies young and old. Buildings were generally without glass windows, and the door open in winter for a light. We preached and warned the people and taught them as well as we could.
>
> While ministering in these settlements, and exposed to a heavy snowstorm, Brother John Murdock was taken sick with a heavy fever; this caused us to stop early in the day among strangers, in a small log cabin consisting of one room; we held a meeting in the evening, and then had a bed made on the floor, before the fire. Before morning Brother Murdock was much better, but I was seized with a most dreadful chill, followed by a heavy turn of fever; morning found me unable to speak or rise. As the bed was in the way, they lifted it up by the four corners, with me upon it, and placed it in the back part of the room upon another bed.[19]

He called his traveling companion, and whispered to him. Murdock, unobserved by the members of the household, laid hands upon him in the ceremony of healing. He rose at once, dressed, and they started on their journey, climbing a large hill in the midst of a great snowstorm without ill effects. Once in Saint Louis, they were conveyed "free of charge" across the Mississippi by friends with whom they had tarried and preached (for these men were traveling "without purse or scrip").

We arrived [he continued] at length at Vandalia, the then capital of Illinois. Here we were invited to a hotel, where we sojourned free

---

[18] Father of the twins adopted by Joseph and Emma Smith.
[19] *Autobiography of Parley Parker Pratt,* pages 78, *seq.*

of charge, and preached to a good audience in the Presbyterian meetinghouse. Next morning resuming our journey we crossed the Okah river on a bridge, but the bottoms for two or three miles were overflowed to various depths, from six inches to three or four feet, and frozen over, except in the main channels with a coat of ice which we had to break by lifting our feet to the surface at every step. This occupied several hours and called into requisition our utmost strength, and sometimes we were entirely covered with water. At length we got through in safety and came to a house where we warmed and dried our clothes. . . . Our feet and legs had lost all feeling, become benumbed, and were dreadfully bruised and cut with ice.

On the next day, we had to cross a plain fifteen miles in length, without a house, a tree, or any kind of shelter; a cold northwest wind was blowing, and the ground covered with snow and ice. We had made two or three miles into the plain when I was attacked with a severe return of my old complaint, which had confined me so many months in Jackson County, and from which I had recovered by a miracle at the onset of the journey—I mean the fever and ague.

I traveled and shook, and shook and traveled, till I could stand it no longer; I vomited severely several times, and finally fell down on the snow overwhelmed with fever, and became helpless and nearly insensible. This was about seven or eight miles from the nearest house.

Brother John Murdock laid his hands on me and prayed in the name of Jesus; and taking me by the hand, he commanded me with a loud voice, saying, "In the name of Jesus, arise and walk!" I attempted to arise; I staggered a few paces, and was about falling again when I found my fever suddenly depart and my strength come. I walked at the rate of about four miles an hour, arrived at a house, and was sick no more.[20]

In those days one was likely to meet Latter Day Saint missionaries almost anywhere. As Pratt and Murdock went on preaching by the way, following pretty closely the National Road, they were pleased to meet at Vincennes where they crossed the Wabash, Elders Peter Dustin and Calvin Beebe, who had left Independence when they did and for the same purpose, traveling and preaching by a different route.

Arriving in Kirtland, Parley found his wife thin and wan, and though she "gradually resumed her wonted cheerfulness," she never became entirely well.

In June, 1832, the first issue of *The Evening and the Morning*

---

[20] *Ibid.*, pages 81, 82.

THE CHURCH GROWS 163

Star was printed, reaching Kirtland sometime in July, to the joy of all who read it. Not only was it the first paper printed in the church, but the first in Jackson County. There was an editorial in it, urging the Saints to see that their children had the advantage of common schools. They had learned that need in Missouri.

In August and September the missionaries began gathering into Kirtland for a conference which convened September 22 and 23. At this conference many of the elders were sent east on missions. In early days of the church, specific missions were not usually assigned. Men appointed to missions by the church were wont to retire to some lonely wood, and there one of their number, as spokesman, asked the Lord for direction as to where they should go. They believed they were given guidance, and the result of their missions seemed to justify that belief. Of course there were many requests for missionaries to be sent, but there was never a lack of men ready to go on what they firmly believed to be the most important business in the world.

About this time Joseph Smith made a short trip east to New York, returning (November 6, 1832) the day of the birth of his son, Joseph, the first living child born to him and his wife. His father was known as Joseph, Senior, himself as Joseph, Junior; the child became Young Joseph, a fond title that was to bring comfort to the hearts of many. He was a brown-eyed boy, very much like his mother, and the father was fond of saying in a jocular way that there was a Hale storm the night Young Joseph was born.

On Tuesday, December 25, 1832, Joseph Smith gave the famous prophecy foretelling the Civil War. South Carolina had the previous month passed the famous Nullification Act. This was met by prompt and decisive action of President Jackson, and was finally temporarily settled by Henry Clay's Tariff Act of 1833, and hostilities ceased.

Joseph Smith was unconvinced that the peace would be permanent and wrote N. E. Seaton, editor of a newspaper in Rochester,

New York, on January 4, 1833: "And now I am prepared to say by the authority of Jesus Christ, that not many years shall pass away before the United States shall present such a scene of bloodshed as has not a parallel in the history of our nation."[21]

Early in November or late in October, two men, who were to figure in the history of the church more largely than anyone at the time realized, came to Kirtland to visit the Prophet. These two men, Brigham Young[22] and Heber C. Kimball,[23] had been baptized earlier in the year. Both were of the shrewd Yankee type, a trifle crude at times, but full of practical wisdom and common sense. They were connected by marriage, and had been baptized with their wives and many of their neighbors at Mendon, New York. Elder Eleazer Miller, had "raised up" there a branch of over thirty souls, some of whom have become famous in the history of the church. They were John, Senior, and Mary Young, Brigham and Miriam Young, Joseph Young, Phineas H. and Clarissa Young, Lorenzo Dow and Persis Young, John P. and Rhoda Greene and their children; Joel and Louisa Sanford, William and Susan Stillson, Fanny Young, Isaac Flummerfelt, his wife and children; Ira and Charlotte Bond,[24] Heber C. and Vilate Kimball, Rufus Parks, John and Betsy Morton, Nathan Tomlinson and wife, and Israel Barlow with mother, brothers, and sisters. Young and Kimball, with some others, moved to Kirtland during the next year, and began to take active interest in the missionary work, and were eventually numbered with the first Quorum of Apostles when they were chosen.

Another of the men who were to be Apostles was baptized in September, 1832, John F. Boynton.[25] He was twenty-one the

---
[21] *Times and Seasons,* Volume 5, page 707; *Church History,* Volume 1, page 261.
[22] Brigham Young was born June 1, 1801 in Whitingham, Windsor County, Vermont. He was a carpenter, glazier, and painter. Baptized April 14, 1832, by Eleazer Miller.
[23] Heber C. Kimball born June 14, 1801 in Sheldon, Franklin County, Vermont. Was a potter. He was baptized in April 1832, by Alpheus Gifford.
[24] Ira Bond and his wife Charlotte were the parents of Myron H. Bond, for many years a prominent minister in the Reorganized Church.
[25] John F. Boynton was born September 11, 1811, in Bradford, Essex County, Massachusetts, and was baptized in Kirtland, Ohio, by Sidney Rigdon in September, 1832.

month of his baptism, and thus became the next to the youngest Apostle. Boynton left the church with others in 1838, went to Saint Louis, was graduated from college, and became a very well-known geologist and lecturer. Although few who knew him ever suspected the hidden chapter in his life when he was a Latter Day Saint Apostle, and his published biographies do not mention it, nevertheless he was always the friend of Joseph Smith while he lived, and never had a word to say against any of the factions of the church throughout his life.

While the men who were a few years later to stand in one of the chief quorums of the church were slowly gathering to her ranks, choice was made of two men as counselors for the President of the church, Sidney Rigdon and Frederick Granger Williams. They were called to this office March 8, 1833, and ordained ten days later.

On February 27, 1833, a unique document was given to the church called "The Word of Wisdom." In this revelation the Saints are warned against the use of tobacco and liquor, and "hot drinks," and advised to eat meat sparingly. The Saints were promised the blessing of health if this counsel were heeded. Coming at a time of the world when the use of these things was almost unquestioned, the document is quite noteworthy. Latter Day Saints were from earliest times ardent advocates of temperance. Abstinence from liquor, tobacco, tea, and coffee in early days was made a test of fellowship. Anyone indulging in such things was brought sharply to account; usage in later years has made its observance a matter of conscience.

About this time also directions were given for making Kirtland a stake of Zion. Hitherto the people had looked forward to going to Missouri and considered Kirtland as only a temporary place of abode. Now steps were taken to build a temple, the plans for which were of divine direction.

In the meantime the church in Missouri was growing, although in the face of more or less opposition from the men among whom they were settling.

Parley P. Pratt gives us the best description we have of conditions in Zion about this time. He had decided to take his wife with him and move to western Missouri. Thankful Pratt had brought with her sixty dollars from the East and with that they planned to have enough money to pay their way. They took a stage to the Ohio River, thence by steamer to Saint Louis, and again by steamer up the Missouri. Times had gone hard with Parley Pratt. He was compelled to take a steerage passage among the poorer class, and dress "more like a laborer than a minister." Yet by some means it became known he was a minister, and he was invited to make a speech on the Nation's birthday. Time always hung heavy on a steamboat, and speaking, whether religious or political, was a popular form of entertainment in those days. Pratt hesitated. He was dressed in "gray satinet." He knew very well that preachers of that day should be clothed in broadcloth. Had not the church raised the money to fit Jared Carter out in black broadcloth before they sent him to Pontiac, Michigan, where he was to meet some of the most influential citizens? He reluctantly consented, asking that all the steerage passengers as well as deck hands be allowed the liberty of the cabin for that day. The request was granted.

"I presented myself before this motley assembly in a plain gray suit of satinet, and bowed respectfully," he tells us. "All tried to be grave, but a smile, a sneer, a look of contempt would now and then escape from some of the more genteel portion of the assembly.... I read a chapter; all was serious attention. I offered up a prayer; all was deep interest. I introduced the Book of Mormon as a record of ancient America; I dwelt upon the history and prophetic declarations, now verified by the erection of free institutions in this great country and their growing influence. I spoke of the general prosperity and resources of this country, acknowledging the hand of Providence in the same."[26] In short, he gave a typical Fourth of July address. At its conclusion the clergyman in the plain gray satinet suit was invited into the cabin to remain for the rest of the voyage, and given free board. He was even offered ten dollars for a Book of Mormon, but unfortunately had none with him.

Arriving at the Colesville settlement, he spent the rest of the summer cutting hay, building, purchasing, and planting land. During August and September he put up about fifteen tons of hay, sowed fifteen acres of wheat, built a log house, and did some fencing. The winter was spent in missionary work.

It was now the summer of 1833. Immigration had poured into the County of Jackson in great numbers; and the church in that country numbered upward of one thousand souls. These had all purchased lands and paid for them, and most of them were improving in buildings and cultivation. Peace and plenty had crowned their labors and the wilderness became a fruitful field, and the solitary place began to bud and blossom as the rose.

They lived in peace and quiet; no lawsuits with each other, or with the world; few or no debts were contracted; few promises broken; there were no thieves, no robbers, or murderers; few or no idlers; all seemed to worship God with a ready heart. On Sundays the people assembled to preach, pray, sing, and receive the ordinances of God. Other days all seemed busy in the various pursuits of industry. In short, there has seldom, if ever, been a happier people upon the earth than the church of the Saints now were.

In the latter part of the summer and in the autumn, I devoted almost my entire time in ministering among the churches; holding meetings, visiting the sick, comforting the sick and afflicted, and giving counsel. A school of the elders was also organized, over which I was called to preside. This class to the number of sixty met for instruction once a week. The place of meeting was in the open air, under some tall trees, in a retired place in the wilderness, where we prayed, preached, and prophesied, and exercised ourselves in the gifts of the Holy Spirit. . . . To attend this school, I had to travel on foot, and sometimes with bare feet at that, about six miles. This I did once a week, besides visiting and preaching in five or six branches a week.[27]

These were the conditions in Zion at that time, as seen by one who lived and labored there.

[26, 27] *Autobiography of Parley Parker Pratt*, pages 86, 87, 99, 100.

XVII.—DOCTRINAL DEVELOPMENT

FROM ITS VERY BEGINNING the church sought to teach the doctrine of Christ as recorded in the New Testament—the "Old Jerusalem Gospel." The pride of its ministers from 1830 until now has been that they are presenting an organization that harmonizes with the New Testament plan. The proposition, afterward embodied in "What We Believe," the epitome of faith, presents the keynote of the doctrinal message of Latter Day Saints, "the word of God shall be the end of all dispute."

Another cardinal principle of the church is its belief in *continual* revelation. The whole "angel message" is predicated upon this belief, and without it the Latter Day Saint Church has no excuse for being. Latter Day Saints believe that as God spoke to men in ages past, so he can and does speak to men now; that Divinity itself restored the Church of Jesus Christ to earth again in 1830, after a long period of apostasy, and that the same Divinity has continued to direct its destinies throughout its history.

Even before the church was organized, and certainly ever since, the church has affirmed its belief in Jesus Christ as the Son of God and the Savior of the world. The first instruction received by young Joseph Smith was: "Hear him!" The burden of the message of the ministry is "Christ and him crucified." The two leading missionary councils of the church, the Twelve and Seventy, are enjoined that they are "special witnesses for Christ."

Latter Day Saints early taught the second advent of Christ, urging that the second coming of Christ was "near at hand." Unlike some of their contemporaries they did not set a date for his coming, although doubtless many of them, if not the majority of the early adherents of the faith, thought the time for the "consummation of all things" was much nearer than they had any particular reason to expect. The emphasis from the beginning was placed upon the preparation of a society worthy to greet Christ at his coming. The preparation of that pure society is still the great object of the church and the immensity of that objective becomes more and more apparent as time passes; a project that is nothing short of audacious, without the aid of divine direction.

In Latter Day Saint preaching one hears much of the "first principles of the gospel," which almost any Latter Day Saint child can enumerate as faith, repentance, baptism, laying on of hands, resurrection of the dead, and eternal judgment, just as Paul enumerates them in the Hebrew letter.[1] These principles have been confirmed many times to the church in "modern revelation." During the time he was assisting in the translation of the Book of Mormon, Oliver Cowdery was reminded that "without faith you can do nothing."[2] The ministry of the church were early instructed to "say nothing but repentance unto this generation."[3] The principles of baptism and laying on of hands, taught in both the Bible and the Book of Mormon, have their confirmation in the experience of Joseph Smith and Oliver Cowdery on May 15, 1829. Latter Day Saints believe that the biblical mode of baptism was by immersion, and that it should be followed by confirmation (laying on of hands by the ministry) for the reception of the Holy Spirit. The laying on of hands by the ministry is practiced in the church for healing the sick, blessing children, (an ordinance which has its genesis in the example set by the Savior) and the ordination of ministers, as well as in confirmation. Baptism in the Latter Day Saint Church is administered only to those who have reached the "age of accountability." The doctrine of the resurrection is clearly taught in the Scriptures as well as in the Book of Mormon, and was confirmed in the early revelations to the church, as well as its companion principle of eternal judgment.

---
[1] Hebrews 6: 1, 2.
[2] Doctrine and Covenants 8:3.
[3] *Ibid.*, 10:4.

Other beliefs have been written deep into the hope of the church. Chief among these has been the cause of Zion, which took hold of the hearts and imaginations of our fathers with such power that they handed it down to generations after them as a priceless heritage. The ideal of a community built in the spirit of Christian brotherhood calls for "personal individual regeneration and for individual preparation, and in the last analysis . . . for group co-operation and righteousness."[4] Growing out of this preaching of Zion, came the term "stewardship." To the Latter Day Saint, theoretically at least, neither his wealth, his talent, nor anything he has is his own, but belongs to his Heavenly Father; he is steward over these possessions, and will eventually answer to him for their use. As one writer has said, "Stewardship is the management of God's investment in man for the purposes of God."

In common with most Protestant churches, the church believed that the privilege of officiating in the ordinances of the gospel had been lost to the world during the Dark Ages, but they believed while honoring the great reformers, that no one but the Almighty himself could confer again upon the world authority to act for God. Belief in this "restoration" of authority is the basis of the name often applied to the whole movement, "the Restoration."

Ministers were early set in the church by this divine authority, and ordained to the Melchisedec priesthood, which ministers in spiritual things; and the Aaronic priesthood, which ministers in temporal things. To this day, one may find in the church the nomenclature of the New Testament ministry: apostles, prophets, seventy, evangelists, pastors, and teachers.[5]

Just as the doctrine of Zion found individualized expression in the doctrine of stewardships, so the doctrine of revelation found its more individualized expression in the belief and exercise of spiritual gifts. The spiritual gifts, akin to those mentioned in the

---

[4] Elbert A. Smith In *Zion Builders Sermons,* Independence, Missouri, 1921, page 87.
[5] I Corinthians 12: 28; Ephesians 4: 11-13.

New Testament, were known only in part by the churches of 1830. The Latter Day Saints believed in and enjoyed them, and the gifts of wisdom and faith have been accompanied from the beginning by the gift of prophecy, of tongues, of miracles, and of healing. As if in anticipation of difficulties which have beset other believers in the spiritual gifts, the church was early instructed "that which doth not edify, is not of God, and is darkness: that which is of God is light, . . . but no man is possessor of all things, except he be purified and cleansed from all sin."[6]

The Saints believed in the resurrection, as did other religious people. But here, as elsewhere, they had a special message. After February 16, 1832, they took to the world the witness of Joseph Smith and Sidney Rigdon:

> This is the testimony, last of all, which we give of him, that he lives; for we saw him, even on the right hand of God; and we heard the voice bearing record that he is the Only Begotten of the Father; that by him, and through him, and of him, the worlds are and were created; and the inhabitants thereof are begotten sons and daughters unto God.[7]

The revelation to which this testimony is an introduction led the Saints to heights of spiritual understanding rarely achieved elsewhere. It told the story of coming glories, and emphasized the fact that all those who inherit the several glories, will be assigned to their respective places, according to their work. Future destiny will not be determined by the arbitrary will of Divinity, but by the things which we choose to do. Every man is to be raised "in his own order,"[8] and every man will be quickened by that glory for which he has prepared, and those who enjoy a lesser degree of light in the ages to come will do so "because they were not willing to enjoy that which they might have received."[9]

There are no secret or oath-bound rites and ceremonies in the church.

---

[6] Doctrine and Covenants 50:6.
[7] *Ibid.*, 76:3.
[8] I Corinthians 15:23.
[9] Doctrine and Covenants 85:6.

XVIII.—The Storm Breaks

The colony in Missouri was ill fated.

"Its foundations were barely begun when the intolerance of frontier farmers shattered the mortar," says a recent historian, E. Douglas Branch. "Missourians were afraid that the Mormons, voting as a solid phalanx, would sometime dictate the politics of the State. They were individualistic, profoundly suspicious of people who were dominated by group loyalties and group egotism."[1]

There were other reasons. Alexander W. Doniphan, than whom there was no man in western Missouri better qualified to speak, gives his opinion of the causes of the difficulty:

"I think the real objections to the Mormons were their denunciation of slavery, and the objections slaveholders had to having so large a settlement of anti-slavery people in their midst, and also to their acquiring such a large amount of land, which then belonged to the Government, and subject to the pre-emption."[2]

Those who differ from the norm always pay the penalty of social ostracism. To the Latter Day Saints, ostracism was immaterial. It "merely hounded them into a conviction of their own superiority."[3] Among them at times undoubtedly more than an arrogant suggestion of group egotism was apparent—a common expression among those who feel they are "chosen" people. With the perspective of later years, it has become fully apparent that two such diverse peoples could not live in peace and unity, especially "where in the rough life of the border there is scant recognition of law and order."[4]

People who have spent their lives in England or in English col-

---

[1] E. Douglas Branch, in *Westward*, page 413.
[2] Alexander W. Doniphan in Kansas City *Journal*, June 5, 1881. *Church History*, Vol. 4, page 360. Doniphan, "Mormon History," *Saints' Herald*, Volume 28, page 230.
[3] E. Douglas Branch in *Westward*, page 413.
[4] James Truslow Adams, in "Our Lawless Heritage," *Atlantic Monthly*, page 736.

onies "where there is not a trace of the sporting spirit,"[5] which leads their American cousins to make a joke of law observance and lawbreaking, have difficulty in understanding the mobs of our past and present public life.

The colonists, long before the Revolutionary War, broke the law of England with impunity. Many a comfortable New England fortune had its foundations laid in the remunerative occupation of smuggling, a quite respectable occupation for church men and statesmen of colonial times. By the time of the signing of the Declaration of Independence "Americans had developed a marked tendency to obey only such laws as they chose to obey."[6]

"The ripest fruits of disregard for law are found mainly when passions are roused, as they were for several decades from 1830 onward."[7] One phase of this remarkable outbreak of religious intolerance was that directed against the Roman Catholics in the more cultured East. In 1834 the Ursaline Convent near Boston was burned to the ground and sacked by anti-Catholics.

The next night a race riot, this time directed against the Negroes, broke out at Philadelphia, in the course of which thirty houses were sacked or destroyed, a church pulled down, and several persons killed. Similar riots occurred within a few weeks at other places, and in a few years the militia had to disperse a mob of a thousand marching on the House of the Papal Nuncio at Cincinnati. The Irish quarter in Chelsea, Massachusetts, was attacked; the chapel at Coburg was burned; that at Dorchester blown up, and that at Manchester, New Hampshire, wrecked; at Ellsworth, Maine, the priest was tarred and feathered, the convent at Providence was attacked, and a riot at Saint Louis resulted in ten deaths.

Similar violence was used against the Mormons, mainly after they were residents of Missouri and before they had adopted the doctrine of plural wives. The feeling against them first manifested itself in tarring and feathering, but by the autumn of 1833, a veritable reign of terror had begun. Houses were destroyed, men were beaten, and even a battle took place. By November mobs had forced about 1,200 Mormons to leave their homes, pursuing them across the Missouri River and burning two hundred of their forcibly abandoned homes. The governor was unable to afford them protection, although admitting they were entitled to it.[8]

[5] *Ibid.*, page 732.   [6] *Ibid.*, page 732.
[7] *Ibid.*, page 732.   [8] *Ibid.*, page 737.

In the month of April, the first mob gathered in Independence, determined as they said, to "move the Mormons out of their diggin's," but the crowd, getting the worse for liquor, "broke up in a regular Missouri row." About that time the members of the church met on the Big Blue at the ferry which was built, owned, and operated by the Saints. Their purpose was to celebrate the birthday of the church. It was a beautiful day, long to be remembered by the Saints, for such peaceful occasions were soon to vanish from their midst. Spring had come with the burst of glory with which it comes in Jackson County. The woods were sweet with flowering shrubs. Every bird, it seemed, was singing to help them celebrate. The little homes in the forest were fast assuming an air of comfort and prosperity. The Saints had been busy hauling rails, which had been cut during the winter, from the woods for fencing, and planting a crop they were never to harvest. There had already been some depredations, houses unroofed, men whipped by young ruffians a little the worse for liquor, and wanting to have some "fun" with the "Mormons."

About the 25th of June, Joseph Smith sent from Kirtland the plat of the new city of Zion, a unique plan, which was never carried out, for in less than a month suppressed excitement burst into flames, and from then on, conditions in Missouri were, as Adams has said, " a veritable reign of terror."

Perhaps more than all else contributing to the mob of July 20, 1833, in Independence, was the publication of an editorial "Free People of Color," in *The Evening and the Morning Star* of that month. A careful reading of this editorial at the present time shows nothing to give offense; but read with the bias of those days, in the spirit of "those who are not of us are against us," one may see why the people were so incensed by it. Actually it was intended to pour oil on troubled waters, by declaring the intention of the Saints to observe strict neutrality on the slave issue, but to the Missourian of that day there was no neutrality. In many quarters the very basis of his civilization was being threatened; he intended to take no chances. And in spite of the efforts of the Saints to move with caution, they were judged not by the words of their mouths, but by the thoughts of their minds and the feelings of their hearts. The Missourians instinctively felt an antagonism to the industrial system upon which their civilization was built, and seized upon this first public utterance, to make it mean an invitation for free blacks to come and settle among them, to be companions to their wives and children!

Upon the 20th a petition was drawn up and signed, asking in no uncertain terms that the Latter Day Saints leave Jackson County. The names signed to this document were those of some of the most influential men in Jackson County, but that by no means intimates that these men were instrumental in the scene which followed. The brick printing office[9] was torn down, together with the dwelling house of W. W. Phelps. Mrs. Phelps with a sick child was thrown into the street, the type and papers in the office were scattered along the streets, as was also the goods from the store of Gilbert and Whitney. Unwound bolts of cloth covered the streets; blacksmith tools from the shop of Robert Rathbun, a Latter Day Saint blacksmith,[10] were strewn about. The press and most of the type were carried to the river and thrown in.[11]

Then as the sun went down, the crowd proceeded to capture Bishop Edward Partridge and Charles Allen and tar and feather them. "If any of the good citizens had anything to do with it, I do not recollect seeing them there," said Robert Weston, who with a boy's curiosity had watched the scene from afar. "I do not think any of the good citizens had anything to do with it, but at

---

[9]The office of *The Evening and the Morning Star* stood a little back of the present location of the present Chrisman-Sawyer Bank, on the corner of Liberty Street, south of Lexington.
[10]Hiram Rathbun, Sr., testimony in the Temple Lot Suit, Plaintiff's Abstract of Evidence, page 221.
[11]Later driftwood harvesters raised the press and sold it to one William Ridenbaugh, who used it to publish the Saint Joseph *Gazette* in 1845. He sold the press to Captain John L. Merrick in 1859, who took it to Denver and started the first paper published in Colorado. "History of the County Press," by Minnie Organ, *Missouri Historical Review,* Volume 4, page 125.

that time we had lots of bad citizens. The fellow that was putting tar on him (Partridge) was Jonathan Shepard and he was not a good citizen by any means, at least I would not consider him so. This man Jonathan Shepard was a good-for-nothing, no-account fellow who never did anything good for himself or anybody else. There was another old fellow there named Bill Connor who was of no earthly account. He was living down here at the time. He was a regular ruffian, and was never happy unless he was in trouble or getting other people in it. He took a very active part in this tar and feather business, and then he wanted to cowhide Bishop Partridge, but they stopped him, and would not let him do it."[12]

Major Doniphan also implies that the trouble was caused by the "more ignorant portions of the community."[13]

But not all authorities are inclined to blame the riffraff of the town for the trouble. One writer who calls himself an agnostic, writes in a sarcastic vein: "The lieutenant-governor of the State, Lilburn W. Boggs, who witnessed this rare exhibition, exclaimed in a paroxysm of religious fervor and patriotic satisfaction, 'Mormons are the common enemies of mankind and ought to be destroyed,' and 'you now know what our Jackson boys can do, and you must leave the country.'" He definitely names George Simpson as the leader of the mob. This same writer gives Boggs, whether rightfully or not, the credit for a plan frequently followed in the next few years, that is to gain possession of the arms of the Saints and then attack them. Warren Watson, the writer mentioned above, says:

> At this crisis Lieutenant Governor Boggs came once more to the front. In great emergencies there is always a demand for intellect and character to dominate and control mere brute force; and the man generally comes forward with the emergency. Boggs had the intellect to conceive a plan charming in simplicity and effectiveness, and he also had the character to put it in operation. The plan was to secure the confidence of the Saints and by pretending to be their friends get

---

[12] Testimony of Robert Weston in the Temple Lot Suit, page 248.
[13] Kansas City *Journal* June 5, 1881; *Saints' Herald* Volume 28, page 198.

possession of their arms. When this comical, and yet laudable, piece of rascality was accomplished . . . once more the "Jackson boys" undeterred by fears of reprisals rushed the attack.[14]

On July 23, 1833, a treaty was signed, under pressure, in which the Latter Day Saints agreed to leave the county, half of them before January 1, 1834, the other half by the first of April. But the Saints had not entirely given up. Edward Partridge, by nature a mild and law-abiding man, who with ten high priests had been appointed to take care of the branches, could not abandon the idea that there was help by process of law in a country that guaranteed freedom of worship to its citizens. Orson Hyde and John Gould had arrived in October to give them messages and aid from Saints in Kirtland. Hyde and W. W. Phelps determined to lay the case personally before the Governor, who, when they saw him, wrote a letter to prominent citizens, attempting to enforce the law.

Encouraged by the Governor's efforts, the people proceeded to plant their winter wheat, making but few preparations for departure. Then the depredations of the mob broke out fresh. Thursday night, October 31, 1833, thirty brawlers went over to the Whitmer settlement near the Blue River, "unroofed and demolished ten houses, and also whipped and pounded several persons in a shocking manner."[15]

Proceeding under the directions of the Governor, some of the Saints went to Independence and presented a letter from him which said:

> After advising with the Attorney-General, and exercising my best judgment, I would advise you to make a trial of the efficacy of the laws. The judge of your circuit is a conservator of the peace. If an affidavit is made before him by any of you that your lives are in danger, it would be his duty to have offenders apprehended and bind them to keep the peace. Justices of the Peace in their respective counties have the same authority, and it is made their duty to exercise it.

---
[14] Warren Watson in *Kansas City Globe Souvenir*, reprinted in the *Saints' Herald*, Volume 37, page 205.
[15] John Corrill, in *The Messenger and Advocate*.

Take then this course, obtain a warrant, let it be placed in the hands of a proper officer, and the experiment will be tested whether the laws can be peaceably executed or not.

In the face of this, they were denied a warrant, and as night was coming on and they had reason to fear the renewal of hostilities with the coming of darkness, word was sent out to each branch to collect and defend themselves, being careful not to be aggressors. The Colesville Saints especially felt it necessary to defend the gristmill, which had been threatened. Pickets were put out to watch it. As darkness deepened two men were seen prowling in the vicinity; they were promptly captured, disarmed, kept all night, but allowed to go home in the morning.

November 2, Saturday night, a number of the young bloods of the neighborhood collected at Wilson's store near the Blue, had a few drinks and went over to a settlement on the Blue and taking the roof off a house, found David Bennett ill in bed. They beat him cruelly, and finally one of the men drew a pistol and shooting high, as he thought, and swearing, said he was going to blow Bennett's brains out. The bullet tore through the top of the sick man's head, cutting a deep gash. Heretofore no opposition had been offered by the Latter Day Saints. But now amid the confusion, women and children running here and there, screaming in terror, someone found a gun, and a moment later one of the mob shouted that he had been shot through the thigh. The effect was immediate. The mob dispersed.

"But the Mormons had shot a man." Far and near the news spread. The Latter Day Saints spent Sunday in council, sent Parley P. Pratt and Joshua Lewis to the circuit judge, John F. Ryland, at Lexington, and waited the outbreak of renewed hostilities. They had not long to wait. On Monday night the 4th of November, the same crowd collected at Wilson's store, went down to the ferry and took the boat (which belonged to the Saints) and otherwise amused themselves. In the meantime a group of brethren assembled at Colesville, hearing that the brethren east of the Blue had been molested, sent nineteen unarmed volunteers to assist them. Two small boys, seeing the men on the road, hastened to the store and told the men assembled there the "Mormons" were on the road. They immediately started in pursuit of them, for the men finding comparative quiet had turned to go back to Colesville. They overtook them near the home of Christian Whitmer, a crippled brother, and dispersed them through the fields and woods. They rode into the cornfield, trampling down the grain, feeding their horses, taunting and tormenting Christian Whitmer, and threatening him, beating any fugitives they happened to find, and shooting recklessly. It may be conceded that up until now most of these depredations were carried on in the spirit of malicious mischief, for if the Missourians had desired to murder the Latter Day Saints, they had ample opportunity to do so. They wished to drive them from the country, but it is doubtful if the majority of them desired battle or bloodshed.

The Colesville Saints about three miles distant could hear the shooting and having reached the point where patience seemed to them to have ceased to be a virtue, they quickly found what firearms they could and marched to the aid of their brethren at the Whitmer settlement. They were fired upon as they approached the cornfield of Christian Whitmer and several shots were exchanged before the mob retreated not waiting to mount their horses and leaving their dead in the field. Two men had been killed, Thomas Linville and Hugh L. Brazaele. Andrew Barber of the Saints was fatally wounded and died the next day. Philo Dibble was critically wounded but survived, though a lifetime cripple.

Of course the news of an "uprising among the Mormons" was heralded far and near, and the number of those killed increased with every telling. As a result, the "militia" got busy and demanded the arms of the Saints. And since it was almost impossible to tell when a group of men were acting officially or unofficially, the Saints complied. When the emissaries to Lexington returned, they found most of the Saints gathered together on the Temple Lot with what few possessions they were able to seize as they fled.

The Saints were camped three days on the Temple Lot, while armed men rode through the settlements rounding up and driving to this spot the few left in their homes. They were then forcibly compelled to agree to leave the county. Through the snow and sleet of November, the pitiful band of exiled Saints made its way to the Wayne City Landing on the Missouri River.

Thursday, November 7th, the shore began to be lined on both sides of the ferry, with men, women, and children, goods, wagons, boxes, chests, provisions, etc., while the ferrymen were very busily employed in crossing them over; and when night again closed upon us the wilderness had the appearance of a camp meeting. Hundreds of people were seen in all directions. Some in tents, some in the open air around their fires while the rain descended in torrents. Husbands were inquiring for wives, and women for their parents, parents for children, and children for parents. Some had the good fortune to escape with their family, household goods, and some provisions; while others knew not the fate of their friends, and had lost all their goods. The scene was indescribable, and I am sure would have melted the hearts of any people upon earth. . . . Next day, our company still increased, and we were chiefly engaged in felling small cottonwood trees, and erecting them into temporary cabins, so when night came on we had the appearance of a village of wigwams, and the night being clear we began to enjoy some degree of comfort.[16]

About two o'clock the next morning, we were aroused from our slumbers by the cry of, "Arise and behold the signs in the heavens." We arose and to our great astonishment all the heavens seemed enwrapped in splendid fireworks as if every star in its broad expanse had been suddenly hurled from its course and sent lawless through the wilds of ether. I can give the reader no better idea of this scene than by allusion to the shooting of a bright meteor with a long train of light following in its course such as many of us have seen in a bright starlit night. Now suppose that thousands of such meteors with their fiery trains were to run lawless through the heavens for hours together, this would be a scene such as our eyes beheld on that memorable morning; and the scene only closed by giving place to the superior light and splendor of the king of day. No sooner was this scene beheld

---

[16] *Autobiography of Parley Parker Pratt.*

THE STORM BREAKS

by some of our camp than the news reached every tent and aroused everyone from their slumbers; every eye was lifted towards the heavens, and every heart was filled with joy at these majestic signs and wonders showing the near approach of the Son of God.[17]

This phenomenon appeared over most of the United States on that night, and before the dawn of the scientific period at an age of religious excitement when the whole world sought a sign, everyone gave it some significance, purely personal. Down in Virginia that night, in a mansion of dilapidated splendor, the wife of a strolling actor gave birth to a son, and the midwife told her that he was born with a cowl, and that the heavens had acclaimed his birth with great signs and wonders, showing he was to be a great man. That baby boy became Edwin Booth, America's greatest actor. In other places religious fanatics and some who were not so fanatical prepared for the coming of the Lord. To the enemies of the Saints, the signs brought fear and wonder; to the Saints they were a signal of approval. An old settler says:

> There was a very remarkable and strange occurrence took place the night after most of them had crossed the river. . . . They camped in the bottom, and built their campfires for perhaps a mile up and down the river, and out into the bottom. It was very cold, but there was plenty of wood. They had large fires, and the whole bottom in the vicinity of their camp presented quite a brilliant appearance, and to add to the brilliancy, awhile before the day the stars (at least it looked like stars) commenced falling like great snowflakes[18] all vanishing before they reached the ground, and it continued from half to three quarters of an hour.[19]

Babies were born that night in the camp in the cottonwoods, and during the weeks that followed;[20] some passed to their reward.

---
[17] *Ibid.*
[18] The author well remembers as a child asking her grandmother, who was in the camp of the Saints that night, "Tell us about the night the stars fell." Her grandmother, Anna Christina Wight, was then about eight years of age, and clearly remembered that even the children were roused and dressed.
[19] Thorpe's *Early Days in Missouri*, Letter No. 15.
[20] A great-grandmother of the author had a son born to her one stormy night among the cottonwoods on the Missouri bottoms. Her bed was made beside a sycamore log, and the only shelter she had from the storm was pieces of rag carpet held up as protection by some of the sisters. Harriet (Benton) Wight was the grandmother of Heman C. and Hyrum O. Smith. Many of her descendants are in the church today. The child born that night grew to manhood and became the father of David Wight, a promising young elder of the Reorganization, and of Estella Wight, who has written much for the youth of the church.

The people of Clay County opened their homes and received the fugitives, notwithstanding the fact that they bade fair to outnumber the original inhabitants of the county.

The fate of the straggling ones who had not known of the camp on the Temple Lot, or somehow got separated from the main body was just as hard. A settlement of from eighty to one hundred and thirty Saints on the Blue, six miles west of Independence, was visited by seventy-five or one hundred mounted men and ordered to leave their homes within two hours under penalty of death. Only a few days previous they had surrendered their arms on condition that they were to be free from molestation. Hastily the small possessions, mostly blankets and bedding that could be carried in four wagons, were loaded; and the whole company started on foot, traveling about six miles in a southerly direction before night overtook them. Destination they had none. They were homeless wanderers. They made their camp as best they could, ate a bit of supper together, and Solomon Hancock, president of the little branch, called them all to prayer as one family. Humbly he stood among the little flock, asking that if it was the Lord's will that this trial come upon them, that they might have strength to bear it.

The next day, they continued southward over a burned off prairie. Most of the children were barefoot, and the hard, sharp stubs of the burnt off bunch grass cut their feet, until by night there was not a child's foot that was not torn and bleeding. They thought they traveled about fifteen miles that day; the third day they made similar progress. They had not seen a soul since leaving their homes, nor a sign of habitation, for the prairie land was not considered habitable in those early times. Toward night of the third day rain began falling, turning to snow and sleet, and they saw not far away a one-room hut. The single man who lived there kindly vacated the one room, and the women and children packed into it as best they could, huddled together, sitting on one another's laps, in order to make room for all. The men leaned up against the house and wagons all night with the rain "streaming down their backs."

After breakfast all took up their walk again. The sleet and rain had stopped, but it was cloudy, cold, and threatening. "The whole land seemed flooded with water," and the little caravan struggled across a marsh through which they had to wade ice cold water from ankle to waist deep. Nearly every person carried a child, and some women carried two, the whole mile and a half with no opportunity to set them down and rest. Little progress was made that day, but they found a dry point of rocks under a bluff where they made camp for the night.

The next morning they awoke to a winter world. The earth was covered with two inches of snow. After breakfast, all assembled for their prayer, as usual, only this occasion was a little different. This was the prayer of desperate men and women turning for their lives and that of their little ones to the only help that was left them. The last morsel of food had been eaten for breakfast; nothing remained. "Brethren," said Solomon Hancock, "the time has now come when we must ask God for our daily bread; for except he provides, our bones must be left here to bleach on these rocks."

"Amen," said many, "unless the Lord provides, so be it."

Then they knelt in prayer. Nearly all the grown people took part in turn. Then they waited. An hour passed. Someone saw on the western horizon a man on horseback riding toward them. He came straight to them, saluted them and said, "Friends, I have heard of your sufferings and have come to assist you. If you can get over to my place, which is five miles to the west, I think you will be able to obtain needful food. I have some potatoes that need to be dug, and if you will give me one half, the rest shall be yours for the digging. I also have a large stall-fed ox which may be yours if you will split me some fence rails; and if you have any money I will see that you get corn meal at a mill not far distant."

What an answer to prayer! Immediately a collection was taken up, the Saints dropping in the hat every penny, even keepsakes. Only a little over five dollars was raised, but with the precious money one wagon was sent to the mill, and the rest started through the snow to the home of their benefactor. The little barefoot children ran through the cold snow as long as they could stand it, then bending a tall bunch of grass to the north, stood on it in the sun until they felt the blood course through their feet again. Then they took another run. Thus the distance was covered, and all went immediately to work.

The women prepared the camp; the old men were delegated to dress the beef, while the young men dug potatoes. At eight o'clock that night all sat down to a real meal. They were almost happy. During the day, some of the neighbors called at Mr. Butterfield's, and brought provisions and clothing.[21] Some of those in better circumstances took families to work for them and sheltered them through the winter. One of them whose name is given as James, sheltered several families at his home, helped them find work, and befriended them in every way he could. He was a Missourian, with a heart of gold beneath his rough exterior, and he often exclaimed with an oath that every time he thought of the treatment his protégés had received in Jackson County his "jackknife opened in his pocket."

The great experiment had crumbled, but it had not failed. The men and women who camped in the bitter November sleet in the cottonwoods of the Missouri River still carried in their hearts their dream of a perfected state of society where there would be no oppression. The spires of Zion rose in their visions, sleeping or walking, while they wandered here and there, driven and despised. But did they name it failure? Perhaps some did. But not the vast majority. The rabid hostility of Missouri and Illinois

---

[21] "Elder John Brush" in *Autumn Leaves*, Volume 4, pages 23, 24.

only succeeded in pressing into the Latter Day Saint fiber strength and tenacity of purpose that could not know failure.

The legacy a man passes on to his sons in land and cattle may vanish, but the legacy of dreams lives on through hundreds of discouragements, through disaster and oppression, and so today the hills of Jackson County, Missouri, are loved by those who never saw them, and the ideals of which they are but the visible sign are handed down from generation to generation, with the thought that sometime there will arise the chosen ones who will redeem Zion, and realize the dream of their fathers, for a state of society where there will be not only spiritual, but economic and industrial freedom. They loved it, the land where they had met the bitterest discouragement of their lives.

Only once after that did Joseph Smith see the land of Zion, and then he crossed the river in secret and in the darkness of night that his feet might stand once more "upon the goodly land."

XIX.—Missions to Canada and the East

*I*N THE MEANTIME, THOUGH tragedy dogged the footsteps of the church in the West, the newly appointed Stake of Kirtland was sending out missionaries who were meeting with splendid success all through the East.

David W. Patten left Kirtland to go back to New York. He converted his family, or some of them, including his mother, his two brothers, Archibald and Ira, his sister Polly, and two brothers-in-law, Warren Parrish and a Mr. Cheeseman, all of whom still lived around his old home at Indian River Falls. Their baptisms by Brigham Young took place on the 20th of May, 1833.

Before he reached home he had stopped to hold meetings with Reynolds Cahoon near a place called Orleans. They were invited one night to preach in a home where there was a sick girl, who had been ill all winter. No hope was held out for her recovery, and she grew weaker and thinner day by day. The girl's name was Lois Cutler, and her father was the Alpheus Cutler who later became so well known in the church. The preaching was of course held in the room where the sick girl lay that she might also hear. The minister spoke of the restoration of the gospel and of the book that was to come forth, and as he told them of the stick of Judah and of Joseph, and held aloft the Bible in one hand and the Book of Mormon in the other, he clapped the two books together and said, "And they shall be one in the Lord's hands."

Then to the surprise of all present, and especially to her own amazement, Lois clapped her pale, thin hands together and said, "And I believe it." At the close of the meeting most of the congregation went home, but the young folks gathered in the old-fashioned kitchen. Their merry voices and laughter came indistinctly to Lois's ears as she lay in bed and listened to the conversation of the elders. At length she asked for administration that she might be healed.

Immediately the prayer ended, the girl wished to get out of bed. Her mother objected that her feet were not dressed. "Dress her feet," said Elder Patten quietly. "Let her get up." She walked about the room as if she had never been sick. And then of course she felt she must join her young companions in the kitchen, but her mother was all solicitude. She could not let her leave the warm room from which she had not stirred for months, but again Elder Patten urged, "Let her go, it will do her no harm!" Mrs. Cutler put a shawl around her shoulders and she went through the cold hall and opened the door of the kitchen. The laughter and talking ceased while all turned to stare. Lois told them she had been healed by the power of God. Naturally, the news spread far and wide, and not only the Cutlers, but many others joined the church in that vicinity, and Patten left a branch of eighteen as he went on his way. Lois herself, her father and mother, and her aged grandmother were among the number. At the baptism, the girl was surprised to hear the officiating minister say, "The Spirit tells me that Lois is the first to be baptized, and if any of you wish to know the reason why, it is because she was the first to believe."

Happily the future is hidden from our view. Little did Lois know on that joyful day that before many years, she and her young husband would be prisoners in the camp of a drunken mob, and that shrinking in terror she would be compelled to listen to their mad carousing, as they hilariously rejoiced over the death of David Patten,[1] the man whose hands she could almost feel in memory again upon her head, as he rebuked the powers of death for her sake. She escaped the mob, and lived for many years, and

---

[1] *Autumn Leaves,* Volume 8, page 315. Lois Cutler married Almon Sherman and was with the colony that founded Clitheral, Minnesota. She united with the Reorganized Church later.

today, her children, grandchildren, and great-grandchildren are numbered with the church.

On this same mission David W. Patten baptized James H. Blakeslee,[2] an eminent preacher and proselytizer of those early days, who in his turn brought many to the church. His wife, Louisiana Edmunds was a sister of Judge Edmunds. James H. Blakeslee was born in Milton, Chittenden County, Vermont, July 18, 1802; was baptized at Ellisburgh, Jefferson County, New York, July 19, 1833. The day following, Patten ordained him to be a priest and the next spring he was ordained an elder by Thomas Dutcher. Of his ability as a preacher the third Joseph Smith says, "Elder Blakeslee has few equals and fewer superiors, for the steadiness of purpose with which he preached and the integrity of his testimony has never been surpassed." The Blakeslees moved to Perth, Canada, in 1835, then to St. Lawrence County, New York, next to Waterville, Oneida County, New York, finally to Utica and did not unite with the main body of the church until they moved to Nauvoo in 1843. In his home at the time of his baptism was a seven-year-old lad who was destined to be Bishop of the Reorganized Church: George A. Blakeslee[3] who was born August 22, 1826, and shared all the wanderings of the family for the sake of the gospel. Grandchildren, great-grandchildren,[4] great-great-grandchildren of James Blakeslee carry on his name and work in the church today.

In September, 1833, the church authorities met in council and determined to purchase another printing press. It was:

> Resolved, that the above firm publish a paper as soon as arrangements can be made, entitled the *Latter Day Saints' Messenger and Advocate.*
>
> Resolved, also that the *Star,* formerly published in Jackson County, Missouri, by the firm of W. W. Phelps and Company, be printed in this place by the firm of F. G. Williams and Company; and be

---

[2]*Church History,* Volume 3, page 756.
[3]*Church History,* Volume 4, page 723.
[4]Two great-grandsons are Blakeslee Smith and Vere Blair, both elders.

MISSIONS TO CANADA AND THE EAST

conducted by Oliver Cowdery, one of the members of the firm, until it is transferred to its former location.[5]

In the month of September, one Freeman Nickerson who had a large and prosperous farm consisting of two hundred acres on Conewango Creek, in the town of Dayton, Cattaraugus County, New York, took a journey to Kirtland with his wife. Elders had preached in his home at various times, and at length he and his wife were baptized. They had two sons working in Canada. They were good boys, and came home very frequently and divided all their earnings with their parents, and although they had tried to explain the gospel to these sons, they had not been very successful. Their purpose in coming to Kirtland was to take the Prophet to Canada to convert their sons! And that is exactly what they did.

On the 5th of October,[6] the Nickersons with Sidney Rigdon and Joseph Smith started for Canada, arriving at Mount Pleasant near Brantford, Ontario, on October 18. Sunday morning, the 20th, meetings were held at Mount Pleasant and also at Brantford; on the 22nd day they held a meeting by candlelight at Colburn, "though it snowed severely." This was at the home of a Mr. Beman (later a Latter Day Saint). On the 25th they left for Waterford, but had only a small meeting. From thence they went to Mount Pleasant and preached again on the 26th. Found the people "very tender and inquiring." Young Freeman Nickerson and his wife gave their names for baptism. Sunday the 27th had another meeting, and baptized twelve, including both of the sons of Freeman Nickerson. The next day they had confirmation, and Communion (Communion in early days was always served at confirmation services) and baptized two. On the morning of the 29th, two more were baptized and confirmed at the water's edge, and in the evening they ordained young Freeman Nickerson an

---

[5] *Church History*, Volume 1, page 372.
[6] Several of these dates are given incorrectly in *Times and Seasons*, Volume 6, pages 866 and 881; also in *Church History*, Volume I, pages 377, 378. Starting with "Monday, 14th" (Oct. 1833) and ending with "Monday, 4th" (Nov.) which are correct for the calendar of 1833, we have reconciled the above dates to coincide with the days of the week mentioned.—Ed.

elder and returned to Kirtland the 4th of November, not an unusual month's work for an old-time missionary pair.

After the return from Canada (December 1), the new press arrived, under the charge of Oliver Cowdery and Bishop Whitney. If the Saints of old had faults, wasting time was not one of them. By the 4th the press was set up and the printers were hard at work setting type for another edition of *The Evening and the Morning Star.*

Joseph Smith rather naively recorded in his journal: "Being prepared to commence our labors in the printing business, I asked God, in the name of Jesus, to establish it forever, and cause that his word may speedily go forth to the nations of the earth to the accomplishment of his great work, in bringing about the restoration of the house of Israel."[7] On December 18, the new press was dedicated in an appropriate manner, and the printers took the proof sheets of the first number of *The Evening and the Morning Star* to be issued from Kirtland, number 15, volume 2.

About this time a man who had been baptized into the church, and cut off for immoral conduct, began to cause trouble. He was an associate of E. D. Howe in collecting material for his exposé of "Mormonism," the first such work published, and the one upon which most others have been based. This man was named Doctor Hurlbut, not that he had any connection with the medical profession, but merely because he was a seventh son his mother conceived the highly original plan of naming him "Doctor," hoping the name might be an omen of coming glory. It wasn't. Doctor was an adventurer, and no name could change him. However, he succeeded in becoming a thorn in the flesh of the Saints for several years.

The troubled ones in Zion were not forgotten, for Elders David Patten and William Pratt were sent as messengers with money, clothing, and provisions. They left the 16th of December, and

---

[7] *Times and Seasons*, Volume 6, page 915; *Church History*, Volume 1, page 379.

were until early March making their way to Liberty, in Clay County.

About this time (December 18, 1833)[8] Joseph Smith, Sr., father of the Prophet, was set apart as patriarch, or father to the whole church. Slightly over two years later, January 21, 1836, in Kirtland Temple, the First Presidency ordained Joseph, Sr., to be patriarch of the church,[9] and in accordance with this ordination and during the same service, they received their patriarchal blessings under his hands. A careful reading of the records indicates that these blessings are such as would be given by a spiritual father to his children—and not infrequently, as in the case of Joseph Smith and John Johnson, the patriarchal blessing was given by a father to his own sons. The work of the patriarchal ministry was not confined to the conferring of blessings. Joseph Smith, Sr., was a spiritual adviser who "fathered" the people, counseling them out of his store of spiritual wisdom.

There were a number of councils held, at one of which the President of the church asked for volunteers to go to Canada, as there had been a number of letters from Nickerson, pleading for help. Six men volunteered and were sent two by two, Lyman Johnson and Milton Holmes, Zebedee Coltrin and Henry Harriman, and Jared Carter and Phineas Young. One of the letters from young Moses Nickerson was printed in the newly established *The Evening and the Morning Star* for February. It was written December 20, less than two months after the baptisms in Canada. "Your labors in Canada," he said in a letter addressed to "Brother Sidney," "have been the beginning of a good work;

---

[8] *Millennial Star*, Volume 18, page 134.
[9] Some confusion is caused by these two "settings apart" of Joseph Smith, Sr., as patriarch. In the private historical collection which belonged to Heman C. Smith is the blessing of his grandfather, Lyman Wight, (original), which shows that Joseph Senior gave patriarchal blessings prior to January 21, 1836. The first paragraph of this blessing reads: "Patriarchal blessing given in Kirtland, Ohio, December 29, 1835, by Joseph Smith, Senior, to Lyman Wight, son of Levi Wight and Sally Corbin, and who was born in the town of Fairfield, Herkimer County, State of New York, May 9, 1796. 'Brother Wight, in the name of the Lord Jesus Christ, I lay my hand upon thee and *seal upon thee the blessings of a father, for thy father is dead and has not the power of priesthood.*'" The significance of this clause is to be conjectured.

there are thirty-four members attached to the church at Mount Pleasant, all of whom appear to live up to their profession, five of whom have spoken in tongues and three sang in tongues: and we live at the top of the mountain!"[10]

Moses was not altogether easily pleased; he said: "If you can send us a couple of preachers out here, as soon as you receive this, you would do us a kindness. . . . . Send those you have confidence in or *none;* the work requires competent workmen."

At the same conference a number of the missionaries were sent east to meet in conference in Saco, Maine, on June 13, 1834. As they were leaving soon after the 20th of February, they would have several months free for preaching and baptizing. Young John F. Boynton was in Saco, Maine, at that time, and in a short note to the brethren in Kirtland, reported that he and an Elder E. M. Greene had baptized one hundred and thirty the previous summer.

On February 22, Lyman Wight and Parley P. Pratt arrived from Liberty, Missouri, the first of the refugees from Independence. They spoke the next day at the Methodist Church of their experiences. Both were good speakers, and a feeling of sorrow and sympathy pervaded the whole village.

---

[10]*The Evening and the Morning Star,* Kirtland, February, 1834.

XX.—Governor Dunklin Takes a Hand

*I*MMEDIATELY UPON THEIR arrival in Clay County, the Saints retained as attorneys the firm of Wood, Reese, Doniphan and Atchison of Liberty, the best legal talent in western Missouri.

Doniphan, later famed as Missouri's greatest soldier, was a Kentuckian by birth, a Whig. He had been well educated with one of the best lawyers in Kentucky. At the time the Saints sought his aid, he was just past twenty-six years of age, tall (six foot four), with large massive head and high forehead, sandy hair and hazel eyes, always smiling. Already he had begun his marvelous dual career as statesman and soldier. He early made it a rule never to prosecute, always to defend. His speeches were not previously prepared; he spoke so simply a child could understand him. Never talking long, he often took only fifteen minutes to close a case. He was always bashful, and looked bashful when he began to speak, but he did not go far with his defense, before men, women, judge, and jury were in tears. His voice it is said could charm birds and squirrels in the woods.

David R. Atchison, his partner, also a tall man (six foot two) was his senior by just one year. He, too, was from Kentucky, a graduate of Transylvania University, a true type of the storied Southern gentleman, cultured, wealthy, educated, a fine conversationalist, gentle, sincere, honest, and frank. He was a Calhoun Democrat, an uncompromising proslavery leader, who never forsook his principles. A born aristocrat, he was democratic by nature, simple and plain in his tastes.

Amos Reese was a man of quick, high temper, but a good lawyer. He wrote many of the papers for the Latter Day Saints while they were endeavoring to get justice in the courts.

Going for advice to Kentuckians, the Saints got it with a true Kentucky flavor. Doniphan favored asking the governor to arm the Saints, make of them a troop of Jackson Guards and return them to their homes with ample power to defend themselves. "Then," declared Doniphan, "if the Mormons don't fight, they're cowards."

He went to Saline County and saw the Attorney General, R. W. Wells, upon the subject, who wrote A. S. Gilbert as follows:

City of Jefferson, November 21, 1833.

Gentlemen:

From conversation I have had with the Governor, I believe I am warranted in saying to you, and through you to the Mormons, that if they desire to be replaced in their property, that is, their houses in Jackson County, an adequate force will be sent forthwith to effect that object. Perhaps a direct application had better be made to him for that purpose, if they wish thus to be repossessed. The militia have been ordered to hold themselves in readiness.

If the Mormons will organize themselves into regular companies, or a regular company of militia, either volunteers or otherwise, they will, I have no doubt, be supplied with public arms. This must be upon application, therefore as a volunteer company must be accepted by the Colonel, and that is a matter in his discretion. Perhaps the best way would be to organize and elect officers as is done in ordinary cases—not volunteers; you could give them necessary directions on these points. If the Colonel should refuse to order an election of company officers, after they have reported themselves to him for that purpose, he would, I presume, be court martialed therefore, on a representation to the Governor of the facts. As only a certain quantity of public arms can be distributed in each county, those who first apply will be most likely to receive them. The less, therefore, that is said upon the subject, the better.

I am with great respect your obedient servant.

(Signed) R. W. Wells.[1]

Three days later, Judge Ryland of Lexington wrote to the Saints, saying he had received a letter from the Governor asking to be informed about the "outrageous acts of unparalleled violence" in Jackson County, and that he was to examine into the outrages. He was holding himself in readiness to go to Jackson County and hold

---

[1] *Times and Seasons*, Volume 6, pages 912, 913; *Church History*, Volume 1, pages 363, 364.

a court of inquiry, etc. "It is a disgrace to the State for such acts to happen within its limits, and the disgrace will attach to our official characters if we neglect to take proper means to insure the punishment due such offenders," he said. A. S. Gilbert replied that he could not get his witnesses together immediately, but would do so as soon as possible, if they could be protected by an adequate guard. Reese concurred that their lives would be in danger if they went back into the county without a guard of militia.

In a previous petition on December 6, Gilbert had asked that the Saints be organized into a company of Jackson County Guards. He now adds an explanation in a long communication under the date of January 8, 1834:

> There is one item in particular in said petition that needs some explanation; the request that "our men may be organized into companies of Jackson Guards, and furnished with arms by the State," was made at the instance of disinterested advisers, and also a communication from the Attorney General to Messrs. Doniphan and Atchison, dated the 21st of November last, giving his views as to the propriety of organizing into regular companies, etc. The necessity of being compelled to resort to arms, to regain our possessions in Jackson County, is by no means agreeable to the feelings of the church, and would never be thought of but from pure necessity.[2]

He suggests that the Saints would much prefer that appraisers be appointed and the land of those who did not wish to be in the same county with the church to be appraised, and they would be glad to purchase at any fair price.

On the 4th of February the Governor answered with another lengthy communication, in which he said, among other things:

> I am very sensible indeed of the injuries your people complain of, and should consider myself very remiss in the discharge of my duties were I not to do everything in my power consistent with the legal exercise of them to afford your society the redress to which they seem entitled. One of your requests needs no evidence to support the right to have it granted; it is that your people be put in possession of their homes from which they have been expelled. But what may be the duty of the Executive after that, will depend upon contingencies.

---
[2] *Times and Seasons,* Volume 6, pages 962, 963. See *Church History,* Volume 1, pages 402, 403.

If upon inquiry it is found that your people were wrongfully dispossessed of their arms, by Colonel Pitcher, then an order will be issued to have them returned; and should your men organize according to law, which they have a right to do (indeed it is their duty to do so, unless exempted by religious scruples), and apply for public arms, the Executive could not distinguish between their right to have them, and the right of every other description of people similarly situated.[3]

He also appointed the Liberty Blues to guard them to Jackson County, that they might appear as witnesses in the investigation there.

On February 24, court convened in Independence, and some of the men of the church were present under guard as witnesses in the case of "The State of Missouri verses Colonel Thomas Pitcher." A mob collected and no effort was made to hold court.

In a letter to his brethren, W. W. Phelps describes the scene which would be laughable were it not so serious:

Clay County, February 27, 1834.

Dear Brethren:
The times are so big with events, and the anxiety of everybody so great to watch them, that I feel somewhat impressed to write oftener than I have done, in order to give you more of the "strange acts" of this region. I have just returned from Independence, the seat of war in the West. About a dozen of our brethren, among whom were Brethren Partridge, Corrill, and myself, were subpœnæd in behalf of the State, and on the 23d (February) about twelve o'clock, we were on the bank, opposite Everit's Ferry, where we found Captain Atchison's company of "Liberty Blues," near fifty rank and file, ready to guard us into Jackson County. The soldiers were well armed with United States muskets, bayonets fixed, etc., and to me the scene was one "passing strange," and long to be remembered. The martial law in force to guard the civil! About twenty-five men crossed over to effect a landing in safety, and when they came near the warehouse, they fired six or eight guns, though the enemy had not gathered to witness the landing.

After we were all across, and waiting for the baggage wagon, it was thought not advisable to encamp in the woods, and the witnesses with half the company, marched nearly a mile towards Independence, to build night fires, as we were without tents, and the weather cold

---

[3] *Times and Seasons*, Volume 6, pages 977, 978. See *Church History*, Volume 1, page 405.

enough to snow a little. While on the way the Quartermaster, and others, that had gone on ahead to prepare quarters in town, sent an express back, which was not the most pacific appearance that could be. Captain Atchison continued the express to Colonel Allen for the two hundred drafted militia; and also to Liberty for more ammunition; and the night passed off in warlike style, with the sentinels marching silently at a proper distance from the watchfires.

Early in the morning we marched, strongly guarded by the troops, to the seat of war, and quartered in the blockhouse, formerly the tavern stand of S. Flournoy. After breakfast, we were visited by the District Attorney, Mr. Reese, and the Attorney General, Mr. Wells. From them we learned that all hopes of criminal prosecution were at an end. Mr. Wells had been sent by the Governor to investigate, as far as possible, the Jackson outrage, but the bold front of the mob, bound even unto death (as I have heard), was not to be penetrated by civil law, or awed by executive influence. Shortly after, Captain Atchison informed me that he had just received an order from the Judge, that his company's service was no longer wanted in Jackson County, and we were marched out of town to the tune of "Yankee Doodle" in quick time, and soon returned to our camp ground without the loss of any lives. In fact, much credit is due to Captain Atchison for his gallantry and hospitality, and I think I can say of the officers and company that their conduct as soldiers and men is highly reputable; so much so, knowing as I do, the fatal result, had the militia come, or not come, I can add that the captain's safe return refreshed my mind with Xenophon's retreat of the ten thousand. Thus ends all hopes of "redress," even with a guard ordered by the Governor, for the protection of the court and witnesses.[4]

The Saints then began a series of appeals to the President of the United States, that were to continue for many years. Governor Dunklin in his next letter the 20th of April, said he was in communication with the Government at Washington, and urged patience.

He says, "Permit me to suggest to you that as you now have greatly the advantage of your adversaries in public estimation, that there is a great propriety in retaining that advantage, which you can easily do by keeping your adversaries in the wrong. The laws, both civil and military, seem deficient in affording your society proper protection; nevertheless public sentiment is a power-

---

[4] *Church History*, Volume 1, pages 407-409. *The Evening and the Morning Star*, pages 276, 277 (Kirtland reprint).

ful corrector of error, and you should make it your policy to continue to deserve it."[5]

On April 21, the elders in Liberty addressed the governor as follows, explaining the plan which had been originated to send help to the distressed brethren in Missouri:

> Liberty, Clay County, Missouri, April 24, 1834.
> Dear Sir: In our last communication of the 10th inst., we omitted to make inquiry concerning the evidence brought up before the court of inquiry in the case of Colonel Pitcher. The court met pursuant to adjournment on the 20th of February last, and, for reasons unknown to us, we have not been able to obtain information concerning the opinion or decision of that court. We had hoped that the testimony would have been transmitted to your Excellency before this, that an order might be issued for the return of our arms, of which we have been wrongfully dispossessed, as we believe will clearly appear to the commander in chief when the evidence is laid before him.
> As suggested in your communication of the 4th of February, we have concluded to organize according to law and apply for public arms, but we feared that such a step, which must be attended with public ceremonies, might produce some excitement, and we have thus far delayed any movement of that nature, hoping to regain our arms from Jackson that we might independently equip ourselves and be prepared to assist in the maintenance of our constitutional rights and liberties as guaranteed to us by our country, and also to defend our persons and property from a lawless mob when it shall please the Executive, at some future day, to put us in possession of our homes, from which we have been most wickedly expelled. We are happy to make an expression of our thanks for the willingness manifested by the Executive to enforce the laws, as he can consistently "with the means furnished him by the legislature," and we are firmly persuaded that a future day will verify to him whatever aid we may receive from the Executive has not been lavished upon a band of traitors, but upon a people whose respect and veneration for the laws of our country, and its pure republican principles, are as great as that of any other society in the United States.
> As our Jackson foes and their correspondents are busy in circulating slanderous and wicked reports concerning our people, their views, etc., we have deemed it expedient to inform your Excellency that we have received communications from our friends in the East, informing us that a number of our brethren, perhaps two or three hundred, would remove to Jackson County in the course of the ensuing summer, and we are satisfied that when the Jackson mob get the intel-

---
[5] *Times and Seasons*, Volume 6, page 1059; *Church History*, Volume 1, pages 416, 417.

ligence that a large number of our people are about to remove into that county, they will raise a great hue and cry, and circulate many bugbears through the medium of their favorite press. But we think your Excellency is well aware that our object is purely to defend ourselves and possessions against another unparalleled attack from the mob, inasmuch as the Executive of this State can not keep up a military force "to protect our people in that country without transcending his power." We want, therefore, the privilege of defending ourselves and the Constitution of our country, while God is willing we should have a being on his footstool.

We do not know at what time our friends will arrive, but expect more certain intelligence in a few weeks. Whenever they do arrive, it would be the wish of our people in this county to return to our homes in company with our friends under guard, and when once in legal possession of our homes in Jackson County, we shall endeavor to take care of them without further wearying the patience of our worthy Chief Magistrate. We will write hereafter, or send an express. During the intermediate time we would be glad to hear of the prospect of recovering our arms.

With due respect, we are, sir, your obedient servants,

(Signed)
A. S. Gilbert,
Edward Partridge,
John Whitmer,
W. W. Phelps,
John Corrill.

P. S.—Many of our brethren who are expected on, had made arrangements to emigrate to this State before the outrages of the mob last fall. We hope the painful emergency of our case will plead an excuse for our frequent communications.[6]

The Governor replied as follows:

City of Jefferson, May 2, 1834.

To Messrs. W. W. Phelps and Others; Gentlemen: Yours of the 24th, ult., is before me, in reply to which I can inform you that becoming impatient at the delay of the court of inquiry in making their report in the case of Lieutenant Colonel Pitcher, on the 11th, ult., I wrote to General Thompson for the reasons of such delay; last night I received his reply, and with it the report of the court of inquiry, from the tenor of which I find no difficulty in deciding that the arms your people were required to surrender on the 5th of last November should be returned; and have issued his order to Colonel Lucas to deliver them to you or your order, which order is here inclosed.

Respectfully, your obedient servant,

(Signed) Daniel Dunklin.[7]

---

[6] *Times and Seasons*, Volume 6, page 1072; *Church History*, Vol. 1, pages 418, 419.
[7] *Times and Seasons*, Volume 6, page 1073; *Church History*, Volume 1, page 420.

City of Jefferson, May 2, 1834.

To Samuel D. Lucas, Colonel Thirty-third Regiment: *Sir*: The court ordered to inquire into the conduct of Lieutenant Colonel Pitcher, in the movement he made on the 5th of November last, report it as their unanimous opinion that there was no insurrection on that day, and that Colonel Pitcher was not authorized to call out his troops on the 5th of November 1833. It was then unnecessary to require the Mormons to give up their arms. Therefore, you will deliver to W. W. Phelps, E. Partridge, John Corrill, John Whitmer, and A. S. Gilbert or their order, the fifty-two guns, and one pistol reported by Lieutenant Colonel Pitcher to you on the 3d of December last, as having been received by him from the Mormons on the 5th of the preceding November. Respectfully

Daniel Dunklin, *Commander in Chief*.[8]

Dunklin answered a letter from Colonel J. Thornton on behalf of the Saints as follows, dating his reply June 6:

City of Jefferson, June 6, 1834.

Dear Sir: I was pleased at the receipt of your letter concurred in by Messrs. Reese, Atchison, and Doniphan, on the subject of the Mormon difficulties. I should be gratified indeed if the parties could compromise on the terms you suggest, or, indeed, upon any other terms satisfactory to themselves. But I should travel out of the line of my strict duty, as chief Executive officer of the Government, were I to take upon myself the task of effecting a compromise between the parties. Had I not supposed it possible, yes, probable, that I should, as Executive of the State, have to act, I should before now have interferred individually, in the way you suggest, or in some other way, in order if possible to effect a compromise. Uncommitted as I am to either party, I shall feel no embarrassment in doing my duty; though it may be done with the most extreme regret. My duty in the relation in which I now stand to the parties is plain and straightforward. By an official interposition, I might embarrass my course, and urge a measure for the purpose of effecting a compromise, and it should fail, and in the end, should I find it my duty to act contrary to the advice I had given, it might be said that I either advised wrong, or that I was partial to one side or the other, in giving advice that I would not, as an officer, follow. A more clear and indisputable right does not exist that the Mormon people who were expelled from their homes in Jackson County, to return and live on their lands, and if they can not be persuaded as a matter of policy to give up that right, or to qualify it, my course, as the chief Executive Officer of the State, is a plain one. The Constitution of the United States declares, "That the citizens of each State be entitled to all privileges and immunities of

---

[8]*Times and Seasons*, Vol. 6, p. 1073, 1074; *Church History*, Vol. 1, pp. 420, 421.

citizens in the several States." Then we can not interdict any people who have a political franchise in the United States from emigrating to this State, nor from choosing what part of the State they will settle in, provided they do not trespass on the property or rights of others. Our State Constitution declares that the people's "right to bear arms, *in defense of themselves,* and of State, cannot be questioned." Then it is their constitutional right to arm themselves. Indeed, our militia law makes it the duty of every man, not exempted by law, between the ages of eighteen and forty-five, to arm himself with a musket, rifle, or some firelock, with a certain quantity of ammunition, etc. And again our Constitution says, "that all men have a natural and indefeasible right to worship Almighty God according to the dictates of their own consciences." I am fully persuaded that the eccentricity of the religious opinions and practices of the Mormons, is at the bottom of the outrages committed against them.

They have the right constitutionally guaranteed to them, and it is indefeasible to believe and worship Jo Smith as a *man,* an *angel,* or even as the only true and living God, and to call their habitation Zion, the Holy Land, or even heaven itself. Indeed, there is nothing so absurd or ridiculous that they have not a right to adopt their religion, so that in its exercise, they do not interfere with the rights of others.

It is not long since an impostor assumed the character of Jesus Christ, and attempted to minister as such; but I never heard of any combination to deprive him of his rights.

I consider it the duty of every good citizen of Jackson and the adjoining counties to exert themselves to effect a compromise of these difficulties, and were I assured that I would not have to act in my official capacity in the affair, I would visit the parties in person and exert myself to the utmost to settle it. My first advice would be to the Mormons, to sell out their lands in Jackson County and to settle somewhere else, where they could live in peace, if they could get a fair price for them, and reasonable damages for injuries received. If this failed I would try the citizens and advise them to meet and rescind their illegal resolves of last summer; and agree to conform to the laws in every particular, in respect to the Mormons. If both these failed, I would then advise the plan you have suggested, for each party to take separate territory and confine their members within their respective limits, with the exception of the public right of egress and regress upon the highway. If all these failed, then the simple question of legal right would have to settle it. It is this last that I am afraid I shall have to conform my action to in the end; and hence the necessity of keeping myself in the best situation to do my duty impartially.

Rumor says that each party are preparing themselves with cannon. That would be illegal. It is not necessary to self-defense, as guaranteed by the Constitution. And as there are no artillery companies organized in this State, nor field pieces provided by the public, any preparation of that kind will be considered as without right; and in the present state of things would be understood to be with a criminal intent. I am told that the people of Jackson County expect assistance from the adjoining counties, to oppose the Mormons in taking or keeping possession of their lands. I should regret it extremely if any should be so imprudent as to do so; it would give a different aspect to the affair.

The citizens of Jackson County have a right to arm themselves and parade for military duty in their own county, independent of the commander in chief; but if citizens march there in arms from other counties, without order from the commander in chief, or someone authorized by him, it would produce a very different state of things. Indeed, the Mormons have no right to march to Jackson County in arms, unless by the order or permission of the commander in chief. Men must not "levy war" in taking possession of their rights, any more than others should in opposing them in taking possession.

As you have manifested a deep interest in a peaceable compromise of this important affair, I presume you will not be unwilling to be placed in a situation, in which perhaps, you can be more serviceable to these parties. I have therefore taken the liberty of appointing you an aid to the commander in chief, and hope it will be agreeable to you to accept. In this situation you can give your propositions all the influence they would have, were they to emanate from the Executive without committing yourself or the commander in chief in the event of a failure.

I should be glad if you or some of the other gentlemen who joined you in your communication, would keep a close correspondence with these parties, and by each mail write to me.

The character of the State has been injured in consequence of this unfortunate affair; and I sincerely hope it may not be disgraced by it in the end.

With high respect, your obedient servant,

(Signed) Daniel Dunklin.[9]

By this time the brethren from Kirtland, organized into what was known as Zion's Camp, were on their way to Missouri. Accompanying the letter was another order for the return of the Latter Day Saints' arms, as they had not been returned:

City of Jefferson, June 9, 1834.

Herewith you have a second order for the delivery of your arms now in the possession of the militia of Jackson County. Colonel Lucas has resigned his command, he informs me. If Lieutenant Colonel

---

[9] *The Evening and the Morning Star*, pages 349, 350; *Church History*, Volume 1, pages 488, 491.

Pitcher shall be arrested before you receive this, you will please hold up the order until I am informed who may be appointed to the command of the regiment.
Respectfully,
(Signed) Daniel Dunklin.

Thomas Pitcher, Lieutenant Colonel Commandant of the 33d Regiment; Sir: On the 2nd day of last May I issued an order to Colonel Lucas to deliver the fifty-two guns and one pistol which you received from the Mormons on the 5th day of November last, and reported to him on the third day of the succeeding December to W. W. Phelps, E. Partridge, John Corrill, John Whitmer, and A. S. Gilbert, or their order. On the 24th, ult., Colonel Lucas wrote and informed me that he had resigned his commission and left the county of Jackson. You as commandant of said regiment are therefore commanded to collect the said arms, if they are not already in your possession, and deliver them to the aforesaid gentlemen or their order.
Respectfully,
Daniel Dunklin, *Commander in Chief*.[10]

Negotiations continued for some time. The Saints in Clay County finally consented to meet their brethren of Zion's Camp and urge them to disperse. The Jackson County representatives agreed to pay certain indemnity for property despoiled and confiscated, but never did, nor did they return the arms taken from the Saints as the Governor ordered.

On November 25, 1834, Honorable J. T. V. Thompson,[11] a senator, wrote from Jefferson City as follows, inclosing an excerpt from the Governor's message:

Jefferson City.

Dear Sir: I will say to you, that your case with the Jackson people has been mentioned to the highest officer of the State, the Governor. He speaks of it in his message and so much of his message will be referred to a committee. I am not able to say what will be their report, but I will write you again.
I have the honor, etc.
J. T. V. Thompson.[12]

---

[10] *Times and Seasons*, Volume 6, page 1088; *Church History*, Volume 1, pages 491, 492.
[11] *Church History*, Volume 1, pages 534, 535.
[12] *Millennial Star*, Volume 15, page 185; *Church History*, Volume I, page 534.

The extract from Governor Dunklin's message referred to in the above letter is as follows:

In July, 1833, a large portion of the citizens of Jackson County organized themselves and entered into resolutions to expel from that county a religious sect called Mormons, who had become obnoxious to them. In November following they effected their object, not however without the loss of several lives. In the judicial inquiry into these outrages, the civil authorities who had cognizance of them, deemed it proper to have a military guard for the purpose of giving protection during the progress of the trials. This was ordered, and the Attorney General was requested to give his attention during the investigation, both of which were performed, but all to no purpose. As yet none have been punished for these outrages, and it is believed that under our present laws conviction for any violence committed upon a Mormon can not be had in Jackson County. These unfortunate people are now forbidden to take possession of their homes; and the principal part of them, I am informed, are at this time living in an adjoining county, in a great measure, upon the charity of its citizens. It is for you to determine what amendments the law may require so as to guard against such acts of violence for the future.[13]

Thus encouraged, the Saints sent a petition to be presented by David R. Atchison then in the Senate. He and J. T. V. Thompson both favorable to the saints attempted to move for reinstatement. But in spite of all friendly efforts all negotiations eventually failed to obtain either reinstatement or indemnity.

---

[13]*Messenger and Advocate*, Volume 1, page 41; *Church History*, Volume I, page 534.

XXI.—The High Council

EFFECTIVE MACHINERY for settling difficulties between members was early in existence in the church, and provision was made for elders' courts, and a court of the Bishop and his associates to act as judges in certain cases. Evidently the appellate court of twelve high priests, presided over by the Presidency, was also familiar to the church for we find the notorious Doctor Hurlbut in June, 1833, appealing from the decision of the Bishop's Court, which "cut him off" from the church for misconduct while in the East on a mission. It is recorded:

> Doctor Hurlbut being dissatisfied with the decision of the council on his case, presented the following appeal:
> I, Doctor P. Hurlbut, having been tried before the bishop's council of high priests on a charge of unchristianlike conduct with the female sex, and myself being absent at the time, and considering that strict justice was not done me, I do by these presents, most solemnly enter my appeal unto the President's Council of High Priests for a rehearing, according to the privilege guaranteed to me in the laws of the church which council is now assembled in the schoolroom, in Kirtland, this twenty-first day of June, 1833.

The rehearing being granted, two high priests John and William Smith "were ordained under the hands of Elder Rigdon," to make out the number that the court might be organized. The decision of the court was that though the Bishop's Court had handed down a correct decision that his "crime was sufficient to cut him off from the church," yet he "should be forgiven because of the liberal confession which he made."[1]

But two days later Doctor Hurlbut was called in question by a "general council" on another charge and cut off. This time he brought no appeal.

---

[1] *Times and Seasons*, Volume 6, page 785; *Church History*, Volume 1, page 296.

Just how common these cases were we do not know, but evidently there was not a permanent high council until February 17, 1834, when at a meeting called at the home of Joseph Smith in Kirtland, the Standing High Council was organized.

The minutes of this meeting state:

> This day a general council of twenty-four high priests assembled at the house of Joseph Smith, Junior, by revelation, and proceeded to organize the high council of the Church of Christ, which was to consist of twelve high priests, and one or three presidents, as the case might require. This high council was appointed by revelation for the purpose of settling important difficulties, which might arise in the church, which could not be settled by the church, or the bishop's council, to the satisfaction of the parties.
>
> Joseph Smith, Junior, Sidney Rigdon, and Frederick G. Williams were acknowledged presidents by the voice of the council; and Joseph Smith, Senior, John Smith, Joseph Coe, John Johnson, Martin Harris, John S. Carter, Jared Carter, Oliver Cowdery, Samuel H. Smith, Orson Hyde, Sylvester Smith, and Luke Johnson, high priests, were chosen to be a standing council for the church, by the unanimous voice of the council. The above-named councilors were then asked whether they accepted their appointments, and whether they would act in that office according to the law of heaven; to which they all answered, that they accepted their appointments, and would fill their offices according to the grace of God bestowed upon them.
>
> The number composing the council, who voted in the name and for the church in appointing the above-named councilors, were forty-three, as follows: nine high priests, seventeen elders, four priests, and thirteen members.[2]

The high council at its first meeting proceeded to try to determine whether disobedience to the Word of Wisdom was a transgression sufficient to deprive a member from holding official position in the church, after it was sufficiently taught him.

The question originated in Springfield Township, Erie County, Pennsylvania, when some of the members refused to partake of Communion because the elder administering did not obey the Word of Wisdom. The two high priests present, Lyman Johnson and Orson Pratt, both soon after ordained apostles, disagreed

---

[2]*Church History*, Volume 1, page 429; Doctrine and Covenants 99:1-3.

as to whether they were justified in doing so. Johnson contended that they were justified, because the elder was in transgression, and Pratt said the church was bound to receive the Lord's Supper under the administration of an elder, so long as he retained his office or license.

The decision (which seems to us to have left the point at issue still in abeyance) was "That no official member in this church is worthy to hold an office, after having the Word of Wisdom properly taught to him, and he the official member neglecting to comply or obey it." This decision stood for many years, the decision of the highest court of appeals in the church on the observance of the Word of Wisdom.

A similar high council was later organized in Missouri.

XXII.—Zion's Camp

THE PURPOSE OF ZION'S CAMP has often been misunderstood, even by friendly historians. This "camp," which was not military, except in the sense that all western immigrations of the day were made in such orderly fashion, was not for the purpose of seizing and holding the possessions of the Saints in Jackson County. The facts were that the attorneys for the Saints had been advised by State authorities, notably the attorney general, that it would be useless to restore these lands to their owners unless some steps were taken to secure the safety of both settlers and property. He suggested, emphatically seconded by Alexander Doniphan, attorney, that if enough of the Saints were concentrated in Missouri to form a regiment of militia, to be known as "Jackson Guards," and given state arms and an arsenal, they would not be molested. Complying with this suggestion, Zion's Camp was organized, but it soon became apparent to the originators of the plan, that more trouble, and not less, would result. Convinced of the futility of the plan, they made known their fears to the church representatives, who promptly disbanded the camp.

But there were other objectives. The Saints at Kirtland were anxious to help their destitute brethren in Missouri, who they knew were more or less dependent upon the charity of the people of Clay County who numbered little more than the refugees whom they had taken in. Food, clothing, seed, implements, and all manner of supplies were needed that spring. These were to be carried to the sufferers by Zion's Camp. Almost all such things were carried overland in those days, even money. The land agent at Lexington was in the habit of putting the gold he received for land in grain sacks, loading it onto a wagon, and with a trusty

Negro servant, starting out through the wilderness to deposit it with the government agent in St. Louis. He was never molested. Zion's Camp carried money, and no small quantity of it, for should their representatives get a settlement such as they profoundly desired with the Jackson County settlers, they would need money to buy out the claims of their enemies there.

Therefore missionaries had been sent out in all directions from Kirtland to gather up men and supplies. There were several women and children in camp, too. The men started, marching from Kirtland on the first of May, 1834, organized of course in the sort of military order then customary to a greater or lesser degree in all westward-going caravans. Accurate diaries were kept on the trip by Joseph Smith and Heber C. Kimball, so their route can be followed quite exactly for a great part of the way. The names of all the men, the few women and children, are a matter of record. Upon their return to Kirtland the members of the first quorum of seventy were chosen from the ranks of Zion's Camp.

A number of men were left in Kirtland to work upon the Temple with Sidney Rigdon in charge. The events of the trip were all quite trivial in their nature until they met Lyman Wight and Hyrum Smith with their company and supplies, gathered from branches at Florence, Ohio; Pontiac, Michigan; Huron County, Michigan, and a branch in Illinois called the Ritchey Branch, as well as from other neighborhoods where scattered members lived. The two camps joined at Salt River, Missouri, where a group of Saints known as the Allred Branch was located. Here they camped in the woods near a spring of water and held preaching services before they moved on. At this point Lyman Wight was put in charge on account of his military experience in the War of 1812.

From the camp on Salt River, Parley P. Pratt and Orson Hyde were sent to wait upon Governor Dunklin at Jefferson City, and request him to call out a sufficient military force to reinstate the

Saints in their homes in Jackson County. The governor readily admitted the justice of the request, but expressed fear that such a procedure would result in Civil War and bloodshed.

The two brethren rejoined the camp as they were entering Ray County and made their report. In the meantime on the 16th at the call of John F. Ryland, circuit judge, a meeting was held at Liberty. He suggested that either one party or the other sell their lands. John Corrill and A. S. Gilbert answered that the Saints were unwilling to sell their lands "which you well know would be like selling our children into slavery."[1]

However, an agreement was drawn up on June 16, signed by Samuel C. Owens, Richard Fristoe, Thos. Hayton, Sr., and seven others offering to buy the Mormon lands. This document was presented at a meeting held in Liberty which has been described by a nonpartisan, Judge Josiah Thorpe:

> There were a good many speeches made, and our friends from Jackson were very rabid. Samuel Owens, James Campbell, Wood Noland, and five or six others whose names I can't call to mind all had more or less to say. Owens being the chief speaker, spoke with force and energy, and in a way to arouse the passions rather than allay them, although it had been decided by all that inflammatory speeches should not be made, and anyone departing from that rule should be called to order and set down; but it was plain to be seen that all that was done or said was all on one side; and very little mercy manifest for the Latter Day Saints. . . . Well, they wrangled and they jawed, until Colonel Doniphan . . . who had been a listener . . . arose and began to shove up his sleeves (his manner when a little warmed up) and commenced his remarks in a rather excited tone, when the chairman or someone called him to order, saying he was giving too strong vent to his feelings; and it was calculated to raise an excitement in the crowd, whose feelings were then almost ready to boil over. The Colonel pulled his sleeve up a little higher and told them "that was what he got up for—to give vent to his feelings." I wish I could give his speech, but, if I recollect, he advocated the right of citizen and individual responsibility, and was opposed to Judge Lynch and mob violence; was in favor of law and order; the law was made for the punishment of evildoers and to protect the law abiding, and should be strictly enforced.[2]

---

[1] *Church History,* Volume 1, pages 492-496; *Times and Seasons,* Volume 5, pages 1488, 1489.
[2] Thorpe's *Early Days in Missouri.*

That changed the trend of the meeting. It was nearly sundown when the meeting adjourned. Now the Jackson County men, armed to the teeth, yet professed to be afraid to stay in Liberty, afraid of the vengeance of the "Mormons." "They were bound to return, and would not be prevailed upon to stay," although they professed to believe if they went, it being in the night, the Mormons would lay in ambush and attack them with a force sufficient to kill the whole outfit, yet they went, taking their lives in their hands, as it were and got safely to the ferry, little thinking what would be their fate before they reached the other shore. There was rather an overload for the boat to take all of them, but they feared to leave any on this side, lest the Mormons might come upon them before the boat could return for them, and so they all got aboard, Everett, the ferryman, assuring them there was no danger. They hadn't got more than half way over before they found that the water was coming into the boat so fast there was no help—they were bound to sink. Owens and one or two others couldn't swim. Campbell (being a good swimmer, having often swum the Missouri River) began to fix and instruct the others how to manage their horses, to let them have their own way and not attempt to use the bridle, and they would take them to the shore. They had kept the oars going while the boat was filling with water, and had gained until they thought they were almost to the other shore. Campbell, feeling no uneasiness for himself, had got them all started, encouraging and telling them how to do, and after watching them until they were some distance and all appeared to be getting along finely, he left the boat, after standing on it until the water was waist deep. The ferrymen, all good swimmers, left every man to himself; strange to say the two best swimmers were drowned—Campbell and Everett; the owner of the ferry. The latter got within twenty or thirty steps of shore, when his wife asked him how he was making it; he answered, "All right," but in a minute or two they heard him no more. . . . It was thought that Campbell and him must have taken the cramp as it was no trouble for either of them to swim the river. Their bodies were recovered two or three days afterward, some distance down the river, lodged in a rock heap. . . . Owen's life was prolonged only to be taken by the Spaniards at the battle of Chihuahua.[3]

This incident added fuel to the flames, for Jackson people[4] in some occult fashion blamed the sinking of the ferryboat on the

---

[3] Thorpe's *Early Days in Missouri*, letter 16.
[4] In a statement signed by three survivors of the accident, Samuel C. Owens, S. V. Noland, and T. Harrington, printed in the *Farmers and Mechanics Advocate*, St. Louis, Missouri, July 3, say under date of June 17: "We are confident that the boat struck something. Our impressions at the time were, and still are, that something had been done to the boat to sink her, as it was known that the committee from this county would cross at that point on last night." This statement gives the loss as five, two of them ferrymen.

Mormons; the Saints with equal fanaticism talked of judgments.[5]

In the meantime the camp of Zion advanced slowly over the prairies until on June 18th they pitched their tents one mile from Richmond, passing through the town early the next day. That evening they went into camp on an elevated piece of ground between two branches of Fishing River.

Here they believed themselves miraculously saved from destruction, as a mob was gathering near Williams Ferry on Fishing River with the intent to cross the river and attack the camp. But a storm came up, and the river swelled by torrents of rain prevented the crossing. Those who attempted to cross were forced to return to their Jackson County homes. In the meantime the travelers with little inconvenience except tents blown down, took refuge in an old meeting house through the night.

The company left the old church,[6] on the 20th, and continued five miles on the prairie. Here the Fishing River revelation was received on the 22d of the month.

The camp then marched toward Liberty on the 23d, taking a circuitous route around the head of the Fishing River to avoid the deep water. When within five or six miles of Liberty they were met by General Atchison and other friends and warned against entering Clay County as per their agreement with Clay County citizens. So the camp turned to the left, crossed the prairie to A. S. Gilbert's residence, and camped on the bank of Rush Creek[7] in "Brother Burket's" (sometimes given as Burghart's) field. Here cholera broke out the night of the 24th and thirteen in all died and were buried one-half mile from the camp by their brethren on the bank of a small stream which empties into Rush Creek. Sometimes the men in the very act of performing last

---

[5]*Times and Seasons*, Volume 6, pages 1089-91, "The angel of the Lord saw fit to sink the boat."

[6]Heman C. Smith, in a letter to Honorable D. C. Allen of Liberty, says he is quite satisfied that the location of this old church was where the present old Baptist Church is situated on the south side of the road between Excelsior Springs and Prathersville (letter of August 7, 1917).

[7]Rush Creek heads about two miles northwest of Liberty and empties into the Missouri River near Missouri City, seven miles southeast of Liberty.

rites over their dead brethren would be stricken themselves. The burials were, of necessity, hasty and without coffins, the bodies simply wrapped in blankets and carried on a horse-sled to their last resting place.

Disease and deformity in that day were to the average religious person, visitations of God's wrath upon erring humanity. The Saints, even their leaders, accepted the belief of the time without question, especially in the cases of such scourges as Asiatic cholera which occasionally swept through the country.

The Saints of the camp, resigning themselves to God's will, did not think of the infested communities through which they had traveled where the heart chilling chant of the Negro slave driving the death-cart, "Bring out your dead. Bring out your dead!" had become a familiar sound on the almost empty streets. A horrible and sickening stench now rose from the dooryards where many loved ones were stealthily buried rather than be surrendered to the public death carts. Spring branches and streams were polluted with the dead. In these places the little caravan of Zion's Camp accepted water and food, or bought it as they traveled along, for, alas, they did not know as we do today "you can eat and drink cholera, but you cannot 'catch' it." In 1884, Robert Koch, the founder of bacteriology, after isolating the bacilli of anthrax and tuberculosis, turned his attention to cholera and discovered the cholera vibrio, and another world-wide scourge bowed its head before science, and disappeared from the civilized world. For the cholera vibrio has many enemies—an hour in the sunshine kills it, acid destroys it, drying makes it sterile, and it can only flourish by getting somehow from the intestine of one human being to another.

Four times during the 19th century, cholera had circumnavigated the globe, leaving its home in the crowded, unsanitary parts of the Orient to make its ravages pandemic. In 1832 it appeared in Missouri—in Palmyra, 105 people died in two weeks. In the three epidemic years 1832, 1833, and 1834, Carrollton lost one in every 16 of her populace. No one in this enlightened age can believe that a God of love would select Asiatic cholera for the punishment of minor camp regulations—for cholera was a terrible thing. He who walked the streets at noonday was often a struggling, screaming victim before nightfall, and at midnight a loathesome corpse. Dr. Victor Heiser in his *An American Doctor's Odyssey* tells of walking along the streets of Manila as late as the year 1905, and seeing a man ahead of him leap into the air, and then fall back sprawling on the ground, and says he knew that even before he reached him, the man would be dead of cholera. "Gentleman, cholera, is a disease the first symptom of which is death," said one doctor to his class. Although the terrific toxin of cholera soon stopped the heart of its victim, yet an eternity of suffering was crowded into the few hours of agony that followed the sudden crises of the disease, and a cholera victim never lost consciousness until the merciful end came.

This was the horror that stalked Zion's Camp on the night of June 24, 1834. In a few days the disease spread into the Gilbert home. Algernon S. Gilbert died and one other of his family.

Here on Rush Creek the camp was disbanded in deference to the wishes of the citizens of Clay County, and Joseph Smith dispatched to Messrs. Thornton, Doniphan and Atchison the following note:

Rush Creek, Clay County, June 25, 1834.

Gentlemen: Our company of men advanced yesterday from their encampment beyond Fishing River to Rush Creek, where their tents were again pitched. But feeling disposed to adopt every pacific measure that can be done, without jeopardizing our lives, to quiet the prejudices and fears of some part of the citizens of this county, we have concluded that our company shall be immediately dispersed and continue so until every effort for an adjustment of differences between us and the people of Jackson has been made on our part that would in anywise be required of us by disinterested men of republican principles.

I am respectfully, your obedient servant,

Joseph Smith, Jr.

The last days of June were spent by the Prophet with his friends in western Clay County, and it was while there he crossed the river into Jackson in secret at night that his feet might stand, for what was to be the last time, upon the "goodly land."

The mission of the men of Zion's Camp was not yet finished. They were to organize a high council in Zion and met at the home of Lyman Wight for that purpose. Lyman Wight was at the time living on the great farm of Michael Arthur, who has been designated as "the friend to man" by the voice of the earlier Saints. He was a Southerner, a slaveholder, and his farm assumed almost the proportions of a plantation. Here he had employed a number of the Saints and provided for their families in true patriarchal style. Lyman Wight was engaged in building him a new brick house. Others, notably Robert Rathbun, were to build the iron work, and Mr. Durfee the woodwork for a new mill, the first mill in Clay County to be run by an inclined wheel, a great improvement over primitive methods.[8]

Michael Arthur championed the cause of the Saints not without cost to himself. He had previously found a ready market in Jackson County for the flour from his mill and the whisky, manufactured on his plantation, but when that fall he sent one of his trusty Negroes across the river with a load of flour and whisky, his Jackson County neighbors mounted the load with axes, cut the barrels to pieces and let the flour and whisky out on the ground (though any mob wasting the latter article in such fashion in 1834, seems incredible).

Arthur's losses in goods and prestige with his neighbors did not deter him from his acts of friendship for the exiled Saints, which were in an especial manner useful to them when he later served in the legislature of the State.

It was in this man's yard that the high priests gathered on July

---

[8]Judge Josiah Thorpe, *Early Missouri Days*, letter 8.

3, 1834, to organize the high council,[9] one of the most momentous acts of the men of Zion's Camp, similar to the high council organized in Kirtland.

David Whitmer was at this time ordained as president of the church in Zion with two counselors, or assistant presidents, W. W. Phelps and John Whitmer. The ordination of Whitmer as "president in Zion" led to much contention in later years as to the exact office he held. Though such a conclusion may be questioned, an examination of the business done by Whitmer and his council suggests such work as was later done by a "stake president" and his counselors. David Whitmer took immediate charge of the scattered Saints of "Zion." Although it was not wisdom to hold meetings in Clay County, he appointed elders to visit in the homes. His teachings were strongly for peace. He asked all the Saints to refrain from voting at the coming election, that those who had so kindly sheltered them might retain the reins of government. All the council seemed agreed that the ministers should "teach the disciples how to escape the indignation of their enemies, and keep in favor with those who were friendly disposed," and the letter composed by the council and addressed to the Saints cannot be too highly commended for the kindly wisdom of its teaching. "Lest any man's blood be required at your hands, we beseech you, as you value the salvation of souls, and are within, to set an example worthy to be followed by those without the kingdom of our God and his Christ, that peace by grace, and blessings by righteousness may attend you till you are sanctified and redeemed." Dated Clay County, August 1, 1834. These were the teachings of the exiled Saints in 1834.[10]

---

[9] *Times and Seasons,* Volume 6, pages 1109, 1110; *Church History,* Volume 1, pages 503-5.
[10] *Times and Seasons,* Volume 6, pages 1123, 1124; *Church History,* Volume 1, page 532 ff.

XXIII.—The Missionary Quorums

The time had now come for the installation of special officers to take charge of the missionary work, which was fast becoming a very large and important part of the church activities. As long before as June, 1829, Joseph had been told that the time would come when twelve apostles would be appointed and sent into the world, even as the twelve apostles in the time of Christ, and the disciples in the church upon this continent.[1]

Joseph Smith told a number of the brethren that there was a special blessing in store for them, and they gathered at Kirtland on the 14th of February, 1835. After preliminary prayer and song, President Smith told of a coming endowment in the priesthood. He then asked all those who went to Zion if they agreed with him. These men were sitting in a body, and all arose. He talked for awhile then on the choosing of the twelve, and after he had spoken at some length, asked who "was willing to have the Spirit of the Lord dictate in the choosing of the elders to be apostles." All signified their willingness. After singing "Hark, Listen to the Trumpeters," a peculiarly appropriate hymn, the meeting was dismissed for one hour.

Upon reassembling they were told that the first business was the selection of the first Quorum of Twelve by the Three Witnesses. Oliver Cowdery, Martin Harris, and David Whitmer accordingly prayed one at a time in turn, and were then blessed that they might be guided in the important work about to be done. After deliberation they then presented the following names:

1. Lyman E. Johnson.
2. Brigham Young.
3. Heber C. Kimball.
4. Orson Hyde.
5. David W. Patten.
6. Luke Johnson.
7. William E. McLellin.
8. John F. Boynton.
9. Orson Pratt.
10. William Smith.
11. Thomas B. Marsh.
12. Parley P. Pratt.

---
[1] Book of Mormon, page 635, authorized edition, Lamoni, Iowa, 1919.

The first three named came forward and were ordained under the hands of the Three Witnesses, and after singing "Glorious Things of Thee Are Spoken," the congregation was dismissed.

The next day was Sunday, and upon the assembling of the congregation, Oliver Cowdery spoke of the nature of the service. They then proceeded to the ordination of Orson Hyde, David W. Patten, Luke Johnson, William McLellin, John F. Boynton, and William Smith; David Whitmer and Oliver Cowdery officiating. On the following Saturday, February 21, Parley P. Pratt was also ordained, or as he says, "took the oath and covenant of apostleship."

There were still two of the chosen twelve absent on missions and when they returned, Thomas B. Marsh on the 25th of April and Orson Pratt on the 26th, they were duly ordained, and the whole quorum received a beautiful and appropriate charge from Oliver Cowdery, following which he took each of them by the hand and said:

"Do you with full purpose of heart take part in this ministry, to proclaim the gospel with all diligence, with these your brethren, according to the tenor and intent of the charge you have received?"

Every one of them replied in the affirmative.

On the 28th the church in council assembled proceeded to select from the number of those who went up to Missouri in Zion's Camp forty-five men who were considered worthy to belong to the first Quorum of Seventy.

On March 1, after attending to the confirmation of some who had been baptized and partaking of the Communion (which in those days always followed a confirmation), the ordination of the men chosen on the previous day took place, and Joseph Young and Sylvester Smith were ordained presidents of seventy.

On March 12, the Quorum of Twelve met and decided to go for a mission in the East "for the purpose of regulating all things necessary for their welfare," which seemed to consist in the process of organizing "conferences" (now known as districts) wherever there were enough "branches" in close proximity to make this advisable. They were to leave Kirtland May 4, and they published their schedule of conferences in advance. Before they started they met in council and selected Thomas B. Marsh, the oldest of their number, to be the president of the quorum.

The seventies also scattered to their missions, going two by two except in very rare instances. On the 28th of December, they again met in Kirtland, and Joseph Smith records the event in his diary in these words:

Monday, the 28th. . . . . . This day the Council of Seventy met to render an account of their travels and ministry, since they were ordained to that apostleship. The meeting was interesting indeed, and my heart was made glad while listening to the relation of those who had been laboring in the vineyard of the Lord with such marvelous success. And I pray God to bless them with an increase of faith and power, and keep them all, with the endurance of faith in the name of Jesus Christ to the end.[2]

These ordinations and the spiritual endowment that accompanied them gave new impetus to the missionary.

---

[2] *Church History*, Volume 1, page 626; *Millennial Star*, Volume 15, pages 548, 549.

XXIV.—The Doctrine and Covenants

On September 24, 1834, a committee composed of Joseph Smith, Jr., Oliver Cowdery, Sidney Rigdon, and Frederick G. Williams was appointed by a general assembly of the church to "arrange the items of Doctrine of Jesus Christ for the government of the church of the Latter Day Saints, which church was organized and commenced its rise on the 6th day of April, 1830. These items are to be taken from the Bible, Book of Mormon, and the revelations which have been given to the church up to this date, or shall be until such arrangement is made."

After working faithfully upon this task until August 17, 1835, the committee announced that their work was ready to present to the people, and another general assembly was called. All the priesthood present in Kirtland were organized and sat with their especial orders. When the assembly was seated, *The Book of Doctrine and Covenants* was presented to the body by Oliver Cowdery, a member of the First Presidency and also of the committee. He was followed by Sidney Rigdon, who explained how they intended to get the vote of the assembly upon the book.

W. W. Phelps bore record to the truth of the book, followed by John Whitmer and John Smith, president of the high council in Kirtland. The high council in Kirtland then ratified it by unanimous vote. Like procedure was followed by Levi Jackman, president of the high council in Missouri. The written testimony and unanimous vote of the Twelve was read, as they were absent in the East engaged in the work of setting in order the various churches. Elder Leonard Rich, president of Seventy, spoke, and the Council of Seventy accepted and acknowledged its truth. Bishop Whitney of Kirtland and his counselors, Acting Bishop John Corrill and his counselors, John Gould, president of Quorum of Elders and the elders, Ira Ames and the priests, Erastus Babbitt and the teachers, William Burgess for the deacons added similar testimony. The book was then accepted by the whole congregation.

If there were any objections they were not recorded.

At the time of the general assembly Joseph Smith and Frederick G. Williams of the First Presidency were away from Kirtland on a mission, and the Twelve were busy organizing the local branches into districts throughout the Eastern States and Eastern Canada. They were fully informed of what was happening, however, and joined with the other two members of the committee of compilation in signing the following testimony:

> *To the Members of the Church of the Latter Day Saints; Dear Brethren*: We deem it to be unnecessary to entertain you with a lengthy preface to the following volume, but merely to say that it contains, in short, the leading items of the religion which we have professed to believe.
>
> The first part of the book will be found to contain a series of lectures as delivered before a theological class in this place, and in consequence of their embracing the important doctrine of salvation, we have arranged them into the following work:
>
> The second part contains items or principles for the regulation of the church, as taken from the revelations which have been given since its organization, as well as from former ones.
>
> There may be an aversion in the minds of some against receiving anything purporting to be articles of religious faith, in consequence of there being so many now extant; but if men believe a system, and profess that it was given by inspiration, certainly the more intelligibly they can present it, the better. It does not make a principle untrue to print it, neither does it make it true not to print it.
>
> The church viewing this subject to be of importance, appointed, through their servants and delegates, the High Council, your servants, to select and compile this work. Several reasons might be adduced in favor of this move of the Council, but we add only a few words. They knew that the church was evil spoken of in many places—its faith and belief misrepresented, and the way of truth thus subverted. By some it was represented as disbelieving the Bible, by others as being an enemy to all good order and uprightness, and by others as being injurious to the peace of all government, civil and political.
>
> We have, therefore, endeavored to present, though in few words, our

belief, and when we say this, humbly trust, the faith and principles of this society as a body.

We do not present this little volume with any other expectation than that we are to be called to answer to every principle advanced, in that day when the secrets of all hearts will be revealed, and the reward to every man's labor be given him.

With sentiments of esteem and sincere respect, we subscribe ourselves,
Your brethren in the bonds of the gospel of our Lord Jesus Christ,

Joseph Smith, Junior,
Oliver Cowdery,
Sidney Rigdon,
F. G. Williams.[1]

Kirtland, Ohio, February 17, 1835.

The written testimony of the Quorum of Twelve appears in Doctrine and Covenants 108A: 5, and is as follows:

The testimony of the witnesses to the book of the Lord's commandments, which he gave to his church through Joseph Smith, Junior, who was appointed by the voice of the church for this purpose: We therefore feel willing to bear testimony to all the world of mankind, to every creature upon the face of all the earth, and upon the islands of the sea, that the Lord has borne record to our souls, through the Holy Ghost shed forth upon us, that these commandments were given by inspiration of God, and are profitable for all men, and are verily true. We give this testimony unto the world, the Lord being our helper: and it is through the grace of God, the Father, and his Son Jesus Christ, that we are permitted to have this privilege of bearing this testimony unto the world, in the which we rejoice exceedingly, praying the Lord always that the children of men may be profited thereby.

A further testimony, giving light on the attitude of the early men toward the revelations, is that of John Whitmer, historian of the church and intimately connected with both the *Book of Commandments* and the Doctrine and Covenants. In his "address" when leaving the editorial chair of the *Messenger and Advocate,* in March, 1836, after bearing testimony to the Book of Mormon, he adds:

I would do injustice to my own feelings if I did not here notice still further the work of the Lord in these last days: The revelations

---
[1] *Church History*, page 578.

and commandments given to us are, in my estimation, equally true with the Book of Mormon, and equally necessary for salvation, it is necessary to live by every word that proceedeth from the mouth of God; and I know that the Bible, Book of Mormon, and book of Doctrine and Covenants of the Church of Christ of Latter Day Saints contain the revealed will of heaven. I further know that God will continue to reveal himself to his church and people, until he has gathered his elect into his fold, and prepared them to dwell in his presence.[2]

This book, now having the indorsement of the entire church, superseded the *Book of Commandments* and became one of the standard books of the church. Additions have been made from time to time.

---

[2] *Messenger and Advocate,* Volume 2, page 287.

XXV.—The Kirtland Temple

PROBABLY NO SPOT is more deeply enshrined in the hearts of Latter Day Saints than Kirtland Temple. Standing, as it does on a hilltop, the Temple may be seen for miles around, gleaming white in the sunshine, a monument to the faith, courage, sacrifice, and devotion of the men and women who lived long ago. Some architects may find it faulty,[1] and time may lay its hand heavily there, but to the true Latter Day Saint there comes the feeling that here he should take off his shoes, for the place whereon he stands is holy.

At a time when they were few in number and poor, at a time when the leaders were straining every nerve to find the means to buy land for a community experiment which threatened to outgrow their meager resources, these people built this great testimony of their faith. It was their tribute of love to their Maker, and they called it "The House of the Lord."

In June, 1833, the Presidency: Joseph Smith, Sidney Rigdon, and Frederick G. Williams, were appointed to draft plans, while Reynolds Cahoon, Jared Carter, and Hyrum Smith were to oversee the actual building operations. By the 25th of June, the Presidency in their letter to Edward Partridge in Zion could report: "We have commenced building the house of the Lord in this place, and it goes on rapidly."

On the 23d of July, while a mob bearing a red flag was advancing upon the Saints in Zion, and six brave men, John Corrill, John Whitmer, W. W. Phelps, Sidney Gilbert, Edward Partridge, and Isaac Morley, were offering themselves a ransom for the rest of their brethren, the Saints back in Kirtland, knowing nothing of

---

[1] In fact, architects praise it. See *Architecture,* August, 1924, pages 265-269. *The Architectural Forum,* March, 1936, pages 178-183.

what had befallen their brethren in the West, were laying the cornerstone of the Temple in that place.

Almost from the very hour of the commencement of the building, the Saints looked forward to a glorious spiritual endowment. Interrupted only by the cold weather of that winter, the work proceeded steadily. Spring came, and with it Zion's Camp left for the West, taking away most of the men from Kirtland, but with Sidney Rigdon left in charge, the work went on with the few who remained.

Heber C. Kimball, who had been with Zion's Camp, returned to find his wife, Vilate, busily engaged at the spinning wheel, for she had taken a hundred pounds of wool to spin on shares that summer. The half she earned by the products of her toil, she used to make clothing for the workmen on the Temple. She did not keep out enough wool "for even one pair of stockings" for herself, but with the assistance of one girl, spun, wove, dressed the cloth, cut it, and made it up into garments for the workers on the Temple. Nearly all the sisters in Kirtland were similarly employed in spinning, knitting, weaving, and sewing.

The walls of the building were partly up when the brethren left for Missouri, on July 26, 1834. "Brother Rigdon," says Heber C. Kimball, "looking at the poverty and sufferings of the church, frequently went upon the walls of the building, both by night and day, and wept, crying aloud to the Almighty to send means," that the building might be completed. The Saints of old time took their religious life seriously.

> After we returned from our journey to the West the whole church united in this great undertaking [says Kimball], and every man lent a helping hand. Those who had not teams went to work in the stone quarry and prepared the stones for drawing to the house.
> The Prophet, being our foreman, would put on his tow frock and tow pantaloons and go into the quarry, the Presidency, high priests, and elders all alike assisting. Those who had teams assisted in drawing the stone to the house. These all laboring one day in the week, brought as many stones to the house as supplied the masons through the whole

week. We continued in this manner until the walls of the house were reared. The committee who were appointed by revelation . . . used every exertion in their power to forward the work.[2]

Missionaries coming in from their missionary field worked on the Temple while they waited to go out again.

Thursday, November 19, 1835, Joseph Smith records in his Journal: "Went in company with Doctor Williams and my scribe to see how the workmen prospered in finishing the house. The masons on the inside had commenced putting on the finishing coat of plastering."

January 8, 1836, he again reports progress: "The plastering and hard finishing on the outside of the Lord's House was commenced on the 2d of November, 1835, and finished this day. The job was let to Artemas Millet and Lorenzo Young, at one thousand dollars. Jacob Bump took the job of plastering the inside of the house throughout at fifteen hundred dollars, and commenced the same on the 9th of November last. He is still continuing the work, notwithstanding the inclemency of the weather."

On the 13th of the month a council was held at Kirtland, composed of the First Presidency of the church, the presidents of the high council in Zion, the presidency of the high council, the twelve apostles, the seventy, and many of the elders. Vacancies were filled in the high councils occasioned by some of the members having been ordained to the office of twelve or seventy. Then a doorkeeper was appointed for the House of the Lord—Thomas Carrico. A committee, Joseph Smith, Sidney Rigdon, W. W. Phelps, David Whitmer, and Hyrum Smith, were chosen to draft regulations to govern the House of the Lord. A resolution was also passed:

> The unanimous voice of the whole assembly, motioned, seconded and carried unanimously, that no whispering shall be allowed in our

---
[2]Heber C. Kimball's *Journal*, pages 81, 82.

councils or assemblies, nor anyone allowed (except he is called upon, or asks permission) to speak aloud, upon any consideration whatever; and no man shall be interrupted while speaking, unless he is speaking out of place; and every man shall be allowed to speak in his turn.³

That night Joseph recorded his impressions of the day's events:

> This has been one of the best days that I ever spent; there has been an entire union of feeling expressed, in all our proceedings this day; and the Spirit of the God of Israel has rested upon us in mighty power, and it has been good for us to be here in this heavenly place in Christ Jesus; and although much fatigued with the labors of the day, yet my spiritual reward has been very great indeed.⁴

Sunday, March 27, 1836, was the time set apart for the dedication of the Temple. It was a time of rejoicing for all. It has been said that the women brought their jewelry and gave it to be sold for the building of this Temple, that their best china and glass were crushed and added to the mortar that covered the outside of the building. The historic building stands on a hill south of the east fork of the Chagrin River, about three miles southeast of Willoughby, Ohio, and about nine miles southwest of Painesville, about six in direct line from Lake Erie. It is visited by many tourists every year.

The building is of stone, plastered outside and in, and is three stories high, exclusive of basement. The first and second floors are auditoriums and very much alike, each fifty-five by sixty-five feet on the inside, exclusive of the vestibule on the east end, through which is the entrance to the building and in which are the stairways. The lower room was to be dedicated for "sacrament offering, and for your preaching; and your fasting, and your praying, and the offering up your most holy desires unto me, saith your Lord."⁵ The second room was to be used for the school of the apostles. There are eight pulpits in each of

---
³*Millennial Star,* Volume 15, page 582.
⁴*Ibid.*
⁵*Church History,* Volume 2, page 33.

these two rooms, four in each end. Those in the west end are for the use of the Melchisedec priesthood and those in the east for the Aaronic. The third story is divided into small rooms, intended as class rooms, as the Saints, especially the priesthood, were engaged almost continually in some kind of schoolwork.

On the long-expected day, the crowd began to arrive before eight o'clock and thronged the doors, until at nine the "presidents" of the church, who were seating the crowd, were reluctantly compelled to close the doors. It is estimated that over a thousand were present, every seat and aisle filled. There was a choir under the leadership of M. C. Davis. Lucy Cowdery,[6] Oliver Cowdery's half-sister, later the wife of Phineas Young, tells in a letter she wrote young Joseph Smith, many years after, of the wonderful experience she had in singing in the choir on this day. No one who took part ever forgot. Even the children remembered. The attendance of children on these important occasions in the life of adults is often underestimated.

> One of my earliest recollections [says Sylvia Cutler Webb][7] was the dedication of the Temple. [She was six years old.] My father took us up on his lap and told us why we were going and what it meant to dedicate a house of God. And although so very young at that time, I clearly remember the occasion.
>
> I can look back through the lapse of years and see, as I saw then, Joseph the Prophet standing with his hands raised toward heaven, his face ashy pale, the tears running down his cheeks as he spoke on that memorable day. Almost all seemed to be in tears. The house was so crowded the children were mostly sitting on older people's laps; my sister sat on father's, I on mother's lap. I can even remember the dresses we wore. My mind was too young at that time to grasp the full significance of it all, but as time passed, it dawned more and more upon me, and I am very grateful that I was privileged to be there.[8]

It is said that the word was given out that babies in arms were not to be admitted because of possible disturbance, but that one mother concealed her babe under her shawl, and that

---

[6]Lucy (Cowdery) Young was admitted to the Reorganized Church on her original baptism in 1879. She says she knew Emma Smith first in 1829.
[7]Sylvia Webb, daughter of Thaddeus, and granddaughter of Alpheus Cutler.
[8]*Saints' Herald*, March 24, 1915, page 289.

the child who had not yet spoken shouted, "Hosanna to God!"[9] The long dedicatory was offered by Sidney Rigdon. At the conclusion of the discourse, Sidney Rigdon presented Joseph Smith as their seer, and he was accepted by rising vote, first by the "presidents," then by the quorums in turn, and then by the congregation. The closing hymn was one we still sing in Latter Day Saint congregations, "Now Let Us Rejoice in the Day of Salvation." And the congregation sat without moving through all the three or four hours of that session. A short intermission was granted for women who had young children to leave for a few moments to care for them. The services were continued in the afternoon, and many wonderful things are related of the spiritual blessings that came to the congregation on that day. In all, the services continued over eight hours. The Saints and friends are praised for their "quiet demeanor" through the exercises. No passing of a collection plate marred the solemnity of that occasion, but a man stood at each door to receive voluntary donations as the people entered. The entire amount of the money gift on this day was nine hundred and sixty-three dollars.

In the days that followed, the people received a spiritual endowment in this Temple which was never forgotten. They went out to the world with new strength, a strength of which they were to stand sorely in need in the trying days that were before them.

---

[9] *Journal of History*, Volume 2, page 420.

XXVI.—After the Endowment

*A*FTER THE ENDOWMENT of the priesthood at Kirtland Temple, most of the elders scattered to various parts of the United States for the purpose of continuing in their mission work. David W. Patten went back to Tennessee, where he had previously enjoyed great success. Heber C. Kimball went east and met with what he considered great blessing in his work. In all the missionary work the Twelve took an active and leading part, and they distinguished themselves not only in preaching, but sometimes otherwise. The elders might spend their spare time studying Greek and Hebrew in the Temple, but when it came to a real man's job, they rolled up their sleeves and showed the people they were no physical weaklings.

Arriving one day at Ogdensburg, New York, just as Brother Heman Chapin was grinding his scythe and fixing his cradle to commence cutting his wheat, Heber C. Kimball asked for a "tow frock and pantaloons" and said he would go into the field and rake and bind all Brother Heman could cut. Brother Chapin replied that no man living could do it. But the next morning he supplied the Apostle with working clothes and a rake, and as soon as the dew was off they took their way to a small field containing about three acres. "We'll commence here," said Chapin. "All right," answered Brother Kimball. "Go ahead, Brother Heman. We'll cut down this piece before dinner." Just as Brother Chapin took the last clip, Kimball had it bound in a bundle, and they went up to dinner. Chapin never said a word or mentioned the subject again, but there wasn't a neighbor in miles around who didn't hear about it. And the next Sunday, though Brother Kimball had preached often in Ogdensburg, he had such a congregation as he had never had before. He had spoken in a language the

AFTER THE ENDOWMENT

farmers understood and admired. Henceforth nothing could shake their loyalty to such a remarkable man.

One of the young Apostles, Parley P. Pratt, felt that even the wonderful temple endowments had failed to solve his problems. His wife was still ill, his debts weighed him down with care and anxiety, and he now had the added responsibility of supporting his mother, who was old and feeble. One night soon after the dedication of the Temple, he retired to his home determined to plan his future course—whether to continue in the mission field—and his heart was still there—or to seek employment and provide for his family, so apparently the sensible thing to do. Morning found him still pondering over his problem. He felt it was too much for him to solve unaided.

Day had hardly dawned before there came a knock at the door, and Heber C. Kimball with other Saints entered. Kimball told the young Apostle that he had a message for him; first, to cease to worry about his wife, her health would improve from that hour and she would bear him a son; to leave his debts in the hands of the Lord, who would provide means to pay them, and care abundantly for his necessities. "Thou shalt go" he was told "to upper Canada, even to the city of Toronto, the capital, and there thou shalt find a people prepared for the fullness of the gospel, and they shall receive thee, and thou shalt organize the church among them, and it shall spread thence into the region round about . . . and from things growing out of this mission, shall fullness of the gospel spread to England; and cause a great work to be done in that land."

A Brother Nickerson was in Kirtland for the dedication of the Temple and offered to pay Brother Pratt's expenses to Canada; so they started out together. After a long and tedious journey in a public stagecoach, as the roads were very bad, and the lake not open, they arrived at the "Falls of Niagara," from whence they continued on foot. At the end of the second day's journey from the falls, they neared the flourishing city of Hamilton at the head of the lake. It was the eve of the Sabbath Day, and they gave out appointments for meeting the following day, then Nickerson left his traveling companion and proceeded on to his home. Pratt, now alone, preached the following day and was kindly entertained by those among whom he found himself.

But his destination was Toronto. Monday morning, he went on into Hamilton, and made inquiry about the road. The road around the lake north was very muddy, almost impassable, he was told, but the lake had just opened, and the fare by boat was only two dollars! Only two dollars! Pratt had not a single penny, and not a soul in Hamilton had he ever seen before! He had been in difficult places before and seeking the Lord in prayer had been shown the way out, but to come to this dilemma after such glorious promises, was totally unexpected. He thought again of the prophecy. Why had he believed so blindly? He had been married for ten years and was childless, and for six years of that time his wife had been tubercular. Doctor after doctor told him the disease was incurable! That foolish promise alone should have warned him! Something seemed to whisper, "Try the Lord. Nothing is too hard for him." Outside the city in the lonely forest, he poured out his soul to God and was comforted. He went into town again and soon was accosted by a stranger, who abruptly asked his name and where he was going. When told, the stranger inquired if he needed money; in reply to the affirmative answer, he gave him ten dollars and a letter of introduction to a friend in Toronto, who the stranger said was interested in things religious. The name was Taylor—John Taylor.

Satisfied now that his troubles were over, he took the first boat to Toronto and sought the home of Mr. Taylor. Mrs. Taylor was cordial and friendly, and called her husband from the machine shop. They gave him tea, but were not at all interested in what he had to say. After a pleasant talk, there seemed nothing to do but depart. He asked if he could leave his luggage there, and went out on the street. Fortunately he had money to get lodging in a public house and pay for a hall for a night or two to preach in. In the morning he made a systematic round of all the ministers. None accorded him hospitality; he asked the sheriff for the courthouse and was refused; he sought to rent a room at the public market and failed. Completely baffled, his mind again turned to the prophecy, and its wild and unbelievable promises that had sent him away from his sick wife and his honest debts and stranded him in a strange city where, manifestly, he could not do what he had been directed to do.

Again he turned to the only refuge left him—the pine woods outside the city. Kneeling again in prayer, he asked for guidance, and arose with resolution. He would leave the city. He walked back to Taylor's, and had his hands upon his luggage, when he was delayed by some casual question of Mrs. Taylor's. Before he could answer, a knock at the door interrupted, and he heard a lady caller enter the hall. He stood, luggage in hand, waiting for the caller to leave, so he could thank his hostess for her kindness and depart.

He could not help but hear Mrs. Taylor's conversation in the next room. The man was a stranger from the United States. He said the Lord had sent him to preach in Toronto. But he could find no room to preach, so was leaving. Yes, it was too bad. He *might* be a man of God.

Then to his astonishment he heard the caller answer. She had been washing that morning, and was very weary, but was "impressed" that she *must* go out. She could not rest, so started to walk to her sister's across the city. As she passed Taylor's something urged her to go in. "I'll call on my way back," she said to herself, but she was forced by some inward compulsion to stop at once. "Tell the stranger," he heard her say, "he is welcome to my home. I am a widow; but I have a spare room and a bed, and food in plenty. He shall have a home at my house, and two large rooms to preach in just when he pleases. Tell him I will send my son John over to pilot him to my house, and I will go and gather my friends and relatives to come in this evening and hear him talk."

Pleasantly domiciled in the home of Mrs. Walton that evening he sat with a crowd of friends around a large table, and in amazement heard his hostess say, "Mr. Pratt, we have for some years been anxiously looking for some providential event which would gather the sheep into one fold, build up the true church as of old, and prepare the humble followers of the Lamb, now scattered and divided, to receive their coming Lord when he shall descend to reign on the earth. As soon as Mrs. Taylor spoke of you I felt assured, as by a strange and unaccountable presentiment, that you were a messenger, with important tidings on these subjects; and I was constrained to invite you here; and now we are all here anxiously awaiting your words."

The way was open and the experiences that followed in the next two months were marvelous to all. Mrs. Walton had spoken truly. A group of students of the Bible had been meeting for two years, and were expecting the events numerated by Mrs. Walton. John Taylor was one of this group, and many others, Isaac Russell, later one of the first missionaries to England; Joseph Fielding, a young Englishman who with his two young sisters, Mary[1] and Mercy,[2] lived about nine miles from the city. The whole group were baptized, although on Pratt's first visit to the Fielding home, Mary and Mercy fled to a neighbor's, leaving their brother to meet the dreaded "Mormon" preacher alone. To them, the name "Mormon" had "such a contemptible sound," and besides they wanted "no new revelation to take the place of the old Bible." Pratt coaxed them home again only by a solemn promise

---

[1] Mary Fielding married Hyrum Smith, after the death of his wife Jerusha, and
[2] Mercy Fielding became the wife of Robert Thompson, well known in early church history.

that he would preach nothing but the Bible gospel. These two sisters, before many months passed, were willing to sacrifice their all for the message which they eventually received with all their hearts.

When Pratt left these kindly friends two months later, they pressed into his hand as he bade them farewell, several hundred dollars, which enabled him to pay his debts on arrival in Kirtland. Eventually he saw every part of the prophecy made by Kimball fulfilled.[3]

The experience of Pratt in Toronto was by no means an isolated one. Such happenings could be duplicated indefinitely in the days that followed the great endowment in Kirtland Temple.

That same summer in another part of Canada (Leeds County, Ontario) young John E. Page, who was sometime to be an apostle, was holding preaching meetings in a place called Plum Hollow. One night a Baptist minister by the name of John Landers came to hear him. The whole strange story was not new to Landers, for two years before his wife's brother, John Cairns,[4] had heard James Blakeslee preach and been baptized by him. Landers heard just one sermon from his brother-in-law, and it had the ring of truth. He told Cairns so. He had a curiosity to hear more.

When John E. Page came along, he went to hear him. At the conclusion of the sermon, Page held up the Three Books: Bible, Book of Mormon and Doctrine and Covenants, and said that he

---

[3] *Autobiography of Parley Parker Pratt*, page 141, seq.
[4] John Cairns was born in Glasgow, Scotland, October 21, 1808, and was baptized in 1834 in Leeds County, Ontario, by James Blakeslee, and ordained to be an elder at his confirmation. He preached in Canada from that time on until 1842, and then moved to Nauvoo from whence he was sent by Joseph Smith to Scotland, his native land. Returning from that mission in 1845, he attended conference in Nauvoo, only to be bitterly disappointed. He quietly took his family and moved to St. Louis, endeavoring to forget about the church. Here he entered into business with profit to himself financially, and was highly esteemed in the community, serving six years upon the city council and acting as President of the Board of Health for some time. In the early days of the church he was considered one of its best in debate, and took part in several debates in this country and his native Scotland. In the eventide of a very busy life, he retired to Hannibal, Missouri, and there his heart returned often to his "early love," the gospel. Always a careful student, he went over thoroughly the claims of the now divided membership, and on July 24, 1885, applied to the Reorganized Church, "Now, fully satisfied that the true Spirit and Power of God is with the Reorganization, I respectfully ask to be received among you." He was received upon his original baptism. On September 11 of the same year, he passed away at Hannibal, Missouri. See *Saints' Herald*, Volume 32, page 477.

knew they were all sacred books, and agreed in teaching the same doctrine. The young man spoke with such conviction that Landers was strangely stirred. He invited the stranger home that night, and the first question he asked him was: "How can you say that you *know* those books are true?"

Page told him that four years before in Ohio a man by the name of Emer Harris came preaching as he was preaching now, and awakened an interest in his heart, but when Harris had explained that his own brother had seen the golden plates, Page had answered that his brother's seeing them would not be enough for him, he wanted to see them *himself,* that he could never go out and testify to the world upon *belief alone.* Then he proceeded with an unusual story as Landers retold it in later years:

He said one night he seemed suddenly to be placed in a new meetinghouse, seated for worship. He saw in a corner of the room where the seats came together, three ancient-looking men, two on one side of the corner and one on the other.

They had the plates from which the Book of Mormon was translated between them. He stood directly in front of them and saw them turn over the leaves, leaf by leaf, until they came to a thick mass of leaves that had a seal on them.

While looking upon them he heard the voice of the Lord say to him, "This is shown you, and you are to bear witness of it all your days where you preach the gospel of the kingdom to all the world."[5] When he had finished, Landers said tolerantly: "Well that may be satisfactory to you, but your *knowledge* will not suffice for me. If I had such a vision, I should know."[6]

Page did not answer. He looked intently at the Baptist minister before him for a moment then arose and walking over to his side, laid his hand upon his head, and told him, "The time will come, when you will have as great, as certain a testimony as I have."

---

[5] A letter from Landers to Mary (Page) Eaton, *Autumn Leaves,* Volume 3, page 198.
[6] Autobiography of John Landers, *Autumn Leaves,* Volume 3, page 68.

That night the young missionary took out his writing materials and entered in the journal, which he kept all his life, this item: "September 13, 1836. I stayed that night with Mr. Landers, a Baptist elder, who, I think, will eventually believe the gospel."

The night of the fourth sermon, Landers handed in his name for baptism, rising publicly at the conclusion of the service to say: "What have I been about all my days with the Bible in my hands!" He was baptized with nine others on the seventh day of October, 1836.

The next month he was ordained an elder and immediately started on a mission with his nephew, preaching every night. One night he preached in a private house, and at the conclusion of the sermon, a man asked him about the doctrine of his church and the coming forth of the Book of Mormon. He told him *what he had been told and sat down.* His brother's son and fellow traveler arose and started to speak in tongues. Immediately Landers seemed to stand upon the Hill Cumorah. He saw the box containing the plates:

> I stood at the southeast of the box, and the cover was removed from the southeast to the northwest corner, so that I was enabled to look into the box. The box was made of six stones, a bottom stone, a top one and four side stones· at the corners and edges they were joined by a black cement. The bottom of the box was covered by the breastplate; in the center of the box and resting on the breastplate were three pillars of the same black substance that was used to cement the stones.
>
> Upon the pillars rested the plates which shone like bright gold. I saw also lying in the box a round body, wrapped in a white substance, and this I knew to be the ball or directors, which so many years ago guided Lehi and his family to this land. The top stone of the box was smooth on the inner surface as were the others, but on the top it was rounded.[7]

---

[7] Autobiography of John Landers, *Autumn Leaves*, Volume 3, page 68. John Landers was born August 20, 1794, in Leeds County, Ontario, and died January 22, 1892, at Lamoni, Iowa. He united with the Reorganization at Amboy in 1860. His granddaughter Christiana Salyards is well known for her books and quarterlies, which are distinguished by a high order of scholarship, and show a most unusual amount of painstaking research.

He lived for nearly a century, and from that time spent his life in telling of what he had heard, seen, and *knew* to be true.

And so, as the months passed, a multitude of witnesses were being gathered together from everywhere "a warning voice" was lifted to tell the story.

XXVII.—The Panic of 1837

ZION HAD NOT BEEN forgotten. The Saints fully expected soon by some means or other to return to their lands in Missouri. A new phrase crept into the conversation and writings of the Saints, "The redemption of Zion." We still hear it with an enlarged significance. But could our fathers see the land they loved and longed for, "the goodly land" for which they yearned, thronged with the Latter Day Saints today, they would think that the "redemption of Zion" for which *they* prayed had come about, and feel that they had not sacrificed and sorrowed and died in vain.

Occasionally a family or two, in spite of adverse conditions "started for Missouri the place designated for Zion, or the Saints' gathering place." One such incident as recorded in Joseph Smith's Journal says:

> They came to bid us farewell. The brethren came in to pray with them, and Brother David Whitmer acted as spokesman. He prayed in the Spirit, and a glorious time succeeded his prayer; joy filled our hearts, and we blessed them and bade them Godspeed and promised them a safe journey, and took them by the hand and bade them farewell for a season. May God grant them long life and good days.[1]

The next day

> The High Council met . . . to take into consideration the redemption of Zion. And it was the voice of the Spirit of the Lord that we petition the Governor; that is, those who have been driven out should petition to be set back on their own lands next spring, and that we go next season to live or die on our own lands which we have purchased in Jackson County, Missouri. We truly had a good time, and covenanted to struggle for this thing until death shall dissolve the union; and if one falls, that the remainder be not discouraged, but pursue this object until it is accomplished, which may God grant unto us in the name of Jesus Christ our Lord. Also, this day drew up a subscription for enrolling the names of those who are willing to go up to Missouri next spring and settle; and I ask God in the name of Jesus, that we may obtain eight hundred or one thousand emigrants.[2]

---

[1] *Church History* Volume 1, page 586; *Millennial Star*, Volume 15, pages 342, 343.
[2] *Ibid.*, page 586.

But an unforeseen calamity awaited them, and not them alone but all their countrymen:

> We were much grieved [says Heber C. Kimball] on our arrival in Kirtland to see the spirit of speculation that was prevailing in the church. Trade and traffic seemed to engross the time and attention of the Saints. When we left Kirtland (but a short time before), a city lot was worth about $150; but on our return, to our astonishment, the same lot was said to be worth $500 to $1,000, according to location; and some men, who, when I left, could hardly get food to eat, I found on my return to be men of supposed great wealth; in fact, everything in the place seemed to be moving in great prosperity and all seemed determined to become rich.[3]

About this time it was planned to organize a banking society among the Saints. Joseph Smith thought, as he later implied, that "an institution of the kind, established upon just and righteous principles" would be a "blessing not only to the church but the whole nation," and many another of the leading men of the church took stock and prominent part in organizing the affair. While it was not a church institution, so many of the prominent church officials were involved that it was naturally associated in the minds of the people with the "new sect" as it was then called. It was on the 2d of November, 1836, that the brethren "drew up certain articles of agreement, preparatory to the organization of a banking institution." Oliver Cowdery was sent to Philadelphia to procure plates for printing the notes and Orson Hyde to Columbus to apply for an act of incorporation. Oliver secured the plates at "great expense," but Orson Hyde was disappointed. "The legislature raised some frivolous excuse on which they refused to grant us those banking privileges they so freely granted to others." It was true. Banks were springing up like mushrooms all over the State and issuing their paper money wholesale.

At a meeting of January 2, 1837, the Kirtland Safety Society was formed as contemplated, not as a bank, but to all intents and

---

[3] *Life of Heber C. Kimball,* page 111.

purposes doing the business of a bank. They could not afford to have new plates made, so they used the ones that Cowdery had bought in Philadelphia at such "great expense," putting *anti* before the word "banking," thus, "Kirtland Safety Society Anti-Banking Company," thus fulfilling the letter of the law. And they paid their price for this ingenious device for saving money by being accused as long as books will be published of having deliberately invented this misleading name for purposes of deception. A little investigation would have shown that the plates were made and paid for while the members of the company still believed they were to have a banking charter. There was no reason why they should contemplate refusal. No one else was being refused.

For a time the Kirtland Bank paper circulated freely and, according to contemporaneous history, was taken without question by the whole community. But the whole venture was ill-starred from the start. The Nation was upon the verge of one of the greatest of those financial crashes which have characterized its history. Before the summer was over, the prosperity of the country, as Kimball plaintively asserts, was found to be "artificial and imaginary." The Kirtland notes began to be refused and rapidly depreciated in value. One by one almost all banks throughout the country suspended specie payment, and gold and silver rose in value in direct proportion with the depreciation of paper currency, which became practically worthless.

"Yes, I know about that bank . . ." said I. P. Axtell, Esq., director in the First National Bank of Painesville in 1889 and a member of the Whig convention as early as 1844. "These parties went into the banking business as a great many others in the State of Ohio and other States. They got considerable money out at first, and their enemies began to circulate all manner of stories against them, and as we had a great many banks then that issued what was known as 'wildcat money,' the people began to get alarmed at so many stories, and would take other banks' issue instead of the Kirtland; and so much of it was forced in at once that the bank was not able to take it up. Had the people left these Saints alone there is no reason that I know of why the Kirtland Bank should not have existed to this time, and on as stable a basis as other banks. . . . Yes, they were as good citizens as those of any society. It was the *fanatics in religion* that tried to drive those men out. There were a great many conservative men in our country at that time who held these fanatics back, and if it had not been for this they would have gone in and killed them all. But our intelligent and honorable citizens prevented this. . . . I know Mr. Pratt very well. He was a smart and a square man all around. These men were neither knaves nor rogues."[4]

Said Robert Lucas, Iowa's first Governor and Governor of Ohio in 1836: "I think it due to that people to state that they had for a number of years a community established in Ohio, and that while in that State they were (as far as I ever heard) believed to be an industrious, inoffensive people; and I have no recollection of having ever heard of any of them being charged in that State as violators of the laws."[5]

By August, 1837, Joseph Smith felt that he was in honor compelled to warn people against the circulation of these notes. In the August number of the *Messenger and Advocate,* he says under the caption of *"Caution to the Brethren and Friends of the Church of Latter Day Saints"*: "I am disposed to say a word relative to the bills of the 'Kirtland Safety Society Bank.' I hereby warn them to beware of speculators, renegades, and gamblers, who are duping the unwary and unsuspecting by palming upon them those bills which are of no worth here."

But long ere this, the church, in common with the rest of the country, was in the grip of one of the worst depressions ever known. "The panic of 1837" was one of the most disastrous crises

---

[4] *Saints' Herald,* Volume 27, page 85. *Church History,* Volume 2, page 96.
[5] *Millennial Star,* Volume 17, page 151. *Church History,* Volume 2, page 97.

the Nation ever experienced. The Kirtland Bank was organized in November, 1836, and by the close of the next month the decline had begun. There was some nervousness at the beginning of the year 1837 among deposit banks. By March of 1837, failures among business houses were a common thing.

The big banks struggled against the current, but on the 9th of May, 1837, $652,000 in specie was withdrawn from vaults of the city banks in New York. And on the evening of the same day it was learned that the principal deposits banks could not sustain themselves, while some local banks had but a few thousand dollars. The next day every bank in New York City suspended specie payment.

This was followed by a general suspension of business all over the country. Few banks survived. A general apathy covered the entire country. At least nine tenths of the factories and manufacturing plants closed down. Gold and silver went into hiding and almost disappeared as a circulating medium. In the largest city of the country, New York City, six thousand masons, carpenters, and other artisans of the building trades were without employment. Men thronged the eating houses, begging a chance to serve as waiters for enough to eat.

Boats and barges and all other shipping lay idle at the docks. One half to two thirds of all clerks and salesmen were out of work. Mothers begged on the street for food for their families, while almshouses and other charitable institutions were running over. Amid such surroundings the bankrupt law was revised and thirty thousand individuals, with aggregate debts of many millions, an average of about $7,000 each, took advantage of it. States abrogated their debts. Even the Federal Government was threatened with bankruptcy.

Not only those interested in the Kirtland Bank, but bankers in general were under the ban. The citizens hated banks, which they blamed for their misfortunes; they hated bankers, and mobs, lynchings, and riots against them became common. While solemn legislative assemblies passed drastic laws against banks in general, the people vented their rage on the bankers themselves. Even the church leaders who had engaged in the Kirtland Banking Association found their lives scarcely safe on the street, so great was the wrath of some of their brethren.

Of Joseph Smith's reputation in Kirtland, E. L. Kelley writes to Joseph III from Painesville, Ohio, on February 19, 1880, after a week of inquiry in the village of Kirtland and vicinity:

> So far among the acquaintances of Joseph Smith, Jr., I have failed to find one who will say that he was not a good citizen and an honest man. "Joe Smith," say they, "was an honorable man and a gentleman in every particular, let the histories say what they may."

In regard to the Kirtland period of the church, Samuel Murdoch wrote to the Dubuque (Iowa) *Times,* April 13, 1893:

> Kirtland is situated in the county in which I was raised from youth to manhood, and at the time Joseph Smith and his Mormons settled there I was nearly a man grown, and some of them were my immediate neighbors, with whose children I was often schoolmates, and I often met their prophet, Joseph Smith, although I was not personally acquainted with him.... From the time they settled in my county until they left it, I must say that during all that time, I never heard Joseph Smith called a thief, a drunkard, or a vicious man, even by his worst enemies, and my recollection of him to this date is that he was a tall graceful, good-looking man, continually wearing a smile[6] upon his face for everyone, and that he was a kind-hearted, generous friend and companion and that it was his winning manners by which he succeeded more than anything else.

It was in the hour of this catastrophe that the mission to England came to divert the minds of the faithful ones from their calamity. Had they not been able to unite in some common purpose, wreckage was almost inevitable.

---

[6]A dispatch from Springfield, Illinois, dated January 4, 1843, and printed in the New York *Herald* of January 18, contains this description of Joseph Smith: "The prophet is a large, portly, and fine looking man, six feet without shoes, looks about forty or forty-two [he was thirty-seven], and weighs 220 pounds, eyes light blue, approaching to gray, light brown hair, peaked nose, large head. I think a very little self-esteem, but more of the intellectual than the animal—dressed in box coat, black, blue dress coat and pants, black silk velvet vest, white cravat, a large gold ring on the finger next to the little one of his left hand, a black cane, and wears a continual smile on his countenance."

XXVIII.—The First Foreign Mission

On Sunday, the 4th of June, 1837, as Heber C. Kimball was seated above the Communion table in the stand on the Melchisedec side of the Temple, Joseph Smith spoke to him quietly and said, "Brother Heber, the Spirit of the Lord has whispered to me: 'Let my servant Heber go to England and proclaim my gospel and open the door of salvation to that nation.' "

Heber C. Kimball was one of the least educated of all the members of the Quorum of Twelve, but he was also at that time one of the most humble. He had been surprised at his call to the apostleship, for he had never considered himself worthy. Now he was completely overwhelmed, but he never faltered. Daily he went to the east room in the attic story of the Temple and poured out his very soul to God, asking for his protection and power that he might fulfill honorably the mission appointed him. "O Lord," he prayed, "I am a man of stammering tongue and altogether unfit for such a work. How can I go to preach in that land, which is so famed throughout Christendom for light, knowledge, and piety, and as the nursery of religion; and to a people whose intelligence is proverbial?"[1]

At that time another member of the Quorum of Twelve, Orson Hyde, was somewhat estranged by reason of the financial trouble in Kirtland. His brother-in-law, Lyman E. Johnson,[2] had failed in a business attempted during the times of prosperity. Altogether, hard times had befallen most of the Saints. Some of them decided that Joseph Smith was a "fallen prophet." When Hyde heard of Kimball's preparations, he went to the Presidency and asked that he might accompany his brother apostle on the mission.

---

[1] Heber C. Kimball's *Journal*, page 10.
[2] Lyman Johnson, one of the Twelve.

Joseph Fielding,[3] a priest who had relatives in England, was also ordained to accompany him.

Naturally, on so long a mission it took some time to get ready; therefore nine whole days were consumed in preparation. Heber and his companions (Willard Richards had determined to go on the day previous to Kimball's departure) accordingly left Kirtland on June 14, 1837, "without purse or scrip" on the first mission of the church to a foreign land. With them were Brother Kimball's faithful wife, Vilate, Joseph Fielding's sister, Mary, and some others of the church members who were to accompany them as far as Fairfield, the lake port of Kirtland. Mary gave them five dollars with which to pay the fare of the party from Fairfield to Buffalo, for they found a boat leaving for that port in about an hour. Leaving their friends to return to Kirtland, the three missionaries went aboard with young Robert B. Thompson and his wife,[4] who were on a mission to Canada. At Buffalo they expected that there might be funds from Canadian Saints who were interested in the English mission, but were disappointed. They walked slowly down the tow path of the canal, talking over what they should do. There was but little money remaining, and they must make some plan for the future. Finally they definitely decided to go on, "believing that God would open the way." They accordingly took passage on a "line boat," a slow, local boat, where fare was cheaper than on a packet. At Utica they left the canal and took a train for Albany.

The money was now exhausted, but Willard Richards was close to his father's home in Richmond, Berkshire County, Massachusetts. Here he remembered that his brother William owed him forty dollars. Hoping he might be in a position to pay, Willard Richards and Heber C. Kimball started to walk the intervening thirty miles, arriving there on the 20th of June. They had now

---

[3] Joseph Fielding, see page 234, also Mary Fielding.
[4] Mercy Fielding, see page 234.

been one week on the way. Securing the money, they took passage in a steamboat for New York City, where they arrived on the evening of June 22. Here they met Fielding and Pratt, who had preceded them, also John Goodson, Isaac Russell,[5] and John Snyder, who had come by way of Canada to join the mission.

There was a ship ready to sail to England but the missionaries had no funds, absolutely none. They hunted up the only Latter Day Saint in New York, Elder Elijah Fordham, who, as he had no house of his own, took lodgings for them with his sister-in-law. But they soon found they could not afford such expensive accommodations, or indeed any accommodations at all. They engaged a small room in an unfinished storehouse belonging to Fordham's father, who was said to be a wealthy man and paid for the building by assisting him for two days in raising another warehouse he was building. Here, on the floor, the prospective missionaries slept while waiting for the Lord to "open the way."

On Sunday, the 25th, they "fasted, prayed, administered Communion, held council for the success of the mission, and *had a joyful time.*" Their afternoon was made none the less enjoyable by the visit of two "sectarian" ministers, and the time was passed in the occupation so dear to the heart of early missionaries of the church, discussion.

In the meantime, the pitiful plight of this great unwarned city solicited their attention. They bought postage with a small part of their funds and mailed one hundred and eighty tracts of Orson Hyde's *A Timely Warning,* to as many priests and ministers of New York City; gave many others away, and conversed about the gospel wherever they could get a listener. They told Brother Fordham that if he were only faithful, a branch would be "raised up" in New York City before their return.

---

[5]Isaac Russell, son of Wm. Russell, was born April 13, 1807, at Windy Hill, Cumberland County, England. Emigrated to Canada with his parents at the age of ten years; baptized in the spring of 1836 by Parley P. Pratt in the Charlton settlement about eight miles north of Toronto. After listening to Pratt's first sermon there, he arose suddenly and said, "This is the gospel I wish to live and die by." Isaac Russell died September 25, 1844, near Richmond, Missouri.

At last enough money was obtained for their fare, eighteen dollars each. The passengers had also secured provisions which they would cook for themselves during the voyage, as was then customary.

The *Garrick,* upon which they had secured passage, was a new packet of the Dramatic Line, built for the Dramatic Company, of which E. K. Collins, who afterward made such a gallant fight to keep the Stars and Stripes on the Atlantic, was the moving spirit. Collins had ordered four new ships built in 1836, of Brown and Bell of New York, sparing no expense in material and workmanship. They were called (from whence came the name of the line) *"Roscius," "Siddons," "Shakespeare,"* and *"Garrick."*[6]

On the first of July, the *Garrick* stood in New York Harbor, her crisp new house flag (blue over white with a white L in the blue) floating in the air. Not far away was the packet *South America.* This was the *Garrick's* maiden voyage, and a wager of ten thousand dollars was up on which was the faster vessel. The wager was a guarantee that the ships would not delay in getting to their destination. The missionaries were full of excitement, anxious to be off. There had been many inconveniences in New York; they had been compelled to spread their blankets upon straw on the floor, but they "did not feel discouraged, believing that God would open up the way."

The one Latter Day Saint in New York accompanied them to the dock and wished to go with them, but was told that since the Lord was about to open up the work in New York City, he might be more useful at home, so he pressed ten dollars into their hands, and the boat was off. It was a wonderful trip. Only two of them, Richards and Fielding, were sick for a day or two. Orson Hyde preached on the aft quarter-deck on the 16th to a congregation of from two to three hundred—English, Irish, Scottish, French, German and Jews.

---

[6] *A Century of Atlantic Travel,* by Bowen, page 23.

Just at daybreak on the morning of July 20, the *Garrick* arrived in the River Mersey, opposite Liverpool, eighteen days and eighteen hours out from New York. The *South America* came in just a few lengths behind, every inch of canvas on both vessels spread. During the entire trip, she had not been out of sight of the *Garrick* but had never passed her. The race, as may be supposed, was the exciting feature of the voyage.

The mission had arrived in Liverpool. They had little money and no friends. For some time they wandered up and down the strange streets, watching the crowds and looking for a cheap place to lodge. At length Hyde, Richards, and Kimball found a small room belonging to a widow in Union Street, which they took for a day or two. All the time they were in Liverpool was spent in council and "in calling on the Lord for direction."

At length they said the Spirit of the Lord spoke to them, saying, "Go to Preston." They accordingly went. The place indicated was a large manufacturing town in Lancashire, thirty-one miles from Liverpool. It was four o'clock, election day, in Preston, the afternoon of July 22, 1837. Queen Victoria had just ascended the throne three days before the landing of the missionaries, and a general election had been ordered. Bands of music were playing, banners were flying, men, women, and children walked the street, decked with ribbons denoting their political choice. The elders watched the scene, feeling strangers indeed. At last a banner floated open as it passed them, and they read in gilt letters, "Truth Will Prevail." That seemed to them a prophecy of what was to come.

The elders took a room in Wilford Street with a widow by the name of Ann Dawson, as many widows earned a scanty living in that place by letting rooms. In the meantime young Joseph Fielding went in search of his brother James, who was pastor of a primitive Baptist congregation in Preston. He returned with an invitation for all the elders to visit his brother, who had already heard much about the church from his brother Joseph and two sisters, Mary and Mercy, who had not many years before left him for Canada.

Upon the day after the arrival in Preston, they all went to hear the Reverend James Fielding discourse in his own pulpit in Vauxhall Chapel. While the missionaries sat and prayed that they might be given a hearing, the Reverend Fielding went on with his sermon, closing by speaking of their brethren from America and inviting them to occupy his pulpit that afternoon. So it happened on July 23, his first Sabbath Day in England, Heber C. Kimball spoke in Vauxhall Chapel, Preston, the first sermon of the Restoration in a foreign land. A large congregation gathered at three o'clock that afternoon, perhaps prompted partly by curiosity, but they kept on coming. Orson Hyde followed him with a short testimony. That evening John Goodson and Willard Richards spoke, and the next Wednesday night Orson Hyde and Willard Richards. By this time people had begun to be convinced of the truth of the message and ask for baptism. Then it was that the Reverend James Fielding, his hospitality strained to the breaking point, refused them the further use of the chapel. From then on meetings were held each night in private homes until on Saturday night when it was decided to baptize those who had requested it the following morning in the River Ribble, which ran through Preston. Reverend James Fielding, when he heard of this, worked himself almost into a frenzy, even calling at the lodgings of his erstwhile friends and "forbidding" them to baptize those from his congregation. He was told they were of age and must choose for themselves. At nine o'clock in the morning of the second Sunday in England, nine persons were baptized in the River Ribble, a young man by the name of George D. Watt being the first. Among the group was Ann Elizabeth Walmsley and her husband, Thomas. Ann Elizabeth had been a victim of that dread malady, consumption, and was wasted to a mere skeleton, but at her baptism she was healed and lived to be a very old woman.

THE FIRST FOREIGN MISSION

Well started now on their mission, they felt need of further direction. The day after the first baptism they met in council at their lodging, and "continued in fasting and prayer, praise and thanksgiving," until two o'clock in the morning. It was determined at this meeting that Elders Richards and Goodson would go to the city of Bedford; Russell and Snyder to Alston in Cumberland, Isaac Russell's birthplace, where he still had relatives; and Kimball, Hyde, and Fielding would remain in and around Preston. In two or three days all had departed on their missions.

It happened that on the 2d day of August, Elder Kimball in visiting the new members, the Walmsleys, met a young girl by the name of Jeannetta Richards, a very intelligent young lady, the daughter of an independent clergyman in Walkerfold. She attended the services and two days later was baptized in the Ribble and confirmed at the water's edge, the first confirmation in England, for others had not yet received this rite.

On the 6th of August in the morning, Orson Hyde preached in the market place, and in the evening at the home of his landlady, Ann Dawson, now a member of the church. Some twenty-eight who had been baptized were confirmed and organized into a branch. Thus was passed the third Sabbath Day in England.

As the end of the week neared, Kimball received two letters from Walkerfold, one from Jeannetta Richards, the other from her aged father, inviting him to visit them and speak in Reverend Richard's church. Accordingly on Saturday afternoon he took the coach for Walkerfold, arriving there about dark. He was cordially met by all the family, had tea, and talked with them until a late hour. The old gentleman was much loved in his parish, having ministered to the people there for over thirty years. In the morning, Brother Kimball went into the pulpit with the Reverend John Richards, who prayed and gave out the hymns, and then presented the speaker from America. Soon after the elder began, the congregation was in tears. Similar meetings were held on

Monday and Wednesday, but on Thursday, when six of his young people gave in their names for baptism, Reverend Richards told the elder kindly that he must close his church to him.

Heber C. Kimball then started preaching in private homes. The old minister continued his kindness and cordiality and even attended the meetings, torn between his devotion to the church in which he had spent his life and his love for his daughter, Jeannetta. The next Sabbath morning Kimball, not to be outdone in cordiality, attended the church and listened once more to the Reverend Richards. He was surprised at the conclusion of the sermon to hear the old minister give out another appointment for him at the church. The next day he baptized two more of the congregation.

Eventually a branch was organized in Walkerfold.

Willard Richards was unmarried when he went to England, but not even zealous young missionaries are immune to the arrows of Cupid.

Two entries in Richards' journal tell a part of the story, time, March and September, 1838:

"I took a tour through the branches and preached. While walking in Thornley, I plucked a snowdrop, far through the hedge, and carried it to James Mercer's and hung it up in his kitchen. Soon after, Jeannetta Richards came into the room, and I walked with her and Alice Parker to Ribchester and attended meeting with Brothers Kimball and Hyde at Brother Clark's.

"While walking with these sisters, I remarked, 'Richards is a good name; I never want to change it; do you, Jeannetta?' 'No, I do not,' was her reply, 'and I think I never will.'"

"September 24, 1838, I married Jeannetta Richards, daughter of the Reverend John Richards, independent minister at Walkerfold, Chaigley, Lancashire. Most truly do I praise my heavenly Father for his great kindness in providing me a partner according to his promise. I receive her from the Lord and hold her at his disposal. I pray that he may bless us forever. Amen."[7]

At that time in England much excitement was caused in the religious world by one Robert Aiken, who had been for years preaching very successfully against "the corruptions of the established church." In his crusade against the Anglican Church, he had established chapels in many communities, in Liverpool, Preston, Manchester, Burslem, London, and elsewhere. Strangely enough, his preaching on the ancient prophecies and their latter-day fulfillment was suggestive of Alexander Campbell and Sidney Rigdon in the Western Reserve. He even predicted a latter-day church rising in fulfillment of the prophecies.

Soon after the missionaries came to England, many of the "Aikenites" united with the church, and Robert Aiken himself came to Preston to lecture against the "Mormons." The elders answered in their own meeting, and as Kimball says in his journal, "This discourse seemed to have a very good effect, and that week we had the pleasure of baptizing fifty into the kingdom of Jesus, a large number of whom were members of Mr. Aiken's church." Soon after, Aiken surprised even his own followers by returning to the orthodox Episcopal fold.

Wherever the missionaries went, they were in demand for preaching in the temperance halls, for temperance workers soon saw that "as soon as men obeyed the gospel they abandoned excesses in drinking; none of us drank any kind of spirits, porter, small beer, or even wine; neither did we drink tea, coffee, or chocolate."

On the first Sunday in September, 1837, the Saints in Preston commenced holding meetings in what was known as the "Cock Pit." It was a large place, capable of seating eight hundred persons. It had formerly been used for the purpose indicated by its

---

[7] Upon the first visit of the author to Nauvoo, Illinois, I saw a broken tombstone by the side of the walk, and examining it, read: "Jeannetta Richards, daughter of Reverend John Richards of Walkerfold, Chaidgely, Lancashire." Old residents told me she had "been buried in her bridal clothes" soon after she came to Nauvoo. Whether or not the tradition is correct, I do not know.

name, but had been converted into a hall.

Heber C. Kimball was much pleased with the new quarters. He describes it:

> The space for cock fighting was an area of about twelve or fifteen feet in the center, around which the seats formed a circle, each seat rising about a foot above another, till they reached the walls of twenty-five feet from the Old Church, probably the oldest church in pied by the singers, and our pulpit was the place where the judges formerly sat who awarded prizes at cock fights. We had to pay seven shillings per week for the use of it and two shillings per week for lighting, it being beautifully lit up with gas. The building was about twenty-three feet from the Old Church, probably the oldest church in Lancashire.[8]

Sometime in September, John Snyder returned from Cumberland, where he had been with Isaac Russell, and reported thirty baptisms there, though they had met with considerable opposition. In a few days he and Elder John Goodson left for America, leaving five of the seven missionaries to carry on. The church continued to grow at an almost incredible rate. On one occasion Fielding and Kimball took a five-day trip away from their headquarters at Preston and baptized one hundred and ten persons. They organized four branches, Downham, Chatburn, Waddington, and Clitheroe. The first night Kimball preached at Chatburn, standing on a barrel in a barn, he baptized twenty-five after the services. In confirming them and conversing with them, the service was continued until after midnight.

On Christmas Day, 1837, three hundred Saints convened in conference at Preston. One hundred little children were blessed. At length the time approached for the first missionaries, with the exception of the two younger men, Willard Richards and Joseph Fielding, to leave England. The last conference was to be held on April 8, 1838. By nine o'clock in the morning six or seven hundred people had assembled, there being about two thousand

---

[8] *Life of Heber C. Kimball*, page 166.

THE FIRST FOREIGN MISSION

members in all England, the result of eight months' missionary effort. There were branches at Preston, **Walkerfold, Penwortham,** Thornley, Ribchester, Chatburn, Clitheroe, Bashau Eaves, Waddington, Leyland Moss, Leyland Lane, Eccleston, Hunter's Hill, Buxton, Whittle, Dauber's Lane, Bamber Bridge, Longton, Southport, Downham, Burnley, Bedford, Alston, Brampton, Bolton, and Chorley. The branch in Preston numbered about four hundred, that in Bedford forty, and the one organized by Isaac Russell in Cumberland sixty.

"At five o'clock in the evening of that day," says Kimball, "we brought the conference to a close, having continued without interruption from nine o'clock in the morning, and appointed seven o'clock the same evening to deliver our farewell addresses. At the appointed time we repaired to the 'Cock Pit' which was crowded to excess."[9]

At nine o'clock on the morning of the 9th, the three, Kimball, Hyde, and Russell, took train from Preston to Liverpool, amply provided by the English Saints with money enough to take them back to Kirtland. The vessel upon which they sailed was their old friend the *Garrick*. Here Kimball won the lasting favor of the captain. For although Heber had become a successful preacher, he was still very much the farmer, and when the steward's very fine Durham cow, which was on the ship to furnish milk for the cabin passengers (a great luxury), took ill, Heber, by the application of home remedies, restored her to health, and the cabin passengers to their milk diet. "From that time forth, the steward sent us turtle soup, wine, and every luxury the ship afforded, and made us many presents," he tells us.

The *Garrick's* record as a fast sailer was still challenged, this time by the packet *New England*. As they passed Sandy Hook the *New England* was four or five miles ahead but the *Garrick* ran in an hour ahead of her, so that the word was passed out that it

---

[9] *Ibid.*, page 206.

was lucky to have Latter Day Saint missionaries on a boat.[10] The *Garrick* came in sight of New York on May 12, after a voyage of twenty-two and a half days.

Arriving in New York, they went in search of Elijah Fordham and found Orson Pratt also, who with his brother Parley had been busy in New York. They had organized a branch of eighty members since the missionaries sailed for England.

Many of those converted on this first mission to England are well known to the church. James Whitehead, whom many living still remember, was baptized in the River Ribble by Heber C. Kimball on October 18, 1837.[11] In a fortnight after, he was ordained a teacher, and before a month passed was a priest and sent out to preach and baptize. The descendants of those who joined the church on that first English mission who are still in the church, would probably make quite an army could all be assembled.

The mission in England continued, during the lifetime of the Prophet, to be a fertile field for missionary work. On the 19th of December, 1839, Apostles John Taylor, Wilford Woodruff, Elder Theodore Turley, and others sailed for England, followed three months later by Apostles Brigham Young, Heber C. Kimball, Parley P. Pratt, Orson Pratt, and George A. Smith, and Elder Reuben Hedlock. Their work was something like a repetition of that of their predecessors. In 1840 the first number of the *Millennial Star* was published in England, and for many years it was one of the main publishing places, first of the church and then of the faction in Utah, who still, after over ninety years' continuous publication, issue the *Millennial Star*.

After the church became well established in Nauvoo, the Saints in England flocked to "Zion" in large numbers.

---

[10] Preachers on a boat are usually accounted an ill omen by old sailors.
[11] From a sermon by James Whitehead in Lamoni, Iowa, May 22, 1887, reported by D. F. Lambert for the *Lamoni Gazette* and later printed in *Autumn Leaves*, Volume 1, page 199.

XXIX.—The Mission to New York City and the "Voice of Warning"

In July, 1837, Parley Pratt came to New York and looked up its one member, who was also an elder, Elijah Fordham. The missionary was a saddened man, for a few months before, the beloved wife of his youth, Thankful, had been laid to rest near the Temple, several hours after the birth of her longed-for child. She had enjoyed almost perfect health since the prophecy given to Pratt before he went to Canada, and had gone back there with him in July, 1836, and spent several months with the Saints, sharing for the first time his missionary work. After making provisions for his baby son, Pratt sought to lose himself in his work.

While he was attempting to get a hearing in New York, he wrote day and night on a book which he hoped would help him in his missionary work. He called it the *Voice of Warning,* and though he had to go in debt with the publisher to get four thousand copies printed, he hoped that he would soon be able to pay for the printing and have much needed help in his work. This book has been reprinted in many editions since that day, and translated into many different languages. Thousands have been converted by reading the *Voice of Warning.*

Never before had he encountered the difficulty in getting a hearing that he did in New York. From July to January, with the help of Elijah Fordham, he "preached, advertised, printed, published, testified, visited, talked, prayed and wept in vain." He was used to opposition, but no one opposed him. The people simply did not care to hear. Six members in six months! The case seemed hopeless. The six had been organized into a branch, and after renting "chapels" time after time, and seeing them empty, the little group satisfied themselves with a small upper room in Goerck Street.

One night in January, Pratt announced a prayer meeting that was to be his farewell to New York. He had concluded to give up the mission and go to New Orleans. The few members and several of their friends had retired to this little room for the last meeting. Each prayed in turn, when suddenly the room seemed filled with light, and one after another spoke in tongues and prophecy, mostly concerning the mission in New York.

Says Pratt of this occasion:

> The Lord said that he had heard our prayers, beheld our labors, diligence, and long-suffering towards that city, and that he had seen our tears. Our prayers were heard, and our labors and sacrifices were accepted. We should tarry in the city and not go thence as yet, for the Lord had many people in that city, and he had now come by the power of his Holy Spirit to gather them into his fold. His angels should go before us and co-operate with us. His Holy Spirit should give the people visions and dreams concerning us and the work of the Lord. He would make bare his arm to heal the sick and confirm the word by signs following, and from that very day forward we should have plenty of friends, money to pay our debts with the publishers, means to live, and crowds to hear us. And there should be more doors open for preaching than we could fill; crowds, who could not get in, should stand in the streets and about the entrance to try to hear us and we would know that the Almighty could open a door, and no man could shut it.

Pratt gave up going to New Orleans and concluded to try again, though he says, "I was almost ready to say in my heart with one of old: If the Lord should make windows in heaven, could these things be?"

In the meeting that night was a man by the name of David Rogers, a chairmaker whose heart was touched. He fitted up a large room, and seated it with the chairs from his warehouse, and invited Pratt to preach there. To his surprise the place was crowded. He then, with the help of one of the members, a joiner, secured another place for a regular meeting place, and seated it. That also, was generally crowded.

One night at the conclusion of a service, a man came to him and introduced himself. He was a Methodist minister by the name of Cox, and wished Pratt to come to his house near the East River and preach. He soon joined the church with all his family and many of his congregation. While preaching here a lady asked for preaching in her home in Willett Street, "For" said she, "I had a dream of you and of the new church the other night." There was still another invitation for preaching in Grand Street.

Within three weeks from the little prayer meeting in the upper room Pratt had fifteen preaching places in the city, all of which were filled to overflowing. A Free Thinkers' Society asked him to deliver a series of lectures in Tammany Hall, which he did. His practice now was to give eleven appointments for sermons each week, and spend his spare time in visiting! Not a long time passed before he added to his program almost daily baptismal services. The baptisms that winter were in the East River.

As had been promised, wonderful healings followed. One crippled woman arose and walked, instantly healed, another who had been in bed for four years with palsy was restored to health. This woman had complete paralysis of her right side also. She was restored to perfect health. A child of Wandle Mace, who was suffering from brain fever and was given up to die by physicians, was healed and in a few hours was playing about the floor. Upstairs above the Maces lay a woman who had been ill in bed for six months, and her child with her suffering from the same disease. Her mother was at the Maces when the baby was healed, and was so amazed that she rushed upstairs and told her daughter that there was a man below who healed the sick as in days of old, by laying on of hands in the name of Jesus. Mrs. Dexter, for that was the sick woman's name, had not a moment of skepticism. She exclaimed, "Thank God, then *I* can be healed." Pratt was called upstairs and both Mrs. Dexter and her child were healed in the hour, and a few days later she walked two miles from her home in Redford to the East River for baptism, and walked home again, in spite of the snow and rain, "the sidewalks being shoe deep in mud and snow." Mr. and Mrs. Wandle Mace, and Mr. and Mrs. Theodore Curtis, and Mrs. Dexter's mother were also baptized that day, all witnesses of the three miracles in Redford Street.

When the missionary left New York in April, 1838, he left branches of the church not only in New York, but in Brooklyn, Jersey, Sing Sing, and parts of Long Island, and had also baptized a group at Holliston, Massachusetts.

XXX.—Far West

IN THE MEANTIME, THE condition of the Saints in the West was becoming rapidly more precarious. They had been well received and kindly treated by the citizens of Clay County, but both the citizens and the Saints understood that the arrangement was to be but temporary. All were looking to a satisfactory readjustment of the Jackson County trouble and the reinstatement of the Latter Day Saints in their homes on the south side of the Missouri. But the months wore into years, and nothing was done. The election returns from Clay County in 1830 show but five hundred and sixty-seven voters. Should the Latter Day Saints settle among them, as it now appeared they might do, the original settlers would be completely outvoted, and that by "Yankees," too, and the Clay County settlers were Southerners to a man, with the exception of "Yankee Smith" and his sons at Smithville.

Considering the circumstances, there were few complaints against the "Mormons," and it is significant that none of them were ever arrested for crime in either Jackson, Clay, or Ray County, although any pretext would have been seized to do that. "The Mormons were in the main, industrious, good workers," said Judge Thorpe,[1] "and gave general satisfaction to their employers, and could live on less than any people I ever knew. Their women could fix up a good palatable meal out of what a Gentile's wife would not know how to commence to get half a dinner or breakfast. They had a knack of economizing in the larder, which was a great help to the men, as they had mostly to earn their bread and butter by day's work with wages about half what they are

---

[1] Thorpe's *Early Days in Missouri*, Letter No. 15.

now. The women were generally well educated, and as a rule quite intelligent, far more so than the men."[2]

Alex. W. Doniphan said, "While the Mormons resided in Clay County they were peaceable, sober, industrious, and law-abiding people, and during their stay with us, not one was ever accused of a crime of any kind."[3]

At length on June 29, 1836, the non-Mormon portion of Clay County population drew up a series of resolutions asking that the Latter Day Saints remove from their midst. The Latter Day Saint population was increasing so rapidly that they already outnumbered the settlers, and although they did not (out of courtesy) attempt to vote, if the time ever came when they should do so, they would gain complete political control of the county.

The settlers cited three reasons for this action:

(1) They are eastern men, whose manners, habits, customs, and even dialect are essentially different from our own.

(2) They are nonslaveholders, and opposed to slavery, which, in this peculiar period when abolition has reared its deformed and haggard visage in our land, is well calculated to excite deep and abiding prejudices in any community where slavery is tolerated and practiced.

(3) They are charged, as they have heretofore been, with keeping up a constant communication with the Indian tribes on our frontier, with declaring, even from the pulpit, that the Indians are a part of God's chosen people and are destined by heaven to inherit this land, in common with themselves.

The document was courteous. They did not even certainly charge the Saints with these misdemeanors but went on to say:

We do not vouch for the correctness of these statements, but whether they are true or false, their effect has been the same in exciting our community. In times of greater tranquillity, such ridiculous remarks might well be regarded as the offspring of frenzied fanat-

---

[2] This statement is doubtful, especially one that follows, saying many of the Mormon men could neither read nor write. An examination of the "testimony" given in Richmond in Senate Document 189, although many of the witnesses against the church sign with a mark, none of the Latter Day Saints do. It is well known that many prominent men in early Missouri history could not read or write. Judge Elisha Camron, for instance, "scarcely knew how to read or write." (See *History of Clay County*, by Woodson, page 85.)

[3] Kansas City *Journal*, June 5, 1881; *Saints' Herald*, Volume 28, page 197.

icism; but at this time our defenseless situation on the frontier, the bloody disasters of our fellow citizens in Florida and other parts of the South, all tend to make a portion of our citizens regard such sentiments with horror, if not alarm.

They admitted "that they had not the least right under the laws of the country and the Constitution to expel them by force," but they did "earnestly urge them to seek some other abiding place where the manners, the habits, and customs of the people would be more consonant with their own. For this purpose we would advise them to explore the Territory of Wisconsin. This country is peculiarly suited to their conditions and their wants."

This action was brought to the attention of the church leaders by a committee. Alexander W. Doniphan, who from the beginning had been their friend, adviser, and attorney, was now a member of the state legislature and sponsored a bill organizing the counties of Caldwell and Daviess from what was then chiefly unoccupied lands in the northern part of the State and part of Ray County. This part of the country was mostly prairie and was popularly supposed to be worthless, the few settlers already there being on the creeks and rivers. Therefore, the proposition was very pleasing to the Missourians. The bill was passed by the House December 23, 1836,[4] and by the Senate four days later.[5] It was understood that Caldwell was to be occupied and organized entirely by the Latter Day Saints. The county offices were to be in their hands, and they were to have a representative in the General Assembly of the State.[6]

Everybody thought this a complete and satisfactory solution of the Mormon problem, which then, as often since demanded attention and settlement. The Missourians were satisfied, because they had a poor opinion of the prairie soil of the proposed new county, which they declared was fit only for Mormons and Indians, and doubted whether it could ever be made really valuable. Moreover, they wished to rid themselves of the presence of the despised sect, whose members were

[4] *Missouri House Journal*, 1836-37, pages 188, 204.
[5] *Ibid.*, page 155.
[6] Stevens' *Missouri the Center State*, Volume 2, page 555.

clannish and exclusive, as well as unpleasantly peculiar. The Mormons were satisfied, because they wished for peace and security and desired above all to enjoy their religion undisturbed and undismayed.[7]

John Whitmer and W. W. Phelps had explored the new country and liked it. In the summer of 1836 and the fall of that year the Latter Day Saints flocked from Ray and Clay Counties and took up land, or, in the few cases where the land was already settled, bought out the original owner. "Nothing could have been fairer or more equitable than the acquisition of the territory afterwards called Caldwell County by the Mormons."[8]

The county seat was located at Far West, and courts were held in the schoolhouse. Justices of the peace were appointed in the different townships, and all the political machinery of the county was controlled by the Mormons. The militia of the county, all or nearly all Mormons, organized and mustered, and a regiment was formed under the laws of the State, of which Lyman Wight was colonel.[9]

> Settlements were now made up and down Shoal Creek and thickly along the southern tier of townships of the county. Mills were built, shops were opened, stores established, and the foundations for a thrifty and successful community were securely laid. . . .
> The townsite was entered August 8, 1836. The north half was entered in the name of W. W. Phelps, the south half in the name of John Whitmer; but both Phelps and Whitmer merely held the land in trust for the church. . . . The townsite was a mile square, giving plenty of room for the building of a large city. It was laid out in blocks 396 feet square, and the streets were alike on a grand scale. The four principal avenues were each 132 feet wide, and all the others 82½ feet wide. They diverged at right angles from a public square in the center designed as the site of a grand temple.
> Nearly all the first houses in Far West were log cabins. In a few months, however, some frames were built, a portion of the lumber being brought from lower Ray and a portion being whipsawed. Perhaps the first house was built by one Ormsby. This was in the summer of 1836. It is said that John Whitmer's house was built January

---

[7] *History of Caldwell and Livingston Counties, Missouri* (1886), Saint Louis National Historical Company, pages 116-118.
[8] *Ibid.*
[9] Lyman Wight held a commission from Lilburn W. Boggs, as colonel of the 59th Missouri Militia.

19, 1837. In the fall of 1836 a large and comfortable schoolhouse was built, and here courts were held after the location of the county seat, until its removal to Kingston. The Mormons very early gave attention to educational matters. There were many schoolteachers among them, and schoolhouses were among their first buildings. The schoolhouse in Far West was used as a church, as a town hall, and as a courthouse, as well as for a schoolhouse. It first stood on the southwest quarter of town, but upon the establishment of the county seat it was removed to the middle of the square.[10]

The whole movement had the indorsement of the church leaders as soon as they heard of the action taken by the citizens of Clay, a letter signed by Sidney Rigdon, Joseph Smith, junior, Oliver Cowdery, F. G. Williams, and Hyrum Smith, saying among other things:

We are sorry this disturbance has broken out—we do not consider it our fault. . . . We advise that you be not the first aggressors. Give no occasion, and if the people will let you dispose of your property, settle your affairs, and go in peace, go. You have thus far had an asylum, and now seek another as God may direct. Relative to your going to Wisconsin, we cannot say; we should think if you can stop short in peace, you had better. You know our feelings relative to not giving the first offense, and also of protecting your wives and little ones in case a mob should seek their lives. . . . Be wise, let prudence dictate all your counsels; preserve peace with all men if possible; stand by the Constitution of your country; observe its principles, and above all else show yourselves men of God, worthy citizens, and we doubt not the community ere long will do you justice and rise in indignation against those who are the instigators of your sufferings and afflictions.[11]

They were in general [says Judge Thorpe], quite industrious, working people, and soon a great change was made in the appearance of the country; huts of every description, from a log cabin to a board shanty, with fields and gardens were to be seen in all directions, mostly along the strips of timber which were found along the creeks and branches.[12]

By far the majority of Mormon settlers in this quarter were poor. Many of them were able to enter and improve but forty acres of land, and nearly all their houses were cabins. Like other pioneers, they had come to the country to better their conditions. To worship as they pleased and to be with their brethren were of course considerations. Every head of a family was guaranteed a home, and if he were unable

---
[10] *History of Caldwell and Livingston Counties.*
[11] *Messenger and Advocate,* Volume 2, pages 353-359; *Church History,* Volume 2, page 73.
[12] Judge Thorpe's *Early Days in Missouri.*

to buy one, it was given him from the lands held by the trustees of the church. Among so many, however, there could but be those of some wealth, as well as craftsmen of various kinds, skilled mechanics, and artisans. There were many persons of education and accomplishment. Schoolteachers were plenty, and schools were numerous.[13]

The despised prairie land proved to be wonderfully fertile, and in a short time government land bought before the Mormons came at one dollar and twenty-five cents an acre was held for ten dollars. Caldwell County was fast becoming settled, so there was no room for the incoming tide of converts from the East and South. The Mormon settlements spread into Daviess, Livingston, Clinton, and Carroll Counties.

It is claimed that all the Mormon settlements outside of this county were made with the prior consent of the inhabitants then living where the settlements were made; the consent was obtained, in nearly every instance, by the payment of money, either for the lands of the pioneer Gentiles or for some articles of personal property they owned. Money was scarce at that day, and although the pioneers did not approve of Mormon doctrines, they did approve of Mormon gold and silver, and they were willing to tolerate the one if they could obtain the other. But afterward certain of the Gentiles claimed that the Mormon occupation had been by stealth and fraud, and perhaps in some instances this was true.[14]

A colony of them entered Carroll County adjoining Caldwell on the southeast and established the little town of DeWitt, which the Saints used as a river port for Far West and their entire community. Still others went into Daviess and Clinton and settled there. In Daviess they established a flourishing colony in Colfax Township and another on the banks of the Grand River, a short distance from the present village of Jameson. Here a city was built and called Adam-ondi-ahman, or shortened, as it generally was by the Saints, to Diahman. Diahman thrived and soon completely outstripped in size the county seat of Gallatin.

Once more, with inextinguishable optimism, the Saints built

---

[13] *History of Caldwell and Livingston Counties*, page 119; *Church History*, Volume 2, page 112.
[14] *History of Caldwell County*, pages 118, 119; *Church History*, Volume 2, page 112.

homes and planted crops. Because of their many misfortunes, many of them were poor "yet they manifested a spirit to share with each other what they did have, and no one felt above any other."[15] Those who had cows, gave all their spare milk to their neighbors who had none, and cheerfully ate their corn bread without butter, those who had "dried fruits, wheat flour, or any other luxuries set them aside for the sick and feeble."[16] But that summer "good crops of corn and potatoes were raised, and when the following winter came all were well provided for, and the season was passed in comfort and peace."[17]

Every Thursday evening, prayer and testimony meeting was held in Far West, and every Sunday there were alternately preaching and Communion services. The Saints attended these meetings regularly. But few of them had teams, and those who had were forced to keep them working their crops all week, so rested their horses on the Sabbath day, and walked to church. "Sunday after Sunday," says one of these settlers, "quite a crowd of men, women, and children could be seen wending their way to the Central City."[18]

The most unfortunate thing that occurred at Far West was a rift in the ranks of the Saints themselves, resulting in the disaffection of some of their best and most honorable and energetic members, including all the Three Witnesses to the Book of Mormon, several members of the Quorum of Twelve, and others. Many of these came back later; others never did, though most of them, if not all, always retained their faith in the cardinal principles of the church. Examining the papers now after the lapse of nearly a century, it seems truly pathetic that these matters, trivial as they now seem, could not have been amicably adjusted. Instead, however, feeling ran to ridiculously frenzied extremes. Cowdery,

---

[15] "Elder John Brush," *Autumn Leaves,* Volume 4, page 66.
[16] *Ibid.* [17] *Ibid.*
[18] *Ibid.*, page 127. John Brush, Nehemiah Brush, his father, and Faucett, his father-in-law, entered eighty acres of land on Plum Creek. "Several miles on either side of them was neither friend nor foe." They all walked to Far West to church regularly.

in a letter to Joseph Smith, suggests that he thinks, had the President of the church been present, matters could have been adjusted.

The following is from Cowdery's letter to Bishop Edward Partridge dated Far West, Missouri, April 12, 1838, "I could have wished that these charges might have been deferred until after my interview with President Smith; but as they are not, I must waive the anticipated pleasure with which I had flattered myself of an understanding on those points, which are grounds of different opinions on some church regulations, and others which personally interest myself." The letter proceeds to answer in detail the charges preferred against him by Seymour Brunson, that he had sold his lands in Jackson County, which Cowdery reminds him "are alodial in the strictest construction of the term, and have not the least shadow of feudal tenures attached to them, consequently . . . may be disposed of by deeds of conveyance without the consent or even approbation of a superior. . . . This attempt to control me in my temporal interests, I conceive to be a disposition to take from me a portion of my constitutional privileges and inherent right . . . . I only, respectfully, ask leave, therefore, to withdraw from a society assuming they have such right.

"So far as relates to the other seven charges, I shall lay them carefully away and take such course with regard to them as I may feel bound by my honor to answer to my rising posterity.

"I beg you, sir, to take no view of the foregoing remarks, other than my belief in the outward government of this church. I do not charge you, or any other person who differs with me on these points, of not being sincere, but difference does exist, which I sincerely regret."[19]

The bishop's court sustained his defense on these points, and it is unfortunate that he did not choose to answer the other charges as frankly and freely. Unprejudiced writers now generally agree

---

[19] This letter is contained in full in *Americana*, September, 1910; pages 915-17, in an article by Brigham H. Roberts in which for the first time the papers in these important cases were published.

that the "authorities of the church moved hastily and without proper leniency,"[20] and thus lost to the church a man whose character through his entire lifetime stood absolutely unimpeached.

Similar judgment may be passed upon the handling of the case of David Whitmer. David Whitmer did not answer to the charges against him, as he refused to acknowledge the legality of the court. He even refused an appeal, declaring that if he did so he "would be acknowledging the correctness and legality of those former assumed councils, which I shall not do."[21]

Brigham H. Roberts, a historian of the Utah Church is authority for saying that the minutes of the High Council show:

After reading the above letter (refusing to take appeal for reasons named) it was not considered necessary to investigate the case, as he had offered contempt to the council by writing the above letter.... The counselors made a few remarks in which they spoke warmly of the contempt offered in the above letter, therefore thought he was not worthy to be a member in the church. And to this effect was the decision of the council.[22]

Should this information be correct (and there is no reason for doubting it), David Whitmer was expelled from the church without trial.

These unfortunate evidences of human misunderstanding in high places in the church are a matter of profound and eternal regret to those who revere the memory of these good men. The evil created by differences of opinion over trivial things did not go to their grave with these good men, but still exist, perpetuated by those who came after them.

The difficulties in Missouri were mainly an echo of those in Kirtland, following the bank failure and other financial troubles of 1837. No matter how stringent the times, nor how impossible it is for even the strongest banks to weather a national crisis, some

---

[20] In *Journal of History*, Volume 4, page 357 *seq.*, Heman C. Smith discusses in detail these cases in "Book of Mormon Witnesses."
[21] See *Americana*, September, 1910, pages 915-17 Article by Brigham H. Roberts.
[22] *Ibid.*

will always be found in every community to accuse the officers of any bank, which has failed, of dishonesty. The men and women who lost money in the Kirtland disaster were no exception. The church made a valiant and courageous effort to meet the indebtedness of the Kirtland Bank, although it burdened the progress of the church for many years, but at the moment there was no safety in the vicinity. The lives of the church leaders were threatened, and they were compelled to go to Missouri.

In Daviess County, the Whig and Democratic parties were almost equally divided. Everyone felt that the "Mormons" would cast the deciding vote, perhaps elect one of their own men, as they well could do. There was no secret balloting. Large sheets of paper were ruled into columns, a broad one for the name of each voter, and as many narrow ones as there were candidates, their names being written at the head of the column. The voter came and declared for whom he wished to vote, and the clerks, one, two, or three, as the necessity of population demanded, recorded the vote. Voting and counting votes was slow business, but the voters were few, and no one was crowded for time. At Gallatin, in Daviess County, there was an election on August 6, 1838, for sheriff. One of the candidates was Colonel William P. Peniston, a strong anti-Mormon, and he well knew that all the Latter Day Saints would cast their vote against him.

Judge Morin, who lived at Millport, told the Saints that an effort was to be made to prevent them from voting, that Peniston might be elected sheriff. He advised them to "stand their ground, and have their rights." But, hoping for better things, the men of the church, some of them, rode into Gallatin to vote on election day, all of them unarmed.

Now election day riots were no novelty in pioneer communities, either before or since the coming of the Latter Day Saints. About eleven o'clock in the morning, when whisky had had time to circulate pretty freely, Peniston mounted a barrel and began a harangue saying that if the Mormons were allowed to vote, others would lose their franchise.

One Dick Welding, properly drunk, added boisterously, "The Mormons weren't allowed to vote in Clay County no more than d—n Negroes." Samuel Brown of the Saints replied with unmistakable pertinency that people who could not read and write should not be allowed to vote. Welding resented the "insult" with a blow, which Brown parried with his umbrella, while Perry Durphy held the arm of his assailant. A general riot followed. Two Canadian boys, Abraham and Hyrum Nelson, were in the crowd. Someone knocked Abraham down, and his brother ran to his defense and began knocking down his attackers with the butt of his riding whip. Riley Stewart struck Dick Welding, and when Stewart was attacked, John Lowe Butler came to his assistance. Butler was a Kentuckian himself, for Apostles Patten and Woodruff had been converting a number of people in Tennessee and Kentucky, and the church now had its share of fighting Kentuckians. Very few of the "Mormons" had voted. They now withdrew a quarter of a mile from town and discussed matters. Butler was still angry. "We are American citizens," he said. "Our fathers fought for their liberty, and we will maintain the same principles." But seeing the mob, armed, approaching them, they bethought themselves of their unprotected wives and children and rode home, collected their families from their small cabins, secreted them in the hazel brush, and stood guard all night in the rain.

Thus was the match set to the fire that was to sweep the country in the next few months.

Report of the riot having been received at Far West in a much exaggerated form, Joseph Smith with two hundred others went on to Adam-ondi-ahman to investigate, but finding all quiet, turned around and called on a justice of the peace, Adam Black. This man had sold his farm to the Saints and had then united with the mobbers to drive the Saints out. Joseph knew this was contrary to his oath as a magistrate and accordingly asked him to sign a statement not to join with their enemies. Black later went before a justice and swore that he had been intimidated and forced to sign the statement, and a warrant was issued for the arrest of Joseph Smith, Lyman Wight, and others. They surrendered, and after a preliminary hearing before Judge Austin A. King were placed under bond to appear for trial September 7.[23, 24]

Continual depredations now ensued, property and crops were destroyed, men were assaulted, women attacked. The Latter Day Saints were afraid of their lives; the other settlers professed to be afraid also. Unfounded rumor on both sides played an important role. The Latter Day Saints appealed to General Atchison, who commanded a division of state militia. The other inhabitants appealed to Governor Boggs. General Atchison came to Far West and Adam-ondi-ahman, and reported to Governor Boggs, who had called out the militia. His report was highly favorable to the Latter Day Saints. He visited Millport, where an armed force was gathered under Austin, and also visited Diahman, where the Latter Day Saints under Wight were camped. He ordered the mob at Millport to disperse, established his camp between Millport and Diahman, and soon as quiet returned sent most of his militia home. Atchison thought the "Mormons" would be all right if they were let alone.

But instead of going home, the mob from Millport went to the little town of DeWitt, on the Missouri River, and besieged it. Joseph Smith and others went to their aid. General Parks was sent to view the situation and reported to General Atchison that two or three hundred "Mormons" were besieged by a much larger

---

[23]"Early Days on Grand River," by R. J. Britton, *Missouri Historical Review*, January, 1919.
[24]The legal papers growing out of Black's complaint and others are in the files of the Missouri State Historical Society, and were reprinted in the *Journal of History*, Volume 3, pages 485, 486. Spelling and punctuation have been reproduced as nearly as possible. They present an interesting commentary on the state of things educational in western Missouri

force of Missourians with a fieldpiece, the latter force expecting and receiving constant reinforcements from neighboring counties. The Saints in DeWitt appealed to Governor Boggs by special petition and messenger, but he refused to interfere. Realizing that further resistance would be useless, the Saints agreed to leave DeWitt if they were paid the appraised value of their property. The appraised value was less than the real value but this proved unimportant, since nothing was ever paid for the property thus stolen. The Saints packed their personal effects in wagons and started to Far West. Some were so weakened by hunger and exposure that they died on the way. This was on the 11th of October, 1838.

Encouraged by this success, the mob renewed their attack on Adam-ondi-ahman. General Parks hastened to Colonel Wight's home on "Tower Hill," and while in consultation with him, Agnes Smith[25] wife of Don Carlos Smith, who was absent upon a mission to the South (for even in the midst of trouble they had not forgotten to send out missionaries), came in with her two crying babies. She had been driven from her home in the night and had waded the river to take refuge at Colonel Wight's. Then it was that General Parks advised Wight to act in his own defense against the mob gathered at Millport. Wight was a regularly commissioned colonel in the militia. General Parks was his superior. The failure of the commanders of the militia sent to Daviess and Carroll Counties, among whom were Atchison, Doniphan, and Parks, was not due to indifference on their part, but to the fact that the troops under their command were bitter against the Mormons, and Atchison said he was afraid, everyday that passed, his men would desert his command and join the mob. From this movement of the "Diahman Boys" against the mob collected at Millport, arose the charge of treason against Lyman Wight and some others.

---

[25] Mother of Iva Donna Coolbrith, once poet laureate of California.

A Captain Samuel Bogart, of the State Militia of Ray County, had, it is said, obtained permission to police the northern part of Ray County. He and the men with him went from one little cabin home of the Saints to another, intimidating them, ordering them off, and even threatening to attack Far West. Wounded citizens began coming into Far West from that region and the cattle of the Saints were being used to provide food for Bogart's army.

Houses in Far West were soon full to overflowing, and hundreds of refugees were obliged to make their beds on the open prairies near the city. It was November again. One night six inches of snow fell upon the beds of the weary campers.[26]

At length a messenger brought a report that Bogart's band was to attack Far West the next day. In the general confusion, no one on either side knew who were militia and who were not. The Saints have always declared they thought Bogart was without legal authority for his acts of depredation. At any rate when this report came to Far West, acting under orders from General Parks to defend themselves, Captain David W. Patten (one of the twelve apostles), known among the Saints for a long time now as "Captain Fear Not," led a small company of the Far West Militia against the Bogart force, who were subsisting upon the Saints on and near Crooked River. Surprising them at daybreak October 25, they attacked the camp and being fired upon returned the fire. Says Judge Thorpe, "The alarm was so sudden, the camp in such a confused condition, that they made no formidable resistance until the company was right in among them, cutting right and left causing a perfect stampede, every man for himself. A few jumped down the bank of the creek, stopped long enough to fire a few shots back, and then retreated for dear life, each making the best of his way for home."[27] It was a costly

---

[26]"Elder John Brush," *Autumn Leaves,* Volume 4, page 130.
[27]Judge Thorpe's *Early Days in Missouri.*

victory for the Saints. Gideon Carter lay dead on the field, and David W. Patten and Patrick O'Banion, a young Saint, died that day.

As for Captain Samuel Bogart, his interest in the eviction of the "Mormons" waned, and he took no more active part in the struggle. However, he was yet to win distinction for himself in quite another way. By the time another twelve months had passed, the "Mormons" were safely out of Caldwell County, and an election was being held in November, 1839, to re-elect officers of the county to take the place of the evicted "Mormons." Then it was that Bogart remembered the leading role he had played in the "Mormon War," put himself up as a candidate, and was elected, too; the new citizens were not unmindful of services rendered. He never occupied in his office, or perhaps even knew he was elected. Just when the election day fun was reaching its height at the former site of the Saints' Far West, Bogart got into a quarrel with a young Batty, quickly flashed a pistol and shot him dead. Before the crowd could recover enough to apprehend him, he had cut across the country for home, selected his best horse, and reached Crooked River at Dale's Mill just as night fell. The stream was in flood, but he plunged in, holding onto his horse's tail, got safely ashore, and headed south toward Richmond. He visited a friend and borrowed two hundred dollars in gold with which he said he wished to enter a valuable tract of land. Rousing the ferryman at the Missouri River, he told him the same story, gave him a twenty-dollar gold piece, and told him to stay on the opposite side until noon the next day, by which time he would have the land entered in his own name. He never stopped going until he reached the new Republic of Texas, where "he attained considerable prominence," according to Missouri historians. He was indicted by a grand jury at Far West but was never arrested.[28]

---

[28]*History of Clinton and Caldwell Counties, Missouri,* by Johnson and McGlumphy, Historical Publication House, Topeka (1923).

In the meantime, Judge King, who had never forgotten the killing of his brother-in-law, Hugh Brazeale, in the brush with the "Mormons" in Whitmer's cornfield on the Big Blue, seized this opportunity to write to General Parks under the date of October 27, two days after Crooked River:

> Our relations with the Mormons are such that I am perfectly satisfied the arm of civil authority is too weak to give peace to the country. Until lately I thought the Mormons disposed to act only on the defense, but their recent conduct shows that they are the aggressors and that they intend to take the law in their own hands.[29]

The letter of Judge King and the reports that reached him from Crooked River now induced Governor Boggs to take action, and he placed General Clark in command over the head of Generals Atchison and Doniphan, General Atchison having refused the command. The instructions of Boggs were as follows:

> I have received information of the most appalling character, which entirely changes the face of things and places the "Mormons" in the attitude of an open and avowed defiance of this State. Your orders are, therefore, to hasten your operations with all possible speed. The Mormons must be treated as enemies and must be exterminated or driven from the State if necessary for the public peace.[30]

General Atchison indignantly left the militia he was commanding at Log Creek upon receipt of the Governor's orders, threw up his command, and returned to his home in Liberty, leaving General Lucas in command of his troops. Doniphan remained with his troops for a few days longer, replying to Governor Boggs that he "disregarded" that part of his order, "as the age of extermination is over."[31]

But before General Clark could arrive to take over his command, there occurred the most atrocious act of the whole "war," the attack on the undefended mill of Jacob Haun on Shoal Creek.

---
[29]*Missouri General Assembly Documents, Orders, Correspondence,* etc., pages 53, 54.
[30]"Facts Relative to the Expulsion of the Mormons from Missouri," by J. P. Green, *Argus,* 1839.
[31]Kansas City *Journal,* June 5, 1881, *Saints' Herald,* Volume 28, page 197.

Haun had come from Wisconsin several years before and built a very good mill on Shoal Creek. Clustered around it by the fall of 1838 were a good blacksmith shop and a half dozen small houses. Several families arriving from Ohio had camped there for a day or two, still living in their covered emigrant wagons. The Saints organized themselves for defense in case of an attack, but David Evans who had been put in charge, succeeded in arranging with the mob that they would be unmolested as long as they were peaceable, and life at the mill assumed its customary quiet routine until they were suddenly attacked on the afternoon of October 30 by an armed mob. While the women and children scattered to the timber which skirted Shoal Creek, the men grabbing their guns ran to the blacksmith shop and, though a mere handful, made a last desperate effort at defense. There were not many more than twenty men in the little camp, and the mob, most of them members of the Livingston County Militia (but General Clark insists acting without orders), numbered two hundred.

David Evans, seeing how completely they were outnumbered, attempted to surrender by running up a white flag. His signal was ignored. The blacksmith shop was surrounded, and the mob commenced firing through the chinks of the logs at the men huddled within. The few rounds of ammunition possessed by the beseiged Saints were soon exhausted. Evans opened the door, and all rushed out, most of them falling from the deadly fire of their enemy as they ran.

Coming upon the field, empty now save for the wounded and dead, the attackers killed their wounded victims. Upon the ground lay Thomas McBride, seventy-eight years of age, who had served under Gates and Washington in the Revolutionary War. A man named Rogers, approaching the old veteran where he had fallen, fatally wounded on his way to the blacksmith shop, asked for his gun. The veteran handed it to him, and the man, finding it loaded, deliberately put it against the old man's breast and fired, then proceeded to cut off his head with a corn knife and otherwise mangle and hack to pieces the body of his victim. William Reynolds (who called himself Runnels) entered the blacksmith shop, and finding only dead bodies, was about to retire when he noticed a ten-year-old boy, Sardius Smith, hiding under the bellows. He drew his rifle and shot the little fellow, and for many years boasted of his exploit, telling how the poor child "kicked and squealed" in agony, and justifying his act by saying, "Nits will make lice." The fate of Charley Merrick hiding under the bellows with the little Smith child was even more cruel. He ran out of the shop, was shot, and lay in agony for three weeks before he finally died.

Says one woman, who was widowed in this massacre, "When they had done firing, they began to howl, and one would have thought that all the infernals had come from the lower region. They plundered the principal part of our goods, took our horses and wagons, and ran off howling like demons."

"We pretty well cleaned the place out," said the victors.

One by one, as night fell, the survivors came out of the woods, looking for their relatives and friends. Three or four men remained, some of them wounded; the rest were women and children. Seventeen lay dead, fifteen wounded. Says Mrs. Amanda Smith, whose husband and 10-year-old boy were with the dead, and whose 7-year-old boy was badly wounded:

> It was sunset; nothing but horror and distress, the dogs filled with rage, howling over their dead masters; the cattle caught the scent of blood and bellowed; a dozen helpless widows, thirty or forty fatherless children screaming and groaning for the loss of husbands and fathers; the groans of the wounded and dying.

All gathered at the Haun home, and soon Sister Haun and others of the women had collected what they could to bandage the wounds of those still living and spent the night going from one to another, ministering as they could with their limited supplies. Morning came and it was apparent that something must be done with the dead. They could not lie unburied in the hot October sun, and there were not able-bodied men enough to bury them. There was a dry hole where someone had attempted to dig a well. Assisted by the women, the few able-bodied men placed the bodies one by one upon a plank, carried them to the well and slid them in. Some hay was thrown on top, and a layer of dirt. Meanwhile Colonel Jennings hastened away from the mill as twilight approached, and halted his battalion at Woolsey's where he prepared to pass the night. A few hours later, he imagined he heard cannon and a great tumult in the direction of Haun's Mill, betokening as he thought the advance of a large "Mormon" force against him. Rousing his men, he hastily broke camp, and moved rapidly eastward, never halting till he put the west fork of Grand River between him and his imaginary pursuers.

Two days later the men got up courage enough to return to the scene of their triumph, and taking possession of the mill, gathered the crops of the men they had killed, ground the corn, butchered the hogs and cattle, and a week or more later, when nothing was left for the widows and orphans who were still at the mill for want of any other place to go, they departed.

Olive Ames of San Bernardino, California, well known to the Saints of that State, was a survivor of that massacre. Polly Wood of western Iowa was another. Saints of Michigan, many of them, remember Hiram Rathbun, Sr., of Lansing, who was shot and crippled for life at Haun's Mill, although he was a mere boy at the time. There are doubtless others now in the church, who have heard the story from the lips of their parents or grandparents.

The following day Clark surrounded Far West and upon November 1 secured the leaders of the church as prisoners. It was the general consensus of opinion of the officers that these men would be shot. Judge Thorpe remembers that Colonel Doniphan had said he was prepared to defend the prisoners with his own life if necessary.[32] The leaders were given a hasty trial by "court martial" (although some, Joseph Smith and Sidney Rigdon and perhaps others, were not members of the militia) and sentenced to be shot at sunrise in the square of Far West on November 2, the next morning. A messenger was sent to General Doniphan with the following order:

Brigadier-General Doniphan, Sir: You will take Joseph Smith and the other prisoners into the public square of Far West and shoot them at nine o'clock tomorrow morning.
Samuel D. Lucas,[33]
Major-General, Commanding.

Doniphan replied promptly:

It is cold-blooded murder. I will not obey your order. My brigade shall march for Liberty tomorrow morning at eight o'clock, and if you execute those men I will hold you responsible before an earthly tribunal, so help me God![34]
A. W. Doniphan,
Brigadier-General.

Samuel D. Lucas immediately countermanded the order and entered into a lengthy correspondence with Fort Leavenworth in an attempt to justify his course.

Years after, when Young Joseph attempted to compliment the now famous General Doniphan upon his courage, he disclaimed any special bravery. He was a young man then, just a few months past thirty. He said, "I did not think anything about whether it was brave or not. I came of a long-lived stock and was young, and thought that I could not afford to go through what might be a long life with my hands stained with the blood of my fellow men."[35]

General Clark proceeded with his work, and having forced the Saints to agree to leave the State by the first of May, 1839, and

---
[32] Thorpe's *Early Days in Missouri.*
[33] *History of Caldwell and Livingston Counties,* page 137.
[34] *Ibid.*
[35] *Church History,* Volume 4, page 578.

sent about sixty more prisoners to Richmond, he considered his task well performed.

The Saints memorialized the state legislature to reimburse them for their property, but nothing came of it. Later they sent a delegation to Washington, where with the aid of Judge Richard M. Young, United States Senator from Illinois, the matter was put before Congress, but it received only assurances that the Federal Government could not interfere in state affairs.

There was so much criticism in the public press of the action of the Missouri authorities in expelling in so arbitrary a manner several thousand of the State's citizens that the legislature which met in November, 1838, appointed a joint committee to investigate the Governor's conduct of the "War."[36] Governor Boggs, in a communication transmitting papers and information, defended his course.[37] After some wrangling, the legislature passed a resolution forbidding the publication of any documents, orders, or correspondence, either printed or copied, in relation to the affair.[38] This restriction was in force for two years. The legislature then proceeded to pass an appropriation of two thousand dollars to alleviate suffering in Daviess and Caldwell Counties, but Latter Day Saints had little benefit therefrom. One of the prime movers in their behalf was their old friend Michael Arthur of Clay County, who wrote to the legislature, of which he had once been a member, as follows:

Liberty, November 29, 1838.
M. Arthur, Esq., to the Representatives from Clay County.
Respected Friends: Humanity to an injured people prompts me at present to address you thus: You were aware of the treatment (to some extent before you left home) received by that unfortunate race of beings called the Mormons, from Daviess, in the form of human beings, inhabiting Daviess, Livingston, and a part of Ray County; not being satisfied with the relinquishment of all their rights as citizens

---
[36] *Missouri House Journal*, 1838-39, pages 24, 32.
[37] *Ibid.*, pages 78, 79.
[38] *Missouri Senate Journal*, 1838-39, page 36.

and human beings, in the treaty forced upon them by General Lucas, by giving up their arms and throwing themselves upon the mercy of the State and their fellow citizens generally, hoping thereby protection of their lives and property, are now receiving treatment from those demons that make humanity shudder, and the cold chills run over any man not entirely destitute of any feeling of humanity. These demons are now constantly strolling up and down Caldwell County, in small companies armed, insulting the women in any and every way, and plundering the poor devils of all the means of subsistence (scanty as it was) left them, and driving off their horses, cattle, hogs, etc., and rifling their houses and farms of everything therein, taking beds, bedding, wardrobe, and all such things as they see they want, leaving the poor Mormons in a starving and naked condition.

These are facts from authority that cannot be questioned, and can be maintained and substantiated at any time. There is now a petition afloat in our town, signed by the citizens of all parties and grades, which will be sent you in a few days, praying the legislature to make some speedy enactment applicable to their case. They are entirely willing to leave our State so soon as this inclement season is over; and a number have already left, and are leaving daily, scattering themselves to the four winds of the earth.[39]

General Clark had in the meantime arrested some forty men, supposed to be implicated in attacks on Millport, Gallatin, and Crooked River, and had taken them to Richmond. These were given some sort of a hearing before Judge King at Richmond. Joseph Smith and six others were remanded to Liberty Jail and others held at Richmond. Here they were held in the most squalid and miserable surroundings all winter, while authorities wrangled over what should be done with them. Chained together, the men slept on the rough stone floor with only straw for a bed, and insufficient blankets to keep them warm. Some of them were quite ill, Joseph Smith with the "face ache," almost too miserable at times to note what was going on, while Sidney Rigdon took a fever and lay in chains, growing steadily worse, until he lost about eighty pounds' weight and was reduced to a state of emaciation. Doniphan, still their attorney, fearful for his life, asked the court for a writ of habeas corpus. Doniphan, noted for eloquence him-

---

[39]*Church History*, Volume 2, pages 268, 269.

self, told the story in his old age, "and the remembrance of it lit up his aged face with a glow of animation."

Elder Rigdon had few if any friends there, about one hundred were gathered, the most of them "Mormon eaters," as they were called, and terribly excited against those under arrest and in custody. After the counsel had argued the legal conditions of the case, Elder Rigdon desired General Doniphan to inquire of the Judge if he might speak in his own behalf. The Judge said, "Certainly." Elder Rigdon arose and began; and says the General, "Such a burst of eloquence it was never my fortune to listen to. At its close there was not a dry eye in the room; all were moved to tears."

At its close the judge said, "The prisoner is discharged the custody of the court. Mr. Rigdon is free to go his way."

The effect of Elder Rigdon's words was such that one of the leading men of the crowd picked up his hat, and, turning to the bystanders, said, "We came here determined to do injury to this man. He is innocent of crime, as has been made to appear. And now, gentlemen, out with your money and help the man to return to his destitute family." He circulated the hat, and money was showered into it till he placed a hundred dollars in Elder Rigdon's hands, with the remark, "Now, old gentleman, make the quickest time possible to your family, who need you and your help."[40] This was January 29, 1839.

Another incident of those days that Doniphan was fond of relating is vouched for by Leonidas M. Lawson, a former resident of Clay County, Missouri, who says in the *American Magazine* for December, 1910:

In the year 1863, I visited General A. W. Doniphan in his home in Liberty, Clay County, Missouri. This was soon after the devastation of Jackson County, Missouri, under what is known as Order No. 11. This devastation was complete. Farms were everywhere destroyed, and the farmhouses were burned. During the visit, General Doniphan related the following historical facts and personal incidents.

On one occasion General Doniphan caused the sheriff of the county to bring Joseph Smith from the prison to his law office, for the purpose

[40] *Saints' Herald*, August 2, 1884; Volume 31, page 490.

of consultation about his defense. During Smith's presence in the office, a resident of Jackson County, Missouri, came in for the purpose of paying a fee which was due to the firm of Doniphan and Baldwin, and offered in payment a tract of land in Jackson County.

Doniphan told him that his partner, Mr. Baldwin, was absent for the moment, but as soon as he had an opportunity he would consult him and decide about the matter. When the Jackson County man retired, Joseph Smith, who had overheard the conversation, addressed General Doniphan about as follows:

"Doniphan, I advise you not to take that Jackson County land in payment of the debt. God's wrath hangs over Jackson County. God's people have been ruthlessly driven from it, and you will live to see the day when it will be visited by fire and sword. The Lord of hosts will sweep it with the besom of destruction. The fields and farms and houses will be destroyed and only the chimneys will be left to mark the desolation."

General Doniphan said to me that the desolation of Jackson County, forcibly reminded him of this remarkable prediction of the Mormon prophet.

The *American* goes on to quote from a Mr. A. Saxey:

In the spring of 1862, my regiment went south, and it was during that time that Order No. 11 was issued; but I was back there again in 1864, during the Price raid and saw the condition of the country. . . . I went down on the Blue River. We found houses, barns, outbuildings, nearly all burned down, and *nothing left standing but the chimneys.*[41]

Doniphan sometimes remarked, "A nicer lot of men I never knew [speaking of the Saints], kind, neighborly, and upright."

Finally, in April, 1839, the prisoners at Liberty were taken to Gallatin for trial. General Doniphan, after the court had proceeded a few days, became convinced that he could not get a fair trial in Gallatin, and secured a change of venue to Boone County. While on the way there in the custody of the sheriff, the prisoners were permitted to escape, probably by collusion with other authorities who had become tired of the contest and did not know what to do with their prisoners.

Those at Richmond were also taken to Boone County and lodged in jail, from whence all but one escaped on July 4, 1839.

---

[41]*American Magazine*, December, 1910.

That one, Luman Gibbs, came to trial and was acquitted.

During all these troubles, missionaries were at work in every nook and corner of the United States, and Saints were pouring into Missouri, only to be turned back as they approached the former home of their friends. Charles Ross, who was a Gentile moving into Missouri, described the method of these guards in his testimony in the Temple Lot Suit:

> When I came to Keytesville, I heard there was a wounded Mormon there. After I got there, there was a guard there, and they examined everybody that came up, and if they had wagon boxes on their wagons, they were not allowed to go through without some kind of an examination. We had some niggers and some hounds with us, and they said we were not Mormons and let us go through.[42]

The trek across the State in the dead of winter by these poor exiles was attended with suffering, privation, and often death. Many families were separated. Some of those widowed in the Haun's Mill massacre were among the number. Mrs. Amanda Smith whose husband and son were killed on that occasion says, "I started the first of February for Illinois without money (mob all the way), drove our own team, slept out of doors. I had five small children; we suffered hunger, fatigue, and cold."

In Far West, preparation was made for the evacuation of the city. They buried their printing press in the night—in the dark of midnight, and piled a straw stack over it. When their prophet was taken prisoner, all his papers were in the hands of his secretary, James Mulholland, a young Canadian and a recent convert. Isaac Russell of Toronto, one of the earliest converts in that city, had become a pioneer missionary in Canada. Shortly before he left the United States as one of the first missionaries to England, Russell had preached in the little village of Churchville, Ontario, where quite a number came into the church, among them William and Wilson Law, Sampson Avard, and an Irish family by

---

[42] Charles Ross testifying in Temple Lot Suit. Plaintiff's Abstract of Evidence.

the name of Scott. Mulholland had married Sarah Scott, the youngest of the Scotts, and therefore shared their home. The family had just arrived in Far West on September 2, but the young scribe knew the value of the papers entrusted to his care, among which was the precious revision of the Scriptures. He feared he would be assailed by the mob as so many men had been and wished to protect the church papers. Ann, the eldest of the Scott sisters was thirty-three years of age, unmarried and unqualifiedly devoted to the church. To her, Mulholland entrusted the papers, thinking the mob would be less liable to molest her. She took no chances. She made two cotton bags of sufficient size to contain them, and sewing a band around the top ends long enough to button about her waist, carried them under the folds of her dress in the daytime "when the mob was around" and slept with them under her pillow at night. When Emma Smith was leaving Far West for Illinois, Ann Scott gave the papers into her keeping and she carried them in the same way with her across the State of Missouri and over the icebound Mississippi.[43]

It cannot be denied that there were two sides of the controversy, but an impartial observer [writes a local historian], in the light of history is forced to the conclusion that the expulsion of the Mormons from the State was neither justified nor necessary, and was a mistake of the gravest kind on the part of the authorities.[44]

---

[43] *Autumn Leaves,* Volume 4, page 18. "Spiritual Experiences," by Ann Davis [nee Scott] of Lyons, Wisconsin.
[44] *History of Caldwell County,* by W. H. S. McGlumphy.

XXXI.—Nauvoo*

*I*T WAS IN THE LATE WINTER of 1838-1839 that the followers of Joseph Smith straggled across the Mississippi to Quincy, a ragged, poverty-stricken band, bitter with the memory of Haun's Mill and Crooked River, but burning with a religious zeal that persecution could not quench and opposition only fanned into flame. The people of Quincy had long been on strained relations with those on the other side of the river. The Missourians claimed that their slaves, once crossed into Quincy, were not only harbored by the people of Quincy, but even helped on their way to freedom in Canada. The feeling reached fever pitch when in 1836, a Doctor Nelson, a brilliant preacher who had a private school in Palmyra, Missouri, and who was by sentiment a strong abolitionist, made an unwise remark in a camp meeting and had to flee for his life. He ran through high grass and brush to the river and was nearly caught, but finally reached Quincy, wet and exhausted. Following this, many fiery messages were exchanged, and relations anything but amicable had since obtained.

Here was another opportunity to reach a hand to the oppressed from Missouri, and the Quincy patriots, who like the Saints were mostly from the East (Maine and Ohio), offered no uncertain asylum to the Saints as they straggled across the river.

Among them was Emma Smith. She knew not where her husband was, nor whether he was dead or alive. In her arms were her two smallest children, Alexander and Frederick. The older two, Julia and little Joseph, clung to her skirts, as she crossed the frozen river on the ice. It was the 15th day of February, 1839,[1] and bitterly cold.

---

*Adapted and expanded from "In Old Nauvoo," by author, *Vision*, Volume 45, page 3.
[1] *Historical Record*, Volume 8, page 735.

Before leaving Missouri, she had visited her husband in prison at Liberty, Missouri. Neither knew whether or not it would be their last meeting. On that occasion, he had placed his hands upon little Joseph and blessed him. Although so very young at the time, the boy did not forget that blessing pronounced upon his head "by lips tainted by dungeon damps, and by the Spirit confirmed through attesting witnesses."[2]

It remained for one of his father's fellow prisoners to remember some of the words spoken on that occasion. Lyman Wight, writing to the editor of the *Northern Islander* published by Jas. J. Strang, from Medina, Texas, in July, 1855, wrote, "Now, Mr. Editor, if you had been present when Joseph Smith called on me shortly after [we] came out of jail to lay hands with him on the head of a youth and heard him cry aloud 'You are my successor when I depart,' and heard the blessing poured on his head.[3] I say had you heard all this, and seen the tears streaming from his eyes, you would not have been led by blind fanaticism or a zeal without knowledge."[4]

Emma with her family found shelter at the home of Judge Cleveland in Quincy where she was made welcome and kindly cared for throughout the rest of the winter. Others of the Saints found homes with prominent families in Quincy, and received kindly treatment from all.

Not far from Quincy, Illinois, there resided upon his broad acres a wealthy Virginian by the name of George Miller. During the so-called "Mormon war," Mr. Miller, who was a lover of a good argument, took a business trip to Missouri, and there in a tavern one night engaged in a very lively discussion on the merits of the treatment accorded the Saints (of whom he was

---

[2] *True Latter Day Saints' Herald*, Volume 14, page 105.
[3] This may not have been the same occasion, referred to by Young Joseph, but I am inclined to think that it was, and that Wight referred to the blessing, as not taking place in the cell room of the jail, but in some other portion of the building, where the men had been permitted to meet their visitors. There may have been another occasion when Wight assisted in such a ceremony.
[4] From Lyman Wight's letter-book, in Heman C. Smith collection.

hearing for the first time). With the support of one other, and with every other man in the crowded room against him, he denounced roundly the persecution to which this people had been subjected. He had never seen a "Mormon," never until that night heard of one, but as he rode home he thought over the argument that had occurred at the tavern, and became more and more satisfied with himself for his outspoken defense of this peculiar sect.

Later he heard that numbers of them were refugees in Quincy, and he somewhat impulsively determined to ride over to Quincy and invite a family of "Mormons" to be tenants upon one of his farms. He readily enough secured "Father" and "Mother" Smith, the parents of the Prophet himself, and some of their family who were at home. He became greatly interested in his tenants, driving in his carriage nearly every Sunday afternoon to listen to "Father" Smith tell of his experiences. One Sunday, returning from such a trip, he met another carriage, and in it, a large man whom he seemed instinctively to know, though he had never met him, was the "Prophet Joseph Smith." There and then before a word ever passed between them his heart went out in an allegiance to the stranger in the other carriage—an allegiance that was never to waver while life lasted. This man is characterized by Dr. H. W. Mills in his article *"De Tal Palo Tal Astilla"* (A Chip off the Old Block) in the annual Publications of the Historical Society of Southern California for 1917 as having "indomitable energy, self-confidence, self-reliance in his own line, and courage that will not be denied and does not know the word 'can't'." George Miller soon joined the church, and after the beloved Bishop Edward Partridge died, succeeded him in 1841 as Presiding Bishop of the church.

Nor were the politicians in the older State of Illinois averse to the incoming tide of voters. On the eve of the most exciting election in the history of their state, the game of politics was being played in earnest. Almost evenly divided politically between

Whig and Democrat, they welcomed the host of "Mormon" voters with wide-open arms. Stephen A. Douglas, "The Little Giant," cultivated the friendship of the Prophet and became a welcome guest at Nauvoo and in the Smith home. Lesser politicians followed his example.

Judge Richard M. Young, Democratic Senator from Illinois (1837-1843), presented in Congress the petition of the Saints for redress, took care to have the name "Commerce" changed to Nauvoo, saw that George W. Robinson, Rigdon's son-in-law, received appointment as postmaster, and urged the necessity of having the Nauvoo mail carried twice a week from Carthage, saying that the "additional expense would not be more than one hundred and fifty dollars, as the mail is carried on horseback." In the same letter he asks that his respects "be presented to Mr. Smith."[5] Young was a tall, handsome Kentuckian with "the polished manners of a Chesterfield,"[6] and the help he gave Elias Higbee was friendly and ardent while Higbee was in Washington, seeking redress for the Missouri troubles. He even advanced money from his private funds to aid the Saints' commission while it was in the city. He is one of the list of prominent men of whom Joseph Smith recorded in his journal, "They will long be remembered by a grateful community for their philanthropy to a suffering people, and whose kindness on that occasion is indelibly engraved on the tables of our hearts in golden letters of love."[7] Another named in that list was the fiery, redheaded young lawyer, Ralston, from Quincy, who was accused in the Whig press of the day as "coquetting with the Mormons." This was the man who helped to defend Joseph Smith in his trial before Judge Douglas at Monmouth.

Associated with Ralston was Orville H. Browning, also of Quincy, afterward Honorable O. H. Browning, secretary of the

---

[5]*Church History*, Volume 2, page 450.
[6]"Forgotten Statesmen of Illinois," by Doctor J. F. Snyder, *Publication No. 11* of Historical Library of Illinois (1906).
[7]"Proclamation [of First Presidency] to the Saints Scattered Abroad," January 15, 1841. *Times and Seasons*, Volume 2, pages 273-277.

interior under President Johnson, a "scholarly lawyer and statesman,"[8] and the man to whom Joseph Smith wrote his last letter[9] just a few hours before he was shot to death. He asked Browning to come to Carthage to assist in his defense. In the case at Monmouth before Judge Douglas, Browning spoke so well that the mother of the Prophet felt he was "moved upon by the Spirit that was given to him in answer to the prayers of the Saints."

In the brief period of a few weeks after his arrival in Illinois, Joseph Smith had made choice of the malaria-ridden lowland about the deserted village of Commerce, an experimental community, then consisting of several empty farmhouses surrounded by unweeded farmlands. The two great political parties vied in favors to the incoming tide of voters. The year 1840 was a presidential year, the most exciting campaign that Illinois had ever seen. The Illinois Legislature, trembling on a hair-trigger balance between Whig and Democrat, voted the infant city, now rechristened Nauvoo, a charter unique in the annals of city government. John C. Bennett, then quartermaster of the State of Illinois, lobbied the charter through political shoals with a suavity born of experience. Among those favoring the charter in the lower house was an awkward, long-limbed, but aspiring lawyer by the name of Abraham Lincoln, whose heart, notoriously tender towards all human suffering, was so deeply moved by the stories of massacre and suffering related, that he rushed forward to the bar at the

---

[8] "Famous Men I Have Known in the Military Tract," *Transactions of Illinois Historical Society* (1908), page 157.

[9] "Lawyer Browning   Carthage Jail
"Sir: June 27th, 1844

"Myself and brother Hyrum are in jail on charge of treason, to come up for examination on Saturday Morning, 29th inst. and we request your professional services, at that time, on our defence, without fail.
"Most Respectfully
"Your Sevt.
"Joseph Smith

"N. B. There is no cause of action for we have not been guilty of any crime, neither is there any just cause of suspicion against us—but certain circumstances make your attendance very necessary.   J. S."
Addressed to "Lawyer Browning, Durney Adams County, Illinois."
From original letter in Daniel Macgregor collection.
Joseph Smith and His Progenitors, by Lucy Smith, pages 344, 345, Lamoni Edition.

final passing of the bill to congratulate Bennett personally and wish the new city success.

In the fall of 1840, the first company of English immigrants arrived on the "North America." Through these the church authorities became first informed of the abuse of immigrants by the ship companies and set about with characteristic Latter Day Saint passion for organization to correct matters.

On account of economic conditions in Europe at the beginning of the nineteenth century there was a period of unprecedented emigration. Between 1841 and 1851 the United Kingdom was reduced by over two millions. Unscrupulous ship owners were not slow to seize upon the opportunity, and until conditions came to be a public scandal, overcrowded their ships, made no effort at furnishing sanitation or comfortable quarters, and otherwise abused their unfortunate passengers. Ships furnished only water and "firing," that is fires upon which the emigrants cooked food brought from home. The ships were often so crowded that each family had a chance at a fire only once in several days, and when a ship was in port, even though it might be for a week at a time, all fires must be out. Every effort was made to keep the emigrants below decks, where they were herded in miserable and loathsome quarters. When Parliament eventually made an investigation, it was found that a ship seldom reached America without the loss of from 1 to 10 per cent of its emigrant passengers with typhoid fever, caused by polluted water. One harbor master at Quebec, in his report to Parliament, claimed that it was easy for him to distinguish at distance of gunshot, "an immigrant ship by the odor alone."[10] Such conditions were intolerable to the average English convert, therefore something must be done.

One fact only dominated the situation for the church, English Saints must be transported to Zion some way, and that without

---

[10] *Story of Emigration from the United Kingdom to North America*, 1763-1912 page 107.

delay. An agent for immigration was appointed in England, who managed the outfitting of Latter Day Saint companies by co-operative buying. As time went on, ships were chartered when necessary. Each company, before sailing, elected officers and adopted regulations to govern the trip. From morning prayer to "lights out," everything was carried on with military regularity. Joseph Smith reported to a conference in Nauvoo that they were bringing European converts to Nauvoo at the average cost of from three pounds fifteen shillings to four pounds per person, depending upon the length of the voyage. Speaking of the Saints some years later, the Cambridge *Independent Press* said, "There is one thing which in the opinion of the House of Commons, the Latter Day Saints can do, *viz.*, teach Christian shipowners how to send poor people decently, cheaply, and healthfully across the Atlantic."[11]

Once in Nauvoo, enthusiastic church members wrote to friends at home that they could live for one-eighth what they had in Old England, with beef and pork at a penny a pound, Indian meal sixty pounds for a shilling, and butter four pence a pound. True, they needed to live for less, for the infant industries of Nauvoo were taxed to the utmost to provide employment for all who came. Skilled tradesmen found themselves in a strange country, dependent upon the charity of their brethren, but that charity was cheerfully given, and they were in "Zion."

The church became proud possessors of a small steamboat, "Maid of Iowa," built in 1842 at Augusta, Iowa, by Levi Moffitt and Dan Jones, which helped to transport the immigrants up the

---

[11] *From Liverpool to Great Salt Lake Valley*, by Frederick Piercy, Liverpool, 1855, page 18, quotes the *Morning Advertiser* of June 2, 1853, as follows: "On Tuesday," says the London correspondent of the Cambridge *Independent Press*, "I heard a rather remarkable examination before a committee of the House of Commons. The witness was none other than the supreme authority in England of the Mormonites [Elder S. W. Richards] and the subject upon which he was giving information was the mode in which the emigration . . . is conducted. . . . He gave himself no airs but was so respectful in his demeanor, and so ready in his answers, that, at the close of the examination he received the thanks of the Committee in rather a marked manner. . . . There is one thing which in the opinion of the Emigration Committee of the House of Commons, they [the L. D. Saints] can do—teach Christian shipowners how to send poor people decently, cheaply, and healthfully across the Atlantic." Although this investigation was at a somewhat later date, the system was developed early and carried out with efficiency from the beginning of immigration to "Zion".

river to Nauvoo under the able captaincy of Dan Jones, the proselyting Welshman.[12]

So thousands came to Nauvoo, although it took their last shilling to pay their passage. Those who had no shillings left to buy "Indian meal," found "shorts" at Newell Knight's mill on the river and got through the winter by making porridge of that. Many were the homesick hearts in those days of readjustment, but ere long prosperity began to dawn on the little city by the river. Before that day, not a few victims of "fever and ague" found rest in the growing cemetery east of Nauvoo. It was not easy to be courageous. England might be "Babylon," but it was home, and many an English housewife sighed over her first shilling's worth of corn meal as she thought of the snowy-white loaves of the jolly English bakers and the cozy neighborliness of snugly built English villages far from a wide, frozen river and a wilderness of woods. Just as fervently, New England Saints in their rude log cabins thought of old elms tapping on many-paned windows, of rains whispering in the leaves of ancient "laylock" bushes, of winged armchairs in front of roaring fires on winter nights, and enormous kitchens with the black bulk of fragrant kettles against the red glow of embers.

Little wonder, then, as Hortensia Merchant wrote,[13] "there was almost every kind of house" in Nauvoo; for when the new settler was at last able to build for himself, the long dreams of the homeland went into the wood, brick, and stone. Old-world houses, filled with the finest examples of English cabinetmakers' art, stood side by side with green-shuttered New England mansions of purest colonial type.

---

[12] Augusta, Iowa, a little village situated on the Skunk River in Des Moines County, Iowa, about ten miles southwest of Burlington, and sixteen miles in a straight line northeast of Nauvoo. Here in 1835 Levi Moffet, one of the first settlers, built the first water-power "flouring" mill in the state of Iowa.

[13] In a letter written from Nauvoo, January 15, 1844. See "Testimony of the Past". by Alma Fyrando, *Journal of History*, Volume 3, pages 252, 253. Hortensia Merchant was the wife of Lucius Merchant. They left the western migration at Winter Quarters and spent the remainder of their lives near Magnolia, Iowa. They became members of the Reorganized Church.

Perhaps the first problem that confronted the Saints was the reclamation of the swampy lowland, upon which part of the city was built.

The whole community had been stricken almost at once with malaria. Only one person in every ten was well. Hardly a family but lost at least one member and in one case, five adults from one family died within the week.[14] The home of Joseph Smith, "the old Homestead" was filled with the sick, while the family occupied a tent in the yard.[15] Other homes were similarly filled with dead and dying, for the scourge struck them before they were fairly established in their new home. The hunger, cold, and privation suffered through the past winter and spring in Missouri had so undermined their resistance, that almost no one was immune.

Gradually this land was drained, the Saints were persuaded to use water from deep wells instead of surface water, and the scourge of fever began to disappear. Advertisements for pills and powders that would surely cure "chills and fever" no longer appeared with such frequency on the last page of the *Times and Seasons*. Some strange ideas had been advanced. Doctor Bennett, who was always working with laboratory experiments, had urged the people to eat raw "and use for culinary purposes" a plant he called "tomato," but which most people knew as "love apple," and which grew in their flower gardens, though it was popularly supposed to be poisonous.

He declared there was some element in this strange fruit that would give health to those who used it, and he even wrote a series of articles upon its culture in the *Times and Seasons*. He pointed out the superiority of the plan of saving seed by drying the fruit whole rather than waiting for the plant to self sow, and

---

[14] "Testimony on the Book of Mormon," by Ebenezer Robinson, *Saints' Herald*, 1886, page 779.
[15] "What Do I Remember of Nauvoo," by Joseph Smith, *Journal of History*, Volume 3, page 133.

said that tomatoes might well be raised in shallow boxes in their windows in early spring, thus insuring an early supply of this life-giving "fruit," but he deplored vehemently the tendency of some gardeners to train the tomato to a stake, or frame, when "the God of heaven" had so apparently intended it for "an incumbent plant."

As early as 1839, the church authorities met in council to consider a church publication, but the prospect seemed almost hopeless. There was no money in the treasury. The man among them most eminently suited to take care of the printing interests of the church was Ebenezer Robinson, who had come to the church as a journeyman printer of nineteen, employed in the publishing house in Kirtland. Here he became acquainted with the church, and with Joseph Smith who as he was wont to declare "translated the Book of Mormon, by gift and power of God, as I verily know" and united his interests with the church. He went to Missouri; was one of the sixty-six confined in Richmond prison, where with others he was forced to sign over all his property "to defray the expense of the Mormon War." Released in late January, he made his way on foot to Illinois, where he arrived with just one dollar in his pocket. He did not find his wife as he expected, and so worked at setting type in the office of the *Quincy Whig,* until he could bring his family from Missouri. By June this man was camping in an old log cabin above the "Stone House" on the Mississippi, and had no money to start a business. Don Carlos Smith, the youngest of the Smith brothers, was also a printer, but he, too, had lost everything in the Missouri exodus.

However, the two young men were called into a council of church authorities and told that if they would publish a paper in the interests of the church, they could have all the profits arising from it (if any). The press, which had been buried in Missouri, was soon in their possession, with what remnants of type and printing material had been saved. The paper-to-be had already been christened by the council *Times and Seasons.* Smith and Robinson set to work with a will. The basement of an old warehouse near the river was obtained. This cellar was damp and dark and as it had no floor there was a constant trickle of seepage water from the river. Neither thought of the danger to his health. While they cleaned "the Missouri soil" from the press and type, they looked about for a loan. Dr. Isaac Galland sold them $50 worth of type on credit, and they borrowed $50 from another brother, with which they purchased paper and printed a prospectus to send out to the Saints throughout the United States.

In the meantime, type was set for the first number and two hundred copies printed, when both the young editors came down with malaria fever, almost simultaneously. Paper enough for two thousand copies of the paper had been wet down, and it mildewed and was spoiled. Francis Higbee wet down more paper, and tried to run off the edition, but failed. Weeks and months passed. Money was coming in plentifully for subscriptions, but no paper was forthcoming. A plan at last was evolved. With part of the subscription money an 18x22, story-and-a-half printing office was built, and the press moved into the lower floor, while obliging neighbors and brethren carried Robinson and his wife (who had been stricken with malaria the day after he was) into the upper rooms on their beds. A printer was hired, and from his bed, Robinson directed the printing of the first number of *Times and Seasons,* in November, 1839. By February the young editors were both far enough recovered from their illness to be at work again, and by spring, a lot next the printing office having been given them by the church, they each built a comfortable log cabin[16] and the *Times and Seasons* was a going concern. It was printed monthly, and the subscription price was one dollar the first year.

As was fitting in a religious periodical, the news and editorials

---

[16] "Testimony on the Book of Mormon," by Ebenezer Robinson, *Saints' Herald,* 1886, page 778, *seq.*

often assumed a note of melancholy piety, so universal in that day. New Year editorials especially were adapted to mourning for the good old times and deploring the reckless speed of 1840.

> In looking back over the years [says the *Times and Seasons* in January, 1840], we see the world of mankind appear to grow worse and worse, wickeder and wickeder. They seem to be determined more than ever to build themselves up in wealth and fame upon the ruin of each other. Steamboats and railroad cars are caused to strive, to outvie others in speed, that they may gain advantage over them, while thousands of lives are endangered thereby, and accident after accident is happening in consequence thereof.

In spite of the enormous growth in membership of the church, but few members of the church owned a copy of the Book of Mormon. The three thousand copies printed by E. B. Grandin in Palmyra, New York in 1830, were early exhausted. Another edition was printed at Kirtland in the winter of 1836-37, but that also was long out of print, and the demand for the book was increasing, and yet because of the panic of 1837, followed by the Missouri troubles which had practically stripped the Saints of every earthly possession, the initial cost of such a venture seemed absolutely prohibitive.

One morning in May, 1840, as Ebenezer Robinson was walking across to the printing office from his home, thinking of the miracle by which the first edition had been printed and given to the church, and the present great need of another such miracle, he says he was spoken to, and told "in plain and distinct language what course to pursue in getting the Book of Mormon stereotyped and printed." He hurried into the office and as soon as Joseph Smith entered, he made his proposal with all the eagerness of a boy. "Brother Joseph, if the church will furnish $200, and give us the privilege of printing two thousand copies of the Book of Mormon, Carlos and I will get $200 and get it stereotyped and printed." Joseph sat with his face in his hands for several minutes, then answered, "We'll do it. How soon will you want the money?" "In two weeks."

Robinson and Don Carlos went immediately to work to raise their part. A brother would loan them $120 until April at 35 per cent interest to be incorporated in the note, all to draw 6 per cent if not paid at maturity. The proposition didn't look too good, but they accepted it. Later the man increased the original loan by $25, but not another dollar could they raise. Then church authorities came to them and explained that they had utterly failed to raise any part of their share. The project was not abandoned, but the money laid by hopefully.

Now subscriptions were coming in, but they were often in the form of eggs, poultry, butter, grain, and other produce, which the "firm" had advertised that they would cheerfully accept in payment of subscriptions in lieu of cash. But they had to pay their debts in hard coin, so the $145 began to dwindle a little. Both felt they could not let it disappear in this fashion, so Carlos suggested that Robinson go to Cincinnati and buy some much-needed type and paper with the money. He answered, "Yes, I will go, and I will not come back until the Book of Mormon is stereotyped," for he says, "it was as a fire shut up in my bones both day and night that if I could get to Cincinnati the work would be accomplished." He mentioned this hope to Hyrum Smith, who branded it as "Impossible!" All others but Joseph agreed; he merely said, "God bless you!" and went over the two former editions with him and compared them. Joseph Smith's own experience had made him chary of the word "impossible!"

June 18, 1840, Robinson boarded the steam packet "Brazil" that plied between the Galena lead "diggings" and Cincinnati, with a Kirtland edition of the Book of Mormon in his pocket. When the paper was bought and loaded on the "Brazil," he had remaining $105.06¼ cents. He was almost inclined to abandon the idea. But he went to a stereotype foundry and told them the size of the book and asked the price. The man named a price per 1,000 ems. Robinson felt depressed as though something was not right and turned away, but thought to ask if there was another stereotype foundry in Cincinnati. There was. Gleason and Shepherd in Bank Alley off Third Street. He went there at once. Three men were conversing at a desk. One approached and held out his hand, saying, "My name is Gleason." Without any further introduction, Robinson said bluntly, "I have come to have the Book of Mormon stereotyped!" A man stepped up from the rear of the room, and Robinson was astounded to hear him say, "When that book is stereotyped, I am the man to stereotype it." He later introduced himself as Shepherd the other member of the firm.

He took the book, went over to a case of type, of the size named by Robinson, set up one line, counted it, counted the lines in a page, multiplied the two numbers together, and then multiplied by the number of pages. "It will cost $550," he announced. Robinson offered to pay $100 down, $250 within the next three months and $200 three months after delivery. The contract was drawn up and signed, with the proviso that if Robinson remained in Cincinnati and read proof, and otherwise assisted, his time at twenty-five cents an hour would be deducted.

He next arranged for board with one Oliver, Shepherd's molder and finisher and paid $5 on that. Shepherd offered to take him around to a bookbinder on Main Street. Here he signed another contract, for 2,000 books bound in leather for $250 (twelve and one-half cents each), $80 while work was being done, balance six weeks after the books were finished. Another contract for $250 was signed, and when the paper house said city references must be furnished by strangers, Shepherd stepped up and said, "I am Mr. Robinson's backer."

Night found the young Nauvoo publisher with an old Spanish sixpence in his pocket, contracts for over one thousand dollars folded up in his trunk, and a lighter heart than he had felt for over a year. From then on, he felt no doubt of the outcome though things looked dark at times. Mr. Shepherd bought three new fonts of type and hired three compositors, while Robinson went to his room and wrote a notice for the *Times and Seasons.* To every elder taking $100 worth of subscriptions paid in advance, the firm would give 120 books.

Several weeks passed, his board was due, and just when things seemed darkest, there came a twenty dollar bill on the State Bank of Indiana, from Don Carlos. This was a specie paying bank, and the bills were at a premium of 13 per cent. With the $22.60 so received, he was able to meet present expenses; then his brother Joseph L. Robinson whom he had baptized at Boonville, Oneida County, New York, when on a mission in the fall of 1836, sent him a draft on the Leather Manufacturing Bank of New York for $95, which he also cashed at a premium of 13 per cent. Later a letter from a perfect stranger, John A. Forgeus of Chester, Pennsylvania, (later of Little Sioux, Iowa) enclosed a draft on a Philadelphia bank for $200—an unsolicited loan. In short, all the contracts were met before they were due, except the paper, and he bought that for cash when needed from another house, as the one with which he had contracted had not the desired grade. The bookbinder was paid his $80 before he began work at all. Two thousand copies of the "Nauvoo edition of the Book of Mormon" were printed as the work was stereotyped. Before the last twenty-four pages were stereotyped, the books were all finished, except these last twenty-four pages. When everything was paid for, and the missionaries furnished the books promised, there were nearly a thousand books left for sale at a clear profit; they had the plates, which had been promised to the church; and Robinson purchased three fonts of type, materials for a stereotype foundry and a bookbindery, and a winter's supply of news and book paper, making a large down payment on it all. In October he took the "Brazil" for Nauvoo, feeling that the Saints of latter days were still dealing with a God of miracles.

When Robinson sold the printing interests sometime later (his partner having died in 1841), he went to Cincinnati to make final settlement with Shepherd with whom he had dealt from time to time; on the subject of their first meeting, Shepherd said, "Mr. Robinson, do you want to know what made me do as I did when you came here? It was not business, it was not what I saw in you, but it was what I felt here," putting his hand upon his heart.

And thus, by that something that touched the heart of a hard-headed business man, the Saints were again able to purchase for themselves a book that had changed their entire lives, and which some of them had long yearned to possess.[17]

The young people of Nauvoo constituted a problem of great anxiety to the priesthood, who hoped with many forebodings that the young might "carry on the work when they laid it down," but the proposition seemed doubtful. They neglected the church books and gave themselves up "to frivolity." Sometimes an elder was strongly urged "by the spirit" to remonstrate with the mothers from the pulpit for permitting their daughters "to neglect the spinning wheel for the piano." The *Times and Seasons* plaintively asked, "What would our Pilgrim forefathers think of the effeminate luxury in which we live?"

The young people themselves were stirred to contrition, and one night at the home of Heber C. Kimball, "the follies of youth and the temptations to which they are exposed generally, and especially in our city, became the subject of conversation." According to account, this gathering of young folk had the good grace to "lament the frivolous manner in which they spent their time, and their too frequent attendance at balls, parties, etc." At this, Brother Kimball offered to call a meeting and "give them such instruction as the Spirit of the Lord might suggest to him, which if followed would doubtless lead to a reformation in the conduct" of the young of the church. To the credit of the young

---

[17] "Testimony on the Book of Mormon," by Ebenezer Robinson, *Saints' Herald*, 1886, page 778.

people, if we may believe the historical chronicles, this suggestion was "received with delight and acted upon with alacrity," and early in January, 1843, "The Young Gentlemen and Young Ladies' Relief Society" came into being. Its first project was the building of a house for a lame English brother by the name of Maudsley.

The women of the church had also united for benevolent purposes into what was known as the "Ladies' Relief Society of the City of Nauvoo," which was organized on Thursday, the 24th of March, A. D. 1842. Seventy, elders, and priests were organized into social groups. The seventy had always possessed a great amount of friendliness and cohesion. In 1838, they with their families had moved in a body from Kirtland,[18] being several months on the road. In Nauvoo they had their own hall, a library of their own, and a museum in which they planned to put curiosities gathered from the far parts of the world in which they expected to travel. For instance, such treasures as the "tooth of a whale, some coral, the bone of an albatross's wing, the skin of its foot, the jawbone of a porpoise, and the tooth of a South Sea whale" were presented by some interested person. There was a Dramatic Society[19] with no mean membership. Thomas A. Lyne had played second tragedian in the first American cast of *Richelieu,* and he and his brother-in-law, George J. Adams, once put on a performance of *Richard III* in Philadelphia in order to get money to hire a hall in which to preach. There was a company of militia, as provided by law, called the Nauvoo Legion.

The Legion in 1840 had a membership of over one thousand! And why not! For Nauvoo in her day was the largest city in

---

[18] Under the leadership of the Presidents of Seventies, the Seventies went into camp on July 5, 1838 at Kirtland, and started on the 6th. The camp numbered 515 persons. They located together at Adam-ondi-ahman. This camp is known as "Kirtland Camp."

[19] This society was no amateur affair. Joseph Smith, son of the Prophet remembers their performance of *King Lear, As You Like It, Wilhelm Tell, Damon and Pythias.* Some of the actors were nationally known. From the Adams family of Nauvoo came Maude Adams, daughter of Annie Adams Kiskadden, granddaughter of Barnabas Adams; who made her debut in lieu of the property baby in the old Salt Lake theater, after a portion of the Saints had gone west.

Illinois. When Nauvoo was founded, Warsaw, her most formidable rival in the neighborhood, had a population of about three hundred, Carthage about the same. The whole population of Hancock County was six thousand.

Honorable Orville F. Berry has described Nauvoo as she was in the days of her glory. He says:

> If you have never been to Nauvoo and have the means and desire to confirm your belief that the men who selected the location of Nauvoo made no mistake, it will pay you to take a trip to the city, or, more particularly to this unique locality or situation. The word "Nauvoo" comes from the Hebrew and signifies "beautiful situation," or "beautiful situation for rest." It is situated on the east bank of the Mississippi River, in Hancock County, Illinois, near the headwaters of the Des Moines River, twelve miles above Keokuk, Iowa, ten miles above Hamilton, Illinois, eighteen miles above Warsaw, Illinois, fifty miles above Quincy, Illinois, nine miles below Fort Madison, and one hundred miles below Rock Island.
>
> Most of these cities, especially the larger ones, were organized prior to the Mormon settlement, and a careful study of their situation would indicate the wisdom of the choice of the Mormons at Nauvoo. I have traveled the Mississippi River practically from New Orleans to Saint Paul, and I say without any reservation that few, if any, locations along this mighty river can compare with Nauvoo. . . . The river, over a mile in width, in perfect symmetry, swings around a rockbound shore in a semicircle, then drops away into the first chain of the rapids. The river approaches in a westerly course below it and goes over the rapids southward, presenting to the view a long reach of wooded bluffs from Fort Madison to Keokuk. In this bend is a most beautiful second bottom, just above the high-water mark, containing eight or nine blocks; then begins a gradual ascent to the Temple Block, and then another, and then comes the level land and prairie to the eastward. The curve in the river is something like a horseshoe. A straight line at the back of the city from shore to shore would be four miles, while the distance measured along the river would be twice that long. Just across between Nauvoo and Montrose is an island about a mile in length and from seventy-five to three hundred yards in width. The island makes a heavy growth of timber and makes a beautiful break in the river. This is the place selected in 1839 by the Mormons when they were driven from the State of Missouri. . . . Nauvoo at that time bade fair to become the leading city of all the West; and in four years from the time the Mormons first settled in Nauvoo it was a city of three thousand inhabitants. The Gentiles, so called, meaning thereby all persons not Mormons, especially in Hancock and surrounding counties, became alarmed at the growing power, and especially the political power, of this strange

people, and, as Smith charged, became intensely jealous of their material, political, and religious progress. From facts obtained by the writer from interviews with old settlers and persons familiar with the facts about Hancock County, it cannot be doubted that they wielded a wonderful political power.[20]

Even in the early days, Nauvoo was not a place of prosperity and happiness only. The grim Reaper was too busy among them. Edward Partridge, gentle and incorruptible Bishop of the church, died May 27, 1840, and Joseph Smith, Sr., patriarch of the church, the following September 14. Don Carlos Smith and Robert B. Thompson, youthful editors of the *Times and Seasons,* crossed the dark valley within three weeks of each other, August 7, and August 27, 1841. But as these stalwarts fell, others stepped forward to take their places, undeterred by the fact that the persecution centering on the men in high places was an active aid to the Reaper in his work. Hyrum Smith took the place vacated by his father; George Miller became Bishop in the stead of Bishop Partridge; Ebenezer Robinson and John Taylor took over editorial responsibilities, and the gospel continued to be preached.

Jacob Scott,[21] who had come from Canada, only to lose a small fortune in Missouri, and who was originally a schoolmaster from Belfast, Ireland, wrote to his daughter in Canada in script as clear cut as the finest engraving and told her about Nauvoo:

Nauvoo, March 17, 1843. We had a long and cold winter, pretty good sleighing for nearly four months. Isaac works occasionally at the cabinet and carpenter business; such as tables, panel doors, window sash, frame sleighs, etc. Great preparations are made and making to prosecute with ardour the temple and the Nauvoo House this spring and ensuing summer. . . . The legislature of Illinois have granted the privilege to the citizens of Nauvoo to make a canal through the city for mercantile and machinery purposes. There are two steam grist and sawmills and one water mill, one iron foundry, one pottery,

---

[20]"The Mormon Settlement in Illinois," by Honorable Orville F. Berry, in *Transactions of the Illinois Historical Society for 1906.*
[21]Scott, see pages 115-116: Born in Armagh, Ireland. Father of Ann Davis, formerly of Lyons, Wisconsin; I. F. Scott, formerly of Randallville, Columbia County, Wisconsin, and Mary Warnock, formerly of Farmington, Iowa. He was baptized March 22, 1837, in Churchville, Ontario, by Isaac Russell and died in Nauvoo, January 2, 1845. His descendants are in the church today.

quite a number of stores (I do not know how many), cabinetmakers, shoemakers, masons, tailors, silk weavers, cotton ditto, white smith, black ditto, doctors, lawyers, bricklayers, brickmakers, tinsmiths, watchmakers, barbers, bakers, stonecutters, laborers, etc. I think there are more than one hundred handsome brick houses in Nauvoo now— . . . we planted last spring some corn, potatoes, and garden vegetables, all of which did remarkably well, turnips also very good. We sowed fall wheat last fall which looks very promising. The boys have taken quite a number of saw logs to mill this winter. I intend building another dwelling house. Land is rising in price about Nauvoo, fourfold (the Saints are gathering in so fast from different States and Europe). Provisions here are very cheap, corn as low as twelve and one-half cents a bushel, potatoes twelve cents, wheat from twenty-five to thirty-five cents per bushel, flour two dollars a barrel, pork twenty-five cents per hundred pounds, bacon two dollars per hundred pounds, best hams three cents per pound, all other eatables in proportion. Perhaps there is not any city on this globe improving as fast as Nauvoo. It is supposed there are at present ten to twelve thousand inhabitants in the city alone, and the country around it and Montrose is swarming with the Saints. The church has now *rest* on every hand and increasing in numbers daily. It is supposed there are at present two thousand from England, Scotland, Wales, and the Isle of Man, waiting between New Orleans and this place until navigation opens, and two thousand more are expected out next spring and summer from the same places.[22]

By 1843, the pride of Nauvoo centered in the white stone temple, already visible for miles up and down the Mississippi that circled the hill upon which it stood. Day by day oxen plodded through the streets of Nauvoo and labored up the hill with great blocks of stone to be put in place by eager workmen. Daily Alpheus Cutler, the master stonemason, rang the great bell at the tithing office at seven o'clock, twelve, one, and six to tell the workmen when to begin and cease from work. "Many times in later years, in the lonely watches of night," old-time Saints were to fancy, "they heard it ring as in long ago." There was no laborer in all Nauvoo, however poor, that was not proud to give his tenth day's work to the temple, feeling that in doing so he was handing down to his children a priceless heritage of tradition. Elder Elijah Fordham of New York, spent eight long months carv-

---

[22] From a letter in the private collection of Paul M. Hanson, Thurman, Iowa.

ing with infinite patience the twelve lifelike wooden oxen that were to support the great baptismal bowl in the basement. "The Temple," writes Jacob Scott, "exceeds in splendor and magnificence any building I have ever seen."

The temple was built of gray limestone, one hundred and twenty-eight feet long, eighty-eight feet wide, sixty feet high, and two hundred feet to the dome of the tower. It had thirty hewn pilasters costing three thousand dollars each. The whole cost of the building was around a million dollars. Says Thomas Edward O'Donnell, associate professor of architecture, University of Illinois, Urbana, Illinois, "Of all structures erected by religious colonies, the largest and most unique was, no doubt, the famous Mormon Temple at Nauvoo. Although never fully complete on the interior, the exterior was essentially complete when the Mormons departed. From the standpoint of architecture alone, it was a great loss to the state when the structure was burned. The architectural and decorative features involved in this Temple were wholly different from anything in the state, and were it standing today, it would be one of our most unique historical structures."[23]

The temple was burned by an incendiary on October 9, 1848.[24]

---

[23] "An Outline of the History of Architecture in Illinois," by Thomas Edward O'Donnell, in *Transactions of Illinois Historical Society for 1931*.

[24] Conflicting dates are given for this event, but this one seems to be correct. It is supported by Joseph Smith III, who in his "Memoirs" (*Herald*, Volume 82, page 177) says that it occurred "on the night of October 8." The Liberty *Tribune* for October 20, 1848, carried a story of the burning received by "telegraphic dispatch dated October 9." The *Millennial Star* for February 1, 1849, Volume 11, page 46, carried a story copied from the *Nauvoo Patriot* (date of issue not given) setting the date of the fire as "Monday, November 19, 1848." Yet in the January 1 issue, page 15, is a letter from Nathaniel H. Felt to Orson Pratt in England, dated from St. Louis, November 16, 1848, which says: "The incendiary torch *has been* applied." This letter, if correctly dated, would make the date of November 19 impossible and the date of November 10 (given in Volume 3, page 22 of the *Comprehensive History of the Church*—a Utah publication) improbable. The date of "Monday, November 19" is impossible in the year 1848, since November 19 fell on Sunday in that year; but October 9 did fall on Monday. For the confession of the man who set the fire, Mr. J. B. Agnew, see *Autumn Leaves* for December, 1905, page 549. He gives no date.

XXXII.—This Gospel of the Kingdom

THE BUILDING OF NAUVOO went forward with incredible rapidity, until it became the largest city in the state. "The blood of the martyrs" was then, as it has ever been, "the seed of the church." The people, hounded by common suffering into group solidarity, assimilated eagerly the motley population that literally poured into the new "City of the Saints." Missionaries without purse or scrip went out from Nauvoo into every nook and cranny of the United States, and even into foreign lands; and in every community where they "raised the warning voice," some were sure to be converted and in time take up their journey to "Zion" in the West. Old newspapers give warped accounts of these meetings. One "Ariel" (for nom de plumes were popular in the forties) writes in the *Spirit of the Times* on September 3, 1841, from Bordentown, New Jersey, telling of attending one of their meetings, as he "was curious to see what kind of creatures they were." The meeting was held by John E. Page, one of the Apostles, at a place called Jacobstown, and "from what I could pick up respecting the doctrines of these people, they do not believe in *endless damnation;* they hold *baptism by immersion* essential; . . . *Infant baptism* is rejected as unnecessary, because young children are incapable of knowing the heinousness of sin, and therefore need no repentance. . . . The Mormons inculcate *temperance* and appear to act up to the principle. They pretend to work *miracles,* healing the sick, etc., by the laying on of hands of the elders. These notions are certainly *novel* and perhaps may be a key to the remarkable success which Mormonism has met with in New Jersey. Certain it is that the disciples of Jo Smith are multiplying in a wonderful manner. We were informed that some fifteen or twenty families, including among them some very respectable, wealthy, and intelligent farmers, have joined the Mormons within a short time past. The Mormons, by their craft, have seduced members from the sheepfold of Methodism and other sects, and it is no wonder these religious denominations are anxious to prevent this state of things and get up camp meetings and protracted meetings to dispel the delusion of Mormonism."

In the fall of 1838, Benjamin Winchester held a debate with a Methodist minister in Monmouth County, New Jersey, and as a result on October 1, 1838, he baptized Josiah Ells, his opponent, into the church. The following December, a branch was organized in that place with Josiah Ells as president. Ells was born March 4, 1806, in Lewis, Essex County, England. He was licensed as a Methodist preacher in England when a young man of twenty-four. Later he came to the United States and preached in the same communion in Philadelphia until 1835, when he removed to Monmouth County, New Jersey.

On New Year's Day, 1840, he first met Joseph Smith, while the latter was in Washington, attempting to get redress for wrongs in Missouri. Joseph Smith induced him to come to Nauvoo, where he accordingly went about the first of April of the same year. The Prophet thought so much of his ability, that he appointed him to meet Reverend Doctor David Nelson of Quincy (the same who had fled from Missouri sometime before after making a rash remark about slavery, and found an asylum in Quincy). Nelson was a man of some note and had written a book, *The Cause and Cure of Infidelity*, much read a generation or two ago. When Ells arrived in Quincy, he found not only a number of clergymen but Governor Carlin himself in attendance. Doctor Nelson had not gone far in the debate before he declined to go on, explaining that his opponent had treated him courteously, but that he could not continue. Joseph Smith, who had accompanied Ells, got up and asked if any clergyman wished to continue the debate. Apparently none did, and the incident was closed.

Miraculous conversions, a source of joy to many throughout their lifetime, and of pride to their children for generations to come, continued to be part of church life in Nauvoo. Visitors flocked to the city of Nauvoo from every part of the United States and Canada. Joseph Smith entertained them all; the Mansion House was built to help accommodate those who wanted first-hand information about the Prophet; then the Nauvoo House was planned for the same purpose. Its need was urgent.

In Kingsville, Ontario, a young normal school student by the name of John Shippy attended some meetings held by John Landers. Landers' cousin, Richard Harrington, was the leading Baptist minister of the town, and young John Shippy's father was a Baptist minister, so he felt safe in doing so. Young Shippy was only fourteen, but he was deeply and permanently impressed by what he heard. He wanted to be baptized, but he was a minor, and his parents would not consent. He did not forget, but treasured what he had heard in his heart, resolving that when he was his own master, he would find out more about the doctrine that so strangely fascinated him. When he was seventeen his father "gave him his time," and he started joyfully for Illinois, working his way as he went. Starting in the spring of 1840, he heard of some Shippys in Laporte, Indiana, and stopped there. He found much to interest him in Laporte and temporarily forgot his quest. On December 28, 1841, he married a young widowed distant cousin, Sophronia (Shippy) Lemon and "settled down." But in 1842, another Latter Day Saint missionary came into the neighborhood, and he was promptly baptized by George W. Chase.

Interest revived, and he again resolved to see the Prophet, and set out for Illinois a second time in the spring of 1843. He visited the branch in Chicago and was ordained a priest and continued on on foot, stopping by the way at Walnut Grove to look up the first minister in whom he had been interested, John Landers. He stayed at the home of Joseph Smith for several weeks, during which time he became more and more satisfied with the choice he had made. On the morning he was due to leave, he rose from the breakfast table and putting several bills into the hands of his host to pay for his accommodation, he said good-by. Joseph stood with the bills in his hands, as if in deep thought, looking earnestly at the young man before him. Then he told him that he should be ordained an elder and return home, preaching by the way, handed him back his money, and told him Godspeed. He was ordained by Willard Richards, started to Canada, preaching and baptizing by the way.[1] Many in the church today trace their baptism to John Shippy, who spent many years in the active ministry, both in the old organization and the Reorganized Church. His descendants and those of his brother Benjamin whom he soon baptized have contributed valuably to the church for many years.

Another Canadian visitor was Samuel Hall, and the story he tells is stranger than fiction. Born of devout Catholic parents, he looked forward to becoming a priest with great hope and expectancy, and was happy when he was at last pronounced qualified of God and the church to enter the hallowed walls he had been taught to revere. He was set to work with older priests in Montreal, Canada, and here he says, "none but God could know of the terrible and soul-crushing disappointment I was doomed to suffer, for suffer I did, both by day and by night, as the hot, scalding tears wet my pillow." He appealed to the "aged and venerable bishop" for a solution of his problems, but received no

---

[1] Facts given in a personal interview by Miriam Shippy Claus of Detroit, daughter of John Shippy.

help. It was a "stunning blow." He tried to "stop all thought." He prayed for death, and asked time and again if God's church had been taken from the earth.

One day while walking down the street in this despondent mood, he picked up a small leaflet. Going to his room as soon as he could, he took it out and read it, then reread it. In his sheltered life, he had never heard of Joseph Smith. It was all new and strange to him. Here, with "bated breath," he read of a great apostasy, of the restoration of the gospel at the hands of an angel, with all its gifts and powers. He threw himself upon his knees and asked God if it were true. On the little pamphlet was the announcement of a conference to be held in Nauvoo, Illinois. Joseph Smith would be there. All lovers of truth were invited to be there and judge for themselves. They were advised to ask of God as the Apostle James had recommended. He prayed earnestly and felt the message to be true, but the decision that he now faced was momentous. Once it was made, whether this strange restored church proved true or false, he could not turn back. If it were true, he would find happiness; if not, his lot would be a sad one, for then he must flee to some remote corner of the earth and drag out his days unknown to friends and family, for he dare not return.

At length he obtained leave of absence to visit New York, and from there quietly made his way to Nauvoo, bidding a mental farewell forever to all the past. Whatever happened from henceforth, he must begin life anew. In his valise were the few scant pieces of clothing he had obtained, his Bible, his Catholic prayer book, and a few dollars in money. He was not long on his way before he began to hear terrible tales of Joseph Smith. His heart sank within him, but he must go on.

Conference was already in session. He left his valise at the hotel and inquired for the church. Directed to the large assembly in a grove, he found service already in progress. The speaker was an "earnest, plain-spoken man." Hall pressed his way into the crowd until near enough to hear, and as it is recorded: "to my utter astonishment and delight I heard, as I had never heard before; aye it was as a living stream of life and light. It seemed as if every word came from the very bosom of eternity to my inmost soul; yes, *every word to me!*" When the speaker finished, Hall turned to a man near him and said, "That is Joseph Smith." "Yes," was the answer, "and he is a prophet of God." "I know he is," Hall heard himself saying.

Hall waited patiently in the crowd that gathered about the speaker, until he could get a word with him, then without parley asked for baptism. The answer was breathtaking, in its simplicity. The Prophet did not stop to ask his name, his qualifications for membership, or from whence he came. Instead he said, "This is the Lord's doings; come with me." Down to the river they went, and Hall was baptized, and coming out of the water, he was confirmed and ordained an elder on the banks of the river.

As he arose, Joseph said, "Brother Hall, you are now a legally qualified servant of Jesus Christ, a minister of life to this generation; go and preach the gospel, and you will be blessed in blessing many." "When shall I go?" asked Hall. "Go now," was the answer.

"Shall I stay until the close of the conference, and then go?"

"No," he said, "go now."

"Very well. I will go and get my things at the hotel and start off."

"No, no," urged the Prophet, "go *now,* just as you are. Your things are safe, you will not need them, and you will lack nothing. Go right along down south and tarry not by the way until you preach the gospel. I bless you. Good day!" and he walked away, leaving the newly baptized Hall gazing after him in bewilderment. Was man ever in a stranger situation? But he had set his feet on a path upon which there was no return. He put his coat and vest across his arm and started at a brisk walk in a southerly direction, as directed. Here he was a fugitive from the Catholic Church, the only church of which he knew anything, in a strange country, having heard but a portion of one short sermon, not a cent in his pocket, his clothing wet. The sun dried his clothes, and as night approached he put on his coat and vest. About sundown he approached a crossroad just as two men in a wagon came long the other road and overtook him. They offered him a ride, which he accepted. All the time they were eyeing him sharply. "Your pants look as if you had been in the water," said one. "Yes," Hall admitted. "I have been baptized by Joseph Smith for the remission of my sins, and I never felt so well satisfied in my life as I do now."

"Oh, so you are a Mormon," said the other, eyeing him curiously, "I never saw one before. What do you think of Joe Smith? How does he look and act? What is he doing? Where are you going? What are you going to do?" Hall told them freely of his life and recent experiences, and they were intrigued. They were going to stay at a small town a few miles farther on on business, and would pay his fare at a hotel if they could hear him preach. On arrival, they did as they agreed, hired a hall, and even went through the streets, as the custom was, ringing a bell and calling out, "Come out and hear a late Catholic priest on Mormonism at the hall."

The meetings lengthened out to a week's stay, then a month, and at the end of that time Samuel Hall baptized thirty-four persons, and organized a branch of the church. Best of all, he had found peace. "I was no longer a friendless stranger, alone in the world, but at home in my Father's house."

And so the gospel spread, and converts poured into Nauvoo, to cast their all into the great work "entrusted to all." They felt the world well lost for the "pearl of great price they had found."[2]

---

[2]"A Leaf From the Life Book of Elder Samuel Hall," by Elder D. S. Mills, *Autumn Leaves*, Volume 4, page 537.

XXXIII.—Enemies in Camp

Nauvoo prospered, and with that prosperity came ease and comfort and a measure of peace to most of the Saints in Nauvoo. The Higbees—whom Lyman Wight had found as fishermen on the Ohio River at Cincinnati, who had been won as friends by the rough pioneer Apostle when he helped them with their nets, and who listened to him preach when the day's work was over, as he stood clad in his working clothes, barefooted, as they were, and told them of the gospel—were men of prominence in Nauvoo, who sent their sons to study law in college.

Joseph Smith himself—as interested in education and as eager to learn as he had been years before in Kirtland, when Oliver Cowdery returning from New York had brought him a Hebrew Lexicon, and he had spent the entire day examining it and learning the alphabet—now saw prospects of a fulfillment of his dearest dream, education for everybody. The plan he visioned was for public schools that would take Latter Day Saint children from the elementary grades through the university, a public school system on so grand a plan that no child would be handicapped as he had been by insufficient learning. A board of regents was chosen, and while no buildings were erected, a faculty was selected and some classes were held.

Soon after coming to Nauvoo, John Cook Bennett, quartermaster of the State of Illinois, joined with the church and was heralded as a great convert by the Saints. Immediately he was accorded all prominence, both in the city and the Legion, and was even chosen to act in Rigdon's place as counselor during his illness. He wrote lengthy articles for the *Times and Seasons* and chose as his nom de plume the suggestive title, "Joab, general in

Israel." In Kirtland the church had its Judas in Doctor Hurlbut, and in Missouri, Sampson Avard, it seemed, came in to play the villian's role, but neither of these could be compared with John Cook Bennett, a cautious and cunning soul to whom openness and straight dealing did not appeal. When a young man in Ohio, Bennett had shown some promise. He studied medicine with his uncle, Doctor Samuel P. Hildreth of Marietta, Washington County, Ohio, and was said to have a diploma, as well as recommendations from some of the principal physicians of Marietta. He married a daughter of Colonel Joseph Barker near Marietta. The young couple soon united with the Methodist Church, in which he became a local preacher, but was never satisfied long in one location or position. He lived at different times in Barnesville, McConnelsville, and Malta, Ohio; Wheeling, West Virginia; Colesville, Pennsylvania, and places in Indiana and has been traced as a resident of at least twenty towns in the Middle Atlantic States. He had a great ambition to dominate any situation in which he found himself, and by means of subtle flattery was almost always able to succeed in insinuating himself into the good graces of any class of people where he saw a chance of good living and a fair measure of popularity for himself. He had, even before his unfortunate meeting with the Latter Day Saints, been able to push himself into places and situations much beyond his actual abilities and from which he extricated himself by simply disappearing, only to turn up elsewhere. He was said to have connected himself with several colleges and universities, become more or less prominent, and then, getting himself into deep water in one way or another, vanished. He was not without a certain sort of ability, and was likely to turn up anywhere in almost any kind of role. He was, among other things, a Christian preacher. At the time he began a siege of flattery upon the Latter Day Saints, having noted their rising popularity, he was quartermaster of the State of Illinois. Bennett's wife for a time followed him from town to town, but at length, after repeated infidelities on his part, returned with her several children to her father in Marietta and persistently refused to give him the "bill of divorcement" he craved. His career was marked all the way by immoralities which he sought to excuse, when they became known, by most ingenious philosophies. Among his many and versatile characteristics was a capacity for intrigue, with which the honest and straightforward men of the church could not successfully cope.

Bennett became the first mayor of Nauvoo and was prominent in military affairs but, ere long, fell into moral delinquency and was expelled from the church. On May 17, 1842, he resigned as mayor, and Joseph Smith was elected.

In the meantime, on the 6th of May, ex-Governor Boggs, while at his home on Pleasant Street[1] in Independence, was shot through the window by an assassin. Though severely wounded, he recovered. He filed a complaint, charging Joseph Smith with being an accessory to the attempted murder, charging the actual shooting to Orin Porter Rockwell, who was alleged to have been employed in Independence at that time. Both Smith and Rockwell were indicted, and Governor Reynolds made requisition on Governor Carlin of Illinois for their surrender. Governor Carlin issued the necessary warrant, and both men were arrested in Nauvoo. They immediately secured a writ of habeas corpus from the Municipal Court at Nauvoo,[2] and were discharged from cus-

---

[1] The Boggs property was across Pleasant street from the Campus, with the house facing east on Spring street.
[2] It has often been charged that the city of Nauvoo made an improper use of the writ of habeas corpus when they claimed under their city charter the right to arrest process issued by the State's circuit court by habeas corpus proceedings, and proceeded to pass judgment upon the sufficiency of writs under which arrests were made, and even to go behind the writs and try the cases upon their merits.
But these critics fail to consider that the Latter Day Saints were claiming these rights by virtue of advice from Illinois statesmen. Both Cyrus Walker, the Whig candidate for Congress, and Joseph P. Hoge accorded them this right, and even Governor Thomas Ford himself when answering the request of Missouri to rearrest Joseph Smith, took refuge behind the aforesaid proceedings of the Municipal Court at Nauvoo to the extent of saying "no process, officer, or authority of the State of Illinois has been resisted or interfered with." It was on this basis that he refused to call out the militia to rearrest Joseph Smith.
Governor Ford, however, in his inaugural address of December 6, 1842, pointed out what he considered as objectionable features in the Nauvoo charter. He then

tody. This angered the Missouri executive, who persuaded Carlin to issue a warrant for their rearrest. Both Smith and Rockwell kept in hiding for some months, but at length, by advice of counsel, Joseph Smith surrendered himself, was taken to Springfield where the Circuit Court of the United States of the District of Illinois was sitting, and with Justin Butterfield, one of the most powerful attorneys in Illinois, as counsel, appealed for a writ of habeas corpus. His release was ordered by the court (Judge Nathaniel Pope) on the ground that he could not be extradited and tried for a crime committed in Missouri, when he was not out of Illinois during the time the crime alleged was committed.

In those days, the holding of circuit court in any town was the event of the year. The circuit judge usually rode horseback from the town in which court was held to the next, followed by most of the district lawyers, also on horseback, who rode circuit with the judge in order to pick up cases. The best hostelry in town was newly decorated and cleaned for the occasion, and needless to say, the judge's choice of a hotel invariably voiced the mind of knowing lawyers as to their choice of a transient home. The lawyers always scrambled to get coveted seats next to the judge in the long dining room, or perhaps near the foot of the table, where they might have a better chance of picking up a client. Prospective jurors, and even men under bond to be tried for criminal charges, sat at the long common table and gathered in

---

recommended its modification. In a letter to Nauvoo, he placed the blame where it belonged when he said, "You have also assumed to yourselves more power than you are entitled to in relation of habeas corpus under your charter. I know that you have been told by lawyers for the purpose of gaining your favor that you have this power to any extent. In this they have deceived you for their own base purposes. Your charter supposes that you may pass ordinances, a breach of which will result in the imprisonment of the offender. For the purpose of giving more speedy relief to such persons, it was given to the municipal court of Nauvoo to issue writ of habeas corpus in all cases arising under the ordinances of the city. It was never supposed by the legislature, nor can the language of your charter be tortured to mean that a jurisdiction was intended to be conferred which should apply to all cases of imprisonment under the general laws of the State, or of the United States, as well as the city ordinances."

Joseph Smith replied: "Whatever power we have exercised in the habeas corpus has been done in accordance with the letter of the Charter and Constitution as we have confidently understood them; and that too with the ablest counsel; but if it is so that we have erred in this thing, let the Supreme Court correct the evil. We have never gone contrary to constitutional law as we have been able to learn it."

the evening afterward in the taproom. The whole town turned out to attend court, and many were the witty sallies and bits of high-flown eloquence that marked the occasion of court week. Justin Butterfield was noted for his wit, and he started his plea in defense of Joseph Smith by saying that it was a momentous occasion in his life to appear before the Pope (bowing to Judge Pope) in defense of a prophet of God (bowing to Joseph Smith) in the presence of all these angels (bowing to the ladies in attendance). From then on he had his house with him.

Missouri authorities, not wishing to be outmaneuvered, revived the old charge of murder and treason. They repeated their requisition for the extradition of Joseph Smith and succeeded in arresting him at Dixon. By kidnaping him, the officers attempted to rush him across the river into Missouri, but the Saints prevented this; and the sheriffs again were compelled to bring their prisoner before the Municipal Court of Nauvoo, where he was again released. The sheriffs now asked Governor Ford to call out the militia to apprehend Smith and escort him to the Missouri border. This the governor (Ford) declined to do, and the matter had to rest there. Joseph Smith in 1841 appeared before Judge Douglas on this charge and was exonerated.

Rockwell was subsequently arrested in Saint Louis and taken to Independence. While waiting trial he broke jail but was recaptured. Alexander W. Doniphan undertook his defense and pleaded his case in the midst of an inflamed populace. No evidence was found to connect him with the crime, so he was tried for breaking jail, and after listening to Doniphan, the jury found him guilty and assessed a penalty of five minutes in jail. In the interviews in later years, Doniphan expressed his genuine conviction that Rockwell was innocent of the assault upon Boggs.

The difficulties of the Saints with the State of Missouri had occupied two years. The trial before Judge Pope occurred on December 31, 1842. It was June 23, 1843, when Joseph was kidnaped and arrested and an attempt made to take him across the river. He was released from custody on July 2. The appeal was immediately made to the Governor, who declined the order, for a military force to escort Smith to Missouri borders on July 26, 1843.[3]

Owing to this constant anxiety, and the periods of time when Joseph Smith must keep in hiding, many things happened in Nauvoo without his personal consent or knowledge. During this period, the reins of government more or less slipped from his fingers. Some things were tolerated that when brought to his attention later, he denounced publicly or by letter. While willing to undergo any process of law in Illinois, where he had confidence in the courts, neither he nor his attorneys thought he could exercise the same trust in the courts of Missouri.

By the time the Missouri matter was finally checked, the trouble with Bennett had grown to such an extent that he had been expelled from the church. Joseph Smith says:

> It may be asked why it was that we would countenance him so long after being apprised of his iniquities, and why he was not dealt with long ago. To this we would answer that he has been dealt with from time to time; when he would acknowledge his iniquity, ask and pray for forgiveness, beg that he might not be exposed, on account of his mother, and other reasons, saying he should be ruined and undone. He frequently wept like a child and begged like a culprit for forgiveness, at the same time promising before God and angels to amend his life if he could be forgiven. He was in this way borne with from time to time until forbearance was no longer a virtue.[4]

Bennett declared open warfare on the Saints and proceeded to publish a book containing affidavits against Joseph Smith's character and other damaging material. In some cases these affidavits were from women whose names had been linked in Nauvoo with that of Bennett himself.

---

[3] See also *Governor's Letter Book of Illinois*.
[4] *Times and Seasons*, Volume 3, August 1, 1842, page 869.

XXXIV.—A Mission to the South Sea Islands*

*I*N THE TOWN OF NEW Bedford, Massachusetts, was the commodious home of a Latter Day Saint by the name of Phillip Lewis. Here in July, 1843, might have been found four men, Addison Pratt, Benjamin Grouard, Noah Rogers, and Knowlton Hanks, Latter Day Saint missionaries bound for the islands of the sea. Passage had already been secured on board a Yankee whaler outbound for nowhere in particular. The boat was the "Timeoleon," and she had no schedule. She might be gone for years, but she would come back with sperm oil. Almost certainly she would, sometime in the next year or so, touch Tahiti. Captain Plasket wanted four hundred dollars to set the men down in Tahiti. Lewis paid three hundred dollars of the amount; and the remaining one hundred dollars, together with another eighty dollars for contingent expenses, was raised by the Saints of New Bedford, Salem, and Boston.

From the hour of its inception, the plan for carrying the gospel to the South Seas had gone rapidly forward. Twelve days from the date of their appointment, the missionaries were all set apart at a memorable meeting in the Presidency's office. Grouard and Pratt were ordained seventies at the same time, and Noah Rogers, already a seventy, was made president of the mission. The other member of the party was Knowlton F. Hanks. By June 1 they were off for New Bedford, visiting branches and conferences by the way.

Knowlton Hanks had been ailing for sometime, but Nauvoo had not been a healthful place, and his friends had talked of the benefits of a long sea voyage and the life-giving warmth of a winter in the tropics. He felt that once at sea his health would improve. The rough trip on the packet from New York to New

---
*Adapted from *The Cruise of the Timeoleon*, by the author; *Vision*, Volume 44.

Bedford had given him a deep-seated cold, which, together with the persistent cough he already had, was giving him serious trouble. Every few moments his body was wracked with coughing. Finally he suggested going to Boston where the members of the Quorum of Twelve would be in conference, and ask for administration.

Pratt never forgot that trip on the stagecoach with Hanks to Boston. The sick man had insisted on giving his seat inside the coach to a lady and taking a less comfortable one outside with Pratt. Terrible fits of coughing shook his emaciated frame, and in the periods of fatigue that followed them, Pratt feared his companion might never live to reach Boston. Supporting him in his arms, he prayed silently that they might safely reach their destination. But even the rites of the church failed to do very much. He begged them not to write to Nauvoo for fear he might be recalled. He wanted to go on, and if he must die, he said whimsically, let it be as near his mission field as possible.

All through July, August, and September the men waited. On the 9th of October, they were summoned to the boat. The blasphemous chanties of the crew mingled with the prayers and farewells of the New England Saints who had gathered to see them off. It was an ungodly ship and a wicked crew, despaired of by even the zealous Addison Pratt, who wrote in his first letter home that he feared "there was little hope for them." The captain would have no prayers or sermons on board, and the missionaries had to content themselves with almost daily religious discussions. There were eight fellow passengers, not including the ship's mascot, an enormous land terrapin, captured on a previous voyage in the Galapagos Islands. There were Doctor Winslow, his wife, their three children, and their Irish maid, and a Mr. and Mrs. Seth Lincoln, whom the missionaries properly characterized in their first letter to Nauvoo as "Baptists who might someday be Latter Day Saints."

The first few days were stormy, and Hanks stayed in his berth, but later came fair winds and a smooth sea, and he joined the group on deck, talking of home and the "new religion," and laughed, as they all did, watching little Charles and Lizzie Winslow ride the great terrapin about the deck. But not many days passed before he became so ill he could no longer leave the cabin. The time was divided into watches of three hours, each of the three men taking turn by the sickbed. Anxious hours passed into days and weeks; still he lingered, growing daily thinner and weaker. It was about evening on the second day of November that Pratt, watching by his side, felt the end was near and lengthened his watch another three hours. Finally he turned the watch over to another of the brethren, but two hours later was summoned hurriedly to the bedside to see Hanks fold his own hands upon his breast and pass away.

There was but one more service to be done. Silent for once were the oaths of the crew as all was made ready for the saddest duty known to seafaring folk. A plank was laid on the starboard gangway, a piece of canvas on it. The body, wrapped in a sheet, was placed there, an eighty-pound bag of sand at the feet, and the old sailmaker sewed up the canvas shroud that was to be its only coffin. "The top-gallant masts were furled, the courses hauled up, and the main and mizzen topsails were hove aback, the noble ship stopped her headway," says Pratt, "and lay in gentle motion, as if to witness the solemn scene." The American Flag hung at half-mast, and all stood uncovered while Noah Rogers offered prayer. Then the plank was gently tilted, and the canvas-covered body slipped feet foremost into the waves. The log book chronicled latitude 21 degrees 34 minutes north, longitude 26 degrees 11 minutes west of Greenwich.

So Knowlton Hanks, the first missionary to die abroad, left his three brethren to finish their mission alone. A bit of old sail had been his coffin, the deep sea his grave, and a line in a whaleman's yellowed logbook his only epitaph.

The course taken was a devious one, visiting in turn waters known to be good whaling grounds. The first port of call was at Cape Verde Islands for salt, then along the coast of Brazil to the whaling grounds near the coast of Trinidad. They then shaped their course for the Cape of Good Hope, then towards Cape Chatham, the southwest point of Australia. On March 8, 1844, they arrived off Cape Chatham, cruised along Bass Straits, but could not land immediately, so sailed off to the south of Van Dieman's Land (Tasmania).

On March 19, it commenced blowing in squalls of rain, sleet, and snow. On the 20th, as the weather lighted up between squalls, they could see the southwest point of what is now Tasmania. But the gale continued, increasing to a fury. Wind roared and whistled through the rigging, seas ran mountain high, crashing over the deck, but the sturdy old "Timeoleon" weathered the gale with only a few boards off the bulwarks, and the loss of two whale boats. Without attempting to land they shaped their course for the west point of New Zealand, a favorite resort for whalemen. Here was not only sperm oil, but large settlements of English speaking people, beautiful climate, and productive soil. The missionaries listened to the alluring talk of the crew and determined to go ashore at New Zealand and start a mission there, instead of Tahiti.

To be at last free of the dirty whale ship—the decks slippery with blubber and blood, the smell of burning blubber and cracklings that lingered in the tropic air for weeks, a sickening odor, by which sailors were wont to say they could scent a whaler twenty miles to windward—would be joy unspeakable! The missionaries got ready their luggage and prepared to disembark in New Zealand. But the weather continued stormy, until Captain Plasket, disgusted, bade good-by to New Zealand waters, without attempting to land, and sailed for Tahiti.

Thus the entire missionary destiny of a whole church was

changed by equinoctial storms, head winds, and the decree of the rough master of a Yankee whaler!

For seven dreary months the passengers had walked the dingy decks of the old whaler with only a few hours ashore, and those few hours now months in the past.

What had once seemed an unusual and rather pleasant experience became a humdrum prison sentence to Noah Rogers and Addison Pratt. Life at sea was no novelty to Benjamin Grouard, for though he was but twenty-four years of age, he already had ten years' experience with the sea. He loved it.

Nearly a month had passed since they had seen land—the Three Kings off the northwest coast of New Zealand on the last day of March. The wind now blew fresh and fair, and the captain announced that he would land at the island of Heitaroa, three hundred miles south by west of Tahiti. Except for a few barrels of fish, he had taken no supplies since he left Cape Verde Islands, and Heitaroa was renowned among seamen for pigs and fruit. But on the last day of April, to his intense disappointment, they sighted Tubuai, an event not only unanticipated, but one which Captain Plasket had earnestly striven to avoid. He sent off a boat, on the long chance of being able to get supplies there, and found, to his surprise, he could get all he needed. Accordingly, the next day, May 1, 1844, a landing was made.

They were given a royal welcome, and as soon as the natives learned there were missionaries aboard, they began to plead with them to stay, for there had been no white missionaries on that island for many months. Addison Pratt at once agreed to remain with them. The captain and Doctor Winslow left gifts and supplies, and each in his own way sought to make the future pleasant for Pratt. The captain told the young native king, with mock sternness, that he was leaving them a missionary, but if he were not treated well the "Timeoleon" would return and take him away again. Doctor Winslow, an avowed free thinker, told Pratt that if he ever wanted to leave the island, he must feel free to draw on him for any amount necessary and consider it a gift if he were never able to repay! So the "Timeoleon" sailed away and left Addison Pratt, the first South Sea Island missionary, alone among strangers.

On May 14, Tahiti was sighted forty miles away, and the next day the "Timeoleon" anchored in the bay and had permission of the French Government to land. The island was in the midst of a revolution. The French had deposed Queen Pomare, and the natives were under arms some ten miles from Papeete. Doctor Winslow, after looking over the situation, reshipped his goods to the Sandwich Islands (Hawaii), but the Lincolns, Rogers, and Grouard decided to remain and make the best of it.

The first sermon was preached by Benjamin Grouard in the house of Kim the pilot, in Taunoa, his text from Isaiah 18: 1-3. Among his congregation were Mr. and Mrs. Seth Lincoln, his fellow passengers on the "Timeoleon" and three other Americans or Englishmen, who soon became the first fruits of the church in Tahiti. The latter three were a Mr. Richmond, William Jefferson, and John Hawkins, the five being baptized in the order named. John Hawkins was baptized late in September or early in October. In his ordination, he was promised that he would live to a good old age, and do a good work among the natives. He always remembered this promise, and although a day came when there was a price on his head "for taking up arms against the French," he had no fear of death; and after he came into the custody of the French and the hour approached for his execution, he, still thinking of his ordination promise, was sure he would have a long life. He was pardoned on the very day he was to die, and lived to fulfill the prophecy spoken over his head.[1]

---

[1] "Events in the Life of Elder John Hawkins of Tahiti," by Joseph Burton, *Autumn Leaves*, Volume 16, page 396. John Hawkins was born at Maidstone, County of Kent, England, October 6, 1817. He left England June 20, 1837, arriving in "Van Diemans" Land, October 20. Left there February, 1840, for Tahiti, arriving there June 3, 1840.

The Lincolns immediately opened their home to the missionaries. Friends were slowly made among the natives on account of the misrepresentations of the English missionaries, who spared no pains to avoid the elders and to teach the natives to do the same.

Just previous to John Hawkins' baptism in October, Noah Rogers decided to leave Grouard in charge of the small group of members in Tahiti and try his luck on other islands of the group. He went to the island of Huahine and sought out those of his own race. Nearly every white man on the island, he was told, kept either a gambling den or a saloon, except the missionary, and he would not even talk to Rogers. Here also Rogers found every door closed by the London Missionary Society, so he went on to another island and still another, always with the same result.

In the meantime Seth Lincoln had been ordained and placed in charge of the small group in Tahiti, and Grouard felt that he might safely visit Addison Pratt, who was still on the island of Tubuai and reporting wonderful success. Very early in the year, he accordingly went to Tubuai and found Pratt in excellent spirits and good form. In fact, he admitted that while he left Nauvoo weighing only one hundred and fifty-four pounds, "steelyards drawing two hundred pounds now would scarcely weigh him."

Pratt had a great story to tell. The first baptism was on July 6, 1844, his first convert being a shipbuilder on the island. This was followed on July 22, by nine more baptisms, and on July 29 a branch had been organized with eleven members. On August 5 Communion was administered for the first time, with fresh coconut water instead of wine.

Pratt had found an excellent home in Tubuai with one of the natives and his wife. All the royal family on that island had been baptized, and Pratt had the honor of marrying the young king (who was a widower) to his present queen. This royal alliance, however, had some drawbacks, for Pratt soon found himself the chief adviser of the king, a sort of unofficial, but none the less authoritative, prime minister. He was even wakened up at night at times to be consulted upon a crime wave of petty thievery on the other side of the island, or weightier matters of state having to do with foreign relations, notably the French Government and the London Missionary Society.

Sensing his unpopularity with the latter institution, Pratt avoided embarrassing entanglements with difficulty. In vain he sought to emphasize the fact that he was a minister and not a statesman; the natives could not be convinced that he was not the last court of appeal on all questions. Practically the whole island had joined the church. The shipbuilders were now nearly finished with their work, and they actually talked seriously of loading the whole branch on the vessel when she was finished and sailing away to Zion! They planned to go up the Columbia River and across the Rocky Mountains to Nauvoo.

Over a year had passed now. It was February, 1845, and not a letter since they left New Bedford. Ships called and sailed away, bringing no news from home, each departure leaving them lonelier than before. Finally a ship captain told them he had heard that Joseph Smith was dead and the church scattered.

"We do not believe it," wrote Addison Pratt, "but if one half of the church is dead, and the other half has denied the faith, I know the work is true, and by the help of God, I am determined to spread the gospel to the ends of the earth, the Lord giving me strength to do it."

But in spite of all his brave assurance, he admitted that just one letter from home would mean more to him than all the letters he had ever had in his life before. After the sun had set and before darkness fell, he often wandered away from his new friends to dream of those he had left at home. As he walked along the beach and thought of the seas that rolled between him and those he loved, he says the question came unbidden, "Has death made any inroads there?" But his only answer was the roar of the breakers on the reef.

In the meantime, Noah Rogers visited Moorea, Huahine, Raiatéa, Bora-bora, Tahaa, and thence to Mote, one of the Harvey Islands, then to the island of Manga, where he found no missionary and offered to stay, but was shown letters bidding the natives to receive no missionaries or teachers unless they came with letters from the English missionaries at Tahiti. The natives understood that all who did not have these letters were *pope havaare* (*lying Catholics*), and had therefore passed a law that no white man should live among them. From there Rogers went to Rurutu, where he heard the same story. He was obliged to return to Tahiti without success.

Grouard had gone to the islands lying to the eastward and had not returned, but there was a letter from him saying that he was on Anaa, one of a chain of thirty or more low coral islands, where there were no vegetables, but plenty of coconuts, fish, and pigs. He wrote that he was happy in his work there and had baptized twenty of the leading men on that island and more were investigating.

Finally on July 3, 1846, Rogers took passage on the "Free Brother" (or "Three Brothers") for home, leaving Addison Pratt in charge of the mission. After a passage of one hundred and thirty days, he arrived in Nantucket on November 6, 1846, the first Latter Day Saint elder to circumnavigate the globe. He proceeded at once to Philadelphia, where he baptized two of the passengers whom he had converted on the trip over, and then went on to Nauvoo, arriving there December 29, just in time to join in the long westward trek of the Saints driven from Nauvoo. December in Nauvoo and the awful hardships of that terrible trip across Iowa in the dead of winter were too great a change from the tropical skies of Tahiti, and his was the first grave made by the "Mormon" pioneers at Mount Pisgah, although, sadly enough, it was not to be the last one.

Addison Pratt continued to labor in Tubuai and Tahiti until March 28, 1847, when he sailed from Papeete on the "Providence." Arriving in Salt Lake City, September 28, 1848, he united his destiny with the faction there. Benjamin Grouard loved the people of Anaa and the low islands. He continued to serve there, being in charge of the mission after the departure of Addison Pratt. He carried on alone, looking forward to reinforcements. In December, 1844, he had written his wife that he had engaged passage on a whaler, which had gone out to fill up, and would return home in ten months "if the Lord wills."[2]

But for some reason he was still on the islands, wandering and teaching from island to island. Wherever he went from village to village, he was followed by a group of eager natives. When he stopped to rest, he preached to them by the roadside and baptized as he went along. He not only preached, but taught them the duties of everyday life, helped them establish their boundary lines, drew up their business contracts, and taught them to do various kinds of manual work. He showed them the simplest methods of farming, helped the women to learn to cook, and taught the children to read and write. It had been years since he had seen any kind of money. His clothing wore out; he went barefoot, dressed in two simple garments, trousers and shirt. He ate the native food of the people among whom he labored, fish and coconuts. Any simple native hut was his home, and all his people obeyed his every wish as if it were law.

He went to Tubuai and built a schooner of eighty tons burden with not a penny in hand to buy any kind of material when he started it. He cut all the timber with his own hands, *tumanu* wood, whipsawed it and designed the vessel, and with the help of the natives completed it in eighteen months. "Home" was now the cabin of his little ship; he enjoyed it, for he had been a sailor since he was fourteen. His field of service was greatly increased for, commander of his own little boat, he was able to go from island to island as he desired until Pratt and four other

---

[2]*Times and Seasons*, Volume 6, page 980.

elders returned from Salt Lake City on May 24, 1850. Doubts assailed Grouard when he heard the stories brought by those who had been with the faction in the West, but he guarded the truth zealously, so that when Apostle T. W. Smith visited the remnant in Anaa thirty years later, they knew only the purest principles of the gospel[3] and the fact that Joseph Smith was a prophet of God. Even the exacting T. W. Smith received them gladly on their original baptism. But long before that time (May 16, 1852), Grouard, Pratt, and the other missionaries had left the islands by the edict of the French Government, forbidden to longer carry on their work there.

Grouard met only disappointment on his return. Of that return he said later to D. S. Mills: "At last I was going home. Home, did I say? Good heavens, I had no home. I was alone in the world. Shipwrecked, worse than I was shipwrecked once upon an uninhabited island." With that shipwreck, Grouard's religious life abruptly ended. He never united with any faction of the church, but went to the gold fields of northern California, built up a comfortable fortune for himself, and made a good home in Santa Ana, where he died March 28, 1894.[4]

---

[3]This was but natural, for from their arrival in the islands the first missionaries had insisted upon the polygamous chieftains being married to their first wives and abandoning the practice of polygamy before baptism, consequently new doctrine brought by Addison Pratt was a radical reversal of Grouard's teaching. For early teaching in regard to polygamy, see "Events in the Life of Elder John Hawkins of Tahiti," by Joseph Burton, *Autumn Leaves*, Volume 16, page 546.

[4]While in the Islands in 1846, Benjamin F. Grouard married a daughter of a high chief of Anaa. When he returned to the United States in 1852, he brought his wife and three sons and settled in San Bernardino, California. Homesickness and climate were too much for the island girl, and in 1853 she and the eldest and youngest sons returned to the islands, leaving the middle son, Frank, with the Addison Pratt family. The Pratts moved to Utah when Frank was five years old. Later he ran away from home, and became lost to his father, who believed him dead. Frank became a famous Indian scout under General George Crook. He and his father met again in Sheridan, Wyoming, in 1893, after a separation of thirty-seven years. "I would have known you among ten thousand," said father to son. See *Life and Adventures of Frank Grouard* by Joe DeBarthe, reprinted by the Buffalo *Bulletin*, Buffalo, Wyoming, 1894.

XXXV.—Last Days of the Prophet

THE CHURCH HAD SO OFTEN appealed in vain for redress of their wrongs that, as the presidential election approached, Joseph Smith proposed to feel out some of the candidates with respect to their attitude towards the Latter Day Saints. He wrote Martin Van Buren, Lewis Cass, J. C. Calhoun, and Henry Clay. None of the answers pleased him. Clay's was the most favorable but not decisive enough to give the church any guarantee of protection. The Saints therefore determined to place Joseph Smith and Sidney Rigdon in the field on an Independent ticket. Surely the church people throughout the States had not the remotest idea of electing this ticket. The only explanation of this move could be that these men, smarting under injustice done, feeling unable to support any ticket in the field, resolved to roll up as high a protest vote as they possibly could. The "platform," if so it may be called, of this unique movement had some very wise provisions, however hopeless might be the chance of putting them into practice.

The year 1844 opened with public feeling running high on the "Mormon" question. So numerous had the Saints become in Hancock County that their favor was eagerly sought, and the party to which support was not given was ready to abuse and slander them.

In 1843 the Whig candidate for Congress, Cyrus Walker, had been defeated by the Democratic candidate, Joseph P. Hoge, and when it was learned that if the votes of Nauvoo, a large majority of which were cast for Hoge, had been cast for Walker, he would have been elected, the rage of the Whig press in Illinois knew no bounds.

The newspaper industry in Illinois was then in its infancy and, as has been implied by historians, a by no means reputable infancy. Newspapers were practically all published in the interest of one political party or the other, each editor as firm in his own political faith (Whig or Democrat) as any crusader in his religious belief. Each printed the speeches of its statesmen in full, and knew by heart the argument of its favorite spellbinders. "A man had to commit murder, steal a horse, or break a leg to get into the papers" in those days. "No painting barns, mending chicken coops, or 'Sunday-ing' with some neighbor," could win public recognition. The front page was for editorial comment on purely political matters, and a little country editor was quite ready to challenge debate with the biggest papers in New York City. The editorial method of debate was to turn out the most unbelievable "violence of invective and abuse." He poured forth a perfect lava of detraction, which, were it not for the knowledge of the people that such charges were generally false, or greatly exaggerated, would have overwhelmed and consumed all men's reputations. This was the sort of thing "especially to the taste of the young, crude state, and the inhabitants entered the lists without reserve and with sufficient vocabularies."

"Newspapers at present have little influence. Their readers are few, and these are taught to believe that anything that appears in a newspaper is a lie of course," said Hooper Warren, while DeTocqueville remarked upon the lack of influence of American newspapers. Miss Martineau had never heard anyone deny the profligacy of newspapers in general, or that American newspapers were the worst. "Why the Republic had not been overthrown by its newspapers," Miss Martineau did not understand.

But lightly as they were taken in their time, unfortunately the evil they do lives after them and imparts new joys to the muckraker sniffing through their yellowed pages for sensation. They certainly furnish plenty of it. With horror we read of John Fuller of Michigan saying in August, 1864, "Are you willing to follow in the footsteps of Lincoln, the perjured wretch?" of O'Brien of Illinois, declaring, "We want to try Lincoln as Charles I of England was tried, and if found guilty will carry out the law," or of

C. Chauncy Burr, saying, "We have patiently waited for a change, but for four years we have lived under a despotism, and the wonder is that men carry out the orders of the gorilla tyrant who has usurped the Presidential chair," but when it comes to lesser lights, we are more ready to believe.

We must approach the newspaper history of that time with this knowledge, for otherwise it cannot be understood. The two parties were so equal in the congressional district in which Nauvoo was situated that the Saints held the balance of power, and it was charged (as it naturally would be) that the Mormon leaders controlled the votes of the church, and hence were in a position absolutely to control the election.

Naturally a man in Joseph Smith's position would have a great deal of influence with a people who loved and trusted him, but the charge that he attempted or desired to dictate the vote of the church was certainly groundless, for in this case, although the vote went heavily for Hoge, Joseph Smith himself voted for Walker and said, "that he would not, if he could, influence any voter in giving his vote; that he considered it a mean business for him or any other man to attempt to dictate to the people whom they should support in elections."

If Joseph Smith had been inclined to use his political power to gain favor, he could have done so in the presidential election of 1844 by throwing his influence with one party or the other. Instead he brought the wrath of both parties upon his head by making what seemed even to some of his friends a rather ridiculous gesture of protest.

About this time disaffection, in which the Laws, Doctor Foster, and [some of] the Higbees figured prominently, culminated, and under date of April 18, 1844, the church recorder published notice that several had been expelled for "unchristianlike conduct." . . . Crime and immoral conduct were charged [freely] on both sides. . . . On May 6, 1844, Joseph was arrested by officer John D. Parker on a warrant by the clerk of the Circuit Court at Carthage issued on complaint of Francis M. Higbee, one of the dissenters mentioned above. It appears that Higbee claimed five thousand dollars damage, but his complaint did not specify upon what his claim was based; nor was there any crime charged whatever.[1]

Joseph obtained a writ of habeas corpus and brought the case before the Municipal Court at Nauvoo. Before this court he appeared on May 8 and after investigation was duly discharged. The complainant did not appear, either in person or by counsel, but at the request of the defendant, the court now went behind the writ and decided that Francis M. Higbee and others had conspired to take the life of Joseph Smith.

Immediately after this a "prospectus" was issued and distributed for a new paper, to be called the *Nauvoo Expositor*. On June 7 the *Expositor* appeared. It contained some original material and some of the old John C. Bennett charges. There were a few certified affidavits and some other serious allegations which were unsigned. In the spirit of those times, and because it was felt that the *Expositor* tended and was intended to stir up riot conditions, the city council on June 10, 1844, declared the *Expositor* a nuisance and ordered the mayor to have the establishment and paper removed without delay, in such manner as he should elect. The mayor issued an order to Marshal John P. Green, who with a posse proceeded to the office of the *Expositor* and removed press, type, papers, and fixtures into the street and destroyed them.

The Saints never did a more unwise thing than order the destruction of the *Expositor,* though it was not an unusual way of expressing disapproval when an editor voiced opinions contrary to the established prejudices of a community. Between 1823 and 1867 in the State of Illinois, sixteen instances of violence to either the editors or presses, or both, of men who dared to express views contrary to those held in the community may be counted. Editors said almost anything they pleased before the days of refinement of libel suits, although they well knew if they went too far they would be jerked up by the community in an unpleasant way. They took that chance. Among these sixteen are the famous cases

---

[1] *Church History,* Volume 2, pages 736, 737.

of Elijah Lovejoy, at Alton, and the attempt of General Burnside to suppress the Chicago *Times.*

In every instance save one or two, the editor left town and abandoned his efforts at publication; in none of them were the instigators punished; in but very few was there any adverse newspaper comment whatever, or any attempt made to punish those who participated.

But in the case of the *Expositor,* public opinion was already inflamed and waited only an opportunity to strike. Higbee swore out a warrant against the mayor and practically all the city council. As usual Joseph Smith and all others charged sued out a writ of habeas corpus in the Municipal Court of Nauvoo. But as the situation became more tense, on June 14 Joseph Smith made a report of the entire affair to Governor Ford and stated that if the Governor had any doubts about the legality of proceedings, he had only to signify it, and all who were implicated would go before any legal tribunal in the state capital and submit to investigation; that he need issue no writ, as they would respond upon receipt of his expressed wish.

Upon advice of Judge Jesse Thomas, those named again submitted to arrest and were tried before Daniel H. Wells, then not a member of the church but known as a "Jack Mormon."[2] The press, especially the Warsaw *Signal* (Whig), continued to pour out all manner of invectives. What favor they might have received from the Democrats after the election of Hoge was nullified by the fact that the Democrats could no longer look to the "Mormons" for help at the coming presidential election.

Again the writ for destroying the *Expositor* was renewed and put in the hands of Constable Bettisworth. Fearing for their lives from the mobs surrounding, the Smith brothers, Joseph and Hyrum, took refuge in Iowa, while they entered into correspondence with legal counsel and determined what to do. They had reason to fear mob violence.

---
[2] Nonmember who was favorable to the church.

A letter from Vilate Kimball to her husband, Heber C. Kimball, pictures conditions in Nauvoo:

June 7, 1844.

My Dear Husband: Nauvoo was never so lonesome since we lived here as it is now. I went to meeting last Sunday for the first time since conference. Neither Joseph nor Hyrum nor any of the Twelve were there, and you may be assured that I was glad when meeting was over. . . .

June 11th. Nauvoo was a scene of excitement last night. Some hundreds of brethren turned out and burned the press of the opposite party. This was done by order of the city council. They had published only one paper [*Nauvoo Expositor*] which is considered a public nuisance. They have sworn vengeance and no doubt will have it.

June 24th. Since I commenced this letter, varied and exciting indeed have been the scenes in this city. I would have sent this to you before this time, but I have been thrown into such confusion, I know not what to write. Nor is this all; the mails do not come regularly, having been stopped by high water, or the flood of mobocracy which pervades the country. I have received no letter by mail since you left.

Nothing is to be heard of but mobs collecting on every side. The Laws and Fosters, and most of the dissenting party, with their families, left here a day or two since. They are sworn to have Joseph and the city council or to exterminate us all. Between three and four thousand brethren have been under arms here the past week, expecting every day the mob would come upon us. The brethren from the country are coming in to aid in defense of the city. Brother Joseph sent a message to the Governor signifying if he and his staff would come into the city he would abide their decision; but instead of the Governor coming here, he went to Carthage, and there walked arm in arm with Law and Foster until we have reason to fear he has caught their spirit. He sent thirty men from there day before yesterday to arrest Brother Joseph, with an abusive letter, saying if thirty men cannot do the business, thousands can, ordering the brethren who had been ordered out to defend the city against the mob to deliver up their arms to their men and then disperse.

Yesterday morning (although it was Sunday) was a time of great excitement. Joseph had fled and left word for the brethren to hang on to their arms and defend themselves as best they could. Some were dreadfully tried in their faith to think Joseph should leave them in their hour of danger. Hundreds have left; the most of the merchants on the hill have gone. I have not yet been frightened, neither has my heart sunk within me till yesterday, when I heard that Joseph had sent word back for his family to follow him, and Brother Whitney's family were packing up, not knowing but they would have to go, as he is one of the city council. For a while I felt sad enough, but did not let anybody know it, neither did I shed tears. I felt a confidence in the Lord that he would preserve us from the ravages of our enemies. We expected them here today by the thousands, but before night yesterday things put on a different aspect—Joseph returned and gave himself up for trial. He sent a messenger to Carthage to tell the Governor he would meet him and his staff at the big mound at eight o'clock this morning, with all that the writ demanded. They have just passed here to meet the Governor for that purpose. My heart said, "Lord, bless those dear men and preserve them from those that thirst for their blood!" What will be their fate, the Lord only knows, but I trust he'll spare them. The Governor wrote that if they did not give themselves up, our city was suspended upon so many kegs of powder, and it needed only one spark to touch them off.[3]

This letter, written upon the scene, shows how much rumor had to do with events. The people who were not Latter Day Saints were as much afraid of the "Mormons" as the Saints were of the mob.

Joseph Smith had contemplated leaving Nauvoo and perhaps taking his case up to Federal authorities in Washington. As Emma Smith said, "He ... left home intending not to return until the church was sifted and thoroughly cleansed; but his persecutors were stirring up trouble at the time, and his absence provoked some of the brethren to say he had run away, and they called him a coward, and Joseph heard of it, and then returned and said, 'I will die before I will be called a coward.' He was going to find a place and then send for the family, but when he came back I felt the worst I ever did in my life, and from that time I looked for him to be killed."[4]

Maliciously minded persons have made it appear that Joseph was about to flee to the West, but was "coaxed to return by Emma" and so lost his life. His letter to her shows plainly what his intentions were, and these persons have for years in their publications deleted the part of the letter showing his destination was probably Washington, D. C. The original letter is in the church vault in Independence, Missouri.

---
[3] *Life of Heber C. Kimball*, pages 350-352.
[4] "Visit to Nauvoo in 1856," by Edmund C. Briggs, *Journal of History*, Volume 9, pages 453, 454.

For   Safety, June 23
Emma Smith:
   Brother Lewis has some money of mine—H. C. Kimball has $1,000, in his hands of mine, Bro. Neff, Lancaster Co., Pa.—$400.
   You may sell the Quincy property or any property that belongs to me you can find anything about, for your support and children and Mother. Do not despair— — If God ever opens a door that is possible for me I will see you again. I do not know where I shall go, or what I shall do, but shall if possible endeavor to get to the city of Washington.
   May God Almighty bless you, and the children, and Mother, and all my friends. My heart bleeds. No more at present. If you conclude to go to Kirtland, Cincinnati, or any other place, I wish you would contrive to inform me this evening.   Joseph Smith.
   P. S. If in your power I want you should help Dr. Richard's family.

He came back to Nauvoo, and the night before he left for Carthage, he spoke to the assembled people of his church from a platform on the northwest corner of the block on which stands the Nauvoo House and south across Water Street from the Mansion House.

"Brethren," he is reputed to have said, "before you would see me taken to Carthage and butchered, would you be willing to lay down your lives for me?"

"Yes," shouted the people almost with one voice.

The meaning of the next words were not understood by the people until several days after, for he felt, that by the sacrifice of his own life, he might spare his brethren and he said:

"Brethren, just as you are willing to lay down your lives for me, so I am willing to die for you."

Shortly after he said, "Farewell, brethren, and farewell to the city I have loved. I am going like a lamb to the slaughter."

He bade good-by to friends in Nauvoo. Charlotte Leabo, daughter of Peter Haws, remembered how he came to their home across the street from where his brother Hyrum lived. She was only nine, and she loved him dearly; he had but recently baptized her in the river. She could not understand why he kissed each of the children and bade them good-by, telling them to be good, and that they would see him no more.[5]

All seemed to sense an approaching tragedy, at least those nearest and dearest to Joseph and Hyrum felt impending calamity. Even Joseph's great mastiff, Major, for the first time in his faithful life, refused to obey orders to "go back home," and insisted on staying close to his master, and when imprisoned in an upper room, jumped from a second-story window to follow. At the loss of that master, who never returned, old Major transferred his loyalty to

---

[5] Daughter of Peter Haws, well known in early church history. Mrs. Leabo was the mother of Sister Detta Wilson (Mrs. Nelson Wilson) who did so much to establish the Reorganized Church in Manitoba and other places in western Canada and on the Pacific slope. Mrs. Leabo's brother, Albert Haws, was the first missionary of the Reorganized Church in Hawaii. *Saints' Herald*, 1904, page 41.

the eldest son Joseph, never leaving him night or day, and refusing to permit strangers to approach him. And there was reason to believe that danger did threaten "Young Joseph."

A group of his friends accompanied the Prophet on horseback part of the way to Carthage, unwilling to part with him, for what they felt might be the last time. Josiah Ells was one of these, and he often told of overhearing Joseph say to his brother Hyrum, who rode at his side, "Well, Brother Hyrum, we must go and lay our heads upon the sod. The mob want blood, and blood they will have. And if they do not have ours, they will kill our women and children." They had stopped at a spring for a drink of water, and when all were refreshed, he turned to his friends and said gently: "You, brethren, need not go further and expose yourselves to useless danger." Reluctant and sorrowing, they turned back.

In his published memoirs, *Joseph Smith III,* Young Joseph (as he was called) tells of meeting the actor, Thomas A. Lyne, on the street in Salt Lake City, on June 29, 1885, and of Lyne's account of this incident, he says:

> He [Lyne] was among the group of brethren who started to escort my father, Uncle Hyrum, and others to the county seat, when they were summoned in arrest to answer for the destruction of the printing plant of the *Nauvoo Expositor.* He proceeded five or six miles upon the road to Carthage, when a halt was called and a division of the party ensued. Father had decided it was unnecessary for so many to go with them, and Lyne was among those requested to return to Nauvoo. To this he strenuously objected, but his objections were overruled by father, who beckoned him to one side and told him to return and to be especially wary, wise, and watchful, adding, "Most probably I shall not return. I want you to live, so that you may help to correct the illusions, misunderstandings, and misstatements that will follow after my death—if I die. You will live to pass through many scenes of difficulty and danger, and you will also bear a strong testimony to the truth."

About four miles out of Nauvoo, they had met Captain Dunn and returned with him to Nauvoo, for Captain Dunn, with his company of cavalry, had with him an order for the "state arms" at Nauvoo. The militia at Nauvoo made no resistance, although

Dunn had requested that the Smiths return with him, for fear of an uprising. The Saints showed their usual disposition to be law-abiding. On account of this delay, it was nearly midnight on June 24, 1844, when the party arrived in Carthage, and put up at Hamilton's Hotel.

The next morning, having heard rumors of violence, they saw the Governor, who "pledged the faith of the State," that they would be protected. They then, accompanied by their attorney, H. T. Reid of Burlington, Iowa, who had met them there by request on the morning of the 25th, voluntarily surrendered themselves to the constable, Mr. Bettisworth, who held a writ against them on a charge of riot and for destroying the press, type, and fixtures of the *Nauvoo Expositor*, property of William and Wilson Law, and other dissenters. Soon after the surrender on charge of riot, they were both arrested on charge of treason against the State of Illinois. The affidavits upon which the writs were issued were made by Henry O. Norton and Augustine Spencer. That same afternoon, the two Smiths and other persons charged with riot, appeared before R. F. Smith, a justice of the peace residing in Carthage, and on advice of counsel "voluntarily entered into recognizance in the sum of five hundred dollars each with unexceptionable security for their appearance at the next term of the circuit court. . . .

"Making out the bonds and justifying bail, necessarily consumed considerable time, and when this was done, it was near night, and the justice adjourned his court over without asking the Smiths to answer to the charge of treason, or even intimating to their counsel or the prisoners that they were expected to enter into an examination that night."[6] In less than an hour after the adjournment of court, Constable Bettisworth, who had arrested the prisoners in the morning, appeared at Hamilton's Hotel, at the lodgings of the prisoners and their counsel, and insisted that they

---

[6]Statement of Attorney H. T. Reid, *Church History*, Volume 2, page 746.

should go to jail. Wood and Reid, their counsel maintained that they were entitled to be brought before the justice for an examination before they be sent to jail, and the constable produced a mittimus, signed by Smith, saying that the prisoners had been brought before him, and on account of the absence of material witnesses the trial was postponed. Therefore the prisoners were to be placed in jail.

The attorneys for the defense said, "the recitals of the mittimus is wholly untrue, unless the prisoners could have appeared before the justice without being present in person or by counsel." Reid and Wood appealed to the Governor, but he refused to intervene, nor would they take the prisoners out of jail for examination, assuring the counsel they had already been committed, but at length they were taken before Justice Smith, and their counsel then asked for a postponement until witnesses could be brought from Nauvoo. The justice fixed the examination then for 12 noon on Thursday, June 27.

On the morning of June 27, the Governor disbanded the troops from McDonough and sent them home, took Captain Dunn's company of cavalry and proceeded to Nauvoo, leaving the jail guarded only by the Carthage Greys. The two brothers spent the day quietly visiting with their friends, John Taylor and Willard Richards. Joseph Smith wrote two letters,[7] both of which showed that he intended to be submissive to the law of the state. However, about six o'clock in the afternoon, an armed mob invaded the jail and shot both of them to death.

---

[7] One to his wife Emma Smith and one to Honorable Orville H. Browning, asking him to assist in his defense. See page 291.

XXXVI.—The Deserted City

Thomas Ford, Governor of Illinois, at the time of the trouble which resulted in the death of Joseph and Hyrum Smith, was a man of much ability. He was "one of the ablest jurors in the State, a man of singularly clear philosophical mind, largely endowed by nature with a vigorous, comprehensive intellect, reinforced by fair education and much study. In stature he was small, with thin, homely features, deep-set gray eyes, and a long nose turned slightly at the point to one side. Well supplied with vanity and self-esteem, his prejudices were invincible, and his arrogance at times intolerable and ludicrous. As insignificant in body and soul as he was admirable in mental power, lacking in physical and moral courage, vindictive, obstinate, and spiteful, he hated those he could not control, and when opportunity offered, caused them to feel the sting of his resentment. His spirit of vengeance outlived the lapse of time. He might forget a benefaction but never forgive an injury."[1]

His course with the Latter Day Saints in Illinois vacillated dangerously between his convictions of justice, what sense of gratitude he had, and moral and physical fear, with a strong leaning towards the latter. Hearing of the tragedy at Carthage, he hastened there with all speed, to find the city mostly emptied of inhabitants. "As the country was utterly defenseless, this seemed to be a proper precaution." Even the county records were taken from the courthouse at Carthage and removed to another location in the dead of night.

Gregg well describes the rather ridiculous situation of that night:

---

[1] Doctor J. F. Snyder in "Forgotten Statesmen of Illinois," *Transactions of Illinois Historical Society*, 1909, page 224.

On the morning of the 28th of June, 1844, the sun rose on as strange a scene as the broad Hancock prairies had ever witnessed. At the three corners of a triangle, eighteen miles asunder, two of them resting on the Mississippi, stood a smitten and mourning city and two almost deserted villages, with here and there a group of questioning men, anxious to obtain the news of the night. These were Nauvoo and the villages of Carthage and Warsaw. Toward the two villages the more courageous ones who had fled the evening before were now returning, tired and worn, to find their several homes unsacked and untouched, and their streets untrodden by a vengeful and infuriated foe. The wet and heavy roads leading to the county seat from the east and south were being again traversed by the refugees of the night, now returning where they had so lately fled in terror. The blue waves of the Mississippi rolled peacefully past the stricken city as when, a few days before, its shores resounded to the Legion's martial tread. All the people knew that a great crime had been committed, by whom they dared not guess; and they knew not how, upon whom, where, or in what manner, retribution might fall![2]

Life soon gained a measure of normalcy, and the "anti-Mormon" papers, led as in the past by the Whig Sangamon *Journal* and Warsaw *Signal*, continued their rabid publication, suggesting now the absolute expulsion of the "Mormons." The agitation continued until the Latter Day Saints finally agreed to evacuate Nauvoo by the spring of 1846. "Quit their freedom among freemen and go where the land, the elements, and the worship of God are free." Early in February the first wagons crossed the Mississippi Ford says:

During the winter of 1845-6, the Mormons made the most prodigious preparations for removal. All the houses in Nauvoo, and even the Temple, were converted into workshops; and before spring more than twelve thousand wagons were in readiness. The people from all parts of the country flocked to Nauvoo to purchase houses and farms, which were sold extremely low, lower than the prices at a sheriff's sale, for money, wagons, horses, oxen, cattle, and other articles of personal property which might be needed by the Mormons in their exodus into the wilderness. By the middle of May it was estimated that sixteen thousand Mormons had crossed the Mississippi and taken up their line of march with their personal property, their wives and little ones, westward across the continent to Oregon or California, leaving behind them in Nauvoo a small remnant of a thousand souls,

---
[2]Gregg's *Prophet of Palmyra*, pages 281, 282.

being those who were unable to sell their property, or who, having no property to sell, were unable to get away.[3]

But these newcomers, determined upon gaining possession of Nauvoo "never ceased from strife and outrage,"[4] until only a comparative few remained. In truth, their courage increased as the number of their victims diminished.

The Illinois people were so anxious to have Nauvoo evacuated that they finally attacked the town with an armed mob. On September 12, 1846, occurred the battle of Nauvoo. The valiant defense of the Saints is thus described by Bancroft:

> On the 10th of September the posse, now more than a thousand strong, with wagons, equipments, and every preparation for a campaign, approached Nauvoo and encamped at Hunter's farm.
> At this time there were in the city not more than a hundred and fifty Mormons and about the same number of Gentiles, or as they were termed, "new citizens," capable of bearing arms, the remainder of the population consisting of destitute women and children and of the sick. Many of the Gentiles had departed, fearing a general massacre, and those who remained could not be relied upon as combatants, for they were of course unwilling to risk their lives in a conflict which if successful, would bring them no credit. Nothing daunted, the little band, under command of Colonels Daniel H. Wells and William Cutler, took up its position on the edge of a wood in the suburbs of Nauvoo, and less than a mile from the enemy's camp.
> Before hostilities commenced, a deputation from Quincy visited the camp of the assailants, and in vain attempted to dissuade them

---

[3]Governor Ford's *History of Illinois*, page 412.
This book was written in an effort to justify himself in the eyes of his fellow politicians, and must be so interpreted. He himself in the closing paragraph of his book tells how he has "had to encounter bitter opposition to his administration, and enmities have sprung up personally against himself, which he hopes will not last forever." For "he is possessed of such sensibility that it is painful to him to be the subject of such unmerited obloquy; and for this reason and this alone, he hopes that when those of his fellow citizens who have disapproved of his administration in these particulars have time to look into the merits of these measures, and see how they have lifted the State from the abyss of the despair and gloom to a commanding and honorable position among her sister States of the Union, they will not remember their wrath forever" (closing words of Ford's *History of Illinois*). Despite this rather pathetic close to his book which he wrote while he was living in greatly reduced circumstances at Peoria —in obscurity as his sole legacy to his orphan children—it was noted for its bitter and scathing quality. He died November 3, 1850, leaving his motherless children destitute, according to Isabel Jamieson in her *Literature and Literary People of Early Illinois*. Two of his sons, Tom and Sewall Ford, under the alias of Charley and Tom Smith, were lynched at Wellington, Kansas, in 1874, as horse thieves. Whether or not they were guilty, the law left them as unprotected as their father did Joseph and Hyrum Smith at Carthage. A daughter, Anna, who had married an officer in the Mexican War during her father's term of office, finally died in indigent circumstances at a Deaconess Hospital in Lincoln, Illinois.
[4]Bancroft's *History of Utah*, page 226.

from their purpose. No sooner had they departed, than fire was opened on the Mormons from a battery of six-pounders, but without effect. Here for the day matters rested. At sunrise the posse changed their position, intending to take the city by storm, but were held in check by Captain Anderson at the head of thirty-five men, termed by the Saints the Spartan band. The enemy now fired some rounds of grape shot, forcing the beseiged to retire out of range; after some further cannonading, darkness put an end to the skirmish, the Mormons throwing up breastworks during the night.

On the morning of the 12th the demand of unconditional surrender was promptly rejected; whereupon, at a given signal, several hundred men who had been stationed in ambush, on the west bank of the river to cut off the retreat of the Mormons, appeared with red flags in their hands, thus portending massacre. The assailants now opened fire from all their batteries, and soon afterward advanced to the assault, slowly, and with the measured tramp of veterans, at their head being Constable Carlin and the Reverend Brockman, and unfurled above them the Stars and Stripes. When within rifle range of the breastworks, the posse wheeled toward the south, attempting to outflank the Saints and gain possession of the temple square. But this movement had been anticipated, and posted in the woods to the north of the Mormon position lay the Spartan band. Leading on his men at double quick, Anderson suddenly confronted the enemy and opened a brisk fire from revolving rifles. The posse advanced no farther, but for an hour and a half held their ground bravely against the Spartan band, the expense of ammunition in proportion to casualties being greater than has yet been recorded in modern warfare. Then they retreated in excellent order to the camp. The losses of the Mormons were three killed and a few slightly wounded; the losses of the Gentiles are variously stated. Among those who fell were Captain Anderson and his son, a youth of sixteen, the former dying, as he had vowed that he would die, in defense of the holy sanctuary.[5]

But there was no alternative. On the 17th of September, the ill-prepared remnant crossed the Mississippi and camped on the other side.

Bancroft sums up the situation as follows:

It was indeed a singular spectacle, as I have said, this upon the western border of the world's greatest republic in the autumn of 1846. A whole cityful, with other settlements, and thousands of thrifty agriculturists in the regions about, citizens of the United States, driven beyond the border by other citizens: not by reason of their religion alone, though this was made a pretense; not for breaking the laws,

---
[5]Bancroft's *History of Utah*, pages 228-230.

though this was made a pretense; not on account of their immorality, for the people of Illinois and Missouri were not immaculate[6] in that respect; nor was it altogether on account of their solid voting and growing political power, accompanied ever by the claim of general inheritance and universal dominion, though this last had more to do with it probably than all the rest combined, notwithstanding that the spirit of liberty and the laws of the republic permitted such massing of social and political influence, and notwithstanding the obvious certainty that any of the Gentile political parties now playing the role of persecutors would gladly and unscrupulously have availed themselves of such means for the accomplishment of their ends. It was all these combined, and so combined as to engender deadly hate. It gave the Mormons a power in proportion to their numbers not possessed by other sects or societies, which could not and would not endure it; a power regarded by the others as unfairly acquired, and by a way and through means not in accord with the American idea of individual equality, of equal rights and equal citizenship. In regard to all other sects within the Republic, under guard of the Constitution, religion was subordinated to politics and government; in regard to the Mormons, in spite of the Constitution, politics and government were subordinated to religion.[7]

While preparing for an article upon the question of why the Saints were driven from Nauvoo, Honorable Orville F. Berry called on several prominent men acquainted with the difficulties, first upon Honorable George Edmunds, one of the finest and most able lawyers in western Illinois. He admitted that he had seen Joseph Smith but once, and that many years before on his way to Kirtland from New York, and that he had never seen Hyrum. Berry said, "I would like a brief, concise statement of the immediate cause leading up to the killing of the Smiths." Judge Edmunds answered, "The impression that I have and always have had since I came here is that politics were largely at the base of the trouble. Had the Mormon population voted for Walker, as Walker supposed they would—he having Joseph's promise to vote for him—the trouble with the Mormons would not have culminated when it did." To the request: "Give me your idea of the

---

[6] One of the most prominent political tormenters of the Latter Day Saints being asked, during a political speech, if he were guilty of some gross immorality, is said to have replied, "Yes, but what in h— has that to do with the Kansas-Nebraska Bill?"
[7] Bancroft's *History of Utah*, pages 231, 232.

justice or injustice of driving the Mormons out of Hancock County," he answered, "I can say for the Mormon population, so far as I knew them, that I think I never knew so industrious, frugal, and virtuous a set of people as they were."

Judge Thomas C. Sharp, whose editorial effusions had more than anything else to do with inflammation of public opinion against the Latter Day Saints, and whom rumor connected still more closely with the actual acts of violence, also gave Honorable O. F. Berry to understand that the trouble was mainly political, and protested in his maturer years that he was "not even favorable" to the manner in which the Smiths met their death. Berry sums up his conclusion by saying:

> After a careful examination of the conditions preceding and after the death of Joseph Smith, my belief is that it was not religious controversies that led to the Mormon trouble in Hancock County and adjoining counties, but that it was purely political. The writer believes from well-established facts that have come to him from interviews with men in active life, that a majority of the people here known as Mormons were good citizens, but that it is equally true there were among them men who no doubt used the church to cover up their own wickedness. This has always been true, and will continue to be in some degree. The writer is satisfied from evidence entirely satisfactory to him that Joseph and Hyrum Smith did not teach and preach the doctrine of polygamy.[8]

But be the cause of their expulsion what it might be, the situation was now desperate for many of them. Bancroft continues:

> ... the last of the Mormon host that now lay huddled to the number of 640 on the western bank of the river in sight of the city; if the first departures from Nauvoo escaped extreme hardships, not so these. It was the latter part of September, and nearly all were prostrated with chills and fevers; there at the river bank, among the dock and rushes, poorly protected, without the shelter of a roof or anything to keep off the force of wind or rain, little ones came into life and were left motherless at birth. They had not food enough to satisfy the cravings of the sick, nor clothing fit to wear. For months thereafter there were periods when all the flour they used was of the

---

[8]Honorable Orville F. Berry in "The Mormon Settlement in Illinois," from *Illinois History Transactions of the Illinois Historical Society* 1906, page 92.

coarsest, the wheat being ground into coffee and hand mills, which only cut the grain; others used a pestle; the finer meal was used for bread, the coarser made into hominy. Boiled wheat was now the chief diet for sick and well. For ten days they subsisted on parched corn. Some mixed their remnant of grain with the pounded bark of the slippery elm, which they stripped from the trees along their route.[9]

The most graphic picture of the scene has been given by Colonel Thomas Kane:

A few years ago, ascending the Upper Mississippi in the autumn when its waters were low, I was compelled to travel by land past the region of the rapids. My road lay through the Half Breed Tract, a fine section of Iowa, which the unsettled state of its land titles had appropriated as a sanctuary for coiners, horse thieves and other outlaws. I had left my steamer at Keokuk, at the foot of the Lower Fall, to hire a carriage, and to contend for some fragments of a dirty meal with the swarming flies, the only scavengers of the locality. From this place to where the deep water of the river returns, my eye wearied to see everywhere sordid vagabond and idle settlers, and a country marred, without being improved by their careless hands.

I was descending the last hillside upon my journey when a landscape in delightful contrast broke upon my view. Half encircled by a bend of the river, a beautiful city lay glittering in the fresh morning sun; its bright new dwellings set in cool, green gardens ranging up around a stately dome-shaped hill, which was crowned by a noble marble edifice, whose high tapering spire was radiant with white and gold. The city appeared to cover several miles; and beyond it, in the background, there rolled off a fair country, chequered by the careful lines of fruitful husbandry. The unmistakable marks of industry, enterprise, and educated wealth everywhere made the scene one of singular and most striking beauty.

It was a natural impulse to visit this inviting region. I procured a skiff, and, rowing across the river, landed at the chief wharf of the city. No one met me there. I looked, and saw no one. I could hear no one move; though the quiet everywhere was such that I heard the flies buzz, and the water ripples break against the shallow of the beach. I walked through the solitary streets. The town lay as in a dream, under some deadening spell of loneliness from which I almost feared to wake it; for plainly it had not slept long. There was no grass growing up in the paved ways; rains had not entirely washed away the prints of dusty footsteps.

Yet I went about unchecked. I went into empty workshops, ropewalks,[10] and smithies. The spinner's wheel was idle; the carpenter

---
[9] Bancroft's *History of Utah*, pages 232, 233.
[10] Ropewalks. Referring to Egan's rope factory near the river.

had gone from his work bench and shavings, his unfinished sash and casing. Fresh bark was in the tanner's vat, and the fresh chopped lightwood stood piled against the baker's oven. The blacksmith's shop was cold; but his coal heap, and ladling pool, and crooked water horn, were all there, as if he had just gone off for a holiday. No work people anywhere looked to know my errand. If I went into the gardens, clinking the wicket-latch loudly after me, to pull the marigolds, heart's-ease, and lady's-slippers, and draw a drink with the water-sodden well-bucket and its noisy chain; or, knocking off with my stick the tall heavy-headed dahlias and sunflowers, hunted over the beds for cucumbers and love-apples—no one called out to me from any open window, or dog sprang forward to bark an alarm. I could have supposed the people hidden in the houses; but the doors were unfastened; and when at last ·I timidly entered them, I found dead ashes white upon the hearths, and had to tread a-tiptoe, as if walking down the aisle of a country church, to avoid rousing irreverent echoes from the naked floors.

On the outskirts of the town was the city graveyard; but there was no record of plague there, nor did it in anywise differ much from other Protestant American cemeteries. Some of the mounds were not long sodded; some of the stones were newly set, their dates recent, and their black inscriptions glossy in the mason's hardly dried lettering ink. Beyond the graveyard, out in the fields, I saw, in one spot hard by where the fruited boughs of a young orchard had been roughly torn down, the still smouldering remains of a barbecue fire, that had been constructed of rails from the fencing around it. It was the latest sign of life there. Fields upon fields of heavy-headed yellow grain lay rotting ungathered upon the ground. No one was at hand to take in their rich harvest. As far as the eye could reach, they stretched away—they sleeping too in the hazy air of autumn.

Only two portions of the city seemed to suggest the import of this mysterious solitude. On the southern suburb, the houses looking out upon the country showed, by their splintered woodwork, and walls battered to the foundation, that they had lately been the mark of a destructive cannonade. And in and around the splendid temple, which had been the chief object of my admiration, armed men were barracked, surrounded by their stacks of musketry and pieces of heavy ordnance. These challenged me to render an account of myself, and why I had had the temerity to cross the water without a written permit from a leader of their band.

Though these men were more or less under the influence of ardent spirits, after I had explained myself as a passing stranger, they seemed anxious to gain my good opinion. They told the story of the Dead City; that it had been a notable manufacturing and commercial mart, sheltering over twenty thousand persons; that they had waged war with its inhabitants for several years, and had been finally successful only a few days before my visit, in an action fought in front of the ruined suburb; after which, they had driven them forth at the point of the sword. The defense, they said, had been obstinate, but gave way on the third day's bombardment. They boasted greatly of their prowess, especially in this battle, as they called it; but I discovered they were not of one mind as to certain of the exploits that had distinguished it; one of which, as I remember, was, that they had slain a father and his son, a boy of fifteen, not long residents of the fated city, whom they admitted to have borne a character without reproach.

They also conducted me inside the massive sculptured walls of the curious temple, in which they said the banished inhabitants were accustomed to celebrate the mystic rites of an unhallowed worship. They particularly pointed out to me certain features of the building, which, having been the peculiar objects of a former superstitious regard, they had, as a matter of duty sedulously defiled and defaced. The reputed sites of certain shrines they had thus particularly noticed; and various sheltered chambers, in one of which was a deep well, constructed, they believed, with a dreadful design. Beside these, they led me to see a large and deep-chiseled marble vase or basin, supported upon twelve oxen, also of marble, and of the size of life, of which they told some romantic stories. They said the deluded persons, most of whom were emigrants from a great distance, believed their Deity countenanced their reception here of a baptism of regeneration, as proxies for whomsoever they held in warm affection in the countries from which they had come. That here parents "went into the water" for their lost children, children for their parents, widows for their spouses, and young persons for their lovers; that thus the Great Vase came to be for them associated with all dear and distant memories, and was therefore the object, of all others in the building, to which they attached the greatest degree of idolatrous affection. On this account, the victors had so diligently desecrated it, as to render the apartment in which it was contained too noisome to abide in.

They permitted me also to ascend into the steeple, to see where it had been lightning struck on the Sabbath before, and to look out, east and south, on wasted farms like those I had seen near the city, extending till they were lost in the distance. Here, in the face of the pure day, close to the scar of the Divine Wrath left by the thunderbolt, were fragments of food, cruses of liquor, and broken drinking vessels, with a brass drum and a steamboat signal bell, of which I afterwards learned the use with pain.

It was after nightfall, when I was ready to cross the river on my return. The wind had freshened since the sunset, and the water beating roughly into my little boat, I hedged higher up the stream than the point I had left in the morning, and landed where a faint glimmering light invited me to steer.

Here, among the dock and rushes, sheltered only by the darkness, without roof between them and sky, I came upon a crowd of several hundred human creatures, whom my movements roused from uneasy slumber upon the ground.

Passing these on my way to the light, I found it came from a tallow candle in a paper funnel shade, such as is used by street vendors of apples and peanuts, and which flaming and guttering away in the bleak air off the water, shone flickeringly on the emaciated features of a man in the last stage of a bilious remittent fever. They had done their best for him. Over his head was something like a tent, made of a sheet or two, and he rested on a but partially ripped open old straw mattress, with a hair sofa cushion under his head for a pillow. His gaping jaw and glazing eye told how short a time he would monopolize these luxuries; though a seemingly bewildered and excited person, who might have been his wife, seemed to find hope in occasionally forcing him to swallow, awkwardly, sips of the tepid river water from a burned and battered bitter-smelling tin coffee pot. Those who knew better had furnished the apothecary he needed; a toothless old baldhead, whose manner had the repulsive dullness of a man familiar with death scenes. He, so long as I remained, mumbled in his patient's ear a monotonous and melancholy prayer, between the pauses of which I heard the hiccough and sobbing of two little girls, who were sitting upon a piece of driftwood outside.

Dreadful indeed, was the suffering of these forsaken beings; bowed and cramped by cold and sunburn, alternating as each weary day and night dragged on, they were almost all of them, the crippled victims of disease. They were there because they had no homes, nor hospital, nor poorhouse, nor friends to offer them any. They could not satisfy the feeble cravings of their sick; they had not bread to quiet the fractious hunger cries of their children. Mothers and babes, daughters and grandparents, all of them alike, were bivouacked in tatters, wanting even covering to comfort those whom the sick shiver of fever was searching to the marrow.

These were the Mormons, in Lee County, Iowa, in the fourth week of the month of September, in the year of our Lord, 1846. The city —it was Nauvoo, Illinois. The Mormons were the owners of that city and the smiling country around. And those who had stopped their plows, who had silenced their hammers, their axes, their shuttle, and their workshop wheels; those who had put out their fires, who had eaten their food, spoiled their orchards, and trampled under foot their thousands of acres of unharvested bread; these were the keepers of their dwellings, the carousers in their temple, whose drunken riot insulted the ears of the dying.

I think it was as I turned from the wretched night watch of which I have spoken, that I first listened to the sounds of revel of a party of the guard within the city. Above the distant hum of the voices of many, occasionally rose distinct the loud oath-tainted exclamation, and the falsely intonated scrap of vulgar song; but lest this requiem should go unheeded, every now and then, when their boisterous orgies strove to attain a sort of ecstatic climax, a cruel spirit of insulting frolic carried some of them up into the high belfry of the temple steeple, and there with the wicked childishness of inebriates, they whooped, and shrieked, and beat the drum that I had seen, and rang in charivaric unison their loud-tongued steamboat bell.

They were, all told, not more than six hundred and forty persons who were thus lying on the river flats. But the Mormons in Nauvoo and its dependencies had been numbered the year before at over twenty thousand. Where were they?[11]

Some of them, a large number, had as Colonel Kane said, "last been seen, a mournful train, carrying their sick and wounded, halt and blind, to disappear behind the western horizon, pursuing the phantom of another home!" They were to find that home and build there another great city, but except those of them who came back in later years, their story is not ours.

Back in that deserted city, near the water's edge, stood the Mansion House, not long since completed, home of a tall, dark-haired widow and her five children, an arrogant little beauty of fifteen, the adopted daughter Julia; a solemn brown-eyed boy of nearly fourteen, Joseph; Frederick, past ten, merry and sunny, with the brown eyes of his mother; Alexander, a lad of blue eyes like his father; and the little brother, baby David, loved and loving of them all, who was not quite two, for he was born after the cruel death of his father. Calmly, with a quiet courage, this woman, when nearly all had left, stayed on, (except for a few months' refuge up the river at Fulton City) and reared her family in the deserted city. Her boys played and studied with the boys of the new citizens. She baked cookies for them all. Time passed. Emma had no enemies in Nauvoo. She found herself and her children respected by all. She never spoke of religion, for although she still cherished in her heart the principles of the church her husband founded, she had come to the time when she had lost some of the illusions her friends still cherished, and had reluctantly bade them good-by at the parting of the roads.

---

[11] Smucker's *History of the Mormons*, pages 217-223; *Church History*, Volume 3, pages 173-179.

XXXVII.—The Parting of the Ways

The leading officials of the church, most of whom were on missions, hastened back to Nauvoo, and were soon engaged in an uncompromising struggle over who was to be the new leader. In 1917 there came into the possession of the Southern California Historical Society an ancient manuscript, the journal of George Miller, presiding bishop in 1844 at the time of Joseph Smith's death: "Many gaps occur . . . the pages are yellow with age, and whole segments have gone by the board, frequently a portion of a page is torn off, and other parts so charred as to be utterly undecipherable," so says Dr. H. W. Mills in his *De Tal Palo Tal Astilla,* but in them we can read something of the turmoil that was occurring in Nauvoo among the principal men of the church:

> On my arrival in Nauvoo, I visited Elder John Taylor of the Quorum of Apostles who was sick of his wounds received in Carthage Jail at the time of Joseph's death. Dr. Willard Richards (Joseph Smith's scribe) was there, and after a few remarks in regard to the mob, I asked Dr. Richards, whom Joseph had left to succeed him in the prophetic office. He replied that all was right; that there was a sealed document left which would be opened when the Apostles should get home that would settle all these matters . . . from the hints and innuendos that I heard frequently, I was induced to believe that Joseph had designated his son Joseph to succeed him to the prophetic office, and on this belief I rested.

The Twelve at Nauvoo early assumed charge, but the vote by which they took control simply read, "All in favor of supporting the Twelve in their calling" (Nauvoo, August 8, 1844). This was interpreted, as time passed, to mean that they were in control, and they proceeded to administer the affairs of the church accordingly. On December 5, 1847, certain members of the Twelve met in council at Winter Quarters, Nebraska, and appointed Brigham Young to be president of the church and Heber C. Kimball and Willard Richards to be his counselors.

Less than three weeks later, December 24, 1847, this action of the Apostles was presented to a conference held in a log tabernacle recently erected on the east side of the Missouri River, and capable of seating about one thousand persons. This conference confirmed the action of the group of Apostles.

There were very many good people in all factions, and the majority of those who endured the hardships of the long westward journey of the Utah pioneers were of that class. Some felt there was no other alternative. The letter from Oliver Cowdery to his sister, Mrs. Phoebe Jackson, and her husband Daniel, which has been preserved, shows something of the predicament in which many of the Saints felt themselves to be.

Tiffin, Seneca County, Ohio, July 24, 1846.

Brother Daniel and Sister Phoebe: Phoebe's letter mailed at Montrose on the 2d of this month was received in due time, and would have been replied to immediately, but it came in the midst of toil and the business of court, which has just closed, and I take the earliest moment to answer. It is needless to say that we had long looked for and long expected a letter from you or Sister Lucy. Now, Brother Daniel and Sister Phoebe, what will you do? Has Sister Phoebe written us the truth? and if so, will you venture with your little ones into the toils and fatigues of a long journey and that for the sake of finding a resting-place, when you know of miseries of such magnitude as have, as will, and as must rend asunder the tenderest and holiest ties of domestic life? I can hardly think it possible that you have written us the truth, that though there may be individuals who are guilty of the iniquities[1] spoken of—yet no such practice can be preached or adhered to as a public doctrine. Such may do for the followers of Mahomet; it may have been done some thousands of years ago, but no people professing to be governed by the pure and holy principles of the Lord Jesus can hold up their heads before the world at this distance of time and be guilty of such folly, such wrong, such abomination. It will blast, like a mildew, their fairest prospects, and lay the ax at the root of their future happiness.

You would like to know whether we are calculating to come on and emigrate to California. On this subject everything depends upon circumstances not necessary for me to here speak of. We do not feel to say or do anything to discourage you from going, if you think it

---

[1] Referring probably to a beginning of polygamy and showing that Oliver Cowdery had then heard for the first time of this nefarious doctrine.

best to do so. We know, in part, how you are situated. Out of the church you have few or no friends, and very little or no society—in it you have both.

So far as going West is concerned, I have thought it a wise move —indeed I could see no other, and though the journey is long and attended with toil, yet a bright future has been seen in the distance if right counsels are given and a departure in no way from the original faith, in no instance, countenanced. Of what that doctrine and faith are and were I ought to know, and further it does not become me now to speak.[2]

Many who went West never took part in the practice of the doctrines that proved so obnoxious to their brethren. For thrift, industry, and many of the virtues that make for good citizenship, this faction distinguished itself. Whatever we may say about what later happened to the leaders in Utah, there is no one who cannot afford to view with admiration the courage, faith, and capacity for sacrifice of the band of Saints who crossed the plains. And in that train of pioneers, there were those who later returned to become our own, and many of the sons and daughters, grandsons and granddaughters of those pioneers became stalwarts of the Reorganization.

After the death of Joseph and Hyrum Smith, Sidney Rigdon came back to Nauvoo to present his claims. He maintained that he was the legal guardian of the church, entitled to preside as the only surviving member of the First Presidency, and that according to divine instruction, he was equal with Joseph Smith in holding the keys of the kingdom.[3]

After consultation with the president of the stake, William Marks, he called a meeting in the grove, August 8, 1844, in advocacy of his claim, but the Twelve as represented by Brigham Young assumed control of the assembly. As is usual in such cases, every man in that meeting saw what happened according to his own opinion of the issues involved. Some later, who went

---

[2] *Church History*, Volume 4, pages 272, 273.
[3] Doctrine and Covenants 87:3.

to Utah, with Brigham Young, said they had witnessed the features of "Brother Brigham" transformed into the very likeness of the prophet. Others, perhaps more literal minded, saw quite another thing. In the tattered remnant of George Miller's journal we read what he wrote at the time:

> On the return of the Twelve, a public meeting was called. The Apostles and Sidney Rigdon were on the stand, Brigham Young acting as principal speaker. Sidney urged his pretensions as a kind of guardian and temporary leader. Young made a loud and long harangue, and as I had always taken him to be a blunderbuss in speaking—and on this occasion apparently more so—for the life of me I could not see any point in the course of his remarks other than a wish to overturn Sidney Rigdon's pretensions. As this meeting was a pretty general conference of the elders, the Twelve assumed a temporary leadership, which was pretty generally conceded to them, as they were the quorum next in authority to the Prophet and Presidency of the whole church. N. K. Whitney and myself were put in nomination as trustees in trust for the church, instead of Joseph Smith, deceased, and were voted in by acclamation, and acknowledged as such by all present.

George Miller, it will be recalled, was then Bishop of the church.

Elder Rigdon's claims in consequence were not presented, but he did not consider this a settlement of the point at issue. Returning to Pittsburgh on October 15, 1844, he commenced to publish the *Messenger and Advocate.* In April, 1845, he perfected his organization, assuming the place made vacant by Joseph's death, and appointing other officers, including two counselors, Samuel James and Ebenezer Robinson; Carvel Rigdon (his brother) as patriarch, and a quorum of apostles. A stake was established at Pittsburgh with the usual officers. He also organized a quorum of seventy-three, unique in the history of the various factions, as it not only included seventies, but men belonging to other quorums as well.

In the pages of Rigdon's *Messenger and Advocate* may be found the names of some of the ablest and most logical expositors of

THE PARTING OF THE WAYS

the faith of the Saints, but the group apparently lacked cohesion. The organization maintained a struggling existence for years but never fulfilled its early promise, although the insistence of this faction upon observance of the laws of the land was most commendable, as compared with the teachings of some of Rigdon's erstwhile brethren.

One of the converts of Rigdon, William Bickerton, was able to start a branch, which has endured until the present time. This group has members throughout Pennsylvania, Ohio, Colorado, and several churches in Detroit, Michigan. One of the admirable achievements of this small faction has been the publication of the Book of Mormon in Italian, and the introduction of the gospel among the people of that nationality in America to a remarkable extent, considering the size of the working force.

The man who became leader of the second largest group of that early period was a man comparatively unknown during the lifetime of Joseph Smith. His name was James J. Strang, and he was not baptized until February 25, 1844, but by sheer force of personality he put himself at the head of a large faction as years passed. He made certain miraculous claims which won many to him, and was not without real ability as a leader. He at first declared against the evil of polygamy as practiced in the West, but some time later avowed belief in the doctrine (about 1848 or 1849). The acquisition of the notorious John C. Bennett to his organization may partly have accounted for his changed viewpoint. Strang claimed his ordination to have been at the hands of an angel about the same hour as the death of Joseph Smith in Carthage.

Strang first built up the city of Voree, at a place now called Spring Prairie, in Walworth County, Wisconsin, but as his organization grew, he decided to plant a colony on the Lake Michigan archipelago and the following year headed a prospecting party to Beaver Island. This island, fifteen miles in length by six in width, became the new home of the "Strangites." Strang assumed more and more of the qualities of a dictator and finally permitted himself to be crowned king in July, 1850. In 1854 King James was elected to the Michigan legislature and took oath of office on January 3, 1855. He had a lovable personality, some real ability, and was daring to the point of rashness. A man of his type was bound to create antagonism, and he was shot and mortally wounded in June, 1856, taken to Voree, Wisconsin, and died there. A few of his adherents remain to this day, but there has never been a successful effort made to revive the movement.

Another group under the leadership of Alpheus Cutler[4] dissented from the westward movement, and after some wandering, founded the little town of Manti in Fremont County, Iowa. Here Cutler finally died, but before he passed away he called some of his elders to him and told them of a land far to the north between two beautiful lakes, where they were to take a colony and preach to the Indians. In 1865, the advance guard of this people found the land described by their aged leader, and the whole colony removed there and founded the village of Clitherall, Minnesota. With them was an Indian chief of the Oneida tribe of New York, by the name of Lewis Denna, who had been a missionary in the time of Joseph Smith, traveling many miles on foot from tribe to tribe in Kansas and Nebraska. With Denna's aid, a treaty, which neither party ever broke, was drawn up with the Indians. They lived in peace together for many years, until civilization drove the Indian elsewhere. Most of these people joined the Reorganization as years went by, but a remnant still

---

[4] The author may not thoroughly understand the position taken by Alpheus Cutler, but he did not, I think, claim at first to be the successor to Joseph Smith, but rather one of a certain quorum or committee of seven men, arranged and set apart by Joseph the Seer in Nauvoo. This committee still retained certain prerogatives after the church, as an organization, had been rejected. This group believed all the fundamental doctrines of the church, as well as baptism for the dead and other temple rites and ceremonies. But their outstanding achievement is the operation among themselves of a United Order with All Things in Common. The belief in this has been taught and an attempt made to put it into practice by almost all factions and groups of the Restoration Movement. This group at Clitherall for a few years held everything in common. This venture failed, and they returned to individual ownership for many years, but a few families are again making an attempt to put it into effect at the present time, with admirable results.

exists and has founded a small but successful community venture in Clitherall with a branch in Independence, Missouri. As a group, by their strict morality, honesty, and industry they have richly earned the honor and respect of all men with whom they have business or social contact.

There were movements sponsored by George M. Hinkle, by James Colin Brewster, by James Emmett, by Gladden Bishop, and several times David Whitmer was persuaded to take the leadership of a small group, but these declined rapidly.

Little Joseph was not forgotten, but a certain fear was expressed for his safety, if we are to believe the journal of Presiding Bishop George Miller, for he says:

> Subsequent to these times of intense excitement, I made frequent attempts at conversation with Brigham Young and H. C. Kimball in regard to Joseph leaving one to succeed him in the prophetic office, and in all my attempts to ascertain the desired truth as to that personage, I was invariably met with the innuendo, "Stop, or hush, Brother Miller, let nothing be said in regard to this matter or we will have little Joseph killed as his father was"; implying indirectly that Joseph Smith had appointed his son Joseph to succeed him in the prophetic office. And I believe that this impression was left not alone upon my mind, but on the brethren in general and remains with many until this day.

Good and honorable men were in every one of these groups; in fact, in spite of certain abnormal social conditions that sprang up in a few of these colonies, out-and-out rogues have been comparatively few in any branch of the Restoration Movement, but so strangely is man constituted that seemingly there can be no honest difference of opinion religiously. Men who had walked closely together, been more than brothers, now condemned each other in the strongest of terms. Each was still confident that the work was of God and that there could be no right way but his way. Some found this certainty only to lose it again as they tried first one faction and then another, finding no satisfaction anywhere. Among this type of men early in the fifties the Reorganization, or "new movement" as it was sometimes called, sprang into being almost simultaneously in different sections of the United States.

From the time of the breakup at Nauvoo and for many years after, the groups into which the church was split tended to fluctuate very largely. Members still considered themselves parts of the church, both as individuals and as branches, but their leaders were gone. The question about who should become the head of the church was vital, but it scarcely affected the faith and hope of the people themselves, founded as it had been in the principles of their religion. Later, as the leaders introduced new theories, these were accepted by a portion of their following, and others drifted away to form alliances elsewhere.

The majority of the membership was scattered, but of the groups who clung together, three immediately assumed major importance: Brigham Young in the West, Sidney Rigdon in the East, and James J. Strang in the North. The largest single group followed Brigham Young, the president of the Quorum of Twelve, to the West, but there were defections all the way across Iowa, notably the group under Alpheus Cutler. Many others never went farther than Council Bluffs; many more stayed at Florence; and still others straggled back to the States or California to later unite with the Reorganization, or joined in the exodus of hundreds after the first missionaries went to Utah.

XXXVIII.—The Good Ship "Brooklyn"

The part played by the dispersed wanderers from Nauvoo in the romantic saga of the building of the West will perhaps never be completely told. There are few States west of the Mississippi into which some colony of these despised ones did not go to begin life anew. They had learned their lesson; they now found their resting places far from the haunts of their fellow men. Not only Utah, but Missouri, California, Illinois, Texas, Iowa, Minnesota, Arizona, Wisconsin, Idaho, Nevada, and others must give credit to this "peculiar people" when they call the roll of their pioneers.

Perhaps of all these colonies none had a more romantic history than the one that sailed around South America to California on the good ship "Brooklyn." Samuel Brannan, an elder in New York City and vicinity who later became prominent in California history, conceived the idea of taking his flock by water to California and there meeting the company who had left under Brigham Young, presumably for the same port.

Samuel Brannan, who a decade and a half later was to share the headlines of New York newspapers only with important news from the Civil War, was young then, only twenty-six, but already he had lived much. Born in Maine in 1819, he had been bound out to an Ohio printer, bought his time at seventeen, and became a literary journeyman. An ambitious "literary weekly" having died on his hands in New Orleans, he went to Indianapolis and started a new venture which also failed. Just at what time in his career he became a Latter Day Saint, we do not know. His name first appears among those "blessed in consequence of their labor on the House of the Lord" in Kirtland, on March 7, 1835, so he must have joined the church while still serving his printer's apprenticeship.

The death of Joseph Smith and the proposed westward move of the majority of the Twelve and their followers found him in charge of the church in New York, and publisher of the church paper, *The Messenger.*

A conference was held in American Hall, New York, on November 12, 1845, in which a series of preambles and resolutions was offered by Samuel Brannan, broaching the subject of a removal west in no uncertain terms. A part of them read:

> Resolved, that the church in this city move, one and all, west of the Rocky Mountains, between this and next season, either by land or water; and that we most earnestly pray all our brethren in the eastern country to join with us in this determination, and carry it out effectually, to the delivery of the people of God from the daughters of Babylon, and not one left behind.
> Resolved, that there are no apologies required of those who do not go, but old age, sickness, infirmities, and poverty. "For he that will not forsake father and mother, houses and lands, wives and children for me and my name's sake, is not worthy of me."[1]

Elder Brannan then laid before the conference his amazing plan, and asked all who wished to go with him to come forward and sign their names.

Arrangements were perfected, and a list published of those selected to make the trip.

These names, among whom may be found many of the pioneers of the church in California were: William C. Reamer and family, John Phillips, William Stout and family, Stephen H. Pierce, John Joice and family, John Hairbaird and family, Mary Murry, Daniel P. Baldwin, William Atherton and family, Susan A. Searls, Eliza Savage, Darwin Richardson and family, Simeon Stanley and family, Moses Meeder and family, J. M. Farnsworth and the names he signed, Jones Cook, Isaac Leigh and family, Manena Cannon and family, the Tompkins family, Henry Roulam, William Flint and family, Joseph Nichols and family, Newel Bullen and family,

---

[1] *Times and Seasons,* Volume 6, page 1037.

Julius Austin and family, Ambrose T. Moses and family, Isaac Adison and family, Silas Eldridge and family, Barton Morey and family, Isaac R. Robbins and family, John R. Robbins and family, Jacob Hayes, Charles Russel and family, James Embly and family, William Glover and family, Robert Smith and family, Alandus D. Ruckland and family, John Eagar, Samuel Smith, Isabella Jones, James Light and family, Peter Pool and family, Joseph France and family, John J. Sirrine and family, George W. Sirrine, Samuel Brannan and family. Doubtless some of these did not go, while others not named were on the "Brooklyn" when she sailed from New York on Wednesday, February 4, 1846.[2]

Brannan, the leader of the group, was a man of vivid personality "deep-chested, broad-shouldered, shaggy-headed." His dress was fashionable, almost "dandified," his appearance impeccable in his then fashionable, "sideburns" and "imperial," his face lit up by flashing black eyes. And we are told, "his courage and generosity were boundless." The "Brooklyn," a three hundred seventy ton ship, with Captain Richardson, master, was chartered for the occasion. Into the hold, with amazing foresight, went the press of *The Messenger,* and two complete flour mills, dismantled but lacking nothing, and other supplies for colonizing in California, which was then on the road to nowhere, and completely out of the jurisdiction of the United States.

February 4 dawned cold, dreary, and rainy. Upon the wharf lingered a few friends and several curious and cynical strangers, looking upon the crowded old emigrant ship "Brooklyn" with her strange cargo as she left the wharf bound for a strange land outside the domains of the United States.

On the boat were two men, traveling for pleasure, and the shipload of nearly three hundred Latter Day Saints. There proved to be little pleasure. First, they lay long becalmed in the tropics and then were in a dreadful storm, during which women and children

---

[2] *Ibid.,* pages 1113, 1114; *Church History,* Volume 3, page 181.

were lashed to their berths, for in no other way could they keep from being flung out. Furniture rolled back and forth. The waves swept over the deck and even reached the staterooms below. The only light was from two lamps hung outside in the hall, dim and wavering beacons in the storm. No one present ever forgot the whining and howling of the wind, the creaking of the ship's timbers, children crying, mothers soothing or scolding, the deep voices of the men trying to inspire courage, the cries of the sick, and yet it is said that through it all the most of the passengers were cheerful, and no one doubted for a moment that he would ultimately reach his destination. The old captain who had seen many a storm at sea finally came down, and while the passengers crowded around him, they made out these words above the din of the storm: "My friends, there is a time in every man's life when it is fitting that he should prepare to die. That time has come to us, and unless God interposes we shall all go to the bottom; I have done all in my power, but this is the worst gale I have known since I was master of a ship."

One woman answered him, "Captain Richardson, we left for California, and we shall get there." Another said, "Captain, I have no more fear than though we were on solid land." The captain gazed at the little company speechless, then turning said to another of the crew as he went up again, "They are either fools and fear nothing, or they know more than I do."

The storm passed, but as they passed Cape Horn, they encountered another in which a sailor was washed overboard and Mrs. Laura Goodwin, one of the passengers, while descending the stairs was thrown forward, causing premature confinement and death. The captain, more willing to accommodate the passengers than was the captain of the "Timeoleon" who buried Knowlton K. Hanks at sea, went ashore at the earliest opportunity, which happened to be on the convict island of Juan Fernandez (77 degrees west longitude, 38 degrees south latitude) to bury her. Here Mrs.

Goodwin was laid to rest, leaving her saddened husband and six little children to continue the journey alone. In spite of the sad occasion, being ashore made a break in the monotonous sea voyage. The passengers bathed, washed their clothing, caught fish and eels, cooked and ate them, gathered fruit, and as they left, decorated their dead sister's grave with shells they had gathered, and took the six sobbing, motherless little ones back to the boat.

Supplies on the boat began to get low, and their diet soon consisted of poor bread and salt pork. The drinking water grew thick and ropy with slime and had a dreadful taste. One pint a day was measured out to each passenger to take to his room to use for drinking, washing, everything. The ship's condition grew rapidly worse. Rats, cockroaches, and smaller vermin infested everything—even the diminishing stock of provisions. Every mouthful had to be watched.

The passenger list meantime had been increased by two, a boy named Atlantic, and a girl named Pacific, their names signifying circumstances attending their birth.

Even amid such dismal surroundings the old dream of Zion still unfulfilled was in the hearts and minds of those poor wanderers, and they drew up a covenant, agreeing to give the proceeds of their labors for three years into a common fund from which all were to draw their living as a start towards the United Order. Some fulfilled that pledge through prosperity and adversity.

On July 31, 1846, the old emigrant ship "Brooklyn" labored through the "Golden Gate." A fog covered the harbor of Yerba Buena, shutting all sight of shore from their eager eyes. At length they could distinguish some dim shapes of ships, whalers, and even men-of-war, and flying from the flagstaff, mysterious and welcome sight, was the Flag of their country! There came a salute from the dim gray fort on the shore, and the "Brooklyn" responded. Now they saw a rowboat approaching, and uniformed men scrambled on the deck, not Mexicans, but Americans. The officer in command, with uncovered head said, "Ladies and gentlemen, I have the honor to inform you that you are in the United States of America." And a cheer—three cheers—went up from the wan, thin skeletons aboard the old "Brooklyn," from hearts weary but hopeful, and loyal to their country still. For just three weeks before, California had become United States soil, and the Stars and Stripes went up over Yerba Buena, now San Francisco.

One of the passengers says: "They crowded upon the deck, women and children, questioning husbands and fathers, and studied the picture before them—they would never see it just the same again—as the foggy curtains furled towards the azure ceiling. A long, sandy beach, strewn with hides and skeletons of slaughtered cattle, a few scrubby oaks, farther back, low sand hills rising behind each other as a background to a few old shanties that leaned away from the wind, old adobe barracks, a few donkeys plodding dejectedly along beneath towering bundles of wood, a few loungers stretched lazily upon the beach as though nothing could astonish them; and between the picture and the emigrants still loomed up here and there, at the first sight more distinctly, the black vessels—whaling ships and sloops of war—that was all, and that was Yerba Buena, now San Francisco, the landing place for the pilgrims of faith."[3]

Soon all were happily unloading the ship. Tents were erected, and sixteen families crowded into the old adobe barracks. Cooking of course had to be done outdoors. Soon a place was selected for the colony to settle—on the north bank of the Stanislaus River near the junction with the San Joaquin—and with a faith that was almost pathos, they named the place New Hope. Here they put in crops and prepared to welcome the body of Saints they still believed to be coming overland.

The women of the "Brooklyn" were quite an addition to the population of Yerba Buena, which up until their arrival boasted

---

[3] *Historical Record*, Volume 8, page 876; *Church History*, Volume 3, page 186.

only "two white ladies." "Polygamy was not in their creed, and they maintained good relations with the Gentiles. The men were industrious, public-spirited; the women, chaste; the children well behaved."[4]

In a letter written the first of the next year, Brannan, with characteristic Latter Day Saint optimism says, "Since our departure from New York we have enjoyed the peculiar care of our Heavenly Father; everything in a most miraculous manner has worked together for our good, and we find ourselves happily situated in our new home, surrounded with peace and prosperity."[5] He also spoke of a paper they would commence publishing the following week, "which will be the government organ by the sanction of Colonel Fremont, who is now our Governor."

Brannan proceeded to set up and operate the first California flour mills; in a little redwood structure back of "Old Adobe," he put up his press, and issued the first newspaper in Yerba Buena, *The California Star*. In the first number of his paper, Brannan promised to "eschew with the greatest caution everything that tends to the propagation of sectarian dogma," a promise he kept faithfully. In the *Star*, he immediately launched a campaign for a schoolhouse, and by his efforts the first little red schoolhouse appeared on the Plaza, south of Old Adobe. This building, grandly designated as the "Public Institute," served the infant San Francisco as school, church, town hall, and eventually as tribunal of the vigilance committee and jail. Samuel Brannan, the dauntless Latter Day Saint elder, performed the first marriage ceremony and preached the first sermon in Yerba Buena after the American Flag went up over that city. He has been dubbed the first "Californian," for he printed a special 2,000 edition of the *Star* and sent it East by the first pony express.

But his exuberance over his new-found home was destined to receive a rude jolt.

---
[4]*The First Forty-Niner*, by James A. B. Scherer, New York, 1925, pages 23, 83.
[5]*Millennial Star*, Volume 9, page 306.

Spring came, and still no colony from Nauvoo. Brannan and some of the Saints set out to meet them, leaving the famous post of Captain Sutter on April 25. They crossed the mountains of California, a distance of forty miles, with eleven head of horses and mules, traveling on foot and driving the animals before them in the deep snow, making the distance in record time, one day and two hours. They had to swim rivers and climb mountains on their way. On June 30, 1847, Brannan met the Utah "pioneers" on Green River in what is now Wyoming and accompanied them to Great Salt Lake Valley. When Brigham Young decided to stop there, Brannan was disappointed and angry and soon started back for California. "He will find that I was right and he was wrong and will come to California,"[6] Brannan said when he met, on September 6, 1847, a detachment of what was known as the Mormon Battalion.[7] These men were told by Brannan that Brigham Young had sent word to all who had not money enough to come to Salt Lake to return to California and get work. About half of the men turned back with Brannan.

Smarting with an indignation toward the church leaders in Utah, from which he never recovered, Brannan took his way back to the new country, whose fortunes he had so readily made his own. Good fortune led him to the right place at the right time— the famous Fort Sutter, where the genial Swiss, Captain Sutter, held dominion over a large area of territory on the Sacramento River, five days journey above San Francisco. Sutter had just contracted with the firm of Marshall, Weimer, and Bennett to put him up a sawmill on the south fork of the American River, where Colonia stands, forty miles northeast of the fort. Brannan was

---

[6]*Historical Record*, Volume 8, page 930.
[7]A battalion furnished the United States by the "Mormons" for the Mexican War. The battalion recruited at Council Bluffs, Iowa, from the camp for the Saints, marched to Fort Leavenworth. They arrived at Santa Fe in October; here they were divided. Ninety who were sick were sent to Pueblo; the remainder marched for California. They arrived after much suffering at San Luis Rey Mission on January 21, 1847. After active service, they were mustered out at Los Angeles, July 16, 1847. The main body of these met Brannan on the Truckee River.

suddenly inspired to stop here and set up a store, for the builders had only consented to build the mill on condition that all necessary supplies be furnished them on Sutter's credit until the mill was in running order. The members of the "Mormon Battalion" who were with him, stopped also to work on the mills.

It was the fall of 1847. All the world knows the rest of the story. Gold was discovered at the bottom of Sutter's new mill race on January 24, 1848. And it was Samuel Brannan who carried the news to San Francisco, where Kemble, a youth from the "Brooklyn," was editing the *Star* in his absence. As Sam ran through the Plaza, brandishing a flask of gold dust above his head, and shouting "Gold! Gold! From the American River" the *Star* expired in the flash of a second, as its subscribers, editor, printer, and printer's devil dropped everything and followed Sam Brannan back to the American River.

Brannan's enterprise at the fort flourished, and of course, he also found diggings of his own. Meals now cost $5 each, eggs $1 apiece, and other necessities in proportion. From a humble Latter Day Saint elder, Brannan soon became California's first millionaire, but he never lost the characteristics that had made him successful in his ministry, for the old-time Latter Day Saint elder must possess courage of that rare variety that is willing to do and dare without counting the cost, for the missionary of that day who had great respect for the safety of his own skin was never a missionary long.

There was no law in California except public opinion, but now that lack began to be keenly felt. Lawless gangs from eastern cities moved into San Francisco en masse. When a gang of desperadoes calling themselves "Hounds" robbed and plundered a group of Chilean immigrants, committing murder and rape, Brannan added another to his long list of firsts. Inflamed with righteous indignation, he organized the first Vigilantes for action. "Brannan had just the oratorical gifts needed, deep feeling, profound courage, and a powerful, penetrating voice. His fine eyes flashing fire, his shaggy mane tossing, his utterance half-choked by emotion, with sledge hammer eloquence, he wielded the throng into unity." He had no thought of lynch law, he insisted on a grand jury, and punctiliously provided the culprits with counsel. On June 1, 1851, the first regular vigilance committee was organized in Brannan's office, with Sam as its president and spokesman. Before the end of the month, five or six hundred members had enrolled.

Bancroft says, "Peculiar as he was in some respects, I cannot but regard his connection with the first Vigilance Committee as the brightest epoch in his eventful life and so long as society holds its course in San Francisco, his name should be held in honor and grateful remembrance."

During the slavery struggle, Sam Brannan held his place on the front page news of New York City and the East. He owned nearly all the land abutting on Market Street in San Francisco, and nearly a quarter of Sacramento, and spent money on a lavish and prodigal scale that has seldom been surpassed. He entertained the whole city of Sacramento one day at his new "City Hotel" at a cost of $150,000. When Mexicans wanted to shake off the yoke of Maximilian, they came to Brannan, and Sam paid the bills liberally. The American Legion down there named themselves the "Brannan Contingent." Only with the men in Utah, whom he had once called brethren, was he niggardly, and when, it is said, Brigham Young sent an apostle to collect the "Lord's tenth," he sent back word that he would not relinquish his tithing until Brigham sent back a receipt signed by the Lord, so that he could be sure the money went to its presumed destination. He was excommunicated, as one whose course in life was unfitting a Latter Day Saint.

The remaining days of Sam Brannan's history had little to do

---

[8]*The First Forty-Niner,* by James A. B. Scherer.

with the old life. Eventually he lost his enormous fortune, or nearly all, and when his wife took her children and left him, in one last burst of prodigality he settled upon her every cent of the remainder, and became a drunkard, a pariah, an outcast from society, living in penury and squalor. Sometimes he stole back to his dream city, San Francisco, to bunk in a two-bit flophouse, and watch men whom he had started in business cross the street to avoid him.

"Then the miracle happened," says his biographer. "Mexico actually paid him $49,000, a meager enough interest on his huge loan, but that was not the miracle. Sam, renegade, adventurer, drunkard, spendthrift, rake—took every dollar of that money and paid his debts with it, quit drinking . . . and died at the rounding of his 70th milestone, redeemed through the power of his will."[9]

When he died, May 5, 1889, in Escondido, California, he had not a cent, and lay in the city morgue for some days until a friend bought six feet of earth in Mt. Hope Cemetery and paid for his burial. Here (in division 4, section 2, lot 7) as late as 1925, his grave was marked by only a two-inch stake. An unimportant street in San Francisco bears his name.

As for the colony he had brought " 'round the Horn," learning that their brethren did not intend to locate in California, the valiant little group at New Hope dispersed and scattered, many of them becoming miners in the gold rush. Some went to Utah, but many remained in California to unite with the Reorganization when the first missionaries crossed the great desert to bring them the message of the coming of Young Joseph. Those messengers were E. C. Briggs, Alexander H. Smith, James W. Gillen, and William Anderson.

---

[9] *The First Forty-Niner*, by James A. B. Scherer, page 124. New York, 1925.

XXXIX.—The Texas Colony

Lyman Wight, the Apostle who had been chosen to fill the place of David Patten when he fell at Crooked River, had throughout his entire life cherished the ideal of "all things common." He had left the experiment of "The Family" in Kirtland to join the church. He went through the experiment of Independence in 1833, without disillusionment. His ideals were of the sort that die hard.

Cherishing these things in his heart, for to him these were the principles of "celestial law," he went about his extensive missionary work with his fellow apostles throughout the years the church was at Nauvoo until the middle of June, 1843; upon returning from an eastern missionary tour of nine and one-half months, during which time he had traveled three thousand miles, baptized over six hundred persons, and organized twenty-one branches, he was asked to go to Wisconsin in company with Bishop George Miller to take charge of the sawmills there. These had been purchased by the church at a cost of twelve thousand dollars for the purpose of cutting timber and making shingles and sawing lumber for the building operations in Nauvoo, particularly the temple and Nauvoo House.

A number of families, one hundred and fifty men, women, and children, went north with him. Doubtless the entire company received their living expenses, and allowed the price of their labor to go to the church. At least we know of one man, just home from a long mission, who went with the company "because he was back in his tithing." During their experiences together in this northern wilderness, Black River Falls, Wisconsin, those who comprised this colony became attached to one another and their intrepid leader and formed the nucleus of what has been wrongly termed "a faction" of the church.

The very isolation of the little group from all the rest of the world from the moment of their embarking on this enterprise helped induce that solidarity. The sharing of mutual dangers and meager supplies augmented that union. They left Nauvoo by steamer on July 22, leaving the boat near the mouth of the Black River at Prairie LaCrosse, finished the journey to Black Falls in keel boats. These keel boats were long and narrow, with a runway about twelve inches in width projecting out over the side of the boat and running the entire length, for the polemen to walk back and forth as they pushed the boat upstream, for these boats were propelled by poles. Three men on a side and one in front to steer manned each boat. Several days on these boats completed the ninety miles between Prairie La Crosse and Black River Falls.

Winter supplies for these people were to be furnished by the Temple Committee, but owing to some lack of knowledge of northern conditions, these supplies were not shipped in time to be brought up by boats. The snow was now deep, but the only teams in the settlement, just two, were set to hauling provisions the ninety miles from LaCrosse for one hundred people and their animals. Everyone went on rations, and by nobody satisfying his wants, the food was carefully apportioned to last until the teams returned. And then visitors came, starving Indians—they were so destitute they had eaten the hides they had dried for sale—and asked for food. Lyman Wight called the group together and put the question before them, "Shall we share our food, which now consists of one barrel of flour with these starving Indians, when we know we shall be without bread before our teams return?" The vote was unanimous in the affirmative, even the little children voting to divide what they had. The Indians were given half the barrel of flour and an ox; and were only asked to return when they had eaten, for they must hear a sermon. No Latter Day Saint elder would miss a chance to preach, especially to the Indians! Three days, without bread, the little company waited for the return of the teams with food. And no one complained, for all had shared in the sacrifice.[1]

These were the scenes that formed the bond between members of the old colony. In March, Lyman Wight was called to Nauvoo, taking his wife and three youngest children, leaving the rest to follow with rafts of lumber. The occasion of his return to Nauvoo was that he might present certain petitions to Congress, regarding the church lands in Missouri. He left home on May 21 for Washington, D. C., and while still upon this mission, for some reason he found it necessary to travel three times from Baltimore, Maryland, to Salem, Massachusetts, spending three weeks in Philadelphia, three in New York, and the same in Boston, traveling "most of the time upon the railroad cars."[2]

Wight tells the story of one day, "just in the midst of pleasure and satisfaction whilst riding along leisurely from Salem to Boston, a little boy threw a paper into the car, announcing the death, yes! announcing the death of my beloved friend, the Prophet."[3]

He hardly knew whether to believe the report or not, one moment it seemed true, the next he doubted it; but a few days later, a personal messenger confirmed the message and bade him return with all haste to meet with the rest of the Quorum of Twelve. He took a train immediately to Buffalo, crossed the Lakes to Chicago, thence to Galena by stage, and down the river on a steamboat to Nauvoo, thanks to modern transportation of the day, making the journey in what he considered a very brief time—by the 6th of August he was in Nauvoo!

Before he had gone to Washington, he had obtained permission from the President of the church, Joseph Smith, to plant a colony "between the head of the Red River, the Little Colorado

---

[1] "Reminiscences," by George Montague, *Autumn Leaves*, Volume 9, page 385.
[2] "An Address by Way of an Abridged Account and Journal of My Life from February, 1844, up to April, 1848, with an Appeal to the Latter Day Saints," by Lyman Wight, page 5.
[3] "An Address by Way of an Abridged Account and Journal of My Life from April, 1848," etc.

River, and the Cordilleras Mountains."[4] This mission seemed sacred to him, comprising as he said, "the instructions given by Brother Joseph the last conversation I ever had with him."[4] This "instruction was given me by Brother Joseph with great zeal, setting forth the necessity for such a mission, for the good of the cause of bringing the Lamanites to the knowledge of the truth, paving the way for the redemption of Zion and building the temple in Jackson County, and giving our posterity inheritances in a land where Gentile foot has never trod . . . for the last fourteen hundred years."[4]

After several violent differences with President Young, during which time Wight's plan for a mission to Texas could not be shaken, he took his family and those of his friends who would go, including nearly all the Black Falls Pine Company and went back to Prairie LaCrosse for the winter, as he found so many of his family and others sick of chills and fever in the "marshlands" of Illinois, after being used to the "pure waters of the pine country." He thought it necessary for them to "regain their health" before starting on the trip westward.

Texas was to him a veritable land of dreams. Here he intended to bring up his children in a wilderness which would "never be defiled" by the "customs and practices of the world"; there these children would have their inheritance and build a righteous city. True he expected to receive his inheritance in Jackson County, when Zion was redeemed, but he hoped to see the day "when I can travel from the city in Jackson County to a city that shall be built by my posterity . . . when there shall not be a day's journey between cities, from one place to the other."[4]

He had hoped to have provisions on hand for the trip, but that winter the men had only work enough to provide a scanty living from day to day. Spring found them penniless, with the exception of three boats. What was to be done? The question was

---

[4] "An Address by Way of an Abridged Account of My Life from April, 1848," etc.

put up to the whole group, as it had been done when they fed the starving Indians. Should they "scatter to the four winds" and "live like the rest of the world," or "fill the covenant of this church made at its rise, which was to stand by each other even until death"?

They decided to do the latter, and one by one came forward and laid all they had above actual necessities, of clothing and all else, in one pile to be sold for their maintenance on the trip. All went aboard the three boats on the evening of March 27, 1845, singing, "Let Zion in Her Beauty Rise." At twenty minutes after eleven on the 28th, the old keel boats were loosed from their moorings and propelled by poles and aided by currents, started down the Mississippi River. Each boat had a row of rude berths on each side, and a space left through the center for luggage, stoves, and cooking utensils. A raft of lumber followed the three as far as Prairie du Chien, where it and its load were sold to pay the debts of the company contracted during the winter.

About two p.m., April 13, a final landing was made at Duck Creek, a few miles above Davenport, Iowa. Here a month's delay occurred while the boats were sold and oxen, tents, and wagons purchased. They made many friends in Davenport, some accompanied them on their journey; others gathered to see them off. The move on May 12 was only twenty miles west to obtain feed for the animals, but on May 26, "at the sound of the horn," a well-organized company moved off, eight wagons and one cart, all drawn by oxen, and eighty-two head of cattle, including the teams. The course was southwesterly across the open prairie, many walking. The next day they stopped at Tipton, Iowa, and fitted up four more teams and wagons.

Without following the details of that journey, we find these weary pilgrims on Sunday, November 16, just crossing the Red River, near Preston, Texas, into the land of their destination. Four miles south they stopped, camped, and looked for a location. They had accomplished this long journey in seven months and eighteen days, mostly by ox team, sometimes without roads or landmarks, fording and swimming rivers or building their own ferries. Nine of the number had been laid in unmarked graves by the way. And these people started on this migration, without a single penny in cash!

Lyman Wight himself with one companion went as scout to select a winter's location. They soon found a deserted fort in Grayson County, near Georgetown, and here they moved on the 19th of November, 1845, and waited out the winter, the men finding what work they could.

On Monday, April 24, 1846, the whole camp moved southward, with the Colorado River in mind, crossing the Trinity River above Dallas on the 30th. May 14 their cattle swam the Brazos, while the wagons were taken apart and ferried across in one small canoe. They arrived June 6 and 7 at the spot chosen as their destination, and immediately went to work to build a mill, pushing the work as rapidly as possible, doing all the iron, stone, and woodwork themselves. They were on the east bank of the Colorado, four miles above Austin. On July 30 the mill started grinding, a real novelty in the community. They made money rapidly, and started at once to construct a sawmill, houses, and shops. But they were not satisfied. In October four scouts, Spencer Smith, John Taylor, and Meachim and William Curtis, were sent on an exploring tour and came back reporting a beautiful country on the Perdinales River. Accordingly a colony was appointed to go there and make location, business being carried on as usual near Austin. In January the Perdinales Colony was recalled, but the project was renewed the following March and several families went there. On May first, a mill site was selected four miles below Fredericksburg, now the county seat of Gillespie County and about seventy miles southwest of Austin. Here houses were built, shops erected, and in exactly six weeks from the day the site was selected, a sawmill was in full operation. The mill on the Colorado meantime was grinding large quantities of meal which was transported by team to Austin, New Braunfels, Brownsville, and Fredericksburg, and sold at good prices. The new settlement was named Zodiac.[5]

Soon a stone fort was added to the other buildings, but there were no Indian troubles. Along the banks of the Little Perdinales River stretched a broad road of their building, back from the road lay a series of *irrigated* farms, separated by stone fences. In December two delegates from Brigham Young appeared in Zodiac, threatening Wight and his followers with excommunication if they stayed out of the fold, and Wight made a "Texas-flavored" answer saying, "nobody under the light of heaven, except Joseph Smith, could call me from Texas to go to Salt Lake City!" Joseph Smith had sent him on a mission to Texas, and the fact that Joseph Smith was dead could not change the fact that he was the one man who could tell Lyman Wight what to do; therefore to Texas he had gone, and in Texas he would stay until he felt that he had successfully filled the mission of the one man whom he loved with his whole heart.

On August 9, 1847, the mill on the Colorado was sold at a substantial profit, and all of the colony moved to the Perdinales, leaving only a few men to finish the new county jail in Austin, which the colony had contracted to build for two thousand dollars. The jail was finished on November 16 and on the 17th was accepted by the jail commissioners. The workers then joined the rest of the colony. A new gristmill had already been erected and many new houses.[6]

The colony carried on a flourishing business with its neighbors. Milling, both grist and sawmill, was now flourishing, blacksmithing and furniture making helped to add to the wealth of the little

---

[5]Here the author's father, Heman C. Smith, was born on September 27, 1850.
[6]See "A Pioneer Colony," by Heman C. Smith; *Autumn Leaves,* Volume 8, page 529, *seq.*

community, which meticulously held their property in common, calling naught that they had their own. Rumors began to go around that Wight had in some mysterious way taken "the bulk of the Mormon wealth" to Texas.

They stood well in their community. Old settlers say that Lyman Wight was often asked to address the senate when he came to Austin, and was always well received by the governor and senators. "He was of very commanding appearance, over six feet, about 200 pounds, and very handsome; wore a beard that he kept in perfect condition . . . his hair long, dressed in a Prince Albert coat, wore finely polished boots . . . carried two six shooters and a bowie knife, drove two to four mules to a fine carriage, with glittering harness, trimmed with brass and silver."[7] How much of this description is true, we can only conjecture.

But the Perdinales was subject to freshets, and in July, 1850, the mill was swept away, and the houses were flooded. The second flood in 1851 drove the colony to a new location on the Colorado. Here they encountered the open warfare of the Indians, new mills were erected, ground broken. The members of the colony began to make and sell furniture. Their venture was profitable, but Lyman Wight was a true type of the restless pioneersman. In 1853 he sold his rights in the settlement to Noah Smithwick and moved on.[8]

The wanderings of the colony took them to Medina,[9] where twelve miles below Bandera they founded the community of Mountain Valley, a pioneer outpost in a country that was almost uninhabited save by hostile Indians. Wight petitioned the state and the National Government to send troops to enable his colony to survive. "While Congress is spending six or eight months to

---

[7] A letter from C. C. Booth, 2021 Bennett Avenue, Dallas, Texas, to Rufus K. Hardy of Salt Lake City, under date of December 9, 1930. Booth names his grandfather, one Josiah Clifton, as his informant.
[8] Hamilton's Creek on the east side of the Colorado River almost twelve miles south of where Burnet, county seat of Burnet County stands. Their mill still stood there as late as 1881 and was called "Mormon Mill."
[9] Birthplace of Hyrum O. Smith.

find out whether it is best to reinforce the Army or not," he wrote, "the Indians are killing men, women, and children, and driving off large quantities of stock, and nothing to hinder. We make this one more appeal to the Government, and if this fails, we have but one alternative, and that is to abandon the frontiers altogether."

Lyman Wight was an insatiable pioneer. When death overtook him, still on the trail, he was planning to preach the gospel to the Indians in Mexico and Central America. He died suddenly near San Antonio, Texas, on March 30, 1858. His followers procured a metallic casket in San Antonio and carried him to the old city of Zodiac, not far from Fredericksburg, to bury him in the colony cemetery there.

On the occasion of his death the Galveston News said:

> We believe we have omitted to notice the death of Mr. Lyman Wight, who for some thirteen years past has been the leader of a small and independent Mormon settlement in Texas. As far as we have been able to learn, these Mormons have proved themselves to be most excellent citizens of our State, and we are no doubt greatly indebted to the deceased leader for the orderly conduct, sobriety, industry and enterprise of his colony. Mr. Wight first came to Texas in November, 1845, and has been with his colony on the extreme frontier ever since, moving still farther west as settlements formed around him, thus always being the pioneer of advancing civilization, affording protection against the Indians. He has been the first to settle five new counties and prepare the way for others. He has at different times built three extensive saw and gristmills.

The Wight Colony always lived in communistic style, according to the "Celestial Law," as they termed it. In a letter, written in 1855 from Medina to an old friend, Sanford Porter, whom he had "found in Illinois" evidently on an early mission, and "lived a near neighbor to" in Jackson County, Missouri, Wight describes their manner of life:

> I will give you a short description of our country. We live in a pleasant country. We seldom feed any of our stock in the winter unless it is some that we work, and sometimes we get along very well without feeding anything. As for snow, I have not seen enough in ten years all together to make four inches. It is a fine place to raise

stock. It is mountainous and healthy, good for corn and garden vegetables. Wheat does well in many parts. There is no scarcity of either cattle or oxen throughout the State, although they are rather higher this year in consequence of the many wars and rumors of war. Oxen are worth fifty dollars a yoke, good four-year-old steers, well broke, from thirty-five to forty-five dollars, according to size, stock cows from eight to ten dollars, good milk cows from twelve to eighteen dollars, and store goods are remarkably low. Horses average with everything else. We have no trouble getting a good living in this country. The most difficulty we find is in keeping close enough to the commandments of God. When one has enough, all have the same. Our houses are as near alike as they can well be. Mine was built first. It is one hundred feet one way (with the exception of eighty-six feet) and lacks only thirty-eight feet of being fifty feet the other way. We have a good door in front and an old quilt neatly hung for the back door. We have fine, beautiful sand for floors. Our houses average from seven to eight feet between the sand and the joists, some being lower and some higher as the case may be. We (not I) have a large stock of cattle, plenty of teams, and we carry on a great many branches of mechanical operations besides our farming. And as we believe the time is not far distant when those who remain and are pure in heart shall return to Jackson County, they and their children singing songs of everlasting joy, we cannot dismiss the subject without giving Brother Porter and his family an invitation to come and go with us and see that goodly land once more.

There is one significant thing about Lyman Wight's community efforts, which deserves attention because of its extreme rarity in Utopian experiments. Wight, as acknowledged leader, never desired or sought temporal or spiritual advantage over his fellows. When he received letters from Strang, "King James I, president of the church"; from Brigham Young, telling of ecclesiastical honors acquired since the death of Joseph, and Thompson with his many titles, he was wont to sign his answer with profound sarcasm, "Lyman Wight, and nothing else." In scathing denunciation of those who he thought were acquiring wealth at the expense of their brethren, he wrote of the Melchisedec priesthood:

> But those who aspire after this priesthood, and seek to obtain it while rolling in luxuries, and seeking the applause of men, I would simply ask them these questions, Have you drunk of the cup whereof Christ drank, and have you been baptized with the baptism wherewith he was baptized? Have you followed the commandment that he

gave to the young man and sold all that thou hadst, and give it to the poor? Have you sold the last coat you had, and traveled in your shirt sleeves sooner than you would see the poor left to the ravages of a ruthless mob? Have you traveled on foot hundreds and hundreds of miles and sought a place for the Saints to camp at, night after night, that they might seclude themselves from the hands of wicked and evil designing men, and then roll yourself in a blanket, and lay yourself in an open prairie, under the open canopy of heaven, in the cold night dews? If you have not done all these, you have not yet fulfilled the saying of the Saviour where he says, If you would be greatest you must first become the least and servant of all. . . . I again ask, when did the church flourish? When the Nephites that dwelt upon this land did not call "aught they possessed their own; but it all belonged to the Lord." When did the people mourn and lament, and howl and weep? I answer, when their priests were lifted up in the pride of their hearts, to the wearing of fine apparel and oppressing the poor and the hireling in his wages, riding in fine carriages, with cushioned seats, bristled carpets, leaving the poor to work out their own salvation among those who are their vital enemies; while the rich and opulent were permitted to increase in opulence by tithing and wringing from the hands of the peasant his hard-earnings.[10]

Fearless, honest, unassuming, and absolutely independent, Lyman Wight called no man his master save one, Joseph Smith, his great friend, and to him alone he had looked for guidance. Even from him, he differed occasionally and took no pains to conceal it. "I would rather go to hell of my own accord than be forced into heaven," he was wont characteristically to say. Curiously, in a movement where the majority of group leaders met violent opposition, Lyman Wight, to whom the applause of the world meant nothing, never lacked for it, and that too, in spite of social anachronisms that were blamed for the unpopularity of other factions. Contemptuous of individual wealth, Lyman Wight's communal experiment flourished financially, in spite of frequent transplantings due to his restless leadership.

Lyman Wight never claimed the right to lead this colony as a divinely appointed head. His teachings were always as Strang put

---

[10]"An Address by Way of an Abridged Account and Journal of My Life from February, 1844, to April, 1848," by Lyman Wight, 1848, pages 14 and 15.

it in the *Gospel Herald,* published at Voree, Wisconsin, August 31, 1848:

> Lyman Wight seems to cherish the idea that is ignorantly held out by some others that Joseph, the Prophet's son, will yet come up and take his father's original place in the church.[11]

In his journal, he wrote what he considered should have been the procedure at the death of Joseph Smith:

> The fifties assembled should have called on all the authorities of the church down to the lay members from all the face of the earth, as much as was convenient and after having taken sweet counsel together, in prayer and supplication before God, acknowledged our sins and transgressions which had caused our head to be taken from our midst: and then have called on Young Joseph, and held him up before the congregation of Israel to take his father's place in the flesh.[12]

In the little pamphlet published by Wight in 1848, a copy of which has only recently come to light, he said:

> I have no notice of this blessing (Doctrine and Covenants 43:2) having been transferred to any person or persons, save it be to the posterity of him who standeth at the helm of [in] life. And I remain firm in the belief, that we who have been organized into the well-established and organized body of the kingdom on earth, should go forth abroad into the earth, and come up to Mount Zion, and build up the city of the living God, even on the spot of ground pointed out by the finger of the Almighty Jehovah, and dedicated by his servant, the Prophet. . . .
>
> Many struggles have been made, and many more may be made to build temples unto the Most High God, yet God in his infinite wisdom, will most assuredly build upon that spot which he has pointed out with his own finger. Unto this spot of ground I invite all nations, kindreds and tongues and peoples; they to consecrate all they have and are, for the express purpose of building up the temple of the most High God and enlarging the borders of Zion, and making the stakes strong.
>
> And this end I pray, that God in his infinite wisdom may hasten the day, and speed the time, that Joseph's voice may be heard from the heavens unto his posterity, even as David's of old, saying, my son, build ye an house unto the Most High God.[13]

---

[11]"Prophetic Controversy No. 2," page 17, Voree, *Herald.*
[12]Lyman Wight's Journal, under date of December, 1851, as published in *Church History,* Volume 2, page 791.
[13]"An Address by Way of an Abridged Account of My Life," etc.

In an old letter book[14] of Lyman Wight, still extant, one may read in dimming letters written over a century ago (1855) these words:

> Now Mr Editor if you been pleasant when Joseph called on me shortly after he came out of jail to lay hands with him on the head of a youth and heard him cry aloud you are my successor when I depart and heard the blessings poured on his head I say had you heard all this and seen the tears streaming from his eyes you would not have been led by blind fanaticism or a zeal without knowledge.

Lyman Wight did not live to see Young Joseph "held up before the congregation of Israel to take his father's place," but his sons saw it, and his sons' sons, and today the children and grandchildren of his children dwell in peace upon that "goodly land," from which he wandered for a quarter of a century, ever longing for the time when he might return and claim an inheritance there. Most of the Texas colony joined the Reorganization, a few went to Utah, and several drifted out of the church altogether.

---

[14] Original letter book of Lyman Wight—Heman C. Smith collection.

XL.—The Community at Preparation

Among those who went to Wisconsin soon after the death of Joseph Smith at Nauvoo, was one Charles B. Thompson, a missionary in the days of Joseph Smith. He appears to have been quite successful and wrote an able defense of the Book of Mormon, a few copies of which are still extant.

After going to Voree with Strang, he published a poem strongly favoring Strang's claims and otherwise appeared to be satisfied with his leadership until some time late in 1847. He claimed to receive a revelation on New Year's Day, 1848, in which he was informed that the church was rejected in 1844, as an organization, but that the priesthood, having been conferred prior to 1844, continued with those holding it until Zion could be established. This position was clearly stated in a proclamation issued from Saint Louis on January 1, 1848: "The Lord will have no more church organization until after the redemption of Zion."

He proceeded at once to organize what he called "Jehovah's Presbytery of Zion," in which were most complicated and numerous divisions, subdivisions, and orders of priesthood. He followed up with several proclamations from Saint Louis. The first was addressed to the nations of the world, and in it he claimed to be Ephraim "born again among the Gentiles," promulgating the idea of transmigration of souls. The second was addressed to the scattered members of the priesthood, and here he proclaimed himself as "Baneemy, Patriarch of Zion." The third was addressed to kings, princes, governors, presidents, rulers, etc., and represented Thompson as "Apostle of the Free and Accepted Order of Baneemy and Fraternity of the Sons of Zion." The fourth was directed to "the children of Zion and the remnant of the priesthood," and was signed by the "Chief Teacher of the Preparatory Department of Jehovah's Presbytery of Zion." He later published a book of purported revelations and also the various rules, regulations, and covenants established in his community.

In 1854, Thompson, who was known among his followers, variously as "Father Ephraim" and Baneemy, and perhaps by other titles, went into western Iowa with fifty or sixty families and pre-empted several thousand acres of the best land to be found in that community. Under this arrangement, all property was turned over to the head of the order, presumably as trustee, and the members even covenanted to turn over all private property, including wearing apparel and right to their own services.

Until the summer of 1855 all seemed to go well, and then some ten families withdrew under the leadership of Hugh Lytle, an elder in the order, publishing a card in the *Preparation News and Ephraim's Messenger,* as follows:

> We, the undersigned members of "Jehovah's Presbytery of Zion," have left the fraternity of Preparation; not that our faith in the work has at all abated, or that we intend to apostatize from the original principles of the work, but on account of believing that the system of separate and single family order is best adapted to our present sentiments and inclinations, but in all other respects, we deem ourselves as much in the faith as heretofore.

These families were those of Hugh Lytle, J. R. McIntyre, F. D. Winegar, John Outhouse, John Thomas, Andrew Hall, Jacob Paden, A. Clements, J. M. Outhouse and Henry Brooke.

These members sued in the court for the recovery of their property and lost the suit, but later a compromise was effected by which they secured some compensation.

Things progressed smoothly for a time, but soon dissatisfaction again arose, and as ominous rumors increased, Thompson took advantage of the absence of the greater part of the male population of Preparation, who were on missions in various parts of the United States, and deeded all the property of the order except forty acres which he retained in his own name, to his wife, Catherine Thompson, and the "Assistant Steward of the Lord," one Guy P. Barnum. Having been notified by those at home of Thompson's transfer of title, the missionaries hastened home. A settlement was attempted by the angered communists, and feeling ran high. Thompson, who in addition to his other titles, was "Chief Steward of the Lord," finally fled. An action in chancery was immediately begun to set aside the transfer of real estate to Mrs. Thompson and Barnum, which lingered in litigation for eight years, when the transfers were set aside by the Supreme Court of Iowa (December, 1866), which held that Thompson held only as trustee. The property was ordered sold by the courts and divided among the original contributors in ratio of the amount each put into the order.

Thompson found his way to Saint Louis in 1860, and there published a magazine *Nachashlogian,* designed to be in defense of Negro slavery. However, only the first number was ever printed.

Almost the entire community at Preparation accepted the Reorganization, some of them becoming quite prominent therein.

Neither leaders nor members were ever accused of immorality and Thompson took and always maintained a decided stand against polygamy.

Their unhappy experience with Thompson's stewardship of their property did not affect their faith in the ultimate triumph of the Zionic ideal. But they recognized the experiment as valuable in showing the weakness of this kind of community.

The majority of the descendants of the colony at Preparation may be found today in the Reorganized Church, still cherishing the Zionic ideals of their fathers.

XLI.—Jason W. Briggs and the Beloit and Waukesha Branches

At Potosi, Wisconsin, in 1841, William O. Clark baptized among others a young man of twenty by the name of Jason W. Briggs. By the following year he had been ordained an elder and had taken the gospel to his home in Beloit, Wisconsin, where he soon raised a small branch of perhaps twenty-five members. All the Briggs family became members, including the father, the mother, Polly Damon Briggs, the eldest son, Silas, the daughter, Mary (married to a Stiles), and perhaps others as well as neighbors and friends.

The Briggs family subscribed, as every Latter Day Saint family was encouraged to do, to the *Times and Seasons,* a marvelous paper in those times to come to this pioneer home. They read every word of it and usually they read it aloud in the evenings, so that all might hear. In that family was a lad of eight, and to him that wonderful paper, so precious that it was almost venerated by the family, was a source of never-failing delight. As soon as he had opportunity, he took it in his own hands and spelled out all that he could read, but alas, most of the words were too long and too complicated for him to understand, and he had to wait until the paper was read to the family assembled. He never missed any of it, but especially did he love to hear the "History of Joseph Smith" that was "running" serially through its pages. So strongly was the subject of these family readings impressed upon his mind that he remembered throughout his life the words and teachings as explained to him then, even when the imprint of later teachings had faded. That child was Edmund C. Briggs, destined to become the first, and at one time the only, missionary of the Reorganization.

Either that same year or the next, young Jason preached in the neighboring village of Waukesha, where some of the relatives of the Briggs family resided, and organized another branch in that locality. In 1843 the young elder went to Nauvoo, a long journey, to see things for himself, and came back well satisfied. The next year the family learned from their *Times and Seasons* that the Prophet had been killed! Jason was twenty-three by that time, and Edmund in his tenth year. The little branch struggled on, but gradually, from what they read in the *Times and Seasons*, became fearful that things were changed at Nauvoo.

The local branches of the church, often far apart, handicapped by difficulties in transportation and correspondence, were much more alone and independent than at later dates. When the President of the church was killed, these went on holding meetings, electing officers, preaching the same gospel they had preached since the church was founded. They did not consider that the church had been removed from the earth. They still believed they were part of the kingdom of God on earth, and that the priesthood with which their officers had been endowed was eternal, and would not be lost except by transgression.

I united with the church in 1841, [says Briggs], and I remained with it. I have accounted myself a member of that church from that time on, from 1841 to 1885, but I have been in different organizations at different times, as I have already stated; but when in each of these organizations I supposed I was under the church.

When I found out that they were teaching anything that was not authorized by the church before 1844, as the law is set forth in the Bible, the Book of Mormon, and the Book of Doctrine and Covenants, why, I left at once.

I always supposed when I belonged to those different organizations that they were the true and direct descendant of the original church, and as soon as my error was revealed to me, I left them—left them as soon as I found out they were not under the church.

These people with whom I was associated in Wisconsin were people who were contending for the original doctrine of the church, for the maintenance of the original doctrine of the church, in its purity.[1]

---

[1] Jason W. Briggs in the *Temple Lot Suit*, pages 401, 402.

Having become convinced that the church as led by Brigham Young was in apostasy, the branch at Beloit renounced that organization in 1845 or 1846 and began to fellowship with the faction led by James J. Strang. During this period, Jason went again as a missionary, working in New York and much in Wisconsin, but he soon became satisfied he was following a false leader.

My reasons for leaving Strang [wrote Jason W. Briggs] were that I saw something better in the matter of faith and leadership—I should say in the form of leadership and faith. Then there were some of the doctrines of Strang that did not suit me, and some things that I considered objectionable. After we left Strang, myself and most of the branch at Beloit became associated with William Smith's organization, under the understanding that he claimed the right to lead as guardian for Young Joseph.

But when in October, 1851, he attended a conference at Palestine, Illinois, held by William Smith and others, Jason became thoroughly dissatisfied with their claims. He was discouraged and depressed. He believed with all his heart that the principles he had embraced in 1841 were those of the true Church of Christ, but now thrice since the death of Joseph Smith he had been misled and disillusioned. Brigham Young had gone into polygamy, so had Strang, and now he believed that William Smith was tending the same way.[2] There were other discouraging features in all of these branches. What was there now, but to do as Joseph Smith had done in his perplexity many years before, ask the Lord. On the 18th day of November, 1851, he was praying on the prairie, "about three miles northwest" of Beloit, when he says he received a revelation:

Therefore, let the elders whom I have ordained by the hand of my servant Joseph, or by the hand of those ordained by him, resist not this authority, nor faint in the discharge of duty, which is to preach my gospel as revealed in the record of the Jews, and the Book of Mormon, and the Book of Doctrine and Covenants; and cry

---

[2] William Smith always denied this.

repentance and remission of sins through obedience to the gospel, and I will sustain them, and give them my Spirit; and in mine own due time I will call upon the seed of Joseph Smith, and will bring one forth, and he shall be mighty and strong, and he shall preside over the high priesthood of my church; and then shall the quorums assemble, and the pure in heart shall gather, and Zion shall be reinhabited, as I said unto my servant Joseph Smith; after many days shall all these things be accomplished, saith the Spirit. Behold, that which ye received as my celestial law is not of me, but is the doctrine of Baalam. And I denounce it and proclaim against it. . . . And the Spirit said unto me, Write write, write; write the revelation and send it unto the Saints at Palestine, and at Voree, and at Waukesha, and to all places where this doctrine is taught as my law; and whosoever will humble themselves before me, and ask of me, shall receive of my Spirit a testimony that these words are of me. Even so. Amen.[3]

After two days' thought and study, Elder Briggs presented this document to several friends, among whom were David Powell, H. Lowe, and John Harrington. But, Brother Harrington reminded him, did not the Doctrine and Covenants say that no one save a prophet, seer, and revelator should receive revelations for the church? This was a real obstacle, and after much discussion Brothers Lowe and Harrington determined, in spite of his difficulty, to put it to a test as indicated in the last sentence of the purported message. Another brother and his wife asked to join in prayer with them. All received the testimony of the truth of what had been given Brother Briggs.

During the remainder of the week following, the little group of Saints in Beloit were filled with suppressed excitement, for it had been whispered about, as secrets usually are, and everyone knew that something unusual was happening, and therefore all made sure to attend church the following Sunday, November 24, 1851, at the home of Sister Polly Briggs. There Latter Day Saint meetings had been held for many years. There were thirty members present when church assembled that morning, and Jason proceeded to preach as usual, though as some afterwards remarked "with unusual liberty."[4] When he had finished, he read to them

[3] *The Messenger*, edited by Jason W. Briggs, Volume 2, page 1.
[4] *The Messenger*, Volume 2, page 5.

the communication received the Monday previous, and told them that he now saw light where before only darkness had reigned. He says there were only "one or two instances of levity" as he made this statement for to the average mind a revelation from God is cause for levity. Briggs was gratified to find only unusual solemnity and intense feeling among the majority.

His announcement was followed by the appointment of another meeting for the evening at the home of John A. Williams. That night, after the usual opening exercises, the meeting was declared open for "consultation and testimony" and soon "took on the character of an investigation," and "many facts relative to the erroneous teaching of William Smith and Wood were brought out." One or two of the membership made what seemed to Briggs to be a feeble effort to defend them, but when a motion was made to "withdraw the hand of fellowship from them," the vote was almost unanimous in the affirmative, only two dissenting.

The next day or two were spent by brothers and sisters alike, as they had time, in the arduous labor of copying in long hand the document presented by Briggs, ready to send to each of the places particularly mentioned. In time, on account of the reference therein to polygamy, it was also sent to all they knew who believed in this doctrine, which was particularly odious to Briggs. Shortly after, a statement was drawn up to accompany the message and was signed by all the branch officers and several of the membership.

Soon after, Lowe, Harrington, Powell, and Briggs met at the home of Jason W. Briggs for consultation. They all knelt together in earnest prayer to know what should be their next step and immediately experienced the gifts of tongues, interpretation, and prophecy, and more than all, "increased light." It was determined to send Elders Lowe and Harrington to visit all the branches eastward as far as Waukesha, and then northward, delivering to each branch of former Latter Day Saints a copy of the message and the statement explaining it, and also to communicate to each of them the stand taken by the church at Beloit and the reason for it, which was as stated by Jason W. Briggs:

> A withdrawal of confidence in any and all organizations and pretended leaders or successors to the Presidency of the church, entertaining a belief that the true successor of Joseph Smith would be his eldest son, who would in the "due time" of the Lord be called to act in that capacity, and for which we would wait; and in the meantime preach the gospel, baptize, and form branches, and nothing more. Such a position was believed the only tenable one. And every day and at every interview with each other, this view of the case became more apparent, and the resolution to pursue that course became stronger.[5]

Imbued with these convictions, the men appointed went to each near-by branch, most of whom had been misled by one or more leaders, and wherever they went and had prayer with their brethren of old time, they found the same spirit of which they had partaken in Beloit in the hearts of the people. New hope seemed to arise as it had with themselves, and new courage and confidence took possession of them all. The branches visited on this trip were the Nephi Branch in Walworth County, one at Voree, and one in Waukesha County. Young Joseph was not consulted; there was no need that he should be, for the promise in the revelation to Briggs was definite enough. He would be called; they were to wait for that. They still had faith, remarkable faith, after years of disillusionment.

---

[5] *The Messenger,* Volume 2, page 5.

XLII.—Zenas H. Gurley and the Yellowstone Branch

THE COMING FORTH OF THE church in 1830 partook no more of the miraculous than did the combination of the scattered elements that were to form the Reorganization of the church, with Young Joseph at its head. The fact that here and there over the land several men were to receive almost exactly the same instruction, at the same time, and be guided together to form the organization we all love was quite as wonderful as the beginnings of the angel message in New York in 1830.

Zenas H. Gurley, another of the good men so strangely moved upon, was one in the quorum of seventies in the church in Joseph's time. He was born in Bridgewater, New York, May 29, 1801. In a letter written to Young Joseph, near his sixty-ninth birthday, he thus described the circumstances that surrounded his infancy:

"Sixty-nine years ago the 29th of May last, a little squalling boy made his appearance in Bridgewater, Oneida County, New York. As his father had died five months previously, the friends thought it right that the father's name should be transferred to the son, so they called him Zenas; and as the law had kindly relieved the mother of nearly all her furniture, a hollow log was provided for a cradle in which this Zenas was carefully rocked through infancy, thus preparing him for the hollow world in which he has been rocked most of the time since."[1] For a second name the child received the maiden name of his mother, that of Hovey.

As he grew older, he adopted the trade of a tanner and currier,

---
[1] *Saints' Herald*, Volume 17, pages 406, 407.

but being always of a studious turn of mind, he made the best of his advantages and soon adopted the profession of a schoolteacher. He also became a member of the Methodist Church, considering that more adapted to his ideas than the Presbyterian faith, in which he had been born and reared. Gurley secured a school to teach near Leeds, Ontario, and there he met and married Miss Margaret Hickey. Here were born to the couple six children, the two oldest dying in infancy. He relates that one night in returning home in a skiff (for he lived beside a lake), the boat was nearly upset in a tempest. In his extremity he called out, "Save, Lord, or I perish!" and he saw the flash of a light and heard a voice say, "Your life is spared for this time, that you may warn sinners to repentance." Believing this to be a call to service, he continued his zeal in the Methodist Church, in which he was now a local minister. At one time in vision he thought he heard John the Baptist preach, and so much did the dream impress itself upon his mind that Gurley did not forget the peculiar construction John the Baptist placed upon certain passages of Scripture.

Some time later he was called upon by friends, who knew his careful study of the Scriptures, to go to hear some "Mormon" missionaries and help "put them down." Nothing loath to be an instrument in the hands of God in so good a work, Gurley went to hear James Blakeslee preach. Again, as in his dream, he listened to the voice of John the Baptist, and heard the speaker place the same, as it had seemed to him, peculiar construction upon the Scriptures. That was evidence enough. He was baptized on April 1, 1838, and soon after loading their household goods and little family of four children into a wagon, they made the long trip overland to Missouri, arriving just in time to join the exodus to Illinois.

They came to Nauvoo almost penniless, and while Margaret Gurley took in washing to support the family, they lived upon corn bread made of corn grated on a hand grater and mixed with water, until Zenas found work as a tanner in the growing city. He had been ordained an elder in June by James Blakeslee, and at Far West had been chosen a seventy. He now felt he should go to preach the gospel, but he had no money with which to proceed to the work he felt he was called upon to do. In this dilemma he and his wife thought of their cow. It was their only cow, bought with their joint earnings, and had been a great source of comfort and help. Nearly every family in Nauvoo possessed themselves early of the luxury of a cow, and one English immigrant says, "It is a delight to see the cows coming into the city at night in droves of hundreds, each one with a small bell at its neck, tinkling as they go along." It had been a great day for the little ones in the Gurley home when their cow joined the herd and they had milk to drink with their corn bread!

But it was a day of sacrifice, and if the father must go on a mission, the cow must be sold to get the necessary funds to take care of the family in his absence and outfit him for his journey. Gurley took his way that day (winter of 1840), on foot of course, with his heart a little heavy, as he thought towards evening of the sacrifice his little ones had made. He found shelter for the night with a Mr. Cline (probably William Cline). Almost the first question asked was in regard to provision made for his family, and when Zenas Gurley told what had been done, Mr. Cline immediately sent the Gurleys another cow.

He went on to the village of La Harpe, where a joint revival was in progress, held by the Episcopal Wesleyan and the Protestant Methodist groups in that village, but they got no converts. Gurley arrived in time to attend the last meeting and gave out an appointment. To his own surprise, curiosity drew a large crowd, and after four or five sermons, he sent for Elder Jehiel Savage (who had baptized Margaret Gurley). He was preaching some twenty miles south of La Harpe, but he came to the place, joined his efforts with those of Gurley, and by spring they had baptized some sixty members, including young Alfred Moffet,[2] whom Gurley baptized in April, 1840. At the General Conference of the church in 1841, held at Nauvoo, Illinois, he was appointed one of eight men (John Murdock, Lyman Wight, William Smith, H. W. Miller, Amasa Lyman, Leonard Soby, Jehiel Savage, and Z. H. Gurley) to travel and collect means for the building of the temple.

Then came the trouble of 1844, and being faithful and unsuspecting, Gurley planned as a matter of course to accompany the westward exodus. The loss of his fine team prevented, and having been forced by the mob to leave all his earthly possessions, he took refuge in Jo Daviess County, Illinois, where he made his home until 1849, when he moved to near Burlington, Wisconsin, having in the meantime become dissatisfied with the claims of Brigham Young, and still later adopting those of James J. Strang.

For perhaps a year he threw himself with old-time enthusiasm into the movement sponsored by Strang, who was a man of winning personality and much native ability. November 6, 1849, found him preaching in the mission where he himself had first heard the gospel, at Gananoque, Landsdown, Pittsburgh, and other points in Canada, evidently spending the winter there. By the middle of March, 1850, he was "assisting Brother Silsby in organizing the brethren and getting them ready for Beaver"[3] at Saint Lawrence, New York, but returned to Voree sometime during the spring and summer and attended conference there June 1 and 2. From there Gurley was sent on a mission to the Indians in the northern part of Wisconsin. On his way, he was solicited to go about fifteen miles south of Yellowstone, Wisconsin, and having preached for several weeks in that vicinity, someone told him

---

[2]Father of Mary Moffet, wife of O. B. Thomas, the mother of James A. Thomas, Mrs. Lydia Wight, and Olive Thomas Mortimore, who have contributed to the work of the Reorganized Church at various times.
[3]*Gospel Herald*, Volume 5, page 22.

of a man he knew who had formerly been a friend of his in the old church. In the latter part of the year, he stopped there to rest, and about the second day of his visit, he was asked to preach the funeral sermon of a little child of David and Anna Wildermuth, the first sermon preached in that vicinity by a Latter Day Saint. Mr. and Mrs. Wildermuth were so pleased with his address that they begged him to remain in the neighborhood and hold meetings. He consented, preaching from house to house about the neighborhood. After hearing a few sermons, David and Anna Wildermuth and two of their sons, E. C. and Eli M., and two old ladies gave their names for baptism. They were accordingly baptized in Yellowstone[4] Creek and became the nucleus of a large and prosperous branch in that place.

> From this time [says Gurley himself], the way seemed to open before me. Calls for preaching came in from various places, which I gladly responded to as far as it was in my power, and with the help of H. P. Brown, who came to my assistance some time in the winter following, we succeeded in building up a church of twenty-three or twenty-four, which we called the Yellowstone Branch. A few months afterward I moved my family into this section [this branch was situated about ten miles east of Mineral Point, Wisconsin, in the western part of the State] and continued my labors with the church, teaching them the principles of the gospel as revealed from heaven to us through Joseph the Seer.
> During this time several strange things came to my knowledge that fully satisfied me that unless good and evil, bitter and sweet, could proceed from the same fountain, neither J. J. Strang, B. Young, William Smith, nor any that had claimed to be prophets, since Joseph's death, were the servants of God.[5]

About this time the newly baptized members at Yellowstone heard that J. J. Strang was preaching polygamy. Naturally they were horrified, and not wishing to have their neighbors think they were connected with an institution of the kind, they immediately drew up a statement and had it published in the Mineral Point *Tribune* and a local paper in Galena. Zenas H. Gurley was absent

---
[4] *Church History*, Volume 3, page 745.
[5] *Saints' Herald*, Volume 1, page 19.

from home at the time preaching, but the people were so anxious to shake off the hateful implication of what they heard that they felt they could not wait until his return. This document as given in substance by Eli M. Wildermuth was about as follows:

> *To Whom It May Concern*: This is to certify that we, the undersigned, who are members of the Yellowstone Branch of the Church of Jesus Christ of Latter Day Saints, do hereby protest against the practice of polygamy and other abominations that are practiced by James J. Strang and his followers; and withdraw our fellowship from them and from all so-called pretenders to the successorship or presidency of the church, among whom are the said James J. Strang, Brigham Young, William B. Smith, Colin Brewster, Alpheus Cutler, Lyman Wight, and others, and hold ourselves aloof from them and do not wish to be held responsible for any of their evil teachings or practices.

This document was signed by David Wildermuth and family, H. H. Deam, David Newkirk, Reuben W. Newkirk, and others. This was in 1851.

When Elder Gurley returned and found what had been done he asked David Wildermuth: "What are you going to do next?"

David Wildermuth replied, "I do not know. I believe the first principles of the gospel, which you have taught, and which we have obeyed are true, but I positively will not accept polygamy and other doctrines that are taught and practiced by Strang and others."[6]

This was the sentiment of all the signers of the protest and others associated with them. Almost as he asked the question, "What shall we do?" the answer came to Elder Gurley, and he said:

> Let us take the advice of the Apostle James, as recorded in James 1:5, "If any lack wisdom, let him ask of God," etc. So it was agreed that each member of the branch should ask for wisdom about what to do next.
>
> [Gurley himself tells feelingly of the dilemma that now faced him.] The inquiry arose in my mind, "What shall we do? Here are a few

---
[6] *Church History*, Volume 3, pages 745, 746.

honest Saints who have obeyed the gospel, and are looking to me for instruction. What can I say? What can I teach them?" Thus I meditated for months. God, and God only, knows what the anguish of my mind was. I resolved that I would preach the word, and thank God, preaching brought me out right.

It was after preaching one Sunday evening, in the fall of 1851, while sitting in my chair at Brother Wildermuth's house, my mind was drawn to Isaiah 2:2,3. At that moment the great work of the last days, as it was spoken of by the prophet in that chapter, seemed to pass before me in all its majesty and glory. It appeared that I could see all nations in motion, coming to the mountain of the Lord's house in the top of the mountains. At this time Strang's Beaver Island operation appeared before me. It looked mean and contemptible beyond description. A voice—the Spirit of God—the Holy Ghost—then said to me, "Can this [alluding to Strang's work] ever effect this great work?" I answered, "No, Lord." I felt ashamed to think that I had ever thought so. The voice then said, "Rise up, cast off *all* that claim to be prophets and go forth and preach the gospel and say that God will raise up a prophet to complete his work." I said, "Yea, Lord."

As I left the house, my mind was dwelling upon what had just transpired. Although the Spirit had told me that God would raise up a prophet to complete his work, it did not enter my mind at that time that I would realize the work in its present form. My whole desires were that those dear souls around me might enjoy the gifts and blessings of the gospel as the Saints did in Joseph's time, and be saved from those meshes of iniquity which thousands had run into. A few weeks afterward, while reading a paragraph in the B. of C. which says, "If thine eye be single, thy whole body shall be full of light," the Spirit said unto me, "Rise up, cast off all that claim to be prophets, and go forth and preach the gospel, and say that God will raise up a prophet to complete his work." I answered, "I will do it, God being my helper." From that time I began to look about in earnest for a starting point. I examined the book carefully and saw at once that the teachings of the day were contrary to the law and resolved that although I had but one talent, in the name of Israel's God, I would go forward and leave the result with him.

At this time I was laboring with Brother Reuben Newkirk, a young and worthy brother [Reuben Newkirk was twenty-nine years of age] I explained my visions to him, and he endorsed them at once. The Spirit of God was with us, and day after day was spent in holding council about the matter, until one day (being at work together in a lone place) we joined hands, and in a most solemn manner entered into a covenant, calling God to witness that we would from that hour renounce all that claimed to be prophets and take the Bible, Book of Mormon, Book of Covenants, and the Holy Spirit for our guide. This was a new era in my existence. In Joseph's time I had stood with thousands of the servants of God and counted it an honor to call them brethren, but alas, how changed the scene! One, only one remained of my associates that I could call brother. At times how dark, how dark was the future! . . .

Could I at that time have been permitted to realize what I have enjoyed with you and other dear Saints within a few weeks past, how gladly would I have stemmed the torrent and said with the apostle, "I count all things but loss for the excellency of the knowledge of Christ Jesus our Lord." Well, thank God, he who commenced this work will carry it forward, and I rejoice. My past experience strengthens me for the future. Then we were alone; our brethren around us, having been taught that Strang was Joseph's successor, could only look upon us as apostates when they became acquainted with our opposition. We seemed to be hedged in. Darkness was all around us on every side. Light was only above us. Well, thank God, we proved him to be a present helper. A few days after we had entered into this covenant, while Brother Newkirk was in secret prayer, the Holy Spirit rested upon him. He arose and spoke in tongues, and started homewards, speaking in tongues and praising God. His wife heard him and met him, and shortly after, she received the same gift and blessing. These gifts were the first fruits of the reformation.

About this time Brother David Powell came from Beloit (about fifty miles distant) bringing with him a revelation which had been given to Jason W. Briggs sometime in the previous November, declaring that the Lord would in his own due time call upon the seed of Joseph Smith to come forth and set in order the quorums; in a word, to fill his father's place. He was commanded to write it and send it to all the churches. There were some ideas in the revelation that I could not receive. I was entirely unacquainted with the order of the priesthood as it really is, nevertheless I knew that God would raise up a prophet, but who he was, or where he would come from, I did not know.

About ten or fifteen days after I had heard of this revelation, . . . my boys came running into my room, declaring with great earnestness that their little sister was up to Brother Newkirk's speaking and singing in tongues. For a moment I was overpowered with joy. I exclaimed, "Is it possible that God has remembered my family?" Immediately I went up and when I was within one or two steps of the house I paused. I listened, and oh, the thrill of joy that went through my soul! I knew that it was of God. My child, my dear child, was born of the Holy Spirit. I opened the door and went in. It appeared to me that the entire room was filled with the Holy Spirit. Shortly after, I requested them all to join with me in asking the Lord to tell us who the successor of Joseph Smith was. I felt anxious to know, that I might bear a faithful testimony. We spent a few moments in prayer, when the Holy Spirit declared, "The successor of Joseph Smith is Joseph Smith, the son of Joseph Smith, the prophet. It is his right by lineage, saith the Lord your God."

It is proper here to state that the main body of the church lived from four to eight miles from us, and having learned that we had left Strang, they regarded us as apostates. However, it was not long after the gifts were manifested, and when they came to know that these blessings were indeed with us, they admitted that they were of God, and gradually, one after another, united with us, until the whole church was made to know the truth of our position and rejoice with unspeakable joy. Although the church had been organized more than a year and was striving to live right before God, yet no visible gifts had been manifested among us.

It was now necessary that we should change our organization and position in regard to the Presidency of the Priesthood. The branch had been organized under Strang. The Lord had taught us that this was wrong, consequently we appointed a day for the purpose of acknowledging the legal heir. The day arrived, and it will be long remembered by many that were present. While we were singing the opening hymn, the Holy Spirit was sensibly felt. Several sang in tongues. A halo of glory seemed to be spread over the congregation, and when we bowed before Almighty God in solemn prayer, all felt and all knew that what we were about to do was approbated of God. After singing, I stated to the church what was the object of our meeting, and I requested all who wished to renounce J. J. Strang as prophet, seer, and revelator to the church, and acknowledge the seed of Joseph Smith in his stead to come forth in the own due time of the Lord, to manifest it by raising up. In a moment the entire congregation stood up, and one simultaneous shout of joy and praise went up to God for our deliverance. Nearly all the congregation were under the influence of the Spirit of prophecy, and many important truths relating to the triumphant accomplishment of this great work was then declared.[7]

After this meeting Elder Gurley wrote Jason W. Briggs, simply: "We have received evidence of your revelation."

---

[7] *True Latter Day Saints' Herald,* Volume 1, pages 19-22; *Church History,* Volume 3, pages 206-209.

XLIII.—Reorganizing the Church[1]

THE FIRST CONFERENCE OF THE men thus drawn together in a common cause was unique.

Never before in the history of the church had a conference convened without a leader to "call" it. Others, secure in the leadership of one or another of the various factions, laughed at the little group. Yet to the handful meeting on that 12th day of June at Beloit (Newark Branch), the "tokens of divine care" were visible and "confirmed their faith that what had been promised would surely be fulfilled in the due time of the Lord. And they determined to wait and prepare for that time."[2]

A statement was made to the conference when it assembled that they would take measures to adopt resolutions declaring their rejection of the different leaders and stating that they "stood in expectation of one of the sons of Joseph Smith assuming the leadership of the church at some time in the future, and that was the position"[3] in which the church would stand, accepting the leadership of no other.

They were in conference two days but proceeded carefully, fearful of going beyond their instructions. Their resolutions were these:

> Resolved, that the conference regard the pretensions of Brigham Young, James J. Strang, James Colin Brewster, and William Smith and Joseph Wood's joint claim to the leadership of the Church of Jesus Christ of Latter Day Saints as an assumption of power, in violation of the law of God, and consequently we disclaim all connection and fellowship with them.

---

[1] The use of the word "reorganize" as referring to the church has been much misunderstood, but it is literally correct according to the dictionary use of the word which is "organize again" or "anew"—and organize, among other meanings is to "rehabilitate," "get in working order." The men who reorganized the church did not plan a new organization, but accepted individuals and whole congregations upon their original baptism.
[2] *The Messenger*, Volume 2, page 9.
[3] *Plaintiff's Abstract in the Temple Lot Suit*, page 396.

Resolved, that the successor of Joseph Smith, junior, as the Presiding High Priest in the Melchisedec Priesthood, must of necessity be the seed of Joseph Smith, junior, in fulfillment of the law and promises of God.

Resolved, that as the office of the First President of the church grows out of the authority of the Presiding High Priest, in the High Priesthood, no person can legally lay claim to the office of First President of the church without a previous ordination, to the Presidency of the High Priesthood.

Resolved, that we recognize the validity of all legal ordinations in this church, and will fellowship all such as have been ordained while acting within the purview of such authority.

Resolved, that we believe that the Church of Christ, organized on the 6th day of April, A. D., 1830, exists as on that day wherever six or more Saints are organized according to the pattern in the Doctrine and Covenants.

Resolved, that the whole law of the Church of Jesus Christ is contained in the Bible, Book of Mormon, and Book of Doctrine and Covenants.

Resolved, that, in the opinion of this conference, there is no stake to which the Saints on this continent are commanded to gather at the present time, but that the Saints on all other lands are commanded to gather to this land, preparatory to the re-establishment of the church in Zion, when the scattered Saints on this land will also be commanded to gather and return to Zion, and to their inheritances, in fulfillment of the promises of God; and it is the duty of the Saints to turn their hearts and their faces towards Zion and supplicate the Lord for such deliverance.

Resolved, that we will to the extent of our ability and means communicate to all the scattered Saints the sentiments contained in the foregoing resolutions.

Resolved, that this conference believes it is the duty of the elders of the church, who have been legally ordained, to cry repentance and remission of sins to this generation, through obedience to the gospel as revealed in the record of the Jews, the Book of Mormon, and Book of Doctrine and Covenants, and not to faint in the discharge of duty.[4]

A committee was then chosen to write a pamphlet to use in their missionary work, based upon these resolutions, to be called *A Word of Consolation*. The committee was composed of Jason W. Briggs, Zenas H. Gurley, Sr., and John Harrington.

The missionaries went out from that little conference with re-

---

[4]Church record in office of Historian, Auditorium, Independence, Missouri; *Church History*, Volume 3, pages 209, 210.

newed courage, but there was one thing which puzzled them all. They had been impressed more than once that they should "organize, in preparation for the re-establishment of the quorums and First Presidency of the church," but no one knew how it was to be done.

David Powell and John Harrington took a mission south that summer and visited some of the old Saints, bearing their testimony to the new movement and baptizing one, young Edmund C. Briggs, then eighteen years of age, who had never held membership in any faction of the church. Edmund had grown to be a delicate, sickly youth, and in November, 1851, had been very ill, presumably dying. He was living with his brother, Silas, in Jefferson County, Wisconsin. Becoming alarmed, this brother sent for his mother to come to him. The letter arrived just as Jason was laying his perplexities in regard to the church before the Lord, and he pleaded there the case of his young brother. He says he was promised, "Thy brother Edmund shall not die, but shall live and come into the church and shall stand with you in this work."[5] This prophecy was fulfilled. The members of the church were poor, but they visited as many of the old Saints as they could. Z. H. Gurley visited Wingville and the Blue Mounds settlement and succeeded in getting several to unite with the church, among them George White of Wingville, and John Cunningham, a brother-in-law of H. H. Deam at the same place, and Daniel B. Rasey, an old member of the church at Blue Mounds.

There was but little business done at the conference on October 6. J. W. Briggs presided, as he had in the previous conference, and Samuel Blair, who was made church recorder at that conference, acted as secretary. It was

"Resolved, that the highest authority among the priesthood represents the legitimate President as a presiding authority."[6]

---

[5] *The Messenger*, Volume 2, page 17; *Church History*, Volume 3, page 212.
[6] *Old Church Record*, page 7; *Church History*, Volume 3, page 213.

The committee appointed to draft the *Word of Consolation* reported their work, presenting the pamphlet in manuscript form. Two thousand copies were ordered printed.

Strange as it undoubtedly was, these men one and all testified that during the length of their membership in other factions, the "gifts of the gospel" were never made manifest, but as soon as they made the move to "stand aloof" and "wait for the legitimate President," they were blessed with great spiritual blessings. Although they had presented the pamphlet, *A Word of Consolation,* to the Saints and received their indorsement, they were not yet satisfied. Not one of them but abhorred the doctrine of polygamy, but they were aware that in carrying their message to the old-time Saints they would meet this doctrine very soon, and they desired something definite to meet the questions that would arise. On the evening of the 9th of January, 1853, "ever memorable with the Saints of God," the committee presented their problem. They wanted the word of the Lord on two questions: First, Is polygamy of God? Second, Is any addition necessary to the pamphlet before its publication? In about half an hour, during which it seemed to Zenas H. Gurley that "angels were hovering over them," and that he received such manifestation of the Spirit as he had not received in the twenty-three years of his membership in the church, the following message was received:

> Polygamy is an abomination in the sight of the Lord God; it is not of me; I abhor it. I abhor it, as also the doctrines of the Nicolaitans, and the men or set of men who practice it. I judge them not; I judge not those who practice it. Their works shall judge them at the last day. Be ye strong; ye shall contend against this doctrine; many will be led into it honestly, for the Devil will seek to establish it and roll it forth to deceive.
>
> They seek to build up their own kingdoms, to suit their own pleasures, but I countenance it not, saith God. I have given my law: I shrink not from my word. My law is given in the Book of Doctrine and Covenants, but they have disregarded my law and trampled upon it, and counted it a light thing and obeyed it not; but my word is the same yesterday as today and forever.

As you have desired to know of me concerning the pamphlet, it is written in part, but not in plainness. It requires three more pages to be written, for it shall go forth in great plainness, combating this doctrine, and all who receive it not, it shall judge at the last day. Let this be the voice of the Lord in the pamphlet, for it shall go forth in great plainness, and many will obey it and turn unto me, saith the Lord.

This accounts [says Gurley] for the last three pages in our first pamphlet, and we most earnestly commend that article to the careful reading of all that have ever known the latter-day work, and pray God our Heavenly Father, in the name of Jesus Christ his Son, to break every band that binds them, that they may be enabled to turn to the law from which they have strayed.

Shortly after this communication was given, it was intimated by the Spirit that we must organize. This was strange teaching to me. I replied, "It is impossible for us to organize farther than we have." I knew that we could not create a priesthood. I conversed with several of the brethren on the subject, and we set it down as a mistake.[7]

March came. The time of the April conference at Argyle, Wisconsin, was near, and they had failed to agree upon whether or not certain brothers held a valid priesthood. They had all been so well satisfied with the results of the meeting in January, when they had presented the question of polygamy, that it was suggested they present a similar question at a special prayer meeting and trust in the Lord for an answer. Accordingly they presented the question for prayer, "Were those ordained apostles by William Smith recognized by God?" The manifestations of the Spirit were fully equal to those of the January meeting. Some testified they saw angels.

Some little time elapsed, nearly an hour, I judge, before we received an answer to our inquiry. We were then told that those ordinations were not acceptable—were not of God, and near the close of the communication we were told expressly to organize ourselves, for "ere long, saith the Lord, I will require the prophet at your hand." Such was the manifestation of the power of God, that not a doubt was left on our minds concerning the source from which the commandment came. We all knew it was from God, but how to organize was the question. We knew we could not create priesthood; we had

---

[7] *True Latter Day Saints' Herald,* Volume 1, pages 53, 54; *Church History,* Volume 3, page 215.

two high priests and one senior president of the seventies, but how could these men organize the church? It was impossible, utterly impossible. We counseled upon it and concluded that possibly under the present circumstances it might be right for high priests to ordain high priests, and for the senior president of seventies to ordain seventies, but when done, what would it accomplish?—nothing—just nothing. We were in trouble—deep trouble. To refuse to organize was disobedience—to go forward in the attempt was darkness. There was but one alternative, and that was to seek wisdom from above.

We sought, and in answer were told to appoint a day and come together fasting and praying, and the Lord would show us how to organize. We therefore appointed the day, dismissed the meeting, and went home rejoicing.[8]

Not until evening of the day appointed (March 20) were they able to meet for prayer on this important matter, but when all were assembled, the question for which all desired an answer was made known in almost childlike simplicity. It was:

Will the Lord please to tell us how to organize, that what we do may be acceptable unto him, and who among us will he acknowledge as the representative of the "legal heir" to the Presidency of the church.

After the meeting continued about an hour, a brother came to Gurley and asked if he had received any answer to the question. Gurley answered, "No." "Well, I have," said the brother. He sat down and wrote, and then read it to the assembly as follows:

Verily thus saith the Lord, as I said unto my servant Moses, "See thou do all things according to the pattern," so I say unto you. Behold the pattern is before you. It is my will that you respect authority in my church, therefore let the greatest among you preside at your Conference. Let three men be appointed by the Conference to select seven men from among you, who shall compose a majority of the Twelve [Apostles]; for it is my will that that quorum should not be filled up at present. Let the President of the Conference, assisted by ten others, ordain them. The senior of them shall stand as the representative. Let them select twelve men from among you and ordain them to compose my High Council. Behold ye understand the order of the Bishopric, the Seventies, the Elders, the Priests, Teachers, and Deacons. Therefore organize according to the pattern. Behold, I will be with you unto the end, even so. Amen.[9]

---

[8] *True Latter Day Saints' Herald*, pages 54, 55; *Church History*, Volume 3 pages 216, 217.
[9] *True Latter Day Saints' Herald*, page 53; *Church History*, Volume 3, pages 217, 218. (See footnote on page 218 of Volume 3.)

The man through whom this message came was H. H. Deam. The long-looked-for time of conference came, the day upon which they were to organize, the day long expected and prayed for by the little group. Gurley relates the experience of the day:

> The 6th of April finally came, and nearly all the church came together. On the 5th, as we had been commanded to organize, we thought it advisable to seek for instructions. We accordingly called a prayer meeting, and as we did not get the desired instruction, we continued it on the 6th. We were then told to organize by what was written. We supposed this referred to the books, of course. Our next step was to organize the Conference. This was now a difficult matter. As I have said, it had become a law to us that the one holding the highest priesthood should preside. There were present two high priests and one Senior President of the Seventies. The question now arose, Whose priesthood is the highest? The subject was discussed at length and what was strange to us all a good deal of ill feeling was manifested.
>
> I have often thought of it. It seemed as though each one thought that the salvation of the church depended on the decision being made according to their respective views, so we argued—so we debated, till the close of the second day [a vote was taken to determine between high priests and seventy which was greatest, and the vote stood nine to nine.—Author] when we began to think the work was lost, and would to God that all Latter Day Saints could know the situation of the church at this time; our feelings—our deep distress—our great anxiety. I considered all was lost—lost—lost. We could not organize. Oh, the bitterness of that moment! We could not see "eye to eye." God had commanded us to do what we absolutely could not do. To my mind, and to the mind of others, our effort was a failure. Kind reader, when your eye falls upon these lines, know that at that time the one who is now penning this, asked God to remove him from the earth. Men who hitherto had been united—had seen "eye to eye"—had labored together as one man for the cause of truth, were now opposed to each other, and after a discussion of two days, learned to their mortification and sorrow, that they, to all human appearances, were forever separate. The Spirit the night before had told a few in a prayer meeting that tomorrow they should see "eye to eye." But the day closed, and we were farther apart than on the former evening. Our attempts were a failure. I repeat, Oh, the bitterness of that moment! Never, never can I forget it. Although since that time, darkness, like Egyptian night has at times seemed to shut out all light and exclude all hope, yet the recollection of that event has enabled me to rest satisfied that he who delivered us then still holds the reins in his own hands, and will bring his work to a glorious consummation, in his own way, and in his own time.

The conference adjourned for prayer meeting in the evening. We accordingly came together at early candlelight, and commenced the meeting as is usual on such occasions. For a short time it seemed as though the "prince of darkness" triumphed. After a little, one of the brethren arose and rebuked the Devil. Shortly afterward some sprang to their feet saying, "angels, angels, brethren, are near us!" and in a moment our darkness was turned into light. The transition was instantaneous. The glory of God, such as I never witnessed before, was manifest. The Spirit seemed to rest upon all in the house. Three were in vision, the Spirit testifying through others at the same time that the recording angel was present. And as we afterward learned, two of the three who were in vision saw the roll, while the third saw the angel and the roll. Just before the manifestation, the brother through whom the revelation had come on the 20th of March [Henry H. Deam] . . . arose to his feet and said, "Brethren, some kind of a spirit tells me that I have the commandment written that we need." He then said "I will read it, and I wish the church to pray, that we may know whether it is from God or not." He then took out and read the revelation which was given us on the 20th of March, remarking that he was not positive that the "Senior" should preside. It was then submitted to the church. . . . In reply to the inquiry as to whether the revelation was of God, the Spirit through a number answered that it was. We were then told that the Lord had withheld his Spirit from his elders to show them that they had not sufficient wisdom in and of themselves to organize. . . . We were then commanded to organize according to the revelation given the 20th of March, with the assurance that the Lord would be with us to the end.

The congregation that evening was large. The schoolhouse [at Argyle, Wisconsin] was filled literally full of Saints, and I believe that everyone was satisfied that that revelation was from God, and that the angel that keeps the record of the Lord's work in every dispensation was in our midst.[10]

J. W. Briggs speaks also of that prayer meeting "by early candlelight" on that memorable April night:

It was at this meeting that [there was] an exhibition of power, light, and unity of spirit above any ever before witnessed among us. Tongues were spoken and interpreted; hymns were sung in tongues and the interpretation sung; prophecy and visions were exercised here for the first time to the writer. Many sang in tongues in perfect harmony at once, as though they constituted a well-practiced choir. Angels appeared and were seen by some, and a testimony of their presence given by others affirming one of them to be the recording angel, who

---

[10] *True Latter Day Saints' Herald*, Volume 1, pages 56, 57.

exhibited a partially unrolled parchment as an unfinished record upon which we were assured should be recorded the act we were called upon to perform in the reorganization of the church, confirmation of the foregoing revelation of the 20th of March, given enjoining obedience to the same. The evident proofs of divine direction were so strong that doubt disappeared, while the light was so clear to all that diversity of opinion ceased, and the whole people were truly of one heart and one soul. And on the next morning at the opening of the session, the revelation of March 20 was presented to the conference, and accepted as such by unanimous voice after which the following persons were chosen as the three to select the seven to be ordained into the Quorum of Twelve Apostles: Cyrus Newkirk, Ethan Griffith, and William Cline, who selected the following seven persons, who were accepted by the conference, and ordained according to the instruction previously given: Zenas H. Gurley, senior, Jason W. Briggs, Henry H. Deam, Reuben Newkirk, John Cunningham, George White, and Daniel B. Rasey. The ordinations took place in the afternoon session [on April 8, 1853] in the following order: Henry H. Deam was first ordained by Jason W. Briggs, assisted by Zenas H. Gurley and Reuben Newkirk, then Henry H. Deam, assisted by Zenas Gurley and Reuben Newkirk, ordained Jason W. Briggs; then Jason W. Briggs, assisted by Henry H. Deam and Reuben Newkirk, ordained Zenas H. Gurley; and then Jason W. Briggs, assisted by Henry H. Deam and Zenas H. Gurley, ordained the other four of the seven chosen.[11]

Thus in a simple, humble manner the reorganization of the church took place. The conference closed with another wonderful testimony meeting and the special charge to the new members of the Quorum of the Twelve, who were now to "take the oversight of the flock."

On that last day also the Twelve met to choose their president, and the Quorum, following the Latter Day Saint custom from the beginning, offered the presidency to the oldest man among them, Zenas H. Gurley, who declined, as did Henry H. Deam, next in age, therefore the choice fell upon Jason W. Briggs, who was made president of the Quorum.[12]

---

[11] *The Messenger*, Volume 2, pages 21, 22; *Church History*, Volume 3, pages 222, 223.

[12] It should be noted that Jason W. Briggs presided over the church from 1853 to 1860 as president pro tem., not because of his ordination to the office of high priest under Strang, but by virtue of his apostleship, the honor of presiding having been declined by Zenas H. Gurley and Henry H. Deam.

Twenty seventies were also chosen and ordained. At the special closing prayer meeting, the Twelve were told in prophecy:

"I give unto you the care of my flock on earth; take the oversight of them, as you shall give an account unto me in the day of judgment."

Zenas H. Gurley admits that he had thought it impossible to obey the command of the Lord to organize, "not having authority to ordain apostles, but we learn what every Latter Day Saint must learn, that a command from God is authority to do all that he requires, be it more or less."[13]

---

[13] *The True Latter Day Saints' Herald,* Volume 1, page 58.

XLIV.—WILLIAM MARKS

WHEN JOSEPH SMITH FIRST arrived in Far West, Missouri, in 1838, he had written a letter to the Saints in Kirtland, remembering many of them by name but to one he wrote a whole paragraph:

> I would just say to Brother Marks that I saw in a vision while on the road, that whereas he was closely pursued by an innumerable concourse of enemies, and as they pressed upon him hard, as if they were about to devour him, and had seemingly obtained some degree of advantage over him, but about this time a chariot of fire came, and near the place, even the Angel of the Lord put forth his hand unto Brother Marks, and said unto him, "Thou art my son, come here," and immediately he was caught up in the chariot, and rode away triumphantly out of their midst. And again the Lord said, "I will raise thee up for a blessing unto many people." Now the particulars of this whole matter cannot be written at this time, but the vision was evidently given to me that I might know that the hand of the Lord would be on his behalf.[1]

November 15, 1854, William Marks sat in his new house at Shabbona Grove, Illinois, to write a letter to his old friend, J. M. Adams. He was sixty-two years of age, and he had not triumphed. Prosperity had blessed him with plenty, but he was lonely for the gospel and for his old friends. He wrote:

> I feel that it would be policy for me to stand still for a short time. I have had it in my mind to try and form a settlement of brethren and try to live according to the law of God, but there have been so many attempts made to gather that I am almost discouraged to make any such attempt, although I should like to live where I could enjoy the society of friends and brethren, but I think we had better try to live and try to do as near right as we know how, and the time will come when we will be regarded for our works.[2]

---

[1] *Millennial Star*, Volume 16, page 131.
[2] Letter from William Marks to James M. Adams, Magnolia, Iowa. James Marvin Adams was born at Sandisfield, Berkshire County, Massachusetts, May 11, 1806, baptized by John Knapp, December 4, 1836, at Andover, Ashtabula County, Ohio, ordained an elder on January 29, 1837, and appointed to preside over the church at Andover; ordained a high priest February 21, 1841; with his family, he started for Nauvoo, May 30, 1844, arriving after the death of the prophet.

William Marks was born in Rutland, Vermont, November 15, 1792. He united with the church in Portage, Allegany County, New York, in the early days of the church. We just hear of him when he took over the mortgage owned by the church on the *Messenger and Advocate* and gave Smith and Rigdon "power of attorney in Kirtland" over the interests of "Wm. Marks & Co." of Portage, Allegany County, New York.[3] He was prominently mentioned as early as September, 1837, when he was on the third of that month chosen a member of the High Council at Kirtland. On the 17th of the same month he was appointed agent for Bishop N. K. Whitney, to transact the business of the bishop at Kirtland in order to liberate the bishop so that he might travel as provided in a revelation given September, 1832.[4] Throughout his career in the church in Joseph's day, he was noted for his business ability and his wisdom in counsel.

Sometime in 1838, Brother Marks went to Missouri. After the trouble there, he with Elias Higbee and Edward Partridge opposed the settling of the Saints in a body anywhere. They thought it would be better for them to scatter for a time and build up homes individually where each should choose. It was with this idea of temporary dispersion in mind that in February, 1839, while Joseph Smith was still held a prisoner in Missouri, they refused the purchase of a two thousand acre tract, lying between the Des Moines and Mississippi Rivers, for the sum of two dollars an acre. After Joseph Smith came to Illinois, he and others strongly urged making another settlement together, and Marks and Partridge, though against their better judgment, acquiesced.

On October 5, 1839, a stake was organized at Nauvoo, and William Marks was chosen president of that stake, a position he held throughout all the period of Nauvoo history while Joseph Smith lived. He was also a city alderman and justice of the peace.

---

[3] Historical Record, Volume 8, page 844; see also masthead of *Messenger and Advocate*, after Volume 3, No. 6.
[4] Doctrine and Covenants 83:23.

Though he held his office undisturbed during Joseph's lifetime, he was soon to find things changed when the Prophet was gone, for at the General Conference of October, 1844, a motion to sustain William Marks "in his calling as president of the stake" was lost by a large majority. In this connection, in a speech by Samuel Bent, it was stated that the High Council had already dropped him because he did not acknowledge the authority of the Twelve.

From that time, Marks began a series of spiritual wanderings that brought him disappointment and disillusionment wherever he turned. Driven from his comfortable home in Nauvoo, he succeeded, as had always been his fortune, quite admirably in a financial way, but he was never content without the church which had been so much of his life in the past.

For a time he favored the claims of Sidney Rigdon, but by April 6, 1847, he was in attendance at a Strangite conference at Voree, Wisconsin. He was appointed then to act as a member of the committee on church property. Even before this, March 6, 1846, he had been "called" by J. J. Strang to occupy in his presidency, but William Marks's habit of independent action evidently led him to question the call.

Apparently he was still wavering by April, for the conference held in Voree that month sustained him only conditionally: "Resolved that if William Marks will magnify his office according to the requirements of the revelation of January 7, we will receive, uphold, and sustain him by our faith, confidence, and prayers as one of the First Presidency."[5]

Some sort of adjusting probably was made, for his name is mentioned occasionally as one of the presidency until June 6, 1850.

On April 23, 1852, he wrote his friend James M. Adams, then living in Vienna, Wisconsin, that he had just come from Saint

---
[5]*Gospel Herald*, Volume 5, page 17.

Louis, where he had attended his first conference with another pretender, Charles B. Thompson, and had evidently determined to cast in his lot with him. "I went there," he says, "to meet in solemn assembly which convened on the 15th day of April. I arrived there on that day with but little understanding of the work, and about as much faith, and with a determination to be *very inquisitive,* for I have learned from experience it is a very easy thing to be deceived. I found when I arrived five brethren, and myself made six, and Brother Thompson, our chief teacher, which constituted about the same number that was present at the organizing of the church."[6] He was hopeful that here at last was to be found the old-time gospel again.

In the same letter he tells of a revelation said to have been received by Thompson on March 9 appointing a committee to seek a location for the Saints to gather, and he was one of the "committy." They planned on going "on or near the frontiers of the Lamanites." He planned to start on the mission to see such location sometime about the middle of May. There was to be another solemn assembly on August 15 in Saint Louis. He must be back for that.

His next letter to Adams said he had not heard from Thompson for a long time, but had made the trip to Iowa near the Bluffs and was busy answering letters about the chosen location:

> I would say to you, Brother Adams, that the country is very new and we will have to undergo a great many privations. What buildings there are in the surrounding country are very poor. They were only put up for the present. I think it would be policy if a few families were going from a neighborhood to have someone go and make preparation. It will save great inconvenience. I think this spring will be a good time to secure locations. I am expecting to start about the first of April. I have purchased a horse power sawmill and made an arrangement for a man to go with me and tend it. I found when I was there there was a great lack of lumber. . . . We have seen so

---

[6]Letter to James M. Adams, Vienna, Wisconsin.—Private collection of Heman C. Smith.

much misery and distress by gathering in haste, I think we had better follow a different course with the present work.[7]

What happened to this location is not known. Marks did not go, but seems not to have lost faith in the work. He was again appointed on a locating committee on April 9, 1853. In June he writes to Adams, soliciting money for a press, and says he has just come from Saint Louis. Another letter in November tells of his illness, lasting throughout the summer. He had, however, sent money to Saint Louis to apply on the printing press and asked Thompson to answer at once, but he failed to do so until late in August and had "been negligent in doing so formerly."[8] At length he wrote he had contracted for a press and would soon be leaving for the Bluffs.

And now on November 15 he had again reached the crossroads. "I received the June number[9] from Preparation[10] the other day, and I made up my mind that all intelligence had departed from that source," he said, and stated his determination to live right and affiliate with no organization, in spite of longing for old friends and associations.

The following spring (1855) he again writes Adams a friendly letter and says:

> I must express some of my views that have lately occurred to my mind, as regards my faith. I can see no more that can have any favorable claims to come out and claim to be a prophet. I think our minds can be at rest, and we can have a little peace on that subject. I think that we have followed the requirements of Saint Paul to prove all things and hold fast to that which is good, and I know of nothing better than the pure principles of the gospel. I have recently come to the conclusion to teach repentance and faith on the Lord Jesus Christ and baptism for the remission of sins and the laying on of hands for the gift of the Holy Spirit. Don't believe in any church organization. Teach the pure principles of the gospel, and every man

---

[7] Letter to James M. Adams, June 25, 1853.—Private collection of Heman C. Smith.
[8] Letter to James M. Adams, November 12, 1853.—Private collection of Heman C. Smith.
[9] *Preparation News and Ephraim's Messenger,* perhaps.
[10] Name of Thompson's community in Monona County, Iowa, upon the Soldier River.

stand or fall. Be his own master. We read that all men that worketh righteousness in all nations shall be accepted of God. I received a letter a few days ago from a man living at Aurora, saying he wished me to come there. There were eight or ten wished to be baptized and were gathering a band of brethren. I do not know how this came, for I have said nothing of my views recently except to my wife. I have written to them today my views.[11]

Less than two weeks later he writes again:

As to the church departing from its foundation, I think that can be clearly shown, but the funeral sermon of the church was a thing quite foreign to my thoughts. If this [evidently some spiritual manifestation of Brother Adams] is from the right spirit, it has incalculable meaning. It seems to have put an end to so much false pretension and false prophets and foolery that has been going on for ten or twelve years. Oh, how it would rejoice my heart to see the true light break forth again, that we might know for a surety, for I have been long wandering in darkness and following false prophets until I have become tiresome and weary. I came to the conclusion in the forepart of last winter to reject all organizations and teach the first principles of the gospel and baptism for the remission of sins and the laying on of hands for the gift of the Holy Spirit. I find recently there is quite a number in this region of the country have come to the same conclusion. John E. Page is one, and some eight or ten others at Aurora. They want me to baptize them, and I want you to advise on the subject. . . . I well remember what Oliver Cowdery told me here when on his way to Council Bluffs.[12] He said the work was of God and the end would be accomplished, let men do or act as they pleased.[13]

The next month another letter reads:

I have waited with intense anxiety to hear from you, and I have perused it until I fully understand its contents as respects our views in relation to the course to pursue in teaching the gospel of the kingdom of Christ. I feel well satisfied and have enjoyed great peace of mind since I came to that conclusion. My mind has never been at rest since the breaking up of the church (or the death of Brother Joseph). I have always had fears that all was not right, but I am satisfied now that all the false prophets have arisen that can, with any degree of plausibility, and if there can be any system adopted that

---
[11] William Marks to John M. Adams, May 20, 1855.—Private collection Heman C. Smith.
[12] In October, 1848.
[13] Letter to J. M. Adams, June 11, 1855.

will be calculated to mitigate the condition of the faithful Saints that are scattered about on the face of the land, it will rejoice my heart.

I would state my views, and then I would like to get the views of my brethren on the subject, asking our Heavenly Father to direct us and claim the promise, if any man lack wisdom let him [ask] God.

I had in contemplation when I wrote you the last letter to look out a good location somewhere in the West and enter a large tract of land, if it was thought advisable by friends and brethren, and invite all of the honest in heart and as many as were so disposed to gather around where we could enjoy some society, for it is like living alone, living in the world as many of us do. I have mentioned my views to several of the brethren since I wrote you, and they seemed very much pleased with my views and hope that I would do it by all means, for they would gladly fall in with the idea.

And now, Brother Adams, I want your advice on the best course to pursue, asking our Heavenly Father to direct you in this matter, and I want your answer on this subject as soon as possible, for if I should conclude to make a location this fall it would be necessary to make a move before a great while, and your opinion about where to make the location of it should meet your views.

I am somewhat advanced in years, sixty-four years old, but my health was never better than at present, although I can't endure so much hardship. My strength has been greatly increased since I have come to the present conclusion. While under the influence of Baneemyism, I lost all my strength and former vigor. I never went on a mission without returning home sick and finally reduced so low as to despair of ever being able to do anything more.

Again in September he wrote a short letter, but his assurance in regard to establishing a colony was on the wane.

It looks like a long journey for me to undertake, and I have had some fears rise in my mind of late that possibly it might prove a failure, and if so it would be very mortifying to me, as there have been so many failures. I thought that I would defer it until spring; learn more of the feelings of my brethren on the subject this winter, as I have had little opportunity to see but few as yet. I have felt very much of late to claim the promise, if any lack wisdom let him ask of the Lord, and I feel if I ask in a right frame of mind he will instruct me. I want your faith and prayers that we may be instructed by the Spirit of truth, that we may not make any move that will not be pleasing in the sight of our Heavenly Father. . . . I had a letter from William Smith this morning from Kirtland. It was on business. Said he was preaching there but would not trouble about church matters, as there were so many, lo here and lo there!

By March, 1856, Marks had determined to call a conference at East Pawpaw, Illinois, to talk matters over. The seminary had been given them with the greatest freedom by the trustees, and a general anxiety was manifested to hear. The meeting was called April 10, at 2 p.m. Their idea was to meet and get "a starting point," not organize then, though he had an idea of eventually organizing as in Book of Mormon times with a high priest to preside, but wished to defer until he could get a more general expression of the brethren.

The resolution to meet together for religious services was carried into effect, but the effort was not a success, "for it seemed the needed favor of God through the Holy Spirit was sadly lacking," said W. W. Blair, who participated in the movement. Organization was never effected, or even contemplated.

On April 6, 1859, William Aldrich and J. C. Gaylord, who were close friends of Brother Marks, were at a conference held near Beaverton, Boone County, Illinois, and became interested in the Reorganization movement.

They visited William Marks and urged him to attend a conference at a schoolhouse near Edwin Cadwell's in the vicinity of Amboy. He did not want to go. He felt he had definitely abandoned hope of finding what he sought and preferred not to risk another disappointment. They insisted; he yielded, though "doubtfully and reluctantly."

The services on the tenth consisted of Communion, prayer, and testimony. The meeting was one of the most notable for spiritual gifts in the history of the movement. William Marks had been invited to the pulpit with Elder Gurley. A little twelve-year-old girl spoke in tongues. Then a young married woman by the name of Helen Pomeroy arose and, coming directly in front of Marks, lifted up her hands to him and said:

> Thus saith the Lord; O thou man of God! In times past thou hast sat with my servant Joseph, the Seer; and in times near to come

thou shalt sit in council with his son. When I called my servant Joseph, he was as a lone tree; but when I shall call his son he shall be as one of a forest.[14]

Thereupon William Marks arose, weeping, and said:

This manifestation I know is by the Spirit of God. It is the same Spirit the faithful Saints ever enjoyed when I first received the gospel in the State of New York, and which we also enjoyed in Kirtland, Missouri, and at Nauvoo, when we lived uprightly before the Lord. I know by the evidences I see and feel here today that God loves and owns this people and the work they have in hand.[15]

When he sat down, Zenas H. Gurley explained the position Marks had held in the church formerly, and he was received into fellowship with his former priesthood. From that moment of decision, William Marks threw his all into the movement, living a life of "consistent self-sacrifice and unswerving devotion to truth." His sacrifice included loss of his wealth, and the failure of his family (except two of his children) to go with him into the church. The testimony of this unusual man was the same to the last. He died at Plano, Illinois, on May 22, 1872, at the age of seventy-nine. By his side in his last hours, "Young Joseph," now president of the church, watched tenderly, and his were the hands that closed his eyes "after the light of the valiant spirit had departed from them."[16]

---

[14]*Memoirs of W. W. Blair*, page 16.
[15]*Ibid.*
[16]*Ibid.*—Preface by Joseph Smith.

XLV.—A Mission to Young Joseph

FIVE YEARS HAVING PASSED, November of 1856 came, and still Young Joseph held aloof. The Saints in Wisconsin continued to send out missionaries and held two conferences a year. There was much happiness, a great deal of readjustment, and some sorrow. A few became tired of waiting and wanted to choose a president other than Joseph, but the growing majority still clung to their original plan. They would wait till the "due time of the Lord." Occasionally they were cheered by a message that the time was not far distant, but years went by.

Samuel Powers and his wife had joined the ranks. Long years before, these people had heard the gospel preached by Jehiel Savage in Canada, but for some reason had never joined the church. They finally moved to Wisconsin and lived near Beloit, where they again came in touch with the church and this time were baptized by Zenas H. Gurley. In July of 1854, Aaron Smith, James J. Strang's first convert, one of his chief witnesses and counselor, having heard of the new movement came down to Zarahemla (the name of the church for the branch or "stake" at Argyle, Wisconsin) and was there baptized.

But as the time approached for the fifth anniversary of the first conference of the Reorganization, the people began to think that they should do something themselves to convince the expected successor. A proclamation was drawn up with much fasting and prayer. All the best rhetoric at the command of these men went into its making, and when it was finished and read to the faithful little group, it seemed truly a masterpiece. With hopeful hearts they outfitted two missionaries. They were young men, as the first missionaries of the church had been young. Samuel Gurley, eldest son of Zenas, was but twenty-five, and Edmund Briggs, Jason's young brother, was a few years his junior. These two young men made the trip from Wisconsin to Nauvoo with the highest of hopes, stopping on the way to visit other Saints of old time. One of those visited was a merchant in a country store near Amboy, in Lee County, Illinois. His name was William W. Blair. He was not a member of the old church but a son of an early pioneer of Illinois, James Blair, who had settled near Amboy as early as 1831, built a log cabin there, and sent for his family from New York. William Blair was, as he grew older, skeptical on religious matters, but finally became interested in the preaching of the Latter Day Saints, then engaged with William Smith, John Landers, Edwin Cadwell, Jason W. Briggs, Ira J. Patten, Aaron Hook, and Joseph Wood and was baptized on October 8, 1851, just a month before Jason W. Briggs became disgusted with this faction and withdrew. At first he was very happy in his new association, but as time went on, he began to feel he had made a mistake, and before he had been with them a year, he and Edwin Cadwell publically withdrew. He then investigated Baneemyism (the faction of Charles B. Thompson) but was soon satisfied it was not the work of God. In 1855 he united with the little group who with William Marks had determined to stand apart from all factions and teach the simple gospel principles as they had been taught before 1844, leaving the results with their Master. These men were John E. Page, John Landers, William Marks, John Gaylord, Russell Huntley, and some others.

It was shortly after nightfall in November of that year, as Mr. Blair was putting away his goods for the night, that two young men entered his store. The moment they came in, he was impressed that they were "Mormon elders," but they merely said they had come to make him a call. He invited them home with him for supper, and on the way they told him they were elders from Zarahemla, Wisconsin, sent to hunt up all the old Saints and tell them that the time was near at hand when the Lord was going to call Young Joseph Smith to take his father's place as president of the church.

"These things were strange and somewhat novel to me," says Blair, "and I had no confidence whatever in their truthfulness." However, no sooner was supper out of the way than he took the visitors into the parlor, where he could be alone with them, and The Three Books were brought out. The two young elders and the young storekeeper (himself not yet thirty) canvassed the question of successorship until 3 o'clock in the morning, when they retired. It was Saturday night. There was no store to keep the next day, so immediately after breakfast they had prayer for guidance and continued the discussion. The entire morning passed; it was 11 a.m., and still Blair opposed them persistently. They were young and inexperienced and disappointed and crestfallen. Blair seeing this told them that they manifested a gentle and kind spirit, but he could not indorse their teachings:

> I would not say they were wrong [said Blair], for I did not know. I only knew I could not as yet see their claims to be true. I felt and said that if their views and teachings were of God, then I hoped to be able to know it, but as yet I had no confidence in them. Soon after this, Elder Briggs rose up, took the Book of Mormon off the stand and opened it hastily, looking intently upon it as if he were reading it to himself. After a moment's waiting, his countenance and his entire being seemed highly animated, and he soon began speaking as if reading from the book. As soon as he began speaking, the Spirit came in mighty power—the same Spirit that bore witness to me of the truth of the gospel five years before—bearing testimony that they were the servants of God, and that their mission and tidings were of God. The first words uttered by Elder Briggs were these: "I, the Lord, will have mercy upon whom I will have mercy; and I will forgive whom I will forgive," words which are found nowhere in the Book of Mormon. Then he began speaking in prophecy, declaring the coming of Joseph, my future mission in the church, with many other things connected with the church and myself. When he ceased speaking, Elder S. H. Gurley arose and spoke in prophecy, testifying many things through the Spirit. My doubts were now dis-

pelled and my mind was fully satisfied that the Lord would, in his own good time, call Young Joseph to the Presidency of the church.[1]

The young missionaries went on their way to Nauvoo, and though it would be December before they could make the trip, the Blairs made preparation to visit Zarahemla (Argyle, now Blanchardville).

Of this unforgettable occasion, Blair spoke many years later:

> I remember going up to Zarahemla in 1857, where I found a little band of Saints upon the bleak hills of Wisconsin. It was one of the poorest, most God-forsaken regions I ever did go to, I think. I had a very dreary time in getting there; a very cold time. But I found God among the Saints; the love of God was there; and the doctrines of eternal life were there with all their power. God gave the blessings of the Holy Spirit to that people. The gift of tongues in prayer, in singing, and in speaking were there. In various other ways was Christ among them, the gift of the prophecy and vision was among them; *and it was like heaven on earth among that little band of Saints at Zarahemla.*[2]

W. W. Blair continued acting with the church until October 7, 1857, when having become dissatisfied with his baptism under William Smith, he was rebaptized by Zenas H. Gurley and on the next day was ordained a high priest.

The mission of Gurley and Briggs to Nauvoo was not so successful, but at length the disappointment righted itself, faith triumphed, and they still believed that in "the due time of the Lord" Joseph would be called.

They found Young Joseph living on a farm near Nauvoo with his bride of a few months. Not more than three or four weeks before, the young man had been visited by George A. Smith of Utah, and Erastus Snow. Now at his door were two more men with a most strange story. They said they had been commissioned from the Reorganized Church at Zarahemla, Wisconsin, to de-

---

[1] "Biography of W. W. Blair," *Church History*, Volume 3, page 726.
[2] Sermon of William Wallace Blair, in the Saints' Chapel in Lamoni, Iowa, on April 6, 1886. *Saints' Herald*, Volume 33, page 279.

liver the word of the Lord to him. Here is the document which they brought with them:

The Church in Zarahemla, Wisconsin, to Joseph Smith:

Our faith is not unknown to you, neither our hope in the regathering of the pure in heart enthralled in darkness, together with the means to the accomplishment of the same; viz., that the seed of him to whom the work was first committed should stand forth and bear the responsibility (as well as wear the crown) of a wise masterbuilder —to close up the breach, and to combine in one a host, who, though in captivity and sorely tried, still refuse to strengthen the hands of usurpers. As that seed, to whom pertains this right, and heaven-appointed duty, you cannot be unmindful nor indifferent. The God of Abram, Isaac, and Jacob covenanted with them and their seed. So the God of Joseph covenanted with him and his seed, that his word should not depart out of the mouth of his seed, nor out of the mouth of his seed's seed, till the end come. A Zerubbabel in Israel art thou. As a nail fastened in a sure place, so are the promises unto thee to make thee a restorer in Zion—to set in order the house of God. And the Holy Spirit that searcheth the deep things of God, hath signified to us that the time has come. For, through fasting and prayer, hath the answer from God come unto us, saying, Communicate with my servant Joseph Smith, son of Joseph the Prophet. Arise, call upon God and be strong, for a deliverer art thou to the Latter Day Saints. And the Holy Spirit is thy prompter. The apostles, elders, and Saints who have assembled with us, have beheld the vacant seat and the seed that is wanting. And like Ezra of old with his brethren, by the direction of the Holy Spirit have we sent faithful messengers to bear this our message to you, trusting that you will by their hands notify us of your readiness to occupy that seat, and answer to the name and duties of that seed. For this have our prayers been offered up without ceasing for the last five years. We are assured that the same Spirit that has testified to us, has signified the same things to you. Many have arisen perverting the work of the Lord. But the good and the true are throughout the land waiting the true successor of Joseph the Prophet, as President of the church and of the priesthood. In our publications—sent to you—we have shown the right of successorship to rest in the literal descendant of the chosen seed, to whom the promise was made, and also the manner of ordination thereto. We cannot forbear reminding you that the commandments, as well as the promises given to Joseph, your father, were given to him, and to his seed. And in the name of our Master, even Jesus Christ, as moved upon by the Holy Ghost, we say, Arise in the strength of the Lord and realize those promises by executing those commandments. And we, by the grace of God, are thy helpers in restoring the exiled sons and daughters of Zion to their inheritances in the kingdom of God and to the faith once delivered to the Saints.

Holding fast that which is good and resisting evil, we invoke the blessings of the God of Israel upon thee and upon all Saints, for whom we will ever pray.

J. W. BRIGGS,
Representative President of the Church
and the Priesthood in Zarahemla.

Zarahemla, November 18, 1856.[3]

Joseph, telling of it, says that the conversation was stormy, and that he told them firmly that he would discuss religion with absolutely no one; he would tolerate politics, weather, anything else, but they must not bring up the subject of religion in his house. He says:

The reception that these brethren met with was not a flattering one. Elder Gurley stated their mission and presented the document containing the message to me. I heard what he had to say; I read the message that they brought, but could not accept it as they had hoped. It was not to me the word of the Lord. Elder Briggs vehemently urged the matter upon me, and announced the culmination of the message in tones of thunder, and almost dictatorily directed me to accept the message and do as directed therein or reject it at my peril.

I met his vehemence indignantly, and almost turned these messengers out of doors. But, through the calmer, humbler efforts of Elder Gurley and the interposition of my wife, the storm abated; I invited them to stay over night, and that when the morning came, I would accompany them to town and would give them a final answer. In the morning I went with them to Nauvoo, introduced them to my mother and stepfather, went with them into a room, where quietly and peaceably Elder Gurley and I talked the situation over. I gave them my answer which was this: What they came to bring might be the word of the Lord; I could not say that it was not. I had, however, no testimony that it was. That I was prepared to do what God required of me, if he would make it known to me what it was; that I believed that he could reveal himself if he would; that I believed that my father was called of God to do a work; and that I was satisfied that that work was true, whether I ever had anything to do with it or not; that I did not then know whether I should ever be called to take any part in that work; but that if I were, I was ready, and that it would have to be made clear to me, in person, as well as to others what that work was; that I could not move upon the evidence given to others only. That they might be assured that I should not go to Salt Lake to affiliate with them there. And finally, that if it

---

[3]*Church History*, Volume 3, pages 260, 262.

should be made clear to me that it was my duty to cast the fortunes of my life and my labor with the work and the people that they were representing, I should without hesitation do it, but that I could not then do so.[4]

With that understanding they parted. Gurley returned to Zarahemla. Briggs stayed in the vicinity of Nauvoo, preaching and working his way at farm work. He had resolved not to return to Wisconsin until Joseph came to the church.

---

[4] *Life of Joseph Smith the Prophet,* pages 756-769; *Church History,* Volume 3, pages 262, 263.

XLVI.—Granville Hedrick and the Crow Creek Branch

There had existed since Nauvoo days, scattered through some four counties northeast of Peoria, Illinois, a group of old-time Saints. Among these were Granville Hedrick,[1] David Judy,[2] Jedediah Owens,[3] John Hedrick, Zebulon Adams, and Adna C. Haldeman.[4]

Alma Owens,[5] son of Jedediah, said that his father and these other men began holding meetings in 1855, at first confining themselves to prayer meetings, but as there is record of a business meeting as early as 1852, probably if there were preliminary prayer meetings they were of still earlier date.

Only three elders were present at this meeting in the winter of 1852, but they took some important action which was so much

---

[1] Granville Hedrick joined the original church not long before the death of Joseph and Hyrum, in the vicinity of Woodford County, Illinois, under the ministry of Hervey Green. He became dissatisfied and went to the lead mines near Galena where sometime after Joseph's death he was rebaptized by William O. Clark. He never had the privilege of meeting Joseph Smith personally. After uniting with the church for the second time, he saw conditions were not right in Nauvoo at that time, and united with the faction under the leadership of Gladden Bishop. Sometime after that he became interested in spiritualism, but eventually returned to a strong belief in the first principles of the gospel (from which he had really never wavered, being disgusted only with certain things he saw of which he disapproved). He gathered about him those old-time Saints who lived near him to form the nucleus of what is now the Church of Christ on the Temple Lot. His character as a man was above reproach in the communities in which he lived.

[2] David Judy was born in 1802, baptized in May, 1832, by Elder Drake and died at Mackinaw, Illinois, April 14, 1886. His obituary in the *Saints' Herald*, Volume 33, page 271, says he "was with the church at the death of Joseph and Hyrum; after that event he became identified with the Hedrickites [Church of Christ] with whom he was connected at his departure. He was a good man, and had the respect of all." He was living near Far West in 1838 at the time of troubles there.

[3] Jedediah Owens was a member of the old church as far back as 1838, as he then owned land in Ray County, Missouri. He was named as one who took part in the battle of Crooked River, October 25, 1838, in which David Patten was killed. He was living in Montrose, Iowa, in 1839, and affiliating with the church with its headquarters at Nauvoo.

[4] Adna C. Haldeman was early affiliated with this group, a meeting being held at his home in 1853; but he was also present in 1859 at the conference of the Reorganization held in Israel Rogers' barn, and appointed one of a committee to get subscribers for the *Herald;* in 1863 he is evidently entirely removed from his affiliation with the Reorganization whatever it was; for he was ordained to the apostleship in the Church of Christ on 17th of May, 1863. His brother Silas Haldeman was the grandfather of Clarence Wheaton, now one of the prominent apostles in the Church of Christ.

[5] Alma Owens, son of Jedediah Owens said in his testimony in the Temple Lot Suit that he did not unite with the church himself until 1864.

in line with what many of their brethren were taking at the same time that their meeting is worthy of note. The meeting was at the home of Granville Hedrick, on Half Moon Prairie near Washbourne, Illinois, and old Father Judy preached, after which:

> The minds of those present were deeply concerned because of iniquity which had found its way into the church which had emigrated to California and Salt Lake, previous to the time of the above meeting. Great attention had been given to ascertain if the church then at Salt Lake practiced such high and wicked crimes as was alleged to them, and after being fully assured that such were the facts, it was concluded upon by those elders who assembled in said meeting to withdraw their fellowship from all such as departed from the principles of righteousness and truth and to maintain a firm position upon God's own revealed plan of salvation.[6]

The spring of 1853 saw another council meeting, this being held at the home of Adna Haldeman. In this meeting "several of the brethren and members of Christ's Church" declared themselves "free from all wicked factions and united upon the pure principles of the Church of Jesus Christ of Latter Day Saints." From that time meetings were held with more or less frequency until June, 1857, when at one of their meetings William W. Blair, now with the group of Saints in Wisconsin, was in attendance and spent much time explaining the views of the Reorganization, with the result that Granville Hedrick and Jedediah Owens rode with him in his carriage to the fall conference at Zarahemla and there received the hand of fellowship.

Hedrick was the recognized leader of this group and a man of undoubted integrity and unimpeachable character. The stand he had taken against what he believed to be corruptions in the church was frank and outspoken. He had at his own expense published a small pamphlet at Bloomington in 1856, called *The Spiritual Wife System Proven False and the True Order of Church Discipline Illustrated*. The few copies of this book still

---

[6]Original *Crow Creek Record*.

extant are now so rare as to be very valuable. In it he calls in no uncertain terms for "all who are pure in heart" to "take some special measures for their deliverance from the awful crash of destruction which is hanging over the heads of the apostates of the Church of Jesus Christ, and speedily step forward upon the rock of their deliverance, which is the Book of Mormon, Bible, and Doctrine and Covenants, which the Saints must come to, and not only say, but do. . . . These three above named inspired volumes were received by the whole church of Christ as established anew by Joseph Smith, to be the rock, and pillar, and groundwork of their faith and doctrine in Christ Jesus, in the first days and years of this identical church of Jesus Christ, hence we have the foundation of this church before us, of which I profess to be a member. . . . You received the Bible, the Book of Mormon, and the Doctrine and Covenants to practice and build upon the sacred things written in these inspired books. This was your faith at the first. Have you departed from that sacred order of things, which was laid for the foundation of your faith in Jesus Christ? I ask, have you departed from it?"[7]

While in Zarahemla, Owens and Hedrick took part in the conference of those building the Reorganization. The next conference was to meet at Crow Creek, Woodford County, Illinois, and Jason W. Briggs and Granville Hedrick were appointed to write a pamphlet "setting forth the true position of our doctrine."

The pamphlet was never written, nor was the conference held at Crow Creek, for before that time a rift had arisen in the relations of the two groups, or more properly the representatives of each, which was never fully bridged, although numerous efforts have been made in later years to accomplish this. On the 25th of December, 1859, two high priests, five elders, and seven members met at Granville Hedrick's home at Crow Creek and passed an interesting series of resolutions:

---

[7] *The Spiritual Wife System Proven False*, by Granville Hedrick.

No. 1. Resolved: that the Bible, Book of Mormon, and the first edition of the Book of Doctrine and Covenants were given for the foundation and standard of faith and doctrine of the Church of Christ, in which all the principles of the doctrine are contained that are necessary to build up the Church of Christ and regulate all the affairs of the same.

No. 2. Resolved, that the doctrines of
Baptism for the dead (proxy),
Tithing as a tenth,
Polygamy,
Lineal priesthood in the office of the presidency of the church,
And, plurality of Gods, with the exaltation of man to the same, are all unscriptural.

The crux of the difficulty centered in lineal priesthood in relation to the presidency of the church. Granville Hedrick, in particular, believed that a meeting of church members should be called to elect a president.

At the same meeting, Jedediah Owens and David Judy were ordained high priests under the hands of John Landers and Granville Hedrick, and Granville Hedrick was chosen by vote and ordained under the hands of John Landers, Jedediah Owens, and David Judy to the office of presiding high priest of the Crow Creek Branch. He had previously been set apart (April, 1857) as presiding elder of the branch.

It was with this people that John E. Page (an Apostle in the church in Joseph's day) found a haven after he had been tossed on seas of uncertainty following Joseph's death, although his wife states that Elder Page expressed disappointment with that affiliation on his deathbed, and asked that his funeral sermon might be preached by his friend, John Landers, who had lately become a member of the Reorganization.

On the 17th day of May, 1863, John E. Page ordained Granville Hedrick, Jedediah Owens, David Judy, and Adna C. Haldeman "apostles of the Church of Jesus Christ of Latter Day Saints."

On the 18th day of July, 1863, Granville Hedrick was ordained president of the high priesthood, "first president of the church, to preside over the high priesthood, and to be prophet, seer, revelator, and translator to the Church of Christ." This ordination was received under the hands of John E. Page, David Judy, Jedediah Owens, and Adna C. Haldeman and others.

Since that time the little church has maintained its existence and gone through more than one change of organization and belief, none of which, however, has affected their belief in the Book of Mormon and the first principles of the church.

As time passed, they became convinced that the Scripture provides for the supreme authority in the church to be the Quorum of Twelve, and their organization is now in accordance with that belief. Their conferences are presided over by this council in order of their age, each presiding in turn. Their conferences at the present time are elders' conferences, with a privilege of referendum to the people of the church in important decisions. Having become convinced that the name of the church had been altered, they called themselves the Church of Christ— this name having been adopted by them many years ago. They take the Bible and Book of Mormon as their standards of faith and practice, but all modern revelation stands upon its merits, although they prefer the *Book of Commandments* to the Doctrine and Covenants.

This group moved to Independence in 1867 and procured by purchase the place dedicated in 1831 for the building of the temple. Throughout the years they and their successors have maintained title to this piece of property. They have gone through poverty and adversity, suffered more than their share of schisms within their own ranks, have been reduced to a mere handful at times, but they have never wavered in their conviction that it is their God-given privilege to hold this place until the time comes to build the temple.

The membership of this faction in 1953 was two thousand two hundred and twenty-five.[8]

---

[8] World Almanac, 1954.

XLVII.—"The True Latter Day Saints' Herald"

A SPECIAL CONFERENCE WAS HELD June 10-14, 1859, at Amboy, Illinois. On June 11, William Marks was recognized as a member of the church by virtue of his original baptism. He had been a high priest in the early church and was so recognized in the Reorganization. Brother Marks was immediately appointed on a committee to publish a hymnbook. This conference is also noteworthy because a letter was here presented from a man named Isaac Sheen, an old-time member of the church who had been engaged during the "dark and cloudy day" in the publication of an antislavery paper and in the activities of the Underground Railway in Ohio. Brother Sheen was considered a writer of parts, and he often contributed to the better-known magazines. He wished to know all the particulars about the organization, and W. W. Blair was appointed to reply.

The fall conference was held in the grain barn of Israel Rogers in Kendall County, Illinois, commencing October 6. Brother Rogers did stalwart service during these years, for he was a man of some substance and utterly devoted to the work of the church. He was born April 4, 1818, in Renssalaer County, New York. In 1840, while working on the Black River Canal in Booneville, New York, he overheard some of his fellow workmen talking of the restoration of the gospel. He investigated, and after a few sermons became convinced and was baptized by Elder Joseph Robertson.

In 1841 he had come west with his branch from New York, intending to go to Nauvoo, but something impressed him to stop at or near Sandwich, Illinois, in DeKalb County, where he bought and improved a good farm. He prospered financially, and after the death of Joseph, his hospitable home became the stopping place for missionaries of all factions. All were entertained, fed, and given shelter, but Rogers refused to unite with any until about 1850. Hearing that William Smith was preaching in Amboy, claiming to be guardian until Young Joseph came of age, he went there, and fellowshiped with him. He was ordained his counselor, but very soon became dissatisfied and retired to the operation of his farm. "These were dark days," he says. In 1859, E. C. Briggs, and W. W. Blair came to his farm. He received them at first rather coolly, but his wife[1] became greatly interested. He soon was won to the cause in spite of himself.

In the fall of 1859 at the conference held in Rogers' grain barn, the entire conference membership was fed and entertained by Brother and Sister Rogers.[2]

Another prominent old-time Latter Day Saint who joined the church sometime during this period was James Blakeslee, an eminent preacher and proselytizer of the early days. He was born at Milton, Chittenden County, Vermont, July 18, 1802, and was baptized on July 19, 1833, by D. W. Patten at Ellisburgh, Jefferson County, New York. Joseph Smith (the third Joseph Smith) said, "As a preacher Elder Blakeslee had few equals and fewer superiors, and for the steadiness of purpose with which he preached and the integrity of his testimony he has never been surpassed." He had been an untiring missionary throughout his entire life. He also was connected with other factions, those of Rigdon and Strang, but found there only disappointment, although while with them he traveled and preached as he had previously done. Once in 1847 he had written: "I have traveled and preached most of my time for the last fourteen years, and now I am so poor as to this world's goods, and my children so far in the rear in their education, that I am under the necessity of staying at home and laboring with all my might to feed, clothe, and educate them, and

---

[1] Mahala Salisbury.
[2] "My mind is turned back twenty-two years when my house would have held the whole church and more. I could feed the whole, and took pleasure in doing so, and that feeling has not gone from me yet."—Israel Rogers, *Saints' Herald*, Volume 29, page 130.

this with my own hands, and which I am willing to do."

Less than three months after, he was in the missionary field again, preaching to large congregations with his usual zeal.

We first find mention of his name in connection with the Reorganized Church at the Conference of 1858.

The letter which the conference of the preceding June had requested Brother Blair to write to Isaac Sheen must have produced satisfactory results, for at this conference he entered heartily into the work of the church, notwithstanding the fact that the church he had known in Nauvoo had numbered thousands and this little group could now be comfortably seated in a grain barn.

There are some men to whom publication and printing are almost second nature. Such a man was Isaac Sheen, and he immediately began urging the church to publish a paper. He felt that in no other way could the mission of Young Joseph—as yet unconnected with the church—be made known far and wide.

Among the humble group in the barn that day were men who had managed their own affairs with superior business ability, men who had moved ever so cautiously during the whole process of reorganization. They did not intend to hasten rashly into any losing venture, so the motion by which the first church paper entered the world was conservatively worded, "Resolved that this church publish a monthly church paper and continue it for six months." With Sheen as sole editor, *The True Latter Day Saints' Herald* was first issued from Cincinnati, Ohio, January, 1860, and succeeded beyond the highest hopes of even the sanguine Isaac Sheen. The first numbers had to be reprinted as time went on to supply the demand.

The *Saints' Herald* is still the official paper of the church, as it has been for over ninety years.

The little paper in its early years was a harbinger of hope to many an old-time Saint who had become disheartened and discouraged in the dark days following the death of Joseph. The price of the *Herald* was one dollar, and the postage upon it in that early time was six cents outside the State of Ohio, and three cents in the State.

In March, 1863, the plant was moved to Plano, Illinois; from there in November, 1881, to Lamoni, Iowa; and from Lamoni to its present location in Independence, Missouri, in May, 1921.

This little paper was indeed as Charles Derry once termed it, "The Herald of a coming day."

XLVIII.—William Marks Receives an Important Letter

Eight years had now passed since Jason W. Briggs had been told to wait for Young Joseph, but Joseph had not yet come. The church grew in numbers, missionaries were sent out from time to time, but nothing was heard of him upon whom their hopes were centered. There was to be a conference at Amboy on April 6, 1860. Early in March, William Marks at Shabbona Grove, Illinois, received the following letter:

Nauvoo, March 5, 1860.

Mr. William Marks; Sir: I am soon going to take my father's place as the head of the Mormon church, and I wish that you and some others, those you would consider the most trustworthy, the nearest to you, to come and see me; that is, if you can and will. I am somewhat undecided as to the best course for me to pursue, and if your views are, upon a comparison, in unison with mine, and we can agree as to the best course, I would be pleased to have your co-operation. I would rather you would come previous to your conference in April at Amboy. I do not wish to attend the conference, but would like to know if they, as a body, would endorse my opinions. You will say nothing of this to any but those who you may wish to accompany you here.

With great regard, I subscribe myself

Yours most respectfully

Joseph Smith.[1]

There was but little time between then and conference. Marks wrote to Israel Rogers and W. W. Blair, asking them to accompany him. It was the 19th of March when Marks visited Rogers at his home in preparation for this visit. It was agreed that Rogers should go and get Blair and they together meet Marks at Burlington, Iowa. He wished to go that day so that they could start for Nauvoo the next day. Brother Marks accompanied him to the station before he drove home, and as they stood talking in the depot, intent on this mission, Brother Rogers says a rather remarkable incident happened:

---

[1] *Life of Joseph Smith the Prophet*, by Tullidge; *Church History*, Volume 3, page 264.

The train suddenly pulled out and left me. Of course, this worried me greatly, as I was very anxious to see Brother Blair that day so he could accompany me on the morrow. While I stood wondering what I should do, to my astonishment I saw the train returning, backing right to the station; this enabled me to jump aboard. When I inquired the cause of the train returning, I was informed that it could not get over the grade. The second time, however, it went over the grade without trouble.

I found Brother Blair at home, attending his sick nephew. He had failed to receive Brother Marks's letter and therefore was quite unprepared to accompany me. He, however, was not surprised. He had a letter from Z. H. Gurley in Blanchardville, Wisconsin, dated January 29, 1860. It read: "I rejoice in God that the work goes on so finely, and I know that if we are united and do what the Lord commands us, the year 1860 will not pass before the Prophet is among us."[2] He consented to go, however, and preparations were hurriedly made, but long before we reached the station, we heard the train whistle. We continued with all speed possible, and though we reached the station fully fifteen minutes late, to our joy we found the train there still apparently waiting for us. This enabled us to meet Brother Marks at Burlington, according to appointment.

From Burlington, they took the steamboat, "Aunt Letty," down the river to Nauvoo, arriving there at four o'clock in the evening on Tuesday, March 21. As they walked down the street towards the Mansion House, they met a tall, brown-eyed young man. "That," said Rogers, "is young Joseph." He had never seen him or his picture, but knew him.

Arriving at Emma's home, they made known their mission, and she sent for her son. He came that evening. The first words of Marks after greetings had been exchanged were exceedingly frank: "We have had enough of man-made prophets, and we don't want any more of that sort. If God has called you, we want to know it. If he has, the church is ready to sustain you, if not, we want nothing to do with you."

The next morning at ten o'clock they left for home after prayer with the family at Joseph's request. No hearts could have been happier than theirs that day, for they carried a great secret. Young Joseph was coming to the church conference at Amboy, Illinois, on April 6!

---

[2] *Memoirs of W. W. Blair*, page 28.

XLIX.—Young Joseph

Even before Joseph's death, Young Joseph, the eldest son of the Prophet, was well known to the Saints in Nauvoo. When his father died he was not yet twelve, an earnest, quiet boy, known and loved by his father's associates. Those who worked on the temple remembered the slender, brown-eyed lad who almost daily rode up the Temple Hill on his father's black horse "Charley" to watch the progress on the building. He was encouraged to come by Alpheus Cutler and Reynolds Cahoon, the temple committee, and the workingmen stopped to explain the progress of the building as he stood by their side and watched them chiseling and carving the stones that were to take their place in the great pilasters of the temple. With a boy's curiosity he watched these great stones being drawn one by one to the top of Temple Hill by teams of oxen and felt himself to be a part of the great movement in which his father played so prominent a part.

No one who lived in Nauvoo and attended meeting in the grove failed to know Young Joseph, for when his father was home, he always insisted upon taking the boy with him into the preacher's stand, although Young Joseph always preferred to sit by his mother in the congregation, as he was privileged to do when his father was away. He loved his father, but shrank from being elevated above his playmates. At the laying of the cornerstone to the temple, he was seated by his father's side on the speaker's stand. One Sunday while he sat there on the stand in the grove beside his father, he heard himself designated publicly as his father's successor.

Many old-time Saints remember this occasion. One of them, John H. Carter, gave his testimony, under oath, in the Temple Lot Suit.

Joseph Smith came on the stand leading his son, young Joseph, and they sat him down on a bench at the prophet's right hand, and Joseph got up and began to preach, and talk to the people, and the question he said was asked by somebody: "If Joseph Smith should be killed or die, who would be his successor?" And he turned around and said, pointing to his son: "There is the successor," and he went on and said, "My work is nearly done," and that is about all he said in regard to his son. He said in answer to a question that was asked as to who should be his successor in case he should be killed or die, and he pointed to his son, young Joseph, who was sitting there at his side, and said he: "There is your leader."[1]

Many others testified to this same event.

Young Joseph always spoke of the Nauvoo days before his father's death as "happy days." If there were difficulties, he did not know them. But the days of happiness passed, and the scene of his life hurried on to that tragedy at Carthage, which left him standing by his father's blood-stained form, feeling the weight of the world on his shoulders. He was only twelve and the chief dependence of his mother in an unfriendly world.

The city his father built melted away as magically as it had risen. He watched the people go. Many went westward, including some of his best friends, his cousins; some to the north, some to the south, some to the east, never again to meet as brothers. One-time cherished friends became enemies; unity became chaos.

Emma Smith and her sons stood aloof from it all in the ruins of a deserted city and the silence of a deserted home. Nauvoo, once the most magnificent city in Illinois, was now a dusty village of long rows of empty houses and unoccupied shops and stores; the Mansion House that had once echoed with the cheerful laugh and witty repartee of great visitors to the strange new city was now empty save for the chance traveler or the rough riverman. Young Joseph thought little of the tragedy that had befallen the church, but the tragedy that had befallen him was very real. He wanted to study, to be a great scholar, and he had no earthly

---

[1] Plaintiff's Abstract in *Temple Lot Suit*, pages 180, 181; *Succession in Church Presidency*, by Heman C. Smith, page 48.

heritage except poverty and a name that his father's professed friends had coupled with ignominy and shame. He longed to lift up his head and walk free of this burden of disgrace as other men did. Out of this first great mental conflict of his life came this firm resolution: "If the father shall be judged by the son, then with the assistance of God I will so order my life that it shall be a living testimony, refuting the accusations against him."

Of his religious life he writes:

We were baptized into the Church of Jesus Christ of Latter Day Saints by Joseph Smith in 1843, confirmed by A. W. Babbitt and another at a meeting of the church held in front of the Temple in Nauvoo. This baptism we believe to have been valid, and a legal act of admission to the church or body of Christ. . . .

In Liberty Jail the promise and blessing of a life of usefulness to the cause of truth was pronounced upon our head by lips tainted by dungeon damps, and by the Spirit confirmed through attesting witnesses.

This blessing has by some been called an ordination, from the usual predilection to confound names and terms. . . .

Subsequent to our baptism in 1843, upon two occasions was the same blessing confirmed by Joseph Smith, once in the council room in the brick store on the banks of the Mississippi, of which we have not a doubt there are witnesses who would confirm the present testimony; once, in the last interview Joseph Smith had with his family before he left Nauvoo to his death. A public attestation of the same blessing was made from the stand in the grove in Nauvoo.

James Whitehead, at that time one of Joseph Smith's scribes, tells of this same event, on the witness stand in the Temple Lot Suit:

I recollect a meeting that was held in the winter of 1843, at Nauvoo, Illinois, prior to Joseph Smith's death, at which the appointment was made by him, Joseph Smith, of his successor. His son Joseph was selected as his successor. Joseph Smith did the talking. There were present Joseph and Hyrum Smith, John Taylor, and some others who also spoke on the subject; there were twenty-five, I suppose, at the meeting. At that meeting, Joseph Smith, the present presiding officer of the complainant church, was selected by his father as his successor. He was ordained and appointed at that meeting. Hyrum Smith, the patriarch, anointed him, and Joseph, his father, blessed him and ordained him and Newell K. Whitney poured the oil on his head, and he was set apart to be his father's successor in office, holding all the powers that his father held. I cannot tell all the persons that were present, there was a good many there. John Taylor and Willard Richards, they were two of the Twelve, Ebenezer Robinson was present and George J. Adams, Alpheus Cutler and Reynolds Cahoon. I cannot tell them all; I was there too.[2]

Whitehead told this incident many, many times; often he added as he did in a sermon in Lamoni, Iowa, May 22, 1887, "I lift my hands to heaven before God, and declare unto you that this is the truth, for it is a positive fact."[3] He continues the narrative and says that Joseph then, turning to this humble secretary, gave him a trust to keep. Of it Whitehead said many years later: "I loved that man, he was a kind benefactor, he was a father to me. I shall never forget the kindness of that man, and I shall never be satisfied until I go where he is again.... After Joseph had blessed his son Joseph, he said to me: 'I have one request to make of you.'

"I said 'Brother Joseph, what is it?'

" 'My request is that you stand faithfully by my son Joseph.'

"I said, 'God being my helper, and by the assistance of the Holy Spirit, I will stand by your son Joseph as long as he stands faithful to the gospel of Jesus Christ.' "[4] Whitehead was true to that trust.

The autobiography of Joseph tells further some of the causes leading to his action in rejecting other factions and accepting the Reorganization. He says:

> It was during this summer [1853] and fall that I had the first serious impression concerning my connection with the work of my father. That spring, if my memory is correct, there was a large emigration to Utah, a part of which was camped at Keokuk, twelve miles below Nauvoo, on the Iowa side of the Mississippi River. A delegation of them visited Nauvoo, and with one of them, whose name, if I learned it, I do not now remember, I had a long conversation re-

---

[2] Plaintiff's Abstract of Evidence in *Temple Lot Suit*, page 28; *Succession in Church Presidency*, by Heman C. Smith, page 47.
[3] Sermon of James Whitehead in Lamoni, May 22, 1887. Reported by Daniel J. Lambert, published in *Autumn Leaves*, Volume 1, page 202.
[4] *Ibid.*, pages 203, 204.

specting Mormonism. I had talked with many upon the matter, but had never taken the subject into very earnest consideration. This person urged that I was possibly doing a great wrong in allowing the years to pass by unimproved. I stated to him that I was ready to do any work that might fall to my lot or that I might be called to do. I had no fellowship with the leadership in the Salt Lake Church and could not then give my sanction to things there; my prejudices were against them. In the summer and fall, several things occurred that served to bring the question up; my sickness brought me near to death; my coming of age and my choice of a profession were all coincident events; and during my recovery I had opportunity for reflection, as for weeks I could do no work. One day, after my return to health was assured, I had lain down to rest in my room; the window was open to the south and the fresh breeze swept in through the trees and half-closed blinds. I had slept and woke refreshed; my mind recurred to the question of my future life and what its work should be. I had been and was still reading law under the care of a lawyer named William McLennan, and it was partially decided that I should continue that study. While weighing my desires and capabilities for this work, the question came up, Will I ever have anything to do with Mormonism? If so, how and what will it be? I was impressed that there was truth in the work my father had done. I believed the gospel so far as I comprehended it. Was I to have no part in that work as left by him? While engaged in this contemplation and perplexed by these recurring questions, the room suddenly expanded and passed away. I saw stretched out before me towns, cities, busy marts, courthouses, courts, and assemblies of men, all busy and all marked by those characteristics that are found in the world, where men win place and renown. This stayed before my vision till I had noted clearly that choice of preferment here was offered to him who would enter in, but who did so must go into the busy whirl and be submerged by its din, bustle, and confusion. In the subtle transition of a dream I was gazing over a wide expanse of country in a prairie land; no mountains were to be seen, but far as the eye could reach, hill and dale, hamlet and village, farm and farmhouse, pleasant cot and homelike place, everywhere betokening thrift, industry, and the pursuits of a happy peace were open to the view. I remarked to him standing by me, but whose presence I had not before noticed "This must be the country of a happy people." To this he replied, "Which would you prefer, life, success, and renown among the busy scenes that you first saw, or a place among these people, without honors or renown. Think of it well, for the choice will be offered to you sooner or later, and you must be prepared to decide. Your decision once made you cannot recall it, and must abide the result."

No time was given me for a reply, for as suddenly as it had come, so suddenly was it gone, and I found myself sitting upright on the side of the bed where I had been lying, the rays of the declining sun shining athwart the western hills and over the shimmering river, making the afternoon all glorious with their splendor, shone into my room instinct with life and motion, filling me with gladness that I should live. From that hour, at leisure, at work or play, I kept before me what had been presented, and was at length prepared to answer when the opportunity for the choice should be given.[5]

In after years, when the church had its headquarters in Lamoni, Iowa, Joseph Smith looked out of the windows of the editorial rooms in the old Herald Office building, and there saw the very prairie scene he had looked upon in this vision.

Continuing with his own statement, Joseph says:

In the fall of this year [1856] three events transpired that had much to do with deciding my course religiously and aiding me to answer the question, what part in my father's work, if any, I was to take. For a number of years I had been more or less intimate with the family of Christopher E. Yates, a friend to the Saints, who at the time of the disturbances in Hancock County, for his outspoken denunciation of mob violence and mob law, had suffered the loss of a fine barn, a lot of grain, hay, and a number of horses by fire, set by incendiaries out of revenge as it is supposed, and who had removed with other citizens into Nauvoo and bought property there. With one of his sons, Putnam, circumstances had made me well acquainted. He had crossed the plains a number of times, had been in Salt Lake City and other parts of Utah, and in California. He and I had frequently discussed Mormonism, that is, some parts of it, and he had persistently insisted that I could do a great and an excellent work by going to Utah, and, as he put it, "taking the lead away from Brigham, breaking up that system of things out there," or "fall in with the style of things there, become a leader, get rich, marry three or four wives and enjoy myself." Though not a religious man himself, he thought it might be a duty that I owed the people of Utah. He further thought that from his experience in Utah, and the expressions he had heard among the people there, I would be received with open arms and could succeed.

To this I replied as best I could, until the question: Why not go to Utah? There are the men who were with my father, or a great many of them. There, a large part of the family; there, also, seem to be the only ones making profession of belief in Mormonism who appear to be doing anything. Does not duty demand that I go there and clear my name and honor of the charge of ingratitude to my father's character? Is not polygamy, against which you object, a

---
[5]Tullidge, *Life of Joseph the Prophet*, pages 756-758; *Church History*, Volume 3, pages 254, 255.

correct tenet? Is not your objection one of prejudice only? These and a thousand others of similar import were suggested, and added their weight to the difficulty of the situation. In the height of it, the words suggested to one who had gone before me came to me with force: "If any lack wisdom, let him ask of God." Why not I? Was I not in a position to need wisdom? And was I not destitute of sufficient to enable me to properly decide? I had for three or four years been investigating spiritual phenomena; had read some of the productions of Andrew J. Davis; had also read a little of Doctor Emanuel Swedenborg's philosophy; but I found no good in spiritualism; the phenomena were physical and gross; no response from the departed spirits of any of the family, though severally appealed to in turn, ever came; and the manifestations, though strange and material, were altogether inadequate for the deductions spiritualists drew from them. I did not give credence to the philosophy. My human intelligence was at fault, I could not decide. I believed that he who had enabled my father to decide which of all should receive his attention, could, if he would, enable me to decide whether I should, or should not, have anything to do with Momonism, and if so, what. I proceeded upon this conclusion.

A year or two before this we had raised an excellent crop of wheat upon a piece of land lying in the south of our meadow, and this man Yates had assisted in doing some of the work. While engaged in it we had some conversation about Utah. After this, I did not see him for some months. One day, while pondering these questions (and here, unlike some, I cannot certainly state whether morn or even, only that the sun was shining), I suddenly found myself sowing this piece of land to wheat. My brother and this Mr. Yates I saw harrowing the wheat after my sowing. In passing over the land I met Mr. Yates as he drove to and fro, and our conversation was upon this Utah subject; and the same arguments and statements were repeated by him. To these I was urging again my reluctance to move, and the question was again presented, Why not go to Utah? I paused, rested the bag of grain that I was carrying across my shoulder, upon my knee, and turned to answer him. I heard a slight noise like the rush of the breeze that arrested my speech and my attention. I turned my gaze slightly upward and saw descending towards me a sort of cloud, funnel shaped, with the wide part upward. It was luminous, and of such color and brightness that it was clearly seen, though the sun shone in its summer strength. It descended rapidly, and settling upon and over me, enveloped me completely, so that I stood within its radiance.

As the cloud rested upon the ground at my feet, the words, "Because the light in which you stand is greater than theirs," sounded in my ears clearly and distinctly. Slowly the cloud passed away and the vision closed. A few days after this occurred, I met this man Putnam Yates, and had a conversation with him in which he again urged upon me the idea of going to Utah; and my answer was in exact accordance with what I had seen. The other question, "Is polygamy of God?" was as distinctly and definitely answered to me, as was the one referred to above; and the answer was, "No," and I was directed that I was to have nothing to do with it, but was to oppose it.[6]

Concerning his decision to accept the call to the Presidency, he writes as follows:

During the year 1859 the question of my connection with my father's work was finally determined. I became satisfied that it was my duty. The queries heretofore referred to were one by one being settled; until the final one, where and with whom should my life labor lie? was the only one left. This was determined by a similar manifestation to others that I had received to this effect: "The Saints reorganizing at Zarahemla and other places, is the only organized portion of the church accepted by me. I have given them my Spirit, and will continue to do so while they remain humble and faithful."

This was in the fall of 1859, and in the winter I resolved to put myself in communication with the brethren of the Reorganized Church.[7]

In concluding this chapter with these excerpts from the autobiography of Young Joseph, it is perhaps well to recount a further statement of his regarding his position as President of the church. He says:

We have always felt reluctant to speak in attestation of the position as President of the Church, for three reasons:

1st. Every aspirant for that position since the crime that left the church a prey to aspirants, has been loud in his own defense, and has each, in turn, run into vice and folly, thereby causing the cause to be evilly spoken of.

2nd. Words are but cheap, protestations are but the breath of one's lips, and wisdom is never very open-mouthed, and the unsupported testimony of any man must fall.

3rd. If the Lord has promised, and the work is his, the Spirit which bore testimony to it at the beginning will continue its ministrations.[8]

---

[6]*Church History*, Volume 3, pages 256-259; Tullidge, pages 760-763.
[7]*Church History*, Volume 3, page 263; Tullidge, page 772.
[8]*The True Latter Day Saints' Herald*, Volume 14, number 7, page 105.

L.—AMBOY, 1860

ON THE MORNING OF April 4, Joseph Smith and his mother crossed the Mississippi with an old friend of the family, James Gifford. Although the skiff was small, the day cold and rainy, and the passage rough, the difficulties did not deter Young Joseph Smith from an avowed purpose. He was enough the son of his father, and of his mother also, to adhere to a chosen purpose in spite of obstacles. Arriving in Amboy, they were ushered into a prayer meeting at the home of Stephen and Experience Stone. As they came into the little gathering the entire assembly, as if moved by one common impulse, arose and stood weeping for joy. Joseph spoke briefly, saying that if the same Spirit that prompted his coming should prompt his reception, he was "with them."

The next day conference met in a rented meeting place, known as Mechanics Hall. The morning was devoted to organization and preaching. At 1:30, the long-expected hour having arrived, Joseph Smith came forward, and Zenas H. Gurley, Sr., who had waited so long and so earnestly for this day, spoke with voice choked with emotion:

"I present to you, my brethren, Joseph Smith."

Acknowledging the introduction, the young man said:

> I would say to you, brethren, as I hope you may be, and in faith I trust you are, as a people that God has promised his blessings upon, I came not here of myself, but by the influence of the Spirit. For sometime past I have received manifestations pointing to the position which I am about to assume.
> I wish to say that I have come here not to be dictated by any men or set of men. I have come in obedience to a power not my own, and shall be dictated by the power that sent me.
> God works by means best known to himself, and I feel that for some time past he has been pointing out a work for me to do.
> For two or three years past deputations have been waiting on me

urging me to assume the responsibilities of the leadership of the church, but I have answered each and every one of them that I did not wish to trifle with the faith of the people.

I do not propose to assume this position in order to amass wealth out of it, neither have I sought it as a profit.

I know opinions are various in relation to these matters. I have conversed with those who told me they would not hesitate one moment in assuming the high and powerful position as the leader of this people. But I have been well aware of the motives which might be ascribed to me—motives of various kinds, at the foundation of all which is selfishness, should I come forth to stand in the place where my father stood.

I have believed that should I come without the guarantee of the people, I should be received in blindness, and would be liable to be accused of false motives. Neither would I come to you without receiving favor from my Heavenly Father.

I have endeavored as far as possible, to keep myself unbiased. I never conversed with J. J. Strang, for in those days I was but a boy, and in fact am now but a boy. I had not acquired a sufficient knowledge of men to be capable of leading myself, setting aside the leading of others.

There is but one principle taught by the leaders of any faction of this people that I hold in utter abhorrence. That is a principle taught by Brigham Young and those believing in him. I have been told that my father taught such doctrines. I have never believed it and never can believe it. If such things were done, then I believe they never were done by Divine authority. I believe my father was a good man, and a good man never could have promulgated such doctrines.

I believe in the doctrines of honesty and truth. The Bible contains such doctrines, and so does the Book of Mormon and the Book of Covenants, which are auxiliaries to the Bible.

I have my peculiar notions in regard to revelations, but am happy to say that they accord with those I am to associate with, at least those of them with whom I have conversed. I am not very conversant with those books [pointing to a volume before him], not so conversant as I should be and will be. The time has been when the thought that I should assume the leadership of this people was so repulsive to me, that it seemed as if the thing could never be possible.

The change in my feelings came slowly, and I did not suffer myself to be influenced by extraneous circumstances, and have never read the numerous works sent me which had a bearing on this subject for fear they might entice me into wrong doing. It is my determination to do right and let heaven take care of the result. Thus I come to you free from any taint of sectarianism, taints from thoughts of the varied minds I have come in contact with; and thus hope to be able to build up my own reputation as a man.

It has been said that a Mormon elder, though but a stripling, possessed a power unequalled by almost any other preacher. This arises from a depth of feeling and the earnestness with which they believe the doctrines they teach; and it is this feeling that I do not wish to trifle with. . . .

Should you take me as a leader, I propose that all should be dealt by in mercy, open as to Gentile or Jew, but I ask not to be received except as by the ordinances of the church.

Some, who had ought to know the proprieties of the church, have told me that no certain form was necessary in order for me to assume the leadership—that the position came by right of lineage, yet I know that if I attempted to lead as a prophet by these considerations, and not by a call from heaven, men would not be led to believe who do not believe now. And so I have come not of my own dictation to this sacred office.

I believe that we owe duties to our country and to society, and are amenable to the laws of the land, and have always considered it my duty to act upon this principle; and I do say that among the people where I live I have as many good and true friends as I could desire among those of any society.

The people of Hancock County have been strongly anti-Mormon, and there I know of no enemies. I have been engaged in business with anti-Mormons, I have mingled with them, and have not only been obliged not to make any remarks which might give offense, but also to smother my own feelings, if I had any. I hold no enmity to any man living who has fought this doctrine, nor do I know any who hold enmity towards me. I hope there are none.

In conclusion, I will come to you if you will receive me, give my ability, and the influence my name may bring, together with what little power I possess, and I trust by your prayers and faith to be sustained. I pledge myself to promulgate no doctrine that shall not be approved by you or the code of good morals. . . .

I do not care to say any more at present, but will simply add that if the same Spirit which prompts my coming, prompts also my reception, I am with you.[1]

At the conclusion of this address, a motion was made by Isaac Sheen that Brother Joseph Smith be received as Prophet, Seer, Revelator, and successor to his father. A wave of assent swept the house, after which Emma Smith Bidamon, widow of Joseph Smith, the founder of the church, was received into fellowship on her original baptism. Young Joseph was then ordained President of the High Priesthood under the hands of Zenas H. Gurley, Wil-

---

[1] *The True Latter Day Saints' Herald*, Volume 1, number 5, pages 102-104.

liam Marks, Samuel Powers, and William W. Blair.[2] Elder Gurley, his face lighted with pleasure, brought to a close the period of waiting by saying:

"Brother Joseph, I present this church to you in the name of Jesus Christ."

And the young man answered with his characteristic sincerity:

> May God grant in his infinite mercy that I may never do anything to forfeit the high trust confided to me. I pray that he may grant to us power to recall the scattered ones of Israel, and I ask your prayers.

The selection and ordination of Joseph Smith overshadowed all other activities of this conference, nevertheless important selections were made to fill other positions in the growing movement. The Standing High Council was reorganized with twelve high priests, Isaac Sheen was ordained president of the high priests' quorum, and five of seven presidents of seventy were selected and ordained on that memorable April 6. Two other presidents of seventy were selected to be ordained later. Next day Israel L. Rogers was ordained Bishop of the church. Before the conference closed, quorums of elders, priests, teachers, and deacons had been organized, their officers ordained, and missions assigned.

---

[2] The probability is that the ordination prayer was by Zenas H. Gurley, Sr. Isaac Sheen, who was editor of the *Herald* in 1860, wrote to George P. Dykes in December 26, 1868, and said that he forgot to say who the spokesman was, but that he had no design in the matter, and the omission having never before been called to his mind, he could only say, "I think that Zenas H. Gurley was the spokesman. . . . This I know, that when I moved before that conference that Brother Joseph be ordained President of the High Priesthood, *I did it with an overflowing inspiration of the Holy Ghost. I know that he was called of God to that office,* and I presume that many of the Saints who were there had the same evidence. After the conference voted unanimously, that he should be ordained. I led in prayer for him, his brethren, and mother, and the oppressed of Utah, and the Holy Spirit promoted me therein powerfully." From *Sheen's Letter,* an 8-page pamphlet. Date and place of publication not given, but probably Plano about 1869.

LI.—FRIENDS AND OTHERWISE

THE PRESS, THE VERY agency that had so much to do with his father's troubles in Hancock County, was divided on the importance of what had happened. The Amboy *Times* was the first to publish the news, and took a conservative and very fair stand on the subject. The editor of the *Times* was at the conference, and it was he who reported (in long hand) the speech of Young Joseph. In his paper he writes:

THE MORMON CONFERENCE

We devote considerable space to the proceedings of this body, believing that they are of great importance to us, even as a nation. There is a great body of these people scattered through the States, who, unwilling to follow the fortunes and doctrines of Brigham Young, have been quietly waiting for the time to come when they could organize under a lineal descendant of Joseph Smith, as their prophet. That time has at length arrived. Joseph Smith, junior, occupies the position which his father once held. A new era in the history of Mormonism has dawned—an era which we hope will greatly improve the name of this despised people.

Whatever ideas we may entertain in relation to the doctrines of the Mormons, we must look with approbation and satisfaction upon any movement on their part which looks towards a radical reformation in their practices as a people.

For many years past Brigham Young has been looked upon as the embodiment of Mormonism, and those professing to be Mormons have been regarded as no better than he. Henceforth, they, or at least one branch of them, are to be judged by a different standard. The eyes of the world will now be turned upon Young Joseph. Hitherto this man has borne a good name. His talents are of no mean order; and it is earnestly to be hoped that he will use them for good, and not a bad purpose.[1]

The news was received in various ways about Nauvoo. George Edmunds, Jr., asked Joseph Smith to remain in Nauvoo for five

---

[1] Amboy (Illinois) *Times* (date not known); *The True Latter Day Saints' Herald*, Volume 1, page 101; *Church History*, Volume 3, page 253.

years and see if the Saints would not move in and again build up the city. Others urged the same course, but there were other more unpleasant features. The citizens in Carthage under the leadership of Jesse C. Williams, Henry P. Harper, Jacob B. Strader, and David Mack, had adopted resolutions earnestly protesting against the return of the Mormons to Hancock County, and even stating they would not be allowed to settle there (August 21, 1860). Similar resolutions were adopted at meetings in Montebello and Basco Township in the same county and about the same time in Nauvoo. Then Joseph received word from Judge Roosevelt of Warsaw that if he should be sent a certain letter ordering him to leave the county or to remain at his peril, to present the names of the men who signed the letter to the grand jury at its first sitting, and he would find a host of friends about whom he knew nothing. The letter never came, but Joseph understood later that such a letter had been presented to several by two men influential in driving out the Saints in 1845-46. Judge Roosevelt had told them he would not sign it and advised them to put it away or they would get into trouble. Thomas C. Sharp, in a mellower maturity, wanted nothing to do with it; he had lived through one Mormon War and chose not to get into another.

Friends all over the county were prompt in their denunciation of such measures, but in spite of that, one interior township passed a sweeping resolution that no Mormon be permitted to preach or pray in that county. The Carthage *Republican* opened its columns to articles against the resettlement of Nauvoo, and some of the personal friends of Young Joseph implored him to leave the county. He wrote a reply and evidently had it printed in the *Democratic News*.[2] It was also reproduced in the *Herald*. The straightforward and fearless attitude of the young leader is plainly revealed in this letter:

---

[2] I have not located this paper.

In taking the head of the Mormon[3] Church, I am running counter to the opinions of many people; but believing that "there is a destiny which shapes our ends," I am content to let those who are astonished and opposed to such a measure, stand the test of time, and an opportunity for reflection, satisfied that investigation will result in my favor.

To those familiar with the books upon which our faith is founded, the Bible being the groundwork, I have no apologies to offer, and to those not familiar with them, and to those who do not believe them, none is due.

I know that many stories are now being circulated in reference to what will be the result of the step I have taken. I know that many believe that I will emigrate to Salt Lake. To those who know me, it is needless for me to say that I am not going to do any such thing while the doctrine of polygamy and disobedience to the laws are countenanced there; to those who do not know me personally, and to whom my principles are unknown, I must say, withhold your censure until such time as I shall, by some flagrant act of disobedience to the law of the land, or some striking breach of morality, deserve the just indignation of society; when I do either one or the other, I am ready for the opening of the vial of wrath of outraged society, and shall cheerfully receive the condemnation I shall merit.

Numbers of the readers of the Democratic press know me personally, and have been warm friends to me; they know my sentiments in regard to those obnoxious features in Utah Mormonism, and I trust in their knowledge of me as a pledge to them of what my future actions shall be.

Religious toleration is one of the principles of our government, and so long as any denomination shall keep within the pale of the law, so long is it entitled to the consideration and protection of the government, but when those bonds are exceeded, the claim is forfeited and society ought to ignore it, and the law proclaim against it.

A man is known by his acts; I have been judged heretofore by mine and am willing still to be so judged, asking all to do so fairly and impartially, laying their prejudices aside, relying not upon rumor for their knowledge, but investigating for themselves.

I leave the result in the hands of him who "doeth all things well," hoping no man will judge me without knowledge.

Joseph Smith.[4]

The summer, fall, and winter of 1860 passed away; Young Joseph Smith went about his business undisturbed. During the year following, he continued to preach in Nauvoo and vicinity,

---

[3] Joseph Smith in a footnote explains that he uses this word in the commonly accepted sense.
[4] *The True Latter Day Saints' Herald*, Volume 1, pages 169, 170 (evidently reprinted); *Church History*, Volume 3, pages 275, 276.

both in Illinois and Iowa, went anywhere in Hancock County he chose, unarmed and alone, or in company with others. Many of the more prominent citizens expressed to him their opinion that mob violence would never again be tolerated. Some even said they were convinced that the treatment of the Mormons had left a curse upon the country that would never be removed until they were permitted to return.

The temple had burned in 1848 and was a genuine loss to the community as well as the State, for says one authority:

> Of all the structures erected by religious colonies [in Illinois], the largest and most unique one was, no doubt, the famous Mormon Temple at Nauvoo. Although never fully completed on the interior, the exterior was essentially complete at the time the Mormons departed. From the standpoint of architecture alone, it was a great loss to the State when the structure was burned. The architectural and decorative features involved in this Temple were wholly different from anything in the State, and were it standing today it would be one of the most unique historical structures.[5]

The French and German population into whose hands the ruins ultimately came, sold them, and under the supervision of one Sellers, the temple ruins became a quarry where stone for many buildings in Nauvoo was dug, until there was scarcely any of the original structure remaining.

A few Saints came back to the old city and attempted to make a home there—Thaddeus Cutler, Henry Cuerdon, Thomas Revell, William Redfield, and some others. Benjamin Austin and family already lived there, having moved in soon after 1860. The first meetings in Nauvoo were held in his small rented home, then the services were moved to the corner of Water and Granger Streets, into the house once owned by William Marks. Later, as the congregation grew, new quarters had to be found, and a room was fitted up in the Brick Store, used as a store and office by Joseph

---

[5] "An Outline of the History of Architecture in Illinois," by **Thomas Edward O'Donnell** Associate Professor of Architecture, University of Illinois, at Urbana, *Illinois Historical Transactions,* 1931.

Smith. They soon numbered seventy-five in Nauvoo. Emma Smith Bidamon had united with the church on the same day as her son Joseph. Two other sons soon united their fortunes with the church, first David, then Alexander. Frederick died April 13, 1862, expressing belief but without baptism.

In 1865, the editorship of the *Herald* was assumed by the President of the church, and Joseph Smith moved his family to Plano in January, 1866. The *Herald* had been moved to this place in 1863 from Cincinnati accompanied by Isaac Sheen and his family.

After his removal, the branch in Nauvoo gradually dwindled and eventually disappeared, but in recent years a flourishing church has again been built up there.

LII.—Welding the Fragments

*A*S THE NEWS SPREAD, by missionaries, by word of mouth, by letter from old friend to old friend, and by the pages of the *Herald*, that Young Joseph had come to the church, members flocked to the standard from everywhere. In the beginning of the year 1860, not knowing the events that were transpiring in the West, a group of old-time Saints in Pittsburgh, Pennsylvania, began holding meetings to "converse upon the past" and interchange ideas about what might happen in the future. They had renounced all other leaders; some of them had been without contact with any branch of the church since 1845, when they went east with Sidney Rigdon. Some of the most prominent of these were Josiah Ells, Richard Savery, James McDowell, Joseph Parsons, and Matthew Smith.

Most of these joined the Reorganization eventually, and many of their children and grandchildren occupied prominent places in its history, among them Richard Savery Salyards, grandson of Richard Savery, for many years secretary of the church and closely associated with his father-in-law the third Joseph Smith. He was throughout his long life, an able defender of the faith.

Josiah Ells was the man, whom, with John Cairns, Joseph Smith had chosen from among all the strong debaters of the church to meet the great preacher, Reverend Dr. David Nelson of Quincy. He was a man of independent thought and action, for only men of this rare type were able to withstand the adverse currents that had lately swept over the wreckage of their one-time faith.

Ells was with the group who accompanied the Prophet part way to Carthage before he was assassinated, and who, with Samuel Bennett, was sent by William Marks to bring John Taylor, who had been fearfully wounded, home from Carthage after the tragedy. They made the trip at midnight, risking their lives to do so, and found the Carthage people reluctant to let Taylor go, as they believed their city would be sacked and destroyed once he was gone.

After the breakup at Nauvoo, Ells went to Pittsburgh with Sidney Rigdon and was chosen one of his counselors, but was never active in that movement, and when the meetings began to be held in 1860, he had stood alone for many years. These meetings had not continued long before W. W. Blair came to Pittsburgh, found this remnant, and told them a reorganization of the scattered fragments had been effected and that Joseph, the eldest son of the Seer, had been chosen President. Shortly before, speaking in one of the prayer meetings held by these old-time Saints, Josiah Ells had testified by the Spirit that before long they would hear something "respecting the kingdom." Therefore Ells and his wife were ready to accept the message when it came. He appointed a meeting, but no one came except himself, his wife, and one other. Undaunted, he kept on meeting, while one by one the old friends ventured out until at length the nucleus of the Pittsburgh Branch was formed. Ells became one of the early Apostles of the Reorganization.

Out in Etna, Scotland County, Missouri, a young carpenter by the name of John H. Lake lived with his wife, Maryette, and her widowed father, Duty Griffith. One day the old gentleman received through the mail a copy of a little magazine called *The True Latter Day Saints' Herald,* and while old Mr. Griffith rejoiced with his daughter that Young Joseph had at last come to take the Seer's place, young Lake looked on with horror, for he now discovered that not only was his father-in-law an old-time "Mormon," but he had actually been living with a "Mormon wife." He hardly knew what to do. He could not in honor desert his wife and their young baby Oracy. He thought that if only he were not so poor he would take his wife and child and go to California, so far away that no one would ever learn of this skeleton in the family closet. Once there, he would see to it, he said grimly, that there would be "one woman who would keep her mouth shut." But he could not get away. The only thing was to live down his disgrace as best he could, study the question, and be able to show his wife how foolish it all was. He commenced his studies with diligence, and six months later was baptized with nine others by John Shippy. He became an Apostle in the Reorganization and baptized hundreds into the church he had once so bitterly scorned.

In Dodge County,[1] Nebraska, in February, 1861, a young Englishman named Charles Derry sat reading the *Herald*. He was born in Bloxwick, Staffordshire, July 25, 1826, and had heard the gospel when he was but nineteen, but rejected it because of an unwise reference to the Baptist communion. Later, on October 3, 1847, he was baptized, and before the winter was over was himself a missionary, traveling without purse or scrip over his native land. For seven years he traveled thus, blessed by the gifts of the gospel and growing more and more convinced of the divinity of his calling. Then in 1854 he was counseled by the church authorities in England to emigrate to Salt Lake City. With joyful hearts the young missionary and his wife, Alice Stokes, who had been a member of the church in the days of Joseph, planned to "obey counsel." On the way the young mother died, and Charles Derry arrived in Salt Lake City with two babes, a girl of four and a boy of two. Nor was that all, for the whole experience was a bitter disappointment, and in 1859, with sorrow and "grief more poignant than death," Charles Derry and the young wife he had recently married left that church and, traveling by ox team, took up their way eastward again to Fontanelle, Nebraska. With his brother George and his mother, both of whom he had baptized before he left England, he found a temporary home, and told them his sad experience, thus successfully prevailing upon them to go no farther west.

---

[1] Maple Creek near Fontanelle.

In his despair at finding conditions so far from what he had expected, his mind turned to the opposite extreme, and he tried to call himself an infidel. Sometimes as he worked in the field or at the anvil of his blacksmith shop, these old experiences in England would suddenly loom up before him, and he would try to account for them in the godless world his new philosophy was endeavoring to construct. He found it hard to relegate them to the realm of chance. When he met an old Latter Day Saint he felt the bond of brotherhood again, and although he told himself he was now an infidel, yet there seemed something about that old-time gospel bond that still held.

One Sunday afternoon, February 20, 1861, he walked slowly over to such a friend's home for a visit and a talk about old times. As soon as he entered, this man, whose name was Clark, handed him a little paper—the eleventh number of the first volume of the *True Latter Day Saints' Herald*. "Heigh, Brother Derry, here's a paper for you!" he said, and Derry opening it started to read it aloud. He read it all, and as he read, the same sweet pervading influence that had warmed his heart so often in old England, stole over his heart, speaking conviction to his very soul. He borrowed the paper, took it home, and read it to his wife, and then fell upon his knees for the first time in years, as he was "wont to do ere dark clouds obscured his vision." While in prayer it seemed to him the darkness of his western experience rolled away, and the awful experiences he had suffered became nothing but memories. At this time, Charles Derry wrote the hymn, "O Lord! Around Thine Altar Now" (which has been in our hymn books since 1870), a prayer of thanksgiving for the new light that had come into his darkened life.

Derry could not wait for the church to come to him, he must needs go to it. The next Sunday with a sack of cookies in his hand, and not a cent in his pocket (for he had been forced to leave most of his possessions in Utah, in order to make his escape, and getting a new start had been difficult indeed) he started on foot through eighteen inches of snow for western Iowa. As he passed through Fremont, the snow was found to be melting and becoming an uncomfortable slush, but he pushed on and that night, by consent of the owner, slept in a wagon at Elkhorn Bridge. He was twenty miles on his way. The next day the United States mail coach overtook him and gave him a ride into the small village of Omaha. He wended his way to the Missouri River, where he was told the crossing was unsafe as the ice was expected to go out any moment. Four inches of water already covered the river surface. After a little hesitation, he offered a silent prayer for safety and started across the treacherous river, making the Iowa side in safety. Within twenty-four hours the ice went down the river. Seven miles through the mud brought him to Council Bluffs (then Kanesville), a somewhat larger place than Omaha. Before leaving home, someone had given him the name of one Latter Day Saint who lived in Kanesville. The name was Isaac Beebe, a stranger to him, but still his only clue to finding the people he sought.

As he walked up the main street, tired, muddy, and travel-worn, he saw a man cutting wood in a yard. He approached him and asked if he knew where Isaac Beebe lived. The woodcutter straightened himself up to his full six feet of height and said, "Right here in this body." Derry told him that he had traveled as much as sixty miles through snow, slush, and mud in the last two days, and requested the privilege of shelter for the night, saying he had a few cookies left for his supper, and with an appraising eye on the woodpile, he would cut the rest of the wood to pay for his bed, as he had no money.

"Come in; we are told to entertain strangers, for thereby we may entertain angels unaware." The stranger assured him he was no angel, but only Charlie Derry, but he was made at home, given supper and lodging, without resorting to the woodpile to earn his way. He was told that two Reorganized elders, W. W.

Blair and E. C. Briggs, were only ten miles east. Early on the morning of March 1, the next day, he continued on his journey through the muddy roads. Travel was slow. When he had gone ten miles, he felt so tired he determined to ask for an opportunity to rest himself at the next house. He soon came to a cabin by the roadside and made his request, and was received in kindly fashion by the lady of the house. He soon learned that this was the home of the Campbells, and that the missionaries were expected momentarily. In about a quarter of an hour they arrived. He was among friends. At the home of the Campbells and that of Jairus M. Putney,[2] he found a Saint's welcome. He attended the services held by the two elders and witnessed baptism in Keg Creek.

When they left that neighborhood, he went with them to Farm Creek, and was entertained at the home of Calvin Beebe, a brother of the man he had met in Kanesville. The following Sunday, March 3, after a sermon by W. W. Blair, he felt he could no longer delay, and was baptized in Farm Creek near the Beebe home, just two weeks from the day the little *Herald* fell into his hands.

The confirmation took place immediately, and with his hands still on Brother Derry's head, Brother Blair asked what office he held in the other church. Derry replied, "I have not come for any office, but simply to be a member in the kingdom of God." But Brother Blair said: "It is my duty to ordain you an elder." Whereupon, without taking his hands off his head, he proceeded to also ordain him to the office of elder.

The community in which he found himself were brethren in truth. When he returned, Philip Gatrost went with him, with team and wagon to bring his family to western Iowa. By the following April—one month later—he was in the mission field,

---

[2] March 1, 1861, W. W. Blair records in his *Memoirs*, page 47, that he "met at Brother Jarius M. Putney's ten miles east of Council Bluffs, Charles Derry, formerly a Brighamite, but who until late had abandoned all religions. He seems to be a good man and claims to be seeking after truth."

preaching and baptizing.[3]

On December 3, 1861, in Little Sioux, Iowa, Silas W. Condit baptized a young Irish schoolteacher named James W. Gillen. He was a handsome young fellow with a winning personality. And he needed it, for he had made his own way in the world since he was twelve. Born in County Derry, Ireland, March 18, 1836, he had been left fatherless before he was six months old. When he was four, his mother with her five children emigrated to Canada and found a home in Montreal. She died, leaving "Jimmy" an orphan of nine years. His brothers and sisters stayed together until he was able to earn a living, but this was not long, for he started to learn the nail maker's trade when he was but twelve. From then on he looked out for himself. He worked at his trade and in a foundry until 1853, and learned the trade of making paper. Then he hired out as a farm laborer, with the privilege of attending school in the winters. For three winters he continued his studies in Essex County, New York, until he was able to enter an institute at Fort Edward, New York, for six months. Smitten with the westward fever, he went to Boone County, Illinois, passed a teacher's examination before Judge Fuller, superintendent of schools, and taught school in Illinois for two years. He then went on west to Harrison County, Iowa, in 1858, where he purchased two hundred and seventy-six acres of land and entered the employ of the Hannibal and Saint Joseph Railroad at Saint Joseph as shipping and receiving clerk. The next year on the opening of the Platte Valley Railroad to Atchison, he went with the first train to Winthrop and remained as shipping and receiving clerk until the commencement of the Civil War, when he returned to teaching school in Harrison County. He was not long in the church before he became an elder, later married Nancy A. Moore,[4] daughter of an old-time

---
[3] Autobiography of Charles Derry, *Journal of History*, Volume 1, page 423, seq., and Volume 2, page 15, seq.
[4] Their son, J. Arthur Gillen, occupied as president of the Quorum of Twelve from 1922 to 1934.

Latter Day Saint family, and became one of the most loved of early Latter Day Saint missionaries, occupying in the Quorum of Twelve for many years.

On a farm near Plum Creek, seven miles north of Sidney, Iowa, lived a man by the name of John Leeka. John Leeka and his family had joined the church at Bentonsport, Van Buren County, Iowa, under the ministry of Joseph Ball and Truman Gilette in March, 1840. Sometime later he had moved into Nauvoo and resided there until the exodus in 1846, which they joined, going west under the leadership of Brigham Young as far as the Missouri River, though they had been advised by Emma Smith not to do so. In western Iowa his confidence wavered, and saying nothing to anyone he quietly folded his tent, took his family into the unsettled country near by, and turned his attention with success to business. He soon felt that all forms of religion were to be rejected, although he treated all professors of Christianity with respect and kindness.

The Civil War came, and Brother Leeka remembered a prophecy made long ago in Nauvoo about the coming of civil strife. It was rumored in the neighborhood that a young woman named Hendrickson had a paper with a copy of that prophecy in it. He sent to borrow it. Sister Hendrickson, with all the generosity of a Latter Day Saint on such occasions, sent it willingly and with it a half dozen others. John Leeka read the prophecy and all about the coming of Young Joseph. He sent for Charles Derry, and he and his wife with others were baptized.

In 1860 Brother W. W. Blair was preaching in a simple little school building in the new country around the town of Galien, Michigan, where the family of James Blakeslee had settled. One day, a stranger came in, but his behavior did not betoken much interest. His face wore a studied attitude of indifference, as though he just "dropped in." He was a large, powerfully built man, with the visible imprint of superior cultural advantages upon his rugged face, now beginning to show the trace of age. The sermon began, and the stranger looked about, straightened up and began to pay earnest attention; soon great tears coursed down his cheeks, and his powerful frame trembled with emotion. Blair turned to Brother Blakeslee as he sat down and asked who the stranger was. Blakeslee did not remember ever having seen him before, but immediately at the close of service approached him, as it was the morning hour on Sunday, and asked him home to dinner. He was surprised when the stranger readily accepted the invitation. He introduced himself as Ezra Thayre,[5] and before the next Sabbath, he and his kindred had been baptized. Ezra Thayre had known Joseph Smith, as a boy; had employed him when Thayre was a bridgebuilder in New York; he had known Oliver Cowdery as a schoolteacher in Palmyra; had joined the early church; and still had the Book of Mormon he purchased from Joseph Smith in Auburn, New York. He told how as Joseph Smith stood before him in that log house back in New York, holding his copy of the Book of Mormon in his hand, and told his story in a "boyish and uncultured way," "such a power" seized upon him as enabled him "to know that every word that that lad said was true." He wanted that very book and no other, and so purchased, and still had it.[6]

Instances like these might be multiplied almost indefinitely. As the months went by, the news of the coming of Young Joseph went into every corner of the country where a Latter Day Saint of other days had found his way. And in almost all of these centers a faithful few welcomed the message and the renewed hope brought by the Reorganization.

In July, 1861, Young Joseph issued his first epistle, that he might further facilitate the work of gathering. This epistle recites the events leading to his acceptance of his prophetic calling, and then closes with this stirring appeal:

---
[5] Ezra Thayre, see page 83.
[6] *Saints' Herald*, Volume 33, pages 278, 279, sermon of W. W. Blair at Lamoni, Iowa, April 6, 1886.

I would not that men should hastily run without tidings, nor do I ask that any should place the stake of their salvation upon an earthly arm. "Cursed is he that putteth his trust in man, and maketh flesh his arm." I ask and desire that all may place their stake of salvation upon the author and finisher of our faith—upon the promises and principles of the Gospel, pure as preached from the Saviour's lips, for in him was no guile, and in his teachings there was no deceit.

In the name of the God of Abraham, of Isaac and of Jacob, I now call upon all the scattered Saints, upon all the broad earth, to arise and shake off the sleep that hath bound them these many years, take on the armor of the just, calling on the name of the Lord for help, and unite once more for the emancipation of the honest in heart from the power of false doctrines and the shackles of sin.

In the name of bleeding Zion, I call upon all those who have been wandering in by and forbidden paths, and have been led astray by wicked and designing men, to turn from their scenes of wickedness and sins of convenience—to turn from their servitude to Satan, in all his seductive devices; from vice in every phase, and from the labor of sin, the wages whereof are ever death—unto their true and delightsome allegiance, to the principles of the gospel of peace—to the paths of wisdom—to the homage of that God that brought the children of Israel out of bondage; to turn and remember the new covenant, even the Book of Mormon; to lay hold anew upon the rod of iron which surely leads to the tree of life; to remember that those who live to the Lord keep his commandments, and that the promises are unto the faithful, and the reward unto those that endure unto the end.

And in the name of the Lord of hosts, I call upon all the inhabitants of the earth to repent, believe and be baptized, for the time cometh when the judgments of God are to be poured out upon all nations, and the besom of God's wrath shall smoke through the land; when men shall know that there is a God in Israel, and he is mighty to punish or to save; that the prayers of those under the altar have been heard, and a swift retribution is to come, when the despoiler will be despoiled; when those who denied justice shall be judged, and the measure meted unto others shall be meted unto them; when the prisoner shall go free, the oppressed be redeemed, and all Israel shall cry, "Glory to God in the highest be given, for he that is long-suffering and slow to anger, has arisen, and shall bring again Zion." Amen and amen.   Joseph Smith,
President of the Church of Jesus Christ of Latter Day Saints.[7]
Nauvoo, Illinois, July 19, 1861.

From that time the Saints began to gather in from all places, and the certainty that the movement would succeed became more and more apparent.

---

[7] *The True Latter Day Saints' Herald,* Volume 2, pages 123, 124; *Church History,* Volume 3, pages 294, 295.

LIII.—England and Wales

The church still followed the custom of having two conferences a year, and in 1862 the fall conference, known as the semiannual conference, convened October 6, 1862. There were two important questions before the conference: the proposal to buy and locate a printing press, and the sending of a first foreign missionary. Both passed the conference. The mission proposed was, as it had been in the old church, a mission to England, and was to consist of three: Jason W. Briggs, Samuel Powers, and Charles Derry who had been ordained a seventy at Little Sioux, Iowa, in September, 1861.

An unusual number of baptisms occurred at that conference including that of a twelve-year-old boy by the name of Heman C. Smith, who was baptized with his parents—Spencer C. Smith, the schoolteacher son-in-law of Lyman Wight and for so many years his secretary and scribe, and the daughter of Lyman Wight, Anna C.—as well as many of the Lyman Wight colony who had come north before the War. All communication had been cut off with their loved ones in Texas, but they waited hopefully the lifting of the war cloud to tell them also the joyful tidings of the return of Young Joseph. Young Heman C. was anxious to have it known that he was "prompted to this action by my own convictions and not by solicitation on the part of my parents or anyone else."

Heman C. Smith was confirmed by William W. Blair and James Blakeslee, and his mother's heart was thrilled by the promise of Brother Blair that, "If faithful, your voice shall be heard in the mountains to the salvation of many souls, and thousands shall yet rejoice that they have heard your voice." Time has tested the truth of this prophecy.

These three were baptized by William H. Kelley, who was a son of an old-time Latter Day Saint, Richard Yancy Kelley, at one time an elder in the church and one of the leading members of the church in southern Illinois, and the grandson of Benjamin Franklin Kelley, one of the first to accept the gospel message in Johnson County, Illinois. Richard continued his work in southern Illinois without question after the death of the Martyrs, until 1847, when, making a trip to Kanesville to examine for himself certain unsatisfactory rumors, he returned disillusioned. His home even then, however, was open to the missionaries of all factions. J. J. Strang, Brigham Young, Sidney Rigdon, Gladden Bishop, and Alpheus Cutler sent elders to that community. All were gladly received as brethren and shared the Kelley hospitality, but after careful examination, he refused to join with any of them until, in the year 1859, E. C. Briggs and W. W. Blair came and told of the little band waiting until the "due time of the Lord" to bring to them Young Joseph. With them he united, and his third son, William, was soon engaged in the missionary work. A younger son of Richard Y. Kelley, Edmund L., then at school, joined the church in 1864 and became the beloved Bishop of the church, so well known as "Bishop Kelley" for nearly thirty years.

Young David H. Smith, youngest son of the Martyr was present at that conference. He was a sensitive, beauty-loving young man, and had written many songs and poems even in his childhood and youth. Now he had turned his abilities to the benefit of the church, and wrote a number of the early-time hymns, often set to music by a young friend of Nauvoo, Imogene Austin.[1] He loved to attend conference, and often earned his way by drawing or painting pictures for the citizens of Nauvoo, usually from original subjects. He was deeply moved by the first foreign mission of the church and wrote a poem, much quoted by the early Saints, "The Three Missionaries."

On December 6 of that year, Charles Derry started on his mis-

---

[1] Mrs. Miriam [Shippy] Claus, now deceased, of Detroit, Michigan, remembered visiting with her parents, Mr. and Mrs. John Shippy in Nauvoo and often told how after dinner the young folks, including David and Imogene Austin, went to the river and spent the afternoon putting music to one of David's poems.

sion "without purse or scrip," as he had always gone, leaving his family in a log cabin near Glenwood, Iowa, as comfortably situated as he was able to do. There were no church allowances in those days, but seven men of that vicinity jointly pledged themselves to see that the family of the Reorganization's first foreign missionary did not suffer. These men, Jairus M. Putney, William Brittain, John Leeka, Elijah Gaylord, Noah Green, John Pack, and Joseph Carven assumed their part in that first mission cheerfully, and as Charles Derry said later, "right nobly did they keep their pledge."

With just thirty-five cents in his pocket, Charles Derry said good-by to his family in the little twelve-by-twelve log cabin in western Iowa and started for the East. He spent a week in Nauvoo, also visited Israel Rogers, who had been ordained the first Bishop of the Reorganized Church at the Amboy Conference of 1860, and had since controlled with admirable economy the funds of the church. From Brother Israel Rogers, Derry received seventy dollars with which to pay his way to England. Brother Rogers told him that much to his regret Brother Powers and Brother Briggs felt unable to fill the mission because of their temporal affairs. The two had prayer together, and Derry departed for New York City, spending his money as frugally as he could for a very good reason; he was thinking of the loved ones back on the Iowa prairies. Arriving in New York, he had only four days to wait before a ship, the steamer "City of Baltimore," was sailing for England. Derry engaged passage on her, steerage for forty dollars. Other help had been given him by Saints along the way and by traveling as cheaply as he could, and subsisting upon the least expensive food he could buy, he was able to send forty dollars to his family and had ten dollars for himself when he went on board.

The first missionaries in 1837 had not been more lonely than he; they had each other; he had no one, despite the fact that this was his homeland. He went to the lodging house from whence he had departed with such high hopes just nine years before to go to Zion. Mrs. Powell's lodging house of Great Crosshall Street had another landlady, but Brother Derry engaged lodging at sixpence a night (he to board himself) and enjoyed the first good night's sleep since he left New York, for it had been a very stormy passage. With his ten dollars he bought actual necessities and had enough left to order one thousand of Joseph Smith's first epistle to the church. While waiting for them to be printed, he visited George Q. Cannon, then president of the Utah faction of the church in England. He requested the privilege of visiting the branches and preaching but was refused. He offered some pamphlets, but Cannon refused them also and called the leaders of the Reorganized Church "apostates."

In a few days the *Millennial Star* came out, with the statement by the editor that he had been told by the "whisperings of the Spirit" to warn the Saints that apostates would soon be in their midst seeking to lead them from the truth. The *Millennial Star* went to every good Mormon home in England, and wherever Charles Derry knocked at the door of an old friend and tried to tell them of his experiences, he succeeded only in convincing them that Brother Cannon was a wonderful prophet. Before he left Cannon's office, Elder Derry also made a prophecy, that in the name of Jesus Christ the Reorganized Church would make their message ring from one end of the land to the other. That remained to be fulfilled. As soon as his literature was ready, he began distributing it among the Saints, the old-time Saints, of Liverpool. Many of them, having read the *Star,* would have none of him; others had left the church when the doctrine of polygamy was first introduced in England but a few years since and wanted nothing more to do with Mormonism in any form. His money was now all but exhausted.

He had bought what food he had, spending his money sparingly, often going without meals. One morning, his money now entirely gone, he was leaving his lodging place without breakfast when the landlady said, "Mr. Derry, you have had no breakfast!" He answered that he was temporarily without money to buy breakfast, but that he expected to receive some that day (he had no idea from whence it would come). She insisted that he come into her part of the house and have breakfast, but he with equal insistence said he did not wish to impose upon her kindness. However, she soon brought him a plate full of toast and butter, and a pot of "tea in good old English style" and bade him eat and be welcome. He had made it a practice to call on every old "Mormon" who he heard was dissatisfied at the introduction of polygamy in the church (which was at a later date in England than in the United States). This morning he made his way to the shop of a Mr. Collinson who was a shoe merchant in Bold Street. He told Derry that he had seen so much that he had turned away in disgust and felt he wanted nothing more to do with it. Elder Derry went on with his story, but his hearer neither assented nor objected, only as he was leaving pressed five shillings into his hand, and asked him to call again. Returning homeward, happy at this manifestation of Providence, he frugally spent one penny for oatmeal and boiled it for his supper. "My heart rejoiced in God," he wrote in his journal, "that I had not prayed to him in vain."

On February 13, he left Liverpool for Chester and found an old friend, Joseph Coward, who had emigrated to Utah, lost a fortune, and returned, disgusted and disheartened. He wanted no more of the church. Charles Derry walked on to Wrexham, Crassford, Overton, Lightwood Green, Elsmere, Shrewsbury, and Wolverhampton, and on the 18th found himself at West Bromwich, where he had been baptized and where he had married his wife, Alice Stokes, and made his home during his early married life.

My mind had been very unsettled in every town I had visited, and no prospect of doing anything by way of preaching had presented itself, but here in West Bromwich I felt to make a stand. The news quickly spread that Charles Derry had returned from Utah. . . . Some said I was "broken," that is worn down. Poor souls, they knew not what I had suffered in mind and body since I last saw them. . . . I then went to a Brighamite meeting in West Bromwich, but found their minds very much poisoned against me. One man named Southwick saw me as I came in and remarked aloud to me, "Charley, thee be'st a weak team, lad." I acknowledged the corn, but I realized that the Lord was strong.

Everyone took special pains to cast a slur or utter a sneer in their testimony, but they fell powerless. I arose to bear my testimony, but I was commanded to sit down. I did so, and the president told me I should have the privilege to say what I pleased at the close. I thanked him and kept my seat till the close; then I arose to claim the privilege promised. The president then demanded what I wanted to say. I told him he would hear by the time I got through. He then insisted upon limiting me to two minutes. I had to submit, but I put in my two minutes, nor did I waste words. None dared a reply, but all seemed to shun me, or to utter some contemptuous sneer. And this in the branch in which, nineteen years ago, I had been baptized, and from which I had been sent out to preach the Gospel. Yet I thank God not a soul among them could point to any wrong I had done.

The way was hard. He could only go from house to house to tell his story where they would receive him. Sometime in March a Mr. Withers obtained the rent of a room in Park Foundry for the sum of eighteen pence a week, for which Derry was to have the use of the place on Sunday and one night a week. He went to the landlord to obtain the key, but the man had changed his mind. Another religious denomination had interfered. The missionary had gone to some expense fitting up the place with seats and had advertised his services, but to no avail. He could have the place the next Wednesday. But when John Pardoe and Charles Derry went there upon the following Wednesday, they were again refused entrance. There was no choice but to occupy a "piece of waste land" near by and preach in the open air. Soon after, he visited a man by the name of Charles Tyler who had left the Mormon Church. He said Derry would find a friend in his brother, Henry Tyler.

Brother Derry was then taken ill but struggled on. By the 25th of March he had obtained another room, but was unable to occupy it until the 31st. For nearly a month he was very ill, but finally was able to resume his work and to baptize upon May 3 the first fruits of the English mission, Henry Tyler, the man whose friendship had been pledged to him by Charles Tyler.

At the April conference of 1863, Jason W. Briggs's mission to England was reaffirmed; Samuel Powers was released, as he was unable to go, and Jeremiah Jeremiah appointed in his stead. On the 11th of May, calling at the post office, Charles Derry found there four *Heralds,* but they were not prepaid. It would cost him four shillings and nine pence to get them. He had no money. His homesick heart longed for the church news, but he turned away disappointed. Passing a pawnshop later, he went in and pawned his overcoat and with the proceeds went back for the *Heralds.* It was still a bit chilly without his coat, but he did not regret his choice. The little papers warmed and cheered him.

Mrs. Henry Tyler had now become interested in the work, also William Tyler, his wife, and his niece; Charles Tyler, William Morgan and wife of Oldbury, and George Morgan. On May 3 Mrs. Jane Fox of Birmingham Heath, gave in her name for baptism. He felt no longer alone.

The day after Mrs. Fox presented her name for baptism, as he sat writing letters, Mrs. Stokes, his landlady, asked him if those were the two men he was expecting, and looking out of the window he saw Jason W. Briggs and Jeremiah Jeremiah. He records in his journal: "My heart was truly glad to see them. I invited them in, and Mrs. Stokes prepared dinner, after which I took them around to see my friends. I am now no longer alone. I have two able men to bear the burden with me, and my hopes for the future are greatly enlarged. We all slept at Stokes'."

On the morning of the 17th, he baptized John Pardoe, Joshua Lyall, and Richard Stokes, who were confirmed by the three elders. In the afternoon the first branch of the Reorganized Church in England was organized with six members,[2] Sarah Withers and Jane Fox besides the four previously named. Elder Henry Tyler was chosen to preside, John Pardoe ordained an elder, and Richard Stokes a deacon.

The next day, after consultation, the three missionaries concluded to publish the *Word of Consolation,* written so many years ago in the early days of the Reorganization. Some changes had to be made to adapt it to present events. Charles Derry read it over aloud, and all suggested changes. During the day, somehow, the two others learned what had become of Brother Derry's coat. Brother Jeremiah's hand went into his pocket at once and produced two shillings, and six pence, to which Brother Briggs added two shillings, and the coat was soon off the pawnbroker's shelf. "My heart swelled with gratitude to my brethren," says Charles Derry, in speaking of it.

On the 20th of May, 1863, their revision being complete, they ordered one thousand copies of the *Word of Consolation* printed by a Mr. Hudson, for two pounds and ten shillings. Jeremiah Jeremiah had already started to Wales, his objective.

On the 23rd came an encouraging letter from John H. Morgan of Lydney, Gloucestershire. He assured them of his joy in receiving Brother Derry's letter and of hearing of the Reorganized Church and the Presidency of Joseph, son of the Martyr. He had been looking forward to this day and was with them, heart and hand. He was sure if they visited them, they could organize there.

In the meantime, meetings were continued with a few additions in West Bromwich until the 31st, when the first Communion service was held. The branch now numbered ten. On June 3, Charles Derry visited Thomas Angel in Dudley, and on the 7th preached his first sermon in Blakely, a branch he had himself organized many years ago. His effort was to teach them that polygamy was no part of the gospel. He had good crowds here,

---

[2]There is said to have been a branch organized in Sheffield prior to this and before the coming of Derry. But I have found little account of it.

all wanting to see Charley Derry again. Particularly was he received in a kindly way by John and Mary Heywood, former converts of his.

Soon word was received from Jeremiah Jeremiah in Wales, that he was in need of help, and Jason W. Briggs hastened there on the 10th of June. On the way to Wales, Briggs went into Gloucestershire and remained ten days, organizing a branch with ten members at Lydney, from whence Brother Morgan had written. Briggs left Brother Morgan holding meetings in that vicinity "with every prospect of building up a large branch."

Jason Briggs hastened on to meet the call of Brother Jeremiah from Merthyr Tydfil, Wales, where he found Jeremiah with eighteen ready for the formation of a branch. They "placarded that and the neighboring town and called a large number together two Sundays, in an open space in the city." By the first of August the *Word of Consolation* had been translated into Welsh and was on the press. Brother Jeremiah went to Monmouthshire, while Briggs visited old members of the church not now connected with the Utah people. A conference was called July 19, and eight elders and two priests were appointed to fill Sunday appointments.

About the middle of July, Brother Derry was challenged by a William O. Owen. Owen had been to Utah, and had become convinced that a great imposition had been practiced upon him, had returned to England, and was exposing "Mormonism" from town to town in lectures. Charles Derry, having more confidence in his colleague, sent to Wales for Briggs.

The debate began at Birmingham, July 18. Before it was finished, Briggs became ill and had to retire, leaving Derry to finish. On the 25th of August, Derry had another debate with Owen on the unique question of "Are the Abominations of Utah the Legitimate Fruits of Mormonism. Proper?" Needless to say Owen affirmed. Derry denied.

While in Birmingham, Derry heard of another Latter Day Saint, Thomas Taylor, who had returned disappointed from Utah. Derry visited him on September 13, but he did not appear particularly interested. Leaving Briggs in Birmingham, he took a trip through the adjacent counties, and at Lydney found a branch raised by Morgan and Briggs. From there he went to Wales to help Elder Jeremiah.

On the 18th of November, a special conference convened at Pennydaren, presided over by Brother Briggs, who had been spending much of his time in the vicinity of Birmingham, having held nine public discussions at Birmingham, West Bromwich, Wednesbury, and Wolverhampton. There he found some of the old Saints who had not yet heard of the Reorganization and were now much interested to learn of the coming of Young Joseph.

A conference met at Pennydaren in Wales the day after Christmas, 1863, a little over a year since the appointment of the first missionaries to England. A number of elders and six branches reported. So great had grown the demands of the work that seventeen more elders and two priests were appointed to missions. Also the publication of a mission paper was provided for at this conference. Up to this time the restored gospel, under the banner of the Reorganization, had met with its greatest success in Wales. "I never experienced more disinterested kindness than I received from the Welsh and English Saints, whom it was my privilege to meet in Wales," says Charles Derry, who was constantly going from place to place preaching and teaching.

In Birmingham, Elder Derry visited Thomas Taylor, whom J. W. Briggs had previously seen but once. He records of him:

> On the 2d of March, Brother Charles Sheen went with me to see Mr. Thomas Taylor, in Birmingham, formerly a member of the church, but having been to Utah and finding there had been a great departure from the truth, he had returned to his native land, disgusted and discouraged. When he heard the truth as God had revealed it at the first, he acknowledged it with gladness. He treated me very kindly and aided me with means.

In March of 1864 the mission paper, appropriately named the *Restorer,* appeared, edited by Jason W. Briggs at Number 305 High Street, Pennydaren, Merthyr Tydfil, Wales. That all of the Saints might enjoy it, the paper was printed partly in Welsh and partly in English.

In the meantime, Charles Derry continued to call upon Thomas Taylor in Birmingham, whose interest he thought was constantly increasing. One George B. Follows wrote to him and came sixteen miles to see and hear him. He was baptized, ordained an elder, and sent into the mission field. James Wiltshire, whom Derry had recently baptized, was preaching in Gloucester. The conference at Pennydaren on May 15 showed a continued uptrend in missionary work, and the numerous workers were advised by the president of the conference, "The winter is past with its rain, cold, and sleet, and the weather is beautiful, and when we are denied all other places, Nature's temple is open, and upon some spare ground, on some highway, or beside some hedge, let us lift up our voices and call men to repentance, and those that 'have departed from the faith' to return to the law of God."[3]

Charles Derry closed his work in England and sailed from Liverpool to New York on board the "James Foster, junior," on June 21, 1864. Three days later J. T. Phillips, a new missionary, appointed to Wales by the General Conference, arrived.

The next conference, held at Pennydaren on July 24, took up the matter of the division of the English mission into districts, with proper district presidents in each case. The elders reported that in following the advice given in May to hold meetings outdoors a great increase in membership had resulted.

On August 11, 1864, another Welsh missionary, Thomas E. Jenkins, arrived from the States and published an address to the Saints in Welsh in the *Restorer*. On September 18, 1864, a branch was organized in Birmingham, over which none other than Wil-

---

[3]*The Restorer,* Volume 1, page 40; *Church History,* Volume 3, page 402.

liam O. Owen, Briggs's opponent in debate, now a member of the church, was chosen to preside. On October 6, Jason W. Briggs, accompanied by Elder E. Griffiths, sailed for New York.

Except for one interval from this time to the present, the English mission has always had one or more American missionaries and in addition has produced many able men from their own land, among them the Thomas Taylor mentioned in this early history, who with Charles H. Caton and Joseph Dewsnup, formed the first bishopric in Europe. The mission has also contributed some important representatives to the general church, notably John W. Rushton, F. Henry Edwards, and Arthur A. Oakman. The mission has been weakened materially by emigration to America, a fund having been created and maintained at one time for the purpose of transporting those who wished to come to this land. While the result has not contributed to the strength of the English and Welsh mission, it has helped the branches in the United States, hardly one of which has not benefited by the addition of members from Great Britain.

In 1869 George M. Rush opened the work in Scotland and continued there for two years, contending against much opposition and prejudice, but succeeding in building up a membership. The work in Scotland also suffered greatly from emigration.

In 1933 and 1934 under the direction of Apostle John W. Rushton, the gospel was preached in Ireland with success, but never followed up.

The influence of British Saints upon the church since 1840 until now has been tremendous. A list of persons descended from early and later English emigrants to the Zion in America who have affected the history of the church from its highest councils down, would probably run into the thousands. Perhaps that is too conservative a statement. With the renewed interest in missionary work now commencing, the future of this mission will possibly exceed the brightness of its past.

LIV.—The First Mission to the West

*T*HE GENERAL CONFERENCE OF 1863 at Amboy, Lee County, Illinois, originated another important mission of the church. Two men were sent to carry the message of the reorganization of the church with Young Joseph at its head, to their brethren in the West, notably Utah, Nevada, and California. The difficulties to be met were even greater than those faced in foreign fields.

The motion as it passed the conference read: "Moved, that E. C. Briggs and C. G. McIntosh prosecute a mission to Utah, Nevada Territory, and California."

On the 21st of April, with a promptness that was a credit to the earliest days of church missionary fervor, Edmund C. Briggs left the vicinity of Plano to "fulfill" his western mission. He expected three or four elders to accompany him and "co-operate with him in his mission."[1]

Evidently but one went, Alexander McCord. The western Iowa district aided liberally in outfitting the Utah missionaries who, with a team of mules and a light spring wagon, made the distance of eleven hundred miles to Salt Lake City. Briggs writes of the opening days of his mission in Utah:

> We arrived here on the 7th inst. [August, 1863]. We had a pleasant trip, though tedious and lonely, over the bleak and dry sandy plains. We came most of the way alone and without fear of danger, though reports of danger were all the time brought to us. At Fort Bridger we were required to take the oath of allegiance to the Government of the United States of America, which we willingly did, and on our arrival here we at once drove up to . . . Brigham Young's house. His clerks told me he was not at home. We then put up at the Mansion House, kept by Mr. Tuft and his mother, a widow, who treated us kindly, and on Tuesday, 11th inst., we had an interview

---

[1] *The True Latter Day Saints' Herald,* Volume 3, page 231.

with Brigham Young. . . . I at once introduced the subject of our presence, and under whose directions we came, and what we expected to accomplish by coming, and with all I bore testimony of the sure calling and true standing of President and Prophet Joseph Smith, the son of the Martyr. He said he knew more of that family *than they knew of themselves,* that Emma is a "wicked, wicked, wicked" woman and always was, that Joseph is acting under the influence of his mother, that she is at the bottom of this work, and our mission here, that the heavens have nothing to do with that family at the present, but they shall be felt after in time, but they are under the influence of the Devil now; that all Joseph wants is to associate with the murderers of his father, etc. He said, "I do not want any of your preaching here or your doctrine, and I will immediately write and advertise you and warn the people not to receive you or your doctrine into their houses, and while I have influence over the Bowery you can't hold meetings."

And then he threw out some intimations to us, and gave us to understand we should be watched, that he wanted us to be gentlemen, and other low insinuations. We then told him we had come to do good, and that we were not in the least daunted or fearful, though intimidations had been thrown out at us before since we arrived here by him and his adherents, etc. We then bid him good day, and since then all manner of stories are afloat against us. Every crime you can think of we are charged with, and I suppose some of the people believe them, but we console ourselves without noticing them enough to contradict them, with the blessed promises of our dear Saviour, who said, "Blessed are ye when men shall revile you, and persecute you, and shall say all manner of evil against you falsely for my sake."[2]

The first appointment for meeting in the territory was given out for Sunday, August 23, at the residence of Honorable Judge Waite, who opened his house to Brother Briggs's services whenever he wished to hold meetings. Most of his work, however, was done in house-to-house visiting among true friends in the territory, many of whom he found hated the prevailing evils of that place more than ever he could, never having experienced them.

Soon after, Alexander McCord went to Ogden, from whence he returned by the middle of October with the report that he had baptized three in Ogden, all members of the church in Joseph's

---

[2] *The True Latter Day Saints' Herald,* Volume 4, pages 89, 90.

time—John Taylor, who had joined the church in Missouri in 1831, his wife, and Stephen Maloney. In writing to the *Herald* on October 15, E. C. Briggs says:

> I can only say now, our prospects are glorious at present of doing a great work here in restoring this people back to God, from whom they have strayed in the dark and cloudy day, and to obedience to the laws of the land which they have so ingloriously denounced heretofore. I hear good news from all parts of the territory.
> We have baptized now about twenty in all, and many more are with us in faith. The Saints here feel to rejoice with unspeakable joy, inasmuch as the Lord has visited them again with the gifts of the gospel, and with that peace of mind or love that casteth out all fear.[3]

Five days later, on the 20th of October, in a long letter telling of his success there, Briggs wrote:

> I write to inform you that the work is prospering here, equal to any expectation I have ever had.[4]

One of those he had converted and rebaptized, George P. Dykes was sent on to California, where by the following spring over fifty-five people had been baptized and six branches formed: Sacramento, with Cornelius Bagnell as president; San Francisco, T. J. Andrews; Folsom, Jeremiah Thomas; Dry Creek, Thomas Phillips; and Watsonville, George Adams; while three missionaries were in the field. Dykes had gone to Nevada, leaving E. H. Webb and Henry H. Morgan, son of John H. Morgan of Lydney, England, to carry on in California.

When E. C. Briggs arrived in California by October 6, 1864, he found a thriving church of three hundred and fifty-seven members waiting for him. The semiannual conference convened on that date (the California Saints having a different conference because of their distance from headquarters), and in the names of elders reporting are found many who later became well known in the history of the church: E. C. Brand,

---

[3] *The True Latter Day Saints' Herald*, Volume 4, pages 123, 124.
[4] *Ibid.*, page 146.

T. J. Andrew, H. V. Moore, Joseph Outhouse, Jonathan Newman, Nathaniel Booth, —— Freeman, E. H. Webb, Harvey G. Whitlock, Glaud Rodger, H. H. Morgan, Cornelius Bagnell, W. H. Wilson, Hiram Falk, G. W. Oman, O. T. Davis, —— Wycoff Abednego Johns, William Potter, Henry Burgess, Aaron Garlick, George Adams, and George P. Dykes.

Many of these were members of the church in the days of Joseph and had come around Cape Horn in the good ship "Brooklyn," or had escaped from Utah and fled to California. During the summer, branches had been organized at Petaluma, Brighton, El Monte, San Bernardino, Alameda, and Stockton. Three seventies were ordained at this conference, Glaud Rodger, Abednego Johns, and H. H. Morgan. A branch was organized in Nevada. Work on the Pacific Slope was set to go forward.

The 12th of December came, and still "not a single hall, or commodious house" was to be procured in all Utah for the purpose of preaching the original doctrines of the church and advocating the succession of Joseph Smith III. Notwithstanding this undoubted drawback, Elder Briggs felt to rejoice over the "triumph of our glorious cause in this desert and salt land." Those who did open their homes to him were beginning to feel the cruel mandate of ostracism, or even drastic measures of excommunication. Eighteen, at least, had been "cut off" from the dominant church there, some for entertaining the missionaries, some for attending meetings, and some for merely reading the *Herald*. In spite of all such difficulties, says E. C. Briggs, "our glorious cause is onward with intense rapidity, despite these oppositions and curses."

At length, on January 26, 1864, the first branch composed of thirty-nine members was organized in Salt Lake City, to be called the Great Salt Lake City Branch. On April 6, the first conference convened, and Utah was divided into three districts, northern, central, and southern. The Salt Lake City Branch by this time numbered one hundred, Provo fifty-two, and Ogden thirty.

In time reinforcements arrived on July 21 in the persons of Daniel B. Harrington and C. G. McIntosh and wife. Alexander McCord started for the East on August 5. A vigorous campaign was begun against the so-called apostates. The property of the Saints was threatened, in many cases even destroyed, and the terrible experiences of the newly converted members then residing in Utah were so appalling that they might well be discredited were they not authenticated by unimpeachable testimony. Such was the feeling against them that they were no sooner baptized into the Reorganization than they began to plan to go either to the East or to California. Many times their previous experiences had already bred in them such hatred of the place that they could not endure the thought of remaining longer than was absolutely necessary. A large company of them, fearful to remain in Utah after the United States soldiers left, went with them under military protection. The result was that for many years the work was hindered in Utah by reason of the immediate migration of all newly baptized members.

These unfortunate conditions ceased to exist in Utah many years ago, and while the membership of the two factions still feel the aftermath of the bitter feelings of past years, and differences of doctrine exist which can probably never be bridged, a feeling of tolerance has grown upon both sides which should be cultivated insofar as is possible without compromise of the convictions of either.

The church has always maintained a mission in Utah, and although the success of early years, when the missionaries found a congregation almost ready made, has not been repeated, there has always been a substantial gain through the Utah Mission.

LV.—The Fight Against Polygamy

That otherwise good and religiously inclined men and women actually believed that God commanded obedience to the doctrine of polygamy seems to us quite incredible, and but few can be found today who will even attempt to defend this doctrine without an effort to minimize and excuse the practice. Such is the inevitable fate of any peculiar behaviorism after being tried in the crucible of public opinion.

But in 1860, and even after that date for some years, polygamy with all its unlovely implications was, as Joseph Smith once called it, " a depressing cloud on the horizon of the past" that had to be lifted before the missionaries of that day could go forth to preach the simple gospel truths as in the days of the first Joseph. The Reorganized Church folk might be ever so virtuous, but so far as public opinion went, a Latter Day Saint was a Mormon, and a Mormon was a polygamist, or if not actually one, he believed it was all right to have more than one wife.

A Latter Day Saint could not enter public life, he could not apply for a job, his children could not attend college or even ordinary grade school, without being marked. People did not admit lightly that they were Latter Day Saints. Such an admission took courage and a great deal of it. Looked at with horror by religious people, with distaste by people of culture, and as a subject for coarse and lewd jokes by the vulgar, the lot of a person who became a Latter Day Saint in 1860 was harder than one who dared to take the step in 1830. Moral courage is as rare as physical courage.

Then, too, there was always the danger of deception. Polygamy had been kept a secret in the West for many years. Who knew when the Reorganization would spring something new?

Therefore, the first affirmation the church had to make was, "We advocate good morals and good citizenship; polygamy is not and never has been a tenet of the church." When Joseph Smith came to the church, he said it had been revealed to him "what stand to take against the sin in the West," and he took that stand with those who loyally helped him, his two younger brothers and others. Whenever there was action taken in the world, in the State or in the Nation against this evil, the Reorganized Church was in the front of that fight, until the world finally came to know that there was a "nonpolygamous" group of Mormons. The church said that polygamy was wrong of itself, always had been and always would be, regardless of where and how it started and that it was never a part of the restored gospel. As for its origin, they kept an open mind. They asked for proof and took the privilege of examining what was submitted. Those who wished to fix the responsibility on Joseph Smith, or shift it from themselves, accepted and advocated this theory, especially Brigham Young and other principal men in the Utah Church who by 1852 had entered into polygamous alliances; but the evidences in support were considered wholly insufficient by many thousands of the members of the original church and by many honest inquirers after the facts, as well as the sons and descendants of Joseph Smith who, notwithstanding their desire to protect his reputation, were undoubtedly sufficiently courageous to face the facts. As the claim was made so many years after his death, and was not and is not supported by any undisputed act done or word spoken by him during his lifetime, the burden of proof, by all rules of evidence, has rested upon the proponents of the claim, and they have never proved their case. An eminent jurist, Federal Judge John F. Philips, reviewed the evidence presented by the polygamous Utah Mormon Church, in legal proceedings wherein the origin of the doctrine and practice of polygamy was a vital issue, and he held[1] that Brigham Young and not Joseph Smith was the author and instigator of that obnoxious and heretical doctrine.

The *Nauvoo Neighbor,* a weekly newspaper published during

---

[1] Reorganized Church *vs.* Church of Christ, *et al.,* 60 Fed. 937.

the later years of Joseph Smith, in its issue of June 19, 1844, published official minutes of meetings of the Nauvoo City Council when, sitting as a quasi-judicial body, that tribunal investigated the circumstances connected with the issuance of a scurrilous sheet called the *Nauvoo Expositor* in its only issue of June 7, 1844. Both Hyrum Smith and Joseph Smith gave their testimony and both denied and branded as a lie that a revelation had been received by the latter providing for polygamy. This document[2] can be seen at the City Library of New York, and it is highly important, as this testimony was given but a few days before these men were murdered by a mob. Young Joseph stated that as the years passed, his confidence in his father's innocence increased, and even since his death and as late as 1933, new evidence in rebuttal of the Utah claims has come to light.

If it was necessary to clear the church of the accusation of polygamy when our men went before the world, it was doubly necessary that those having once tasted of its bitter fruits be careful not to be caught in its snare again. It was necessary to convert those honest in heart, who had actually placed a confidence in it for there were such, strange as it now seems. True, the majority of the factions had a deep and abiding hatred of the doctrine, but in the largest of them all, belief in this nefarious practice had actually at times been made a test of fellowship, while isolated cases of plural wives were seen in two other groups.

To those outside the church and those within, the Reorganization declared in no uncertain terms the uncompromising stand they had taken, and pointed to the Book of Mormon and its plain declaration that polygamy was an abomination.

This doctrine was, Young Joseph had said, the only doctrine in any faction that he held "in utter abhorrence."[3] To men of refined sensibilities like the sons of Joseph Smith, the very lit-

---

[2]*Nauvoo Neighbor,* issue of June 18, 1844.
[3]Speech at Amboy, Illinois, April 6, 1860.

erature emanating from the West, crude, coarse, and repulsive as it was, involving their father as it sought to do, was a lifelong cause of sorrow and indignation.

The history of the doctrine has no place in the history of the church except as it affected the lives of the members; polygamy was never put forth as a belief of the church until announced by Brigham Young eight years after Joseph Smith's death. That it existed many years previous cannot be denied; nor does the candid student fail to admit that all abnormal behaviorisms in human society are a matter of evolution, but they realize that evolution may proceed from a comparatively harmless beginning. Given an age of speculation (religious speculation not confined to Latter Day Saints) and a gross materialistic leadership such as that of Brigham Young, the riddle is not difficult to solve.

Whatever its origin, the Reorganized Church has taken a firm position against it, upon which the attitude of Young Joseph himself may be taken as representative.

Having been asked by a friend:

"If it were proven conclusively to you that your father was a polygamist, what difference would that make in your position on polygamy?"
"None," was the answer. "Polygamy would still be everlastingly and eternally wrong. Should I ever become so convinced, it would merely mean one more sorrow that I must carry to the grave."

Hating the doctrine[4] as he did, believing as he did that those who implicated his father in it had marred his life, his mother's and his brothers', this new leader was constantly urging tolerance upon those who looked to him for counsel.

We are striving to secure a unity of belief among the one-time Latter Day Saints, our only intention towards them being for their good. To make this intention apparent to them is our duty, and to present the good in such form that they are attracted to it rather than repulsed from it is also our duty. Our relation to them, then, is one of friendship to the men composing them; though there may be and

---

[4] Joseph Smith (Young Joseph) had such a deep abhorrence of this particular doctrine that he confesses to have become physically sick at meeting at a dinner table with a Utah relative and his several wives.

ought to be no compromise upon our part with those measures of either or all of them that we believe to be erroneous or wicked.

The men composing these various organizations have been at one time, if they are not now, lovers of the principles of the gospel as taught by Christ; they were honest in the convictions which resulted in their obeying it, and they have taught the necessity of obedience to it as strenuously as do we. We in this respect stand upon common ground, and so far should meet as brothers. If they advocate and practice what is to our understanding wrong, we to them occupy a similar position, because we teach and practice what is to their understanding erroneous. With the three or four of them that are left, we are now at variance on points of doctrine; but that variance is rather upon matters of comparatively later origin and does not involve what all agree in calling the fundamental principles of the gospel of Christ, however that gospel may to us be affected by the teaching of those things to which we do not agree.

At present but one of these organizations, the one in Utah, outnumbers the Reorganization, and from all the indications seen now, the latter is rapidly increasing. . . . As a natural result, judging from past history, the increase of numbers, and the growing importance which the increase of numbers gives, there will be a strong tendency to become conservative; and arrogant conservatism is but another name for intolerance. Our labor should be to secure our relations with these factions from assuming the intolerant form.[5]

In the past this advice so far as applies to the question of polygamy in the West may at times have been forgotten; it may be forgotten again in the heat of controversy, but it cannot be denied that the wiser men of the Reorganization have striven from the first to take a tolerant, kindly attitude towards those who have held opposite views, even while, as the third Joseph has said: "We are and have been the acknowledged and avowed enemy to the doctrine of polygamy, and we are *called to preach* in opposition to it."

As the occasion for such preaching becomes less, no one rejoices more than the Reorganized Church. Polygamy is not a pleasant subject; our ministry turn with relief from it to the two great affirmative objectives of the church, the redemption of Zion and the evangelization of the world, beside which all else pales to insignificance.

---

[5] From a series of *Herald* editorials published 1871, 1872. Republished in *Church History,* Volume 3, page 679.

LVI.—Reinforcements

While the two major missions were progressing so satisfactorily, other missionaries pressed out into every place where they knew old Saints to be, bringing them the story of Young Joseph. Acceptance was general, though many still remained apart, disfellowshiping all religions.

W. W. Blair early visited Manti, Iowa, where he found a little band of Saints under Alpheus Cutler, many of whom joined with the Reorganization. Here he organized a branch of twenty-two, some who had been members in the days of Joseph the Martyr, and others who were new to the work of the restoration of the gospel. Wheeler Baldwin became branch president, and among those in the branch were the Redfields, Wilcoxes, and others. In a short time the branch increased to forty in number. Now and then in his journeys W. W. Blair met with those who were able to confirm his faith in the calling of Young Joseph to his place at the head of the church. This happened while he was visiting Mr. and Mrs. Reals in Manti, on the 12th of March, 1863. Their statement was:

> During a visit of Joseph Smith and family in June, 1839, at Mr. Anson Matthews', near Table Grove, McDonough County, Illinois, we heard him [Joseph] say that he sometimes thought his enemies would kill him. "And if they do," said he, *"this boy* [putting his hand on Young Joseph's head] will finish the work in *my place.*"[1]

Some of the Saints had joined none of the factions, but remained quietly in their places and waited. Among such were the Lamberts, Richard and Jane, of Rock Creek Township, Hancock County, Illinois. When Joseph Smith was killed they both were very young. Richard Lambert was but eighteen when he

---

[1] *Memoirs of W. W. Blair.*

came from England in 1840, and Jane, who came the next year, was only sixteen. A few years later they married, made a little home nine or ten miles southeast of Nauvoo, and brought up their twelve children unmolested by anyone. As early as 1860 John A. McIntosh brought them the message of the coming of Young Joseph, and one by one they accepted it. One of the sons, Joseph R., was baptized in Nauvoo by James Burgess. He was to become prominent later as a member of the Quorum of Twelve.

Sometime during these years, Thomas P. Green, a local doctor of Jeffersonville, Wayne County, Illinois, with his entire local organization united with the church.[2] Undisturbed by the preaching of any and all the leaders who sprang up after the death of Joseph Smith, he had gone on preaching the first principles of the gospel, listening to no new or strange doctrines. As years went by, he organized many new branches in his vicinity and even held twenty-one debates with other denominations. When he came into the Reorganization movement, he brought with him sixty-one members. At a conference in St. Louis, June 25 and 26, 1860, he related so eloquently his experiences through this time of waiting that the house was in tears.

In the summer of 1863 a young soldier just invalided home to Wisconsin from the War was baptized. This young man was Henry A. Stebbins. His uncle, Henry Pease, had been prominent in the beginning of the Reorganization in Wisconsin. Five years later Henry Stebbins began his life of service in the church. He was for many years church recorder, having care of the membership rolls of the church and at the same time keeping up his ministerial work to the very time of his death in 1920.

On the 28th of August, 1864, William W. Blair went from Cincinnati, Ohio, to Syracuse in the same state and began a series of very profitable meetings, preaching each evening and

---

[2]Now the Brush Creek Branch of Illinois, which some years ago celebrated its centennial.

visiting and holding prayer and social meetings during the days. Here he baptized David Griffiths and his wife, Martha Davis Griffiths, who had been first baptized during the ministry of the great Welsh proselytizer, Captain Dan Jones. They came to America in May, 1855, after David Griffiths had served for several years as a deacon in Merthyr Tydfil Branch in South Wales. They were not long in the United States before the birth of their son, Gomer T., on June 2, 1856, and during Blair's visit to Syracuse, he blessed this youngster at the same time that his parents were baptized. This little Welsh lad grew to manhood to take his place in the highest councils of the church, eventually serving for many years as president of the Quorum of Twelve Apostles.

In the spring of 1865, so many left Utah to return to the States that only "skeletons" of former branches remained. Elder Thomas Job, still resident in Utah was not discouraged; he went on preaching, and during the summer organized two more branches, one at Goshen and one at Spanish Fork. Among those baptized in Utah during the previous year was James Caffall, who had been a missionary in England almost from the date of his baptism (1845) until he came to America in 1850, settling in Saint Louis until 1861 and then migrating to Utah. He had not long been in Utah until he became doubtful of the preaching of the authorities in Salt Lake City. Becoming acquainted with the teachings of the church under Young Joseph, and finding there what seemed to him more of the spirit he had known in the church in his native land, he became a member and joined the emigration eastward in 1865. He also was destined to become a powerful representative of the church, going back to England some years later to revisit the scenes of his former ministry with what seemed to him a more glorious message.

The Civil War ended, and with its ending there came from Texas, by a long trip overland, one Andrew Huffman, of the old Texas colony. Harriet Wight, the widow of Lyman Wight, early in 1860 had heard that Young Joseph had come to the church, and she had written for particulars, but before any word could come, communication was cut off between these people and the North. Several of the sons of Lyman Wight and others of the old colony had donned the Confederate gray. Back in New York, unknown to them, their cousins wore the blue. The war cloud was real to these people. Just before the War, Spencer Smith and others had come north. There had been no communication between the two parts of the old colony, and a long life together where they had shared all things common made them a little more than brothers. Andrew Huffman, as soon as he could get through the lines, came to look for these brethren who had left Texas six years before and never since been heard of. He did not know where they were, but he remembered that just before the War he had heard that Young Joseph, whom he had often heard Lyman Wight say would lead the church, had come into his own. He went to Nauvoo.

There he heard that the remnants of the old colony had settled in western Iowa and were now members of the Reorganized Church. He hurried there, taking with him letters from Joseph, asking that Spencer Smith and Hugh Lytle accompany him back to Texas to preach to their friends and relatives there. By July he had reached the loved ones in western Iowa, and Spencer Smith's wife, Anna, wrote immediately:

Manteno, Shelby County, Iowa, July 9, 1864.

Oh, My Dear Mother and Relatives: After long years of trial and separation, how it thrills my heart with joy and satisfaction to have the unspeakable pleasure of addressing that dear name of mother and relatives so dear to me, and if it were possible, rendered doubly dear by affiliation and separation. I will not attempt to tell you of the many feelings of anguish and how much I have suffered on your account. . . . Spencer is thinking of accompanying Andrew home.[3]

---

[3]Original letter Heman C. Smith collection.

Then followed an account of deaths in the family in New York, of three young cousins lost in the War, and another "very near starved to death in Libby Prison." A postscript added on the 12th of July, says:

> Spencer is all ready to start for your place in the morning. I hope he will do much good among my relatives. The man who is going with him (Hugh Lytle) is a very good man. He blessed my babe.[4]

Going by way of Nauvoo, they arrived in the familiar old town of Bandera, Texas, on August 14, 1865, but immediately upon arrival, both Spencer Smith and Andrew Huffman were prostrate with fever. Hugh Lytle began preaching alone on Sunday, August 20. He preached twice every Sunday and on every Wednesday night. On the 27th he baptized seventeen, and on the following Sunday, fifteen more. Some were received upon their original baptism, and before a month had passed a branch was organized with thirty-eight members, twenty-two of whom had belonged to the old organization and come to Texas with Lyman Wight.

Between the date he left home and the next 28th of January, Spencer Smith had been able to get but few letters to his family, and had received fewer from them. His wife reported with pleasure that what letters she had received had arrived promptly "within four to six weeks after date." Hers were often four months in reaching him, and many of them he never received.

With his companion, Hugh Lytle, conditions at home had been still sadder, for Anna Smith writes on August 23, 1865:

> I suppose that ere this reaches you Brother Lytle will be informed of the departure of his companion to the spirit land. Oh, comfort him as much as you can! For it must be a dreadful blow to him, but he will have the consolation of knowing that he is in the pathway of duty and on the Lord's errand.[5]

Truly our pioneer fathers were made of stern stuff.

---

[4]Original letter Heman C. Smith collection.
[5]*Ibid.*

Early in 1866, Hugh Lytle returned to Iowa, having baptized forty-one in Texas. Later in the year, Spencer Smith returned home, camping hopefully in the vicinity of Linn's Mill, three miles from Medoc, Missouri. He expected to find old friends, for on the way north they had spent one winter in Jasper County, Missouri, and he had taken charge of Linn's Mill on Spring River, five miles below Carthage, but he was disappointed to find all his friends had moved away or been killed in the War. Smith had always liked that country and thought could he but have had spiritual privileges there, he would be sorry he had moved on to Iowa.

He had been from home a year. Conditions had changed greatly. "The Pacific Railroad is finished through here, and the cars are running eight miles from here. The country used to be overstocked with grain and provisions. Wheat used to sell for from forty cents to fifty cents per basket. It now sells for a dollar and a quarter, and other things in proportion," he wrote.

And so by magic of modern transportation, western Iowa, one of the strongholds of the church, moved several days closer to headquarters and was no longer a pioneer community.

The progress in the general church was onward. One notable event was the choosing of William Marks as first counselor to the young President in 1863. Joseph had always found wisdom in counsel with Brother Marks, and the aged counselor now began to realize the truth of the promise made years before that he would be a blessing to many people.[6]

As from all directions men flocked to his standard, Joseph Smith, with rare tact, constantly urging temperance, tolerance, and long-suffering, made of them a united priesthood. There were difficulties, but they were few considering the situation from whence they were being slowly extricated. Of these men he gave a wonderfully correct characterization when he said:

---

[6] See Chapter XLIV.

The men of the present are, a great many of them, men who were pioneers in the work in the early days of its commencement; some are the children of those who have fought the good fight of faith and have lain down to rest from their warfare, while some are those who have believed our report and have become identified with the work during the days of the Reorganization. These men have, many of them, suffered grievously for the sake of the cause of the Master and are not yet done with their willingness to sacrifice for the same cause; and all are men who desire the advancement of the cause in truth and righteousness. Their purpose is not to suffer defeat if they can prevent it by honorable means. They regard the men of the past as brothers, and they feel that they have the right to examine the records left for their use and direction and exercise their own right of decision upon them. To inquire into the measures of their predecessors and to decide for the interests of the church, according to the light afforded by the history of the past, the light of the present and their prescience of the future, these men of the present believe to be their duty.

They are, as a class, fearless and free in their discussion of every question with which they have to deal, and there are men of marked piety and ability among the number, able and willing to defend the principles of the faith and doctrines of the church, as left us by the first elders and as found in the books, but unwilling to defend any in wrongdoing. For that reason they do not propose to defend what they feel assured was wrong in the past. They are willing to stand for the right, but will not exonerate the evil doer; he must abide the consequences of his evil doing, let him be whom he may. They are earnest and mean to redeem the character of the church from opprobrium, so far as their lives and influence can do so. . . .

That all the men of the Reorganization are not of the character above described is but natural. Coming out of all the factions, and being gathered up from the various cities, towns, and hamlets where they had waited the passing away of the "cloudy and dark days," it is but reasonable to suppose that there should be men of every possible shade of religious belief that could have obtained during those disastrous years in which righteousness seemed to have been forgotten among the children of Zion. These men, uniting with a common object in view, needed intercourse, long and trying intercourse with each other, in order that an assimilation should be possible. Bravely has this work of assimilation gone on, and well and bravely have the men of the present borne the test required.

Sometimes the people were too anxious to "gather"; he held them back. "Slowly, slowly, they stumble who run fast," he counseled them, continuing patiently on, striving to teach by precept and example that before a people can build the city beautiful they must learn to live together in peace and harmony.

We must be true men, true in all the walks of life, making better citizens, better sons, better husbands, better fathers, better daughters, better wives, better mothers, better men, better women, better Saints.

We must build our houses solidly, to stand for more than a day; we must build our fences, to secure good neighbors; we must strive for the best roads, best bridges, best wells and springs, best towns, best everything of public utility and benefit; doing all our work with a view to its stability.

Our spiritual labor must be of like permanent character. We must preach the principles of life and enforce them by our example. We must carry the news to the ends of the earth, and we must be glad in it ourselves. We must be faithful, sober, upright, and intelligent, and so shall we gain the desired end—happiness here, eternal life hereafter.[7]

Thus he endeavored to impress upon his people that, important as the building of the city of Zion might be, more important than all else was the building of a people to live there.

---

[7] From a series of editorials in *Saints' Herald,* called "The Situation," published in the latter part of 1871 and the early part of 1872; republished in *Church History,* Volume 3, chapter 34, page 686; *The True Latter Day Saints' Herald,* Volume 19, pages 85, 86.

LVII.—Plano Days

For many years, the work of the church centered in the little village of Plano on the Fox River, in Kendall County, Illinois. Here the *Herald*, after it was moved from Cincinnati, was published under the active supervision and editorship of Joseph Smith, the President of the church. From the church press in Plano were issued other books and tracts dear to the hearts of the Saints, who were eager for literature in relation to Young Joseph and the rapid spread of the church.

About the year 1865, a young war widow came to reside in Plano with Elijah Banta and his wife of Sandwich, Illinois. She was born in Ohio, and had followed the fortunes of the church with her parents and large family of brothers and sisters through the Missouri days and those at Nauvoo. She was just old enough when she left Nauvoo to know that Mormonism had marked her family with a great tragedy, which nothing, it seemed, might ever efface. She had resolved never again to have anything to do with it.

Educated women were uncommon in the days of Marietta Hodges (later, and better known as Marietta Walker). She had been from childhood engaged in school work, first as a student in the boarding school for girls kept by a Mrs. Avis in Saint Louis, then in 1859 a student and graduate of Oxford College for Women at Oxford, Ohio. Later having been called to Texas to take charge of a sister's motherless children (one of whom was Lucy Lyons, later Resseguie), she presided over Westmoreland College in San Antonio, Texas.

She was married on the eve of the War to a young southern soldier, Robert Faulconer, and in the second year of the War his death left her with a fatherless baby daughter, Lucy. As soon as she could get through the lines after the War, she found a haven in the home of her sister, Mrs. Banta, who had joined the Reorganization. She resolved anew to have nothing to do with the church, but at length, having met Joseph Smith, whom she had known when they were both children in Nauvoo, her prejudices were eventually overcome, and she threw herself unreservedly into the work of the church, becoming as time went on probably the most outstanding woman of the Reorganization. To her Joseph Smith wrote on her seventy-seventh birthday:

> The secret of much of the attraction which drew me to the home of Elder Banta was this: As the Savior at the house of Lazarus found Mary and Martha and there spent hours of relaxation, it is no disparagement to the example set by him, that I, striving to follow in the precepts that he had given, confess here and now that at Brother Banta's I found a Lazarus, a Mary, and a Martha, and I owe much of my usefulness, not only that year, but afterwards, to the feasts of intellectual conversations and bright interchange of thought upon intellectual matters that I found with the Mary of the household. The result of these conversations in general are with me still. I acknowledge my indebtedness here to you, that while I enjoyed the splendid hospitality of Brother Banta and his companion, I valued the comfort of the chats upon gospel work and intellectual affairs with yourself and your mother.[1]

The small band of willing missionaries were pushing their way into every community where they knew old Saints to have lived. Canada was now a fertile field for missionary efforts, and as soon as the war cloud lifted, the first missionaries went into the Southern States. Perhaps the first missionaries to the Southeast were W. A. Litz and Calvin A. Beebe, who wrote jointly from Cokerville, Monroe County, Alabama, on March 7, 1866, to say:

> On our arrival here January 6 we were well received, and doors were opened to us to preach almost in every house. Our meetings were well attended and the best of order preserved. In fact, we can never speak in too high terms of praise of the people we have found

---

[1] *Zion's Hope*, Volume 43, page 105.

here. In the two months we have been here, we have, by the blessing of God, baptized twenty-five, who are rejoicing in the truth of God, and many more are believing who will, we suppose, obey soon. We expect on tomorrow to organize a branch here and to baptize some more.

The following day four more were baptized, and a branch called the Lone Star Branch was formed. In the meantime Levi Graybill and Benjamin Ballowe had opened the work in Tennessee.

The first two missionaries soon extended their work to Georgia and Florida.

Late in the same year, after a visit home, W. A. Litz and W. L. Booker left Nebraska City in November and were joined on the way by Thomas Waddell of Saint Louis. Brother Waddell, who was well liked by the southern Saints, succeeded in baptizing a number of converts in Alabama and Florida, and wrote home at times, reporting wonderful progress. Between May and August of the year 1866, he baptized seventy and organized two branches. He wrote: "I am happy to know that the Lord has blessed my labors wheresoever I have been." That was his last letter to the *Herald*. On the 30th of September he took ill with typhoid fever, from which he never recovered. At the home of W. W. Squires he died, the first missionary of the Reorganized Church to die at his post in the mission field. Those who had loved him laid him to rest under the tall southern pines, a few miles above Milton, Florida, on a bluff overlooking the east side of Black Water Bay. Years later another missionary replaced the decayed headboard with a cedar slab, upon which he carved an inscription, noting name and date of death.

While the new missionaries carried on so joyously, an old veteran of the faith was laid to his rest in Ogden Cemetery. That old-time missionary was none other than Thomas B. Marsh, president of the first Quorum of Twelve, who died in January, 1866. Elder Thomas Job, then a missionary in Utah, wrote that T. B. Marsh was at the Reorganized Church conference in Salt Lake City and bore a strong testimony to the truth and necessity of the Reorganization. And when a revelation from Young Joseph was read to him, he said it was the voice of God and again testified that he knew it. He desired the missionaries to write to Young Joseph, asking that he send and bring him back from there. He vowed that he had faith that he could bear the journey and join the young Prophet.[2] But before his wish could be granted he was called to his long home.

Through all the years since the revision of the Scriptures had been finished by Joseph Smith the first Prophet it had been carefully guarded by his wife, Emma Smith. The church had long looked forward to its publication, and April 10, 1866, a motion was passed in the General Conference at Plano, that "the church publish the New Translation immediately."

On the second day of May, following this conference, William Marks, W. W. Blair, and Israel Rogers went to Nauvoo to procure the manuscript for what was then, rather erroneously, called the "New Translation." Emma Smith firmly refused any payment for her careful watch care over the manuscript through the years, saying if she received a copy of the book, she would consider herself amply repaid. If, she told them, she had wished to *sell* the book, she could have done so years ago and for a substantial price. During the twelve months following, every effort was made to make a perfect copy for publication from the manuscript and the old Bible[3] from which the revision was made.

The church was poor and had not the funds for this work, which was really a large task for so small a group, but a plan

---

[2] *The True Latter Day Saints' Herald*, Volume 9, page 139.
[3] This Bible was in the possession of Vida Smith Yates, Independence, Missouri, and was a gift to her from her father, Alexander H. Smith, who received it from his mother, but since this book was written it has been given by Mrs. Yates to her cousin, Israel Alexander Smith, her father's namesake. I. A. Smith, a son of "Young" Joseph and a grandson of the Prophet, was President of the Church from 1946 to 1958.

was formulated whereby all of the presidents of branches and districts were authorized to solicit subscriptions for publishing the New Translation (in reality a revision), and each person who made a donation was to receive one of the books at cost. While the money was being collected, the copy was being prepared. By a year from the following autumn the book was ready to be stereotyped, and W. W. Blair and Ebenezer Robinson (the same Robinson identified with the early printing concerns of the church) were looking after the work in Philadelphia. At the same time, they were preaching to those who had once been identified with Sidney Rigdon and succeeded in baptizing ten while they stayed there. The last *Herald* of 1867 brought to the waiting Saints the glad news that the first five hundred of the first edition of five thousand copies of the "Inspired Translation of the Holy Scriptures" had been received and were ready for mailing.

One student of the Scriptures once jocularly remarked, "I don't know what right Joseph Smith had to change the Bible, but he certainly improved it." Another more earnest critic says:

> This much, at least, may be said of many of the changed readings found in the Bible of the Reorganized Latter Day Saints: Its author had the courage deliberately to alter the text and make it say clearly what many Bible students succeed in getting by theological legerdemain. This Bible contains the usual thirty-nine books of the Old Testament, and the usual twenty-seven of the New. No apocryphal books are admitted, but the Book of Mormon is accepted as inspired equally with other books of the Bible.[4]

During these formative years, the question of tithing had to be approached very gently. Some believed in it, but many having seen its abuse in other factions were opposed so strongly to its teaching that they would almost have left the church rather than have seen it enforced. They had seen such abuses as one tenth of the meager city relief given to poor widows in England taken from them, and to those people the safest way out of the

---

[4] P. M. Simms in *The Bible From the Beginning*, pages 145-147. Mr. Simms failed to observe that the "Song of Solomon" is omitted from the Old Testament in the Inspired Version.

difficulty was just to say nothing at all about tithing. But as time went by and confidence was restored, the financial affairs of the church were put on a sounder basis.

Then in 1870, Israel L. Rogers, the church's first Bishop, offered to give the church all that it owed him, $4,097.26, placing it on the books as his tithing, and offering as a pledge of his faith in the financial law to pay tithing annually from then on. The interpretation of the Reorganized Church in 1867, *viz.*, that the law first requires one tenth of one's net worth and then one tenth of the annual increase, has been the interpretation of the church from that time on, though many have preferred to tithe their entire income. Tithing has been voluntarily contributed from the first, but as prejudices have died down and confidence increased, the custom in the church has come more and more into favor, until few today think of questioning the scriptural method of financing the Lord's work.

The priesthood was fast assuming more orderly formation, and in 1870 a resolution was passed "that the presidents of the seventies be requested to inquire into the conditions of the seventies," and steps were taken to organize into quorums. Joseph Smith, in editorials in the *Herald,* defined in detail the duties of the Twelve and the Seventy, and with inspiring words rallied them to a sense of the importance of their mission.

> Purse and scrip are laid aside. It is the Lord's work. He has promised to provide for them. Self-denial is to become a pleasure, danger is forgotten, fear overcome and cast out; revilings accepted with humility, and scoffings without reproach; the goods of this world measured only by their usefulness to the advance of truth; wisdom taken as a companion—a lovely handmaiden of the Lord; and with the blue dome as their rooftree, the Lord their refuge in sunshine and in storm; his hand their guard, his Spirit their comfort and their guide; Christ their pattern, his followers their brethren, and all the world their neighbors, they pass out, away from the scenes dear to them into the great harvest field, there to wield the sword of truth as ambassadors for Christ, and him crucified.[5]

---

[5] *The True Latter Day Saints' Herald,* Volume 9, page 130.

Nor was that picture of the old-time missionary overdrawn. Constantly encouraged to make their work of that pattern, they honored their calling and held it sacred. Joseph Smith early outlined in minute detail the manner of serving communion, administering to the sick, and other rites and ceremonies of the church, and with one accord his directions were followed, making much for unity. Throughout his long service as President of the church, no dissension rose over these parts of the service, although its membership came from so many different "factions." Thus his time and that of the officers of the church could be given to other more weighty things. And so it happened as time passed that he who had taken the lead of a suspicious, divided priesthood came to the place where Brother Joseph's opinion on most matters almost had the weight of law, and the customs established during those years still reign in the hearts of those who lived and walked with him. Truly, "he being dead yet speaketh."

Plano continued to be the headquarters of the church for many years. A little stone church had been built there in the summer of 1868, dedicated November 15 of that same year, and a branch gathered there, but the authorities of the church still looked forward to some sort of colonization. Not in Independence —not yet—but a preparatory gathering somewhere in "regions round about."

In 1860 the church numbered, all told, less than five hundred. In eight years' time the number had grown to more than ten thousand.

Without any organized capital, the church had printed and sold or given away some ten thousand volumes of three- to five-hundred pages each, besides stereotyping and printing five thousand copies of the Inspired Translation, and many tracts and papers.

On May 1, 1869, appeared the first issue of the *Herald*

printed on the church's own fine new Taylor Cylinder Power Press, operated by steam. The church was justly proud of that new acquisition. In July, a child's paper appeared, sponsored largely by Marietta Faulconer, later Mrs. S. F. Walker. The name, appropriately, was *Zion's Hope*. Although changed in form, it is still issued by the Herald press.

In January, 1888, the first issue of a new monthly magazine, *Autumn Leaves*, for young people appeared for the first time. Marietta Walker was editor. This magazine continued under the same name until the name was changed to "Vision" with the issue of January, 1929. The magazine was discontinued with the issue of August, 1932, another victim of the depression.

The years bringing achievement brought their inevitable sorrows. One by one the faithful old soldiers who had carried on through the years fell from the ranks in death: William Marks, Josiah Butterfield, Samuel Powers, James Blakeslee. And the faithful old missionary, Zenas H. Gurley, who had been so prominent in bringing about the Reorganization of the church, died at his post in the mission field, dying as he had lived, in the work he loved best.

LVIII.—Switzerland and Germany

ONE OF THE FIRST TO BE baptized in the Utah mission was Frederick Ursenbach, a Swiss brother who had come to Utah with a considerable amount of money, expecting to spend his fortune and himself in the interests of the church. He was disappointed, and at his earliest opportunity united with the Reorganization and was ordained a high priest at the first conference of the church in Utah, April 6, 1864.

This decision made Ursenbach unpopular in Utah, and the earning of a living there became impossible. All his life he had earned a comfortable livelihood as an expert buyer of fine wines. Necessity obliged him to return to Southern Europe and his life-long occupation, which he felt so incompatible with his office in the church that he could not officiate as a missionary, but in 1868, he urged the church to send a missionary to Switzerland, where he had found a number of old Latter Day Saints, anxious to return to the old faith. At his own expense he had translated and printed a little tract called *The Gospel,* which he distributed freely.

But four years passed before a man was found for the mission. At the April conference of 1872, John Avondet, an old Latter Day Saint, and a native of Pinerolo, Italy, was selected. He spoke German well enough to carry on the work in Switzerland. Brother Avondet sailed from New York City for Liverpool on the "City of Limerick," arriving in Switzerland on the 24th of the same month and proceeded at once to look up the old "Mormons," but they would have nothing of him, claiming they had been so badly deceived in the past that they would not be caught in the snare again. He gave out an appointment but only strangers came. Even the visit to his own parents, brother-in-law, nieces, and nephews was a disappointment. They treated him kindly but wanted nothing to do with religion.

He wrote to Brother Ursenbach in Lausanne, who at once came and spent two days with him, "the first real happiness" he had enjoyed on his mission, said Avondet. On leaving, Ursenbach left one hundred francs (about twenty dollars) with the missionary to help carry on the work. As he was "without purse or scrip" and much in need of money, the help was appreciated.

Avondet soon left Switzerland for his native land, and during the winter of 1872-73 worked in his mother's vineyard at Prarostino, Pinerolo, Italy. He wrote to the church that he had not called for any financial help of the church as he "saw it was not necessary" since he could earn his living working in the vineyard daytimes, and preach the gospel evenings and Sundays. That summer he baptized the first fruits of his mission to his native land, two sisters by the name of Gardiol. The mission was a difficult one. He found many dissatisfied old members of the church, but they were afraid of another deception, and had all returned to the church of Waldenses.

In the meantime a Swiss brother by the name of John L. Bear appeared at the fall conference of 1872 at Council Bluffs and volunteered for the Swiss mission, and was appointed. Brother Bear was well educated in the German tongue, a good and fluent writer in a German script that looked like copper plate. He had left Switzerland for Utah thirteen years before, become dissatisfied there, and joined the movement dissenting from the dominant church there under the leadership of Joseph Morris. In the Morrisite massacre, his young wife and infant child had been murdered, and he left the state with the United States Army, under General Connors, when he established the military post at Soda Springs, Idaho. The soldiers whose sympathy was stirred by the conditions of the Morrisites took as many of these unfortunate people with them as wished to go, laid out a little city in the wilderness, and gave each his own plot of ground. Soon the place became an important outfitting post for caravans west and the exiles prospered. Bear married again, and built up another home. The colony held church and Sunday school regularly and preached the Morris revelations with other church doctrine.

For some years they had heard rumors of a new organization of the church called Josephites, and one day in the spring of 1868, a neighbor told Bear there were some of this peculiar kind of Latter Day Saints, converted in Utah, but making their way eastward, camped on the road above Soda Springs. Bear wondered if he knew any of them, and overcome with a sudden nostalgia for old friends, he walked up the road and was happy to see Albert Bishop and family whom he had met in New York in 1860, when all were on their way to the "promised land," also William Summerfield, William Woodhead, and several others. Bear asked for some tracts, but a careful search by everyone of their luggage failed to find a single one. Then someone brought out an old *Herald* published by Sheen in Cincinnati. Some of the brethren came down and preached that night in the Morris camp, and Bear, having read the *Herald* promptly, liked it and sent a subscription in for it. The next year Edmund C. Brand and Lars Edler came to Soda Springs, and on November 29, 1869, Bear was baptized, confirmed, and ordained an elder. Bear was devoted to his new-found faith. He wrote in laborious long hand a tract setting forth the mistakes of Morris and inviting his Swiss friends into the Reorganized Church, making a copy for each family. Many came into the church.

He now lived on a farm near Agency City, Missouri, and he and his wife Barbara Dielhelm, read in the *Herald* of the need of a missionary to Switzerland, and though they were very poor, both felt that here at last was something they could do for the church, and therefore, Bear volunteered for service. It was January before sufficient money could be procured to send him on his way. At last the Bishop wrote him to come on. With what little money he had he bought a cheap satchel and a rough, blue jacket, as he had neither coat nor overcoat. Thus equipped he was about to set out on foot, when, as he was bidding good-by to his wife and four little ones, Barbara, his wife, handed him sixty-five cents that she had saved for just this occasion. That was all she had. He refused to take it, protesting, "What will you do without a single cent?" She insisted, he still refused, and she began to weep, begging him to take it, she had saved it especially for him. Reluctantly, he took it and started for Plano. Joseph Smith kept him over the week end, and insisted that he preach—a happy occasion. In Sandwich a poor widow gave him a dollar, and Brother Rogers took him to Chicago and bought him a third-class ticket which provided him with steerage accommodations, a hard berth with a straw "tick." He had to part with his dollar to secure the loan of a straw pillow and a blanket till he got to Liverpool. Thus auspiciously began the mission of our second Swiss missionary. After a rough passage on the "Atlantic" of the White Star Line, Bear arrived in his native land.

The old Saints there knew and trusted him, and he found in Zurich more invitations to preach than he could fill. All spring he preached in private houses, and on April 13 baptized the first members of the Reorganized Church in Switzerland, one of Bear's brothers and a nephew. He longed for tracts in the German language but had not the money to have them printed. One *Voice of Warning* of his own, an old edition in German, he loaned over and over again, until it was practically worn out. Some wished to buy it, but he could not let it go.

Laboriously he translated into German *The Truth Made Manifest* and some four tracts against polygamy for circulation among the Utah people. He loaned them in manuscript form. If one was lost, he had all the toil of translating it over again. Thus the first missionaries to Switzerland and Italy worked patiently and baptized now and then their hard-earned converts. In those early days in Switzerland, John L. Bear lived a life of sacrifice and came back to the States to live and die a poor man. He sustained himself when his funds were exhausted by his own labor, and his greatest misfortune while there was the time when he engaged to thresh wheat from 4 a. m. to 9 p. m. at night for the sum of one franc (about eighteen cents) a day, and being long unaccustomed to the use of a threshing flail his arm became so lame "he could not write a word, for a whole week." In order to supply tracts for the mission, he knew he must not lose a single moment from his translating and copying. He had a good education and knew he translated them correctly, and was a good and fast writer, but the matter of supplying postage to send his tracts to investigators at a distance was a real difficulty. The impossibility of securing money for this purpose he felt hampered him a great deal.

During all this time he and Avondet wrote often to each other and longed to meet. At last on February 15, 1874, this wish was gratified, and they met in Geneva, Switzerland, and held earnest counsel over the condition of the mission. Both were now financially at the end of their resources. They wrote a joint letter to the church, asking to be supported in their mission or recalled.

> We are satisfied that the church can be built up here; that many will embrace it, when we can spend our time in spreading the truth; if the church cannot sustain us immediately, then we are not able to stand any longer, and ask to be released, which would give us pain indeed to give up our mission when the Spirit testifies unto us that a great work can be done here; but we are in this position now, that we can see no way for us, if the church does not take immediate action in our behalf and the work of God in these countries. We also concluded that if the church in America would help us, we would like to travel together, if you give your consent to it; we think we could do

more good in going together than single. . . . When the work is started, then the mission will supply itself.

This communication found the church in the United States partaking of one of those periods of national economic depression that are part of its history. The men were recalled, and given a vote of thanks for their work.

With mingled sadness at leaving the mission, and joy at the thought of coming home, they made preparations for leaving the little group of Saints in Zurich. A newly baptized man, an old Latter Day Saint by the name of Taylor, a man who could speak both French and German was placed in charge of the newly organized branch of sixteen. Tearfully they bade farewell to the few Saints and started for England, where after six weeks' delay, money came for their passage, and they embarked on the "Ohio" of the Red Star Line on the 9th of December, 1874. After a terrible passage on which the "Ohio" lost several of her lifeboats in a storm, they arrived at Philadelphia on the 22nd. At St. Louis the brethren parted, Elder Avondet arriving home on Christmas Day, Brother Bear three days later.

The latter walked ten miles from St. Joseph to his farm, arriving at 8 o'clock in the morning of December 28. He found his family in straitened circumstances; nothing to eat but a little bread and potatoes enough for one meal which his wife had saved for months ahead to have for him at his coming. His cattle and horses were so thin he could hardly drive them to the creek for water, for a drought the previous summer had taken their entire crop. The Bishop, shocked at seeing him so thinly clad in midwinter, had given Brother Bear some money, telling him to buy himself some warm clothing. With this he paid the bill his family had at the mill, and purchased flour and oats. In a day or two he was cutting cord wood in an attempt to recoup his fortunes.

Conditions gradually improved, and at length they were renting a larger and more desirable farm and prospects were brighter. Only one cloud dimmed the horizon; the Saints he had left behind in Switzerland were constantly importuning him to return. Then on November 7, 1878, his faithful wife died, and with her last breath said, "The Lord will take care of these children; you go and preach the gospel." German and Swiss friends urged him to go once more to Switzerland and Germany, but he could not make up his mind.

The letters from his far-away homeland had a strong appeal as they told of their isolation and longing to hear the gospel again: "With great longing we looked for your letter, which was delayed so long we soon would have believed that we were forsaken of the whole world and forgotten; yet thy good father heart beats in the far distant land for us, thy children, who are here alone. . . . May God give unto us the joy to see thee once more in our midst, to instruct us and build us up." And then the words of his wife on her deathbed would come to him. At last he concluded to put the whole matter up to the President of the church and the Bishop. They much desired him to go, and that settled the question with him. He began to look about for homes for his children.

Homes were offered at once to the two oldest girls and two oldest boys, but two remained, Mary, four years old, and Lillie, two. Too young they were to be of much help to anyone, and small enough to be a care. At last Sister Hartman Nesser, a poor woman with children of her own, but interested in the Swiss mission, came from Stewartsville and offered to take the baby. The Bishop was willing to pay $25 annually for the care of the child. No satisfactory place offered for the four-year-old, and he wanted to take her with him. He felt that if he did not the child would be abused and asked to work beyond her strength, but he was overruled by others, and regretted throughout the time of his mission that he had not followed the dictates of his own conscience and taken the little one with him.

How different this time was his trip to the old country! He was permitted to travel second class, for financial conditions were improving with the church, and a family of Saints in New York entertained him until time to board the vessel. Joseph Squires and his family and another family of Saints in Brooklyn saw that he was supplied with every comfort for the journey, and Brother Squires took him to the pier when he sailed April 24, 1880, on the "Devonia" of the Cunard Line. In a short time he was preaching and baptizing again in his native land. This time he was better supported by Saints at home, at one time receiving $17 from a Brother Bierlein in the United States. He carefully invested the money in having a tract printed *The Church of Jesus Christ in the Days of the Apostles* and the *Present Churches, Their Doctrine and Authority*. In one page at the end he summed up the difference between the Utah Church and the Reorganization, and on another the Epitome of Faith, making fifty-three pages in all. The five hundred copies cost him $20, and one of the first of the pamphlets brought to him a candidate for baptism, John Bossard, whom he baptized in the River Rhine.

In the spring of 1882 he left Switzerland again for the States.

Never again did he return to the little group he had baptized in Switzerland, although he did much work among the German and Swiss Saints in the United States. Intermittent missionary work has been carried on in Switzerland since the mission was opened, with a faithful few local men carrying on the work when help from the main church was unavailable.

Strangely enough the work in Germany had its beginning on the faraway continent of Australia, when Cornelius A. Butterworth baptized a fine German brother by the name of Max Kippe in Hastings, Victoria, in the year 1895. Immediately as a labor of love for his family in Germany, who understood only German, Max Kippe translated the Doctrine and Covenants for his brother

SWITZERLAND AND GERMANY

Alexander, and he was by his brother's efforts converted[1] although not baptized until 1906 when missionaries from the States, J. A. Becker and C. C. Joehnk, were appointed to Germany and Switzerland. C. C. Joehnk then baptized Alexander Kippe and his wife into the church. Alexander Kippe besides years of splendid leadership in Germany contributed to the church a translation of the Book of Mormon into German. German-born missionary talent was soon available to the church, Alexander Kippe, Carl Greene, Johan Smolney and others. Despite wartime conditions and restrictions, the work in Germany has prospered, and the Saints there have been blessed and protected, and there exists in that war-torn land a base for extensive missionary development.

---

[1] See *Herald*, Volume 93, page 744, "Australia—Historic Hastings Branch a Link With Alexander Kippe," by Herald G. McGurk.

LIX.—Pioneering for the Gospel in the West

The Conference of 1866 had appointed Alexander H. Smith to take charge of the California mission, with power to choose his associates. He chose William Anderson and William H. Kelley, but for some reason William H. Kelley did not go. Leaving Nauvoo on foot on the twentieth of May, 1866 for this mission, Alexander Smith bade farewell to his family and started westward with exactly a quarter of a dollar in his pocket. The Mississippi rolled almost in front of his door. He knew very well that it would cost him twenty-five cents to cross that river, therefore he had compromised with the scriptural provision by retaining just twenty-five cents for boat fare, but as he walked along the street he began to think about it and decided that his faith was small and that he must at least start in the right way. He went back to the old Mansion House and gave the quarter to his wife and went on his way with a lighter heart. On the way down the street he met an acquaintance, and when Alexander told him he was going to California, the friend immediately offered to ferry him across the river, as he had a skiff!

James W. Gillen accompanied the two missionaries as far as Utah, and Charles Derry went with them to Columbus, Nebraska, where all four preached for awhile. The Bishop had done his best, but when Henry J. Hudson of Columbus saw the outfit and the team, he said in his characteristic way to Alexander, "What! Are you going to cross the plains with those *rats?*" There were fifteen members of the church in Columbus, and among them they raised sixty dollars and purchased a strong team of mules. Then, finding the two missionaries still short of comforts, two buffalo robes at a cost of twenty dollars each, and many other supplies were added to the outfit, until they had spent a hundred and twenty dollars. And those fifteen Saints were not rich except in faith and kindness of heart!

When all was ready, Brothers Derry, Hudson, and Galley crossed with the missionaries to the west side of the Loup Fork, where all knelt on the bank of the stream and with earnest hearts and tearful eyes dedicated the three missionaries to the keeping of their Heavenly Father, gave them a hand in parting, and watched the missionaries disappear towards the setting sun.

Soon after, forty wagons of Saints, converts from Utah, returning to the States, came up in fine spirits and full of faith, reporting an excellent trip with the loss of only two mules and one ox! A fine record for an emigration train.

Gillen remained in Utah, but the two others, after preaching awhile and greeting old friends, particularly Doctor John Bernhisel, continued on their way west. While in Salt Lake City, Alexander spoke in Independence Hall, September, 1866. It always had been difficult to get a place to speak in Utah, but Mark Forscutt, another veteran of the Morrisite massacre, hired the hall that night at a cost of five dollars, paid from his own pocket. On Wednesday night Alexander spoke again by invitation in Fox's Gardens. For over a year the missionaries were away on this mission and met with their usual success. A call for missionary help had come also from Oregon, to meet which, in time, Joseph C. Clapp was sent.

Many years before, on their memorable mission to Kentucky, Wilford Woodruff and David Patten had converted a young man by the name of Benjamin Clapp, and his wife Mary. Wilford Woodruff baptized young Clapp, and Patten ordained him at the time or soon after. Clapp was a prominent pioneer missionary in the days of the Martyr, and was the man who "opened" many a southern mission field. The young couple went to Missouri and here on August 24, 1837, was born a son, who was blessed and named by the Prophet at Far West. In that blessing, the child received the name Joseph Carlos (after Joseph Smith and his brother Don Carlos) and the promise that he would "bear the gospel banner and even upon the islands of the sea lift up the standard of truth."

As the years passed, and the scenes of Far West, Nauvoo, Winter Quarters, and Salt Lake City came and went, something happened to young Joseph Carlos. He became the bold independent frontiersman of the day, but in place of his once loved religious faith, he saw a sinister, creeping thing that sought his life. He left Utah, then ventured back at peril of his life, and rescued his mother and sisters and took them to California. Had his hand not been so quick on the trigger he would never have lived to open the mission in the Northwest for the Reorganization. Not once, but many times his life was saved from assassins by a seeming miracle. No one but his mother remembered the prophecy back in Far West, and least of all did Joseph Clapp himself like to think of it; for, he says when at length he heard of the Reorganized Church, "Before I united with the Reorganization, I had concluded that all that was good in 'Mormonism' was slain and buried with the Prophet, but not so now, for light and truth shone out in every sermon, and was manifest in every prayer, and seemed to be the inspiration of every hymn. . . . I wished for the pinions of an eagle, that I might fly to every hamlet and tell of the rich treasures that I had found." And so Joseph Clapp received the gospel anew, and while the hands of the elders were still upon his head in confirmation, he was ordained to the office of an elder.

The ordination, baptism, and confirmation took place at a conference in California. That night the newly made elder returned heartsick to his abiding place. Doubts assailed him. True, his mother had often told him of the promise made by the Martyr. "You will yet preach this gospel," she affirmed stoutly, even in the days of his wild youth. "There is not enough power in earth or in hell to prevent it, for the voice of the Lord was that you should lift up the standard of truth upon the islands of the sea," and the words of the elders when they ordained him were almost exactly the same that he had heard from his mother so often; on the other hand, it seemed he had not a single qualification for an elder. "I had never written a line in school; I had never done an example in mathematics, I had never had a lesson in English grammar, and could not parse a sentence; and then I imagined myself standing before the people to preach." And yet he said, "I wanted to get into the fight, and I wanted to get into the very worst of it, so that I might show a little valor and love for the Master who had shown so much for me." In this mood he retired to a little closet, where his bed had been made on the floor (because of the press of conference guests), but he could not sleep for the thoughts that assailed him. Lighting the candle that sat on the floor at the head of his bed, he drew his Doctrine and Covenants out from under his pillow and read, although it was very late. The words seemed like a personal revelation; dropping to sleep he had an experience that he never forgot, convincing him of his call. And although doubts often assailed him, doubts that had only to do with his own unworthiness, he yet lived to fulfill the prophecy made when he was blessed as a babe, a humble, consecrated man of God.

When chosen for the Oregon mission, he had but a few years of experience in California, traveling with older men, but he was the type of pioneer who knew the West and could "rough it" with the best of them. He understood the various Indian dialects well enough to converse with them; he knew their habits and customs well enough to live with them and earn their respect; he was a skilled horseman, "could ride anything that could stand up"; and if there was any one thing he could do better than another it was to drive a "line team," four or six horses, in an immigrant or baggage train. A poor equipment for a preacher? If the introduction of the gospel into Oregon had waited for a more refined and cultured set of qualifications, it might have waited for years, and literally hundreds of Saints would have died without hearing the glad news! Missionaries of that time went without purse or scrip, and to tell the truth, if they had not gone that way, they would not have gone at all, for there was no money to send them. Young Joseph Clapp started off on foot. An old man, Hervey Greene, a veteran missionary of the days of the Martyr, went a little way with him, and when he was about to turn back, they withdrew into a small clump of willows and had prayer. Never did Joseph Clapp forget that Godspeed on his missionary life. That eloquent prayer "rang in his ears" even down to old age; that patient old face with the tears coursing down it as he gave his parting blessing stood between him and temptation and discouragement many times.

In Oregon, that fall, he picked apples, he pitched hay, he walked for miles in the wet and the rain, but in the spring he was able to report thirty-one baptisms, ordination of three elders, the organization of the Sweet Home Branch, and other church work. Once when he wished to get to a certain place, he joined an immigration train and drove a line team (as he often had in crossing the western plains). Every night on the way, a big fire was built, and the preacher-teamster told the story of the gospel, while the entire company gathered around the crackling pine flames to listen. By the time the train arrived at its destination "quite a number were converted," so he baptized several, organized a branch, helped them all stake out their claims and went his way. One night, riding an unbroken young horse, through the winter rain from one place to another, he felt the need of rest and shelter, more for the horse than for himself, he said, but he was turned down at every door, although he was in a settlement of religious people. Night was lowering; he knew not what to do. Then out of the past, his father's missionary experiences rose to mind. How often he had heard that father say, that although often turned away from a Christian's door, he had never failed to be made welcome at an infidel's. An idea presented itself, and he acted upon it promptly. At the very next place, he dismounted and asked politely if they knew where any infidels lived. The lady who answered the call was a little surprised, but answered, there was one, only one, in the neighborhood—an old infidel by the name of Cogswell living about six miles away on the Mohawk River. Clapp thanked his informant, left her staring in astonishment while he made off in the direction indicated.

Surely enough, here he found welcome, intelligent conversation, an urgent invitation to stay several days and preach, money and a ferry ticket for the morrow, and a lunch when he started on his way!

One astounding experience that almost precludes the notion of coincidence is typical. A dilemma presented itself to the young missionary while going through the small town of Lebanon. His clothing was dilapidated; he had urgent need of a pair of trousers; his were worn out. He was possessed of only $3.50 and that was *Herald* subscription money. Well, he would have to spend it, and repay it later. He would get a pair of cheap cotton trousers, and go home! When he got there, if he ever did, he would stay! There were three stores in town; but only one pair of trousers that Brother Clapp could wear—a fine black pair at $8.

He wandered out in the street, and for lack of anything else to do he went into the post office and inquired for a letter. He did not know why he did so. He never had received mail at Lebanon, Oregon; he never expected to, but there was a letter —a letter from a stranger in southern Oregon, by the name of Buell, and in the letter was a five dollar greenback! A year later, by arduous journey, he reached the part of the country from whence the letter came and paid the man Buell a visit, and learned the sequel.

Mr. Buell was an old Latter Day Saint. He had gone north to Strang, been ordained an apostle; and later, disappointed, left for the West in disgust and sought to forget it all. He was succeeding fairly well; was an ardent member of the Methodist Church; a "class leader." No one suspected his past life, and he was glad of that. But one day he opened his Methodist paper to read a letter from a fellow Methodist preacher in northern Oregon. The letter said that the writer had met a young "ignoramus" by the name of Joseph Clapp who told them "the gospel had been lost to the world; that it had been restored by angels, and with it came the gifts of the gospel as in former days"—the last seen, went on the writer, "this young ignoramus (using the expression again) was making his way towards Lebanon." As he read, the embers of a fire Brother Buell had long thought smouldered and gone out, flared again. He wrote a letter, and addressed it to Lebanon, asking where he could get some literature. When his boy was already started with the letter, he called him back, and impelled by some mysterious impulse inserted therein a five-dollar bill, sealed it again and sent it on its way. Brother Buell was soon a member and an elder in the Reorganization. Thus the gospel story was first told in the northwest attended by suffering, sacrifice, and mysterious evidences of providential blessing—to an extent almost incredible to the church of today.

LX.—"TE ATUA SPEAKS AGAIN"*

ON THE 6th OF November, 1873, Glaud Rodger and Charles Wesley Wandell sailed from San Francisco on a mission to Australasia, on the barque "Domingo." Both were experienced missionaries. Rodger had preached for many years in his native land, Scotland, and later in England, and Wandell was a missionary in Nauvoo days and had been once to Australia for the Utah Church, but on his return from that mission he had visited Salt Lake City, became disappointed and left the church, only to join the Reorganization shortly before his appointment to Australia. By revelation he was called to the office of seventy, even before his baptism.

"We cast off from the pier at Stuart Street wharf at three o'clock in the afternoon, and at sunset were outside the Golden Gate and upon the bosom of the broad Pacific," says Wandell.

The weather was fine, and the little ship made an average of one hundred and sixty miles a day. They saw the North Star gradually drop from sight and watched with eagerness for the appearance of the Southern Cross that would herald their approach to the part of the world they longed to revisit. Wandell had with him some hymnbooks, the *Lute of Zion, Fresh Laurels,* and the *Sabbath-School Bell.* From these he spent much time selecting hymns for use in Australia. It was pleasant work, and he enjoyed it.

Early on the morning of the third of December, they crossed the equator. That very day a leak that had appeared in the ship's bow became so bad that they had to shorten sail to keep the ship from plunging. The captain went below to examine, found the apron split and a stream of water coming in. He

---
Te Atua, Tahitian for "God."

administered first aid with oakum and nailed a piece of board over it to keep it there but concluded it was unsafe to proceed on their way. So they bore up for Tahiti, a little over a thousand miles away, making the island by the 13th of December.

Here the missionaries visited Queen Pomare and amused themselves by watching the natives eating strange fruits, and Wandell busied himself by finding all he could about the history of the islands. On Friday, December 19, as the two missionaries took a stroll on the Queen's Road outside of town they were accosted by two men. These natives could not speak a word of English, but the missionaries made known as well as they could that they were ministers bound for Sydney. The excitement of the two natives became greater at this word, and they clung to them, talking and gesturing, using over and over the word *Parato* (Pratt—Addison Pratt). Frightened at their persistence and unable to understand them, the missionaries got away from them as quickly as they could.

As they went on they met the road overseer, who spoke good English, and he told them there was a settlement of "Mormons" at Tiona (Tahitian for Zion), five miles west of town. And the ship was to sail the next day! Too late now to do anything! They fell back on the Latter Day Saint missionary's last court of resort—they prayed about it. The ship was detained until Christmas day, six days longer.

Early the next morning (the 20th and Saturday) they started before breakfast for Tiona. They stopped at the house of a man designated as a Mormon, and after having been given a drink of coconut milk, they were guided to Tiona and met David Brown, the principal man in the little colony, who spoke "sailor English." Brown had been a sailor. He was an East Indian by birth but learned to speak English on board a whaler. He had been converted by the natives, having been on the island only ten years.

The little settlement of Saints at Tiona was all excitement. Meeting was announced at three o'clock, and the glad Saints greeted each other with *"Te Atua speaks again"* (God reveals himself once more), while they prepared chicken breadfruit, and coconuts for their guests.

The history of the church since the missionaries had been ordered from the islands was the theme of the afternoon's discourse, and particularly the coming of Young Joseph, all of which the Tahitian Saints accepted without question. In the evening the Saints gathered in the room of the missionary pair and sang the familiar old hymns of Zion, "The Spirit of God Like a Fire Is Burning," and others, all in Tahitian. The whole day following was spent in church services. Fifty-one were baptized, confirmed and reordained.

From the Saints the missionaries learned of the persecutions of the island brethren. At the time the missionaries were forced to leave the islands (May 15, 1852), there were between fifteen hundred and two thousand Saints scattered over about twenty islands. All meetings were prohibited, even family worship. At the time Addison Pratt and others left the islands, there were a great many of the Anaa brethren in prison in Tahiti and thirty-eight confined in Anaa. Their crime was that they had held meetings after being forbidden by the authorities. Singing, reading, or even praying was prohibited. Some were whipped so severely they had to go to the hospital for treatment.

Not only the Latter Day Saint missionaries, but all Protestant missionaries, were included in this prohibition. The Saints in Tahiti were forced to work on Queen Pomare's Road. Six of the native brethren lost their lives at the time of this persecution.

In spite of all these persecutions, the teaching of the missionaries had not been forgotten, and the branch at Tiona was kept intact all through the years they waited, watching each ship that touched at the harbor of Papeete for tidings of the church and of *Parato,* who had left them so long ago.

The time passed quickly now until Christmas Day, the time to go. That day is well described by Wandell:

> We finished our writing, met with the Saints at the meetinghouse, and then tried to get away, but a feast was preparing, and there was no letting us off before that was over. So at eleven o'clock in the forenoon we sat down to the feast under the grateful shade of a patriarchal breadfruit tree. A raised platform was fixed for Brother Rodger and me, upon which was set for our use boiled breadfruit, raw bananas, coconut milk, fried chicken, scrambled eggs, etc., all of which was laid upon a tablecloth of spotless purity.
>
> Our table was at the head of an oblong circle, some thirty feet across, covered with tara (taro) leaves (a large, broad leaf), which gave it the look of green carpeting. Around the edge of this circle the feast was set; the center of the circle being graced by a canoe-shaped wooden vessel which held a barbecued hog.
>
> However, before we had time to compose ourselves for the work in hand, a difficulty arose in the shape of several dogs, chickens and a pig, which incontinently broke through this charming circle of friendly Saints, and made a splendid charge on the edibles around them! But in all such contests man will come off victorious; so one brother whipped off his bandana, festooned it around one of the pig's forefeet, led him outside to a sapling, and there triumphantly tied him! The dogs and chickens were also finally got outside, and a patrol established to keep them there. So, order was restored and then, after lifting the voice in thanksgiving to the great Author of all our mercies, we set to in good earnest to do the amplest justice to what was before us.
>
> Brother Rodger and myself were told that we could help ourselves to such as was set particularly for us, or we could call for anything in the feast. In order to show them that we entered heartily into their arrangements and felt to be one with them, we immediately called for some of the pig in the canoe. We were rewarded by a general smile of gratification, and the first cut of the pig.
>
> The feast proceeded. It was wonderfully strange to us; all the circumstances conspired to make it so. We had started in good faith for Australia, and here we were at Tiona, in Polynesia! Why should the good barque "Domingo" spring a leak in fine weather, and in that particular part of the ocean which necessarily made Tahiti our only available refuge? Was it not one of those special providences which occasionally occur to keep us in remembrance of the unceasing watch care which Jehovah has for the cause of Zion? And who are these whose fine open countenances show the kindly spirit within? They are Latter Day Saints; not all of them old-timers, for it is probable that not more than a half a dozen of them ever heard Addison Pratt

or any white elder. They have come into the church through the labor of the native elders since Brother Pratt was compelled by the French to abandon this mission.

The greater part of the Saints have now for the first time heard the voices of elders from America; and how their trusting hearts are drawn to ours! We are to them almost as though we had come from the courts of heaven! . . . At parting they embraced and kissed us— . . . hung upon our necks and wept like children. . . . That we could remain unmoved amid such a scene was impossible. Indeed, we were quite overcome, and found it necessary to get away as soon as we consistently could. Brother Reipu had been selected to see us safe on board; but he was so overcome by his feelings that a less sensitive brother had to take his place. One sister followed us for fully a half mile; then kissing our hands, returned weeping towards Tiona.

On Christmas Day, the "Domingo" "hove up her anchor and stood out to sea," and the missionaries looked forward to the next adventure in the mission that so far had such an unexpected and auspicious beginning.

In spite of that auspicious beginning, it was June 17, 1878, before a missionary, William Nelson, sailed from San Francisco for the South Sea Islands, and he was a volunteer, using his own money for the enterprise. He was ordained an elder the day he sailed, and his experience as a missionary was slight, but he was zealous and willing. His arrival on July 23, 1878, was a joyous occasion for the native Saints. But he found the government would not permit him to stay without special papers, and he was forced to return the next year. Nothing daunted, he secured papers, returned and stayed for several years.

But at length the mission received sufficient notice to have sent them Thomas W. Smith and his wife, Helen, who sailed for the islands on the "Tropic Bird" on October 1, 1884. From that time until now, the South Sea Island Mission has been provided with help from America and has grown steadily. Several of the South Sea Island brethren have visited the States—Metuaore, Paia, Horahitu, and Mervin. One boy spent years in college in Lamoni; a child adopted by the Lakes visited America with them, but upon their return died and was buried in his native land. Two of the young ladies were trained at the Independence Sanitarium and became graduate nurses.

On the islands lies buried a brave young missionary, Charles Lake, who knowing he could not live, chose to die at the post of duty; also Clara Kellogg Ellis, who laid down her life in those faraway islands in the service of her fellow men. These are enshrined in the hearts of true Latter Day Saints, even those who never saw them, as they remember that "greater love than this hath no man."

LXI.—Australia

Thursday, January 22, 1874, the "Domingo" with the American missionaries aboard entered Sydney harbor. Wandell was acquainted with the members of the Utah Church in Sydney. He had been an earlier missionary there; the Utah Church had kept up a mission there for a number of years. In fact, a missionary had been sent to Australia from England during Joseph's lifetime; but whether or not any work was done, or what became of the young nineteen-year-old William Barrett who was sent there, has not been recorded.

Leaving Rodger to take care of the luggage, Charles Wandell wandered into the city to look for old friends and was not long in locating them. John Bennett took him to the hatters at once and bought a hat for him before he went with him to call on other Saints, for the Australians were always punctilious about the appearance of the missionaries. The next house at which they called was that of Richard Ellis, whom they found ready to receive the missionary, for Sister Ellis declared she had seen him in a dream and knew he was coming! From there he went to Brother Pegg's and to Brother Nichols', happily renewing old acquaintances. The next day Brother Ellis paid for the drayage of their luggage to Nichols', where they had secured a room.

The two missionaries occupied the time in distributing tracts and visiting until they felt sure the mission would be successful, then hired the United Temperance Hall for three months. The first baptisms occurred on February 8, and were two, Richard Ellis and Albert Aspinwall. Two meetings were held the same day in their new hall, with more names given in for baptism the following Sunday. They felt that they were off to a very fair start.

The next year, after an illness of several weeks, Charles Wandell died in Saint Vincent's Hospital. He had remained with Richard Ellis and family until he could no longer climb the stairs. He believed himself to have bronchitis, but upon his removal to Saint Vincent's learned that the malady was heart disease, and incurable. "He was happy, and had no fear of death; he also bore his testimony to the truth of the work, and that you were the legal successor of your father."[1] He was buried by the Saints in Leichhardt Cemetery, and standing beside the grave, Elder Rodger gave a short talk about death and the resurrection; then the little group of Saints sang a song of Wandell's own composing, "Weep, Weep Not for Me, Zion."

For many years Charles Wandell had kept a journal. On March 2, 1875, he had made a last entry in it:

> The swelling of my limbs, caused by heart disease, has developed a dangerous sore in my left leg. The point is to keep this sore from mortifying and killing me at once. Know all men that I want all of my bound books and other church books to be the property of the Australian Mission of the Church of Jesus Christ of Latter Day Saints.
> I want my clothes, all of them, to be given to the elder whom the church may send out to take my place. The trunk goes with the clothes. I here (March 2) feel it my duty to state that I believe Young Joseph Smith to be the true leader and President of the Church of Jesus Christ of Latter Day Saints. . . . He must increase. . . . I feel more than ever convinced that a splendid work will yet be done here. Also I here record my unlimited faith in the atonement of Jesus Christ as the world's Saviour. It is in view of the completeness of that atonement that I am enabled to think so calmly about it. God and Christ are true, and so is a universal Providence.
> . . . All is calm and serene. The eternal future is bright, and one night last week the angels sang a beautiful song. . . . I am truly and greatly blessed.

Thus with calm assurance this Latter Day Saint missionary, far from home, in a strange land, ill unto death, wrote the last words his pen would ever form.

Glaud Rodger was alone from then on. Having left Sydney, he says for four months he lived among strangers, never during

---

[1] Letter to Joseph Smith from Richard Ellis.

all that time seeing the face of a Latter Day Saint. The time was lonely and filled with discouragement. "It was then, dear brethren, that I saw the wisdom of sending the elders two and two." At last two men, heads of families, were brought into the church in Waratah.

The papers took notice of Rodger's advent in Waratah, in such manner as the following:

> Mr. Rodger preaches regularly every Sabbath at the old School of Arts upon the "Fullness of the Time" and "The Approach of the Second Advent of the Lord." He is very impressive in his style of delivery and vividly portrays the prophetic statement, denouncing the coldness and apathy of the Christian Church throughout the world at the present day. Arguing from appearances, he draws his deductions from Scripture that the end of the present dispensation is close at hand. In his views there is nothing of the speculative character, the foundation of his belief being based upon the orthodox teaching contained in Scripture. Polygamy is not a doctrine of this section of the church, but is severely denounced as impolitic and unscriptural.[2]

Another paper said:

> We have had two additions to our list of religions lately, *viz.*, the Latter Day Saints and the Unitarians. The former is represented by an elderly and sincere-looking gentleman named Rodger, who can be heard on Sunday at Mr. Fryar's room opposite the goods shed. I had a long conversation with him the other day. Although there is no fear of his converting me to his theological views, I was rather taken up with him. . . . Mr. Rodger told me that his church does not believe in or practice polygamy and is not to be confounded with Brigham Young's order. The former gentleman is a minister of the original church of Saints, over whom the son of Joseph Smith is at present president. The great aim of the body is to found a community in which all the virtues—and, if possible, none of the vices—of modern society shall flourish. To accomplish this, they have established settlements in Iowa and Missouri, where they teach and practice the doctrines of their faith.[3]

Other newspapers were less kind, but the missionary carried on alone and received the encouragement at times of additions to the very slowly increasing ranks. He wrote to America that

---

2 and 3 Unfortunately the original source of these clippings is not known.

the work in Australia was slow but permanent. He rightly appraised its character, as time has amply proved. Today the work of Glaud Rodger stands as firm and everlasting as the day he left Australia. He has never been forgotten. His name still lives in Australia, as it has been bestowed upon the children and grandchildren of those whom he brought into the church, and the story of his many hardships and sacrifices is handed down in Australian families as part of the traditional heritage of children he never saw.

Glaud Rodger was born in Scotland, and from there one brother had gone some years before to seek his fortune in Australia. When Rodger had been appointed to that faraway country, his dearest dream was to find this brother, from whom he had been long separated, and tell him of the gospel. As soon as he could leave the southern part of his mission, he took his way upon foot northward over the route since become dear to many a missionary to that land, except that the hospitable homesteads scattered through the Australian bush, to whose welcome shade present missionaries look forward with anticipation, were not there. Instead were the homes of strangers. He found his brother at Bungwahl engaged in the timber business with another Scotchman by the name of John Wright. The meeting with this brother was finally made doubly joyful by the baptism into the church of not only his brother but the Wrights. This was the same John Wright who later established a mill and shipbuilding establishment at North Forester (Tuncurry), and whose name and memory, with that of his capable wife, is remembered by so many American missionaries. As years went by, Glaud Rodger established the church on the north coast, and also went to Victoria with the message, hunting up the old Saints as he went.

Many and beautiful are the stories told of this lone missionary and his faith and sacrifice. Near the little village of Glen Eden, in Victoria, a hill may be seen that is sacred to his memory. The hill stands now quite denuded of forest, but in that day it was covered with timber, the typical Australian bush. Upon the very top of this hill, in his lonely ramblings, Glaud Rodger built himself an altar of stones, and whenever he was homesick or discouraged he climbed this hill to his altar of prayer. Glaud Rodger, like Charles Derry, the first missionary to England, was fond of expressing his deepest feelings in verse, so when he was leaving Victoria for home, he wrote a poem and hid it under the rocks of this altar. He told the young people of Glen Eden that to the one who first found this altar and the poem, his farewell in verse would belong. No prize was ever more coveted. The young folks of the community vied with one another in the search for Brother Rodger's altar as if for some buried treasure, and the young woman who ultimately found it treasured the poem throughout her life as one of her most sacred possessions.

Sometime in May, 1879, Glaud Rodger arrived in San Francisco from his long mission, and later wrote: "I have left the colonies clear of any incumbrance; no debt for my successor to meet; a good little library, and many friends both in and out of the church."

James W. Gillen followed as his successor, sailing from San Francisco, June 4, 1879, for Australia. Thomas W. Smith and his wife Helen, Joseph and Emma Burton followed them and in time many other American missionaries, and not one but returned to tell in terms of love of the people in that faraway mission "under the Southern Cross." For years the people in that island continent have maintained a printing office; they have supported their own missionaries and supported them well and at times have sent money to help with the spread of the gospel elsewhere. The work still moves forward as it did in Rodger's day, "slowly but permanently." There is a feeling of assurance about the Saints in that land; one feels that those who are Saints today will be Saints tomorrow, and their children and grandchildren

Saints the day after. Australia has paid her debt to the American Saints, who sent out with some sacrifice the first missionaries to her shores, by sending back in turn her younger men, several of whom are now or have been missionaries in the United States. Two of the younger Apostles of the church, George G. Lewis and C. George Mesley, have been back to take charge of the work in their native land. John Blackmore, William Patterson, Albert Loving, Harold Velt, and Walter Johnson have contributed their share to the church in America, while one of the noblest and most loved of them all, John T. Gresty, sleeps in America, as Charles Wandell does in that faraway land.

LXII.—Scandinavia

One of the most important missions of the church has always been the Scandinavian Mission. Two missionaries destined to open this field for the Reorganization arrived in Copenhagen, Denmark, on May 16, 1875. Elder Magnus Fyrando, a native of Sweden, and Hans N. Hansen of Denmark, had the honor and arduous responsibility of "opening the door" in Scandinavia.

Magnus Fyrando had joined the church when he was nineteen (the church as he heard it preached contained only the purity of the gospel). Before he was of age, he was preaching the message as he then understood it in his native land, Sweden. His face bore scars which remained as long as life lasted, of beatings he had received at the hands of mobs in his youth, while preaching in his native tongue. His young wife, Elsie Olsen, was as devoted as he. Had she not walked seven miles in wooden shoes, her lunch tied in a napkin, that she might hear a sermon? The young couple had, at cost of all their earthly possessions, paid their way to the Zion they hoped to find in the mountains. On the way, their first child was born at a camp of the Saints near the Sweet Water River. Little remained of their clothing except bare necessities. Elsie Fyrando made her baby's first dress of her only sunbonnet. Arriving at their destination, they lived in a tent and a dugout; they plucked herbs and wild tea for drink; their kitchen equipment was an empty peach can and a tin plate; and their first meat a gift of an ox head, from an old German friend. Elsie Fyrando made soup three times on the bones. But physical discomfort was not all. Finally they made their way eastward, and hearing the gospel preached again by the Reorganized elders, they joined the church near Omaha.

Fyrando immediately visited Sweden, where he previously

had done missionary work for the faction of the church in Utah, while Hansen visited the place of his birth. Meeting again in Copenhagen, they made, without success, a concerted effort to get a place to preach. Therefore, Brother Fyrando went back to Sweden where he had friends, while Hansen found employment at manual labor in Copenhagen. He had not forgotten his mission and spent every hour outside of those of his day's work in finding and talking to old-time Saints. At last he considered that the interest warranted his beginning to hold regular meetings. At his own expense he rented a hall and called his companion back from Sweden, that they might fulfill the well-established custom of "two by two." With an audience of thirty, they held their first public meeting, August 18, 1875. But after only a few efforts they were obliged to give up their work in the hall, and Fyrando returned to Sweden.

Nearly a year passed, and in the spring of 1876 prospects began to brighten and the month of March found both missionaries in Aalborg,[1] Denmark, preaching to good-sized congregations.

Quite an interest has been manifest, and it appears as if the Lord had now opened the way for his gospel to be preached in this country. Last Tuesday we had the privilege of administering the ordinance of baptism to two that are the first fruits of labors that yet have been gathered; but we hope and believe that several more will come soon. Those baptized are both heads of families, good, earnest men, previously belonging to the Brighamite Church. One of them was an elder who opposed us as long as he could, but when he saw his error, he laid it aside and received the truth.

As there is now quite an interest manifest and the prospects are that a good many will come into the church, we see the necessity of having a hymnbook of our own in the Danish language, as we hitherto, as also the Scandinavian Saints in America, have used the Brighamite book, which is not suitable to our faith. We would therefore propose to Scandinavian Saints in America to help us with means to

---

[1] Aalborg in the province of Jylland is noted as the place where the second branch of the church in Denmark was organized. This was under the church in Utah, but George Parker Dykes, who baptized the eight members who composed this branch on October 27, 1850, and organized them into a branch on November 8 following, was among the first fruits of the Reorganized Church in Utah.

get up a book, with from one hundred and fifty to two hundred selected hymns, arranged similar to the *Saints' Harp*. We would like to have the book as soon as possible, for we need it, and would therefore ask those interested to put forth a helping hand as soon as possible.[2]

This book was later published, also Book of Mormon and Doctrine and Covenants.

During the summer, Elder Fyrando visited Norway and Sweden, staying two weeks in Christiania, distributing tracts and making some friends, although he could find no place, public or private, in which to preach. He walked six or eight miles from the city and found a hall he could lease for three months at a cost of twenty *kroner* per month, amounting for the three months to twenty dollars, but he had not the money and turned away. As he was a stranger to the country and to the language as well, he found it difficult to do much, so after three weeks in Sweden, where he had a "very good time," he returned to Copenhagen. He also had found it necessary to spend his time at manual work in order to keep up the rent on their halls and pay his own board and lodging. At one time, while in Copenhagen, he received a call to Aalborg to administer to a man who was believed to be dying. He had no money. Fortunately it was summer. He pawned his blankets to get money to answer the call of a distressed brother!

That year the little mission received reinforcements in the person of Peter N. Brix, who was in the field and working hard by July, 1877. He was ordained an elder and appointed to that mission in the spring of 1876.

On the way to their mission, the first missionaries had rejoiced in a prophecy they heard in Philadelphia on their way to embark on their journey. They remembered every word and believed it. They were told, "You shall have a safe and speedy journey, be blessed in your labors: the angel of the Lord shall

---

[2] *The Saints' Herald*, Volume 23, page 283.

minister to you, and the same angel shall minister to your loved ones at home. You shall be enabled to fulfill your mission, you shall return to your family, and not one of their number shall be missing."

Thus encouraged they went on, nothing doubting. And when, during the year 1876, a letter came from Phineas Caldwell, president of Magnus Fyrando's home branch, saying, "If you want to see your son, come home at once," his faith was sorely tried. The letter came on a Saturday when he and Brother Brix were seventeen miles from Aalborg, Denmark, with appointments out for the next day; a hall already rented at what seemed to them with their limited means, great expense. Fyrando felt that he could not preach; he urged Brother Peter N. Brix to go alone. He could not force himself to think of aught else except that his only son (he had buried the three others in the dreadful days in Utah) lay at the point of death, perhaps already dead, thousands of miles away, and he had not the money to go to him. Brix left the house and went down the walk, but just as he went out the gate, the words of that prophecy came again to Brother Fyrando's mind, "you shall return to your family, and not one of their number shall be missing." Hurriedly calling back his missionary companion, he went with him and preached. He finished the two years of his mission, and never doubted that he would find his son there upon his return home.[3] Although Fyrando had visited much in Sweden and spent many days in tracting and visiting, he found it impossible to do any preaching on account of the strict laws of the country, but made many friends. He left Copenhagen, April 20, 1877, in company with five of the brethren from Denmark. (Scandinavia has suffered, as have the English and Utah Missions, because of heavy emigration to the United States of members, particularly those members who could have aided in the support of missionaries.) The little company arrived in New York, May

---

[3]"Magnus and Elsie Fyrando," by Alma M. Fyrando, *Journal of History*, Volume 3, page 306.

8. "I was sorry," said Fyrando, "to leave the mission and Brother Brix alone. . . . It is hard to be alone." Hans Hansen had been released and returned to America the previous year.

That space forbids the story of the many sacrifices and unselfish service of our missionaries to Scandinavia is regrettable. Incidents of a character that should inspire faith in those who read them would make a large volume. Two missionaries from America lie buried there, for in October 26, 1900, Mads P. Hansen, after only a brief experience in the mission field, died at Arendal, Norway, leaving his missionary companion, N. C. Enge, alone. With the 40 *kroner* (about $11) he found in the missionary's pocket, Brother Enge had to meet funeral expenses. Such was the poverty of our early missionary efforts.

The next winter February 9, 1901, N. C. Enge baptized his first Norwegian converts, a Mr. and Mrs. Olson. It was they who cared for Brother Hansen in his last illness. They walked six miles in the snow to be baptized by Brother Enge in the sea— only to find after the ceremony that a recent law had been passed that anyone baptizing a member of the Lutheran Church [the state church] without first notifying their Lutheran minister, was subject to fine. Brother Enge went to the authorities, confessed his "mistake" and out of his meager funds paid a fine of 25 *kroner,* about $6.64.

In December, 1915, in Eidevold, Norway, the first church building of the Reorganized Church on the continent was finished. The second, probably was built in Germany.

The Scandinavian mission field has been kept up for many years. During much of the time a Scandinavian paper, *Sandhedens Banner,* was published in the interest of the mission. *Sandhedens Banner* appeared first in October, 1844, as a periodical for Scandinavian people. It was issued from Lamoni, Iowa, with Peter Andersen as editor. Of the many who have sacrificed much and given much of their lives to that mission, may be mentioned Peter Andersen and Peter Muceus, also Peter N. Brix, who died in Aalborg, Denmark, and Mads P. Hansen who died in Arundel, Norway. Among other more recent missionaries were Marce Sorensen, John Wahlstrom, N. C. Enge, H. H. Hanson, J. J. Christiansen, C. Oscar Johnson, C. A. Swenson, Peter T. Andersen, O. W. Okerlind, E. Y. Hunker, and V. D. Ruch and wife.

LXIII.—Canada

Work in Canada went forward rapidly under the direction of that veteran missionary John Shippy and others. One of the outstanding early missionaries in Canada was Arthur Leverton, and it was he who had baptized a young man by the name of John J. Cornish, who was known and loved by Saints everywhere. When first ordained to the ministry, Cornish could not read his own text. He not only learned to read the Bible but other books, and his progeny in the gospel, those he converted, and those his converts brought into the church, now number a mighty army, among which are some of the best-known ministers of the church.

Many are the faith-inspiring stories told of this man's ministry. Favorite among them is the following well-authenticated account of a baptism in London, Ontario, many years ago:

One Wednesday night after prayer meeting Sarah Lively and Mary Taylor offered themselves for baptism. It was late when we closed our meeting, and by the time we got to the Thames (south branch), it must have been almost eleven or half past eleven o'clock at night. A number of the Saints with others went to witness the baptism, probably about twenty Saints and about ten others. Among the number of the outsiders was one who endeavored to persecute us to a great degree, and the night being dark, with very dark, heavy clouds, and also a little misty rain, it was so that we could scarcely see each other's forms. The way being rough, with little hills and valleys, the Saints occasionally fell into the water and got wet. This provoked the persecutor to make more fun than ever. By and by we reached the river, and after we got through with our opening exercises, I stepped to the water with the hands of one of the candidates in mine. The moment my foot touched the water there came a sound from heaven as of a rushing wind, and with it came a very bright and brilliant light, more bright and glorious than my eyes had ever before seen. We were all filled with the Spirit, and the Saints immediately fell upon their knees and thanked God that he had shown unto the persecutors that we were acknowledged from on high. I gave a glance around as I was walking into the water, to see the light, and also the position of the people on the bank. The light came down from heaven, and it was in a circle, and it was about large enough to take in the thirty people, and also a part of the river, just that part where I baptized. I stood about one foot inside of this bright circle, and I cast a look outside of it, and it was just as dark one foot from the outer edge of it as it was ten rods or a mile away. When I came leading the sister to the bank, I noticed that all, both Saints and outsiders were on their knees, with the exception of the one who persecuted us the most. After the two were baptized one of the outsiders cried out, "Oh, pray for me! This is enough to convince anyone that the latter-day work is true." In time everyone who was at the baptism came into the church.

At another time, while I was confirming a sister, the Spirit declared that from that time if she continued faithful, she would have the gift of visions. She immediately saw the Saviour, and she was wrapt in the glory of the Spirit.

J. J. Cornish.

London, Ontario, July 12, 1877.

We, the undersigned, hereby certify that we are the parties baptized as described above on December 27, 1875, and that the circumstances related in the foregoing letter are correct to the best of our knowledge, so far as they relate to that event.

Mrs. R. May,
Mary E. Bushnell.

We, the undersigned, hereby certify that we were present at the baptism referred to in the foregoing letter, and that the description as given is true to the best of our knowledge.

A. C. Dempsey,
Elijah Sparks,
M. A. Sparks.[1]

In the same city of London, there lived a good Methodist couple by the name of John and Elizabeth Parker, who had been faithful church members for over twenty years. Their son-in-law, William Clow, had been a witness of the scene described above, and had joined the church. Mr. and Mrs. Parker also joined, and began slipping little tracts into the letters sent to another son-in-law, a local Methodist minister in Toronto, who had married their second daughter, Janet. Mr. Luff did not scorn these offerings but read each one, and was perhaps more deeply impressed than he cared to admit. He answered some

---

[1] *Church History*, Volume 4, pages 181, 182.

times in a light vein and when his wife visited her parents some months later said jokingly that he wondered if when she came back he would not have a "Mormon" wife. At the same time he told her if she felt she should join the church, he would never oppose her, although he might be a Methodist minister all his life. She thought she need not worry, but in due time the letter came telling of her conversion and baptism.

Meantime Mr. Luff continued to officiate in his capacity in Toronto, and planned seriously to enter the regular ministry, as he was being urged to do. His health made a rest imperative, and he went to his father-in-law's where his wife still was. He found, as was common among Latter Day Saints, that the gospel was in the minds and conversations of all. He felt they were all praying especially for him, but he would not leave the communion in which he had found so many blessings without being sure of what he was finding in its stead, although his eight months' study had made him somewhat dissatisfied with his own church. He shut himself in the Parker family parlor one entire day and read the Book of Mormon, and as he read, at times, a peaceful assurance came over him. He could not describe it. But he did know, he said, that *no one* could offer opposition to that book, while under that influence.

"Are they of God?" he asked himself again and again. He was not of an emotional type, and what affected others often left him cold, but over and over in his analytical mind he went over various points of doctrine. Prayer meeting night came, and there was a goodly number present. When liberty was given to speak, Mr. Luff arose. He expressed confidence in God, pleasure in beholding the happiness of those there who were attempting to serve Him, but as to their religion he could not, like them, say he *knew* it to be of God. He did know one thing. God had blessed him where he was and though he was anxious to obtain all the good possible, yet he could not think of renouncing that church and entering another until he was sure he could please God better than remaining where he was. He wished them well; hoped their joy might never be less, but he did not feel like speculating with his soul.

That testimony was a distinct disappointment to those who heard, for all had been praying and expecting something entirely different. The meeting progressed. At one time all knelt in prayer, and Joseph Luff silently asked for an answer that night to his questions, at the same time seeking pardon if such a petition was presumption on his part, further he wished that the answer might be given through Robert Parker,[2] his wife's ten-year-old brother, a member of the church and absolutely without guile.

No human being heard that prayer. The congregation arose from their knees, and singing and testimony continued. Soon "Robbie," as he was then called, stood up and spoke as a child of his age would speak, but before he had said many words his face became pale and tears flowed down his cheeks as he turned and facing his brother-in-law raised his hand and said:

> Verily, thus saith the Lord God unto you, O son of man, Go now and obey my gospel, for this is indeed my church. It is my will that you shall be baptized at the hands of one of these my servants, for you have received of my Spirit, saith the Lord.

What could anyone in such a position do? Joseph Luff arose and told his experience, admitting that he was not entirely satisfied on all points, but willing to go ahead and obey, trusting for more light. Brother Cornish who was presiding walked over to him and spoke in tongues. The interpretation was given. The whole company was in tears. After the service he spoke of baptism, and was told there would be a baptism two days later. Joseph Luff did not wish to wait, so the entire congregation re-

---

[2]R. J. Parker, later a missionary of the church.

paired at once to the River Thames, about a quarter of a mile away, where about half past ten at night he was baptized by John J. Cornish.

A few days later he returned to Toronto. One of the first things he learned was that his name had been presented for admission to the regular ministry at the annual conference of the Methodist Church. Those who presented it were horror-stricken at the news from London! Brother Luff says:

> I can never tell how I felt. Up to the last Sunday before leaving home, I had occupied the Methodist pulpit; and, though teaching no particular doctrinal tenets, had been reckoned as one who endorsed all that was embodied in the creed. Now I felt that I was to be a target for every shaft. Where should I begin? How should I convince my thousands of friends that I was not only honest but had divine warrant for my course? My heart beat with unusual vigor when stepping from the cars, and along the streets where I had been a thousand times before. . . . The load of that city seemed to be on my heart, and I carried responsibilities as never before. But there I was back again, and, with an oft repeated "God help me" on my lips, I returned to my home and business.[3]

This was the beginning of the history of the Reorganization in the city of Toronto, as well as the story of one of the church's grand old men, whose name is known wherever the church is known.

Canada has continued until this day to be a fertile field for church activities.

---

[3] *Autobiography of Joseph Luff,* Herald Publishing House, Lamoni, Iowa, 1894.

LXIV.—Lamoni and the Order of Enoch

During these scenes of missionary activity, the church at home was also progressing. The spring conference of 1873 saw an important reorganization of the leading quorums of the church by revelation. Since the very foundation of the church has always rested upon the belief of Latter Day Saints that God could communicate his will to the people who were his children upon the earth now as in former years, they naturally rejoiced at the long revelation of 1873, which seemed to seal their faith with the assurance that their chosen leader was the prophet son of a prophet father. There had been three brief revelations before, one in 1861 on the subject of tithing, one in 1863 calling William Marks to the presidency and urging that elders be sent two by two, and a third in May, 1865, about ordaining men of every race and promising that the Quorum of Twelve should soon be filled.

In spite of the fact that the members of the Quorum of Twelve had in the past not been chosen by direct revelation, the feeling had obtained throughout the church that they should be so selected, and the revelation of 1873 confirmed that opinion. William H. Kelley, Thomas W. Smith, James Caffall, John H. Lake, Alexander H. Smith, Zenas H. Gurley, Jr., and Joseph R. Lambert were chosen to make ten in the Quorum of Apostles. The names of Daniel B. Rasey and Reuben Newkirk, since they could no longer travel in the field, but had for many years devoted themselves to their secular affairs, were dropped from the Quorum. Jason W. Briggs, E. C. Briggs, and Josiah Ells of the old Quorum remained.

The wisdom of this revelation was manifest by time, as all but one of these ten men spent the remainder of their lives in the service of the church, leaving behind them honorable records full of achievement. The other one, Jason W. Briggs, though he became disaffected from the church, was an able man and lived a life of honor and integrity.

From the very first the "gathering" had been talked and variously urged. Some were slightly impatient with delays, and it became apparent that some place where land was cheap must be selected for the homes of the incoming tide of Saints from all over the United States, England, and now, from Scandinavia. An Order of Enoch was organized, and at the conference of 1875 a "removal committee," who made trips of investigation to various parts of the country. Chicago and vicinity, Nauvoo, Stewartsville, Far West, Saint Joseph, Council Bluffs, and other places were considered.

The Illinois press had concerned themselves with the coming of Young Joseph to the church in 1860. They now became interested in the proposed move, and some of their comments show the change wrought in public opinion in the course of a decade and a half by this young man, Joseph Smith, and the movement he led. The *Plano Mirror* of June 22, 1876, carried this comment:

> There is a vigorous effort on the part of the Latter Day Saints to change the location of the headquarters of the church from Plano to some new Zion, where the whole church can be concentrated in a community of its own. This is a favorite scheme with the leaders of the church, and they seem now to be in earnest. There is a call to the "Saints" in the last *Herald* from President Joseph Smith, chairman of the board of removal, urging the matter. . . .
> Should these people leave Plano, they will be a loss to the village; they are good citizens and number two hundred in Plano and vicinity. Elder Smith is a good man, and however much others may dissent from his Mormon views, all who know him respect him.

On the 18th of December, 1877, President Smith was somewhat surprised to take from the post office an official-looking document from Nauvoo. It was a petition. He remembered the one he received in 1860, stating in no uncertain terms that

Young Joseph was not wanted in Hancock County since his affiliation with the "Mormon" people.[1]

He opened the document and read:

> We, the undersigned citizens of Nauvoo, and surrounding country, most cordially invite the head or leaders of the Reorganized Church of Jesus Christ of Latter Day Saints, to establish the headquarters of their church in said city of Nauvoo.
>
> We believe that the odium rightfully attached to the Brighamite Mormons in the infamous practice of polygamy is detached from the Reorganized Church of Latter Day Saints; we believe you will receive a cordial welcome and reception from all philanthropic people of our country, and we further believe by establishing the headquarters of your church in the aforesaid city of Nauvoo, with our united efforts we can build, or make it one of the most populous cities in the military district.

Then followed a list of names, much of it in double column, three and a half yards long, containing the names of the leading men in the city.

And to cap it all, that veteran lawyer and newspaper man of Carthage, Thomas C. Sharp, whose militant and fiery editorials in the *Warsaw Signal* had done much to arouse public opinion against Joseph Smith and who stood trial for complicity in his death but was acquitted, published an interesting comment in his paper, the *Carthage Gazette,* taking back, of course, none of the acts of his past—politicians are not made that way—but offering this tribute to Young Joseph:

> The Nauvoo *Independent* says that a petition, signed by some four hundred persons, has been forwarded to Joseph Smith, Jr., requesting him to make Nauvoo the headquarters of his reformed church of Latter Day Saints. Some of our old anti-Mormon citizens are a little nervous over this matter—we are not. Young Jo is a different man from old Jo, and don't seek to gather all the faithful together, that he may use them politically and financially as the Brighamites do. There is nothing objectionable in Young Jo's church, that we have heard of, except his creed, and as to creeds we have nothing to say.[2]

---

[1] See page 454.
[2] Carthage *Gazette,* December 26, 1877; *Saints' Herald,* Volume 25, page 24, January 15, 1878; *Church History,* Volume 4, pages 207, 208.

LAMONI AND THE ORDER OF ENOCH

At length the removal committee chose none of the places mentioned, but rather went into a comparatively new country in southwestern Iowa, where the Order of Enoch had already bought land and where there was plenty of room for development.

This place was named Lamoni[3] and was often referred to in the first few years as "The Colony." The company which settled it (the Order of Enoch) did so under the auspices of the Burlington & Quincy Railroad. The town in Fayette Township, Decatur County, was laid out in 1879. At this time there was in the vicinity only one farmhouse, owned by a Mr. Shepard, on an eighty-acre farm just north of town. His widow afterward sold this farm to F. Drummond, who erected the house finally owned and occupied by E. H. Dancer just north of town. Mr. Dancer came to it in 1877. The nearest farm was owned by E. Ferguson, one-half mile east of what is now Lamoni. The first Latter Day Saints to settle in Lamoni were S. F. Walker and his wife, the Marietta Faulconer of Sandwich days. The couple had homesteaded in Nevada and come back to help make the proposed colony a success. Zenas H. Gurley, Jr., kept the first "stock of goods" in what is now Lamoni, at "Hopkins corner." Elijah Banta was the first agent of the company; David Dancer followed, and the Order of Enoch operated in this way until the last of the land was sold. The railroad coming through in 1879, a town was laid out and called Lamoni. Before that time a post office called Sedgewick, near the town, received the mail of the "colonists." Later Alexander H. Smith brought his family from Nauvoo, and settled just across the Missouri line near Andover. He brought with him his invalid brother David, in the vain hope that country life might restore him to health.

Not far away a group of Saints had settled some years be-

---

[3] *History of Ringgold and Decatur Counties,* Lewis Publishing House, Chicago, 1887, page 782, seq.

fore at a place called "Pleasant Plain," laid out as a village as early as 1854, but always called "Nine-Eagles" on account of a Pleasant Plain in Jefferson County, Iowa. Some years later, Pleasanton was officially adopted as the name of this settlement and post office.

Some of the church authorities visited the little colony on the way home from the fall conference in western Iowa, and at the same time attended the Decatur District conference in 1875. (This colony bought land in 1870-1871.)

> It was a very enjoyable trip [Joseph Smith wrote], and resulted in satisfying the excursionists that the land was excellent, the crops this year good, the people agreeable, the conference a pleasant one, and the country a delightful one to live in. Everybody, myself included, had a strong attack of the farming and pastoral fever. Now don't rush into that region all at once, but go cautiously, carefully, and with all things prepared before you; as the law directs. . . .
> There are a hundred fifty-three members in the Lamoni Branch this fall, with a constant prospect of increase, as an interest is awakened all over the district. At their last conference it was resolved to build a chapel for worship, and a building committee was appointed, with instructions to proceed at once to the completion of the work. . . .
> We are also authorized to say that no one, be he Saint or otherwise, who will not consent to the righteousness of God and the rules of right dealing between man and man, is wanted there—nor will such be welcome there, either to those in or out of the church. But men—honest men—true men and women will find warm hearts and good neighbors. There is neither justice of the peace nor constable in this township where the Saints are settled; neither has there been a law-suit there during the five years of their settling there.[4]

In 1877 Joseph Smith made a tour of land not far from Independence, and also visited Independence itself.

He first visited Davis City, arriving there on a Saturday afternoon in August. He found many Saints in the little town. After remaining over Sunday, preaching in the afternoon, he left with a Brother Fowler, whom he had formerly known in Amboy, to go to the "colony," as folks about there called it.

---

⁴*Saints' Herald*, Volume 22, pages 625, 626; *Church History*, Volume 4, page 120.

But a shower came up, and he took refuge for the night in the first house on the prairie "within reach," which happened to be the home of Brother Fowler. He writes of it thus:

> The country where the Order of Enoch had located the scene of their operations has been frequently described, but we found a changed land to that we visited and rode over some six years ago. Then, a wilderness of arable land, untouched by the plow; and dotted only here and there by a farm or a grove, greeted the eye; now, a cheerful scene of busy farm life, a wide spread of growing corn and wheat and rye and oats and waving grass was seen everywhere, broken now and then by an interval of untilled land, showing the places yet open to the settler; where the cattle roamed freely, the occupants, literally, of a "thousand hills." It was rightly called a rolling country; very fair to look upon, and giving to the careful and industrious husbandman a just reward for his labor. . . .
> We found the Saints by no means discouraged or cast down. Their faith, grand and glorious, was a well-spring of power to them; and they were grappling with difficulty as strong men to wrestle, calm, watchful, wary, and ready. . . .
> Brother M. A. Meder, of California, whom we had come to meet, had not yet arrived, so we procured a team, and began a tour of examination to see the country. We spent Monday, Tuesday, and Wednesday, the 16th, 17th, and 18th, visiting near localities, and on the 19th we started from Brother George Adams', one of the most westerly farms in the colony, en route for Independence via Eagleville, Bethany, Pattonsburg, Maysville, and Stewartsville. . . ..
> At Stewartsville we became the guests of Brother J. T. Kinnaman, one of the sweet singers of Israel—one whom Solomon would have placed with Asaph and his band had he lived in his day. We tarried here over Saturday and Sunday, preaching twice in Crab Orchard Schoolhouse to houses full of people, Saints, and inquirers.[5]

After a visit to Independence, he went back by wagon to Lamoni with T. W. Smith. He continues:

> And though the way was long, the hills steep and rugged, we managed to cheer the way by conversation about the country and its possibilities for the Saints, about doctrine and its effects, and with argument about things that we did not see alike. . . .
> Prices for farms range from five to thirty dollars per acre; now and then improved farms being offered for twelve dollars and fifty cents. Brother J. T. Kinnaman paid nineteen hundred dollars for one

---

[5]*Church History*, Volume 4, page 186.

hundred and fifteen acres, including some twenty of timberland. Brother McKee of California paid twenty-three dollars per acre for his farm. These were both improved farms, though the improvements were not the best.

In the editorial department of the *Herald,* Joseph Smith detailed in all these places farming conditions, including crops, price of land, and other factors, and almost immediately the country between Independence and Lamoni began to be settled by Latter Day Saint farmers. Thus very slowly the long-expected "gathering" began to take place.

While a great deal of time was taken to consider where best to move the business interests of the church, they were eventually taken to Lamoni. The last number of the *Herald* issued from Plano, October 15, 1881, contained the following editorial comment:

> President Joseph Smith left Plano on October 7, with his family and household effects for Lamoni. . . .
> This issue closes the stay of the *Herald* in Plano, Kendall County, Illinois. It came here in 1863, and was kindly received by the leading citizens of the place. It began its career here with a list of three hundred subscribers, many of them free; and some of them taking several copies. It had a press and fixtures costing about two hundred and seventy-five dollars, and occupied one room about eighteen by twenty feet square. It had Brother Isaac Sheen for its editorial force, and Brother William D. Morton, senior, as its foreman, compositor, and pressman, with a Washington Medallion number four hand press as its machinery. It will reach Lamoni, Decatur County, Iowa, and begin a new departure (on the old way) with an eight horse power engine, two cylinder power presses, and a jobber press, with type and other fixtures to match, an office two stories high, thirty by sixty-five feet in size (engine room attached), an editor, bookkeeper, superintendent, and five compositors.[6]

The Kendall County Record, published at Yorkville. county seat of Kendall County, Illinois, noticed the departure of President Smith as follows:

> Elder Joseph Smith, the President of the Reorganized Church of Latter Day Saints, took his final departure from Plano last Saturday

---
[6] The *Saints' Herald,* October 15, 1881, page 322.

night. The publishing house will follow inside of a week. The concern goes to Lamoni, Iowa, where the central organization will be stationed. Mr. Smith leaves Plano, but carries the good will of Plano's citizens with him. He has lived here for the past fifteen years, and has always borne the reputation of a good citizen. Always to be found on the side of right, he maintained his position to the end, and goes to his future home with sad farewells and good wishes of his many friends. The organization will be continued in Plano.[7]

The prejudice against the Saints was fast disappearing. Two years before there had been a local conference held in Far West District, and Alexander H. Smith attended, visiting the spot from which as a babe in his mother's arms he had been driven in winter before an angry mob. He says:

It was with peculiar feelings that I joined in the business of the conference; and these feelings were intensified when I was called upon to speak, and subsequently to baptize in the immediate neighborhood of my birthplace, whence forty years ago my father and mother were driven by mob violence. I could not help thinking that God in his own time and way was preparing for the return from exile those who are faithful, to their land of promise, and my heart was soft, my trust strengthened in the work.

In 1881 Joseph Smith preached in the courthouse in Carthage in the very room where his father and uncle were arraigned in 1844. Newspaper comments were favorable, and that old-time enemy of the church in Nauvoo, Thomas C. Sharp, commented in a manner that had only a hint of the fire-eating editor of the Warsaw Signal in the 1840's:

The lectures of Elder Joseph Smith, of the Reorganized Mormon Church, at the courthouse, on Friday and Saturday evenings, and on Sunday morning and evening, were attended by crowded audiences. We were not present at any of the lectures, but learn from those who were that there was nothing said at which any person could take offense. He simply argued religious questions from a Mormon standpoint, but repudiated polygamy. Mr. Smith has the reputation of being a gentleman and a good citizen, and received from our people the courteous treatment which every such man, irrespective of his religious views, is entitled to.

---
[7] *Kendall County Record,* Yorkville, Illinois (date unknown); *Church History,* Volume 4, page 373.

During the year 1880, it was determined to take action to clear title to the temple property in Kirtland. After the temple had stood empty for some time, title had been secured by one Russell Huntley, who deeded it to Joseph Smith and Mark H. Forscutt. It was thought best for the church to get judgment against everyone having apparent shadow of title. As was expected, the suit was not contested, but the court action successfully cleared the title. About three years later, April 6, 1883, the first General Conference of the Reorganized Church in Kirtland Temple was held.

In 1884 the Brick Church of beloved memory was built by the congregation in Lamoni, the largest chapel built by the Reorganization to that date, and an ambitious structure for so small a group. During the summer following, the "Ladies Mite Society" of Lamoni took their patiently earned savings and bought the "old church bell"[8] that, although it went with the "Brick Church" to a fiery grave in January, 1931, still in memory chimes its call to worship in the hearts of the Latter Day Saint youth who grew up within the sound of its mighty voice. How the most sacred sorrows and joys of Lamoni Saints have attuned themselves through the years to the melodious swing of that great bell!

The years brought their share of shadows with sunshine. Death invaded the ranks, as it must inevitably do. The faithful Scotchman, Glaud Rodger, who introduced the gospel into Australia, died in his mission field at Elko, Nevada, on August 3, 1884, and March 1, 1886, Peter N. Brix, one of the early Danish missionaries, passed away in Aalborg, Denmark, adding to the shadow of death, the sorrow of the absence and burial of the dear one far from home and home folk.

By 1887 Lamoni had attained to the dignity of a population of 400. But to the Saints the greatest tragedy of all was the

---

[8] *Saints' Herald*, Volume 32, page 591 (1885).

withdrawal from the church of Jason W. Briggs and of Zenas H. Gurley, Jr., son of the Zenas H. Gurley who was so interested in the foundations of the Reorganized Church. The causes leading to these withdrawals seem quite inadequate, for a great deal of the difficulty arose from personal misunderstandings. In later years Briggs said on the witness stand in the Temple Lot Suit:

> There were no changes in the doctrines of the church that my action was based on in separating from the church. . . . There was nothing changed that I would consider vital at all in the doctrine. . . . I did not withdraw because of any change in doctrine or because anything new was brought in, but it was in the interpretation put upon certain lines of policy and doctrine; and while others were allowed to discuss those lines of policy, I was not permitted to do so.

This did not refer to any action of the body so restricting him, but to one of the editors of the *Herald* with whom he had some difference as to what could properly be put into the columns of the *Herald*.

During the first eight years after the removal of the church to Lamoni, the Bishop of the church was George A. Blakeslee, a son of the old-time missionary, James Blakeslee. Upon his death in 1890, Edmund L. Kelley, son of Richard Yancy Kelley who was an elder in the church in Nauvoo days, came to the church as Bishop. He remained the financial guardian of the church through a period of much financial uncertainty.

Edmund L. Kelley had attained a good education for that time in the West, and mostly by his own efforts. His father had died, leaving a large family, and he was therefore compelled to make his own way in the world. He had attended Iowa University during parts of the years 1863 and 1864, then gone to Poughkeepsie, New York, to attend the Eastman Business College, from whence after graduation he went to New York City seeking employment, and finding none along his own line, hired out as a boat hand on the steamer *"Herald"* running between New York City and Rondout on the Hudson until he could get a position teaching school. The first of January, 1866, he took the principalship of a boys' school in Williamsport, Pennsylvania, and at the close of the term returned to the West and worked for Edwards and Greenough during the summer months on the Chicago Directory. From then, much of his time was spent in teaching school, returning for another term of college in Iowa City in 1870, then back again to schoolteaching. In May, 1871, he accepted his first mission for the church, and in the first part of May, 1871, preached his first sermon, near Wilmington, Illinois.

In September he quit missionary work and entered the college at Iowa City again to study law, and was able to finish his work and open a law office in Glenwood, Iowa, the following year. He served as counselor to Bishop Blakeslee throughout his term of office, and succeeded, by call through the President of the church, to the office of presiding bishop upon Brother Blakeslee's death.

LXV.—The Saints Return to the Goodly Land

*A*LMOST WITH THE INCEPTION of the Reorganized Church came the desire and longing to go back to Jackson County, Missouri, "the goodly land" so loved by the church fathers; and slowly the Saints began to drift back. Nothing untoward happened; they found the old enmities born of political and social antagonisms of half a century ago were long since dead and almost forgotten.

Since the exodus of the Saints, the people of that community had been torn asunder by fratricidal strife. Border warfare waged in and about Independence, loved ones were killed, slaves freed, property scattered. Men of wealth found themselves penniless. Order Number Eleven[1] had forced the southern families from their comfortable homes, taking only what little property they could carry with them. Those who returned found their homes desolate; many of the fine old plantation houses were burned. Even as, many years ago, the despised Mormon women, with their children clinging to their skirts, had done, so southern women with their children and the few possessions they could carry in their hands, stepped from their doorways to count by half dozens on the hills about them the fires that they knew were the homes of their neighbors. Most of the women were alone; their husbands were soldiers. The exodus south of these fugitives in obedience to Order Number Eleven marked the cruelest episode in local history since 1833. True, there were but few who had taken part in causing the Saints' exodus; however, there were some.

"I did not know much about many people," said one of these citizens on the witness stand in the Temple Lot Suit. "My con-

---

[1] *Order No. 11*, page 212

ceptions were [those] of Missourians and other southern people. Yankees were not allowed to come into this country before the war by anyone who knew anything about it, nor these Mormon people either, and those people who were here and supposed to be abolitionists and northern people kept that matter a secret and did not tell many people about it."

He declared that "people entertained opinions and animosities and prejudices against these people, which under circumstances dissimilar from those which followed the war, would have rendered it impossible for these people to have come into this community and live in peace and safety. . . . I did not participate in any such feelings as that, and there were a great many people who did not. Still there were a great many people, who, if it had not been for the experiences they had passed through in the war, would not have permitted this people to return here. . . . Now, after the war . . . we were in a condition not to have too much to do with resistance and rebellion; we might have a great many opinions on one thing and another, but we were very chary about expressing them."[2]

Whether this rather frank appraisal of conditions, or the additional reason expressed, that "people were only too glad to find a man with any kind of a religion who believed in it and who lived up to it" was the underlying cause or not, those who returned to Independence found little of the old feeling against them and their religion.

In 1877 Joseph Smith visited Independence and found a few Saints there. He wrote of his visit to Independence in the *Herald*:

> At Independence, we found a few Saints in charge of Brother George Pilgrim, the husband of a niece of Elder John E. Page, one of the early apostles of the latter-day work. We found a welcome at the house of Brethren J. W. Brackenbury and ———Beagle, Saints lately from Kansas, the former an old schoolmate, when the Saints were happy in Nauvoo, the beautiful city. On the morning following

---

[2] John T. Crisp in Temple Lot Suit.

our arrival, Brother Brackenbury . . . showed us a portion of the city and its vicinity. Of course, as our stay was short, we saw but little and can only judge by what we saw. The city is handsomely situated and sits not like Rome on seven hills, but on hundreds of hills, surrounded by hundreds more. A constant succession of vale, hill, farm valley, villa, dell, grove, plain, meadow, spring, wood, reaches in every way from this Jerusalem of modern Israel. Wood, water, and stone are everywhere to be had and beauty of prospects lies in every direction. We slept one night in the city, walked over the Temple Lot, sang and prayed with earnest souls there, and left them anxious, waiting, and willing. . . .

We found Brethren Parker and Clow with their families from Canada, at Independence, together with some of the Hedrickite, Brighamite, Whitmerite, Framptonite, Morrisite, and Strangite brethren, all with the Josephites indulging a hope that the time for favoring Zion, the land of Zion, had fully come.[3]

That John W. Brackenbury should be one of the first to return was a strange coincidence, for this man, then a child, had been one of the miserable campers in the willows by the river in November 1833, and with his widowed mother and brothers and sisters had gone through all the troubles of the church from that time on. He was a son of Joseph Blanchett Brackenbury, one of the very earliest missionaries of the church, who had died in his mission field in New York, leaving his wife with this family of little ones. Undismayed, she had followed the fortunes of the church, taking up her little farm in Zion with the rest.

The return to Independence presents a different picture from that of the expulsion. It is true that when the first family returned in 1867, they were threatened in some quarters, but this did not represent the disposition of the community. That attitude is better shown by the fact that meetings were held in the courthouse in 1870 and afterwards. In 1873 a church, or branch, was organized in the courthouse and met there for a time. The minister in charge of the Baptist Church permitted the use of their font for baptism.

---

[3] *Saints' Herald,* Volume 24, page 264.

The return was very slow at first. By 1878, when the district was formed, there were only thirty-five members. A year later, though this number was only thirty-eight, they resolved to build a brick chapel on East Lexington, forty by sixty feet, which it was thought would do them for years. This building was sufficiently finished to be used by the first of February, 1881, so they removed from the hall in the Chrisman-Sawyer Bank Building. When this church was dedicated, July 1, 1884, the membership had increased to about three hundred and fifty, and by 1887 to four hundred and eighty, and the need for larger quarters was seen.

The usual question of location came up for discussion. Some wanted the new church to stand near the Brick Chapel on East Lexington, stating that the town would never grow to the west, but Joseph Luff favored a lot proffered by one of the Saints, Daniel Bowen, which stood directly north from the Temple Lot, and upon this piece of ground the final choice rested. Here was erected the "Stone Church," which was dedicated April 6, 1888, and which still houses the central congregation of the church, although there are over thirty other churches in the Independence and Kansas City areas.

General Conference of the church was held in Independence, April 6 to 13, 1882, and also April 6 to 15, 1885. Both of these conferences appear to have been held at the opera house on the east side of the square where Bundschu's building now stands. April 6, 1888, the basement having been completed, the cornerstone of the Stone Church was laid, and the Conference assembled in the basement. Before the year was out the upper auditorium was ready for use.

At the Conference that year President Smith said:

> The circumstances under which we are gathered are pleasant. The ground upon which we meet is historic, and it should be sacred to us. I am pleased to note that there has been a striking improvement among our people. . . . If we shall patiently wait and quietly move

along we shall succeed without disruption. Only that which is honest and straight will be permitted to abide. I feel to congratulate the brethren upon the thought that the constant endeavor of the great majority who have been preaching has been to maintain righteousness and truth, both in word and in conduct. We can afford to be patient with those who differ from us, and more so with those who are of us.[4]

W. W. Blair of the First Presidency said:

To me the whole outlook of the work is very promising. What a contrast this day is with our situation in 1856 to 1860, so great that we can hardly imagine the change. Then our number was few indeed, and there were foes everywhere. The only source we could look to for aid was above. Old Saints said that the efforts of the Reorganized Church would be a failure, and, indeed, it had to face all the factions and their antagonism. But we were conscious that we were in the right and that all would work out well, for we looked above and trusted in God. The inspiration of the Spirit was with us, and we were comforted by the testimony that the standard should not be permitted to fall, for God had lifted it up and it should triumph gloriously. Now the work stands higher than it ever did before, though we are largely misunderstood by the world and a good deal misrepresented. Still there are many who begin to think that there is some truth with us.[5]

Many Saints had moved into Independence, including the family of Alexander H. Smith. Frederick G. Pitt was pastor of the congregation.

The headquarters of the church were still at Lamoni, but the number of Latter Day Saints in Independence increased slowly as the years passed. Church activity was continued much as usual. It was a period of intense missionary activity.

---

[4] *Church History*, Volume 4, pages 588, 589.
[5] *Ibid.* page 589.

LXVI.—Island Missions

ONE HAPPY EVENT of this time was the establishing of the Hawaiian Mission. In 1889, upon a business trip to the States, Gilbert J. Waller, a Honolulu businessman of English birth, became interested in the gospel and was baptized in Oakland, California. He immediately began to agitate the question of a mission to the islands. Elder Albert Haws[1] had been appointed to that mission at the Conference of 1890, but no one was chosen to accompany him, and as a suitable person could not be found, he undertook the work alone, leaving San Francisco, September 12 on the ship "Australia." On the same ship he found two other Latter Day Saints from California, Brother and Sister C. H. Luther.

As the Reorganized Church was practically unknown on the Islands, great difficulty was experienced at first in securing a place in which meetings could be held, the people generally being opposed to anything connected with Mormonism. The efforts to secure any church building, meetinghouse, or school in which to hold services were unavailing, and it was very apparent from the start that the work would meet with strong opposition from the different religious bodies established here, prominent among which were the Roman Catholics, the Episcopalians, and the so-called "Missionary Party," the representative on these Islands of the Calvinistic or Presbyterian faith. This powerful religious body, which owed its birth to the labors of the New England missionaries who, nearly a century ago, came to these Islands from the far-off shores of New England and here planted their faith, exercised at this time, and had done so for years back, a mighty influence over the native Hawaiians. In fact, the ruler of this Island Kingdom and the government itself were largely under its control.

Those in charge of the Utah church, which has a large following on the Islands amongst the Hawaiians, the work having been established here about a half century ago [this was written in 1901] when Elder G. Q. Cannon and others visited these Islands and labored in the interest of their church also proved unfriendly, refusing to permit Elder Haws to preach in their house of worship, and endeavoring to prejudice the natives against the Reorganization.

---

[1] A son of Peter Haws, well known in Nauvoo in the early days of the church.

With such opposition arrayed against them at the start, the few who were desirous of establishing the work here realized the need of divine guidance and aid which was sought for and obtained. Indeed, to them it seemed apparent that the Master had been providing for emergencies by bringing one of their number to a knowledge of the work, who was possessed of some means and who was willing to use the same when necessary for the establishment of the work. As no place could be obtained free for the holding of meetings, it was necessary to rent a hall for the purpose, funds for which and other exigencies were provided.[2]

The first meeting for prayer and Communion was held at the room of Elder Haws on Beretania Street, and those present were Albert Haws, Mr. and Mrs. Luther, and Gilbert J. Waller. The succeeding meetings were held in the law office of a Hawaiian lawyer by the name of Kaulukou. This man was not a professor of any kind of religion but freely offered the use of his office evenings for a Bible class, which was held several nights a week. This first meeting place of the church was at the corner of King and Bethel Streets. Here on February 1, 1891, Elder Haws preached the first sermon, much to the pleasure of the congregation, who were mostly Hawaiians. Some prayer services were also held at the homes of those who were interested during this time, but at length it seemed advisable to procure a larger place of meeting, and one of the halls of the Odd Fellows Lodge was rented for one month at a cost of fifteen dollars.

One of the advantages enjoyed by the Hawaiian Mission was the splendid literary support afforded the missionary. This work was made possible by the financial support of Gilbert J. Waller. Almost immediately two tracts were printed in Hawaiian. Another advantage enjoyed by the Hawaiian Mission was the early inclusion among the membership of a man who was an able interpreter, Joseph M. Poepoe who eventually became an elder. He was a man of outstanding ability, prominent in government af-

---

[2]*Church History*, Volume 4, pages 661, 662.

fairs, and rendered invaluable service not only as an interpreter but as a translator. The Doctrine and Covenants and Book of Mormon were early made available to the Saints in their native tongue, as well as other articles and tracts. After Joseph M. Poepoe passed on, other able men took his place as interpreter and occasional translator, among whom may be mentioned Isaac N. Harbottle and James Puuohau. The work, growing slowly at first, has progressed through the years in a very satisfactory manner. Missionaries have been kept there constantly since 1890, but it is no disparagement to the work of any of them to say that the reputation of Gilbert J. Waller for honesty, integrity, and good citizenship has done more for the church in Hawaii than anything else. Endowed with those qualities that distinguished him as one of nature's noblemen, he gave a wonderful demonstration of what a Latter Day Saint businessman can do for the church, when he combines good citizenship and unimpeachable integrity with his religious zeal.

In the Society Island Mission the work went steadily forward during these years, being greatly facilitated by the use of the gospel boat. Apostle Thomas W. Smith was the first to mention having a boat of our own, when in 1886, after spending one and one half years, he wrote, "What is needed here is a small schooner, belonging to the church, but I have no hope of receiving gifts from America for that purpose."

Elder Smith undervalued the interest of his American brethren, or perhaps we should say sisters. When in 1891 Elder Devore, then in the islands, renewed the subject, Mrs. Marietta Walker and James Caffall took up the matter and made it an interesting objective. Bishop Kelley supported the move, and the *Herald* editors were with him. A subscription list was opened in the "Mother's Home Column," of which Marietta Walker was editor. Assisted by her niece, Lucy Lyons Resseguie, Mrs. Walker collected and published a book of poems, which she named

Afterglow. The money derived went into the fund for the gospel boat. The Sunday school took it up, and many a middle-aged man or woman of today thinks back upon the pleasure derived from pennies, not spent for candy, but put into a special bank to be sent to Bishop Kelley to help buy the gospel boat. There was hardly a child in the church who did not feel a personal interest in the "Evanelia." All rejoiced when, in less than three years, three thousand dollars had been collected (mostly in very small amounts), and "our boat" could be purchased. Bishop Kelley went to San Francisco in person to secure the boat. How fortunate it was then that Joseph F. Burton, the missionary, had been Captain Burton for so many years. They decided to build a boat. Nothing but the best material went into her making. Everything about her furnishings were the special gifts of friends and Sunday schools throughout the country.

Captain Burton volunteered to take her across the sea to the Islands. Captain Burton and his wife, a young missionary named Hubert Case and his bride (who was Alice Montague, daughter of an old missionary, George Montague), and the crew, Jeptha Scott, mate, and Frederick Nieman and William McGrath, sailors, made up the seven passengers aboard. On September 14, 1894, she was launched at San Francisco with an American Flag flying proudly above her, and the ceremony was celebrated in true sailor fashion, but on September 22 the Saints had their own little dedicatory service of singing and prayer, and the next day she sailed away to the Islands where three missionaries and two thousand Saints eagerly waited her coming.

They had named her "Evanelia," the Polynesian name for Gospel Ship. The "Evanelia" was the great interest of the Saints at that time and their chiefest anxiety. Zealous Saints even named their baby girls Evanelia. On November 30, after thirty-five days at sea, she rode triumphantly into harbor at Papeete, and Elder Gilbert and Metuaore were first on board to congratulate

Captain Burton and admire the little gospel boat.

Bishop Kelley had warned the people who used the boat against loading her with merchandise, and for awhile his advice was heeded. The little boat went to and fro in service of the church, but at length temptation became too great and the money to be derived from carrying cargo too seductive, and she was put into the merchant trade. On July 26, 1896, overloaded, she sank in a calm sea.

A few years later another tragedy, the tidal wave of January, 1903, hampered the work in the South Sea Islands. The missionaries on the Islands then were Joseph F. Burton and Emma, his wife, a wonderful missionary pair justly revered by the church, and J. W. Gilbert and wife. Mr. and Mrs. Joseph F. Burton were at Papeete, but Mr. and Mrs. Gilbert were at Hikueru and passed through the worst of the storm. In a coconut tree they found shelter from the rising water, but the wind, after lashing the tree furiously, finally felled it, and they were forced, wading waist deep in water, to find another refuge. Finally they climbed into the high stump of another tree and managed to cling there until morning, when the receding waters revealed a scene of horror. Everywhere were dead and dying, and they could see sharks devouring the bodies of many of their dead in the sea. Nothing but sorrow and suffering were to be seen anywhere. There was almost no food or drinking water on the entire island. Of the sixty-six sailboats in the harbor, all but one or two were destroyed. No one had shelter or clothing. It was then that Elder Gilbert, rising to the occasion, as the leader of a thousand thirsty people, started in primitive fashion to distill water for drinking purposes from sea water. Had it not been for his ingenuity and thoughtfulness, many more might have perished in a still more horrible manner. The loss of the church in the islands was very great. More than five hundred perished in the storm.

The island Saints recovered from this calamity, as they had

many another. They were accustomed to adversity, particularly in the earlier years of the work, when they were proscribed and vigorously persecuted by the government of the Islands (French) and yet, refused stanchly to renounce their faith. They are among the most generous, faithful, and kindly adherents of the church. The Society Island Mission has always maintained a small force of missionaries there; and a record of the names and the work accomplished by each of this small army of noble men and women who have freely sacrificed their life and time in this difficult mission would make a book in itself. Their names are held in grateful remembrance by those whom they served.

A mission was opened in the Isle of Pines, but abandoned after several years because of financial stringency and lack of missionaries. Even in the short time during which the gospel was preached there, a lasting imprint was made upon the history of the church.

LXVII.—Development and Progress

At the beginning of 1873 President Joseph Smith was without counselors, William Marks having died in May of the previous year. At the General Conference of 1873 the Quorum of the First Presidency was filled for the first time in the Reorganization by the ordination of Elders W. W. Blair and David H. Smith as counselors to the president of the church. David's service was limited by ill health and he was released at the General Conference of 1885, but President Blair continued to serve until his death in 1896.

Following this, for a few years, President Joseph Smith had for his counselors two men who were especially set apart for other work, Patriarch Alexander H. Smith and Bishop Edmund L. Kelley. At the Conference of 1902, the Presidency was filled with two men who could devote their entire time to the work, R. C. Evans and Frederick M. Smith, eldest son of the president. The two former counselors were now able to revert to their own work.

The only other change in counselors to President Joseph Smith was in 1909, when Elder Elbert A. Smith was chosen to succeed Elder R. C. Evans, who became a bishop. "Brother Elbert," as he was known throughout the church, was the son of David H. Smith and, like his father, was greatly gifted and came to be loved among the Saints throughout the world.

Of the ten men who occupied in the Quorum of Twelve in 1873, only seven were left, and at the Conference of 1887 four more men were chosen by revelation to occupy in the quorum—James W. Gillen, Heman C. Smith, Joseph Luff, and Gomer T. Griffiths. These four men proved by the length and quality of their service to the church the wisdom of their calling.

The Quorum of Twelve was filled for the first time in the Reorganization in 1897, and in 1901 and 1902 the replacement of those who had grown old in service by ministers who were in vigorous manhood gave the quorum new strength in the councils of the church. Three of those added were from missions abroad: Peter Andersen, a Dane; John W. Rushton, an Englishman; and Cornelius A. Butterworth, an American who had moved to Australia and married an Australian woman, and who was to give the remainder of his life in service in that distant mission. The other three new members of the Twelve were experienced American missionaries: Elders Frederick A. Smith, Francis M. Sheehy, and Ulysses W. Greene.

Apostles Joseph Luff and Heman C. Smith were relieved of apostolic responsibility in 1909 in order to give more time to their work, Luff as Church Physician and Smith as Church Historian. The vacancies which thus occurred, and four others which came in 1913, were all filled without delay so that the Quorum of Twelve was complete throughout the remainder of President Joseph Smith's administration.

The work of the seven presidents of seventy became stabilized by direct revelation in relation to the perpetuation of the quorums of seventy and their own council.

In 1890 the Standing High Council, the highest court of the church which had become greatly depleted, was reorganized so that it could function as intended by the law of the church. This important body has been maintained from that date at full strength.

Prior to the year 1900 there were few bishops in the church, but in that year the First Presidency recommended the ordination of ten bishops for service in the United States and England. Seven of these brethren were ordained during the year and the other three within a short time thereafter. One of these three was Elder Thomas Taylor of England. Bishop Metuaore was ordained in 1901 for service in Polynesia and Bishop Lewis in 1902 for service in Australia. The ordination of these standing ministers was expected to stabilize the financial aspects of church work throughout the United States. The ordination of the three bishops in missions abroad, coupled with the selection of apostles from missions abroad, was intended to do the same thing in these missions. As part of the same period of expansion, tracts were ordered printed in languages other than English.

The first formal meeting of the bishops of the church as a group was at the General Conference of 1905. In later years those holding the office of bishop constituted the Order of Bishops.

Perhaps no event in this period of church history had as great appeal to the Saints as the forming of "stakes" in Lamoni and Independence. There had been a stake at Kirtland in the early days, and the word, however peculiar its connotation in this connection might be to others, had very close associations to old-time Saints. Early in 1853, a stake had been authorized at Zarahemla. It was premature; nothing further was heard of it except that the *Word of Consolation* only a short time later said: "there is no stake to which the Saints on this continent are commanded to gather." In 1901 they were instructed by revelation to organize two stakes—one at Lamoni and one at Independence. The organizations were very impressive. Mothers took their children that they might say in future years they had been present at this history-making event. Independence Stake was organized Wednesday, April 24, 1901, and Lamoni Stake Tuesday, April 30. George H. Hulmes became president of the Independence Stake and John Smith president of the Lamoni Stake. Roderick May, bishop of Independence District, and William Anderson, bishop of Decatur District, and their counselors were chosen to form the bishoprics of the new stakes and were so ordained. Twelve men were also chosen and ordained in each stake as high counselors.

With the completion and orderly assignment of priesthood affairs, the church had grown also. The conference where each member cast his vote after the manner of a general assembly had very soon grown unwieldly, and it was necessary for the General Conferences to become representative bodies. For more than fifteen years the rules of representation provided that the Melchisedec priesthood of the church should be ex officio members of the Conference, and that the delegate vote of the Conference should consist of representatives chosen on the basis of one delegate to every hundred members, with one delegate for each isolated branch having less than one hundred members.

There were many events of exceptional interest through the years. The original manuscript of the Book of Mormon—those precious yellowed pages intrusted to David Whitmer by Oliver Cowdery just before his death that the old man would have guarded with his life if necessary—was always a point of interest. Many were the visitors who went to Richmond, Missouri, where the white-haired, remaining witness of the Book of Mormon lived, to listen with joy to his testimony and look on the pages written by the hand of Oliver Cowdery and others back in that long-ago day when the history of the church had yet to be lived and suffered. Once a committee met at Richmond to correct the current edition of the Book of Mormon by the original manuscript. All future editions followed that corrected copy. At length, after the death of Whitmer (1888), the manuscript came into the hands of the Reorganized Church (April 1903), together with a history written by John Whitmer, first church historian, a few pages of manuscript revelations, and the original manuscript of the characters taken to Professor Anthon and Doctor Mitchell.

Sunday schools were always encouraged by the church, although some members were dubious about them. The third Joseph Smith, son of the Martyr, remembers being one of sixty boys in a Sunday school class in old Nauvoo. "I remember," he says, "the meetings in the grove on the hillside near the temple, and going there to Sunday school. Here I was a scholar in a class of about sixty boys under the teaching of Almon W. Babbitt, who, as my memory now recalls him, was a kind, friendly, pleasant teacher. . . . He was a man of good presence, and quite able to teach."[1]

Edwin Stafford speaks of the same Sunday school: "I well remember the first time my brother and myself attended Sabbath School at Nauvoo, from the fact that this was the first time we had ever done so since becoming members of the church; there existing in the minds of the Saints with whom we had associated before going there, a prejudice against Sunday Schools, styling them sectarian institutions. It was held in the grove just west or south of west of where the temple was in process of erection; and it seemed as if the grove was filled with the different classes of which such schools consist. The Superintendent was Brother William Marks, President of the Stake of Nauvoo."[2]

Very shortly after Joseph Smith (Young Joseph) came to the church in 1860, he established a Sunday school in Nauvoo, and one was started in St. Louis as early as 1864. By 1869 the church was publishing a paper for Sunday school, by the name of *Zion's Hope*. The president of the church, Joseph Smith, was its first editor, though much of the work devolved upon Marietta Walker (Frances) and Mark H. Forscutt (Uncle Mark).

In those early days a small book of lessons or questions was published for use in the Sunday schools, and branch presidents were urged to encourage Sunday schools and organize them wherever possible. The General Sunday School Association was organized in April 1891, and operated efficiently for years, with every Sunday school in the church a member, and even the Home Department taking active part in its legislative sessions. The Association took over the publication of the Sunday school papers and lesson helps, and operated at a profit to the church.

---
[1]"What Do I Remember About Nauvoo," *Journal of History*, Volume 3, page 142.
[2]"Incidents in the Life of One of Earth's Pilgrims," by Edwin Stafford, *Autumn Leaves*, Volume 1, page 506.

DEVELOPMENT AND PROGRESS 573

A young people's society, designated by the ambitious title of "Zion's Religio Literary Society," was the outgrowth of several "Student Societies" and other young people's organizations. In 1893 an association was formed that paralleled the Sunday School Association. Although never so large or financially prosperous, this organization was a force for good among the people of the church for years.

The women of the church have long had an organization of their own, although it has functioned under various names, the earliest being the "Prayer Union" and the "Daughters of Zion." Subsidiary organizations such as the Laurel Club of Independence and the Mite Society of Lamoni gave excellent local service.

Another aspect of the growth of the church has been its institutional development. On November 12, 1895, the cornerstone for Graceland College, the church's own school, was laid, and in 1897, January 1, the building was dedicated. College classes in the meantime had started in September 1895 and have continued to this day. Frederick M. Smith, eldest son of Joseph and third president of the church, was the first graduate, coming from the large and more efficient university at Iowa City to complete his work at the church college. He was graduated in 1898.

It was difficult to finance the college during its early years and in 1904 the General Conference actually voted to close the institution at the end of the school year. However, it was found that this could not be done without incurring losses which the Conference had not considered, and the Board of Trustees, with the support of the Presidency and Presiding Bishopric, took it on themselves to keep the college operating until Conference could be held. In 1905 the desired approval was received and thereafter the college grew steadily in the quality of its educational offering and its influence in the affairs of the church.

Ten years after Graceland opened her doors, the church was directed in 1906 by special command to build a "sanitarium, a place of refuge and help for the sick and afflicted,"[3] with Dr. Joseph Luff of the Twelve in charge. Independence was the place of its location. Excavation for the building was begun in August 1907, and the building was formally opened on December 16, 1909, entirely free from debt. This hospital has been in constant operation ever since.

The School of Nursing is an important department of the hospital. It was opened in 1910 and immediately set a high standard for its graduates. For many years it has been accredited by the Missouri State Board of Nurse Examiners and given full accreditation by the National Nurse Accrediting Service. The school offered a basic three-year course in nursing and was opened to young women between the ages of seventeen and thirty-five who were high school graduates ranking in the upper half of their graduating classes.

In the year 1906 provision was made for the realization of a project long planned and discussed by the Daughters of Zion, the women's organization of the church. A committee, selected from some of the prime workers in this movement, was appointed to serve in conjunction with the bishop of the church and his counselors to provide for a home for children when it could be accomplished without accruing debt. Those women named were Mrs. B. C. Smith, Callie B. Stebbins, Ruth Lyman Smith, Eveline Burgess, and Emma Hougas. In a short time plans were perfected, and the Children's Home in Lamoni was opened August 15, 1911. It functioned for a number of years.

Homes for the aged have been provided by the church at Lamoni, Iowa; Independence, Missouri; Kirtland, Ohio; and Holden, Missouri. For many years these were administered by the Presiding Bishopric, but as occasion demanded, this responsibility was handed to local boards.

---

[3] Doctrine and Covenants 127:1.

DEVELOPMENT AND PROGRESS

Bishop Edmund L. Kelley moved to Independence in 1905. Something less than a year later Joseph Smith and his older son, President Frederick M. Smith, also moved to Independence. Here the president of the church devoted himself more and more to his occasional public ministries and his work on the *Herald* and such prophetic guidance as became his privilege and duty. More and more, particularly after 1909, the burden of administration was passed to Frederick M. Smith and his other counselor, Elbert A. Smith. This meant that when the time came for the transition to be completed, Brother Joseph's successor was already experienced in overall church administration and the Saints were aware of his capacity for work of this nature. The fact that they were together at Independence during President Joseph Smith's last years meant that the eyes of the church turned more and more to Independence as the Center Place and the thoughts of the church were inclined toward the gathering here and in the regions round about.

LXVIII.—Frederick M. Smith

As Joseph Smith grew older, he became increasingly concerned that the church might not be scattered and confused at his death, as it had been in 1844. He made careful plans that all should be left in order and that all should understand that he had been directed to choose his son, Frederick M. Smith, as his successor. He even prepared and left for the instruction of the priesthood and church a careful "Letter of Instruction" (March, 1913) explaining in detail the procedure that should be followed in event of his death.

His son had been called to occupy in the Presidency with his father in 1902, and in 1909 President Smith presented again to the church his gavel, which he had used for thirty years. He seldom presided from that time, turning the work over largely to his son, a particularly good parliamentary leader.

In Frederick M. Smith was realized the dream of his father and his grandfather. They had both passionately longed for an academic education. Young Frederick M. Smith had that ambition as they had and was able to realize it as they were not. In addition to that training, his father had counseled with him over the problems of the church for several years. When at length the expected burden of responsibility fell upon his shoulders, he was in Worcester, Massachusetts, completing work for his doctor's degree.

On the 10th of December, 1914, the third Joseph Smith passed away. For days his family and friends had gathered around him, cherishing every word, seeking to satisfy his slightest wish. He had written directions for his funeral, and fearing the love of those who had followed him so long might lead to an extravagant display, he urged simplicity. He asked that no new clothing be bought, that he be buried in the same sort of casket that was used in the church's Home for the Aged, and, especially, that no money be spent on flowers, but that all who felt thus to honor his memory, give the amount they would have spent in that way, to the poor. His wishes were followed as nearly as the love of his people would permit. The casket was of simple design, with but one wreath. At the foot was placed an urn and into it as they passed for one last look at that loved face, the thousands who loved him in life put the money with which they would have liked to show their devotion in a last tribute of affection. It was later distributed to the needy. The service was significant of his life, a long life of placing others first.

The editor of the Kansas City *Journal* for December 12, 1914, paid this tribute to the departed leader:

> He was the Prophet, but first of all he was the Christian gentleman and the good citizen. As such he lived; as such he died; and as such he will be remembered by all outside the household of his faith. His followers themselves can have no legacy of remembrance more honorable than this appraisement of the people among whom he lived and labored so many years.
>
> Kindly, cheerful, loyal to his own creed, tolerant of those of others, standing for modesty, simplicity, good citizenship, embodying in his private and public life all the virtues which adorn a character worthy of emulation—such is the revelation which Joseph Smith leaves to the world, as the real interpretation of an ecclesiastical message translated into terms of human character.

The church then turned to his son, and he was ordained President of the High Priesthood of the church May, 1915. As one poet of the church had written in 1909.

> Through half a century thou hast been our chief,
> Our hearts will not allow thy work is done,
> Yet one thought makes more tender coming grief
> Thy Work will still continue in thy son.

Frederick M. Smith did not make so deliberate a choice of his position in life as had his father. He was brought up from early childhood to feel that such was his destiny. Everyone he met on the street in Lamoni as a boy and young man knew he would sometime be President of the church. It was not always pleasant.

His every act was scanned with a view to its influence upon his future position. His life did not belong to him, with which to do as he willed; it belonged to the church. Of course he could have refused to accept this responsibility, but he did not though at times he must have considered such a course, for as he grew older he developed a great deal of independence of thought and action. With a natural leaning towards science and mechanics, he cultivated also, largely for the sake of his future position, an interest in philosophy and economics. As Frederick M. Smith had a fund of knowledge on almost every subject he often surprised his visitors, so quickly did he pick up the topic of almost any conversation and enter into a discussion of the latest thought upon the subject.

Like his father, his character was unimpeachable. The low, coarse, crude, and vulgar were naturally distasteful to him. He always stood on the side of any movement for civic righteousness or betterment, as his father did, not only as a matter of ethics, but also as a matter of taste. At the same time he was a lover of all clean sports, as fond of fishing and outdoor life as he was of playing football in his college days.

His church statistical record shows that he was baptized July 20, 1883; ordained an elder on July 12, 1897; was secretary of the fifth quorum of elders in April, 1898, and was appointed to a mission in Ohio and western Pennsylvania at that time.

He was a member of the Board of Trustees of Graceland College from 1901 to 1912. He was identified with other church work at the same time, giving valuable assistance in association with the historian, the librarian, and the Lamoni Stake Bishopric before being ordained as his father's counselor on April 18, 1902.

He was united in marriage on August 3, 1897, with Miss Ruth

L. Cobb, daughter of Elijah and Alice (Lyman) Cobb, who was then an instructor on the faculty of Graceland College. He continued his studies and received his bachelor's degree in 1898, enjoying the distinction of being the first graduate of the college, and the only member of his class. He remained to teach mathematics there in 1899-1900. He and his family moved to Independence in 1906. He attended the University of Missouri in 1908-1909. From the University of Kansas, he received his Master's degree in 1911.

In 1914 he and Mrs. Smith went to Worcester, Massachusetts, where he carried on graduate studies under the guidance of Dr. G. Stanley Hall. His studies were interrupted by his father's death on December 10, but he returned to Clark University and received his doctor's degree in 1916.

Ordination as president of the church came to him on May 5, 1915. From the first his administration reflected the vigor of his strength and a forward-looking, progressive attitude. He was eagerly concerned for the building of the kingdom and regarded the organization and effective functioning of stakes as an important step in this direction. Under his guidance the Independence Stake was divided in 1916, to create the Kansas City, Holden, and Independence stakes. A year later the Far West and Nodaway districts were combined to form the Far West Stake with Richard S. Salyards as president and Beauford J. Scott as bishop. In 1920 the Independence Stake was reconstituted as the City of Zion under the immediate supervision of the First Presidency, the Presiding Bishopric, and the Standing High Council.

The General Conference of 1920 was one of the most important held in many years. Two recommendations of the First Presidency were particularly noteworthy: the extension of missionary endeavor and the building of the Auditorium. In line with his recommendations concerning evangelism, President Smith went to Europe later in the year, accompanied by Apostle T. W.

Williams. Together they visited England, Germany, Holland, and Palestine to evaluate the needs and prospects in these countries. Apostle Gillen joined them in the British Mission, where he remained in charge.

The Saints responded enthusiastically to the call to build the General Conference Auditorium. Money was subscribed liberally. But economic conditions and dissension in the church made it impossible to build as soon as had been hoped. Construction began in 1926 and was sufficiently advanced for the General Conference of 1927 to meet in the lower auditorium. A few months later the church officers and department heads moved into the Auditorium. But when depression struck the nation and the world in 1929 all further construction was postponed. It was not until 1956 that the work was resumed on a large scale.

The 1920's saw other threats to the life of the church. President Smith shared his father's conviction that the members of the Twelve and Seventy should be relieved, as far as possible, of the burdens of local work so as to be free to push evangelism into new fields. His attempts to achieve the reorganization of the quorums which this entailed met with resistance, and this was augmented when his attempts to set up clearer lines of ministerial responsibility were regarded as leading to an unwarranted and undesirable concentration of power in the First Presidency. These and related differences came to a head at the Conference of 1925, and the church was so divided that many lost heart. It was not until the whole fellowship of the Saints began to work together to "pay the debt" as the nation emerged from the depression that the precious sense of unity under God began to be felt throughout the church once more.

In the year 1930, the community and the church joined hands to raise funds, which resulted in the erection of a building adjacent to the old Sanitarium building. During the depression, work on this was stopped, but the building was kept in a good state of preservation during that period.

In 1941, negotiations carried on with the United States Government resulted in the receiving of a grant in the amount of $288,000.00 which made possible the completion of four floors of the building for hospital facilities, and in addition to this a complete heating plant for the entire new building and the old building as well.

The grant was allotted outright to the Independence Sanitarium and Hospital, and the ownership and management of the institution and all assets belonging thereto are controlled entirely by the church through the Board of Trustees consisting of the three members of the First Presidency, the three members of the Presiding Bishopric, the chairman of the Church Medical Council, and two ex-officio members, *viz*, the mayor of the city of Independence and the judge for the eastern district of the Jackson County administrative court. For nearly thirty years President Smith worked in close official and personal harmony with his cousin and counselor, President Elbert A. Smith. They were aided from 1922 until 1938 by President Floyd M. McDowell, whose special abilities lay in the field of education with special emphasis on the work of the young people. After Elbert became Presiding Evangelist, President McDowell thought it well to resign and to devote himself fully to departmental ministries. Israel A. Smith, the next younger brother of President Smith, was called to be a counselor in the First Presidency as was Presiding Bishop L. F. P. Curry. The arrangement was a temporary one at first, but it was confirmed in the revelation of 1940 and the Presidency thus constituted continued until the death of President F. M. Smith. When Bishop Curry became a member of the First Presidency, Bishop G. Leslie DeLapp succeeded him as Presiding Bishop of the church.

At the very heart of President F. M. Smith's hopes for the church was the passionate longing for Zion which moved his forebears. If he cherished one ideal for the church more than another, it was that he might see rise in Zion buildings beautifully and permanently planned and built—such inspirational buildings as he had visited in his travels in the old world, buildings that would be worthy of his dream of Zion.

But he shared the unfortunate lot of those who dream magnificently, those whose "reach" constantly exceeds their "grasp." He died on March 20, 1946, with his building program scarcely begun. He chafed under the obstacles and delays that continually blocked the achievement of his goals for the church. Two world wars and a major economic depression diverted his powers to other fields. He toiled on, hoping and dreaming to the last, tortured toward the end with ill health, living always under the shadow of a great loneliness, for on May 4, 1926, his wife died as the result of an accident. She was the one great love of his life. Unreconciled to her loss, he was faithful to her memory to the end of his life.

"His most impressive monument is the great domed auditorium at Independence, one of the landmarks of the region," said the *Kansas City Star* the morning after his death.

But perhaps more impressive and greater by far will be the monument to his memory that will be built by the youth of the church in the lives they will live, and the contributions they will make to the spiritual and economic brotherhood that was his life's ideal. In the youth of the church, he placed his trust. He believed in them and urged them to seek the best in education that the country affords. By precept and example he encouraged them to eschew the cheap and tawdry, the low and the vulgar. To them he passed on his dreams of the best and the most beautiful for the building of Zion.

LXIX.—Israel Alexander Smith

THE CHOICE OF A NEW PRESIDENT in the church follows the definite pattern of all priesthood choice and ordination as set forth in the law. From the office of deacon up to that of president choice is made by divine call and concurred in by those over whom the one to be ordained shall minister. However, in the case of president that call to serve has traditionally come to one of the descendants of Joseph the Prophet. There is much to commend this procedure, since some orderly method of succession must be followed in order to prevent schism and contention in the body. However, as has been said, ultimate choice rests with the people.

Many years ago two young men were bearers of a message[1] to a young man in Nauvoo whom neither had ever seen. In those days the Reorganized Church seemed, except to those who had a part in it, to have a very tenuous hold upon life. But the young man[2] who wrote this document at Zarahemla, Wisconsin, which was sent by the little group there with faith, prayers, and overwhelming confidence in the stranger to whom it was addressed, thought he wrote with inspiration. And who can say that he did not? One who reads that epistle, couched in ancient Biblical language, and compares it with the subsequent life of him to whom it was sent, is impressed with the clarity of its prophetic vision.

"Our faith is not unknown to you . . . ." it read "that the seed of him to whom the work was first committed should stand forth to bear the responsibility (as well as wear the

---
[1] *Church History*, Volume 3, page 260, from "Autobiography of Joseph Smith," as published in *Life of Joseph the Prophet*, by Tullidge, pages 772-783.
[2] Jason W. Briggs.

crown) of a wise master builder. . . . As that seed, to whom pertains this right, and heaven-appointed duty you cannot be unmindful nor indifferent. The God of Abraham, Isaac, and Jacob convenanted with them and their seed. So the God of Joseph covenanted with him and his seed, that his word should not depart out of the mouth of his seed, nor out of the mouth of his seed's seed, till the end come. . . . We cannot forbear reminding you that the commandments, as well as the promises given to Joseph, your father, were to him, and his seed."

There was more to that letter, and the years saw it all fulfilled. Joseph the son of Joseph did become a "wise master builder"; he did indeed "combine in one a host, who, though in captivity and sorely tried, still refused to strengthen the hands of usurpers." He became as was there set forth truly "A Zerubbabel in Israel." "As a nail fastened in a sure place, so are the promises unto thee to make thee a restorer in Zion—to set in order the house of God." Time proved no truer words were ever set on paper. He was all of these things. The imprint of a power beyond that of the young man who penned them is there.

Then, too, the deathbed blessing by his father of Joseph the Prophet points out that his blessing should be for his children "after him." For these and other reasons the people of the church looked to a younger brother of Frederick M. to succeed him at his death. This man was already his brother's counselor, Israel Alexander Smith. However, as has been so often set forth by Joseph the Third, lineage alone does not constitute a call to assume this high and holy office.

In accordance with the law of the church, as found in the Doctrine and Covenants, giving to each president of the high priesthood the right to designate his successor, and in harmony with the precedents whereby both Joseph Smith III and his son Frederick M. Smith were selected, Israel A. Smith had been named by Frederick M. Smith to be his successor in a statement made to the Joint Council of First Presidency, Quorum of Twelve Apostles and Presiding Bishopric on October 20, 1938. As an additional safeguard, however, it was deemed advisable by the Quorum of Twelve Apostles to submit the question to the Presiding Patriarch of the Church who, under the law, has comparable prerogatives. Presiding Patriarch Elbert A. Smith, in whom the people had unbounded confidence, made a statement to the General Conference in harmony with the prior recorded designation by the then deceased president, Frederick M. Smith. On these two facts the several quorums of the church and finally the General Conference acted, and on April 6, 1946, the one hundred and sixteenth anniversary of the organization of the church, Israel A. Smith was unanimously elected to the office previously held by his grandfather, Joseph Smith, Jr., his father, Joseph Smith III, and his brother, Frederick M. Smith. On the following day, April 7, 1946, he was ordained President of the High Priesthood, with all the duties and prerogatives that go with that office.

In such manner was choice made of Israel Alexander Smith to lead the church in his brother's stead, and even then his name must receive the approval of all the quorums of the church, and finally of the General Assembly of the membership and by unanimous vote as in the case of his predecessors. He was ordained president of the High Priesthood with all the duties and prerogatives that go with that office.

Israel A. Smith was born on February 2, 1876, at Plano, Illinois, and was named for the first bishop of the Reorganization, Israel L. Rogers, and for the boy's Uncle Alexander, who in turn received his name during one of the darkest eras of church history from one of Missouri's greatest lawyers, soldiers and statesmen, General Alexander W. Doniphan. Not in name only was Israel a true Latter Day Saint. Throughout a life spent in the legal and business world outside the church, he made no apology or excuse for his belief, however unpopular it might seem. He had a firm belief in the restoration of the gospel by the hands of an angel, and in the divine authenticity of the Book of Mormon.

Early in his childhood, his parents moved from Plano to Lamoni, Iowa. Here he grew to young manhood in the spacious but modest home, "Liberty Hall," which his father had built on the outskirts of Lamoni. He attended Lamoni schools and was duly baptized by "Uncle" Henry A. Stebbins at the age of ten years on June 25, 1886. He took part in the activities of the home, for his thrifty Norwegian mother, with the aid of the children, grew much of their living: There were cows for the boys to milk and chores of all kinds to do to keep the long table in the dining room bounteously provided for the family and for the inevitable guests of which there were many. "Brother" Joseph, the genial host who presided at that table, brought home a constant stream of missionaries—young men on their first mission and old-timers full of years and marvelous experiences. Listening to these men was a favorite entertainment for young Israel both at his father's table and fireside and on that memorable "first day of General Conference." They were of deep and abiding spiritual significance to the boy who listened to them.

As he grew older, he discovered what he wanted to be and do in life. And this goal, chosen early in life, remained his constant aim and ambition. He wanted to be a lawyer. This had also been his father's choice in early life, and perhaps his admiration for his father influenced his decision. Soon after his graduation from the Lamoni high school, his father asked him what he wished to be. His answer was prompt: A lawyer. Kindly his father explained to him that the family budget would not permit of law school. His older brother was already in college; no more funds were available. "I have always thought of you as the lawyer of the family," he told him. Two years in Graceland might be arranged. Israel took them gladly as preparatory work, but he still intended to be a lawyer.

A succession of "jobs" followed; they were only a means to an end. He worked in the office of a wholesale drug company in Des Moines; he was employed for a time by the Bell Telephone Company in Ohio, West Virginia, and Pennsylvania. He sold insurance. He was a salesman for a paper company.

In 1908 he married a Lamoni girl, Miss Nina Grenawalt, and that year found him working as an assistant in the editorial offices of the Herald Publishing House for the princely sum of $11.00 a week. This was very well; it gave him time to study: evenings, every available moment. He took a correspondence course. He studied in a local attorney's office, eagerly acquiring all the legal knowledge he could. In the meantime he served as a member of the Thirty-fourth General Assembly of Iowa in 1911-1913. Two years later he took examinations and was admitted to the bar of Iowa (1912) and one year later to the bar of Missouri.

His father was now advanced in years and totally blind. He was in urgent need of a secretary to look after his large correspondence and also to act as secretary for him while he dictated his memoirs. During this period, Israel was his father's constant companion until he passed away December 10, 1914.

After his father's death, he devoted himself a great part of the time to his chosen profession, and attained recognition in the legal world and gained the respect and honor of his associates. He did not amass wealth. He probably never would have. He was too much the son of "Brother Joseph" and "Sister Bertha," who of old at "Liberty Hall" nearly always had in their care some unfortunate with whom nobody else could afford to be bothered. Clients he had in plenty, but so many of them needed a friend and found it in him. The tide of human sorrow and suffering that flows through a lawyer's office found in him a sympathetic ear and an understanding heart. All too often there was no fee, and none was asked or expected.

There were sorrows of his own, too. Two sons had blessed his home. Both wanted to follow their father's steps in the legal profession. He determined that they should not have to struggle as he had done. To send them to school exacted great financial sacrifice cheerfully made. Joseph Perrine, the eldest, died on March 2, 1936, after a brief illness at Missouri University in his junior year. The younger, Donald Carlos, finished his college course before the Second World War claimed the youth of the nation. He, now the only son, saw active service as an officer in the Navy, and was retired in 1945 with the rank of lieutenant commander.

Perhaps Brother Smith's most signal service in his chosen field was his participation as a delegate in the Missouri Constitutional Convention which convened at Jefferson City, Missouri, on September 21, 1943, and adjourned on September 29, 1944. As commissioned by vote of the people of Missouri, this convention drafted a new constitution, since approved and now in effect. Within a few days of his choice as a delegate, he was also chosen to serve a four-year term as President of the Pioneer Lawmakers Association of Iowa, over which association he presided at their 29th biennial session in March, 1947.[3]

When Israel Smith came to the Presidency of the church, he also held membership or office in the following organizations:

[3] See *Annals of Iowa*, July, 1947, complete minutes of "Pioneer Lawmaker's Association," pages 3-45.

American Bar Association (president 1943-44); Missouri Historical Society (trustee 1947-48); National Municipal League; Iowa Pioneer Lawmakers Association (president 1943-47); American War Dads; Honorary Member Kiwanis International; Optimist International (past president); Jackson County Tuberculosis Society (trustee). President Smith was a graduate with the degree of Bachelor of Laws from Lincoln Jefferson University, and was admitted to practice before the Federal Court of Missouri and the Supreme Court of the United States in 1921.

While he was pursuing all these activities outside the church, the church was not forgotten. He served in whatever capacity he could, quietly and efficiently, whenever he was asked to do so. He was ordained a high priest on April 11, 1915, at Lamoni; set apart as counselor to Bishop Benjamin R. McGuire, April 15, 1920, and ordained a bishop on July 4 of that same year. His associate in the Presiding Bishopric was James F. Keir, and the deep friendship which developed during that association endured until Bishop Keir's death January 20, 1956.

Israel A. Smith stepped into the leadership of the church at a particularly propitious time. World War II had ended the previous year. The burden of debt under which the church had labored through the depression years had been lifted, and church finances were on a sound basis. In the nation there were prosperity and full employment, instead of the postwar depression which had been predicted by many prophets of gloom. The atomic age had been ushered in by the bombing of Hiroshima in 1945.

Many of the differences and even antagonisms of earlier years had been softened by time or forgotten. Brother Israel took quite seriously the task of bringing peace and unity to the church. In his acceptance speech he said: "It is one of the challenging duties of the presidencies of the church to bring about complete harmony and unity among the quorums and councils of the church.

"Every good and desirable thing, all our hopes, and the blessings of heaven await the faithful discharge of these responsibilities. I trust I may be of assistance in securing this unity" (*Saints' Herald,* January 28, 1957).

In an interview with Roger Yarrington in the same issue of the *Herald,* President Smith said further: "I wanted to bring about an era of harmony in the councils of the church. We had passed through a period of disagreement, and that disagreement needed to be replaced with harmony before the work of the church could progress.

"Brother Garver and Brother Edwards were my counselors, and met with me here in this office. I told them I didn't know how long our administration would be, but if we could bring about harmony we would be making a real contribution regardless of our time in office.

"I've had the pleasure of hearing both of those men tell me that they consider that objective accomplished" (*Saints' Herald,* January 28, 1957, page 87).

Under these conditions, and under this kind of leadership, the church was ready for a period of rapid growth, expansion, and progress. There was a steady, consistent, and sustained annual increase in baptisms during all of the twelve years Brother Israel served the church as its prophet and leader. With this expanding membership there came also an expansion of the church's building program. The decade from 1946 to 1956 was marked by the expenditure of $7,588,830.00 by local branches and congregations for new houses of worship and for modernizing and remodeling existing buildings. A new building was provided for Resthaven; additions were made to the facilities at Graceland and at the Independence Sanitarium and Hospital. The buildings vacated by the moving of Resthaven were converted for use by the new School of the Restoration, which offers both residence and correspondence courses to ambitious members of laity and priesthood who want to improve their education but do not have time or opportunity to attend a full-time college.

Under the direction of the Presiding Bishopric, plans were laid for the eventual completion of the Auditorium. It was a matter of some pride with Brother Israel that the front entrance and foyer were finished in time for the 1956 Conference, and a matter of regret to all of his associates that he did not live long enough to see the first Conference in the completed General Conference Chamber in October of 1958, although work on it was well advanced before his death.

It was both fitting and proper that Brother Israel should have felt a deep concern for the interests of the church and its members in missions abroad. In July of 1947 President F. Henry Edwards and Bishop G. Leslie DeLapp went to Europe to survey conditions there and lay the groundwork for a more stable missionary effort. In October of 1947 President John F. Garver and Bishop Walter N. Johnson embarked for Australia to survey the mission field there. In June of 1950 President Smith and Bishop Mark Siegfried left by plane for Hawaii, Tahiti, and Australia. In each place they found a joyous and loving reception, and left behind them a people encouraged and strengthened by a kindly prophetic ministry.

President Garver's death on March 3, 1949, left a vacancy in the Presidency which was filled during the 1950 Conference by the ordination of W. Wallace Smith as Counselor on April 4, 1950.

The Conference of 1950 also called for the organization of stakes in the Detroit and Los Angeles areas, and for the organization of the Center Place as a stake, thus relieving the Presidency of direct responsibility for its administration. In the early summer of 1950, these three stakes were organized under the direction of the First Presidency.

Another progressive move which characterized the tenure of Israel A. Smith as President of the Church was the calling of various educational gatherings, conferences, and institutes. A Book of Mormon Institute was held in Independence during January of 1951, and the Women's Department Institute in October of that same year. An institute devoted to the study of the Doctrine and Covenants was held from September 25 to October 3,

1952, at which time the Herald House introduced a new edition of the Doctrine and Covenants containing explanatory headings for each section, and divisions of paragraphs into lettered subdivisions. An Institute on Evangelism followed in April of 1953, and an Institute on the Teaching Mission of the Church that fall. Meanwhile the Bishopric had also sponsored a Professional and Business Men's Conference in February of 1953.

In October of 1950 the first High Priests' Conference was held in historic Kirtland Temple—a gathering marked by an outpouring of peace, unity, and spiritual power. On the closing Sunday morning, the entire assembly was shocked and saddened by the news that Nina G. Smith, beloved wife of the President, had died quietly in her sleep. She had been his faithful, loving, and uncomplaining companion through many years when his time and strength and resources had been devoted unstintingly to the church. Her loss was felt keenly not only by her husband, but by his three younger brothers whom Israel and Nina had taken into their home and reared as their own after the death of the boys' mother.

After his wife's death, Brother Israel was a lonely man. He threw himself even more intensely into his church work. His son and daughter-in-law, Donald and Darlene, moved into the old family home on Short Street, and continued to make it home for him. Here he could enjoy the pleasant association of his grandchildren, or retire to the privacy of his own apartment, with its library and study, if he so desired. Although he worked hard, he learned to conserve his strength, to delegate authority, and to share responsibility. His friendship for Bishop James F. Keir, who had lost his wife some months before, became even more significant to him.

In May of 1951, President Smith made a short trip to Mexico, where he made a close study of the legal, political, and economic conditions that might have a bearing on future missionary endeavor in that country. In the summer of 1952, in company with Bishop Henry L. Livingston, he journeyed to Europe, where he visited many branches of the Saints to their great blessing and uplift.

During his tenure, both as counselor and as Prophet, Brother Israel was always ready to defend the good name of his grandfather against the attacks of those who through malice or ignorance charged him with the crime of polygamy. In *Herald* articles and in personal correspondence, he brought to bear his legal and analytical mind to disclose error, to condemn slander, and to defend the right. Few men knew as much as he of the historical proof of his grandfather's innocence of polygamy, or could quote and cite so many original sources in support of his arguments.

As Prophet, Israel A. Smith gave five revelations to the church, Sections 139 to 143, beginning with April 9, 1946, and ending with April 7, 1954. Section 144 on the calling of his successor was adopted on October 6, 1958. Though many of these had to do with changes in the official personnel of the church, there were also flashes of spiritual truth and insight which will be quoted as Scripture in many sermons which are as yet unpreached.

After a little more than twelve years in the prophetic office and ministry, during which he endeared himself to the Saints in all parts of the world, Israel A. Smith was fatally injured in an automobile crash on Highway 69 south of Pattonsburg, Missouri, on June 14, 1958. He met death in the line of duty, for he was on his way to Lamoni to participate in a stake conference when the accident occurred in a blinding rainstorm. He died a few hours later in a hospital in Bethany, Missouri.

His funeral service was held from the Stone Church on June 17, 1958, with his pastor, Elder Glaude A. Smith, delivering the sermon, and the Radio Choir singing the hymns. His remains were laid to rest in Mound Grove Cemetery beside his wife, and close to his father, his brother, and his son.

LXX. W. Wallace Smith

*A*LTHOUGH THE DEATH OF President Israel A. Smith was sudden, tragic, and unexpected, it was not altogether unanticipated. After a man has passed his eighty-second birthday, he knows that his time is running out. Always mindful of the needs of the church, Brother Israel was concerned that when death should come to him—whether early or late— the church might continue its orderly path, without confusion or doubt. Therefore on two occasions he had 'left documentary instructions directing the procedure to be followed.

When about to undergo a major operation in February of 1948, Brother Israel executed a document designating W. Wallace Smith as his successor, stating that this call was made known to him at the time Wallace had been called into the Council of Twelve, in 1947, and containing the further provision that the document should be returned to him in the event that he survived the operation. He survived the operation; the document was returned, and few people were even aware of its existence.

On May 28, 1952, he signed another document on the eve of his departure for Europe, and after it was witnessed by Bishop G. L. DeLapp and President F. Henry Edwards, it was placed in the custody of Brother Edwards, in strict confidence, where it remained in safekeeping until 1958.

After the death of President Israel Smith, according to previous instruction President Edwards delivered this document to Paul M. Hanson, President of the Council of Twelve. He in turn communicated it to the Twelve, and to a council which included the Presidency, the Twelve, the Presiding Bishopric, the Presiding Evangelist, the President of the Quorum of High Priests, and the Senior President of Seventy. This council agreed to announce the contents of the document, but to withhold complete publication of it until it could be formally presented to the October Conference.

In due time the Conference received the document, accepted its recommendations and on motion of Apostle Arthur Oakman and second by Z. Z. Renfroe, Senior President of Seventies, provided for the ordination of William Wallace Smith as President of the High Priesthood, the Prophet, Seer, and Revelator to the church.

On Monday evening, October 6, before a capacity audience in the Auditorium, W. Wallace Smith was ordained under the hands of Paul M. Hanson, president of the Council of Twelve, Apostle D. T. Williams, Presiding Bishop G. Leslie DeLapp, and Ward A. Hougas, President of the High Priests' Quorum, thus becoming the fifth president of the church. Paul M. Hanson was the spokesman.

Immediately the President was plunged into the work of the church and of the Conference. Almost his first official act was to present to the Conference a document designating F. Henry Edwards and Maurice L. Draper as his counselors, honorably releasing Elbert A. Smith as Presiding Evangelist and calling Roy A. Cheville to take his place, and also honorably releasing Paul M. Hanson, Daniel T. Williams, and Edmund J. Gleazer from the Council of Twelve, and calling Charles D. Neff and Clifford A. Cole to fill two of the vacancies. The document was accepted as the revelation of God, ordered printed in the Doctrine and Covenants, and smoothly and unitedly the church resumed its forward march under its new leadership.

If there were those who had entertained any doubts as to the new Prophet's ability to carry on in the steps of his illustrious forebears, they were reassured by the new dignity, humility, and spiritual stature which became apparent almost from the moment of W. Wallace Smith's ordination. The qualities of leadership which had first been tested in the apostolic quorum, and then refined as one of the counselors of the Presidency, had now reached the first stage of fruition, and the church faced the future with confidence and hope.

William Wallace Smith was born in Lamoni, Iowa, on November 18, 1900. He was the second son of Joseph Smith III and Ada Clark Smith. In 1906 he moved with his parents to Independence, where he attended the public schools and was graduated from William Chrisman High School in 1919. After two years at Graceland College, 1919-1921, he continued at the University of Missouri, taking his A.B. degree in 1924.

On November 12, 1924, he was married to Rosamond Bunnell, President Frederick M. Smith officiating. There are two children, Rosalee (wife of Dr. Otto H. Elser) and Dr. Wallace Bunnell Smith.

Wallace Smith's first business experience was with the Martin-Welch Hardware Company of Independence, where he was employed from 1924 to 1942, when he became a salesman for the wholesale hardware firm of Richards and Conover. On September 9, 1928, he was ordained to the office of elder, and in 1929-30 was associated with John Sheehy as pastor of the Stone Church.

From Independence he moved to St. Joseph, Missouri, and then during the war to Portland, Oregon, where he was employed by the Albina Engine and Machine Works—a firm specializing in shipbuilding and ship repairs, where he continued until 1947. He served as pastor of First Church in Portland during 1945-46.

His ordination as apostle came on April 8, 1947, and as Counselor to Israel A. Smith on April 4, 1950.

Since he had been a member of the quorum of the First Presidency for more than eight years, President Smith needed no introduction to the problems and opportunities confronting the church. A year after his ordination he and his associates directed the Conference of High Priests at Kirtland. In 1960 the Centennial of the reorganization of the church was celebrated during General Conference and some far-reaching developments in field administration were initiated. Free from the details of field supervision which had previously consumed much of their time, the Twelve became available for surveys of missionary possibilities in the Orient, Brazil, Mexico, Nigeria, and these surveys were followed by the assignment of appointee ministers. As a further step toward the better organization of the church and the assignment of local responsibilities, new stakes were organized at Council Bluffs, San Francisco, and Los Angeles, with four more to be organized at Tulsa, Des Moines, Denver, and Seattle.

The Auditorium was completed and dedicated in 1962. It had been a long and costly business, and almost all of those prominent in the inception and planning of the Auditorium had died. But there were present many who had stood by hopefully during the dark days of the depression, and who—with their children—had again taken up the burden when funds became available, and for these it was a time of fulfillment and great rejoicing. Bishop DeLapp and his counselors had served the church in many ways, and their contribution to the completion of the Auditorium was widely recognized and deeply appreciated.

On April 1, 1962, at the World Conference, President Smith presided over the dedication of the Conference Chamber of the Auditorium. He was assisted by his counselors, Presidents F. Henry Edwards and Maurice L. Draper; Presiding Evangelist Roy A. Cheville; President of the Council of Twelve Charles R. Hield, and Presiding Bishop G. Leslie DeLapp. A chorus composed of the Graceland Concert Choir, the Student Nurses Choir, the Radio Choir, and the Auditorium Chorale sang under the direction of Frank K. Hunter. Franklyn S. Weddle directed the congregational singing, and Bethel Knoche was organist.

The 1962 Conference authorized the reorganization of Center and Central Missouri stakes "to form three or more stakes, and to make adjustments to boundary lines of the contiguous stakes." In the implementation of this action the Blue Valley and Santa Fe stakes were created, and adjustments were made to Central Missouri, Kansas City, and Center stakes. Creation of new stakes continued with the action of the 1964 Conference which authorized the organization of the San Francisco and Omaha-Council Bluffs stakes. Division of the Los Angeles Stake to form the Los Angeles-Ventura and Orange-San Gabriel stakes was approved at the 1966 Conference, while the 1968 Conference authorized organization of the Tulsa, Denver,

Des Moines, and Seattle stakes. Kirtland Stake was approved in 1972 and St. Louis Stake in 1978. During the twenty-year span of the administration of W. Wallace Smith the church's stakes increased in number from seven to eighteen.

Another important development of this period was the opening of more new national jurisdictions for evangelism and Zionic ministries than had been opened in the entire previous 130 years. By 1978 the church was formally engaged in ministry in all of the same countries as in 1958 and in addition had begun work in Argentina, Belgium, Brazil, Fiji, France, Haiti, Honduras, India, Italy, Japan, Kenya, Korea, Liberia, Mexico, New Caledonia, Nigeria, the Philippines, and Taiwan. The growth rate in these new fields was greater than in the United States and Canada. While total membership increased by 24.4 percent during this period, it amounted to 19.8 percent for the United States and Canada, and it was 89.0 percent for all the other jurisdictions.

In 1976 President Smith submitted to the church a document (Doctrine and Covenants 152) in which he indicated the wisdom of his own retirement and designated his son, Wallace Bunnell Smith, as his successor. The "president-designate" was to serve "as an assistant to his father and to the First Presidency... during a period of spiritual preparation and study approximating two years" prior to being considered by the church for approval "as president to succeed his father."

Accordingly, in 1978 the World Conference received a statement on April 2 from President W. Wallace Smith in which he tendered his "resignation as prophet-president to become effective at the completion of the ordination of my successor." Apostle Clifford A. Cole assumed the chair as all three members of the First Presidency left the Conference Chamber. He asked Apostles D. V. Lents and C. D. Neff to be associated with him in presiding over the Conference during the succession proceedings.

A motion of gratitude and acceptance was presented by Apostle William E. Timms and Senior President of Seventy Harry W. Black.* The motion also contained an affirmation of

---

*Both of these brethren were born in the British Isles, whence have come many church leaders over the years.

the call of Wallace B. Smith, who then made a statement of acceptance and retired from the chamber.

An amendment was moved by Elders James Christenson and Howard O. Thornburg to insert, following the words "moved that" in the enabling statement (third paragraph) of the motion, these additional words: "we accept the resignation of President W. Wallace Smith as requested, and that..."

There were several statements of affirmation, after which the amendment and amended motion were passed, and Brethren W. Wallace and Wallace B. Smith were escorted into the Conference Chamber by Apostle Charles D. Neff, President of the High Priests Quorum Goeffrey F. Spencer, Senior President of Seventy Harry W. Black, and Presiding Bishop Francis E. Hansen.

The First Presidency composed of W. Wallace Smith, Maurice L. Draper, and Duane E. Couey continued to preside over the Conference until the ordination on Wednesday evening, April 5, of Wallace B. Smith as president of the high priesthood and of the church. W. Wallace Smith at that time received the title of President Emeritus in harmony with the provisions of Doctrine and Covenants 152 as adopted in 1976. Thus concluded an administrative term of nearly twenty years (October 1958 to April 1978) in which the church experienced great developments in its ministerial programs and extended its outreach into many far-flung national and cultural jurisdictions.

LXXI.—Wallace Bunnell Smith

*I*N A DOCUMENT APPROVED by the 1976 World Conference (Doctrine and Covenants 152), Wallace Bunnell Smith was named "prophet and president-designate" and called to assist his father and the Quorum of the First Presidency during a period of spiritual preparation and study approximating two years. His ordination to the prophetic office and as president of the high priesthood and of the church took place on April 5, 1978, after action by the World Conference accepted his father's resignation and confirmed his call as indicated in 1976.

Wallace Bunnell Smith was born on July 29, 1929, in Independence, Missouri. His heritage in the church included his mother's family, from whom he received his middle name. At the age of sixteen he was ordained to the office of priest on October 21, 1945. As his ministry continued, he was ordained an elder (March 11, 1964) and a high priest (October 3, 1965). His experience in various church functions involved activities as a congregational presiding elder, counselor to the stake president, counselor to the stake bishop, and member of the Center Stake High Council. He was set apart as a member of the Standing High Council on April 5, 1968.

President Smith's education following high school was at Graceland College (1946-48), the University of Portland in Oregon (1948-49), and Kansas University (1949-50) where he received his Bachelor of Arts degree. He took a Doctor of Medicine degree from the Kansas University School of Medicine in 1954 and the following year entered the United States Naval Reserve as a lieutenant in the Medical Corps. He became a flight surgeon and was on active duty until July 1958. Upon leaving the Navy he returned to the Kansas University Medical Center for one year of residency in internal medicine and three years in ophthalmology. He then joined his brother-in-law, Dr. Otto Elser, in the practice of ophthalmology in Independence, Missouri, in which he was engaged at the time of his designation as successor in the prophetic leadership of the church in 1976.

WALLACE B. SMITH

Wallace B. Smith and Anne Marthene McCullough were married on June 26, 1956, at Beaver, Pennsylvania. Anne was born on January 24, 1934, at Beaver Falls, Pennsylvania. She shares her husband's interest in professional health care. Following high school she received her nursing education at Sewickley Valley Hospital and became a registered nurse. Her professional experience as a nurse includes service in the United States Navy, where she held the rank of lieutenant (J.G.), and hospital duty at Sewickley Valley Hospital and the Kansas University Medical Center. She continues her interest in health ministries as a volunteer at the Independence Sanitarium and Hospital, where she has been a member of the auxiliary for many years; she has also served as president, secretary, and treasurer of the auxiliary board.

Sister Smith was baptized in July 1956 at Independence, Missouri. She has been a church school teacher, member of the vacation church school staff, and a member of the leadership team for O'Teens. Her interest in girls is natural—she and President Smith have three daughters. Carolyn Joyce was born on November 1, 1957; Julia Anne on January 27, 1962; and Laura Louise on September 1, 1964.

President Smith responded to the prophetic role in 1978 when he presented inspired direction to the church immediately following his ordination. Of immediate concern was the reorganization of the Quorum of the First Presidency. Presenting what he believes "does truly represent...[God's] will and his instructions for the guidance of the church," President Smith first commended his parents for their years of devoted service. He then designated Duane E. Couey and Howard S. Sheehy, Jr., as counselors and members of the First Presidency. Maurice L. Draper was commended for his long service to the church which was given with uncommon faithfulness and skill. He was called to continue as a consultant to the First Presidency and to teach and write for the benefit of the church. In other directions William E. Timms was relieved from the Council of Twelve Apostles and Harold W. Cackler from the Presiding Bishopric.

To fill vacancies in these councils Roy H. Schaefer and Phillip M. Caswell were called as apostles and Ray E. McClaran was called to serve in the Presiding Bishopric.

The document concluded with an admonition to the Saints for a continued widening of ministries of evangelism and elevation of the level of response to the principles of temporal stewardship. They were reminded that God's "Spirit is reaching out to numerous souls even now." This set the mood for a "Faith to Grow" emphasis developed during the following two years for implementation during the decade of the 1980s.

Pursuing this theme in 1980, President Smith presented a revelation on April 8 in which three apostles with many years of service were commended for their devotion and relieved of their duties in the Council of Twelve. The president of the council, Clifford A. Cole, was freed for ministries of teaching and writing. Apostle Donald V. Lents, by then the "senior" apostle, had served in that capacity under three church presidents—Israel A. Smith, W. Wallace Smith, and Wallace B. Smith. Aleah G. Koury was named, subject to the vote of the members of the order, to serve as secretary of the Order of Evangelists, to which ministry both he and Apostle Lents were called.

To fill the vacancies thus created, Kisuke Sekine, Everett S. Graffeo, and Kenneth N. Robinson were called. The intercultural expansion, so significant in the prior twenty years, was thus reinforced. Kisuke Sekine is the first Oriental to serve in the apostolic council. Kenneth Robinson is an Australian with international experience. Everett Graffeo is an American whose full-time ministry has involved several years experience in the Pacific islands and an assignment as campus minister at Graceland College.

Augmenting the significance for further expansion into intercultural ministries having world dimensions as implied by these apostolic callings, the revelation also contains an urgent appeal for the Council of Twelve "to pursue strategies and methods by which the missionary work may be promoted and my gospel most meaningfully communicated to the world." At the same time, the importance of the "redefinition of terms within the basic law of temporalities" is emphasized, with attention being given to this need on a broad base of consideration and common consent.

In the spirit of affirmative hope the closing words of the 1980 revelation describe the tone of the church's leadership emphasis for the first two years of President Wallace B. Smith's administration: "If you will move out in faith and confidence to proclaim my gospel my Spirit will empower you and there will be many who respond, even in places and ways which do not now seem clear." Thus the First Presidency calls the church to confront the decade of the 1980s with "Faith to Grow."

Appendix

Compiled by Church Historian

IMPORTANT EVENTS IN CHURCH HISTORY

*T*HE DATES OF THE RECEPTION of the revelations are not included, as these can be found in Doctrine and Covenants. Also important changes in quorum personnel are usually omitted, as these are given in lists of quorum personnel herewith, and dates of ordination show when changes occurred:

December 23, 1805, Joseph Smith, Jr., born Sharon, Vermont.
1815, Joseph Smith, Sr., and family removed to Palmyra, New York.
Spring, 1820, Joseph Smith's first vision, Manchester, New York.
September 21, 22, 1823, Joseph Smith, Jr., second vision and shown plates of Book of Mormon.
September 22, 1827, Joseph Smith, Jr., received plates of Book of Mormon.
February, 1828, Martin Harris took transcript of characters to Prof. Anthon and Dr. Mitchell of New York.
April 7, 1829, Oliver Cowdery became scribe for Joseph Smith.
May 15, 1829, Joseph Smith and Oliver Cowdery baptized each other and received Aaronic priesthood.
June, 1829, the Three Witnesses, Oliver Cowdery, Martin Harris, and David Whitmer, were shown plates by an angel.
June, 1829, the Eight Witnesses were shown and handled plates.
June 11, 1829, Book of Mormon copyrighted.
March, 1830, Book of Mormon as printed by E. B. Grandin of Palmyra, completed.
April 6, 1830, church organized at Peter Whitmer, Sr., farm, Fayette, New York, with six members: Joseph Smith, Hyrum Smith, Peter Whitmer, Jr., Oliver Cowdery, Samuel H. Smith, David Whitmer. Joseph Smith, Jr., and Oliver Cowdery ordained each other elders, laid hands upon and confirmed each member of the church, administered Lord's Supper.
June 1, 1830, first conference of the church.
October, 1830, departure of first missionaries: Parley P. Pratt, Oliver Cowdery, Peter Whitmer, Jr., Ziba Peterson. At Kirtland baptized over 100.

January 31, 1831, missionaries had reached Independence, Missouri, and started preaching to Indians.

February 1, 1831, Joseph Smith, Jr., arrived in Kirtland.

February 4, 1831, Edward Partridge was appointed first Bishop.

June 6, 1831, high priests first ordained.

July 1831, Colesville Branch arrived in Zion and settled in what is now Kansas City, Missouri.

August 2 and 3, 1831, land of Zion, City of Zion, and Temple Lot dedicated.

August 4, first conference in Zion held at the home of Joshua Lewis (probably near 35th and the Paseo in Kansas City, Missouri).

September 12, 1831, at conference in Hiram, Ohio, William W. Phelps instructed to purchase press and type.

November 1, 1831, Oliver Cowdery was appointed to take copy of revelations to Independence, Missouri, to have printed. Two days later John Whitmer was appointed to accompany him.

January 25, 1832, Joseph Smith, Jr., was ordained president of high priesthood at Amherst, Ohio.

April 26, 1832, Joseph Smith, Jr., was acknowledged president of high priesthood in council in Independence, Missouri.

June, 1832, *The Evening and the Morning Star*, first publication of the church, was printed in Independence, Missouri.

November 6, 1832, Joseph Smith III born at Kirtland, Ohio.

February 2, 1833, Joseph Smith, Jr., completed corrections of New Testament (Inspired Version of Holy Scriptures).

March 18, quorum of high priests first organized in Kirtland. Sidney Rigdon and Frederick Granger Williams ordained as counselors to Joseph Smith.

June 1, 1833, instructions received concerning Temple in Kirtland.

June 25, a plat for city of Zion with explanation by First Presidency.

July 2, Joseph Smith, Jr., completed corrections of Holy Scripture (Inspired Version).

July 20, printing press in Independence destroyed by mob, stopping publication of *The Evening and the Morning Star* and preventing completion of the *Book of Commandments*.

July 23, cornerstone of Temple at Kirtland laid.

August 2, revelation received to build House of the Lord in Zion, Independence, Missouri, but the Saints were driven out within a few months.

November 7, 8, exodus from Jackson County, Missouri.

December, 1833, *The Evening and the Morning Star* published at Kirtland.

December 18, Joseph Smith, Sr., ordained patriarch.

February 17, 1834, first Standing High Council organized at Kirtland, Ohio.

July 3, 1834, High Council organized in Zion.

APPENDIX

October, 1834, *Messenger and Advocate* first published in Kirtland.

February 14, 1835, Twelve Apostles chosen for first time in Restoration.

February 28, first Quorum of Seventy organized at Kirtland, principally from those who had gone up to Zion in the army of relief in the summer of 1834.

August 17, 1835, general assembly of the church held and Book of Doctrine and Covenants accepted and adopted.

December 26, Joseph Smith, Jr., and other elders commenced study of Hebrew under Dr. Seixas.

January 21, 1836, leading officers of the church anointed and blessed in Temple and received spiritual endowment.

March 27, 1836, Lord's House, or Temple, at Kirtland dedicated. At second service on April 3, for those who could not get in at the first dedication, Joseph Smith, Jr., and Oliver Cowdery retired to the pulpit, dropped the curtain, and received a vision of the Savior, Moses, Elias, and Elijah.

July 1, 1837, the first foreign mission of the church sailed from New York. Heber C. Kimball and Orson Hyde in charge.

July 23, having arrived in England, the first sermon was preached in Preston; a week later nine persons baptized.

October, 1837, *Elders' Journal*, Joseph Smith, editor, first published at Kirtland. Two months later office was destroyed by fire and publication issued in Far West, July and August, 1838. This succeeded *Messenger and Advocate*, published in October, 1834, to September, 1837.

March 14, 1838, Joseph Smith and family arrived in Far West, Missouri.

October 30, mob massacred many at Haun's Mill, in Missouri, including children and Thos. McBride, ex-soldier of the Revolutionary War.

October 31, Joseph Smith and others wrongly arrested during parley to adjust the difficulty.

Winter of 1838-1839, general exodus of Saints from Missouri.

April 22, 1839, Joseph Smith, Jr., arrived in Quincy, Illinois.

May 1, 1839, first purchase of land at Commerce, Illinois, afterwards Nauvoo.

May 10, Joseph Smith arrived with his family at Commerce.

June 11, first house erected by Saints in Commerce was built by Theodore Turley.

September, 1839, most of Quorum of Twelve started for England, where they arrived early in 1840.

October 5, William Marks appointed president of the Stake of Nauvoo.

November, 1839, first number of *Times and Seasons* published at Commerce, Illinois.

First Nauvoo Edition of Book of Mormon published.

April 14, 1840, Orson Hyde left Commerce en route for Jerusalem.

May 27, 1840, first number of Latter Day Saints' *Millennial Star* published in England.

December 16, 1840, charter of Nauvoo signed by Governor Carlin to take effect February 1, 1841.

January, 1841, first British edition of Book of Mormon published.

January 30, 1841, Joseph Smith, Jr., elected sole trustee for church. According to the statute, under which this was done, this was limited to holding of five acres of land for houses of worship, hence it was probably for the erection of the Nauvoo Temple.

April 6, 1841, cornerstones for Temple at Nauvoo were laid. This was pursuant to revelation of January 19, 1841.

October 24, Orson Hyde had arrived in Jerusalem and now ascended Mount of Olives and dedicated by prayer, the land for gathering of Jews.

March 15, 1842, Joseph Smith editor of *Times and Seasons*. After eight months' service he was succeeded by John Taylor, November 15.

March 24, 1842, Ladies' Relief Society organized, Emma Smith, president.

March 21, 1843, the Young Gentlemen and Ladies' Relief Society, Nauvoo, organized.

May 23, 1843, Addison Pratt, Noah Rogers, Benj. F. Grouard, K. F. Hanks, were set apart to go to Pacific Islands. Left June 1, from Nauvoo, sailed from New Bedford, Massachusetts, October 9.

August 31, 1843, Joseph Smith moved into Nauvoo Mansion House; the following month opened it as hotel.

November 3, K. F. Hanks was first Latter Day Saint who died and was buried at sea.

May 1, 1844, the three missionaries to South Sea Islands arrived at Tubuai and by 14th two of them reached Tahiti.

June 16, 1844, first convert on the Pacific Isles was baptized.

June 27, 1844, assassination of Joseph Smith, Jr., and Hyrum, at Carthage, Illinois.

February, 1846, general exodus from Nauvoo.

1851, Doctrine and Covenants published in Welsh, the first in a foreign language.

May 1, 1851, Book of Mormon published in Danish, the first in a foreign language.

November 18, 1851, revelation to Jason W. Briggs; about same time a similar revelation to Zenas H. Gurley, Sr.; both to the effect that the son of Joseph was his true successor.

June 12, 1852, conference at Beloit, Wisconsin, of those looking for the coming of Young Joseph.

1852, Book of Mormon published in French, German, and Italian; also, April 6, in Welsh.

1852, Doctrine and Covenants published in Danish.

April 8, 1853, seven men ordained to Quorum of Twelve in Reorganization.

January, 1860, *The True Latter Day Saints' Herald* published as monthly.

April 6, 1860, Joseph Smith III acknowledged and ordained as president of high priesthood. High council also reorganized, and seventy and presidents of seventy ordained, also presiding bishops.

February 4, 1863, Chas. Derry arrived in England, followed by J. W. Briggs and Jeremiah Jeremiah.

May 18, 1863, Jeremiah opened the mission in Wales.

August 11, 1863, E. C. Briggs and Alexander McCord arrived in Salt Lake City, Utah.

February 6, 1864, Zion's Hope Sunday school organized in St. Louis. A Sunday school was probably organized earlier in Nauvoo by Joseph Smith III.

May 1, 1865, Joseph Smith III was appointed editor of *Saints' Herald*. On this account he removed to Plano in January, 1866.

May, 1865, the Sunday school movement was indorsed by the First Presidency and the Twelve, who urged a Sunday school in every branch.

January, 1866, Thomas B. Marsh, once president of the Twelve, died in Utah. Elder Thomas Job reported that Marsh had accepted Reorganization and planned to move East.

April, 1866, resolutions adopted for publication of Inspired Version of the Holy Scriptures.

About August, 1866, Alexander H. Smith and William Anderson visited Salt Lake City for a few weeks en route to California.

December, 1867, the Inspired Version was announced as being printed and ready for mailing.

1867, a return movement was started to Jackson County, Missouri, by members of Reorganization.

April 2, 1869, Alexander H. Smith and David H. Smith appointed to Utah; left Plano May 20, and Nauvoo early in June; arrived in Salt Lake City in July, and interviewed Brigham Young.

July 1, 1869, first publication of *Zion's Hope*.

April 12, 1870, organization of the First United Order of Enoch approved by General Conference.

April 1, 1872, Joseph Smith III published an editorial in which he stated that Utah would not receive statehood until the constitution prohibited polygamy. That when they did so, that would be evidence of the wrongness of polygamy and admission that it was not divine. This was over eighteen years before the manifesto was adopted, and over twenty years before the adoption of such a constitution.

July 24, 1872, John Avondet opened mission in Switzerland.

June 2, 1873, John Avondet opened mission in Italy and remained until February, 1874.

July, 1873, branch organized in courthouse in Independence, Missouri.

December 3, 1873, Charles Wandell and Glaud Rodger arrived in Society Islands en route to Australia, and found many very greatly interested during the two weeks' stop.

January 22, 1874, Elders Wandell and Rodger arrived in Sydney, Australia.

1874, mission opened in Germany.

November 1, 1874, the *Messenger* first published by J. W. Briggs in Salt Lake City; continued until early in 1877.

May 16, 1875, Magnus Fyrando and H. N. Hansen arrived in Denmark and visited Sweden.

July, 1878, *Saints' Advocate* was published for use in Utah, W. W. Blair, editor, and continued through the eighth volume in 1886.

April 30, 1879, Emma Smith Bidamon, widow of Joseph Smith, Jr., died.

October 7, 1881, Joseph Smith and general officers left Plano for Lamoni, Iowa.

November 1, 1881, first issue of *Saints' Herald* in Lamoni.

April 6, 1882, General Conference met in Independence, Missouri, first time for fifty years.

April 6, 1883, General Conference met in Kirtland Temple, in Ohio, first time in forty-five years.

1884, Spaulding Manuscript found in Honolulu by L. L. Rice and James H. Fairchild.

October, 1884, first issue of *Sandheden's Banner*, Peter Andersen, editor.

1884, Brick Church built in Lamoni, Iowa.

January, 1888, first issue of *Autumn Leaves*, edited by Marietta Walker.

April 6, 1888, cornerstone laid for Stone Church, Independence, Missouri.

September, 1890, mission opened in Hawaii by Albert Haws and G. J. Waller.

January 3, 1891, *Zion's Ensign* first issued.

April, 1891, General Sunday School Association organized by direction of General Conference.

April, 1893, general organization of Zion's Religio Literary Society for young people by a committee of General Conference.

About 1893, general organization of Daughters of Zion. There was a local Daughters of Zion organized in 1879, Providence, Rhode Island. Mite Societies for benefit of poor and the church existed from early days of Reorganization. This organization later changed its name to Women's Auxiliary for Social Service. Then to Women's Department.

March, 1894, decision of John F. Philips in the U. S. Circuit Court, in the Temple Lot Suit. Found Joseph Smith, Jr., innocent of any connection with polygamy and that the Reorganized Church is the true successor to the original church from 1830 to 1844, with like doctrine and practice.

September 23, 1894, the boat "Evanelia" for the South Sea Islands was dedicated.

September 17, 1895, decision of Judge Thayer in the U. S. Circuit Court of Appeal gave possession and legal title to the Temple Lot to the Church of Christ, on technical issue of pleadings, and because of laches or delay in filing suit. This decision in no way affected the question of succession or Joseph Smith's lack of responsibility for polygamy.

September, 1895, Graceland College opened in Lamoni, Iowa, and classes started. (The building was opened January 1, 1897.)

June, 1898, Graceland College graduated its first class, Frederick M. Smith.

1898, Saints' Home opened in Lamoni, Iowa, for benefit of the old folk.

1898, Book of Mormon published in Hawaiian.

1901, stakes organized in Independence, Missouri, and Lamoni, Iowa.

1903, Book of Mormon published in Danish.

April, 1903, George Schweich, the grandson of David Whitmer, delivered to Joseph Smith III and others of the church the Book of Mormon manuscript, John Whitmer's Manuscript History, a copy of Book of Mormon characters taken by Martin Harris to New York, a few sheets of early revelations, and a few other valuable items.

January, 1907, Herald Office in Lamoni destroyed by fire, with great loss of valuable historical manuscripts.

December 15, 1909, Sanitarium dedicated and opened in Independence, Missouri.

April 18, 1910, United Order of Enoch incorporated in Independence, Missouri.

1911, the new manuscript of the Book of Mormon was translated by Alexander Kippe into German and published.

August 15, 1911, Children's Home opened in Lamoni, Iowa.

July 2, 1913, *Stepping Stones* first published.

September, 1914, Graceland opened as junior college with F. M. McDowell as separate Dean.

December 10, 1914, Joseph Smith III died in Independence, Missouri.

May 5, 1915, Frederick M. Smith ordained President.

April 1916, the former Independence Stake divided into Independence, Kansas City, and Holden Stakes.

May, 1917, Far West Stake organized.

April, 1920, Independence declared to be Zion, and the principal headquarters of the church.

July, 1920, Frederick M. Smith and T. W. Williams went to Europe, visited British Isles, Germany, Holland, France, Italy, and Palestine.

May 24, 1921, first issue of *Saints' Herald* in Independence, Missouri.

May 5, 1923, purchase of the Campus, Independence, Missouri, consisting of a large home and twenty acres of land, used for general recreation, education, and worship purposes.

July 29, 1923, first summer service held outdoors on the Campus.

February 2, 1926, excavation started for erection of Auditorium.

April, 1926, seven presidents of seventy reorganized.

April Conference, 1927, held in lower room of Auditorium.

October, 1928, Conference held for first time in upper assembly room of Auditorium.

April, 1930, Centennial Conference of church held in Auditorium.

November 11, 1930, cornerstone laid for new building for Sanitarium.

December 18, 1930, first CBS network broadcast of *Messiah* by Messiah Choir.

January, 1931, Brick Church at Lamoni, Iowa, burned.

June, 1937, Youth Convention accepted name of Zion's League for youth movement.

1941-1942, new Sanitarium prepared for use, with U.S. Government help.

October, 1942, first issue of *Guidelines*.

December 31, 1942, church debt paid and new policy of reserve (started two years previously) established.

March 20, 1946, Frederick M. Smith died at Independence, Missouri.

April 7, 1946, Israel A. Smith ordained president of the church at Independence, Missouri.

April, 1946, First Presidency completed under Israel A. Smith; John F. Garver and F. Henry Edwards ordained as Counselors.

1947, European church headquarters building purchased, Rotterdam, Holland.

January, 1948, first issue of *Daily Bread*.

April, 1948, first Supervisor of Priesthood Education appointed, Floyd M. McDowell.

1948, Department of Ministry to College People organized.

1949, first mission in Alaska organized.

1949, Resthaven purchased for Home for Aged Women.

April 4, 1950, W. Wallace Smith ordained Counselor to President replacing John Garver, deceased.

April 6, 1950, organization of three new stakes authorized: Center Stake, Detroit International, Los Angeles Metropolitan.

1951, new building for German Mission headquarters, Hannover.

March, 1951, Braille Edition of Book of Mormon completed by Myrtle Fortney and Braille Corps of Denver Red Cross.

January, 1954, first issue of *University Bulletin*.

February, 1954, contract let to complete Auditorium foyer and entrance.

September 11, 12, 1954, Washington, D.C., church opened.

November 28, 1954 (Sunday), first baptisms in Korea by Priest Bill Whenham.

August 28, 1955, formal opening of new church building and Latin-American Mission, Weslaco, Texas.

March 23, 1956, new Resthaven building officially opened.

April 11, 1956, premier showing of "Other Sheep," first color motion picture produced by Audio-Visual Department.

June 10-23, 1956, first session, School of Restoration.

July, 1956, Old Saints' Home in Lamoni razed.

August, 1956, first Braille edition of Doctrine and Covenants completed by Edna Koontz and Bonita Gates.

September, 1956, Graceland offers first four-year course in religion.

October, 1956, first issue of *Stride*.

December 1, 1956, *The Hymnal* published.

July, 1957, work begins on finishing the Auditorium Conference Chamber.

April 13, 1958, John and Zelma Gideon and four children—the church's first converts in India—baptized by Elder W. E. Connell.

June 9, 1958, Justin Azim James, first convert in Pakistan, baptized by Elder W. E. Connell.

June 14, 1958, President Israel A. Smith fatally injured.

September 21, 1958, General Conference Chamber dedicated.

October 5, 1958, first Conference convened in completed Auditorium Chamber.

October 6, 1958, President W. Wallace Smith ordained.

November 23, 1958, the 42nd annual *Messiah* performance given—the first in completed Conference Chamber.

May 15, 1959, death of Elbert A. Smith.

June, 1959, Brazil's first baptism and ordination, Ferdinand Frohmut.

June 24, 1959, Dutch translation of the Doctrine and Covenants.

October 8-11, 1959, Kirtland Conference of High Priests.

October 21, 1959, D. Blair Jensen and C. D. Neff survey Orient.

November, 1959, first baptism in Spain, George Ventura.

November 29, 1959, *Messiah* broadcast on television from Auditorium.

1960, first printing of the Spanish Book of Mormon.

1960, centennial celebration of *Saints' Herald* (1860-1960).

April 3-10, 1960, Amboy Centennial Conference.

April, 1960, regional administration first instituted.

April 7, 1960, dedication of the Auditorium organ.

April 17-20, 1961, World Church Women's Institute, Independence, Missouri.

May 14, 1961, Floyd McDowell Commons dedicated, Graceland College.

January 1, 1962, New Zealand organized as separate mission.

January, 1962, *Saints' Herald* becomes semimonthly publication.

April 1, 1962, dedication of the Auditorium.

April 1, 1962, first issue of Australian edition of *Saints' Herald*.

1962, reorganization of Center and Central Missouri Stakes; organization of Blue Valley and Santa Fe Stakes.

January, 1963, first issue of the periodical, *Restoration Witness*.

March 31-April 7, 1963, World Institute in Evangelism, Independence, Missouri.

November 19, 1963, Apostles P. Farrow and D. Couey survey Nigeria.

1964, Omaha-Council Bluffs Stake and San Francisco Bay Stake organized.

January 8-10, 1965, Television and Radio Seminar, Independence, Missouri.

March 21-26, 1965, Worship and Hymnody Institute, Independence, Missouri.

March 28-April 3, 1965, Observance of fiftieth anniversary of Oriole program and Girls' Week.

October 7-10, 1965, High Priests Conference, Kirtland, Ohio.

November 14, 1965, Gobert Edett of Nigeria ordained an elder.

September 12, 1966, Nine-month concentrated training program for appointees opened at School of the Restoration.

Septemnber 23, 24, 1966, First mission conference held in Japan.

November 10, 1966, Church officially registered in Peru.

November 19, 1966, Independence Messiah Choir presented fiftieth anniversary performance.

1966, Book of Mormon published in German language.

March 6-10, 1967, First in a series of three seminars of the Joint Council of First Presidency, Council of Twelve, and Presiding Bishopric.

May 7, 1967, Frederick Madison Smith Library at Graceland dedicated.

June 6-10, 1967, First International Institute for Women's Leaders, Lamoni, Iowa.

August 26-September 1, 1967, College Student Conference, Lamoni, Iowa.

October 29, 1967, First in a series of Auditorium worship services by First Presidency.

November 18-19, 1967, Seminar on the Church and the Future of Higher Education, Independence, Missouri.

1967, First Older Youth Service Corps team to British Isles.

1967, Missions Abroad construction projects completed: Private school in Papeete, Tahiti; community and social center in Matamoros, Mexico; medical clinic in Mosan, Korea; and school for children of the Sora tribes in Orissa State, India.

1967-1968, Fifteen World Church Goals Institutes held in regions.

April 12, 1968, Haiti Mission officially opened.

APPENDIX

1968, the "Commission" system of headquarters staff organization is begun with the assignment of several apostles to Commissioner posts.

1968, beginning with the January *Herald*, a series of articles on "basic beliefs" of the church is published by the Basic Beliefs Committee.

1968, four new stakes are designated by the World Conference: Tulsa, Denver, Des Moines, and Seattle.

October 16, 1968, New Caledonia Mission officially opened.

1968, Martin Luther King Memorial Scholarship Fund is established by Graceland College.

1969, civil war in Nigeria impedes entrance of church officials into the nation.

1969, the number of officially established missions beyond the domestic field by the end of the year is twenty-one.

1969, the *Saints Herald* becomes a monthly family magazine and efforts are made to place the *Herald* in every home of the church, through congregational rather than personal subscription.

1969, publication of *For What Purpose Assembled* marked the beginning of a major emphasis on the church as mission.

1969, the Booz-Allen-Hamilton Management Study was submitted to the First Presidency on October 17.

February 1, 1970, new administrative structure begun at headquarters, designed to enhance decentralization.

February 20, 1970, the first RLDS medical-dental health team arrives in Haiti.

April, 1970, two new publications begin—*The Distaff*, a monthly magazine of the Women's Department, and *Courage*, an independent, church-related, scholarly journal.

April 7, 1970, World Conference considers the higher education implications of the Report of the Commission on Education.

April 7, 1970, World Conference adopts a new format for the Doctrine and Covenants.

September, 1970, Graceland College begins course offerings at the Independence Center.

June 1-5, 1971, a joint conference of over 450 high priests and seventies met at Graceland College, the first such event in church history.

August 8-14, 1971, the first Adult Singles Reunion convened at Graceland.

September 3-6, 1971, "Focus '71," a World Church conference for older youth, met at the Auditorium.

November 12, 1971, the centenary of the organization of the Lamoni Church is celebrated.

November 14, 1971, a copy of a portrait of Joseph Smith, Jr., is presented to the National Portrait Gallery of the Smithsonian Institution, Washington, D.C.

June, 1972, the church is officially registered in Argentina, South America.

September, 1972, *Commission Magazine* is first published by the Commission of Education to replace *Dimensions* and *Distaff.*

September 18, 1972, the John Whitmer History Association is organized.

1972, the New Graded Curriculum for the Church School is introduced into the field jurisdictions.

December, 1972, President W. Wallace Smith attends funeral services for the late President Harry S Truman.

February, 1973, Honduras Mission officially organized.

April 29, 1973, ribbon-cutting ceremony officially opens Graceland's facility in the Independence area.

July 7, 1973, Alice Myrmida Smith Edwards, daughter of Frederick M. Smith, dies.

October 21, 1973, formal opening of Flournoy House, one of the earliest homes in Independence, and the home of the man who sold the Temple Lot property to Bishop Partridge in 1831.

January 29, 1974, Health Ministries Commission releases a four-year summary of health ministries made available by the church to peoples of eleven nations, data showing that over $1 million worth of supplies, equipment, and other medical resources had been given.

May 23, 1974, publication of the *First Supplement to the Hymnal* follows many months of hard work by the World Church Congregational Music Committee.

June 3-7, 1974, newly appointed Women's Ministry Commission convenes at Independence.

July 1, 1974, Dr. Velma Ruch becomes Acting President of Graceland College, replacing Dr. William T. Higdon, who had been ordained to the Council of Twelve the previous April.

September 14-15, 1974, a joint council of First Presidency, Council of Twelve, and Seventy meet to consider the church's theological position on the observation of the sacrament of the Lord's Supper.

September, 1974, Graceland College waives tuition requirements for retired persons over the age of fifty-nine.

November 20, 1974, a historical documents-on-microfilm-exchange was made between the First Presidencies of the RLDS and the LDS churches.

March 14, 1975, Suzanne Selden, R.N., Australia, begins a two-year health ministry tour in Nigeria.

April 7, 1975, Park College Board of Trustees relinquish management of the college to a new twelve-member board, nine of whom comprise the Graceland College Board of Trustees.

April 12-16, 1975, first Asia-Pacific Church Conference held, at Hong Kong.

August 6-13, 1975, first Melchisedec Training School held at Graceland College, for ministerial personnel and their wives.

September, 1975, *Second Supplement to the Hymnal* published by Herald House.

January, 1976, Seminar on the Church and Higher Education held at Park College.

February 15, 1976, Dr. Barbara McFarlane Higdon named Dean of the Park College School for Community Education.

March, 1976, the first International Women's Forum convenes at Independence, Mo.

April, 1976, the Task Force on Aging, appointed in 1974, files initial report with the First Presidency.

April 1, 1976, the History Commission organized by the First Presidency.

June 27, 1976, Governor Bond of Missouri rescinds the infamous 1838 "extermination order" of Governor L. W. Boggs, at Far West Stake Reunion.

July 12, 1976, the new $17.5 million acute care tower of the Independence Sanitarium and Hospital is officially opened.

September 18-October 2, 1976, Health Ministries teams of volunteers extend health care to Omaha Indian Tribespeople at Macy, Nebraska.

July 1, 1976, President-Designate Wallace B. Smith begins his work in the office of the First Presidency.

September 22, 1976, Giovanni D'Asaro is baptized—the first member of the church in Rome, Italy.

November 21, 1976, St. Louis District organized into a stake.

January 1, 1977, "regional organization" extended to church jurisdictions beyond North America.

July 17, 1977, Kirtland Temple certified as a United States National Landmark.

September 30, 1977, first national conference of Native American Indian people.

April 5, 1978, W. Wallace Smith retired and Wallace B. Smith was ordained president of the church.

April 6, 1979, Mackay Hall, Park College, entered in the National Register of Historic Places.

August 19, 1979, Lamoni, Iowa, celebrates its centennial year.

April 9, 1980, first Oriental apostle, Kisuke Sekine, ordained at the Sesquicentennial World Conference.

LEADING OFFICERS OF THE CHURCH

Abbreviations: b. for born; bap. for baptized; ord. for ordained; d. for died; r. for released; res. for resigned. After the death of Joseph Smith, the church was rejected; the process of apostasy was a gradual one. As late as 1855 in parts of Europe the Holy Spirit was still retained. After the death of Joseph Smith, June 27, 1844, numerous factions arose and gathered in Utah and vicinity, Wisconsin, Texas, Western Iowa, and elsewhere. But all of these combined represented only a small fraction of the church membership, as stated by Joseph Smith, Jr., before his death. The death of the President does not mean by law a disorganization of the quorums or an end to priesthood responsibility. In this particular case, however, there was a break and mutual rejection by each faction of the others. Those marked "rj. 1844" were in office at the death of Joseph Smith.

President of the Church:

Joseph Smith, Jr., b. Dec. 23, 1805, Vermont; bap. May 15, 1829; ord. Jan. 25, 1832; killed June 27, 1844.

Joseph Smith III, b. Nov. 6, 1832, Ohio; bap. Nov. 1843; ord. April 6, 1860; d. Dec. 10, 1914.

Frederick M. Smith, b. Jan. 21, 1874, Illinois; bap. July 12, 1883; ord. May 5, 1915; d. Mar. 20, 1946.

Israel A. Smith, b. Feb. 2, 1876, Plano, Ill.; bap. June 25, 1886, Lamoni, Ia; ord. April 7, 1946; died June 14, 1958.

W. Wallace Smith, b. Nov. 18, 1900, Lamoni, Ia.; bap. June 6, 1909, Independence, Mo.; ord. Oct. 6, 1958; Pres. Emeritus, April 5, 1978.

Wallace B. Smith, b. July 29, 1929, Missouri; bap. June 12, 1938; ord. Pres. Designate March 31, 1976; ordained Pres. April 5, 1978.

Counselors in the Presidency:

Sidney Rigdon, b. Feb. 19, 1793, Pennsylvania; bap. Nov. 14, 1830; ord. March 18, 1833; rj. 1844.

Frederick G. Williams, b. Oct. 28, 1787; bap. Oct. 1830; ord. March 18, 1833; rj. and r. Nov. 7, 1837.

Hyrum Smith, b. Feb. 9, 1800, Vermont; bap. June 1829; ord. Nov. 7, 1837; patriarch, Jan. 19, 1841; killed June 27, 1844.

William Law, b. Sept. 8, 1809, probably Ontario; bap. about 1838; ord. Jan. 19, 1841; expelled April 18, 1844.

William Marks, b. Nov. 15, 1792, Vermont; bap. before Sept. 1837, ord. April 1863; d. May 22, 1872.

William W. Blair, b. Oct. 11, 1828, New York; bap. Oct. 8, 1851, and April 17, 1857; ord. April 10, 1873; d. April 18, 1896.

David H. Smith, b. Nov. 11, 1844, Illinois; bap. Oct. 27, 1861; ord. April 10, 1873; r. April 1885.

Alexander H. Smith, b. June 2, 1838, Missouri; bap. May 25, 1862; ord. April 9, 1897; r. April 18, 1902, Presiding Patriarch.

E. L. Kelley, b. Nov. 17, 1844, Illinois; bap. May 23, 1864; ord. April 9, 1897; r. April 18, 1902, Presiding Bishop.

APPENDIX

Frederick M. Smith, b. Jan. 21, 1874, Illinois; bap. July 12, 1883; ord. April 18, 1902; ord. May 5, 1915, president of high priesthood.

Richard C. Evans, b. Oct. 20, 1861, Quebec; bap. Nov. 5, 1876; ord. April 20, 1902; r. April 20, 1909; ord. bishop.

Elbert A. Smith, b. March 8, 1871, Illinois; bap. Nov. 25, 1887; ord. April 20, 1909. Also ord. Counselor to Frederick M. Smith, May 5, 1915; r. ord. Presiding Patriarch April 10, 1938.

Floyd M. McDowell, b. March 26, 1889, Wisconsin; bap. Oct. 1, 1899; ord. Oct. 15, 1922; res. Oct. 20, 1938.

Israel A. Smith, b. Feb. 2, 1876, Illinois; bap. June 25, 1886; app. Oct. 20, 1938; ord. April 14, 1940; r. April 7, 1946; ord. president of church; d. June 14, 1958.

L. F. P. Curry, b. July 20, 1887, Pennsylvania; bap. Jan 21, 1906; app. Oct. 20, 1938; ord. April 14, 1940; r. April 7, 1946; d. Jan. 23, 1977.

John F. Garver, b. Jan. 28, 1878, Indiana; bap. Sept. 26, 1897; ord. April 10, 1946; d. March 3, 1949.

F. Henry Edwards, b. Aug. 4, 1897, England; bap. Nov. 3, 1905; ord. April 10, 1946; ord. counselor, W. Wallace Smith, Oct. 8, 1958; r. April 19, 1966.

W. Wallace Smith, b. Nov. 18, 1900, Iowa; bap. June 6, 1909; ord., April 4, 1950; ord. Pres. of church, Oct. 6, 1958.

Maurice L. Draper, b. Aug. 25, 1918, Arma, Kansas; bap. June 10, 1928; ord. Oct. 8, 1958; r. April 6, 1978.

Duane E. Couey, b. Sept. 13, 1924, Wisconsin; bap. Sep. 18, 1932; ord. April 19, 1966; ord. Presiding Patriarch, March 31, 1982.

Howard S. Sheehy, Jr., b. March 19, 1934, Denver, Colorado; bap. June 14, 1942; ord. April 6, 1978.

Alan D. Tyree, b. December 14, 1929, Kansas City, Mo.; bap. June 12, 1938; ord. March 31, 1982.

Presidents of Quroum of Twelve:

Thomas B. Marsh, 1835, to 1839.
Brigham Young, April, 1840, to 1844.
Jason W. Briggs, April 6, 1853, to April 1886.
Alexander H. Smith, April 15, 1890, to April, 1897.
William H. Kelley, April 13, 1897, to April 19, 1913.
Gomer T. Griffiths, April 20, 1913, to Oct., 1922.
J. Arthur Gillen, Oct. 15, 1922, to April, 1934.
Paul M. Hanson, April, 1934, to Oct. 1958.
Charles R. Hield, October 12, 1958, to April 6, 1964.
Clifford A. Cole, ord. April 8, 1964.
Charles D. Neff, ord. April 10, 1980.

Quorum of Twelve:

Thomas B. Marsh, b. Nov. 1, 1799, Massachusetts; bap. Sept. 1830; ord. April 25, 1835; expelled 1839.

David W. Patten, b. 1800, New York; bap. June 15, 1832; ord. February 15, 1835; killed October 25, 1838.

Brigham Young, b. June 1, 1801, Vermont; bap. April 14, 1832; ord. Feb. 14, 1835; rj. 1844.

Heber C. Kimball, b. June 14, 1801, Vermont; bap. April 1832; ord. Feb. 14, 1835; rj. 1844.

Orson Hyde, b. June 8, 1805, Connecticut; bap. Aug. 31, 1831; ord. Feb. 15, 1835; rj. 1844.

William McLellin, b. 1806, Tennessee; bap. summer 1831; ord. Feb. 15, 1835; expelled, 1838.

Parley P. Pratt, b. April 12, 1807, New York; bap. Sept. 1, 1830; ord. Feb. 21, 1835; rj. 1844.

Luke S. Johnson, b. Nov. 3, 1807, Vermont; bap. June 1831; ord. Feb. 15, 1835; expelled April 13, 1838.

William B. Smith, b. March 13, 1811, Vermont; bap. June 1830; ord. Feb. 15, 1835; rj. 1844.

Orson Pratt, b. Sept. 19, 1811, New York; bap. Sept. 19, 1830; ord. April 26, 1835; rj. 1844.

John F. Boynton, b. Sept. 1, 1811, Massachusetts; bap. Sept. 1832; ord. Feb. 15, 1835; dropped, 1838.

Lyman E. Johnson, b. Oct. 24, 1811, Vermont; bap. Feb. 1831; ord. Feb. 14, 1835; expelled 1838.

John Taylor, b. Nov. 1, 1808, England; bap. 1836; ord. Dec. 19, 1838; rj. 1844.

John E. Page, b. Feb. 25, 1799, New York; bap. Aug. 18, 1833; ord. Dec. 19, 1838; rj. 1844.

Wilford Woodruff, b. March 1, 1807, Connecticut; bap. Dec. 31, 1833; ord. April 26, 1839; rj. 1844.

George A. Smith, b. June 26, 1817, New York; bap. Sept. 10, 1832; ord. April 26, 1839; rj. 1844.

Willard Richards, b. June 24, 1804, Massachusetts; bap. Dec. 31, 1836; ord. April 14, 1840; rj. 1844.

Lyman Wight, b. May 9, 1796, New York; bap. Nov. 14, 1830; ord. April 4, 1841; rj. 1844.

Jason W. Briggs, b. June 25, 1821, New York; bap. June 6, 1841; ord. April 8, 1853; r. April 1886.

Zenas H. Gurley, Sr., b. May 29, 1801, New York; bap. April 1, 1838; ord. April 8, 1853; d. Aug. 28, 1871.

Daniel B. Rasey, b. Nov. 27, 1814, New York; bap. June 1851; ord. April 8, 1853; r. April 1873.

R. W. Newkirk, b. Oct. 29, 1822, Ohio; bap. about 1850; ord. April 8, 1853; r. April 1873.

Henry H. Deam, b. May 5, 1817, Pennsylvania; bap. the fall of 1836; ord. April 8, 1853; r. Oct. 1864.

John Cunningham, b. probably in Pennsylvania; bap. at early date, unknown; ord. April 8, 1853; r. Oct. 1854.

George White, b. in England; ord. April 8, 1853; r. Oct. 18, 1863.

David Newkirk, b. in Ohio; bap. 1851; ord. April 1855; r. April 7, 1865.

Samuel Powers, b. Dec. 17, 1819, Ontario; bap. 1852; ord. April 1855; d. Feb. 16, 1873.

William W. Blair, b. Oct. 11, 1828, New York; bap. April 7, 1857; ord. Oct. 7, 1858; ord. First Presidency April 1873.

James Blakeslee, b. July 18, 1802, Vermont; bap. July 19, 1833; ord. Oct. 6, 1860; d. Dec. 18, 1866.

Edmund C. Briggs, b. Feb. 20, 1835, New York; bap. July 1852; ord. Oct. 6, 1860; Evangelist April 18, 1902.

John Shippy, b. Jan. 26, 1823, Ontario; bap. fall of 1842; ord. Oct. 6, 1860; cut off April 1868. Later rebaptized, ord. elder.

Josiah Ells, b. March 4, 1806, England; bap. Oct. 1, 1838; ord. April 1865; d. Oct. 15, 1885.

Charles Derry, b. July 25, 1826, England; bap. Oct. 3, 1847; ord. April 1865; resigned April 1870.

John H. Lake, b. Dec. 4, 1829, New York; bap. Dec. 13, 1860; ord. April 10, 1873; ord. Evangelist April 1902.

Thomas W. Smith, b. March 7, 1838, Pennsylvania; bap. March 14, 1866; ord. April 10, 1873; d. May 27, 1894.

Alexander H. Smith, b. June 2, 1838, Missouri; bap. May 25, 1862; ord. April 10, 1873; ord. to First Presidency and Presiding Patriarch, April 1897.

William H. Kelley, b. April 1, 1841, Illinois; bap. March 1, 1860; ord. April 10, 1873; r. April 19, 1913.

Joseph R. Lambert, b. Oct 4, 1845, Illinois; bap. Nov. 5, 1863; ord. April 10, 1873; ord. Evangelist, April 1902.

Zenas H. Gurley, Jr., b. Feb. 24, 1842, Illinois; bap. May 13, 1861 ord. April 9, 1874; r. April 1886.

James Caffall, b. July 14, 1825, England; bap. 1864; ord. Sept. 5, 1873; r. April 1902.

James W. Gillen, b. March 18, 1836, Ireland; bap. Dec. 3, 1861; ord. April 13, 1887; r. 1900.

Heman C. Smith, b. Sept. 27, 1850, Texas; bap. Oct. 7, 1862; ord. March 30, 1888; r. April 1909. Elected Church Historian April 16, 1897.

Joseph Luff, b. Oct. 31, 1852, Ontario; bap. May 22, 1876; ord. April 13, 1887; r. April 1909, Church Physician.

Gomer T. Griffiths, b. June 2, 1856, Pennsylvania; bap. April 22, 1877; ord. April 13, 1887; r. Oct. 1922, Evangelist.

I. N. White, b. Dec. 27, 1841, Ohio; bap. March 2, 1868; ord. April 12, 1897; r. April 14, 1913, Evangelist.

John W. Wight, b. Aug. 8, 1856, Texas; bap. Oct. 8, 1869; ord. April 12, 1897; r. April 1913.

Richard C. Evans, b. Oct. 20, 1861, Quebec; bap. Nov. 5, 1876; ord. April 12, 1897; ord. April 20, 1902, First Presidency.

Peter Andersen, b. April 1, 1860, Denmark; bap. Dec. 9, 1880; ord. April 7, 1901; r. April 1920.

Frederick A. Smith, b. Jan. 19, 1862, Illinois; bap. June 24, 1877; ord. April 19, 1902; r. April 20, 1913, Presiding Patriarch.

Francis M. Sheehy, b. June 1, 1851, Connecticut; bap. Jan. 29, 1871; ord. April 20, 1902; r. April 1920.

Ulysses W. Greene, b. June 16, 1865, Massachusetts; bap. Aug. 10, 1882; ord. April 20, 1902; r. Oct. 1922, Evangelist.

Cornelius A. Butterworth, b. Dec. 24, 1864, Iowa; bap. Dec. 13, 1885; ord. April 23, 1902; r. Oct. 18, 1922.

John W. Rushton, b. Feb. 12, 1874, England; bap. Sept. 15, 1888; ord. April 20, 1902; r. April 1947; d. May 8, 1950.

James F. Curtis, b. Jan. 26, 1875, Missouri; bap. June 10, 1883; ord. April 20, 1909; r. ord. Evangelist, April 9, 1938.

Robert C. Russell, b. Aug. 25, 1867, Ontario; bap. Sept. 11, 1894; ord. April 20, 1909; r. Oct. 18, 1922, Evangelist.

James E. Kelley, b. June 11, 1879, Indiana; bap. April 13, 1896; ord. April 19, 1913; d. June 4, 1917.

William Aylor, b. Jan. 9, 1864, Illinois; bap. Dec. 1, 1891; ord. April 19, 1913; res. Oct. 18, 1922.

Paul M. Hanson, b. Jan. 8, 1878, Iowa; bap. Oct. 15, 1893; ord. April 19, 1913; r. October 8, 1958.

James A. Gillen, b. May 24, 1868, Idaho; bap. May 21, 1876; ord. May 19, 1913; res. April 13, 1934.

Myron A. McConley, b. Sept. 17, 1885, Colorado; bap. May 27, 1894; ord. April 8, 1920; r. Oct. 5, 1948; ord. evangelist, Oct. 5, 1948.

Thomas W. Williams, b. Aug. 23, 1866, Utah; bap. March 23, 1875; ord. April 8, 1920; r. April 1925.

John F. Garver, b. Jan. 28, 1878, Indiana; bap. Sept. 26, 1897; ord. Oct. 13, 1922; r. April 10, 1946, ord. Counselor to President Israel A. Smith.

D. T. Williams, b. Dec. 13, 1889, Iowa; bap. Feb. 25, 1898; ord. Oct. 13, 1922; r. Oct 8, 1958; ord. evangelist, Oct. 8, 1958.

F. Henry Edwards, b. Aug. 4, 1897, England; bap. Nov. 3, 1905; ord. Oct. 13, 1922; r. April 10, 1946, ord. Counselor to President Israel A. Smith.

APPENDIX

Edmund J. Gleazer, Sr., b. March 23, 1895, Ireland; bap. Feb. 4, 1912; ord. Oct. 13, 1922; r. Oct. 8, 1958; ord. evangelist, Oct. 8, 1958.

Roy S. Budd, b. May 3, 1890, Missouri; bap. May 8, 1898; ord. Oct. 13, 1922; r. Oct. 1936.

Clyde F. Ellis, b. Dec. 19, 1891, Michigan; bap. June 16, 1900; ord. Sept. 30, 1923, d. June 21, 1945.

George G. Lewis, b. Nov. 17, 1901, New South Wales; bap. Nov. 8, 1909; ord. April 15, 1932; d. Sept. 14, 1948.

C. George Mesley, b. Oct. 15, 1900, Victoria; bap. April 7, 1918; ord. April 10, 1938; res. April 10, 1954.

Arthur A. Oakman, b. March 30, 1905, England; bap. Sept. 5, 1915; ord. April 10, 1938; r. April 6, 1964; ord. evangelist.

Charles R. Hield, b. Aug. 11, 1896, Wisconsin; bap. Sept. 3, 1905; ord. June 19, 1838; r. April 6, 1964.

D. Blair Jensen, b. April 21, 1901; bap. June 13, 1909; ord. April 10, 1946; r. April 18, 1966.

Wm. Wallace Smith, b. Nov. 18, 1900, Lamoni, Iowa; bap. June 6, 1909; ord. April 8, 1947; r. April 4, 1950; ord. Counselor to President Israel A. Smith.

Roscoe E. Davey, b. Feb. 11, 1896, Montana; bap. July 6, 1909; ord. April 8, 1947; r. April 6, 1964; ord. evangelist.

Maurice L. Draper, b. Aug. 25, 1918, Arma, Kansas; bap. June 10, 1928; ord. April 8, 1947; counselor to W. Wallace Smith, Oct. 8, 1958.

Reed M. Holmes, b. June 17, 1917, Washington; bap. June 21, 1925; ord. Oct. 5, 1948; released April 3, 1974, ord. Presiding Patriarch.

Percy E. Farrow, b. July 16, 1902, Ontario; bap. Oct. 13, 1912; ord. Oct. 5, 1948; r. April 18, 1966.

Donald O. Chesworth, b. Sept 21, 1910, Massachusetts; bap. June 25, 1922; ord. April 4, 1950; released April 14, 1972.

Donald V. Lents, b. July 30, 1917, Iowa; bap. Aug. 2, 1925; ord. August 29, 1954; r. April 9, 1980.

Charles D. Neff, b. March 24, 1922, Hardin, Mo.; bap. Nov. 3, 1946, St. Louis, Mo.; ord. Oct. 8, 1958.

Clifford A. Cole, b. Nov. 16, 1915, Lamoni, Ia.; bap. Oct. 5, 1924, Wyo.; ord. Oct. 8, 1958; r. April 9, 1980.

Duane E. Couey, b. Sept. 13, 1924, Wisconsin; bap. Sept. 18, 1932, Milwaukee, Wisc.; ord. April 5, 1960; to F. Pres., April 19, 1966.

Cecil R. Ettinger, b. July 26, 1922, Illinois; bap. Oct. 26, 1930, Taylorville, Ill.; ord. April 5, 1960; released April 3, 1974.

Russell F. Ralston, b. May 20, 1913, Colorado; bap. June 12, 1921; ord. April 7, 1964; released April 2, 1976.

William E. Timms, b. Sept. 23, 1912, England; bap. October 28, 1923; ord. April 7, 1964; r. April 6, 1978.

Alan D. Tyree, b. Dec. 14, 1929, Kansas City, Mo.; bap. June 12, 1938; ord. April 19, 1966; to F. Pres. Mar. 31, 1982.

Earl T. Higdon, b. July 9, 1907, Ft. Scott, Kans.; bap. July 11, 1915; ord. April 19, 1966; released April 3, 1974.

Aleah G. Koury, b. Sept. 26, 1925, Toronto, Canada; bap. Mar. 31, 1935; ord. April 19, 1966; r. April 9, 1980.

Howard S. Sheehy, Jr., b. Mar. 19, 1934, Denver, Colo.; bap. June 14, 1942; ord. April 5, 1968; to F. Pres. April 6, 1978.

J. C. Stuart, b. Aug. 6, 1915, Cashion, Oklahoma; bap. Aug. 2, 1924; ord. April 15, 1972; r. Mar. 31, 1982.

Paul W. Booth, b. July 30, 1929, Caraway, Arkansas; bap. Aug. 21, 1938; ord. April 4, 1974.

William T. Higdon, b. Jan. 4, 1930, Independence, Mo.; bap. June 12, 1938; ord. April 4, 1974.

Lloyd B. Hurshman, b. May 20, 1930, Independence, Mo.; bap. June 12, 1938; ord. April 4, 1974.

Eugene C. Austin, b. March 15, 1929, South Dakota; bap. June 13, 1937; ord. April 2, 1976.

Roy H. Schaefer, b. Aug. 20, 1932, Brooklyn, N.Y.; bap. Oct. 19, 1941; ord. April 6, 1978.

Phillip M. Caswell, b. Sept. 2, 1936, Knoxville, Iowa; bap. May 27, 1945; ord. April 6, 1978.

Kisuke Sekine, b. Dec. 16, 1930, Saitama-ken, Japan; bap. Aug. 8, 1951; ord. April 9, 1980.

Everett S. Graffeo, b. April 14, 1936, Mapleton, Iowa; bap. April 30, 1944; ord. April 9, 1980.

Kenneth N. Robinson, b. Oct. 24, 1941, Perth, W. A., Aust.; bap. Nov. 23, 1952; ord. April 9, 1980.

Joe A. Serig, b. April 18, 1935, Wheeling, W.V.; bap. May 16, 1943; ord. March 31, 1982.

James C. Cable, b. Feb. 6, 1936, Independence, Mo.; bap. June 11, 1944; ord. March 31, 1982.

Presiding Bishops:

Edward Partridge, b. Aug. 27, 1793, Massachusetts; bap. Dec. 11, 1830; ord. Feb. 1831; d. May 27, 1840.

George Miller, successor to Partridge as Presiding Bishop, b. Nov. 25, 1794, Virginia; bap. summer of 1839; ord. Nov. 19, 1841; rj. 1844.

I. L. Rogers, b. April 4, 1818, New York; bap. 1840; ord. April 7, 1860; res. April 1882. (Was first bishop of the reorganization.)

George A. Blakeslee, b. Aug. 22, 1826, New York; bap. before 1844 and in 1859; ord. April 1882; d. Sept. 20, 1890.

E. L. Kelley, b. Nov. 17, 1844, Illinois; bap. May 23, 1864; ord. April 10, 1891; r. April 1916.

Benjamin R. McGuire, b. May 18, 1877; bap. Aug. 21, 1899; ord. April 16, 1916; r. April 19, 1925.

A. Carmichael, b. Sept. 14, 1863, California; bap. Dec. 18, 1873; ord. April 19, 1925; r. April 15, 1932.

L. F. P. Curry, b. July 20, 1887, Pennsylvania; bap. Jan. 21, 1906; ord. April 17, 1932 (acting since Feb. 1931); r., ord. First Presidency April 14, 1940.

G. Leslie DeLapp, b. Nov. 4, 1895, Wisconsin; bap. June 6, 1909; ord. April 14, 1940; r. April 18, 1966.

Walter N. Johnson, b. May 4, 1905, Australia; bap. Jan. 30, 1916; ord. April 19, 1966; released April 15, 1972.

Francis E. Hansen, b. Oct. 30, 1925, Weston, Iowa; bap. June 23, 1935; ord. April 15, 1972.

Counselors to Presiding Bishops:

Isaac Morley, b. March 11, 1786, Massachusetts; bap. Nov. 1830; ord. June 3, 1831; r. at death of Partridge, 1840.

John Corrill, b. Sept. 17, 1794, Massachusetts; bap. Jan. 10, 1831; ord. June 3, 1831; r. Aug. 1, 1837.

Titus Billings, b. March 25, 1793, Massachusetts; bap. Nov. 1830; ord. Aug. 1, 1837; r. death of Partridge, 1840.

William Aldrich, b. Dec. 3, 1806, New Hampshire; bap. Sept. 1835; ord. April 1866; r. April 1873.

Philo Howard, b. April 6, 1819, New York; bap. June 5, 1864; never ordained, but appointed April 1866; d. Jan. 25, 1869.

Elijah Banta, b. Jan. 5, 1823, Kentucky; bap. April 8, 1863; ord. April 1873; res. Oct. 1874; ord. April 1882; res. April 1891. (Death of Blakeslee.)

David Dancer, b. Feb. 20, 1827, New York; bap. May 10, 1868; ord. April 1873; res. April 1882. (Resignation of Bishop Rogers.)

Henry Stebbins, b. Jan. 28, 1844, Ohio; bap. Aug. 23, 1863; ord. April 1875; resigned at resignation of Bishop Rogers, April 1882.

E. L. Kelley, b. Nov. 17, 1844, Illinois; bap. May 23, 1864; ord. April 13, 1882; r. ord. Presiding Bishop, April 10, 1891.

George H. Hilliard, b. Nov. 7, 1858, Ohio; bap. Aug. 3, 1867; ord. April 1891; d. Oct. 8, 1912.

Edwin A. Blakeslee, b. July 18, 1865, Michigan; bap. June 27, 1875; ord. April 1891; res. April 1916.

James F. Keir, b. Feb. 7, 1876, Illinois; bap. July 19, 1887; ord. April 1916; r. April 1925.

Israel A. Smith, b. Feb. 2, 1876, Illinois; bap. June 25, 1886; ord. April 1920; r. April 1925.

Mark H. Siegfried, b. Aug. 16, 1881, Illinois; bap. Oct. 3, 1898; ord. April 19, 1925; r. Feb. 1931.

John A. Becker, b. Oct. 8, 1874, Ohio; bap. Aug. 20, 1899; ord. April 13, 1926; r. Feb. 1931.

G. Leslie DeLapp, b. Nov. 4, 1895, Wisconsin; bap. June 6, 1909; ord. April 17, 1932 (active from Feb. 1931); ord. Presiding Bishop April 14, 1940.

N. Ray Carmichael, b. Dec. 12, 1892, California; bap. Feb. 17, 1901; ord. April 8, 1934; r. April 14, 1940.

Clarence A. Skinner, b. June 17, 1880; bap. May 26, 1891; ord. April 14, 1940; res. April 9, 1946.

Henry L. Livingston, b. April 30, 1902, Oregon; bap. Oct. 23, 1910; ord. April 14, 1940; r. April 18, 1966.

Walter N. Johnson, b. May 4, 1905, Australia; bap. Jan. 30, 1916; ord. April 14, 1946; ord. P.B. April 19, 1966.

Francis E. Hansen, b. Oct. 30, 1925, Weston, Iowa; bap. June 23, 1935; ord. April 19, 1966; ord. P.B. April 15, 1972.

Harold W. Cackler, b. Sept. 30, 1912, Ottercreek, Iowa; bap. June 24, 1923; ord. April 19, 1966; r. April 6, 1978.

Gene M. Hummel, b. Nov. 12, 1926, Lancaster, Ohio; bap. May 11, 1958; ord. April 15, 1972.

Ray E. McClaran, b. Nov. 23, 1930, Kansas City, Mo.; bap. Dec. 20, 1959; ord. April 6, 1978.

Presiding Patriarch:

Joseph Smith, Sr., b. July 12, 1771, Massachusetts; bap. April 6, 1830; ord. Dec. 18, 1833; d. Sept. 14, 1840.

Hyrum Smith, b. Feb. 9, 1800, Vermont; bap. June 1829; ord. Jan. 19, 1841; killed June 27, 1844.

Alexander H. Smith, b. June 2, 1838, Missouri; bap. May 25, 1862; ord. April 9, 1897; d. Aug. 12, 1909.

Joseph R. Lambert, b. Oct. 4, 1845, Illinois; bap. Nov. 5, 1863; ord. April 17, 1910; r. April 20, 1913.

Frederick A. Smith, b. Jan. 19, 1862, Illinois; bap. June 24, 1877; ord. April 20, 1913; r. emeritus April 10, 1938; d. June 25, 1954.

Elbert A. Smith, b. March 8, 1871, Illinois; bap. Nov. 25, 1887; ord. April 10, 1938, r. Oct. 8, 1958.

Roy A. Cheville, b. Oct. 2, 1897, Maxwell, Ia.; bap. Jan. 14, 1914, Rhodes, Ia.; ord. Oct. 8, 1958, released emeritus April 3, 1974.

Reed M. Holmes, b. June 17, 1917, Washington; bap. June 21, 1925; ord. April 4, 1974; r. March 31, 1982.

Duane E. Couey, b. Sept. 13, 1924, Wisconsin; bap. Sept. 18, 1932; ord. March 31, 1982.

Senior Presidents of Seventy:

Joseph Young, 1837 to 1844.

Archibald M. Wilsey, April 6, 1860, to April 6, 1873.

Crowell G. Lamphear, April 10, 1873, to April, 1879.

Glaud Rodger, April 14, 1880, to Aug. 3, 1884.

Edmund C. Brand, April 14, 1885, to Oct. 12, 1890.
Duncan Campbell, April 10, 1891, to April 30, 1901.
Columbus Scott, April, 1902, to April, 1915.
Jas. McKiernan, April, 1915, to April, 1916.
T. C. Kelley, April, 1916, to April, 1926.
James W. Davis, April, 1926, to April, 1942.
Ernest Y. Hunker, April, 1942, to April, 1952.
Zenos Z. Renfroe, April, 1952, to April, 1960.
Russell F. Ralston, April, 1960, to April, 1964.
Harry L. Doty, April, 1964, to April, 1976.
Harry W. Black, April, 1976, to April, 1982.
A. Alex Kahtava, April, 1982.

Presidents of the Seventy:

Hazen Aldrich, bap. at an early date; ord. March 1, 1835; r. April 6, 1837, High Priest.

Joseph W. Young, b. April 7, 1797, Massachusetts; bap. April 6, 1832; ord. March 1, 1835; rj. 1844.

Levi W. Hancock, b. April 7, 1803, Massachusetts; bap. Nov. 16, 1830; ord. Feb. 28, 1835; rj. 1844.

Leonard Rich, bap. early date; ord. Feb. 28, 1835; r. April 6, 1837, High Priest.

Zebedee Coltrin, b. Sept. 7, 1804, New York; bap. 1830; ord. March 1, 1835; r. April 6, 1837, High Priest.

Lyman Sherman, ord. March 1, 1835; r. April 6, 1837, High Priest.

Sylvester Smith, ord. March 1, 1835; r. April 6, 1837, High Priest.

John Gould, ord. April 6, 1837; r. Sept. 3; ord. High Priest.

James Foster, b. April 1, 1775; bap. before 1835; ord. April 6, 1837; d. Dec. 21, 1841.

Daniel S. Miles, ord. April 6, 1837; rj. 1844; d. 1845.

Josiah Butterfield, b. in Maine; ord. April 6, 1837; rj. 1844; d. 1844.

Salmon Gee, b. Oct. 16, 1792, Connecticut; bap. July, 1832; ord. April 6, 1837; dropped March 6, 1838.

John Gaylord, b. July 12, 1797; bap. Aug. 2, 1835; ord. April 6, 1837; expelled Jan. 13, 1838.

Henry Harriman, b. June 9, 1804, Massachusetts; bap. early 1832; ord. Feb. 6, 1838; rj. 1844.

Zera Pulsipher, b. June 14, 1789, Vermont; bap. Jan. 1832; ord. March 6, 1838; rj. 1844.

Archibald M. Wilsey, b. Jan. 18, 1800, New York; bap. 1836; ord. April 6, 1860; ord. High Priest, April 6, 1873.

William D. Morton, b. June 22, 1816, Pennsylvania; bap. Jan. 1842; ord. April 6, 1860; ord. High Priest, April 1873.

George Rarick, b. Dec. 27, 1808, Pennsylvania; bap. about 1831; ord. April 7, 1860; ord. High Priest, April 10, 1873.

Crowell G. Lamphear, b. Aug. 17, 1821, New York; bap. March 1859; ord. April 6, 1860; ord. High Priest, April 1879.

E. C. Briggs, b. Feb. 20, 1835, New York; bap. July 1852; ord. same day, July 1, 1852; ord. Apostle, Oct. 12, 1860.

James Blakeslee, b. July 18, 1802, Vermont; bap. July 19, 1833; ord. April 6, 1860; ord. Apostle, Oct. 1860.

John A. McIntosh, b. April 14, 1806, Kentucky; bap. 1838, also Nov. 27, 1859; ord. July 3, 1860; ord. High Priest, Oct. 8, 1869.

Edmund C. Brand, b. Feb. 26, 1822, England; bap. July 29, 1852; ord. Sept. 12, 1875; d. Oct. 12, 1890.

Duncan Campbell, b. Nov. 29, 1845, Ontario; bap. Aug. 13, 1871; ord. April 1873; ord. High Priest, May 1901.

Charles W. Wandell, b. April 12, 1819, New York; bap. Jan. 5, 1837, also July 6, 1873; ord. Aug. 22, 1873; d. March 14, 1875.

Glaud Rodger, b. July 23, 1820, Scotland; bap. Aug. 11, 1842; ord. April 18, 1880; d. Aug. 3, 1884.

John S. Patterson, b. Jan. 1, 1824, Scotland; bap. July 15, 1866; ord. April 11, 1885; exp. April 1887.

James W. Gillen, b. March 18, 1836, Ireland; bap. Dec. 3, 1861; ord. April 14, 1885; ord. Apostle, April 13, 1887.

Heman C. Smith, b. Sept. 27, 1850, Texas; bap. Oct. 7, 1862; ord. April 14, 1885; ord. Apostle, March 30, 1888.

Columbus Scott, b. Aug. 2, 1850, Indiana; bap. Jan. 9, 1871; ord. April 14, 1885; res. April 1915 after 30 years.

John T. Davies, b. June 1828, Wales; bap. March 1869; ord. April 14, 1885; ord. High Priest, April 19, 1900.

I. N. White, b. Dec. 27, 1841, Ohio; bap. March 2, 1868; ord. April 14, 1888; ord. Apostle, April 12, 1897.

John C. Foss, b. New Brunswick; bap. March 11, 1869; ord. April 14, 1888; superannuated April 18, 1905.

Robert J. Anthony, b. Nov. 12, 1831, Ohio; bap. Dec. 9, 1869; ord. April 1, 1889; d. May 9, 1899.

James McKiernan, b. Feb. 14, 1847, Iowa; bap. Oct. 4, 1870; ord. April 10, 1891; res. April 8, 1916.

Francis M. Sheehy, b. June 1, 1851, Connecticut; bap. 1868; ord. April 14, 1897; ord. Apostle, April 16, 1902.

Hyrum O. Smith, b. Dec. 15, 1855, Texas; bap. Oct. 25, 1866; ord. April 20, 1900; ord. High Priest, April 16, 1913.

James F. Mintun, b. July 9, 1855, Iowa; bap. July 22, 1877; ord. April 20, 1900; ord. High Priest, April 13, 1917.

Warren E. Peak, b. Feb. 23, 1865, Illinois; bap. May 15, 1884; ord. April 20, 1900; ord. High Priest, April 13, 1917.

Romanan Wight, b. Jan. 13, 1851, Texas; bap. Oct. 7, 1860; ord. April 1902; res. April 1909.

T. C. Kelley, b. May 15, 1857, Illinois; bap. Aug. 1875; ord. April 18, 1906; ord. High Priest, April, 1926.

APPENDIX 623

John A. Davis, b. April 4, 1860, Wales; bap. March 1, 1869; ord. April 20, 1909; ord. High Priest, Nov. 20, 1921.

Elmer E. Long, b. Jan. 4, 1874, Ohio; bap. Aug. 18, 1895; ord. April 7, 1916; returned to Seventy, April 7, 1926.

Arthur B. Phillips, b. Feb. 7, 1873, Connecticut; bap. April 5, 1892; ord. April 8, 1913; ordained a Bishop, Dec. 2, 1923.

James T. Riley, b. April 19, 1862, Indiana; bap. May 11, 1897; ord. April 1916; returned to Seventy, April 8, 1926.

James W. Davis, b. Sept. 21, 1879, Michigan; bap. Feb. 17, 1889; ord. April 13, 1918; res. April 1942.

Edward A. Curtis, b. May 1, 1891, Missouri; bap. Jan. 4, 1899; ord. April 1920; r. 1932.

Raleigh L. Fulk, b. July 24, 1880, Illinois; bap. Nov. 19, 1911; ord. Oct. 7, 1923.

Eli Bronson, b. June 15, 1893, Illinois; bap. July 21, 1901; ord. April 1926; r. April 1932.

Roscoe E. Davey, b. Feb. 11, 1896, Montana; bap. July 6, 1909; ord. April 1926; r. April 8, 1947; ord. Quorum of Twelve.

Guy P. Levitt, b. Oct. 29, 1893, Michigan; bap. Aug. 13, 1916; ord. April 1926; res. May 1937.

Ernest Y. Hunker, b. Aug. 22, 1899, Missouri; bap. May 25, 1919; ord. April 15, 1932; r. April 1952 and ord. evangelist; d. Mar. 22, 1966.

Harold I. Velt, b. Oct. 12, 1893, Victoria, Australia; bap. July 13, 1913; ord. April 15, 1934; r. Dec. 30, 1951; ord. evangelist.

Zenos Z. Renfroe, b. Mar. 15, 1894; bap. Aug. 18, 1907; ord. April 10, 1938; selected Senior Pres. of Seventy, April, 1952; r. April 8, 1960.

Percy E. Farrow, b. July 16, 1902, Ontario; bap. Oct. 13, 1912; ord. April 12, 1942; r. Oct. 5, 1948; ord. Quorum of Twelve.

Glen H. Johnson, b. Nov. 13, 1914, Iowa; bap. Oct. 17, 1926; ord. April 9, 1947; r. April 7, 1964.

George A. Njeim, b. Dec. 31, 1900, New Zealand; bap. Aug. 7, 1914, Lebanon; ord. April 13, 1947; released April 6, 1970.

James C. Daugherty, b. Oct. 20, 1913, California; bap. June 10, 1934; ord. April 8, 1948; ord. H.P., April 4, 1968; d. June 22, 1974.

Russell F. Ralston, b. May 20, 1913, Colorado; bap. June 12, 1921; ord. April 6, 1950; selected Senior Pres., April, 1960; r. April, 1964; ord. Quorum of Twelve.

Sylvester R. Coleman, b. Feb. 6, 1919, Missouri; bap. July 15, 1928; ord. April 8, 1954; ord. H. P., Dec. 12, 1965.

Harry L. Doty, b. July 14, 1911, Michigan; bap. July 16, 1919; ord. April 8, 1954; selected Senior Pres., April 1964.

C. Houston Hobart, b. Sept. 15, 1915, Missouri; bap. June 29, 1924; ord. April 10, 1960; r. April 10, 1980.

Luther S. Troyer, b. Oct. 29, 1911, Missouri; bap. June 20, 1920; ord. April 8, 1964; r. April 12, 1972, ordained Patriarch.

Harry W. Black, b. Dec. 23, 1927, Stockport, England; bap. Oct. 13, 1940; ord. April 9, 1964; selected Senior Pres., April 1, 1976.

Louis C. Zonker, b. Oct. 25, 1923, Wellsburg, W. Va.; bap. Mar. 13, 1932; ord. April 21, 1966.

Wayne E. Simmons, b. Feb. 6, 1915, Cameron, Mo.; bap. Feb. 11, 1923; ord. April 5, 1968; released May, 1973.

T. Ed Barlow, b. April 27, 1931, McKenzie, Alabama; bap. July 20, 1941; ord. April 12, 1970; d. Nov. 20, 1979.

A. Alexander Kahtava, b. Oct. 14, 1938, Sault Ste. Marie, Ontario, Canada; bap. July 26, 1959; ord. April 4, 1974.

Victor B. Hatch, Jr., b. March 19, 1929, Stonington, Maine; bap. Aug. 22, 1937; ord. April 1, 1976.

Kenneth E. Stobaugh, b. June 3, 1924, Independence, Missouri; bap. June 12, 1932; ord. April 1, 1976.

Clayton H. Condit, b. Mar. 19, 1928, Clatsup Plains, Ore.; bap. April 1941; ord. April 10, 1980.

Gary B. Beebe, b. July 27, 1935, Glendale, Calif.; bap. Nov. 21, 1943; ord. April 10, 1980.

Ray J. Burdekin, b. July 11, 1933, Casino, N.S.W., Aust.; bap. March 14, 1943; ord. March 31, 1982.

Joe B. Bayless, b. Nov. 18, 1932, Hobart, Okla.; bap. June 8, 1941; ord. March 31, 1982.

Presidents of High Priests' Quorum:

Don Carlos Smith, b. March 25, 1816, New York; bap. June 1830; ord. Feb. 15, 1836; d. Aug. 7, 1841.

C. C. Rich, b. Aug. 21, 1809, Kentucky; bap. April 1, 1832; ord. High Priest in Missouri, Aug. 10, 1837; expelled from Missouri, 1839.

George Miller, bap. summer 1839; ord. fall 1841; rj. 1844.

Isaac Sheen, b. Dec. 22, 1810, England; bap. Aug., 1840; ord. April 9, 1850; d. April, 1874.

Charles Derry, b. July 25, 1826, England; bap. Oct. 3, 1847; ord. April 1874; res. April 19, 1901.

Frederick G. Pitt, b. Dec. 3, 1848, Quebec; bap. June 18, 1871; ord. April 19, 1901; ord. Evangelist, April 17, 1910.

Joseph A. Tanner, b. March 22, 1866, Missouri; bap. Oct. 5, 1879; ord. April 17, 1910; r. Oct. 1928.

John F. Sheehy, b. Dec. 17, 1888, Maine; bap. March 6, 1904; chosen pro tem. Oct. 1928; r. April 1932. (Not ordained.)

Ward A. Hougas, b. March 18, 1895, Iowa; bap. June 26, 1904; ord. April 15, 1932; r. Oct. 12, 1958.

Garland E. Tickemyer, b. Jan. 1, 1913, Longwood, Mo.; bap. July 9, 1922, Blue Lick, Mo.; ord. Oct. 12, 1958; res. April 12, 1972.

Roy H. Schaefer, president pro tem, b. Aug. 20, 1932, Brooklyn, New York; bap. Oct. 19, 1941; app. April 13, 1972; r. April 4, 1974.

Geoffrey F. Spencer, b. October 27, 1927, Teralba, N.S.W., Australia; bap. Jan. 30, 1938; ord. April 4, 1974.

APPENDIX

High Council:

Kirtland

Oliver Cowdery, b. Oct. 3, 1806, Vermont; bap. May 15, 1829; ord. Feb. 17, 1834; Counselor to President, Aug. 1835.

Joseph Coe, ord. Feb. 17, 1834; r. Sept. 3, 1837.

Samuel H. Smith, b. March 13, 1808, Vermont; bap. May 1829; ord. Feb. 17, 1834; removed from Kirtland, March 1838.

Luke S. Johnson, b. Nov. 3, 1807, Vermont; bap. June 1831; ord. June 17, 1834; ord. Apostle, Feb. 15, 1835.

John S. Carter, ord. Feb. 1834; d. Aug. 27, 1834.

Sylvester Smith, ord. Feb. 17, 1834; r. Sept. 14, 1834.

John Johnson, ord. Feb. 17, 1834; r. April 3, 1837.

Orson Hyde, b. June 8, 1805, Connecticut; bap. Aug. 31, 1831; ord. Feb. 17, 1834; ord. Apostle, Feb. 15, 1835.

Jared Carter, ord. Feb. 17, 1834; removed from Kirtland, Oct. 1, 1837.

Joseph Smith, Sr., b. July 12, 1771, Massachusetts; bap. April 6, 1830; ord. Feb. 17, 1834; r. Jan. 13, 1836; Presiding Patriarch and Counselor to President of church.

John Smith, b. July 16, 1781, New Hampshire; bap. Jan. 9, 1832; ord. Feb. 17, 1834; r. Sept. 3, 1837, Counselor to President.

Martin Harris, b. May 18, 1783, New York; bap. April 6, 1830; ord. Feb. 17, 1834; r. Sept. 3, 1837.

Orson Johnson, ord. Aug. 27, 1834; expelled, Sept. 3, 1837.

Hyrum Smith, b. Feb. 9, 1800, Vermont; bap. June 1829; ord. Sept. 24, 1834; Counselor to the First Presidency Jan. 13, 1836; ord. Counselor Nov. 7, 1837. (Note: Oliver Cowdery, John Smith, Hyrum Smith, and Joseph Smith, Sr., were chosen as special Counselors to the First Presidency at various times.)

Joseph Kingsbury, ord. Jan. 13, 1836; r. Sept. 3, 1837.

John P. Green, ord. Jan. 13, 1836; r. Sept. 3, 1837; removed from Kirtland. Also in High Council of Zion in 1838.

Noah Packard, b. May 7, 1796, Massachusetts; bap. June 1, 1832; ord. Jan. 13, 1836; removed from Kirtland, 1839.

Thomas Grover, ord. Jan. 13, 1836; removed from Kirtland Sept. 3, 1837; ord. to High Council in Zion, Aug. 1837; driven from Missouri, 1839; ord. to High Council in Nauvoo, 1839; rj. 1844.

Samuel James, ord. Jan. 13, 1836; no report after 1839.

Henry G. Sherwood, ord. Sept. 3, 1837; removed from Kirtland; ord. High Council in Nauvoo, 1839; rj. 1844.

William Marks, b. Nov. 15, 1792, Vermont; bap. before Sept. 1837; ord. Sept. 3, 1837; removed to Missouri about 1839.

Mayhew Hillman, ord. Sept. 3, 1837; removed to Missouri 1838; ord. on High Council Adam-Ondi-Ahman, 1839.

Harlow Redfield, ord. Sept. 3, 1837; removed to Missouri 1838.

Asahel Smith, b. May 21, 1773, New Hampshire; bap. 1835; ord. Sept. 3, 1837; removed to Missouri, 1838; was member of High Council in Iowa, 1839, 1840.

Phineas Richards, ord. Sept. 3, 1837; no further mention.

David Dort, ord. Sept. 3, 1837; removed to Missouri, 1838; ord. to High Council in Nauvoo, 1839; d. 1841.

Oliver Granger, ord. Sept. 3, 1837; d. Aug. 25, 1841.

Lyman Sherman, ord. Oct. 1, 1837; no later mention.

Zion:

Simeon Carter, ord. July 1834; left Missouri Dec. 1838.

Parley P. Pratt, b. April 12, 1807, New York; bap. Sept. 1, 1830; ord. July 3, 1834; ord. Apostle, Feb. 21, 1835.

William E. McLellin, b. 1806, Tennessee; bap. summer of 1831; ord. June 3, 1834; ord. Apostle, Feb. 15, 1835.

Calvin Beebe, ord. July 3, 1834; driven from Missouri, Dec. 1838; ord. High Council Reorganized Church, April 6, 1860; d. 1861.

Levi Jackman, b. July 28, 1797, Vermont; bap. May 4, 1831; ord. July 3, 1834; driven from Missouri, Dec. 1838.

Solomon Hancock, ord. July 3, 1834; driven from Missouri, 1838.

Christian Whitmer, b. Jan. 18, 1798, Pennsylvania; bap. April 11, 1830; ord. July 3, 1834; d. Nov. 27, 1835.

Newel Knight, b. Sept. 13, 1800, Vermont; bap. May 1830; ord. July 3, 1834; driven from Missouri, 1838; ord. to High Council at Nauvoo, Oct. 1839; rj. 1844.

Orson Pratt, b. Sept. 19, 1811, New York; bap. Sept. 19, 1830; ord. July 3, 1834; ord. Apostle, April 26, 1835.

Lyman Wight, b. May 9, 1796, New York; bap. Nov. 14, 1830; ord. July 3, 1834; r. 1837. Counselor to John Smith as president of a stake.

Thomas B. Marsh, b. Nov. 1, 1799, Massachusetts; bap. Sept. 1830; ord. July 3, 1834; ord. Apostle, April 25, 1835.

John Murdock, b. July 15, 1792, New York; bap. Nov. 5, 1830; ord. July 3, 1834; removed to DeWitt; r. Oct. 1838.

Elisha H. Groves, ord. Jan. 1836; driven from Missouri, 1838-1839.

Jessie Hitchcock, ord. 1836; r. May 22, 1837.

George M. Hinkle, ord. 1836; r. Oct. 1838; removed to DeWitt.

Peter Whitmer, Jr., b. Sept. 27, 1809, New York; bap. June 1829; ord. 1836; d. Sept. 22, 1836.

Elias Higbee, b. Oct. 23, 1795, New Jersey; bap. summer of 1832; ord. 1836; driven from Missouri, 1838.

Samuel Bent, b. Sept. 19, 1778, Massachusetts; bap. Jan. 1833; ord. Oct. 1838; driven from Missouri, Dec. 1838; ord. to High Council of Nauvoo, Oct. 1839; rj. 1844.

George Morey, b. Nov. 30, 1803, New York; bap. early days; ord. Aug. 1, 1837; driven from Missouri, 1838; ord. to High Council Reorganization, April 6, 1860; d. Dec. 1875.

Isaac Higbee, b. Dec. 23, 1797, New Jersey; bap. May 1832; ord. Oct. 1838; driven from Missouri, Dec. 1838.

George W. Harris, ord. and active in Dec. 1838; also ord. Nauvoo, Oct. 1839; rj. 1844.

APPENDIX 627

Nauvoo—in addition to those previously noted:

David Fullmer, b. July 7, 1803, Pennsylvania; bap. Aug. 6, 1836; ord. Oct. 1839; rj. 1844.

Alpheus Cutler, b. Feb. 29, 1788, New Hampshire; bap. Jan. 20, 1833; ord. Oct. 1839; rj. 1844. (Data from Emma Anderson. His tombstone implies b. Jan. 1, 1784.)

William Huntington, b. March 28, 1784, New Hampshire; bap. 1835; ord. Oct. 1839; rj. 1844.

C. C. Rich, b. Aug. 21, 1809, Kentucky; bap. April 1, 1832; ord. Oct. 1839; ord. Counselor to William Marks, April 1841.

Seymour Brunson, ord. Oct. 1839; no data after Oct. 1841.

Lewis D. Wilson, ord. Oct. 1839; rj. 1844.

Leonard Soby, ord. April 1841; rj. 1844.

James Allred. ord. April 1841; rj. 1844.

Reorganization:

Andrew J. Jackson, ord. April 6, 1860; d. 1863.

Dwight Webster, ord. April 6, 1860; d. 1868.

John C. Gaylord, b. July 12, 1797, Pennsylvania; bap. Aug. 2, 1835; ord. April 6, 1860; d. 1874.

Jacob Doan, b. Jan. 7, 1807, North Carolina; bap. June 12, 1859; ord. April 6, 1860; d. 1875.

William Aldrich, b. Dec. 3, 1806, New Hampshire; bap. Sept. 1835; ord. April 6, 1860; d. 1876.

Lyman Hewitt, b. March 3, 1806, Kentucky; bap. Aug. 1845; ord. April 8, 1860; d. 1880.

Zenos Whitcomb, b. Dec. 1, 1810, Hadley, Stemstead Co., C. E.; bap. 1839; ord. April 6, 1860; d. May 3, 1885.

Edwin Cadwell, b. July 7, 1810, Massachusetts; bap. March 1840; Oct. 7, 1860; ord. April 6, 1860; d. 1886.

Oliver P. Dunham, b. Oct. 29, 1807, Connecticut; bap. Dec. 1840; ord. April 6, 1860; d. 1887.

Winthrop H. Blair, b. June 12, 1821, New York; bap. June 13,1859; ord. April 6, 1860; res. 1894.

Hiel Bronson, b. April 1, 1809, Connecticut; bap. Sept. 1833, and Feb. 1862; ord. April 1866; d. 1887.

Jesse Price, b. Aug. 8, 1801, Pennsylvania; bap. Sept. 18, 1863; ord. April 1866; d. 1880.

J. C. Crabb, b. May 7, 1833, Indiana; bap. May 26, 1862; ord. April 1890; r. April 1916.

Charles Derry, b. July 25, 1826, England; bap. Aug. 3, 1847, and in 1861; ord. April 1890; ord. Evangelist, 1902.

David Dancer, b. Feb. 20, 1827, New York; bap. May 10, 1868; ord. April 1890; d. 1898.

Frederick G. Pitt, b. Dec. 3, 1848, Quebec; bap. June 18, 1871; ord. April 1890; ord. Evangelist, April 17, 1910.

James H. Peters, b. Oct. 7, 1838, New York; bap. April 16, 1879; ord. April 1890; d. 1903.

Asa S. Cochran, b. Jan. 24, 1843, Ohio; bap. Feb. 17, 1867; ord. April 1890; r. 1916.

William Anderson, b. Feb. 1, 1840, Scotland; bap. Sept. 11, 1864; ord. April 1890; d. Feb. 1911.

David Chambers, b. June 16, 1841, Scotland; bap. Aug. 22, 1863; ord. April 1890; d. 1897.

Robert M. Elvin, b. June 6, 1846, Scotland; bap. April 15, 1866; ord. April 1890; r. April 1916.

John A. Robinson, b. Dec. 1, 1840, Ireland; bap. Aug. 14, 1871; ord. April 1890; d. 1902.

Calvin A. Beebe, b. April 28, 1836, Missouri; bap. Aug. 4, 1859; ord. April 1890; d. 1903.

John A. Chisnall, b. June 17, 1833, England; bap. Oct. 20, 1869; ord. April 1894; r. 1913.

Charles A. Butterworth, b. Sept. 24, 1846, Maryland; bap. Oct. 14, 1861; ord. April 1897; ord. Evangelist, April 1903.

J. M. Baker, b. Jan. 1, 1854, Ohio; bap. March 28, 1886; ord. 1900; r. 1916.

Willis A. McDowell, b. June 21, 1856, Wisconsin; bap. Jan. 9, 1878; ord. April 1902; ord. Evangelist, April 1913; d. May 31, 1934.

Temme T. Hinderks, b. Aug. 2, 1855, Prussia, Germany; bap. Nov. 24, 1872; ord. April 1903; r. Feb. 19, 1922.

Joseph A. Tanner, b. March 22, 1866, Missouri; bap. Oct. 5, 1879; ord. April 1903; r. 1928.

John A. Grant, b. June 2, 1862, Ontario; bap. March 3, 1887; ord. April 1905; r. Feb. 19, 1922.

George A. Smith, b. April 1, 1850, Ohio; bap. June 15, 1873; ord. April 1905; r. April 1916.

Vinton M. Goodrich, b. April 18, 1859, Ohio; bap. Nov. 14, 1894; ord. April 1911; r. April 1916.

Samuel Twombly, b. Aug. 19, 1861, Illinois; bap. July 15, 1894; ord. April 1911; ord. Evangelist, April 1926.

Charles Fry, b. Feb. 13, 1872, England; bap. March 29, 1886; ord. April 1913; r. Feb. 19, 1922.

Richard J. Lambert, b. Sept. 20, 1874, Iowa; bap. Dec. 3, 1882; ord. April 1913; r. April 1932.

W. O. Hands, b. May 22, 1870, Pennsylvania; bap. June 16, 1889; ord. April 1916; r. Feb. 19, 1922.

Walter W. Smith, b. Sept. 21, 1879, Kentucky; bap. Aug. 19, 1894; ord. April 1916; res. 1925.

David J. Krahl, b. Aug. 22, 1871, Iowa; bap. April 13, 1888; ord. April 1916; r. Feb. 19, 1922.

George H. Hulmes, b. Feb. 24, 1882, Pennsylvania; bap. May 7, 1892; ord. April 1916; r. April 1932.

William R. Pickering, b. Dec. 31, 1849, Missouri; bap. Feb. 20, 1881; ord. April 1916; r. Feb. 19, 1922.

John A. Becker, b. Oct. 8, 1874, Ohio; bap. Aug. 20, 1899; ord. Feb. 19, 1922; res. 1926 Presiding Bishopric; re-ord. April 14, 1940; res. April 9, 1956.

Nathaniel Carmichael, b. Nov. 21, 1862, California; bap. Sept. 18, 1873; ord. Feb. 19, 1922; r. April 1932.

John F. Garver, b. Jan 28, 1878, Indiana; bap. Sept. 26, 1897; ord. Feb. 19, 1922; res. 1925; Apostle.

Roy V. Hopkins, b. July 18, 1881, Illinois; bap. Sept. 18, 1892; ord. Feb. 19, 1922; r. April 1932.

Mark H. Siegfried, b. Aug. 16, 1881, Illinois; bap. Oct. 3, 1898; ord. Feb. 19, 1922; res. 1925; Presiding Bishopric.

Israel A. Smith, b. Feb. 2, 1876, Illinois; bap. June 25, 1886; ord. Feb. 19, 1922; ord. First Presidency, April 1940.

John M. Cockerton, b. March 25, 1864, Oregon; bap. Feb. 21, 1891; ord. Feb. 19, 1922; d. 1923.

Beauford J. Scott, b. Jan. 19, 1859, Missouri; bap. Jan. 6, 1880; ord. April 1925; r. 1932.

Robert T. Cooper, b. Aug. 4, 1870, Pennsylvania; bap. Aug. 30, 1878; ord. April 1925; d. Oct. 29, 1834.

C. Ed. Miller, b. June 8, 1867, Ohio; bap. July 10, 1889; ord. April 1925; res. April 1938.

Denzil O. Cato, b. Dec. 15, 1889, Missouri; bap. May 31, 1900; ord. April 25; res. April 2, 1960.

Merrill A. Etzenhouser, b. May 7, 1884, California; bap. June 4, 1893; ord. April 15, 1926; r. April 1932.

J. Stanley Kelley, b. Feb. 4, 1890, Ohio; bap. Jan. 17, 1898; ord. April 15, 1932; res. April 1942.

Leonard Lea, b. June 9, 1897, California; bap. July 19, 1908; ord. April 15, 1932; res. April, 1954.

Carroll L. Olson, b. May 20, 1903, Minnesota; bap. July 28, 1921; ord. April 15, 1932; r. April, 1972.

Howard P. Andersen, b. April 17, 1900, Missouri; bap. Aug. 17, 1909; ord. April 15, 1932; r. April 2, 1960.

Harry G. Barto, b. Aug. 30, 1895, Iowa; bap. May 29, 1904; ord. April 15, 1932; r. April 9, 1956.

Amos E. Allen, b. March 24, 1893, Missouri; bap. June 9, 1901; ord. April 15, 1932; r. April 3, 1968.

Arthur B. Phillips, b. Feb. 7, 1873, Connecticut; bap. April 5, 1892; ord. April 15, 1932; res. March 31, 1952.

A. K. Dillee, b. Feb. 17, 1881, Kansas; bap. Nov. 13, 1899; ord. April 15, 1932; r. ord. Evangelist, 1942.

Charles F. Grabske, b. May 2, 1892, Michigan; bap. Jan. 10, 1903; ord. April 14, 1936; r. April 3, 1968.

Howard W. Harder, b. Dec. 16, 1890, Michigan; bap. June 19, 1904; ord. April 12, 1942; r. April 3, 1968.

Arthur B. Taylor, b. Dec. 16, 1893, Ontario; bap. July 3, 1903; ord. April 12, 1942; r. April 3, 1968.

James F. Keir, b. Feb. 7, 1876, Illinois; bap. July 19, 1887; ord. April 12, 1942; res. March 31, 1952.

Franklyn S. Weddle, b. Aug. 24, 1905, North Dakota; bap. May, 1914; ord. April 1, 1952.

Myron C. Zerr, b. Sept. 24, 1910, Missouri; bap. Nov. 17, 1918; ord. April 1, 1952.

L. Wayne Updike, b. Sept. 17, 1916, Wisconsin; bap. Sept. 8, 1929, Black River Falls, Wisc.; ord. April 11, 1956; res. April 2, 1960.

Lloyd L. Bland, b. March 15, 1910, Missouri; bap. June 16, 1918, Kansas City, Mo.; ord. April 11, 1956; released April, 1976.

Sanford Downs, b. Jan. 24, 1906, Oklahoma; bap. Aug. 27, 1916, Baker, Ark.; ord. Apr.11, 1956; deceased June 15, 1975.

Reginald A. Smith, b. Jan. 8, 1903, Iowa; bap. Feb. 26, 1911, Independence, Mo.; ord. April 5, 1960; deceased Sept. 28, 1974.

Clifford P. Buck, b. Jan. 10, 1922, Wyoming; bap. July 15, 1934, Wray, Colo.; ord. April 5, 1960; res. April 20, 1966.

Paul A. Wellington, b. April 15, 1919, Kansas; bap. July 3, 1927, Mapleton, Kansas; ord. April 5, 1960.

George K. Shoemaker, b. April 13, 1923, Iowa; bap. May 29, 1935; ord. April 20, 1966.

Donald E. Benton, b. Sept. 13, 1926, Iowa; bap. June 9, 1935; ord. April 5, 1968; res. Sept., 1970.

Bernard B. Butterworth, b. May 2, 1923, Iowa; bap. June 14, 1931; ord. April 5, 1968.

Thomas M. Sherman, b. Sept. 1, 1916, Mo.; bap. Oct. 26, 1924; ord. April 5, 1968.

Wallace B. Smith, b. July 29, 1929, Mo.; bap. June 12, 1938; ord. April 5, 1968; res. April, 1976.

Harold L. Condit, b. April 10, 1918, Hagerman, Idaho; bap. Aug. 23, 1930; ord. April 15, 1972.

Byron Constance, b. Dec. 18, 1926, Cameron, Missouri; bap. June 9, 1935; ord. April 15, 1972.

Otto H. Elser, b. Sept. 24, 1921, HauBersbronn, Germany; bap. Oct. 4, 1929; ord. April 2, 1976.

Dallas B. Fouts, Sr., b. November 2, 1928, New Albany, Indiana; bap. June 12, 1938; ord. April 2, 1976.

Gerald L. Rushfelt, b. Aug. 4, 1929, Kansas City, Kansas; bap. August 15, 1937; ord. April 2, 1976.

Geoffrey F. Spencer, b. Oct. 27, 1927, Australia; bap. June 30, 1938; ord. April 2, 1976.

INDEX

ABBREVIATIONS

ap.—apostle
bap.—baptized, baptism
B. of M.—Book of Mormon
bp.—bishop, bishopric
Ch.—church
conf.—conference
couns.—counselor
D. C.—Doctrine and Covenants
H. C.—High Council
miss.—missionary, mission
pat.—patriarch
pr. bp.—presiding bishop, presiding bishopric
pres.—president
Q-12—quorum of twelve
Reorg.—Reorganized, Reorganization
sev.—seventy
q. of twelve—quorum of twelve

Aaronic priesthood conferred, 77, 78, 79; office work of..................170
Adam-ondi-ahman, built on banks of Grand River in Daviess Co., 266; Joseph Smith investigates reports of riot at, 271; Gen. Atchison comes to, 272; mob renews attack upon 272
Adams, Barnabas, grandfather of Maude Adams..............................303
Adams, George J., put on a performance of Richard III to get money to hire a hall in which to preach, 303; present at blessing of young Joseph.................................445
Adams, James M., letters of William Marks to................415, 417, 421
Adams, Maude, of Latter Day Saint parentage 303
Adams, Zebulon, connected with Crow Creek Branch.......................431
Advent, second of Christ taught......168
Aiken, Robert, a crusader against Episcopal church, 253; lectures against "Mormons" 253; returns to Episcopal fold................................253
Aldrich, Hazen, pres. of sev..............620
Aldrich, Wm., interested in Reorg. movement, 422; couns. to pres. bp., 616; on H. C. Reorg............619, 626
Allen, Amos. E., on H. C. Reorg.....629
Allen, Charles, tarred and feathered by mob..175
Allred, James, on H. C. in Nauvoo..626
"All Things Common"................90, 381
Alston in Cumberland; Russell and Snyder preach in, 251; thirty baptisms, 254; sixty membership, 255; branch organized by Isaac Russell..255
Amboy, conference (1859) near, 422; (1860), Chap. L................................450
Amboy Times, on conference of 1860, 454; editor takes Joseph III's speech in longhand......................454
Amend., Wm., first in Western Reserve baptized for remission of sins (1827)....................................... 29

Ames, Ira, bears testimony of Book of Doctrine and Covenants..............221
Ames, Olive, survivor of Haun's Mill Massacre.....................................279
American Magazine, on prophecy of Joseph Smith..........................283, 284
Anaa, work of Grouard upon....329-331
Andersen, Howard P., on H. C. Reorg. 629
Andersen, Peter, chosen an ap., 568; in Scandinavia 539, 540, 616
Andersen, Peter T., miss. to Scandinavia 540
Anderson, Captain, killed at battle of Nauvoo.......................................347
Anderson, William, miss. to California, 373; 516; visited Salt Lake City 603
Anderson, William, bishop of Lamoni Stake, 569; on H. C. Reorg...627
Angel, Thomas, Derry visits in Dudley 476
Anthon, Prof., certified to characters 59, 60, 571, 599
Anthony, Robert J., pres. of sev......622
Apostles, first called by revelation, 546; called, 568; first chosen, 217, 601; first in reorg., 413, 602; men who have served as, 613-618; start for England......................................601
Argyle, Wisconsin (now Blanchardville) conference of 1853....411-413, 427 (See Zarahemla)
Arthur, Michael, friend of the Saints..215
Aspinwall, Albert, one of first baptisms in Sydney.................................529
Assassination of Joseph Smith at Carthage 343, 345
Atchison, David R., retained as attorney by L. D. S., 193; protects Saints witnesses with Liberty Blues, 196; Saints appeal to, 272; visits Millport and 'Diahman, 272; orders mob at Millport to disband, 272; sends most of his militia home, 272; reports "Mormons" will be "all right if left alone," 272; refuses command of militia called out by Boggs, 276; at receipt of extermination order leaves his command and returns home............276
Auburn, N. J., Joseph, Joseph, Sr., Hyrum, and Oliver preach near...... 83
Auditorium excavation for, 605; first conference held in, 605; work progress 580, 591
Austin, Eugene C., ord. ap................618
Austin, leader of mob at Millport...272
Austin, Imogene, sets music to words written by D. H. Smith......470
Austin, Texas, colony builds jail at..380
Australia, first miss. of Reorg., arrive, 597; history of mission, Chap. LXI 529
Authority, must be restored from heaven 76, 170
Autumn Leaves, published..........506, 604
Avard, Sampson, convert of Russell at Churchville, Ont., 285; trouble with 316

631

Avondet, John, the first missonary of Reorg. to Switzerland and Italy............507, 511, 603
Axtell, I. P., on Kirtland Bank........241
Aylor, Wm., served as ap..............616

Babbitt, Almon W., confirmed Joseph Smith III, 444; taught Joseph III in Sunday School...............572
Babbitt, Erastus, bears testimony to Book of Doctrine and Covenants 221
Bainbridge, New York, home of Josiah Stoal, 39, 40; South Bainbridge. Joseph Smith and Emma Hale married at 40
Baker, James M., on H. C. Reorg....627
Baldwin, Wheeler, appointed on a mission with Wm. Carter, 115; did missionary work near Kirtland......115
Ball, Joseph, converts John Leeka...466
Ballowe, Benj., opened work in Tennessee 501
"Balm of Gilead" Pamphlet in defense of Negro slavery written by Gov. Reynolds 144
Bamber Bridge, branch organized by first Eng. missionaries...............255
Bancroft, on evacuation of Nauvoo, 347; describes Battle of Nauvoo ....346 - 350
Baneemy, Pat. of Zion, Thompson claims to be 387
Bank, Kirtland 240-244
Banta, Elijah, at Sandwich, Ill., 499; couns. to pr. bp. 619
Baptism, controversy concerning, 28; Roger Williams upon 28; administered by Joseph and Oliver, 77, 78; believed and taught, 169; first in England, 249, 250; first for remission of sins in Western Reserve, 26-29; of Sarah Lively (May) in Canada, 541; first on Pacific Islands, 326; administered almost daily 80
Barber, Andrew, L. D. S. killed at battle at Whitmer settlement 179
Barlow, T. Ed., pres. of sev. 623
Barnum, Guy P., "Assistant Steward of the Lord"...............389
Barrett, William, first miss. to Australia 529
Barshe Lees, branch organized by first Eng. miss. 255
Barto, Harry G., on H. C. Reorg....629
Basco Twp., Hancock Co., Ill., citizens protest against return of Saints 455
Batty, — —, murdered by Bogart....275
Bayless, Joe B., pres. of seventy 623
Bear, John L., early miss. of Reorg. to Switzerland 508-515
Beaver Island, colonized by James J. Strang 359
Becker, John A., couns. to pr. bp., 619; on H. C. Reorg. 628
Bedford, Bedfordshire, Richards and Snyder preach in, 251; branch of forty in 255
Beebe, Calvin, on H. C. in Zion, 621; and on H. C. Reorg., 621; early miss. of church, 162; entertains Chas. Derry 464, 625, 627
Beebe, Calvin A., miss. to southeast, 500; on H. C. Reorg. 627
Beebe, Gary B., pres. of seventy 623
Beebe, Isaac, entertains Charles Derry 463
Bellamy, Edward, theories in Looking Backward learned from L. D. S. 153
Beloit Branch, early history, 390-395; conference at 405, 602
Bennett, David, wounded by mobbers 178
Bennett, John Cook, quartermaster of state of Illinois, 291, 315; lobbied for Nauvoo charter, 291; history and character, 315-320; urges Saints to eat tomatoes, 295; joins James J. Strang 359
Bennett, Samuel, sent to bring John Taylor home from Carthage 459
Bent, Samuel, on H. C. in Zion, 622 reports dropping of Marks, 417; H. C. in Nauvoo 626
Bentley, Adamson, reformed Baptist minister, Sidney Rigdon meets, 104; becomes brother-in-law, 104; visits Alexander Campbell with Sidney Rigdon, 104, 105; active exponent of reform Baptist (later Christian) church, 105; with Rigdon perfected and carried on Ministers Meeting, 105; intimacy with Rigdon completely severed 107
Benton, Donald E., S. H. C. 629
Berry, Hon. Orville F., describes Nauvoo, 304; investigates cause of Nauvoo troubles, 348; his conclusions 349
Bettisworth, Constable, writ placed in hands of, 336; Joseph and Hyrum surrender to, 342; insists Smiths go to jail, 342; produces mittimus 343
Bickerton, William, convert of Rigdon and movement he founded 359
Bierlien, — —, assists Swiss. miss. financially 514
Billings, Titus, one of communistic group. "The Family" in Ohio, 90; goes "up to Zion" with group of Saints, 156; couns. to pr. bp. 619
Bishop, Albert, and family go east from Utah 509
Bishop, Gladden, leader of a movement, 361; Granville Hedrick associated with 431
Bishops, presiding, 615; counselors to 618-619
Black, Adam, treachery of, 271; Joseph Smith and others call upon. 271; swore out warrant against Smith, Wight, and others 272
Black, Harry W., Sr. Pres. 70's...............620
Black River Falls, Wisconsin, church buys sawmills at, 374; colony sent from Nauvoo 375
Blackmore, John, from Australia....534
Blair, Wm. W., 425; visited by Briggs and Gurley, 425, 426; visits Zarahemla, 427; at Manti, 491; blesses Gomer T. Griffiths, 493; com. on Inspired Translation, 502; served as ap., 615; couns. to pres., 612; quoted, 426; 561; baptizes

INDEX

Chas. Derry, 464; visits young Joseph 441
Blair, Samuel, secretary and recorder 407
Blair, Winthrop H., on H. C. Reorg. 627
Blake, Captain, old partner of Stephen Mack, befriends Lucy......114
Blakeslee, Edwin A., couns. to pr. bp. 619
Blakeslee, George A., pr. bp., 555, 618; childhood of.................188
Blakeslee, James, early church experiences, 188, 437; conversion and baptism by David Patter, 188; his ability as a preacher, 188; baptizes Zenas H. Gurley, Sr., 397; an ap. in Reorg., 615; pres. of sev., 621; death of, 506; meets Ezra Thayre in Galien, Mich..................467
Bland, Lloyd L., S. H. C..................629
Blue, settlement on 177; attacked by mob, 177; driven south.................182
Bogart, Samuel, active against Saints, 274; Battle of Crooked River, 274; a murderer and fugitive 275
Boggs, Lilburn W., race for land with Partridge, 153; extermination order, 276; shot at Independence, 317; his part in Independence mob, 176; commissions Lyman Wight as colonel of 59th Missouri Militia, 264; calls out militia, 272; Saints in DeWitt appeal to.................273
Bolton, South Lancashire, Branch organized by first Eng. miss........255
Bond, Ira and Charlotte, baptized at Mendon, N. Y..................164
Book of Commandments, to be printed, 151; printed, 151; completion prevented, 600; superseded by D. C., 151; preferred by Church of Christ.................435
Book of Doctrine and Covenants, pub. in Welsh, 602; Chap. XXIV, 220, 223; com. on compilation, 220; endorsed by General Assembly, 220; endorsement of John Whitmer, 222; endorsed by Church of Christ, 434; rejected by present Church of Christ.................435
Book of Mormon, Chap. VII, 55-68; Copyrighted, 66, 599; statements of E. Douglas Branch concerning, 82; first British edition, 602; given to Catteraugus Indians, 89; not written by Spaulding, 57, 65, 73, 108, 109, 111; mss. obtained from David Whitmer, 571; 605; plates of described, 55, 56; presented to S. Rigdon by Pratt. 89, 109, 110; printed, 599; published in French, German, Italian, and Welsh, 602; authorized ed. trans. into German, 605; published in Danish, 605; published in Hawaiian, 605; published in Italian, 359; title page, 66; translation of, 52, 59-66, 72; witnesses to, Chap. VIII, 69-75; Palmyra ed., 298; Kirtland ed., 298; Nauvoo ed..................298-301
Book of Mormon, mss., described by Alex W. Doniphan, 65; handwriting of identified, 65; obtained from D. Whitmer..................571, 605
Book of Mormon plates, in stone box on Hill Cumorah, described, 37; neighborhood gossip concerning, 52; description of, by Joseph Smith, 55; Martin Harris describes, 56; David Whitmer describes, 56; one of first accounts of, 56; Lucy Smith's account in letter to brother, 58; William Smith's description of, 58; family forbidden to see, 59; in constant danger, 59; Emma Smith rides horseback to warn Joseph of danger to, 59; taken away temporarily, 61; "packed up" and taken to Fayette, 63; Mrs. Whitmer is shown, 64; seen by eleven men, 69; seen in vision by John E. Page, 236; seen in vision by John Landers 237
Booker, W. L., miss. to the Southeast 501
Boone Co. Doniphan takes charge of venue to.................284
Booth, Ezra, appointed on mission with Isaac Morley, 115; arrives in "Zion," present at dedication of Zion, 119; "denied the faith," 119; visits Joseph Smith.................150
Booth, Paul W., ord. ap. 618
Bossard, John, Swiss convert........514
Boynton, John F., baptized, 164; left the church in 1838, 149, 165; prominent geologist, 165; loyal friend of Joseph Smith, 165; served as ap., 614; work in Saco, Maine 192
Bowen, Daniel, donates lot for Stone Church 560
Brackenbury, John W., early settler in Independence.................559
Brackenbury, Joseph Blanchett, early miss. 559
Brampton, Cumberland, Branch, org. by first Eng. miss. (probably org. by Isaac Russell).................255
Brand, Edmund C., pres. of sev., 621; senior pres. of sev., 620 visits David Whitmer, 73; reports to semiannual conf., of 1864, 483; miss. work in Idaho.................509
Brannan, Samuel, leader of Brooklyn Colony.................363-373
Brazaele, Hugh L., killed in battle at Whitmer settlement.................179
Brazil steamboat between Galena and Cincinnati, Robinson takes....299
Brewster, James Colin, leader of a faction, 361; Yellowstone branch renounces, 401; Reorg. renounces claims of.................405
Brick Chapel at Independence..........560
Brick Church at Lamoni....554, 604, 606
Briggs, Jason W., and Beloit and Waukesha Branches, Chap. XLI, 390-395; baptism and early life, 390; renounces Brigham Young, Strang and Wm. Smith, 392; receives revelation, 392, 600; on com. to write Word of Consolation, 406; presides at conference, 407; chosen pres. Q-12, 413; address to

young Joseph, 428, 429; with Wm. Smith, 425; sent to Eng., on mission, 469; mission re-affirmed, 475; goes to Wales, 477; debate with Wm. O. Owen, 477; served as ap. after reorg. of twelve, 546; withdraws from church, 546; served as ap. 614
Briggs, Edmund C., childhood in the church, 390; prophecy concerning, 407; baptism, 407; mission to young Joseph, Chap. XLV, 424-430; the first mission to the West, Chap. LIV, 481-485; arrives in Salt Lake City, 603; served as ap., 615; served as pres. of sev., 621; tells Brooklyn Colony of Reorg.....373
Briggs, Polly, mother of Jason and Edmund, 390; meeting held at home of...393
British Saints, influence upon the church 480
Brittain, William, pledges himself to see Derry family does not suffer 471
Brix, Peter N., miss. to Scandinavia, 537, 538; dies in mission field 540
Brockman, Rev., leader of attack on Nauvoo 347
Bronson, Eli., served as pres. of sev. 622
Bronson, Hiel, heard Rigdon deny Spaulding story, 110; on H. C. Reorg. 627
Bronson, Mary, heard Ridgon deny Spaulding story...110
Bronson, Phineas, heard Rigdon deny Spaulding story.............................110
Brooke, Henry, seceded from Thompson 388
Brooklyn, branch organized................260
Brooklyn, voyage of, Chapter XXXVIII 363
Brown, David, at Tiona........................524
Brown, Samuel, involved in Gallatin riot 271
Browning, Orville H., attorney for Joseph Smith, 290; Secretary of Interior under Johnson, 291, 343; Joseph Smith wrote last letter to 291; Lucy Smith's opinion of his oratory, 291; text of last letter......291
Brunson, Seymour, prefers charges against Oliver Cowdery, 268; on H. C. at Nauvoo...626
Brush Creek, Branch, Illinois.............492
Buck, Clifford P., S. H. C.....................629
Budd, Roy S., served as ap.................617
Buel, —, writes to J. C. Clapp........522
Bump, Jacob, plastered inside Temple 226
Bunnell, Rosamond, marries W. W. Smith 597
Burdekin, Ray J., pres. of seventy..................623
Burgess, Eveline, on Children's Home Com...574
Burgess, William, bears testimony to Book of Doctrine and Covenants 221
Burnley, Lancashire, Branch organized by first Eng. miss...........................255
Burton, Emma, miss. to South Sea Islands 566
Burton, Joseph F., miss. to South Sea Islands, 565, 566; captain of "Evanelia" 565
Butler, John Lowe, of Kentucky, L. D. S., involved in Gallatin riot....271
Butterfield, — —, befriends Saints..184
Butterfield, Josiah, served as pres. of sev., 621; death of.............................506
Butterfield, Justin, counsel for J. Smith at Springfield, appeal for writ of habeas corpus........................318
Butterworth, Bernard B., S. H. C...630
Butterworth, Chas. A., on H. C. Reorg. 627
Butterworth, Cornelius A., chosen ap. 616
Buxton, Derbyshire, branch org. by first Eng. miss...255

Cable, James C., ap. 618
Cackler, Harold W., pres. bpric.......620
Cadwell, Edwin, on H. C. of Reorg., 627; conference held near his home, 422; with Wm. Smith, 425; publicly withdraws from W. Smith 425
Caffal, James, serves as ap., 546, 615; sponsors gospel boat....................564
Cahoon, Reynolds, appointed on mission with Samuel H. Smith, 115; preaches at home of Alpheus Cutler, 186; appointed to oversee actual building operations, 224; one of Temple committee............................442
Caldwell Co., Mo., set apart for Saints, 263; L. D. S. in Chap. XXX 261
Cairns, John, brother-in-law of John Landers, baptized by James Blakeslee, 235, 236; biography of 235
California, first baptisms of Reorg. in 483
Cambridge Independence Press quoted 293
Campbell, Alexander, on creeds and confessions of faith, 30; Sidney Rigdon visits, 104, 105; Sidney Rigdon accompanies, 105; becomes bitter enemy to Rigdon....................107
Campbell, Duncan, served as pres. of sev., 621; served as senior pres. of sev. 620
Campbell, James, active against "Mormons" in Jackson Co. meeting at Liberty, 210; drowned in ferry accident......................................211
Campus, first services held on, 605; purchased 605
Canada, first preaching in, 189; call for miss. for, 191; mission of P. P. Pratt in, 231-235; miss. for first mission to England from, 246; boys at Gallatin riot from, 271; converts at Far West from, 285; Jacob Scott quoted, 305; John Shippy converted and sent out as missionary, 310, 311; Hall of Montreal converted, 311; work in Canada, LXIII, 541; baptism of Sarah Lively and Mary Taylor, 541; conversion of Joseph Luff............542-545
Cane Ridge, Kentucky, most famous revival 18, 19
Cannon, George Q., "Prophecy" concerning Derry..472

INDEX

"Captain Fear-Not"—see David W. Patten killed at Crooked River 274
Card, Varnem J., a lawyer in Ohio, affected by Rigdon's oratory........102
Carlin, Constable, heads attackers at Battle of Nauvoo............................347
Carlin, Gov. of Illinois, present at debate between Dr. David Nelson and Josiah Ells....................309
Carmichael, Albert, served as pr. bp. 618
Carmichael, N. Ray, couns. to pre. bp. 619
Carmichael, Nathaniel, on H. C. Reorg. 628
Carrico, Thomas, chosen doorkeeper for Temple..226
Carroll Co., Missouri, Saints settle in, 266; De Witt founded by L. D. S...266
Carter, Gideon, killed at Crooked River 275
Carter, John S., on H. C. at Kirtland 206, 624
Carter, Simeon, bap. and ordained, 91, 100; obtains B. of M. by accident, 100; appointed on mission with Solomon Hancock, 115; on H. C. in Zion..............................625
Carter, Jared, sent as special miss. to Pontiac, 123; baptized 70 persons in, 123; outfitted in black broadcloth, 166; on H. C. in Kirtland, 624; mission to Canada, 191; oversees building operation for Kirtland Temple..............................224
Carter, William, appointed on a mission with Wheeler Baldwin, 115; dropped out.............................115
Carthage, almost empty of inhabitants, 344; county records taken from courthouse, 344; protest against return of Saints to Jackson Co..455
Carthage, courthouse, Joseph III preaches in......................................553
Carthage Gazette comments on Joseph Smith III...............................548
Carthage Greys, left alone to guard jail 343
Carthage Republican opens columns to articles against Saints..................455
Cartright, Peter, describes "jerks" 20; prominent itinerant preacher 21
Carven, Joseph, pledged himself to see Derry family did not suffer....471
Case, Francis and Mary, converted.. 96
Case, Hubert and Alice, South Sea Islands miss., passengers on Evanelia 96, 565
Caswell, Phillip M., ap. 618
Caton, Charles H., one of first bishopric in Eng.............................480
Cato, Denzil O., on H. C. Reorg.......628
Catteraugus, Indians near Buffalo, first miss. to West preach to........ 89
"Celestial Law" in Texas colony......382
Centennial Conference held in Auditorium 606
Chagrin River, Ohio, Mayfield located upon, 90; Rigdon baptizes in 102
Chaigley (correct spelling of Chaidgely)...............................252, 255
Chambers, David, on H. C. Reorg.....627
Chapin, Heman, Kimball assists in cutting wheat..230
Character building, advised by Joseph III...498
Charter members of the church.....599
"Charley," favorite horse of Joseph Smith, Jr., 45; Young Joseph rode 442
Chatburn Branch organized by first miss., to England, 254, 255; Kimball preached in barn..................254
Cheeseman baptized by Brigham Young 186
Chesworth, Donald O., apostle.........617
Cheville, R. A., pres. patriarch........620
....593, 613
Chicago Democrat, letter from Joseph Smith, quoted, 35, 36; description of plates quoted from 55
Chicago Times on David Whitmer.. 74
Chicago Tribune (1886) quotes David Whitmer on Joseph Smith........... 44
Children's Home, opened at Lamoni, Iowa 574, 605
Chisnall, John A., on H. C. Reorg...627
Cholera, Asiatic plague strikes Zion's camp....................................212
Chorley, Lancashire, Branch organized by first Eng. miss....................255
Christ, second coming taught............168
Church of Christ, Temple Lot, Chap. XLVI..............................431-435
Civil War, prophecy concerning, 163; borrowed by John Leeka........466
Clapp, Joseph Carlos, miss. to Oregon 517-522
Clark, Gen., surrounded Far West, 279; forces Saints to agree to leave state, 280; sends 60 prisoners to Richmond 281
Clark, Wm. O., rebaptizes Jason W. Briggs, 390; rebaptizes Granville Hedrick..431
Clay Co., Mo., citizens of, draw up resolutions 262
Clements, A., seceded from Thompson 388
Cleveland, Judge ——, of Quincy, shelters Emma Smith and family..288
Cline, William, furnishes cow for Gurleys, 398; on com. to choose first Reorg. ap.......................................413
Clinton Co., Missouri, settlements in, 266; Colfax Twp., L. D. S. settled, 266; Jameson L. D. S. settled, 266; Adam-ondi-ahman built..................266
Clitherall, Minnesota, founded by followers of Alpheus Cutler..........360
Clithero Branch, Lancashire, organized by first Eng. miss................255
Clow, Wm. sends literature to Joseph Luff, 542; comes to Independence with family............................559
Cobb, Ruth L., mar. F. M. Smith, 578; dies...582
"Cock Pit" in Preston, Lancashire, early meeting place of Saints, described 253

THE STORY OF THE CHURCH

Cochran, Asa S., on H. C. Reorg.... 627
Cockerton, John M., on H. C. Reorg. 628
Coe, Joseph, appointed on mission with Wm. Phelps, 116; served on H. C. in Kirtland 206, 624
Cole, C. A., ap., pres. of 12 617
Coleman, Sylvester R., pres. of sev. 623
Colesville, New York, Joseph Knight, miller and grain buyer of, 39; preaching at 82; branch organized at 87
Colesville Branch, organized in 1830, 87; held up by ice on way to Kirtland, 114; community experiment at Kirtland not a success, 115, 116; arrive in Missouri, 119; at first conference in Zion, 120, 598; conditions in, 124; settled twelve or fifteen miles west of Independence. 130; send assistance to brethren on the Blue, 178, 179; Newel Knight superintends move to Missouri, 115; operates mill in Jackson Co., 135; visited by Joseph Smith 157, 158
Colesville settlement, location of, 81; William McLellin baptized in, 123; Parley P. Pratt ill in, 124, 160; 12 or 15 miles west of Independence, 130; Parley P. Pratt settles in. 167; Saints defend gristmill in 178
Collison, ——, an "apostate" Mormon 473
Coltrin, Zebedee, greets P. Pratt, 98; appointed on mission with Levi Hancock, 115; goes on mission to Canada 191
Coltrin, Sr., welcomes Parley P. Pratt 98
Commerce, chosen for city of Saints, 291; name changed to Nauvoo, 291; first purchase by Saints of land in, 601; Joseph Smith and family arrive in 601; first house by Saints erected in 601
"Common Stock" ideas abandoned..112
Communion, authorized, 81; first at organization of church, 82; served in Canada, 189; first in England, 476; Joseph III gave uniform directions 505
Condit, Clayton H., pres. of sev. 623
Condit, Harold L., S. H. C. 639
Condit, Silas W., baptizes James W. Gillen 465
Confessions of faith, and creeds, issue in denominations, 22; Winchester taught election and reprobation, 26; thinking men assail, 25, 26; origin of, 26; Alexander Campbell advocates destruction of, 30; Barton Stone approves Campbell's attitude on 30
Conference, first conference at Fayette, 83; of June 6, 1831, at Kirtland, O., 118; Conference determines to publish E. & M. Star, also revelations of church, 151; at Amherst, O., 155; in Zion, 120; 600; in Missouri ratifies order at Amherst, 157; in Kirtland, Sept. 22, 23, 1832, 163; in Preston, England, 254; Conference at Winter quarters approves Brigham Young as president, 355; Conference in New York City, 364; Conference at Beloit, Wis., (1852), 405; fall conference 1852, 407; Conference at Argyle (now Blanchardville), Wis., 409-414; Conference at Beaverton, Ill., 422; Conference near Amboy, 422; Owens and Hedrick attend Con. at Zarahemla, 432, 433; special Conference at Amboy, (1859), 436; Conference in Rogers' grain barn, 436; Conference at Amboy, (1860), 450; Conference of 1866; 516; Conference of 1882, at Independence, 560; Conference of 1887, 568; rules of representation at, 571; conference at Pennydaren, Wales 478
Confirmation, first in England, 251; first in the church 82, 599
Constance, Byron, S. H. C. 630
Convent, Catholic, Joseph Smith's comment concerning burning of....47
Conner, Bill, in mob in Independence 176
"Coolbrith, Iva Donna," daughter of Don Carlos and Agnes Smith..273
Cooper, Robert T., on H. C. Reorg....628
Cornish, John J., baptized and labored in Canada, 541; remarkable experience at a baptism 541, 542
Corrill, John, to go on mission trip with Lyman Wight to Zion by way of Pontiac, 115; one of first miss. to Michigan, 122; signs letter to governor, 199; bears witness to truth of Doctrine and Covenants, 220; offered himself ransom for brethren 224
Couey, Duane E., ap., F. P., Pres. Patr. 617, 613, 620
Counselors to pr. bp., those who have served 619, 620
Counselors to pres. of church, those who have served 612, 613
Coward, Joseph, Derry meets in Chester 473
Cowdery, Lucy (later Young), tells of singing in choir at Temple dedication 228
Cowdery, Oliver, friend of Smith family, 52; communicates story of plates to D. Whitmer, 52, 53; buried in Richmond, Mo., 54; witness to Book of Mormon, 55, 70, 71, 72; goes to Harmony, Pa., 53; writes to D. Whitmer to come for Joseph and him, 63, acts as scribe, 62, 63, 64, 72; oversees printing B. of M., 67; baptism, 78, 79; Aaronic priesthood conferred upon, 78; Melchisedec priesthood conferred upon, 81; preaches near Auburn, N. Y., 83; baptizes Parley P. Pratt, 87; sympathetic to Hiram Page delusion, 88; on mission to Lamanites, Chap. X, 88; on Spaulding theory, 65, 73; goes to Tiffin, O., and practices law, 72; preaches to Catteraugus Indians 89; preaches in Rigdon's pulpit at Mentor, O., 89; meets Lyman Wight, 90; travels to Missouri, 81-83; arrives in Independence, 95; on mission to Lafayette

INDEX

Co., Mo., 96; present at dedication of land of Zion, and site for temple, 119; one of first schoolteachers in Jackson Co., 134; in charge of printing press in Kirtland, 189; on H. C. in Kirtland, 206, 620; one of com. to select first q-12, 217; assisted to ordain first apostles, 218; on com. to arrange Doctrine and Covenants, 220; sent to Philadelphia to secure plates for Kirtland Bank, 240; presents D. C. to church, 220; expelled from church, 267; answer to charges, 268; action of court now considered unfortunate, 268; letter to Daniel and Phoebe Jackson, 356; his first knowledge of polygamy, 356; death at home of D. Whitmer, 73; last words of, 73; visits Wm. Marks, 420; prophesies triumph of work, 420; special couns. in pres. 624
Crabb, James C., on H. C. Reorg...627
Creeds and confessions of faith, issue at stake in religious denominations, 22; thinking men assail, 26; origin of, 26; O'Kelley and Methodist seceders "no creed but Bible," 27; Jones and Smith form fellowship renouncing, 27; Alexander Campbell advocates destruction of, 30; Barton Stone approves Campbell's attitude on, 30; Joseph Smith said angel told him they were an abomination............... 76
Crisp, John T., testifies of conditions in Independence............557, 558
Crooked River, Battle of...................274
Crow Creek Branch, Granville Hedrick and the, Chap. XLVI...............431
Cuerdon, Henry, returned to Nauvoo 457
Cumberland, thirty baptisms............254
Cumberland, Presbyterian church, origin of.. 27
Cummins, Maj. Richard W., Indian agent forces miss. to leave Delaware Indians... 96
Cumorah Hill, described..................... 37
Cunningham, John, joined Reorg., 407; served as ap., 612; chosen and ordained as ap.......................413
Curry, Lemuel F. P., pr. bp.............618
Curtis, Edward A., served as pres. of sev..622
Curtis, J. Frank, served as ap..........616
Curtis, Meacham, sent out as scout by Texas colony................................379
Curtis, Theodore, Mr. and Mrs. baptism of..260
Curtis, William, sent out as scout by Texas colony................................379
Cutler, Alpheus, becomes acquainted with church and is baptized, 186, 187; master stonemason at Nauvoo Temple, 306; founded Manti, Iowa, 360; followers founded Clitherall, Minn., 360; dissented from Brigham Young, 360; on H. C. in Nauvoo, 626; Yellowstone Branch, Wisconsin, renounces claims of, 401;

one of temple committee, 442; present at blessing of young Joseph 445
Cutler, Lois, daughter of Alpheus Cutler, healing of, 186; baptism of, 187; in midst of mob, 187; married Almon Sherman...................187
Cutler, Thaddeus, returned to Nauvoo 457
Cutler, William, in command of L. D. S. at Battle of Nauvoo..............346

Dancer, David., couns. to pr. bp., 619; H. C. Reorg., 627; agent of the Order of 'Enoch..............................549
Danish Book of Mormon published..605
Daughters of Zion, women's movement 573, 604
Daugherty, James C., pres. of sev...623
Dauber's Lane, branch org. by first Eng. miss. 255
Davey, Roscoe E., served as pres. of sev., 622; ord. ap..............................617
Davies, John T., served as pres. of sev..622
Davies County, Missouri, Mormon settlements in.......................................266
Davis City, Iowa, visited by Joseph Smith 550
Davis, James W., served as pres. of sev., 622; served as sr. pres.............620
Davis, John A., served as pres. of sev..622
Davis, M. C., led choir at dedication of Temple...228
Deam, Henry H., revelation through, 410; chosen and ordained as ap., 413, 612; declines presidency of Q-12, 413; renounces all factions....401
DeLapp, G. Leslie, goes to Europe, 591; witnesses document, 594; ord. W. W. Smith, 595; couns. to pres. bp., 619; presiding bishop................619
Delaware Indians, Kans., first miss. to West preach to, 95; forced to leave by Indian agent......................... 96
Delegate members of conference......571
Deloit, Iowa, sermon of Wm. Smith at, quoted..58, 59
Democratic News, young Joseph replies to attackers in.....................455, 456
Denmark, miss. work in, Chap. LXII 535-540
Denna, Lewis, Indian miss. with Cutler 360
Derry, Charles, early experiences, 461-464; reads Herald, 462; writes hymn, 462; investigates Reorganization, 462-464; baptized, confirmed and ordained, 464; baptizes John Leeka, 466; ordained a sev. and sent to England, 469; leaves for Eng. mission, 471; arrives in England, 471; makes stand at West Bromwich, 474; pawns coat for Heralds, 475; Briggs and Jeremiah arrive in England, 475; first baptisms of Reorg. in England, 475; first branch of Reorg. organized in England, 475, 476; debates Wm. O. Owens, 477; visits Thomas Taylor,

478; returns to America, 479; served as ap., 615; served as pres. H. P. quorum..................624,627
Derry, George, turned back from going West..................461
Detroit, Mich., mission to..................122
Devore, L. R., miss. to Society Islands 564
De Witt, siege of, by mob........272, 273
Dewsnup, Joseph, one of first bishopric in England..................480
Dexter, Mrs. —, healing and baptism of..................259
'Diahman Boys, militia under Wight..................273
Dibble, Philo, wounded at battle on Whitmer settlement..................179
Dillee, Alma K., on H. C. Reorg........629
Directors, ball of, seen by three witnesses 71
Districts (conferences) organized....219
Doan, Jacob, on H. C. Reorg..........626
Doctrine and Covenants, see book of Doctrine and Covenants
Doniphan, Alexander W., orders a suit of Peter Whitmer, 95; quoted page 262; retained as attorney for Saints, 193; Clark placed over, 276; advises Saints to organize Jackson Guards, 194; defends Saints in Liberty meetings, 210; sponsors bill give Caldwell Co., to Saints, 263; prepared to defend Saints with life, 279, 280; defies order to execute Joseph Smith, 280; gives Joseph Smith III reason for act, 280; relates prophecy concerning devastation of Jackson Co., 284; tells of eloquence of Rigdon, 44, 282, 283; tribute to bravery of Lyman Wight, 44; tribute to Joseph Smith's leadership. 44; identifies Cowdery's handwriting, 65; defends Porter Rockwell, 319; tribute to Saints in Clay Co..................262
Dort, David, on H. C. in Kirtland, 625; on H. C. in Nauvoo..................626
Doty, Harry L.,Pres. of sev., 617,620 Sr. Pres. of Seventy..................623, 620
Douglas, Stephen A., friend and guest of Joseph Smith, 290; as judge exonerates Joseph Smith of "murder and treason," 319; Browning pleads Joseph Smith's case before..................291
Dow, Lorenzo, itinerant preacher......21
Downham, Lanc, branch organized by first miss. to Eng......254, 255
Downs, J. Sanford, S.H.C..................629
Dramatic Society of Nauvoo..........303
Draper, Maurice L., couns. to pres., 613; ord. ap..................617
Dunham, Oliver P., on H. C. Reorg. 627
Dunklin, Daniel, Gov., Phelps and Hyde lay case before, 177; encourages Saints, 177; letter of A. S. Gilbert to, 194; answer to Gilbert, 195; letter of elders in Liberty to, 198, 199; reply, 199; letter to Col. J. Thornton, 200-202; orders mob to return Saints' arms....202, 203
Dunn, Captain —, collects "state arms" at Nauvoo..................341

Durfee. L. D. S. carpenter, built woodwork for Michael Arthur's mill 215
Durphy, Perry, L. D. S. involved in Gallatin riot..................271
Dustin, Peter, early missionary......162
Dykes, Geo. P., converted and rebaptized, 483; sent to California, 483; goes to Nevada..................483

East River, New York City, baptisms almost daily in..................259
Eccleston, branch organized by first England miss..................255
Edler, Lars, miss. to Idaho..................509
Edmunds, Judge George, Jr., saw Joseph Smith once, 348; never saw Hyrum, 348; opinion of cause of trouble, 348; opinion of Saints, 349; asked Joseph III to remain in Nauvoo 5 years..................454, 455
Education, first schools in Jackson Co., 134; in Nauvoo, 315; editorial in Evening and Morning Star urging, 162, 163; school of elders, conducted by Pratt, 167; schoolwork for priesthood in Kirtland Temple, 227, 228; L. D. S. women well educated, 262; many schoolteachers and numerous schools among Saints, 265; first school in San Francisco, 369; Graceland College..................573
Edwards. F. Henry, served as ap., 616; England has contributed, 480; ord. First Pres..................613
Eight witnesses, shown the plates.. 72
Elders Journal, published at Kirtland..................601
Elders, school of, conducted by P. P. Pratt..................167
Elec., doctrine of the..................15, 16
Ellis, Clara K., buried in South Sea Islands..................528
Ellis, Clyde F., served as ap..........617
Ellis, Nancy Rigdon, testimony on Book of Mormon..................108, 109
Ellis, Richard, prominent Saint of Sydney, Australia..................529
Ells, Josiah, Methodist minister, holds debate with Benjamin Winchester, 309; baptized by Winchester, 309; becomes pres. of branch at Monmouth Co., N. J., 309; early history, 309; meets Joseph Smith, 309; appointed by Joseph to meet Dr. David Nelson of Quincy in debate, 309, 459; experience in church. 459, 460; served as ap., 612; accompanies Joseph part way to Carthage, 341, 459; tells of Joseph's prophecy concerning death, 341; renounced all factions, 459; sent by Wm. Marks to bring John Taylor home, 459; went to Pittsburgh with Rigdon, 460; holds meetings, 460; W. W. Blair converts to Reorg..................460
Elser, Otto H., S. H. C...................630
Elvin, Robert M., on H. C. Reorg...627

Emmett, James, baptized on first mission to Michigan, 122; leader of a faction..361
Endowment, spiritual at Kirtland Temple 228, 229, 601
Ensign, Zion's published.....................604
Epistle, first by Joseph Smith, III 467, 468
Erie Canal, Palmyra on, 43; travel upon, 85; Joseph Sr., lived in Waterloo upon, 113; Saints from N. Y. travel to Kirtland by....113, 114
Escape from authorities, Joseph Smith and others....................284, 285
Etzenhouser, Merrill A., on H. C. Reorg. 628
Evanelia, the gospel-boat............565, 566
Evans, David, in charge of defense at Haun's Mill, 277; surrender ignored 277
Evans, Richard C., couns. in pres., 568; served as ap.................................613
Evening and the Morning Star, (Independence), to be published 151; press for printing bought, 151; paper bought for first edition, 156; first number appears, 162, 598; Free People of Color, editorial in, 174; press and type thrown in river by mob, 175, 600; The Evening and the Morning Star (Kirtland) a republication provided for by resolution, 188; first number issued, 190, 600; letter from Moses Nickerson 191
Everetts ferry, sinking of ferry boat at, 211; Everett drowned...............211
Exodus from Jackson Co., 180-185, 598; from Missouri, 280-286, 601; from Nauvoo, Chap. XXXVI 344-354, 602
Extermination, order of Gov. Boggs 276

Factions. Reorg. rejects all, 405; Joseph Smith III attitude toward, 489, 490; renounced by Yellowstone Branch, 401; Yellowstone Branch withdraws fellowship from all.......401
Fairfield, O., port of Kirtland; Saints accompany first miss. to Eng. to...246
Faith taught..168
Family, the experimental community in Kirtland, 90; Lyman Vight left to join church..............................374
Farrar, Canon, statement regarding John Wesley 23, 24
Farrow, Percy E....................................617
Far West, Chapter XXX, 261-286, county seat of Caldwell, Co., Mo., 264; townsite entered, 264; description of town, 264; life in, 266, 267; Whitmers, Cowdery, and others dissent from church, 268; Saints from, investigate reports of riot in Gallatin, 271; Saints flock into, 274; election in, after exodus of Saints, 275; preparations for evacuation, 285; exodus from, 280-286, 601; evacuation of, 286, Joseph Smith and others sentenced to be shot in square, 280; surrounded by militia..................................279
Faulconer, Marietta, later Marietta Walker 499, 500
Fayette, N. Y., Peter Whitmer, Sr., moves to, 52; Oliver Cowdery taught school in, 52; geographical location, 63; Joseph Smith removes to, 63; scene of vision of three witnesses, 73; first conference at, 83; location of preaching points in, 82; Parley P. Pratt and Hyrum Smith walk to, from Palmyra, 87; branch at, 87; first missionaries leave, 82; conference at, 112; preaching at..................................82
Ferry, L. D. S. on Big Blue; Saints meet at, 174; taken by mob, 178; sinking of boat at Everett's ferry 210, 211
Fielding, Rev. James, invites first miss. to use pulpit, 250; turns against L. D. S...................................250
Fielding, Joseph, hears the gospel, 234; ordained to go on mission to Eng., 246; his brother, Rev. James Fielding, visited by miss., 249; miss. trip of, 254; remains in Eng..254
Felding, Mary, hears the gospel, 234; marries Hyrum Smith, 234; gives $5 to finance first foreign mission, 48, 246; accompanies Eng. mission to Fairfield............................246
Fielding, Mercy, hears the gospel, 234; marries Robert Thompson......234
Fishing River Revelation received..212
Flournoy, Jones H., Bishop Partridge buys Temple Lot from........152
Follows, George B., comes 16 miles to see Derry...479
Folsom, California, Branch organized 483
Ford, Thomas, Gov., Joseph Smith offers to go before any court he may designate, 336; pledges faith of state, 342; Wood and Reid appeal to, 343; refused to intervene, 343; disbands McDonough troops, 343; character of, 344; on removal of L. D. S., 345; his history, 346; his children..346
Fordham, Elijah, only L. D. S. in New York City, 247, 257; promise to, 247; carves oxen for baptismal font in Temple, 306, 307; assists P. Pratt in mission in New York City..................................257
Forgeus, John A., sends $200 to help publish Book of Mormon, Nauvoo ed...301
Forscutt, Mark, letter from David Whitmer, 74, 75; helps edit Zion's Hope, 572; hires Independence Hall for A. H. Smith to preach in, 517; Russell Huntley deeds Kirtland Temple to..........................554
Fort Osage (now Sibley) elders stop at 121
Foss, John C., served as pres of sev. 622
Foster, Dr. ——, disaffected, 334; leaves Nauvoo with family..............337

Foster, James, served as pres. of sev. 621
Fouts, Dallas B., Sr., S. H. C. 630
Fox, Jane, of Birmingham Heath, gave in name for baptism.....475
Fox's Gardens, Salt Lake City, Alexander H. Smith preaches in.....517
Free People of Color, editorial in Evening and the Morning Star.....174
Free Thinkers Society, asks P. P. Pratt to deliver series of meetings in Tammany Hall, N. Y.....259
Friendship, Allegheny Co., N. Y., home of Rigdon in later life.....103
Fristoe, Richard, prominent in opposition to Mormons in Jackson Co., offered to buy land.....210
Fry, Charles, on H. C. Reorg.....628
Fulk, Raleigh L., served as pres. of sev. 622
Fuller, Edson, appointed on mission with—Jacob Scott, 115; dropped out 115
Fullmer, David, on H. C. in Nauvoo 626
Fyrando, Elsie (nee Olsen), wife of Magnus Fyrando, early experience in the church.....535
Fyrando, Magnus, miss. to Scandinavia, 535; early experiences in the church, in Sweden and Denmark; prophecy to and its fulfillment 535-540

Galland, Dr. Isaac, helps start Times and Seasons.....297
Gallatin, election day riot at....270, 271
Gardiol, ——, two sisters, first baptisms in Italy.....508
Garrick, the, ship upon which miss. embark for Eng., 248; description of, 248; race with South America, 248, 249; miss. return upon, 255; race with New England.....255
Garver, John F., on H C. Reorg., 628; served as ap., 616; ord. First Pres.; died.....613
Cathering, Saints return to Independence, Chap. LXV, 557-561; Joseph Smith III upon.....497, 498
Gatrost, Phillip, brings Derry's family to western Iowa.....464
Gauze, Jesse, goes to Missouri.....156
Gaylord, Elijah, pledges himself to see Derry family does not suffer 471
Gaylord, John C., served as pres. of sev., 621; on H. C. Reorg., 626; determines to stand apart from all factions, 425; interested in Reorg.....422
Gee, Salmon, served as pres. of sev. 621
General Assembly.....220
Germany, miss. in.....515, 603
Gibbs, Luman, tried and acquitted.285
Gilbert, Algernon S., partner of Knight, goes to Independence, 116; to establish new store in Independence, 116; goes to Independence by boat, 117; arrives in Independence, 118; probable reference to by Latrobe, 126, 127; store attacked by mob, 175; letter to form attorney gen. quoted, 194; discusses organization of Saints into militia, 195; signs letter to governor, 199; died of cholera, 214; offers himself as a ransom for brethren 224
Gilbert, J. W., and wife, miss. to South Seas, experience in tidal wave 566
Gilbert, John H., set type for B. of M..... 67
Gillette, Truman, converts John Leeka.....466
Gillen, James A., served as ap., 616; served as pres. of q. of twelve.....613
Gillen, James W., baptized by S. W. Condit, 465; chosen an ap., 568; early life, 465; miss. to Australia, 533, miss. to Cal., 373; served as as ap., 615; served as pres. of sev., 622; married Nancy D. Moore.....465
Gleason and Shepherd—stereotyped Book of Mormon (Nauvoo) ed.....300
Gleazer, Edmund J., Sr., ap.....617
Glories, revelation on.....154, 171
Goerck Street, N. Y., first meeting place of Saints in New York City..258
Goodrich, Vinton M., on H. C. Reorg. 628
Goodson, John, one of first miss. to Eng., 247; preached in Preston, 250; went to Bedford, 251; left for America 254
Goodwin, Mrs. Laura, died on Brooklyn, and buried on island of Juan Fernandez.....366
Gospel, The, a tract distributed by Ursenbach 599
Gospel Herald, quoted.....385
Gould, John, goes to Independence with aid from Kirtland, 177; served as pres. of sev., 628; bears testimony to truth of Doctrine and Covenants.....220
Grabske, Charles F., served on H. C. Reorg. 629
Graceland College.....573, 605
Graffeo, Everett, ap. 618
Grandin, Egbert B., printed Book of Mormon..... 67
Granger, Oliver, on H. C. at Kirtland 625
Grant, John A., on H. C. Reorg.....628
Green, Noah, pledged himself to see Derry family did not suffer....471
Green, Hervey, baptized Granville Hedrick, 431; bids farewell to Clapp on his first mission.....520
Green John P., baptism, 164; marshal destroys press of Expositor, 335; on H. C. at Kirtland.....625
Greene, Thomas P., and congregation at Jeffersonville, Ill., unite with Reorg.....492
Greene, Ulysses W., served as ap..616
Gregg, describes scene after assassination 344, 345
Griffith, Duty, receives Herald.....460
Griffith, Ethan, one of com. to select the q. of twelve Reorg.....413
Griffith, Selah J., appointed on a mission with Newell Knight, 116; mated with Thomas B. Marsh.....116

INDEX

Griffiths, Gomer T., parentage and blessing, 493; chosen an ap., 568; 615; served as pres. of q. of twelve 613
Grouard, Benjamin F., Chap. XXXIV, 321; ordained a sev. and set apart for island mission, 321; 596; an old sailor, 325; preaches first sermon in Tahiti, 326; visits Tubuai, 327; goes to Anaa and low islands, 329; builds a schooner at Tubuai, 330; forbidden to preach by French, 331; leaves islands, 331; later life and death 331
Grover, Thomas, on H. C. in Kirtland 625
Groves, Elisha H., ordains David Patten, 159; on H. C. in Zion 626
Gurley, Margaret (nee Hickey), married Zenas Gurley, Sr., 397; takes in washing, 397; baptized by Jehiel Savage 398
Gurley, Samuel, sent on mission to young Joseph, Chap. XLV 424-430
Gurley, Zenas H., Jr., first store at Lamoni, 549; made an ap., 546, 614; withdrawal 554, 555
Gurley, Zenas H., Sr., Chap. XLII, 396-404; early history, 396-398; baptism, 397; early miss. work, 398; appointed to travel and collect money for Nauvoo Temple, 399; falls to go west, 399, 400; miss. in Strang's organization, 399; raises branch at Yellowstone, Wisconsin, 400; renounces Strang with entire branch, 401; seeks light on next step, 401-404; receives revelation from J. W. Briggs and accepts it, 403, 404; visits Wingville and Blue Mounds, Wis., 407; on com. to draft Word of Consolation, 408; relates experiences of April, 1853, 411, 412; chosen and ordained an ap., 412, 413; baptizes Samuel Powers and wife, 424; assists in ordaining young Joseph, 452; probably spokesman in his ordination, 453; covenant with R. Newkirk, 402; daughter speaks in tongues 403

Haldeman, Adna C., connected with Crow Creek Branch, 431; present at Reorg. conference in 1853, 431; on com. to get subscribers for Herald, 431; council meeting at home, 432; ordained an ap., 434; assists in ordaining Hedrick pres. of the church 435
Hale, Emma, see Emma Smith.
Hale, Isaac, prosperous farmer, 61; Joseph and Emma return to, 59; attitude toward Joseph, 61; Joseph buying farm from 61
Hall, Andrew, secedes from Thompson 388
Hall, Samuel, Catholic Priest, reads tract in Montreal, 312; goes to Nauvoo, 312; baptized, confirmed, and ordained, 313; goes on a mission, 313, 314; baptizes, 314; organizes branch 314
Halsey, Thankful, -married Parley P. Pratt (see Thankful Pratt)
Hamilton, Ontario, experience of Parley P. Pratt in 232
Hamilton's Hotel, Joseph Smith and party put up at, 342; Bettisworth insists go to jail from 342
Hancock, Levi, appointed on mission with Zebedee Coltrin, 115; served as pres. of sev., 621; Pratt leaves Independence with 161
Hancock, Solomon, appointed on a mission with Simeon Carter, 115; pres. of branch on Blue River, 182; prays for food, 183; on H. C. of Zion 625
Hands, W. O., on H. C. Reorg 628
Hanks, Knowlton F., set apart for South Sea Island mission, 321; dies and is buried at sea 323
Hansen, Francis E., pres. bpric 618, 619
Hanson, Hans N., appointed on first Reorg. mission to Scandinavia, 535; arrives in Copenhagen, 535; returns home 533
Hanson, Paul M., served as ap., 616; served as pres. of q. of 12, 613; released 616
Hark, Listen to the Trumpeters, sung at choosing of missionary quorums 217
Harmony, Penn. (now Oakland), Joseph employed in, 40; meets Emma Smith, 40; not the Harmony of the Rappite community, 40; Joseph and Emma move to, 59; Martin Harris goes to, 60; David Whitmer goes for Cowdery and Smith 63
Harper, Henry P., protests against return to Hancock Co 455
Harriman, Henry, miss. to Canada, 191; served as pres. of sev 621
Harrington, Daniel B., arrives in Utah 485
Harrington, John, received testimony of Briggs revelation, 393; spiritual experiences, 393, 394; on com. to draft Word of Consolation, 406; takes mission south 407
Harris, Emer, first preaching heard by John E. Page 236
Harris, Geo. W., on H. C. in Zion and in Nauvoo 626
Harris, Lucy, cousin and wife of Martin Harris, opposed to Martin's friendship with Joseph Smith, 51; Martin takes 116 first pages of mss. to show her 61
Harris, Martin, befriends Joseph Smith, 50, 51; family of, 51; his story, 51; acts as scribe for Joseph Smith, 60; loses manuscript, 61; took characters to Prof. Anthon, 60, 597; testimony to Book of Mormon, 70-72; appointed on mission with Edward Partridge, 115; present at dedication of site for Temple, 119, 120; H. C. in Kirtland 206, 624

Harris, Nathan, father, Martin, prominent farmer of Palmyra, N. Y. ... 50
Hatch, Victor B., Jr., pres. of sev. 623
Haun, Jacob, builds mill on Shoal Creek ... 277
Haun's Mill Massacre ... 277, 279
Hawaii, mission to, 562-564, 604; Spaulding's manuscript found in 604
Hawkins, John, one of first baptisms in Tahiti, 326; promise made to and its fulfillment ... 326
Haws, Albert ... 340, 562, 563, 604
Haws, Peter, lived across from Hyrum Smith, 340; Joseph bids goodby to children of, 340; Albert Haws and Mrs. Leabo, his children ... 340
Hayden, A. S., tribute to Rigdon, 103, 104; tells of healing of Mrs. Johnson's arm ... 150
Hayton, Thos., prominent in opposition to L. D. S. in Jackson Co., offers to buy L. D. S. land ... 210
Healing of Elizabeth Ann Walmsley, 250; of Mrs. Johnson's arm, 150; of Parley P. Pratt, 161; of Lois Cutler, 186, 187; in New York City, 259, 260; David Patten blessed with gift of, 158; of two children by Patten ... 160
Hebrew, Joseph Smith and others study, 601; presented a lexicon by Oliver Cowdery, 315; Joseph Smith's "heart rejoices in" study of ... 47
Hedlock, Reuben H., leaves on mission to Eng. ... 256
Hedrick, Granville, Chap. XLVI, 431-435; history, 431; first meeting of group, 431, 432; writes pamphlet, 432; conference at Crow Creek, 433; ideas on succession in Presidency, 434; made presiding elder of Crow Creek Branch, 434; ordained an ap., 434; ordained pres. of the church, 434; purchases Temple Lot, 435; visits Zarahemla ... 432
Hendrickson, ——, loans Herald to John Leeka ... 466
Herald, see Saints' Herald.
Hewitt, Lyman, on H. C. Reorg. ... 627
Heywood, John and Mary, receive Derry kindly ... 477
Hield, Chas. R., served as ap., 617; pres. of quo. of twelve ... 613
Higbee, Elias, H. C. in Zion, ... 626
seeks redress in Washington, D. C., 290; conversion by Lyman Wight, 315; opposes Saints settling in a body ... 416
Higbee, Francis, attempts and fails to run off first ed. of Times and Seasons, 296, 297; dissents from church in Nauvoo ... 334
Higbee, Isaac, conversion by Lyman Wight, 315; on H. C. in Zion ... 626
Higdon, Earl T., Ap. ... 618
Higdon, William T., ord. ap. ... 618
High Council, Chap. XXI, 205-207; organized, 205, 600; first case before, 205; organized in Zion, 207, 215, 216, 600; ratifies Doctrine and Covenants, 220; appoints, com. on Doctrine and Covenants, 220, 221, 222; attends council in Kirtland, 226; to supervise stake of Zion, 579; reorganized in Reorg., 453, 602; those who served in Kirtland, 624; in Zion, 625; in Nauvoo, 626; in Reorg. ... 626
High Priests, ordained, 148, 602; ordained by Granville Hedrick, 434; first quorum organized, 602; controversy with seventy, 410-412; Isaac Sheen chosen pres. of quorum, 453; those have served as pres. of H. P. Q. ... 623
Hilliard, George H., couns. to pr. bp. ... 619
Hillman, Mayhew, on H. C. Kirtland, 625; on H. C. in Adam-ondi-ahman ... 625
Hinderks, Temme T., on H. C. Reorg. ... 627
Hinkle, George M., leader of a movement, 361; on H. C. in Zion ... 626
Hitchcock, Jesse, on H. C. in Zion 626
Hobart, C. Houston, pres. sev. ... 623
Hodges, Marietta, see Marietta Walker.
Hoge, Joseph P., defeated Cyrus Walker for Congress ... 332
Holden Stake formed ... 605
Holland, miss. to ... 605
Holliston, Mass., baptisms at ... 260
Holmes, Milton, missionary to Canada ... 191
Holmes, Reed M., apostle, 611; Pr. Patr. ... 617, 620
Holy Scriptures (see Inspired Version).
Home for children ... 574, 605
Homes for aged ... 574, 605
Hook, Aaron, with Wm. Smith ... 425
Hopkins, Roy V., on H. C. Reorg. 628
Horahitu, visited America ... 527
Hospital and Sanitarium ... 573, 574
Hougas, Ward A., pres. of H. P. Q. 624
Howard, Philo, couns. to pr. bp. ... 619
Howe, E. D., publishes Mormonism Unveiled, 107, 108; associate of D. Hurlbut, 190; incensed because wife becomes member of church, 107; first to advance Spaulding's theory, 108; papers sold to L. L. Rice ... 110
Hudson, Henry J., assists western mission financially ... 516
Hulmes, George H., pres. of Independence stake, 570; on H. C. Reorg. ... 628
Hummel, Gene M., couns. to P. B. ... 620
Humphrey, Solomon, appointed on a mission with Joseph Wakefield 115
Hunker, Ernest Y., served as pres. of sev.; evangelist ... 617, 623
Hunter's Hill, branch organized by first Eng. miss. ... 255
Huntington, William, on H. C. at Nauvoo ... 626
Huntley, Russell, determines to stand apart from all factions, 425; deeds Kirtland Temple to Joseph Smith and Mark Forscutt ... 554
Hurlbut, Doctor, mentioned by Rigdon, 110; expelled for immoral conduct ... 190, 205
Hurshman, Lloyd B., ord. ap. ... 618
Hyde, Orson, biography of, 151; baptized, 151, 152; married Marinda

INDEX 643

Johnson. 149; goes to Missouri with aid, 177; lays Jackson Co., trouble before Gov. Dunklin, 177; sent to Columbus. O., to apply for act of incorporation for Kirtland Bank, 240; estranged by financial trouble in Kirtland, 245; goes on mission to Eng., 245, 599; ministry in Eng., 250-252; leaves England, 255; dedicates land of Jerusalem, 602; on H. C. at Kirtland........206, 624
Hymnbook, Wm. Marks, a com. on publication 436
Hymns, Hymn No. 74 in Saints' Hymnal, 462; hymns selected by Wandell, 523; The Spirit of God Like a Fire Is Burning, 525; Hark, Listen to the Trumpeters, 217; Let Zion in Her Beauty Rise, 378; Weep, Weep Not for Me, Zion, 530; Now Let Us Rejoice in the Day of Salvation..................................229

Immigration, first immigrants came to Nauvoo, 292; conditions between 1841-1851, 292; L. D. S. management of, 293; Cambridge Independent Press, comments upon L. D. S. immigration, 253; effect on Nauvoo economically, 293, 294; from British Isles, 480; from Utah 485
Independence, first miss. arrives, 95, 598; established tailor shop in, 96; Pratt returns from, 96; elders appointed to travel there, 115; Joseph Smith starts for, 116; his opinion of Missourians, 118; opinion of the country, 119; site for Temple, dedicated near, 119, 120; miss. party starts return from, 121; Latrobe describes, 126; Washington Irving describes, 128; Warren Watson describes, 130; Joseph Smith leaves Kirtland for second visit to, 156; returns from, 157, 158; mob in, 174; Saints camped on Temple Lot in, 180; Saints forced to leave, 180, 181; Joseph Smith III visits Independence, 558; Independence branch organized, 559; Brick Church built, 560; Stone Church built, 560; Independence Stake organized, 570, 605; Independence Stake divided, 570, 605; declared city of Zion, 570, 605; Sanitarium built, 573, 574, 605; home for old folks established, 574; Joseph Smith moves to, 575; E. L. Kelley moves to, 575; The Evening and Morning Star published at, 151, 600; Herald moved to Independence, 439; plat for city of Zion received 600
Independence Hall, Salt Lake City, Alex. H. Smith preaches in..........517
Independence landing, eleven elders leave from..121
Independence mob, good citizens had nothing to do with it, 175; Doniphan says "more ignorant part of community," 176; Warren Watson names Boggs and others..176
Independence Stake, 570, 605; declared to be Zion.................................605
Indians (Lamanites), mission to, 88; Pratt, Cowdery, Whitmer, and Peterson preach to Catteraugas, 89; preach to Delawares, 95, 96; forced to leave Indians by agent, 96; O. Cowdery hears of Navajoes, 97; followers of Cutler make and keep treaty with, 360; Lewis, Denna miss., 360; Lyman Wight colony share food with, 375; Lyman Wight colony have trouble with, 381, 382; Wyandottes visited by miss... 91
Inspired Version (a revision) of Scriptures; Joseph Smith and Sidney Rigdon go to Hiram, O., to work upon, 148, 149; work temporarily suspended, 152; revelation received while working upon, 154; mss in hands of James Mulholland at siege of Far West, 285, 286; Anne Scott becomes custodian, 286; Emma Smith receives, 286; resolution to publish, 502; com. of Reorg. procure from Emma Smith, 502; manner of publication, 502, 503; stereotyped in Philadelphia, 503; first ready for mailing, 503; P. M. Sims comments upon, 503; five thousand, 503; work on, completed 600
Institutes held 591, 592
Interpreters, 62; (see Urim and Thummim) seen by three witnesses 71
Ireland, preaching by J. W. Rushton..480
Irving. Washington, describes Independence..128
Isle of Pines, mission in....................567
Italian, Book of Mormon printed in..359
Italy, miss. opened in..............508, 603

Jackman, Levi, bears record to truth of Doctrine and Covenants, 220; on H. C. in Zion.................................625
Jackson, Andrew J., on H. C. in Reorg. 626
Jackson Co., Mo., first miss. arrived, 95; miss. cover all roads, two by two, 115; Joseph Smith arrives in, 118; trouble in Chap. XVIII, 172-185; conditions of Saints in, 154; first schools in, 134; petition asks Saints to leave, 175; exodus from, 179-185; 598; Gov. Dunklin attempts to settle difficulties in, Chap. XX, 193-204; Joseph Smith visits at night, 185, 215; Lyman Wight expects his inheritance to be in, 377; Granville Hedrick and his followers return to, 435; Saints return to, Chap. LXV, 557-561; prophecy concerning, by Joseph Smith, 283, 284; desolated by Order No. 11, 284, 557; conditions after war in 557, 558
Jackson, Daniel and Phoebe, letter of Oliver Cowdery to....................356

James, with Peter and John, confer Melchisedec priesthood..................81
James, ——, assists fugitive Saints..184
James, Samuel, on H. C. at Kirtland, 625; couns. to Sidney Rigdon 358
Jefferson, William, one of first baptisms in Tahiti.....................................326
Jeffersonville, Ill., Branch unites with Reorg...492
Jehovah's Presbytery of Zion...........387
Jenkins, Thomas E., Welsh miss., arrives 479
Jennings, Col ——, leader of mob at Haun's Mill................................278, 279
Jensen, D. Blair, ap.............................617
Jeremiah, Jeremiah, appointed to Eng. mission, 475; arrives in Eng., 475; starts to Wales, 476; in need of help in Wales, 477; Briggs goes to assist, 477; opened miss. in Wales 606
Jerks, a manifestation at revivals 20, 21
Jerusalem, Hyde dedicates................602
Joab, General in Israel, nom de plume of John C. Bennett.........315, 316
Job, Thomas, missionary work in Utah 493; writes of death of Thomas B. Marsh.................501, 502, 603
Joe Duncan, a horse belonging to Joseph Smith..45
John with James and Peter confers Melchisedec priesthood....................81
John the Baptist confers priesthood upon Joseph Smith and Oliver Cowdery 77, 78
Johns, Abednego, ordained a seventy 484
Johnson, Elsa, wife of John, of Hiram, O., Joseph Smith and wife at home of, 149; mother of Luke, Lyman, and Marinda Hyde, 149; healing of crippled arm......................150
Johnson, Glen H., pres. of sev............623
Johnson, John, of Hiram, O., Joseph Smith 149; disaffected in 1838, 149; on H. C. in Kirtland, 624; father of Luke and Lyman Johnson and Marinda Hyde, 149; blesses his own sons...191
Johnson, Luke S., brought into church at Kirtland, 101; on H. C. at Kirtland, 2.6, 624; served as ap., 614; baptized by Joseph Smith, 149; disaffected in 1838....149
Johnson, Lyman E., brought into church in Kirtland, 101; served as ap., 614; youngest member of first quorum of 12, 149; baptized by Sidney Rigdon, 149; disaffected in, 149; practiced law in Davenport, Iowa, and Keokuk, 149; death of, 149; missionary to Canada, 191; failed in business.................................245
Johnson, Orson, on H. C. in Kirtland 624
Johnson, Walter N., couns. to pr. bp.; Pres. Bish............................619, 620
Jones, Abner, rejects "sectarian names and creeds"..................................27
Jones, Dan, assists in building Maid of Iowa, 293; Captain of Maid of Iowa, 294; baptizes the Griffiths....493
Joseph Smith and His Progenitors, gives account of finding the plates 58
Judy, David, with Crow Creek Branch, 431; biographical, 431; ordained H. P., in Crow Creek Branch, 431; ordained an ap. in C. of C., 434; assists in ordaining Hedrick pres. of the church..........435

Kahtava, A. Alexander, pres. of sev., Sr. pres...623, 620
Kane, Thomas, describes evacuation of Nauvoo.......................................350-354
Kansas City, Joseph Smith and party camp near spring, 118; in 1831, 130, 131; stake organized.....................605
Kansas City Journal, concerning Joseph Smith..577
Kansas City Star, statement concerning Joshua Lewis........................120
Keir, James F., couns. to pr. bp.; H. C. resigned.................................619, 629
Kelley, Benjamin Franklin, one of first members of church in Johnson Co., Ill...470
Kelley, Edmund L., joined Reorg., 470; became bishop, 470, 618; sponsors move for gospel boat, 564; moves to Independence, 575; couns. to pres. of church..........568, 612
Kelley, J. Stanley, on H. C. Reorg..629
Kelley, James E., served as ap.........616
Kelley Richard Yancey, joins Reorg. 470
Kelley, Thomas C., served as pres. of sev., 622; served as senior pres. of sev...620
Kelley, William H., served as ap., 546, 615; baptizes Heman C. Smith, 469; family history, 469, 470; engages in miss. work................................470
Kendall Co., Record, on departure of Joseph Smith from Plano 552, 553
Kimball, Heber C., baptized, 164; kept journal in Zion's Camp, 209; one of first quorum of apostles, 217; wife works for Temple, 225; tells of work on Temple, 225; tells of Sidney Rigdon's anxiety for Temple, 225; account of work upon, 225, 226; assists Heman Chapin cut wheat, 230; preaches at Ogdenburg, N. Y., 230; delivers prophecy to P. Pratt, 231; speaks of speculation in Kirtland, 240; appointed on mission to Eng., 245; leaves Kirtland for Eng., 246; sails from New York, 248; arrives in Eng., 249; preaches in Walkerfold, 251; baptizes 110 persons on 5-day mission, 254; preaches and baptizes at Chatburn, 254; leaves Eng., 255; arrives in New York, 256; baptizes James Whitehead, 256; leaves on second mission to Eng., 256; served as ap., 614; organizes young people in Nauvoo, 302; couns. to Brigham Young, 355; concerning young Joseph....361
Kimball, Vilate, her work for temple, 225; baptized, 164; accompa-

INDEX

nies Eng., miss. as far as Fairfield, 246; letter to husband..........337
King, Judge Austin A., Wight, Smith, etc., have preliminary hearing before, 272; brother-in-law of Hugh Brazeale, 276; writes to Gen. Park, 276; Saints tried before 282
Kingsbury, Joseph, on H. C. at Kirtland 625
Kippe, Alex, trans. Book of Mormon 605
Kirtland, "The Family" at, 90; first miss. visit, 91; Joseph Smith moves to, 112; eastern Saints move to, 112-115; a temporary stopping place, 115, 116, 165; elders go on mission to Zion, 115, 122; Jared Carter leaves for Pontiac, 123; High Priests ordained at, 148; Joseph Smith returns to, 148; revelation on glories received in, 154; makes trip to Independence from, in 23 days, 157; conference of Sept. 1832 in, 163; Young and Kimball visit, 164; Patten leaves for New York on miss., 186; reprint of Star issued from, 190; made a stake, 165; church leaders blamed for failure of bank, 244; 1st quo. of seventy org. at..........601
Kirtland Bank, plans to organize, 240; Oliver Cowdery procures plates, 240; denied act of incorporation, 240; an anti-banking society formed, 240, 241; notes begin to be refused, 241; I. P. Axtell, Esq., on 241, 242; Joseph Smith warns against, 242; panic of 1837, 242; Saints struggle to meet obligations in full..........270
Kirtland Temple, Chap. XXV, 224-229; plan to build, 165; women assist, 225; Rigdon's anxiety for 225; prophet assists, 225; plastering, 226; doorkeeper for appointed, 226; committee to draft regulations for, 266; dedication of, 228, 229, 599; endowment in, 229; deeded to Joseph Smith and Mark Forscutt by Russell Huntley, 554; title cleared by Reorg., 554; cornerstone laid..........600
Knight, Joseph, miller and grain buyer of Colesville, N. Y., 39, 40; often employed Joseph Smith, 39; his family, 39; Joseph Smith takes his team to go after plates, 41; follower of Joseph Smith, 48; operates mill in Jackson Co..........135
Knight, Newell, appointed on a mission with Selah J. Griffith, 116; superintends removal of Colesville branch, 115, 116; present at dedication of Zion, 119; writes of Joseph Smith's visit to Colesville branch, 157; has mill in Nauvoo, 294; on H. C. in Zion, and in Nauvoo..........625
Knight, Polly, first Saint to die in Jackson Co. 120
Koury, Aleah G., Ap..........618
Krahl, David J., on H. C. Reorg..........628

Ladies Mite Society of Lamoni gives bell to church..........554
Ladies Relief Society of the City of Nauvoo..........303
Lafayette Co., Missouri, Oliver Cowdery and Ziba Peterson preach in 96
Lake, Charles, buried in South Sea Islands 528
Lake Cayuga, near Fayette..........63
Lake, John (and Maryette), 160; Ap..........615
Lake Seneca, near Fayette, 63; Cowdery baptized Pratt in..........87
Lambert, Joseph R., parentage, 492; served as an ap., 615; served as pr. pat..........620
Lambert, Richard and Jane, remain in Hancock Co., 491; unite with Reorg. 491, 492
Lamphear, Crowell G., served as pres. of sev., 621; served as senior pres. of sev..........620
Lamoni Stake organized..........570, 605
Landers, John, a Baptist preacher, heard gospel first from John Cairns, 235; converted and baptized by John E. Page, 235-238; sees plates of Book of Mormon in vision, 237; preaching in Kingsville, Ontario, 310; visited by John Shippy at Walnut Grove, Ill., 310, 311; with Wm. B. Smith, 425; determined to stand apart from all factions, 425; John E. Page requests preach funeral sermon, 434; ordains Jedediah Owen and David Judy, high priests, 434; ordains Granville Hedrick, presiding priest of Crow Creek Branch 434
Lane, George, pioneer preacher and revivalist in western New York....32
Latrobe, Charles J., describes Independence 126-128
Latter Day Saints' Messenger and Advocate, authorized, 188; Whitmer's address in leaving editorial chair, 222, 223; succeeded by Elders' Journal..........601
Law, William, converted by Russell at Churchville, Ont., 285; left Nauvoo in June, 1844, 337; couns. in presidency, 612; Expositor property of 342
Law, Wilson, converted by Russell at Churchville, Ont., 285; left Nauvoo in June, 1844, 337; Expositor, property of..........342
Lawson, Leonidas M., quoted on prophecy concerning Order No. 11 283
Laying on of hands, believed and taught 169
Lea, L. J., High Council; resigns....629
Leabo, Charlotte, formerly Haws, memories of Joseph's farewell..........340
Leeka, John, early history, 466; advised by Emma Smith not to go west, 466; baptized by Charles Derry, 466; pledged himself to see Derry family did not suffer..........471
Legislature of Missouri, passes resolution forbidding publication of any documents, orders or corre-

spondence relating to expulsion of Saints 281
Lents, Donald V., ap.................... 617
Let Zion in Her Beauty Rise sung as Texas colony embarked............. 378
Letter of Instruction left by Joseph Smith III........................ 576
Leverton, Arthur, miss. in Canada..541
Levitt, Guy P. served as pres. of sev. 622
Lewis, George, ordained a bishop....569
Lewis, George G., becomes an apostle, 534, 617; returns to Australia, 534; dies........................... 617
Lewis, Joshua, facts concerning conference at home of, 119, 120; a Missouri convert, 120; location of home, 120; sent as representative of Saints to Judge Ryland........... 178
Lewis, Phillip, finances South Sea Island mission........................ 321
Leyland Lane branch organized by first Eng. miss........................ 255
Leyland Moss, branch organized by first Eng. miss........................ 255
Liberty, Missouri, meeting called by Jackson Co., men, 210; leaders of church remanded to jail in, 282; prisoners taken to Gallatin from, 284; Emma Smith visits husband in 288
Liberty Jail, leaders of church remanded to, 282; Emma and Young Joseph visit Joseph Smith in, 288; Joseph S. suffers from face ache in, 282; Rigdon released from, 283; Joseph prophesies desolation of Jackson Co. while confined in, 283, 284; prisoners taken to Galatin 284
Lincoln, Abraham, voted for Nauvoo charter........................... 291
Lincoln, Seth, and wife, passengers on Timeoleon, 322; baptized in Tahiti, 326; Lincoln ordained and put in charge of Tahiti Branch....327
Linville, Thomas, killed in battle at Whitmer settlement................ 179
Litz, W. A., miss., to the southeast 500
Livingston Co., Missouri, Saints settle in, 266; militia involved in Haun's Mill Massacre................. 277
Livingston, Henry L., couns. to pr. bp................................. 619
London Missionary Society, opposes miss. work in Islands................. 327
Lone Jack, Missouri, Ziba Peterson teaches school in..................... 134
Long, Elmer E., served as pres. of sev. 622
Longton, Staffordshire, branch organized by first Eng. miss........... 255
Looking Backward, Bellamy's theories in, borrowed from L. D. S....153
Lord's Supper, first observed in the church................................ 599
Loving, Albert, a miss. from Australia 534
Lowe, H., receives testimony of Brigg's revelation, 393; spiritual experiences 393, 394
Lucas Robert, Gov. of Iowa and also of Ohio, tribute to Saints............ 242

Lucas, Samuel D., Gov. Dunklin orders to return Saints' arms, 200; orders Doniphan to execute church leaders, 280; countermands order when defied by Doniphan, 280; put in command when Atchison leaves militia on receipt of extermination order....................... 276
Luff, Joseph, served as ap., 568, 615; conversion, 542-545; made church physician 574
Luther, Mr. and Mrs. C. H., L. D. S. passengers to Hawaii............. 562
Luther, Martin, considered himself a forerunner........................... 25
Lyall, Joshua, baptized by Derry....475
Lydney, Gloucester, Briggs organizes branch at......................... 477
Lyman, Amasa, sent out to collect money for Temple..................... 399
Lyne, Thomas A., played in first American cast of Richelieu, 303; played Richard III to get a hall to preach in, 303; meeting Young Joseph, 341; accompanies prophet part of the way to Carthage.......... 341
Lyons, Lucy, later Lucy Resseguie..499
Lytle, Hugh, leads secession from Thompson, 388; miss. to Texas, 494; wife dies, 495; returns to Iowa 496

McBride, Thomas, killed at Haun's Mill 277
McClaran, Ray E., couns. to pr. bp. 620
McConley, Myron A., apostle; evangelist 616
McCord, Alexander, miss. to Utah, 481; baptizes three in Ogden, 482; arrives in Salt Lake City.............. 603
McCready, James, prominent revivalist 18
McDowell, Floyd M., couns. in pres. phd. educ. superv................613, 606
McDowell, James, renounces all factions 459
McDowell, Willis A., on H. C. Reorg. 627
McGee, Wm., leads revolt in Presbyterian church......................... 27
McGrath, Wm., sailor on Evanelia.565
McGuire, Benj. M., presiding bishop 618
McIlwains Bend, elders camp near..121
McIntosh, C. G., sent on mission to Utah, Nevada, and Cal., 481; arrives with wife in Utah.............. 485
McIntosh, John A., brought gospel to Lamberts........................... 492
McIntyre, J. R., secedes from Thompson faction..................... 388
McKiernan, James, served as pres. of sev., 622; served as senior pres. of sev............................ 620
McLellin, William, baptized by Hyrum Smith in Colesville settlement, 123; biography, 123; on H C. in Zion, 625; served as ap........614
McLennan, William, Joseph III read law under............................. 446
Mace, Wandle, child of, healed, 259; baptized 259, 260

INDEX

Mack, David, protests against return of Saints to Jackson Co..........455
Mack, Lucy (see Lucy Smith).
Mack, Solomon, letter of Lucy Smith to, quoted.................58
Mack, Stephen, brother of Lucy Smith, 114; his old partner befriends Lucy Smith, 114; his success in Michigan.................122
Mack, Temperance, widow of Stephen 122
Maid of Iowa, river steamboat owned by the church...........293, 294
Major, faithful mastiff companion of Joseph Smith, Jr., and his son, Joseph, 46; tries to follow Joseph Smith to Carthage, 340; transfers loyalty to Young Joseph........340, 341
Maloney, Stephen, baptized by Alex. McCord 483
Manchester, N. Y.; Hill Cumorah near, 37; one of the first three branches, 87; Pratt preaches in, 87; reaching around...............82
Mansion House, built to help entertain investigators, 310; home of widow of prophet, 354; Joseph moves into 603
Manti, Iowa, founded by Alpheus Cutler, 360; followers of Alpheus Cutler visited by Blair, 491; branch organized by Blair...........491
Mantua, Ohio, Rigdon pastor in........107
Manuscript, Book of Commandments, taken to Missouri..................152
Manuscript, Book of Mormon, first manuscript lost, 61; Alex. Doniphan identifies handwriting, 65; given to printer, 67; history of, 571; comes into possession of Reorg. Church 571, 605
Marks, William, vision of Joseph Smith concerning, 415; letters to J. M. Adams, 415, 417-421; agent for Bishop Whitney, 416; takes over church mortgage, 416; opposes Saints settling in a body, 416; chosen pres. of Nauvoo Stake, 416; dropped from his position by Brigham Young, 417; permits Rigdon to present his claims in Nauvoo, 357; favors Sidney Rigdon, 417; with Strang, 417; with C. B. Thompson, 417, 418, 419; on locating com. for Thompson, 418, 419; renounces Thompson, 419, 420; resolves to renounce all factions, 419; quotes Oliver Cowdery, 420; calls a conference, 422; attends Reorg. church near Edwin Cadwell's, 422; spoken to in prophecy, 422; received by Reorg. 423; receives letters from Young Joseph, 440; Chap. XLVIII; visits young Joseph, 441; assits in ordaining Joseph III, 452, 453; old home in Nauvoo meeting place for Saints, 457; sends men to bring John Taylor home from Carthage, 459; on Inspired Version com., 502; dies, 423, 506; serves as couns. to pres., 546, 612; member of H. C. in Kirtland, 625;

com. to publish hymnbook, 436; Joseph III, at bedside of, 423; superintendent of Sunday school at Nauvoo.................572
Marsh, Thomas B., sent on mission with Ezra Thayre, 115; on H. C. in Zion, 626; served as ap., 613; died at Ogden, Utah, 501, 602; mated with Selah J. Griffith as Thayre did not go, 116; pres. of q. of twelve........................613
Maudsley, ———, building house for first project of young folks.........303
May Roderick, bishop of Independence Stake.................570
Mayfield, Ohio, chosen location for The Family," 90; Rigdon and Cowdery preach and baptize at......102
Medina, Texas, Wight colony at, 381; letter to Sanford Porter describing 382
Melchisedec priesthood promised, 78; authorized, 80, 81; ex-officio members of conference, 571; office of 170
Membership, fifty members, 87; upward of a thousand, 167; of Church of Christ Temple Lot, 435; more than a thousand in Ohio, 99; church in New York several hundred, 99; Colesville church in Missouri, sixty, 119; of Nauvoo Legion, 303; baptized in Kirtland, 91; in England, 254, 255; in California in 1864.................483
Mendon, New York, baptisms at......164
Mentor, Ohio, Rigdon pastor of, 107; Rigdon visited at, by western miss. 89
Merchant, Hortensia, describes Nauvoo architecture.................294
Merchant, Lucius, on character of Joseph Smith.................44
Merrick, Charley, killed at Haun's Mill 278
Merthyr Tydfil, Wales, branch organized 479
Mesley, C. George, from Australia, 534; apostle; resigns.................617
Messenger, The, printed in New York, 364; press of, carried to California, 365; California Star printed upon press of.................369
Messenger, The, (Utah) published by Briggs.................602
Messenger and Advocate (see Latter Day Saints' Messenger and Advocate).................188
Messenger and Advocate, Rigdon's..358
Metuaore, visits United States, 527; ordained a bishop.................569
Miami Canal.................117
Michigan, first miss. to.................122
Miles, Daniel S., served as pres. of sev. 621
Militia, county, each county compelled by law to maintain, 145; Liberty (Missouri) Blues, 146; Blues guard Saints, 196; Carthage (Illinois) Greys, 146; Greys left alone to guard Carthage Jail, 343; Muster days, 145, 146; in Caldwell Co., 146; Nauvoo Legion, 147;

Jackson Co. demands arms of Saints, 179; orders Saints to leave, 180; Col. Pitcher of Jackson Co. militia ordered to return Saints' arms, 203; Saints advised to form Jackson Guards, 195, 196, 198-202; Diahman Boys, 273, 274; Far West militia under David Patten attack Bogart at Crooked River, 274; Livingston Co., militia involved at Haun's Mill Massacre, 277; Joseph Smith and Sidney Rigdon not members of, 280; Nauvoo Legion, 303; Legion gives up its arms 341; McDonough militia disbanded 343
Millennial Star first published, 256, 598; warns about Derry............472
Miller, C. Ed., on H. C. Reorg........628
Miller, Eleazer, baptizes Kimball and Young............164
Miller, George, defends Latter Day Saints, 288; meets Joseph Smith, the prophet, 289; ordained presiding bishop, 289; journal of, 355, 358; trustee in trust for church, 358; becomes bishop, 305; pres. of H. P. Quorum, 624; served as pr. bp., 618; sent up to pineries....374
Miller, H. W., sent out to collect money for Temple............399
Millet, Artemas, plastered outside of Temple............226
Millport, Mo., mob camped at............272
Mineral Point Tribune; members of Yellowstone Branch print statement in............400
Minister's Meetings, Reformed Baptists hold, 105; able to trace Rigdon's movement by minutes of........106
Mintun, James F., served as pres. of sev............622
Missions, not specific, 163; guided by inspiration............163
Missouri, Joseph Smith's impressions of, 119; life of Saints in 121, 154, 267
Missourians, Joseph Smith's impressions concerning............118
Mitchell, Dr., visited by Martin Harris 60
Moffet, Alfred, baptized at La Harpe, Ill., 339; father of Mary Moffet Thomas............399
Moffitt (Moffet), Levi, built Maid of Iowa 293, 294
Montebello Twp., Hancock Co., Ill., citizens adopt resolutions protesting against return of Saints 455
Morey, George, on H. C. in Zion and in Reorg............626
Morgan, George, interested............475
Morgan, Henry H., son of J. H. Morgan of Lydney, Eng., miss. to Cal., 483; reports to semiannual con. in Cal., 484; ordained a sev. 484
Morgan, John H., of Lydney, Gloucester, with Reorg. "heart and hand"............476
Morgan, Wm. and wife, of Oldbury, interested 475

Morin, Judge ——, of Milford, warns Saints of impending trouble 270
Morley, Isaac, one of communistic group, "The Family," in Kirtland, 90; sent on mission with Ezra Booth, 115; arrives in "Zion," 119; offers his life as a ransom for brethren............224
Mormon Battalion, the, met by Brannan 370
Morton, Wm. D., served as pres. of sev. 621
Mount Pleasant, near Brantford, Ont., first meetings in Canada, 189; first baptisms............1£9
Mountain Valley, Texas, settled by Wight colony............381
Muceus, Peter, work in Scandinavia..540
Mulholland, James, Joseph Smith's secretary has his papers............285
Murdock, John, with Hyrum Smith to travel to Zion by, 115; becomes ill, 122; his mission to Detroit and Pontiac, 122; one of first miss. to Michigan, 122; his twins adopted by Joseph and Emma Smith, 155; travels with Pratt, 161; ill with fever, 161; officiates in healing of Pratt, 161; to travel and collect money for a temple............399
Museum, in Seventy's Hall............303

Nachashlogian, magazine in defense of Negro slavery published by C. B. Thompson............389
Nauvoo, Chapter XXXI, 287-307; name changed from Commerce 290; immigrants arrive in, 294; architecture in, 294; health in, 295; publication interests of, 296-298; young people of, 302; Ladies Relief Society of, 303; largest city in Illinois, 303; description by Orville F. Berry, 304; by Jacob Scott, 305; 306; habeas corpus, writ of, as used in, 317; municipal court of, 335, 336; conditions in, June, 1844, 337-339; Joseph Smith bids good-by to, 340, 341; deserted, Chap. XXXVI, 344-354; after the martyrdom, 344, 345; described by Kane, 350-354; Emma Smith remains in, 354; miss. from Zarahemla visits young Joseph in, 427-430; Marks, Blair, and Rogers visit young Joseph in, 440, 441; young Joseph's childhood in, 442, 443; Joseph III baptized in, 444; Geo. Edmunds, Jr., asks Joseph III to remain in, 454; resolutions against Saints returning passed in, 455; a few Saints return to, 457; Joseph Smith III moves from, 458; people ask for Saints to establish headquarters in............548
Nauvoo, Battle of............346, 347
Nauvoo, Charter granted............291
Nauvoo Expositor, published, 335; referred to, 488; press destroyed by order of mayor, 335; not un-

INDEX

usual proceeding, 335; writ for destroying renewed..................337
Nauvoo House, to be built for entertainment of visitors to Nauvoo, 310; building, 305; Joseph speaks to people from platform on corner, 340; timber for..................374
Nauvoo Legion, 147, 303; gives up arms..................342
Nauvoo Neighbor, referred to..........487
Nauvoo Temple, work upon, 306; Alpeus Cutler master stonemason, 306; Elijah Fordham carves oxen for baptismal font, 306, 307; Jacob Scott on, 307; description, 307; cost of, 307; O'Donnell on, 307; burned, 307, 457; timber for, 374; ruins become a quarry, 457; converted into a workshop, 345; desecration of..................352
"Navajos," Oliver Cowdery writes of..................97
Neff, C. D., ap., pres. of 12..........593, 617, 613
Negroes, riot against in Phila., 173; Joseph Smith wept over riot against, 47; slavery in Missouri, Chap. XIV, 138-144; Doniphan gives slavery as main cause of Missouri trouble, 137; Gov. Reynolds writes, Balm of Gilead, in defense of Negro slavery, 144; Free People of Color editorial in Evening and Morning Star..................174
Nelson, Abraham, of Canada involved in Gallatin riot..................271
Nelson, Dr. David, fugitive from Missouri, 287; author of Cause and Cure of Infidelity, 309; debates with Josiah Ells, 309; and John Cairns..................459
Nelson, Hyrum, of Canada involved in Gallatin riot..................271
Nelson, William, miss. to South Sea Islands..................527
Nephi branch in Walworth Co. visited by Reorg. miss..................395
"New Hope," settlement of Brooklyn colonists in Cal., 368, 369; dispersed..................373
New Translation, see Inspired Version.
New York City, miss. to England delayed in, 246; mission to, Chap. XXIX, 257-260; Samuel Brannan resolves to go to Cal. from 363; 364; Brooklyn sails from, 365; branch of six organized in..................257
Nesser, Sr. Hartman, helps Swiss miss. 513
Newkirk, Cyrus, one of the comm. to select first Reorg. q. of twelve....413
Newkirk, David, served as ap., 615; renounces all factions..................401
Newkirk, Reuben W., renounces all factions, 401; served as ap., 614; released as ap., 546; covenants with Gurley to renounce all prophets, etc., 402; speaks in tongues, 403; chosen and ordained an ap...413
Newspapers, reputation of 332, 333; method of suppression, 335; instances of violence to presses of, or editors..................335

Nickerson, Freeman, unites with church..................189
Nickerson, Freeman, Jr, ordained elder..................189
Nickerson, Moses, letter in Evening and Morning Star concerning work in Canada, 191; attends dedication of Temple, 231; pays Pratt's way to Canada..................231
Nieman, Frederick, sailor on the Evanelia..................565
Nine Eagles, post office, later Pleasanton, Iowa..................550
Njeim, George A., pres. of sev..........623
Noland. Wood, makes incendiary speech at Liberty, against Saints..210
North America, first immigrants arrive in..................292
Northern Islander, the, published by Strang, contains letter of Lyman Wight on succession..................288
Norton, Henry O, swears out warrant against Smith for treason....342
Now Let Us Rejoice in the Day of Salvation, sung at Temple dedication..................229

Oakman, Arthur A., served as ap...617
O'Banion, Patrick, killed at Crooked River..................275
Ohio-Erie Canal..................117
Ohio, Canal System..................116, 117
O'Kelley, James, secedes from Methodist Church, war against creeds..27
Olson, Carroll L., on H. C. Reorg...629
Order of Enoch, Chap. LXIV, 546-556; bought land in Iowa, 549; organization of approved by conference; incorporated in Independence..................605
Order No. 11, devastation of, foretold by Joseph Smith, 283, 284; in Jackson Co..................557, 558
Ormsby, ——, built first house at Far West..................264
Outhouse, John and J. M., seceded from Thompson..................388
Owen Alma, Crow Creek branch......431
Owen. Jedediah, with Crow Creek Branch, 431; in Battle of Crooked River, 431; biographical, 431; went with Blair to conference at Zarahemla, 432; ordained H. P., 434; assists in ordaining Hedrick "Presiding High Priest of the Crow Creek Branch," 435; ordained an ap., 434; assists in ordaining Hedrick pres. of the church..................435
Owen, William O., debates with Derry and Briggs in Eng., 477; converted, presides over branch 479, 480
Owens, Samuel C., prominent opponent of L. D. S. in Jackson Co., offers to buy lands, 210; chief speaker against Saints in Liberty meeting, 210; lost life at Chilhauhau, 211; believed Mormons responsible for sinking of ferry boat..................210, 211
Oxen, for baptismal font, carved by Elijah Fordham..................306

Pack, John, pledged himself to see Derry family did not suffer............471
Pacific Islands mission (see South Sea Islands).
Packard, Noah, on H. C. at Kirtland 625
Paden, Jacob, seceded from Thompson 388
Page, Edward, on Joseph Smith..44, 49
Page, John E., converts John Landers, 235, 237; sees plates of Book of Mormon in vision, 237; quotation from Spirit of Times, regarding, 308; determined to stand apart from all factions, 419, 420; dissatisfied with Hedrick affiliation, 434; asks that John Landers preach funeral sermon, 434; served as ap.....614
Page, Hiram, finds a stone, 88; husband of Catherine Whitmer, 88; one of eight witnesses............ 72
Paia visits U. S. A............527
Palmyra, New York, revivals near, 31; description of, 42; Harris family pioneers of, 50; Book of Mormon published at, 67; Parley P Pratt visits, 86, 87; preaching at, 82; Ezra Thayre, a bridge builder in............ 83
Panic of 1837, Chap. XXVII......239-244
Pardoe, John, friend of Derry in England, 474; baptized by Derry..475
Park, George S., founder of Park College 143
Parker, Robert J., speaks to Luff in prophecy............544
Parks, Gen., reports to Atchison on De Witt situation, 272; advises Wight to act in own defense, 273; King writes............276
Parrish, Warren, baptized by Brigham Young............186
Parsons, Joseph, renounces all factions 459
Partridge, Edward, chosen bishop, 100, 600; conversion, 100; biographical, 100; buys Temple tract, 152; buys much land in Jackson Co., 152; tarred and feathered by mob, 175; offered himself a ransom for brethren, 224; death of, 305; George Miller, succeeds; served as pr. bp., 618; visited Joseph Smith in New York, 100; returned to Kirtland, 112; Smith family entertained by, 115; appointed on miss. with Martin Harris, 115; signs letter to Gov. Dunklin, 199; opposes Saints settling in a body 416
Patriarch, Joseph Smith, Sr., ordained, 191; those who have served as presiding............620
Patten, Archibald, baptized............186
Patten, David Wyman, his great faith and gift of healing, 158; hears of gospel, 158, 159; investigation and baptism, 159; his work in Michigan, 159; goes to Kirtland to see prophet, 160; ministry in New York, 186-188; healing of Lois Cutler, 186, 187; baptism of Alpheus Cutler and family, 187; baptizes James Blakeslee, 188; chosen on q. of twelve, 217; mission to Tennessee, 230; ordained an ap., 218, 613; in command of Far West militia, called "Captain Fear-not," 274; killed at Crooked River, 275; sent to Zion with succor, 190; mob rejoices over death............187
Patten, Ira, baptized, 186; with Wm. Smith............425
Patten, John, brother of David, writes of Book of Mormon, 159; baptizes David Patten............159
Patterson, John S., serves at pres. of sev............621
Patterson, Col. Robert, entertained miss. 95, 96
Patterson, Robert, a printer in Pittsburgh, connected by Howe with Spaulding theory............108, 110
Patterson, William, miss. from Australia 534
Pawpaw, East, Ill, Conference held by Wm. Marks............422
Peak, Warren E., served as pres. of sev............622
Pease, Henry, prominent in early Reorg............492
Peniston, Col. Wm. P., candidate for sheriff, afraid of "Mormon" vote, 270; harangues election day crowd 270
Pennydaren, Wales, conferences at..478
Penwortham, branch organized by first Eng. miss............255
Persecution of the Saints in Jackson Co., Missouri, 271-286; in Nauvoo, Caldwell, Daviess, and Livingston Co., Missouri, 271-286; in Nauvoo, Hancock Co., Ill., 339-343; in South Sea Islands, 525; in Utah............485
Peter, James, and John, promise Melchisedec priesthood, 78; confer M. P............ 81
Peters, James H., on H. C. Reorg...627
Peterson, Ziba, one of first miss. to West, 88; with Oliver Cowdery preaches in Lafayette Co., Missouri, 96; opened school in Lone Jack 134
Petition by people of Jackson Co., asking Saints to leave, 175; petition of people of Clay Co., 262, 263; petition by people of Nauvoo, Ill. 547
Phelps, Morris, baptized on first mission to Michigan............122
Phelps, William Wine, baptized and ordained, 116; appointed a miss. with Joseph Coe, 116; preaches in Zion, 119; buys press and type for Evening and Morning Star, 151; dwelling house destroyed by mob, 175; present at dedication of Zion and site for Temple, 119; lays Jackson Co. trouble before Gov. Dunklin, 177; signs letter to Gov. Dunklin, 199; bears record to truth of Doctrine and Covenants, 220; explores what became Caldwell Co., 264; north half city of Far West entered in his name, 264; offers his life as a ransom for brethren..224

INDEX

Phillips, J. T., miss. to Wales, arrives 479
Phillips, Arthur B., on H. C. Reorg., served as pres. of sev............629, 619
Philips, Judge John F., decision in Temple Lot Suit............487
Pickering, William R., on H. C. Reorg............628
Pilgrim, George, early settler at Independence 558
Pineries of Wisconsin, saw mills bought by church at Black River Falls, Wis............374
Pioneer settlement of Phelps and Gorhams purchase, history of by O. Turner, quoted on early story of finding of plates............56, 57
Pitcher, Col Thomas, head of Jackson Co., militia, case of State of Mo., vs., 196; Saints petition for return of arms, 199; governor orders to return arms............199, 202, 203
Pitkin, George, took elders from Hiram to Steubenville in his wagon 156
Pitt, Frederick G., on H. C. Reorg., 627; pastor at Independence, 561; pres. of H. P. Q............624
Pittsburgh, Pa., Rigdon, pastor in, 106; Saints begin independent meetings, 459; visited by W. W. Blair 460
Plano, Ill., headquarters of the church, Chap. LVII, 499; conferences at, 502; church in, 505; last Herald issued from............552
Plano Mirror, on removal of Saints from Plano............547
Plasket Captain of Timeoleon, charged $400 fare for miss., 321; allowed no sermons or prayer on board 322
Plates of Book of Mormon, vision of Joseph Smith concerning, 36; Joseph sees for first time, 37, 38; annual visits to, 38; obtains, 40; David Whitmer's story of, 52, 53; description of, 55, 56; Harris' story, 57; Lucy Smith tells of, in letter to Solomon Mack, 58; William Smith on, 58; testimony of witnesses, 69; three witnesses see, 70, 71; Oliver Cowdery's testimony, 72; Martin Harris' testimony, 73; Chicago Times on Whitmer's testimony, 74; Emma Smith warns Joseph of, 59; Martin Harris assists, 60; taken away, 61; Oliver Cowdery comes to act as scribe, 62; "packed up" and taken to Fayette, 63; Mrs. Whitmer sees, 64; manner of translation, 64; assistant scribes.. 65
Polygamy, Chap. LV, 486; synonymous with L. D. S. in 1860, 486; "stands to take" revealed to Young Joseph, 486, 487; Reorg. view concerning, 486, 487; Young Joseph convinced of father's innocence, 488; Book of Mormon condemns, 488; Joseph Smith III's attitude toward, 487-490; not taught by Grouard, 331; condemned by Strang at first, 359; not in creed of Brooklyn colony, 369; Thompson takes decided stand against, 389; Oliver Cowdery first hears of, 356; Hon. O. F. Berry on, 349; Briggs renounces Strang and Wm. Smith because of, 391, 392; Wm. Smith denies part in, 392; Yellowstone Branch renounces Strang because of, 401; "not of God," 408; John F. Philips on, 602; Joseph Smith's prophecy concerning statehood in Utah, 601; Granville Hedrick publishes tract against, 432; Crow Creek branch opposes 434
Pomeroy, Helen, speaks in tongues to Wm. Marks............422
Pontiac, Michigan, first mission to, 122; Jared Carter sent as miss., 123, 166; cradle of church in Michigan 123
Porter, Sanford, letter of Lyman Wight to............382, 383
Pope, Judge Nathaniel, releases Joseph Smith on habeas corpus at Springfield 318
Powell, David, receives testimony of Jason Briggs revelation, 393; spiritual experiences, 394; brings Briggs revelation to Yellowstone, 403; takes mission south............407
Powers, Samuel, early history of, 424; joins Reorg., 424; serves as ap., 615; sent to Eng. on mission, 469; unable to fill miss., 475; death 506
Pratt, Addison, set apart for island mission, and ordained a seventy, 321, 600; sails from New Bedford, Conn., 322; remains at Tubuai, 326; baptizes first converts, 327; his life in Tubuai, 327, 328; left in charge of mission, 329; sailed from Papeete, 330; natives remember ministry, 524; return on second mission, 331; forced to leave by French 331
Pratt, Orson, becomes miss. 99; arrives in Zion, 123; sent on miss. with brother Parley, 115; served on q. of twelve, 614; on H. C. in Zion, 625; on miss. to Eng............256
Pratt, Parley P., early history, 84; interested in "Reformed" Baptist movement, 84; reforms as miss. to New York, 84, 85; hears of Book of Mormon, 86; visits Palmyra, 86, 87; reads Book of Mormon, 87; walks to Fayette, 87; baptized by Oliver Cowdery, 87; preaches in Smith home in Manchester, 87; one of miss. to Lamanites, 88; presents Book of Mormon to Sidney Rigdon, 89; visits Lyman Wight at Mayfield, 90; his journey to Independence, 95; selected to return, 96; return trip, 97, 98; goes on miss. with brother Orson, 115; arrive in Zion, 123; falls victim to fever and ague, 124; returns to Kirtland, 161, 162; returns with wife and settles in Independence,

166; delivers Fourth of July address on steamboat, 166; appeals to Judge Ryland, 178; one of first quorum of apostles, 217; ordained, 218; prophecy to, 231; introduces gospel in Toronto, 232-235; leaves on mission to England, 256; writes Voice of Warning, 257; his work in New York City, 257-260; serves as ap. 614

Pratt, Thankful, meets husband in Kirtland after absence of eighteen months, 162; has tuberculosis, 161; goes to Zion with husband, 166; prophecy concerning, 231; dies 257

Pratt, Wm. sent with help to Zion .. 190

Preparation, Monona Co., Iowa, history of community 387

Preparation News and Ephraim's Messenger, card of Hugh Lytle and followers published in 388

President of High Priesthood, Joseph, Jr., ordained at Amherst, 155; conference in Missouri ratifies ordination, 157; Joseph Smith III ordained at Amboy, 452, 453; Frederick M. Smith ordained 579, 605

Presidents of H. P. Q. 623

Presidents of seventy, selected and ordained, 453; perpetuation of, 568; those who have served, 617, 620; reorganized, 605; senior presidents 620

President of U. S. A., Joseph Smith a candidate 332

Presiding Bishops, those who have served 618

Presiding Patriarchs, those who have served 620

Preston, Lancashire, England, first miss. go to, 249; first sermon in, 250; first baptisms in, 250; first confirmation in, 250; meetings held in Cock Pit, 253; conference at, 254; membership in, 255; branch organized in 255

Price, Jesse, on H. C. Reorg 627

Presthood, Aaronic, conferred 78-81

Priesthood, Melchisedec conferred 78-81

Printing press, to be purchased and sent to Independence, 151, 598; set up in Independence, 156; thrown in river with type, 175; 600; of George S. Park's Eastern Luminary destroyed, 143; later history of Independence press, 175; determine to purchase new press, 188; arrives in Kirtland, 190; set up and working, 190; buried at evacuation of Far West, 285; dug up and cleaned, 296; of the Expositor destroyed, 342; of Messenger taken to Cal., 365; California Star published upon, 369; new Taylor Cyinder Power Press for Herald, 506; Marks contracts for Thompson, 419; proposal to buy 469

Prohibitionist, Joseph Smith called the first 154

Prophecy, gift of, belief in, 170; concerning devastation of Jackson Co., 283, 284; concerning Civil War, 163; concerning Utah statehood, 601; concerning Wm. Marks, 415; to Wm. Marks concerning Young Joseph, 423; to Parley P. Pratt, 231; concerning mission to New York City, 258; to John Hawkins, 326; Joseph Smith, concerning his own death, 341; concerning Young Joseph, 392; concerning a prophet to be raised up, 402; concerning successor of Joseph Smith, 403, 404; concerning coming of "the prophet," 440, 441; at blessing of Joseph Carlos Clapp, 517; 518; at confirmation of Heman C. Smith, 469; to Joseph Luff 544

Pulsipher, Zera, served as pres. of sev. 621

Putney, Jairus M., welcomed Bro. Derry, 464; pledged himself to see Derry family did not suffer 471

Puuohau, James, interpreter 564

Quincy, Josiah, on Joseph Smith 49

Quincy, Illinois, people of, receive Saints, 287; defend Dr. Nelson, 287; try to divert attackers of Nauvoo 346

Quincy Whig, Ebenezer Robinson, worked in 296

Quorum, meaning as used by L. D. S. 149

Ralston, Russell F., pres. of sev., Ap. 623, 617

Ralston, ———, accused of "coqueting with Mormons," 290; helped defend Joseph Smith in trial before Judge Douglas 290

Rarick, George, served as pres. of sev. 621

Rasey, Daniel, of Blue Mounds, Wis., join Reorg. 407; served as ap., 614; released from apostleship, 546; chosen and ordained an ap. 413

Rathbun, Hiram, Sr., wounded for life at Haun's Mill 279

Rathbun, Robert, his blacksmith shop in Independence attacked by mob, 175; built iron work for Michael Arthur's mill 215

Reals, Mr. and Mrs., testimony on succession of young Joseph 491

Redfield, Harlow, on H. C. Kirtland 625

Redfield, William, returned to Nauvoo 457

Redress, sought by Saints, appeal to Gov. Dunklin by Hyde and Phelps, 177; appeal to Circuit Judge Ryland, 178; appeal by Doniphan to Attorney-general Wells, 194; appeal to pres. of the United States, 197; appeal by elders in Liberty to Gov. Dunklin, 198, 199; appeal to Col. Thornton, to Gov. Dunklin, 200-203; petition to Missouri legislature, 204; memorialize Missouri legislature for reimbursement, 281;

INDEX

Saints send Delegation to Washington, 290; Lyman Wight presents petitions to Congress..........376
Reese, Amos, retained as attorney by L. D. S. 193
Renfroe, Zenos Z., Sr., Pres. of Seventy 620, 623
Reid, H. T., firm of Wood and Reid, of Burlington, attorney for Smiths, 342; insists Smith be examined before sent to jail, 342; 343; appeals to governor, 343; asks for postponement........................343
Regeneration, doctrine of..............16, 26
Religio Literary Society, Zion's 573, 604
Reorganize, meaning of word......405 ff.
Reorganized Church, Chap. XLIII, 405 ff.; first conference, 405; renounces all factions and declares successor to be Joseph Smith III, 405; Word of Consolation, 406, 408, 476, 477; who shall preside over, 409-412; q. of twelve chosen, 413; seventies chosen and ordained, 413; William Marks unites with, 423; 436; mission to young Joseph, 427-430; conference of June, 1859, at Amboy, 436; fall conference of 1859 in Israel Rogers grain barn, 436; James Blakeslee unites with, 437; Isaac Sheen unites with, 438; publishes the True L. D. S. Herald, 438; Joseph III signifies willingness to accept leadership of, 440; Amboy conference of 1860, 450-453; sends miss. to Eng., 469-480; sends miss. west, 481-485; fights polygamy, 486-490; publishes Inspired Version, 502, 503; teaches tithing, 503, 504; sends miss. to Switzerland, 507, 514; opens miss. in Calif., 516, 517; opens miss. in Oregon, 517, 520; island Saints hear of, 524-527; sends miss. to Australia, 529-534; sends miss. to Scandinavia, 535-540; begins gathering at Lamoni, Iowa, 547-550; moves publishing house to Lamoni, 552; returns to Independence, 557-561; organizes stakes, 570; obtains Book of Mormon mss., 571; builds Graceland College, 573; builds Sanitarium, 574; builds Children's Home, 574; builds homes for old people, 574; moves headquarters to Independence, 575; mourns death of Joseph Smith III, 576; Fred M. Smith becomes pres. of, 577; Auditorium begun, 580; growth of........505
Representation, rules of........................571
Resseguie, Lucy Lyons, assists in gospel boat move, 564; formerly Lucy Lyons..499
Resthaven 591, 607
Restorationalists, a sect believing in restoration of wicked, 29, 30; Edward Partridge an adherent, 100; revelation on glories pleases..........154
Restorer, The, miss. paper published in Eng..479
Resurrection, a belief and teaching of the church..................................169

Revelation, continued, a belief of the church..168
Revell, Thomas, returned to Nauvoo 457
Revival, The Great, Chap. II, 18-22; strange manifestations at, 18; at Cane Ridge, Kentucky, 19; described, 19, 20; results of..........25, 26
Reynolds, Gov. of Illinois, wrote pamphlets in defense of Negro slavery 144
Reynolds, William, boasts of killing child at Haun's Mill..................278
Ribble, River, first baptisms in Eng. performed in............................250
Ribchester, branch organized by first Eng. miss. 255
Rice, L. L., found Spaulding romance 110, 600
Rich, C. C., on H. C. at Nauvoo........626
Rich, Leonard, bore witness to truth of Doctrine and Covenants, 220; served as pres. of quorum of sev..621
Richards, Jeannetta, Elder Kimball meets and baptizes, 251; first confirmed in Eng., 251; father invites miss. to visit, 252; marries Willard Richards, 252; dies in Nauvoo, Illinois..253
Richards, Rev. John, of Walkerfold, invites miss. to occupy his pulpit, 251; daughter marries Willard Richards 252
Richards, Phineas, on H. C. at Kirtland 625
Richards, Willard, appointed on mission to Eng., 246; preaches in Eng., 250; goes to Bedford, 251; married Jeannetta Richards, 252; remains in Eng., 254; ordains John Shippy, 311; visiting Joseph and Hyrum Smith in Carthage Jail at time of assassination, 343; serves as an ap., 614; statement concerning succession, 355; couns. to Brigham Young, 355; present at blessing of young Joseph..445
Richardson, master of the Brooklyn 365, 366
Richmond, ——, one of first baptisms in Tahiti..........................326
Rigdon, Carvel, pat. of Rigdon's organization 358
Rigdon, Sidney, "a kind of reformed Baptist," 84; Pratt ambitious to convert, 89; presented with Book of Mormon, 89; baptized, 91; meets Joseph Smith, 100; his age, 100; "great orator," 101, 102, 106, 283; winning power of oratory attested by John Barr, 102; his later life, 103; biography, 104; meets Adamson Bentley and becomes brother-in-law, 104; marries Phoebe Brook, 104; with Bentley calls on Alex Campbell, 105; his "ministerial meeting," 105; accepts "call" to Pittsburgh, Pa., 106; takes notes at Campbell Walker debate, 106; labors as tanner, 107; pastor at Mantua, O., 107; pastor at Mentor, O., 107; Campbell and

Bentley become enemies, 107; "Spaulding" theory, 107, 108; Nancy Rigdon Ellis tells of father's first contact with Book of Mormon, 109; John W. Rigdon's testimony, 109; Rigdon's denial in Boston Journal, 110; testimony of Bronsons, 110; L. L. Rice's opinion, 111; Dr. Fairchild's opinion, 111; on a mission to Missouri with Joseph. 112; returns to Kirtland with Joseph, 121; goes to Missouri, 115, 117; land of Zion dedicated by, 119; temple site dedicated, 119, 120; works on revision of Scriptures, 148, 149; moves family to Hiram, O., 149; 155; baptizes Lyman E. Johnson, 149; tarred and feathered, 155; ill and delirious, 155; goes with party to Missouri, 156; returns to Kirtland, 158; couns. to Joseph, 165; goes on mission to Canada, 189; ordains alternates for H. C., 205; on com. to arrange Doctrine and Covenants, 220; takes part in General Assembly, 220; signs report of com. on Doctrine and Covenants, 221, 222; on com. to draft plans for Temple, 224; in charge of work on Temple, 225; wept and prayed on Temple wall, 225; gave dedicatory prayer at Kirtland Temple, 229; gave advice to Jackson Co. Saints, 265; not a member of Missouri militia, 280; ill in prison, 282; obtains release from Liberty jail, 283; comes to Nauvoo to present claims, 357; leader of a faction, 358; publishes Messenger and Advocate, 358; William Bickerton, a convert, 359; couns. to pres....................612
Riley, James T., served as pres. of sev. 622
Robinson, Ebenezer, editor of Times and Seasons, 305; in charge of printing interests, 296; experiences, 296; cleans press and type and prints Times and Seasons, 296; 297; experience with third edition of Book of Mormon, 298-302; looks after stereotyping of Inspired Version, 502, 503; couns. to Sidney Rigdon, 358; present at blessing of young Joseph................445
Robinson, George W., postmaster at Nauvoo 290
Robinson, John A., on H. C. Reorg...627
Robinson, Joseph L., assists in publication of third ed. of Book of Mormon..301
Robinson, Kenneth, ap. 618
Rockwell, Orrin Porter, accused of shooting of Gov. Boggs, 317; defended by Alex W. Doniphan, 319; no evidence to connect him with crime 319
Roberts, Brigham H., quotes minutes of H. C. in case of David Whitmer 269
Rodger, Glaud, sails from San Francisco for Australasia, 523; forced to go ashore at Tahiti, 524; finds Saints of Tiona, 524; farewell to island Saints, 526, 527; sails from Tahiti, 527; lands at Sydney, 529; miss. work in Australia, 530-534; dies in mission field, in Nevada, 554; ordained seventy, 484; served as pres. of sev...............................621
Rogers, ——, murdered Thomas McBride at Haun's Mill..............277, 278
Rogers, David, fitted up room for Saints to meet in New York City..258
Rogers, Israel, early life, 436; couns. to William Smith, 436, 437; unites with Reorg., 437; conference held in his grain barn, 437; fed and entertained entire conference, 437; visits young Joseph, 440, 441; first bishop of Reorg., 471; finances Derry for Eng. miss., 471; pays tithing 504
Rogers, Noah, set apart for mission to islands, 321; sailed from New Bedford, 422; offered prayer at Hanks burial at sea, 323; landed in Tahiti, 326; visits Huahine, 327; visits Moorea, Huahine, Bora-bora, Raiatea, Tahaa, Mote, and Mangua, 329; leaves islands, 329; first L. D. S. miss. to circumnavigate the globe, 329; his first grave of Mormons, at Mt. Pisgah...................329
Roosevelt, Judge, befriends Joseph III 455
Rushfelt, Gerald L., S. H. C. 630
Rushton, John W., England, contributes to church, 480; chosen and serves as ap., 568, 616; preaches in Ireland 480
Russell, Isaac, Pratt meets in Toronto, 234; one of first miss. to Eng., 247; went to Alston in Cumberland, 251; reports baptism of 30 in Cumberland, 254; left for America, 255; organized branch in Cumberland, 255; converts Jacob Scott, the Laws, Sampson Avard, James Mulholland, Scotts, in Churchville, Ont.............................285
Russell, Robert C., served as ap.....616
Ryland, John F., circuit judge at Lexington, Saints appeal to, 178; asked to investigate, 194; attempts to compromise.................................210

Sabbath observance not customary, 15; directions for keeping............121
Saco, Maine, work of John F. Boynton in 192
Saints Herald, The True Latter Day Saints' Herald, first issued from Cincinnati, 438; moved to Plano, Ill., 439; to Lamoni, 439; to Independence, 439; Duty Griffith receives, 460; Charles Derry reads, 461; Charles Derry pawns his coat to get copies of, 475; reviews farming conditions around Zion, 552; editorial on leaving Plano, Ill., 552; first published as a monthly, 602; Joseph Smith chosen editor, 603; first number from Lamoni, 604; first issue from Independence, 605; falls into the hands of John

INDEX 655

L. Bear, 509; copies of, loaned to John Leeka............466
Saints' home, opened in Lamoni............605
Salisbury, Jenkins, walks from Fairfield to Kirtland............115
Salt Lake City, Utah, Briggs and McCord arrive, 481; first branch of Reorg. in............484
Salyards, Christiana............237
Salyards, Richard Savery............459
San Francisco, branch organized............483
Sangamon Journal, rabid against L. D. S.............345
Sanitarium and Hospital, grant to by U. S. Gov't............581, 606
Savage, Jehiel, preaches at LaHarpe, 398; appointed to travel and collect money for Temple, 399; converts Samuel Powers and wife, 424; baptized Margaret Gurley....398
Savery, Richard, renounces all factions............459
Scandinavia, mission to, Chap. LXII............535-540
Schaefer, Roy H., H. P. Q. Pres. pro tem; ap............624, 618
Schools, first in Jackson Co., 118, 134; of the elders conducted by Pratt, 167; large schoolhouse built in Far West, 265; numerous in Caldwell Co., 266; public schools of Nauvoo, 315 (see Education).
Scott, Anne, custodian of the Inspired Version............286
Scott, Jacob, describes Nauvoo, 305, 306; speaks of Nauvoo Temple, 307; app. on a mission with Edson Fuller, 115; "drops out"............115
Scott, Columbus, served as sev., 622; served as senior pres. of sev.............620
Scott, Walter, "reformed Baptist," meets Sidney Rigdon, 105; first to teach "baptism for remission of sins" in the Western Reserve, 29; bitterly repulses Sidney Rigdon....117
Sedgewick, Iowa, later called Lamoni............549
Sekine, Kisuke, ap.............618
Seneca River, Joseph baptizes Partridge in............100
Serig, Joe A., ap.............618
Seventy, presidents of, Joseph Young and Sylvester Smith, ordained, 218; Leonard Rich speaks for, 220; acknowledge truth of Doctrine and Covenants, 220; senior pres. of, at conference of 1853, 411; work stabilized by revelation, 568; those who have served...620-623
Seventy, "Special Witnesses," 168; selected from Zion's Camp, 218; moved to Kirtland in a body, 303; seventies hall in Nauvoo, 303; their museum, 303; difficulty between high priests and, 411; Joseph Smith defines duties and pays tribute to, 505; work of presidency of, stabilized............568
Sharp, Thomas C., on Nauvoo trouble, 349; wanted nothing to do with protest against young Joseph, 455; comments on young Joseph............548
Sheehy, Francis M., served as ap., 616; served as pres. of sev.............622
Sheehy, Howard S., Jr., Ap., pres.....618
Sheehy, John F., pres of H. P. Q...624

Sheen, Isaac, makes inquiry, 436; ordained pres. of H. P. Q., 624; united with Reorg. 438; editor of Herald, 438; moves to receive Joseph III............452
Shepard, Jonathan, tarred Bishop Partridge............176
Sherman, Lois, see Lois Cutler.
Sherman, Lyman, on H. C. at Kirtland, 625; served as pres. of sev...621
Sherman, Thomas M., S.H.C............630
Shippy, Benjamin, baptized by John Shippy............311
Shippy, John, conversion and ordination, 310, 311; and family visit in Nauvoo, 470; baptizes John H. Lake, 460, 461; serves as an ap....615
Shoal Creek, Jacob Haun builds a mill on, 277; Saints settle upon......264
Shoemaker, George K., S.H.C............629
Siegfried, Mark H., couns. to pre. bp., 619; on H. C. Reorg............628
Simmons, Wayne E., Pres. Sev............623
Simpson, George, leader of Independence mob............176
Sing Sing, New York, branch organized in............260
Skinner, Clarence A., couns. to pr. bp.............619
Slavery, one of causes of Missouri difficulties, 137; Doniphan cites it as chief cause of difficulty, 137; in Missouri, Chap. XIV, 138; Gov. Reynolds writes book in defense of, 144; Thompson publishes magazine in defense of............389
Smith, Aaron, baptized............424
Smith, Agnes, a fugitive, 273; mother of Iva Donna Coolbrith............273
Smith, Alexander Hale, mother carries across frozen river, 287; son of Joseph, 254; joins Reorg. church, 458; appointed in charge of mission to Calif., 516; starts for Calif., 516; chosen as ap., 546; couns. to pres., 568; visits Salt Lake City with Brother David, 603; served as couns. to pres., 612; serves q. of twelve, 615; moves to Independence, 561; moves to Andover, Mo., 549; preaches to old Brooklyn colony, 373; pres. q. of twelve, 613; pres. patr.............620
Smith, Alvin, brother of Joseph, 38; starts building new home, 39; death of............39
Smith, Amanda, survivor of Haun's Mill massacre, quoted, 278; describes her escape to Illinois............285
Smith, Asahel, on H. C. at Kirtland, 625; H. C. in Iowa............625
Smith, Mrs. B. C., on Children's Home committee............573
Smith, David H., born after father's death, 354; unites with Reorg. church, 458; writer of songs and hymns, 470; an invalid, 549; couns. to President Joseph Smith............612
Smith, Don Carlos, absent on mission, 273; a printer, 296; published Times and Seasons with Ebenezer Robinson, 297; died in 1841, 301, 302, 305; pres. of H. P. Q.............623
Smith, Don, Carlos, son of Israel A. Smith, war record............588

Smith, Elbert A., couns. in pres., 613; presiding patriarch, 620; released 620
Smith, Elias, in Vermont rejects creeds 27
Smith, Emma (nee Hale), later Bidamon; Joseph Smith marries, 40; loses first-born child, 61; assists Joseph as scribe, 61, 65; warns Joseph of danger to plates, 59; goes with Joseph to obtain plates, 41; finds home with Johnsons in Hiram, O., 149, 155; carries Inspired Version mss. in flight from Missouri, 286; visits husband in Liberty jail, 288; states why husband left Nauvoo, 338; remains in Nauvoo, 354; goes to Amboy with son, 450; received into Reorg. church on original baptism, 452; turns over mss. of New Translation to Reorg. 502; advises John Leeka not to go west........................466
Smith, Frederick A., apostle, 616; presiding patriarch; released; died 620
Smith, Frederick Granger, Joseph Jr., speaks of, in journal, 45; carried by mother across frozen Mississippi, 287; dies professing belief 458
Smith, Frederick M., Chap. LXVIII; chosen as father's successor, 576; ordained president, 577, 579; baptism, ordinations, marriage, 578; doctor's degree, 579; missionary survey of Europe, 579; death, 582; named successor, 586; Pres. of C..612
Smith, George A., served as ap., 614; leaves on mission to Eng., 256; visited young Joseph........................427
Smith, Heman C., birth, 380; prophecy to, 469; baptism, 469; chosen an ap., 568; served as ap..................615
Smith, Humphrey, an abolitionist....142
Smith, Hyrum, assists father on farm near Palmyra, 38; one of eight witnesses, 69; Parley P. Pratt meets, 87; walks with Pratt to Fayette, 87; appointed a miss. with John Murdock, 115; miss. to Detroit and Pontiac, 122; baptizes William McLellin, 123; brings re-inforcements to Zion's Camp, 209; one of committee to oversee building Temple, 224; on com. to draft rules for house of the Lord, 226; discourages plan to publish third ed. Book of Mormon, 299; Peter Haws lived across street, 340; Joseph prophesies their death, 340, 341; charged with riot, 341; death, 343; Hon. O. F. Berry on his responsibility for polygamy, 349; Judge Edmunds never saw, 348; becomes pr. pat., 305; couns. to pres., 606; on H. C. in Kirtland, 624; served as pr. pat., 620; takes refuge in Iowa, 336; anointed young Joseph as successor, 444; special couns. in pres................612, 621

Smith, Hyrum, O., served as pres. of sev., 622; birthplace of................386
Smith, Israel A., Chap. LXIX; named as successor by Frederick M. Smith, 586; elected as president, 586, 612; birth, 586; marriage, member of Iowa Assembly, 588; death of son, 589; ordinations, 590; society memberships, 590; brings harmony in councils, 591; visits Hawaii, etc., 592; to Mexico, 593; five revelations, 594; death 594
Smith, John, on H. C. in Kirtland, 206, .624; bears record of truth of Doctrine and Covenants, 220; special couns. in presidency...................624
Smith, John, Pres. Lamoni Stake....570
Smith, Joseph, Jr., attends revival, 32; partial to Methodist sect, 33; first vision, 33, 34, 599; family of, 34, 37; second vision, 36; sees plates, 37; works on father's farm, 38; his employers, 39; married Emma Hale, 40; obtains plates, 40; family history, 42; his character, Chap. V, 42-49; as a leader, 44; Lucius Merchant speaks of his kindness, 44; and his morality, 39; his unselfishness, 45; love for children, 45; love of animals, 45, 46; temperance, 46; eager student, 47, 48, 315; tolerant, 47; industrious, 48; Josiah Quincy on, 49; Martin Harris befriends, 51; meets D. Whitmer, 52, 53; meets O. Cowdery, 52; describes plates, 55; William Smith on plates, 58; moves to Kirtland, O., 112, 600; Harris acts as scribe, 59, 60; Emma's illness, 61; Oliver Cowdery comes to Harmony, 62, 599; moves to plates to Fayette, N. Y., 63; saw David Whitmer in vision, 64; Whitmer and Cowdery see plates, Harris sees plates, shows plates to eight witnesses, 69-71; declares a restoration of gospel, 76; Aaronic priesthood conferred upon, 77, 78; baptism of, 77, 599; Melchisedec priesthood conferred, 81; organizes church, 81, 82, 599; preaches near Auburn, N. Y., 83; preaches in his father's house in Manchester, 87; baptizes Partridge, 100; goes on miss. to Missouri with Rigdon, 115; W. W. Phelps visits, 116; takes Miami Canal to Cincinnati, 116, 117; visits Walter Scott, 117; takes steamboat for St. Louis, 117; impressions of Missourians, 118; camped at spring in Kansas City, 118, arrived in Independence, 118; present at dedication of Zion and Temple site, 119; laid a stone at northeast corner of contemplated temple, 120; attends funeral of Polly Knight, 120; attends conference at Joshua Lewis', 120; not a member of Caldwell Co., militia, 146; joined Nauvoo Legion, 147; returns to Kirtland, 148; works on revision of Scriptures, 150, 151;

INDEX

moves to Johnson home in Hiram, 149; heals Mrs. Johnson's arm, 150; corrects and prepares material for Book of Commandments, 151; points out spot for Temple, 120, 152: "the first prohibitionist," 154; receives revelation on glories, 154; tarred and feathered, 155; goes to Independence, 156, 157; ordained pres. of high priesthood at Amherst, 157, 600; his ordination ratified in Missouri, 157, 600; on the "United Order," 157; visited Colesville branch, 157; leaves for Kirtland, 157; delayed by accident to Bishop Whitney, 158; makes short trip to New York, 163; birth of son Joseph, 163; 600; prophesies Civil War, 163; visited by Young and Kimball, 164; sends plat of Zion, 174; visits Canada, 189; organizes H. C., 206; in Zion's Camp, 208; stands for last time "in goodly land," 215; tells of endowment, 217; mentions seventies, 219; on committee to arrange Doctrine and Covenants, 220; not present at general assembly, 221; signs report on Doctrine and Covenants, 221, 222; on committee to draft for Temple, 224; records progress on Temple plans, 226; on committee to draft regulations for house of the Lord, 226; presented as seer at Temple dedication, 229; in favor of bank, 240; warns people against bank notes, 242; calls Kimball to Eng. mission, 245; investigates trouble at Adam-ondi-ahman, 271; visits Adam Black, 271; goes to aid of De Witt, 272; surrenders at Far West, 279, 280; ordered shot, 280; saved by action of Gen. Doniphan, 280; remanded to Liberty jail, 282; warns Doniphan of devastation of Jackson Co., 283, 284; visited by wife and son Joseph, 238; blesses young Joseph, 288; encourages E. Robinson to publish Book of Mormon, 298, 299; elected mayor of Nauvoo, 317; charged as accessory to shooting of Boggs, 317; indicted and arrested and discharged on writ of habeas corpus, 317; warrant issued for re-arrest, 318; keeps in hiding, 318; surrenders and again released on writ of habeas corpus, 318; Missouri authorities arrest at Dixon, 319; released by Nauvoo Municipal Court, 319; Missouri asks Ill. gov. to escort to border; Ford refuses, 319; tried before Judge Douglas and released, 319; his reason for tolerating Bennett, 320; island miss. hear of his death, 328; writes to presidential candidates, 332; did not dictate vote, 334; Higbee brings charges of damage against, 334, 335; released on writ of habeas corpus, 335; Higbee swears out warrant again for destruction of Expositor, 336; sues out writ of habeas corpus in Nauvoo, 336; reports affair to Gov. Ford and offers to stand trial, 336; takes refuge in Iowa, 337; bids good-by to Nauvoo, 310; Major attempts to follow, 341; friends accompany on horseback, 341; returns to Nauvoo with Capt. Dunn, 342; arrives in Carthage, 342; surrendered, 342; arrested on charge of treason, 342; killed by mob, 343, 602; Judge Edmunds never saw but once, 348; Sharpe claims not favorable to manner of death, 349; Hon. O. F. Berry's opinion on trouble, 349; his family remain in Nauvoo, 354; Lyman Wight hears of death, 376; Lyman Wight records last conversation with, 376, 377; writes concerning Marks, 415; his son, young Joseph, 442; pointed son out as successor, 442, 443; baptizes young Joseph, 444; requests James Whitehead to stand by son, 445; born at Sharon, Vt., 599; his couns. ordained, 600; complete correction of Scriptures; commences study of Hebrew, 601; editor Elders' Journal, 601; arrives with family in Far West, 601; arrives at Quincy, 601; elected sole trustee for church, 602; editor Times and Seasons, 602; moved to Mansion House, 602; served as pres. of church 612

Smith, Joseph, Sr., son Joseph tells of plates, 36; father of Joseph Smith, Jr., 42; one of eight witnesses, 72; blesses his sons, 191; on H. C. in Kirtland, 206, 614; serves as pr. pat., 620; ordained pat., 191; 602; gave blessings prior to 1836: 191; lived in Waterloo, N. Y., 113; moves to Kirtland, 113, 114; resides on farm of George Miller, 289; dies in Nauvoo, 305; son Hyrum succeeds him, 305; special couns. in pres..........................624

Smith, Joseph III, born at Kirtland, 163, 164; clung to mother as crossed Mississippi on ice, 287; visited father in Liberty jail, 288; father blesses as successor, 288; Lyman Wight assists in blessing, 288; quotation from Memoirs, 341; remains with mother in Nauvoo after father's death, 354, 443; Lyman Wight expects to see take father's place, 386; revelation to Briggs points out, as successor, 392, 393; Yellowstone Branch acknowledges as rightful heir, 404; mission to, Chap. XLV, 424-430; pays tribute to James Blakeslee, 437; letter to Wm. Marks, 440; visited by Marks, Blair, and Rogers, 440, 441; at deathbed of Wm. Marks, 423;: tribute to Wm. Marks, 423; boyhood in Nauvoo, 442; to succeed his father, 288, 442-445; 491; his religious experiences, 444; bap.

tized by father, 444; testimony of John M. Carter, 442, 443; his own testimony, 443, 444; James Whitehead, 444; vision of, 445, 446; its fulfillment, 447, 448; his questions answered, 447, 448; reasons he came to Reorg., 449; statement regarding position, 449; goes to Amboy to take his place, 450; his speech at Amboy, 450-452; ordained pres. of high priesthood, 452, 602; comment by Amboy Times, 454; Geo. Edmunds, Jr., requests him to remain in Nauvoo, 454; resolutions protesting return of church to Hancock Co., 455; warned by Judge Roosevelt, 455; Sharp's attitude, 455; opposition of Carthage Republican, 455; answers in Democratic News, 455; 456; in Nauvoo, 456; moves to Plano, 458; attitude toward polygamy, 489, 490; sends miss. to Texas, 494; becomes editor of Herald, 499; 603; friendship with Marietta Walker, 499; tribute to miss., 504; John L. Bear spends week end with, 510; appoints his successor, 576; death, 576; prophesies concerning statehood of Utah, 603; visits Salt Lake City, 604; leaves Plano for Lamoni, 604; serves as pres. of church, 612; chose F. M. Smith as successor, 576; directions for funeral, 576; tribute, Kansas City Journal..........577
Smith, Joseph Perrine, son of Israel A. Smith, died..........................589
Smith, Julia (adopted child), twin, dies at Hiram, 155; clings to mother's skirts as she crosses river........287
Smith, Lucy Mack, joins Presbyterian church, 33; mother of Joseph Smith, 42; writes to Brother Solomon Mack of finding of plates, 58; similar accounts in Joseph Smith and His Progenitors, 58; moves to Kirtland, 113, 114; goes with first miss. to Mich., 122; resides on farm of George Miller.....................289
Smith, Nina G., dies..........................593
Smith, Reginald A., S.H.C...............629
Smith, R. F., justice of peace, Smiths appear before, 342; taken before again..343
Smith, Samuel Harrison, baptized, 80; H. C. in Kirtland, 624; appointed on a mission with Reynolds Cahoon................................115
Smith, Sardius, killed at Haun's Mill 278
Smith, Spencer, explores for location for Texas colony, 370; miss. to Texas 494, 495
Smith, Sylvester, on H. C. at Kirtland, 624; served as pres. of sev....621
Smith, Thomas W., made ap., 546; miss. to Society Islands, 564; served as ap..................................615
Smith, Wallace B., Chap. LXXI,S.H.C. 626; ord. pres. desig.;pres...598B,612,630
Smith, W. Wallace, Chap. LXX, ordained ap., 617; to presidency, Pres. Emeritus 595, 612

Smith, Walter W., on H. C. Reorg...628
Smith, William B., tells of revivals near Palmyra, 32; Smith family in Palmyra, 32; tells of Joseph's getting plates, 37; describes plates, 58, 59; served as ap., 612; walks from Fairfield to Kirtland, 115; Briggs fellowships with, 392; holds a conference at Palestine, Illinois, 392; Yellowstone Branch renounces, 401; Reorg. renounces, 405; movement under......................425
Snow, Erastus, visits Joseph Smith..427
Snow, winter of the great..........92, 95
Snyder, John, one of first miss. to Eng., 247; went to Alston in Cumberland, 251; reports 30 baptisms in Cumberland, 254; left for America 254
Soby, Leonard, on H. C. in Nauvoo, 622; sent out to collect money for Temple 399
South Sea Islands, mission to, Chap. XXXIV, 321; Reorg., Chap. LX, 523; LXVI, 562; first miss., 321; sailed from New Bedford for, 322; voyage to, 322, 323; miss. land at Tubuai, 325; Addison Pratt at Tubuai, 325; miss. land at Tahiti, 326; first sermon in Tahiti, 326; Noah Rogers visits other islands, 329; Grouard goes to Low Islands, 329; Rogers sails for America, 329; Pratt sails for America, 330; Grouard's life on islands, 329, 330, 331; Australian miss. delayed at Tahiti, 524; find L. D. S. at Tiona, 524, 525; persecution of island Saints, 525; experiences of Rodger and Wandell in, 526, 527; Wm. Nelson miss. to, 527; Thomas W. and Helen Smith, miss., 527; Charles Lake dies, 528; Clara K. Ellis, 528; gospel boat, 564-566; tidal wave......................................566
Southport, Lancashire, branch organized by first Eng. miss............255
"Spartan band," thirty-five men under Capt. Anderson, at Battle of Nauvoo 346, 347
Spaulding, Solomon, reputed author of Book of Mormon, 108; Rigdon says never heard of..............................110
Spaulding theory, claim that romance of Spaulding was basis for Book of Mormon, 108; first advanced in Mormonism Unveiled, 108; becomes American tradition, 108; reasons for disbelieving, 108; denial by Nancy Rigdon Ellis, 109; 109; by John W. Ellis, 109; by Sidney Rigdon in Boston Journal, 110; testimony of Bronsons, 110; romance found, 110, 111; opinion of Fairchild, 111; opinion of Rice......111
Spencer, Augustine, swears out warrant against Smiths for treason....342
Spencer, Geoffrey F., H. P. Q. Pres.; S. H. C. 624, 630
Spirit of the Times quotation regarding preaching of J. E. Page..308
Spiritual gifts, believed in..........170, 171
Spiritual Wife System Proven False, etc., by Hedrick..................................432
Spring in Kansas City, camping

INDEX 659

place, 118; location of............118
Squires, Joseph, kindness to foreign-going miss..................514
Squires, W. W., Thomas Waddell died at home of..................501
Stafford, Edwin, tells of Sunday school at Nauvoo..................592
Stake at Zarahemla, premature........570
Stakes of Zion, Kirtland, 165; Lamoni, 570, 605; Independence, 570, 605, Kansas City, 605; Holden, 570, 605; Far West, 605; Council Bluffs, San Francisco, Los Angeles, Tulsa, Des Moines, Denver, Seattle 598, 608
Stars, falling of..................180, 181
Stebbins, Henry A., joins Reorg., 492; recorder for many years, 492; couns. to pr. bp...............619
Stewardship defined.................170
Stewart, Riley, L. D. S. involved in Gallatin riot.......................271
Stoal, Josiah, of Bainbridge, N. Y., friend of Joseph Knight, 40; hires Joseph to dig for Spanish gold, 40; at Smith home when plates were obtained, 40; follower of Joseph Smith............................ 48
Stobaugh, Kenneth E., pres. of sev. 623
Stone, Barton, prominent revivalist, 19; a great revival, 18-21; on "election," 26; experiment preaching baptism, 28; compliments A. Campbell on attitude toward creeds and confessions of faith...... 30
Stone Church, at Independence, cornerstone laid, 604; built..........560
Stokes, Richard, baptized by Derry..475
Strang, James J., leader of faction, 359; baptized, 359; his claims, 359; his attitude on polygamy, 359; joined by John C. Bennett, 359; builds city of Voree, 359; founded Beaver Island, 359; crowned king, 360; elected to Michigan legislature, 360; shot by assassins, 360; Jason Briggs fellowships with, 392; Briggs gives reason for leaving, 392; Gurley adopts leadership of, 399; Gurley urges claims in mission field, 399; 400; Yellowstone branch renounces, 401; Gurley has spiritual experience in regard to, 402; Reorg. renounces, 405; Marks occupies as couns. to, 417; Marks leaves 423
Strader, Jacob B., protests against return of Saints to Hancock Co.....455
Stuart, J. C., ord. ap. 618
Successor to Joseph Smith, Jr., 288, 355, 361, 385, 386, 442-445..........491
Successor to Joseph Smith III........576
Succession, difficulty over in Nauvoo 355
Sunday schools, few in United States, 16; at Nauvoo, 572; Joseph III establishes in Nauvoo, 572; publishes Zion's Hopes, 572; Sunday school association............572
Sweden, Chap. LXII, 535; Magnus Fyrando, first miss., 535; miss. of Utah faction in...............535, 536

Sweet Home, Oregon, branch, organized 520
Switzerland, mission in, Chap. LVIII, 507; Frederick Ursenbach in, 507; publishes the Gospel, 507; church sends John Avondet to, 507; Avondet lands, 507; Avondet meets Ursenbach in Lausanne, 508; Avondet goes to Italy, 508; John L. Bear volunteers for service, 510; arrives in Zurich, 510; many calls for preaching, 510; difficulties of mission, 510, 511; meets Avondet in Geneva, 511; group in Zurich left under Taylor, 512; Bear returns on second mission, 514; leaves again for America............514
Sword of Laban, seen by three witnesses 71

Tahiti, Grouard and Rogers land in, 326; first sermon, 326; first baptisms, 326; Rodger and Wandell in, 523; find Saints at Tiona, 524; persecution of Saints in, 525; Wandell and Rodger leave for Australia 527
Tammany Hall, Pratt preaches New York City......................259
Tanner, Joseph A., on H. C. Reorg., pres. of H. P. Q..............627, 624
Tarbell, Squire, married Joseph Smith and Emma Hale.............. 40
Tarred and feathered by mob, Joseph Smith and Sidney Rigdon in Hiram, 155; Edward Partridge and Charles Allen in Independence......175
Taylor, John, stranger in Hamilton, Ont., gives address to Pratt, 232; Pratt seeks home of, 232; reception of Pratt by, 232; one of group of Bible students, 234; editor of Times and Seasons, 305; 604; miss. to Eng., 256; served as ap., 614; with Joseph Smith at assassination, 343; present at blessing of young Joseph..................444, 445
Taylor, John, sent out as scout by Texas colony, 379; he and wife baptized in Ogden...............482, 483
Taylor, Thomas, Derry visits in Birmingham, 478; visits again, 479; one of first bishopric in Eng. 569
Temperance, beginnings in U. S., 14; in Nauvoo, 46; preached by Joseph Smith, 46; J. S. called first prohibitionist, 154; Word of Wisdom, 165; L. D. S. ministers in Eng. demand for preaching..............253
Temple contemplated in Far West..264
Temple contemplated in Independence, Joseph Smith lays stone for corner, 119, 120; Sidney Rigdon dedicates spot upon which it is to be built, 119, 120, 600; Partridge buys tract containing dedicated site, 152 (see Temple Lot); Lyman Wight says will "most assuredly" be built..........................385
Temple (Kirtland), see Kirtland.
Temple (Nauvoo), see Nauvoo.
"Temple Lot" in Independence;

dedicated, 119, 120; Partridge buys land containing, 152; Saints camp upon, 180; bought by Granville Hedrick. 435: Temple Lot suit decisions, 604; prophecy by Lyman Wight concerning 385
Texas Colony, Chap. XXXIX, 374-386; Lyman Wight authorized to colonize by Joseph Smith, 376; leaves Prairie La Crosse, 375; journey to Texas, 378; first location, 379, 380: build Zodiac, 380; build Mountain Valley, 381; relations with community, 381; build county jail in Austin, 380; had all things common, 382; looked for coming of young Joseph, 384, 385, 494; some join Reorg., 469; Huffman goes to Nauvoo, 493, 494; miss. sent to southern remnant of colony, 494, 495; branch organized among Texas remnant 495
Thayer, Judge, decisions in Temple Lot suit 604
Thayre, Ezra B., follower of Joseph Smith, 48; his conversion, 83; appointed on miss. with Thomas B. Marsh, 115; could not prepare in time, 116; joins Reorg 466, 467
Thomas, Judge Jesse, advises J. S. to submit to re-arrest 336
Thomas, John, secedes from Thompson 338
Thompson, O., community experiment at, by Colesville br. not a success 116
Thompson, Charles B., miss. in days of Joseph, 387; goes to Voree, 387; history of his organization, 387, 388; position and claims, 387; founds Preparation, Iowa, 388; part of membership secedes, 388; final dispersion at Preparation, 388; many of his followers join Reorg., 389; publishes Nachashlogian 389
Thompson, Robert B., miss. to Canada, 246; married Mercy Fielding, 234; death 305
Thornley, branch organized by first Eng. miss. 255
Thornton, Col. J., befriends Saints .. 200
Thorpe, Judge Josiah, describes meeting at Liberty, 210; tribute to Saints in Clay Co., 261; on Saints in Caldwell Co., 265; describes Battle of Crooked River, 274; says Doniphan prepared to defend prisoners with his life 279
Three Missionaries, The, poem by David H. Smith 470
Three witnesses, see Witnesses.
Tickemyer, G. E., pres. of H. P. Q. 624
Timely Warning, a, by Orson Hyde, distribution to ministers of New York 247
Timeoleon, a whaler, upon which first island miss. embarked for Tahiti, sails from New Bedford, 321, 322; voyage of 322, 324
Times and Seasons published by Smith and Robinson, 296-298, 601; John Taylor, editor, 305, 602; Joseph Smith, editor, 602; read in Briggs family 390
Tithing, question approached gently in Reorg., 503; its abuses elsewhere, 503; Israel L. Rogers pays .. 504
Tomatoes, Dr. Bennett urges Saints to eat 295
Toronto, Ontario, Parley P. Pratt told in prophecy to go to, 231; Joseph Luff, a Methodist minister of, 542; is baptized, 544, 545; returns to Toronto 545
Total depravity, doctrine of 26
"Tower Hill," home of Lyman Wight, near Adam-ondi-ahman 273
Translation of Book of Mormon, Harris acts as scribe, 60; history, 60; 116 pages lost, 60; Cowdery comes to Harmony to act as scribe, 62; used Urim and Thummim, 62; family present in room during, 64; manner of, 64, 65; finished 66, 67
Treason, Missouri authorities revive old charge of, 319; Smith arrested on charge of 342
Treaty, under pressure of Saints in Jackson Co., with mob, 177; between followers of Alpheus Cutler and Indians 360
Trouble, Missouri, opinion of cause, E. Douglas Branch, 172; Alexander W. Doniphan, 172; James Truslow Adams 172
Trouble at Nauvoo, cause of, Bancroft upon, 347-350; Hon. Orville F. Berry investigates, 348; Edmunds, Judge George, upon, 348; Thomas C. Sharp upon 349
Troyer, Luther S., Pres. 70's 623
Tubuai, miss. first landing on Pacific Isles, 325; Addison Pratt stays on, 325; first baptism on, 326; Pratt's life on, 327; Grouard builds a boat in 330
Turley, Theodore, first to build house in Commerce, 601; mission to Eng 256
Turner, O., story of finding of plates 56
Twelve (Quorum of), see Apostles; first quorum chosen by three witnesses, 217, 218; organized conferences (districts,) 218, 219; duties defined by Joseph III, 504; first chosen by direct revelation, 546; assumed control at Nauvoo, 355; testify to truth of Doctrine and Covenants in writing 220
Twombley, Samuel, on H. C. Reorg. 628
Tyler, Charles, had left Mormon church, 474; interested 475
Tyler, Henry, first fruit of Derry's mission to Eng 475
Tyler, Mrs. Henry, interested 475
Tyler, Wm., and wife interested in work 475
Tyree, Alan D., ap., F.P 618, 613

United Order, efforts to establish, 153, 157; among followers of Alpheus Cutler, 360; in the Brooklyn colony, 367; Edward Bellamy's ideas from, 153 (see also

INDEX

"all things common," Preparation, and Texas colony, and Order of Enoch).
United Order of Enoch, see Order of Enoch.
Updike, L. Wayne, S.H.C.............629
Urim and Thummim, used to translate, 56, 64; "most mysterious things in Old Testament"............56
Ursaline Convent, burning of, Joseph Smith's comment concerning 47, 173
Ursenbach, Frederick, conversion in Utah, 507; urges church to send miss. to Switzerland, 507; prints and distributes tract called The Gospel, 507; meets Avondet in Lausanne 507, 508

Vandalia, Ill., Pratt and Murdock preach in Presbyterian church, ...161, 162
Vauxhall Chapel, in Preston, Lancashire, first sermon in England preached in 250
Velt, Harold I., from Australia, 534; served as pres. of sev.; evangelist 623
Voice of Warning, printed first........257
Voree, Wisconsin, built by James J. Strang, 359; visited by Reorg. miss. 395

Waddell, Thomas, miss. to southwest, 501; dies in mission field......501
Waddington, Eng. branch organized by first Eng. miss........................254, 255
Waite, Hon. Judge, opened home in Utah to E. C. Briggs...................482
Wakefield, Joseph, appointed on a mission with Solomon Humphrey..116
Wales, mission, opened by Jeremiah Jeremiah, 477; Word of Consolation translated into Welsh, 477; conferences at Pennydaren, 478; Chas. Derry's tribute to Saints of, 478; Restorer published in, 479; J. T. Phillips arrives, 479; Thomas E. Jenkins arrives.........................479
Walker, Cyrus, Whig candidate for Congress, defeated by Hoge, Democrat, 332; Joseph Smith voted for, 334; Edmunds thinks if "Mormons" had voted for Hoge, trouble would be averted........................348
Walker, Marietta, comes to Plano, 499; Joseph Smith on her 77th birthday, 500; sponsors Zion's Hope, 506; sponsors move for gospel boat, 564; publishes Afterglow, 564, 565; one of first to locate in Lamoni 549
Walker, Samuel Frye, first L. D. S. in Lamoni..549
Walkerford, Chaigley, Lancashire, baptisms in, 251, 252; branch organized 251, 252
Waller, Gilbert J., assists Hawaiian mission 562, 563, 604
Walton, Mrs. —— befriends Pratt in Toronto...234

Wamsley, Ann Elizabeth, first healing in Eng...250
Wandell, Charles Wesley, sails from San Francisco to Australia, 523; previously a miss. to Australia, 523; called to be seventy before baptism, 523; his ship puts into Tahiti for repairs, 523, 524; finds Saints at Tiona, 524; farewell to Saints at Tiona, 526, 527; lands at Sydney, 529; death...............529, 530
Warsaw Signal pours out invective, 336; rabid against L. D. S.......345, 548
Waterloo, N. Y., family of Joseph Smith, Sr., reside in.............................113
Watson, Warren, on Lilburn W. Boggs 176
Watsonville branch, California, organized 483
Watt, George D., first baptism in England 250
Waukesha, Wis., branch organized by J. W. Briggs...391
Wayne City Landing, Saints cross river 180
Webb, E. H., miss. in California....483
Webb, Sylvia Cutler, of Kirtland Temple, memories of dedication....228
Webster, Dwight, on H. C. Reorg..626
Weddle, Franklyn, High Council......629
Welding, Dick, starts Gallatin riot..271
Wellington, Paul A., S.H.C................629
Wells, Daniel H., Joseph Smith tried before, 336; commanded L. D. S. troops at Battle of Nauvoo...........346
Wells, R. W., attorney general, letter to Gilbert, 194; comes to Independence to investigate outrages..197
Welsh, Doctrine and Covenants published in..602
Wentworth, John, letter from Joseph Smith quoted, 35, 36; J. S. describes plates to.......................................55
Wesley, John, Canon Farrar writes of, 23-25; predicted a restoration..25
West Bromwich, Worcester, Derry makes a stand...............................473, 474
Weston, Robert, on personnel of mob 175
Whitcomb, Zenos, on H. C. Reorg...627
White, George, of Wingville, Wis., unites with Reorg. church, 407; served as ap., 615; chosen and ordained an ap..413
White, Isaac N., served as an ap., 616 served as pres. of sev.........................622
Whitehead, James, baptized by Kimball, 256; tells of blessing of young Joseph, 444; promise to Joseph, the martyr..445
Whitlock, Harvey G., appointed on mission with David Whitmer, 115; reported to semiannual conference of 1864 in California..............................484
Whitmer, Christian, acted as scribe for Joseph, 65; one of eight witnesses, 69; battle in his cornfield, 179; served on H. C. in Zion............625
Whitmer, David, birth, 52; first hears of J. Smith and plates, 52, 53; lived and died in Richmond Mo., 54; Oliver Cowdery writes to, 62; goes to Pennsylvania for Smith

and Cowdery, 63; plowing done in night, 63; one of three witnesses, 69, 70; shown plates, 70; his story, 71; Oliver Cowdery dies at home of, 73; statement of E. C. Brand, 73; letter to M. H. Forscutt, 75; Chicago Times on, 74; death, 74; writes inscription for tombstone, 74; chooses text for funeral sermon, 74; appointed on a mission with Harvey Whitlock, 115; leader of faction, 361; ordained pres. of church in Zion, 216; assists to choose first q. of twelve, 217; officiates with Oliver Cowdery in ordaining first ap., 218; "charges preferred" against, 269; refused to answer charges, 269; expelled from church without trial 269
Whitmer, Mary, wife of Peter Whitmer, Sr., sees plates 64
Whitmer, Elizabeth Ann, youngest of Whitmers, 52; married Oliver Cowdery 73
Whitmer, Jacob, one of eight witnesses 69, 72
Whitmer, John, one of eight witnesses to Book of Mormon, 69, 72; with Oliver Cowdery takes revelations to Missouri, 152; couns. to David Whitmer, 216; bears record in regard to truth of Doctrine and Covenants, 220; endorses Doctrine and Covenants, in editorial, 222; church historian, 222; quotation from his mss. history, 119, 120; offers himself a ransom for his brethren, 224; explores Caldwell Co., 264; enters south half of Far West townsite in his name, 264; his house built in Far West, 264; acted as scribe for Joseph, 65; signs letter to governor 199
Whitmer, Peter, Jr., on H. C. in Zion, 618; one of eight witnesses, 69, 72; one of first miss. to West, 88, 89; starts a tailor shop in Independence, 95; present at dedication of spot for Temple, 119, 120; goes to Missouri 156
Whitmer, Peter, Sr., early history, 52; acquainted with Oliver Cowdery, 52; translation of Book of Mormon mostly at his home, 63-67; church organized at home of....81, 82
Whitmer settlement, attack upon Saints in 179
Whitney, Newel K., brought into church in Kirtland, 101; entertains Joseph Smith and wife in Kirtland, 112; Algernon S. Gilbert partner of, 116; goes to Missouri, 156; store attacked by mob, 175; bears witness to truth of Doctrine and Covenants, 220; trustee in trust for church, 358; poured oil on head of young Joseph 444
Whittle, branch, organized by first Eng. miss. 255
Wight, John W., served as ap........616
Wight, Lyman, held "all things common," 90; baptized, 91; first miss. trip, 99; to "Zion" by way of Pontiac, 115, 122; well liked by Missourians, 132; Levi Graybill on his character, 132; one of first missionaries to Michigan, 122; arrives in Kirtland, from Missouri, 192; meets Zion's Camp with reinforcements, 209; put in charge of Zion's Camp, 209; H. C. in Zion organized at his home, on farm of Michael Arthur, 215, 216; built brick house for Michael Arthur, 215; Adam Black swears out warrant against, 271, 272; L. D. S. militia under, camped at Diahman, 272; writes to Northern Islander on blessing of young Joseph, 288; chosen to fill place of David Patten in twelve, 374; takes charge of Wisconsin saw mills,374; divides with starving Indians, 375; held commission as colonel 59th Missouri Militia from Boggs, 264; Doniphan's tribute to bravery, 44; recalled to Nauvoo, 376; presents petitions to congress, 376; hears of Joseph Smith's death, 376; called to Nauvoo to meet with twelve, 376; commissioned by J. Smith to plant colony in Texas, 376; differed with Brigham Young, 377; took friends to Prairie La Crosse for winter, 377; starts with colony for Texas, 378; journey to Texas, 379, 380; refuses to go to Utah, 380; a description of, 381; characteristics of, 381-383; death of, 382; comment of Galveston News, 382; practiced "Celestial Law," 382; did not claim presidency of church, 384; served on H. C. in Zion, 625; served as ap., 614; brings John Murdock to Independence on horseback, 122; sent out to collect money for Temple 399
Wight, Romanan, served as pres. of sev. 622
Wildermuth, David and Anna, Gurley preached at home of, 400; baptized, 400; renounces all factions, 401; expresses belief in first principles 401
Wildermuth, E. C., baptized 400
Wildermuth, Eli M., baptized............400
Williams, Daniel T., served as ap., 616; Evang. 616
Williams, Frederick Granger, a Kirtland convert, accompanies first miss. west, 91; mention of, 101; couns. in pres. 165, 600, 612, one of com. to arrange Doctrine and Covenants, 220; on com. to draft plans for Temple 224
Williams, Jesse C., protests against return of Saints to Hancock Co.....455
Williams, John A., meetings at Beloit at home of 394
Williams, Roger on baptism 28
Williams, Thomas W., serves as ap., 616; visits Europe with F. M. Smith 605

INDEX

Wilsey, Archibald M., served as pres. of sev., 621; served as senior pres. of sev............620
Wilson, Detta (Mrs. Nelson), daughter of Charlotte Leabo............340
Wilson, Lewis D., on H. C. in Nauvoo............626
Wilson's Store, near Blue River, collecting place for mob............178
Wiltshire, James, preaches in Gloucester............479
Winchester, Benjamin, holds debate with Methodist minister, Josiah Ells, 309; baptizes Ells............309
Winegar, F. D., secedes from Thompson faction............388
Winslow, Dr., and family, passengers on Timeoleon............325, 326
Witnesses, eight, testimony of, 69; shown plates............72
Witnesses, Three, Chap. VIII, 69-71; reaffirm testimony, 55; ask for privilege of being witnesses, 70; Cowdery and Whitmer see vision, 70; D. Whitmer's own story, 71; Martin Harris sees vision, 71, 72; Oliver Cowdery's testimony, 72; M. Harris true to his testimony, 73; character and after life of Whitmer, 73, 74; select first quorum of twelve, and ordain them............217, 218
Women's auxiliary for social service, formerly daughters of Zion, 575; becomes department of women............604
Women, department of, formerly women's auxiliary for social service............604
Women's movement, ladies relief society of the City of Nauvoo, 303; Daughters of Zion, Women's auxiliary, women's department,............573
Wood, Joseph, goes on mission to Michigan with David Patten, 159; Reorg., renounces claims of, 405; with Wm. Smith............425
Wood, Polly, survivor of Haun's Mill massacre............279
Woodhead, William, migrating from Utah............509
Woodruff, Wilford, served as ap., 614; mission to Eng............256
Word of Consolation, com. appointed to draft, 406; presented to church in mss. form, 408; 2000 copies ordered printed, 408; English mss. revived, 476; translated into Welsh............477
Word of Wisdom, given, 165; Saints keep, 133; made a test of ministerial standing, 206, 207; Saints keep in Eng............253
Writ of habeas corpus, Smith and Rockwell released by Municipal court in Nauvoo............319, 335, 336
Wyandotte Indians, near Sandusky, O., first miss. to west preach to....91

Yates, Christopher E., friend of Joseph Smith III............447
Yates, Putnam, Joseph III discusses Mormonism with............447, 448
Yellowstone branch, Wisconsin, organized, 400; renounces all factions............400, 401
Yerba Buena, Brooklyn colonists landed at............367, 368
Young, Brigham, baptized, 164; to become an ap., 164, 217; biographical, 164; baptizes Parrish and Cheeseman, 186; mission to Eng., 256; large group follows, 357; appointed pres. at Winter Quarters, 355; reports on speech at Nauvoo, 358; concerning young Joseph, 361; responsible for polygamy, 489; served as ap., 614; Yellowstone branch, Wis., Reorg. renounces claims of, 405; pres. of q. of twelve............613
Young Gentlemen and Young Ladies Relief Society............303
Young, Lorenzo D., plastered outside Kirtland Temple, 226; baptized............164
Young, Phineas, baptized, 164; mission to Canada, 191; married Lucy Cowdery............228
"Young Joseph," see Joseph Smith III.
Young, Joseph, baptized, 164; served as pres. of sev., 621; served as senior pres. of sev............620
Young people's societies, in Nauvoo, 302, 303; in Reorg. church............573
Young, Judge Richard M., befriends Saints in Congress............290

Zarahemla (Argyle) (now Blanchardville), Aaron Smith comes to, for baptism, 424; W. W. Blair visits, 427; miss. from, 425, 426; Hedrick and Owen take part in conference at, 433; Saints organizing there acceptable to Lord......449
Zerr, Myron, High Council............629
Zion, High Council in, organized, 215, 216; ratifies Doctrine and Covenants, 220; present at council in Kirtland, 220; considers "redemption of Zion"............239
Zion, ideal of, 12; Rigdon "longed for above all other events in history of the world," 103; "stewardship" grows out of, 170; not a failure, 184; members of Thompson's community not discouraged,............388, 389
Zion, land of dedicated, 119; miss. travel toward two by two, 115; settlement started, 119; first conference, 120; first death, 120; directions given for Sabbath observance in, 121; conditions in, 121-124; Partridge buys land for, 152; David Whitmer made "president of the church" in, 216; Independence, made city of,............605,

plat of, received..................................174
See also Independence, Missouri.

Zion's Camp, on way to Missouri, 202; purpose of, 208; Lyman Wight and Hyrum Smith with refreshments join at Salt River, Missouri, 209; cholera epidemic, 212-214; Fishing River revelation, 212; seventies selected from, 218; mentioned in letter to Governor Dunklin, 198, 199; disbanded......................203
Zion's Ensign published........................604
Zion's Hope, child's paper, issued, Joseph Smith, first editor................572
Zion's Religio Literary Society, see Religio.
Zodiac, Texas, built by Texas Colony 380
Zonker, Louis C., Pres, 70's................623